Better Homes and Gardens®

TREASURY of NEEDLECRAFTS

First Edition. Third Printing, 1982.
Library of Congress Catalog Card Number: 81-67152
ISBN: 0-696-00755-X

BETTER HOMES AND GARDENS® BOOKS

Editor: Gerald M. Knox
Art Director: Ernest Shelton
Managing Editor: David A. Kirchner

Crafts Editor: Nancy Lindemeyer
Crafts Book Editor: Ann Levine

Associate Art Director (Managing):
Randall Yontz
Associate Art Directors (Creative):
Linda Ford, Neoma Alt West
Copy and Production Editors: Nancy Nowiszewski,
Lamont Olson, David A. Walsh
Assistant Art Directors: Faith Berven, Harijs Priekulis
Senior Graphic Designer: Tom Wegner
Graphic Designers: Alisann Dixon, Lyne Neymeyer,
Lynda Haupert, Bill Shaw, D. Greg Thompson

Editor in Chief: Neil Kuehnl
Group Editorial Services Director: Duane Gregg
Executive Art Director: William J. Yates

General Manager: Fred Stines
Director of Publishing: Robert B. Nelson
Director of Retail Marketing: Jamie Martin
Director of Direct Marketing: Arthur Heydendael

Treasury of Needlecrafts
Crafts Editor: Ann Levine
Copy and Production Editor: David A. Kirchner
Graphic Designer: Randall Yontz

One of the nicest things about learning a stitchery craft or needleart is being able to say, "I made it myself." And with this outstanding collection of our best-loved handmade projects, you can do just that. Whether you choose patchwork and quilting, appliqué, crocheting and knitting, needlepoint, embroidery, or rug making, you'll find these pages brimming with delightful make-it-yourself projects for you and your home. For a closer look at what you can do with your favorite needlecraft techniques, please turn the page.

Contents

Patchwork and Quilting ______ **6–69**
Patchwork—A Practical and Creative Craft ______ 8–23
Pieced Patchwork—A Kaleidoscope of Patterns ______ 24–39
Traditional—American Quilts and Quilting ______ 40–55
Patchwork Plus—Novelty Projects ______ 56–69

Appliqué ______ **70–167**
Learning to Appliqué ______ 72–89
Displaying Your Skills ______ 90–107
Special Appliqué Techniques ______ 108–127
Patterns from Quilts ______ 128–141
Designs from Nature ______ 142–155
Creative Appliqué ______ 156–167

Crocheting and Knitting ______ **168–233**
Afghans ______ 170–193
For Your Table ______ 194–205
For Your Bedroom ______ 206–221
Accessories ______ 222–229
Basic Crocheting Stitches ______ 230–231
Basic Knitting Stitches ______ 232–233

Needlepoint ______ **234–323**
Needlepoint—An Exciting and Elegant Craft ______ 236–253
Pillows—A Primer of Design and Pattern ______ 254–269

Adventures in Needlepoint—
Unique Projects to Stitch 270–285
Creative Techniques—
New Ways with Needlepoint 286–299
Spectacular Stitchery—Art from Your Needle 300–320
Basic Needlepoint Stitches 321–323

Embroidery 324–409
Folk Embroidery 326–339
Old-Fashioned Stitchery 340–353
Designs from Nature 354–365
Cross-Stitch and Counted-Thread Techniques 366–381
Machine Embroidery 382–391
Special Stitchery Techniques 392–405
Basic Embroidery Stitches 406–409

Rug Making 410–475
Rag and Braided Rugs 412–423
Rugs to Knit and Crochet 424–435
Hooked Rugs 436–449
Special Rug-Making Techniques 450–461
Creative Rug Making 462–475

Index and Credits 476–480

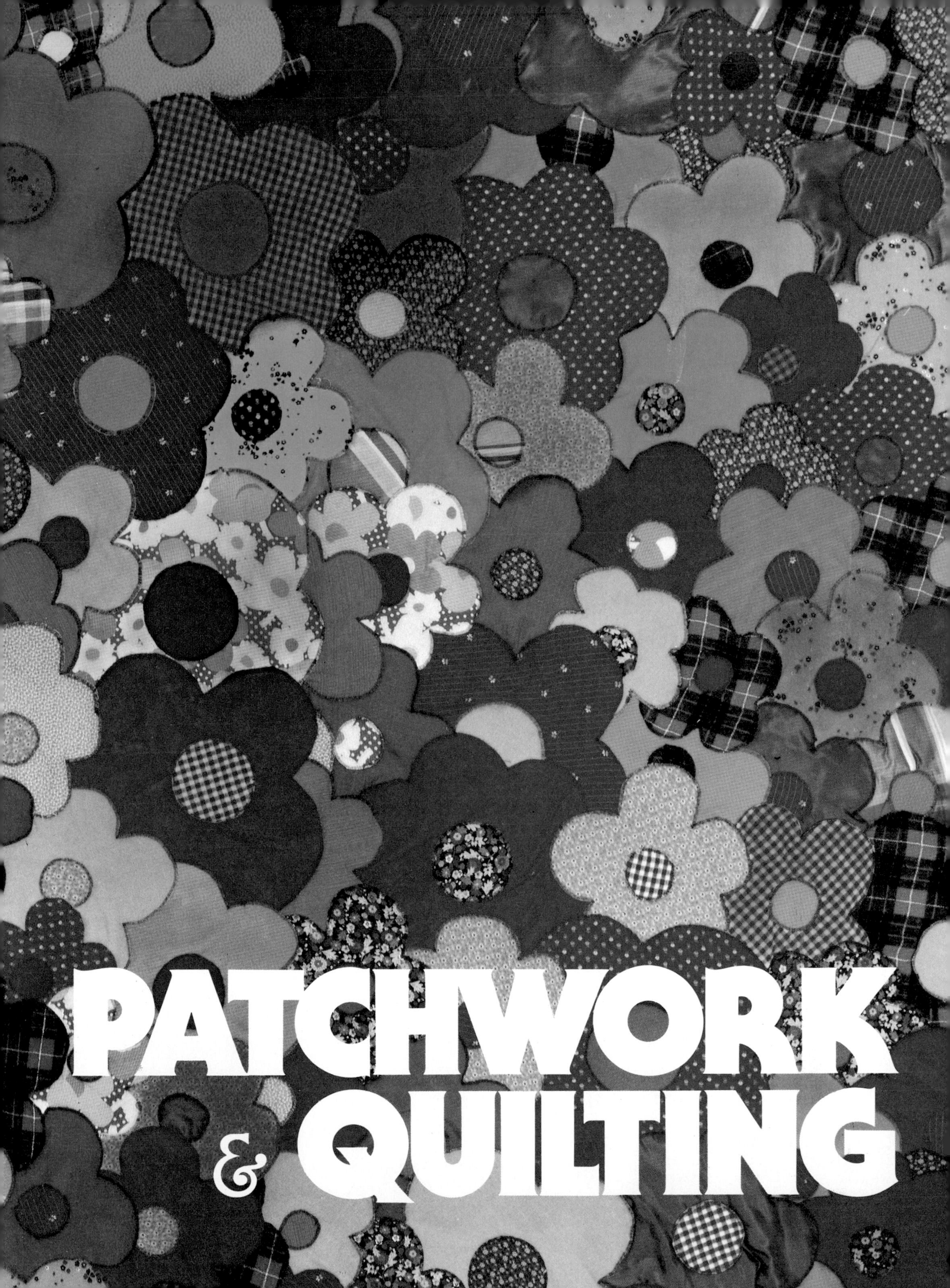
PATCHWORK
& QUILTING

It is difficult for us today to imagine how valuable and important small scraps of fabric were to our pioneer forebears. In a time when little was discarded, frugal homemakers saved the best parts of worn clothing and household items and then artfully stitched them into beautiful, warm quilts. That's how the truly American craft of patchwork was born. If you'd like to try your hand at this heritage craft, this section will guide you, stitch by stitch, through a collection of interesting and useful projects for your home that will make patchwork come alive for you.

Patchwork-

A Practical and Creative Craft

Not all patchwork is complex and time consuming. There are some attractive patterns that even first-time patchworkers can create. This section is designed to introduce you to the basics of patchwork through some quick-and-easy projects that will turn you on without scaring you off. Instructions for items shown here are on pages 14 and 15.

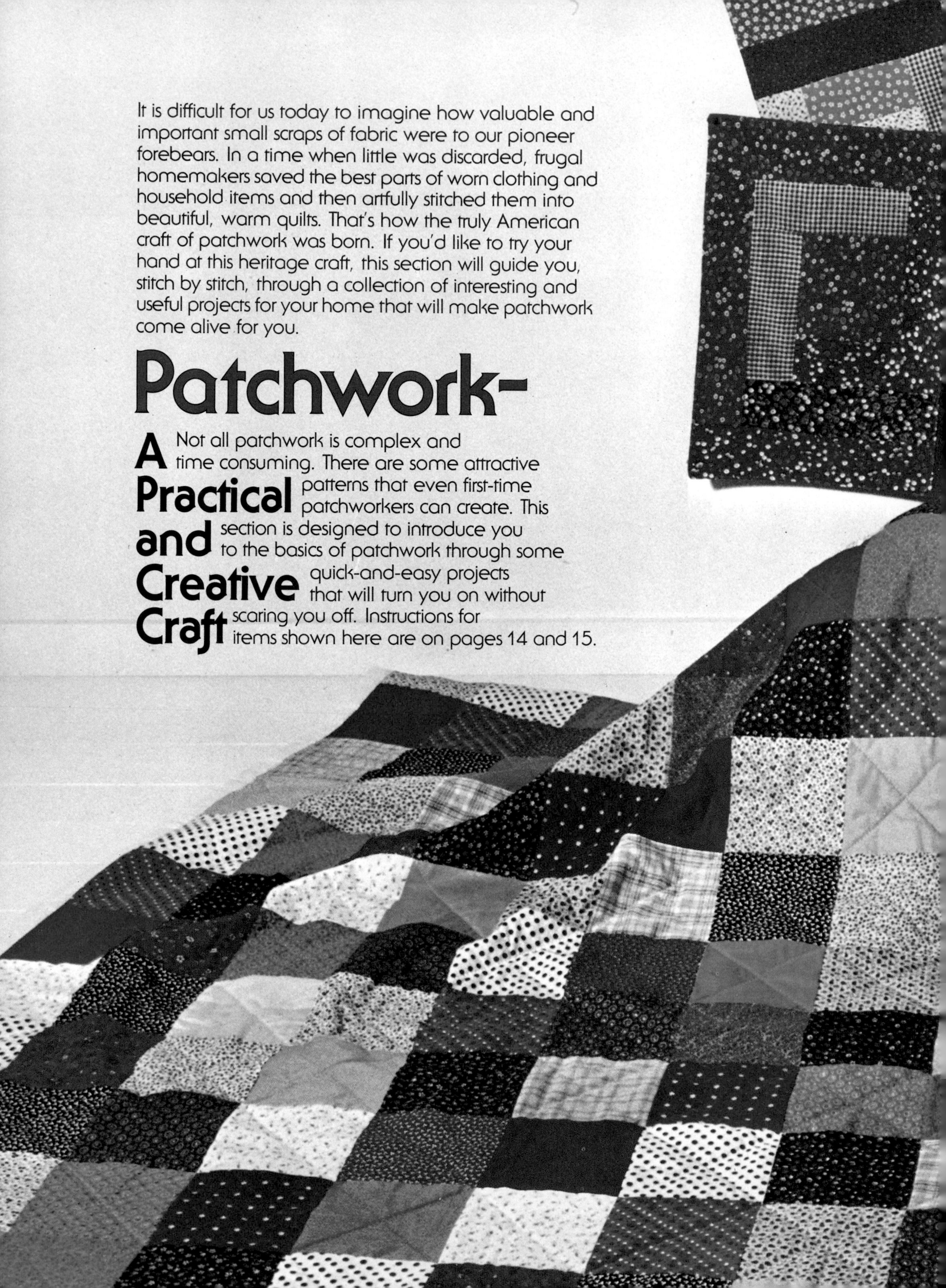

Patchwork Basics

Patchwork can be a simple combination of squares, or maybe a complex arrangement of several geometric shapes. But no matter what the design, all patchwork projects involve the same procedures–drafting a pattern, collecting materials, cutting and piecing shapes together to form blocks, and then joining the blocks to create pieced fabric. Here's what you need to know to make patchwork fabric for quilt tops, curtains, pillows, place mats, or any other item you want to fabricate with dazzling design and color.

Choosing a design is not only the first step in any patchwork project, it may well be the most difficult. It's easy to fall in love with one of the traditional patchwork patterns and attack it with great enthusiasm. But without sufficient experience it's a disappointment when you discover the project you chose isn't within your range of skills, and you either abandon or lose interest in it. So start slowly. Choose a simple patchwork pattern first, and then work up to the more impressive designs. There are dozens of beautiful patchwork patterns worked with nothing more complicated than squares and slashed squares (triangles). Pick one of these and you won't have any trouble—even with your very first project.

Collecting Fabrics

Traditionally, patchwork quilt tops have been made of calico, 100-percent cotton broadcloth, cotton percale, gingham, chintz, corduroy—and even some fancier fabrics such as velvet, satin, or taffeta. When choosing fabric for patchwork, don't lose sight of its washability. If the finished project is better off washable, stay away from satins, felts, velvets, or any fabric that must be cleaned.

Evaluate a fabric's characteristics and learn to avoid those that are difficult to use in patchwork. For instance, burlap or loosely woven fabrics ravel too easily to be practical. Heavy fabrics such as denim, sailcloth, or canvas are difficult to sew. Polyester knits are very stretchy, and linen wrinkles too easily. So, your best bet is to stick to cotton or cotton blend fabrics.

Mixing fabrics and patterns is a matter of personal taste. Some fabrics are natural go-togethers; others are not. For instance it won't take you long to realize that gingham and satin is probably not the combination you want. Keep textures in mind, too. On the one hand, a quilt top might be more interesting if it displays both smooth and textured fabrics. On the other hand, you may determine that the effect you want calls for fabrics all of one texture—or without any noticeable texture.

Print fabrics are perfectly at home in the potpourri that is patchwork. If you want the print to register as a color, choose a very small-scale print. A large-scale print will come off looking more like a texture when used in a large patchwork piece—or as no print at all when cut in small sections.

Though patchwork is a good way to utilize good pieces of worn-out garments or scraps from sewing projects, it takes years to develop a really well-rounded scrap bag. And the design you choose might dictate a definite color scheme—one you can't achieve with leftovers. In that case, you'll have to buy new goods. For fabric bargains, check mill outlets, remnant counters, and discount shops. If fabric is new, make sure it's preshrunk and colorfast. And wash all fabrics and press thoroughly before starting to cut.

Marking Your Fabric

The process of marking fabric starts with making a template of each piece in your patchwork design. A template is a pattern that can be used over and over. You can buy ready-made plastic or metal templates at craft supply shops, or make your own using sandpaper or lightweight cardboard. (Sandpaper will not slip when placed on fabric, so cutting pieces is easier.) Plan to make several templates of each pattern piece because the edges fray with repeated use and can interfere with the precision of your measurements. Accuracy is the secret to successful patchwork.

To make a template, enlarge the pattern to its actual working size. (For information on enlarging, see pages 272 and 273.) Graph paper can make enlarging easier and more accurate. When the piece is enlarged, cover cardboard or sandpaper with carbon paper, face down, and place your pattern over it. Trace over the pattern, remove the graph paper and carbon, and cut the template using sharp scissors.

Before cutting, mark on each template how many pieces of each color and print fabric you'll need. This will speed the cutting process since you won't have to stop to check the master design.

Find the straight grain of the fabric by looking at the selvage, or, on pieces with no selvage, by pulling a thread. Place the pattern piece template on the straight grain of the fabric. For square or rectangular pieces, all edges should be on the lengthwise or crosswise grain; diamond-shaped pieces should be cut with two edges on the straight grain. Right angle triangles should have two sides on the straight grain. All other shapes should have the straight grain running through the center of the piece.

If your patchwork is to be pieced, lay the fabric out so the wrong side is up. If it is to be appliquéd, have the right side of the fabric up so you can see just where the hems of the pieces are to be turned under for stitching. Place your template on the fabric and trace with a soft pencil.

Seam allowances are generally not given on patchwork patterns, so you'll have to add ¼ inch to all edges when cutting. Always remember that the pencil line represents the line for sewing—not cutting. Study the top drawing on this page and note the solid tracing lines and the dotted cutting lines.

If you lay out your pattern pieces ½ inch apart, you can cut down the middle of the space between squares, creating a ¼-inch seam allowance and wasting almost no fabric. Add seam allowances to your template if you like. It's more work at the outset, but it may save you time if you're going to be cutting great quantities of squares.

Cutting Pattern Pieces

Make sure your scissors are really sharp. And always begin by laying the fabric out on a cutting board or a large flat surface.

To make the best use of your fabric, cut any border strips first. If your project pattern calls for long, continuous strips, cut them out of the full fabric lengths, then go on to cut the small pieces. Don't forget the ¼-inch seam allowance on border strips as well as pattern pieces.

Cut each piece individually, one at a time, to prevent the bottom layers of fabric from slipping. The only exception would be in the case of completely nonslip fabric. Then carefully pin two layers together to trim your cutting time in half.

Sort pieces according to color and shape as you cut your fabrics. One way to keep pieces in order is to string them together as shown in the bottom drawing on this page. Tie a knot in the end of a single thread and pull the needle through the center of each block. After stringing all the identical blocks onto the thread, remove the needle. Do this for each different group of size, shape, and color. Then as you need the blocks, simply slip them off the thread one at a time.

continued

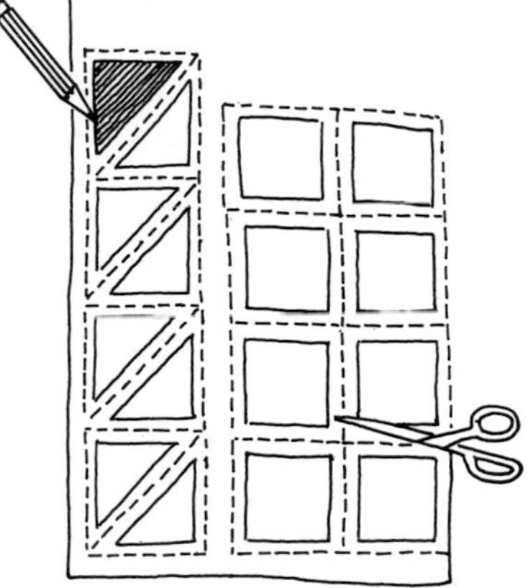

Marking and cutting fabric.

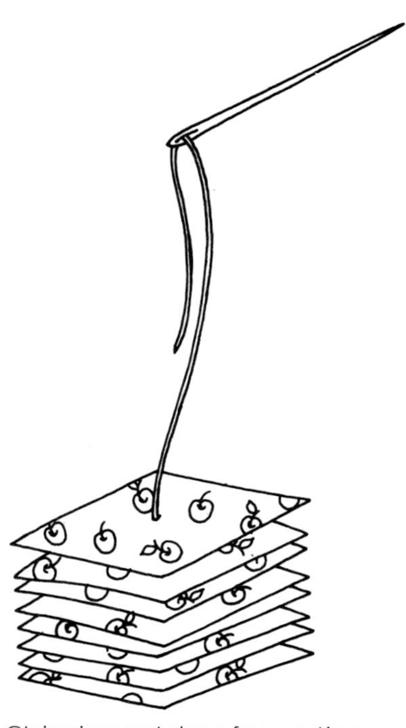

Stringing patches for sorting

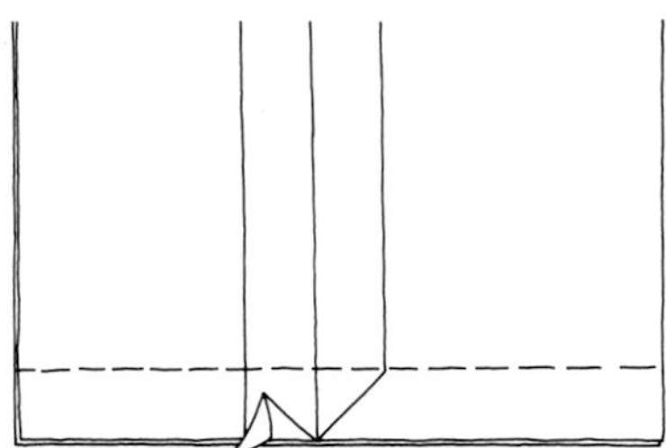

Trimming a seam

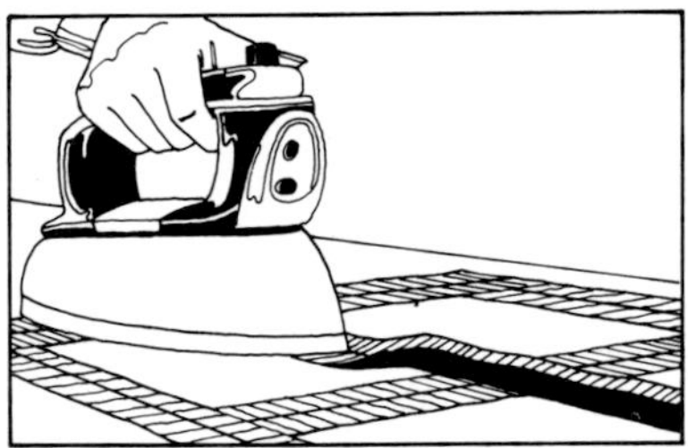

Pressing seams open

Piecing Your Fabric

"Piecing" patchwork fabric means sewing all the small pieces together to form blocks. This doesn't necessarily take a lot of experience and talent. What it takes is accuracy and patience.

Join patchwork pieces by hand or machine sewing. Purists among quilters might frown on machine "piecing," but few people today have the leisure time to hand stitch hundreds of pieces together to form a quilt.

However, there are some things to consider in deciding whether to hand sew or machine sew the pieces together. If the pattern pieces are very small, you may find they're difficult to handle on the sewing machine. The close stitches made by the machine may also make it difficult to hand quilt over them. You might consider a combination of the two methods. Hand stitch the pieces to form the blocks, then machine stitch the blocks together for added strength on long seams.

Hold the pattern pieces firmly in place with right sides together as you piece. There's no need to pin or baste short piecing seams, however the longer seams should be pinned to make sure all pieces line up properly and don't shift in the sewing. To hand sew, use tiny running stitches; if machine piecing, use medium-length stitches. If your sewing machine has a lock stitch, you may find it helpful to use it. That way you can clip the threads at either end of the seam without having the seam open up. Without a lock stitch, you should fasten both ends of the seam by tacking with a back-and-forth stitch.

Seams should be fastened at either end when hand sewing, too. Do this by making several back-stitches.

If you've traced your pattern pieces on the wrong side of the fabric, without a seam allowance, you will have a pencil line to guide you in sewing a straight seam.

Don't stretch seams when sewing two bias edges together. Pull the thread taut to prevent stretching. It's a good idea to finger press the seams open as you go, making sure each seam is open before crossing with another seam. Trim out the excess fabric where seams cross in order to reduce bulk. See the top diagram on this page.

Piece one entire block at a time. Then press. Seam allowances may be pressed to one side or open. If the quilted object is to receive much wear or if some fabric in the block is dark and some light, don't open the seam, but press it toward the darker of the two colors. That way the seam won't show through the light colored fabric and it will be stronger. If quilting close to the seam line through three layers of fabric is going to be too difficult, as it occasionally is with hand quilting, then press seams open.

After you've sewn and pressed all the blocks, compare them to make sure they're all the same size. If block sizes vary, adjust the seams wherever necessary to make them uniform.

Joining Blocks

"Setting together" means sewing the blocks together to form the quilt top or necessary yardage for the patchwork project you're working on. In patchwork, there's always a logical way to set the blocks together. If, for instance, your quilt top is made up of squares, the easiest way to assemble the top is to sew several blocks together to form a row, then sew the rows together to make up the completed top. If all blocks are uniform in size, this method should be no problem. But care must be taken in sewing the rows of blocks together so each block lines up precisely with the one next to it.

Arrange pieces for a project made up of squares or random colors and prints by laying all of them out on the floor and placing them in a pleasing relationship to each other. At this time, add alternate solid color blocks or stripes if you're using them. Borders should be added after all the blocks are joined together.

Making Borders

Borders are sewn to the completed quilt top in one of two ways, depending on how you want to finish the corners. If you're going to overlap the edges, pin the lengthwise strips to the quilt, right sides together, and machine-sew ¼ inch from the cut edges. Then do the same with the widthwise strips.

Mitering the corners is a bit trickier, but the professional-looking result is often worth the extra work. First pin the lengthwise border strips to the quilt, right sides together. Let the ends of the border extend beyond the quilt top a little more than the width of the strip. Machine-sew a ¼-inch seam. Next, pin the crosswise strips to the quilt top, but not to the lengthwise border strips. These strips should be longer than the quilt top is wide. Sew these border strips only to the quilt. Fold the crosswise border strip up so its right side faces the right side of the quilt. Fold the extension of the strip up at a 45-degree angle, then turn the folded crosswise border back down into normal position. Hand stitch the diagonal fold in place joining adjacent border strips.

Another way to form a quilt border is to turn the backing fabric to the front and then stitch it in place. Since this is done after the quilting has been completed, instructions for this method of making a border are given in the quilting basics section, starting on page 42.

Mile-a-Minute Machine Patchwork

This is the quickest and easiest way to make a checkerboard pattern. Here's how to do it:

1. Select two fabrics that are compatible in color or design, washability, and weight. Prewash the fabric and press it flat.
2. Lay out each piece of fabric on a smooth, flat surface. Using a yardstick and tailor's chalk, mark strips 3½ inches wide. Cut on the marked lines. Strips may be cut either with the grain of the fabric or across it.
3. With right sides together, join the strips lengthwise with ¼-inch seams. Alternate the prints or colors so that when all strips are sewn together, you have a "striped" piece of fabric. See the top photo (A) at right. Press all of the seams open.
4. Lay the pieced fabric out so strips run crosswise in front of you. Using a yardstick and chalk, mark the fabric in strips 3½ inches wide. Cut on the lines. Handle the strips carefully to keep stitches from raveling. See middle photo.
5. Pin the strips together again, right sides facing. Reverse every other strip so that alternating blocks of fabric meet to form a checkerboard pattern. Pin the strips together carefully to be sure the seams between the patches meet.
6. Restitch the strips together, using a ¼-inch seam allowance. See bottom photo at right. To keep puckering at a minimum, stitch at a steady, even speed. Press all seams open.
7. For other less-symmetrical patchwork patterns, experiment with placement of strips for different effects.

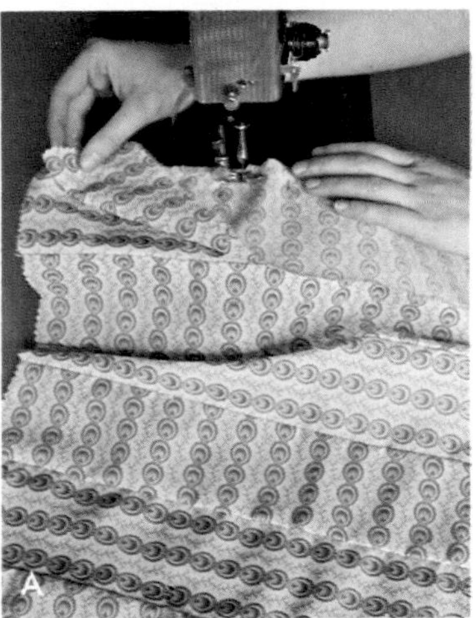

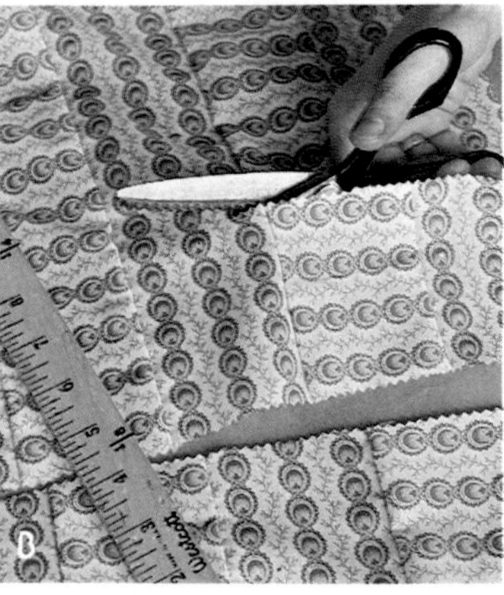

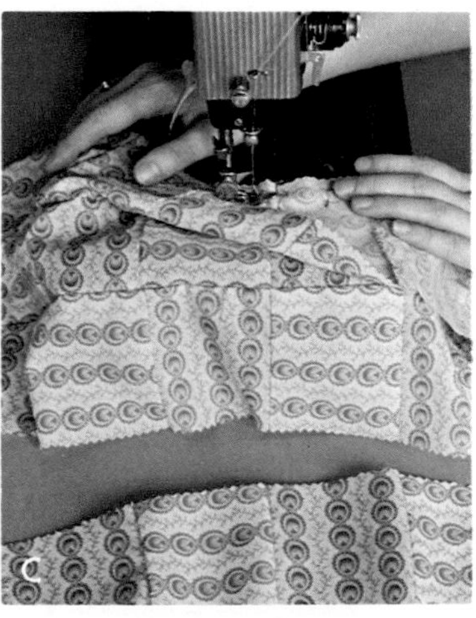

Quick and Easy Patchwork for Beginners

(shown on pages 8 and 9)

Everything shown on pages 8 and 9 is easily within your creative reach, even if you've never done patchwork before. The secret is to start with a simple project and gradually work up to more complex designs. But here are instructions for projects you can accomplish with ease.

Patchwork Quilt

This colorful quilt is a snap. First, decide on the size of the finished quilt, then determine how many squares to cut by dividing that measurement by three or four—the size of your squares. When cutting any kind of patchwork, be sure to add ¼-inch seam allowances to all measurements.

Lay out your patchwork squares on the floor and arrange them in a color and pattern placement that appeals to you. Then sew squares together to form rows. When all the rows are finished, sew them together for the completed quilt top. Use a sheet for backing fabric, or cut and piece yard goods to the proper size. When the backing is ready and pressed, lay it on the floor, wrong side up. Cover it first with quilt batting and put your completed quilt top on it, right side up. Pin and baste according to the instructions on page 43.

The quilt we show on pages 8 and 9 has been machine quilted. Instructions for this method of quilting appear on page 44. Follow them and quilt your project with diagonal lines through each square from corner to corner. When the quilting is done, the edges of the quilt may be finished in whatever method you choose. One of the simplest ways for beginners to finish quilt edges is to sew wide bias tape to the quilt top, right sides together. Trim excess batting and backing, and turn the tape to the back side. Slip-stitch down.

Hearts and Flowers Pillow

What a fitting name for the 16-inch pillow diagrammed below. It's created from small-print floral fabric with a heart appliqué added to the center block.

To make this pillow, enlarge the pattern below. Then gather your materials, being sure all fabrics you select are preshrunk and pressed wrinkle-free.

When cutting fabrics, remember the ¼-inch seam allowance on all edges.

Cut each piece of the patchwork according to the drawing below, then assemble. First, machine appliqué the heart to the large light colored square in the center of the pillow.

Then add the two print pieces to the sides of the center square, and sew on the top and bottom pieces. For the next fabric border, sew the top and bottom strips to the pillow, then add the two side pieces.

For the outside border, sew the small squares to each end of two of the strips and set aside. Sew the remaining outer strips to the sides of the pillow top. Then add the strips and squares to the top and bottom of the pillow. Make sure the squares line up with the strips at the sides. Press all seams open.

Cut backing fabric the size of the pillow cover. Place the two

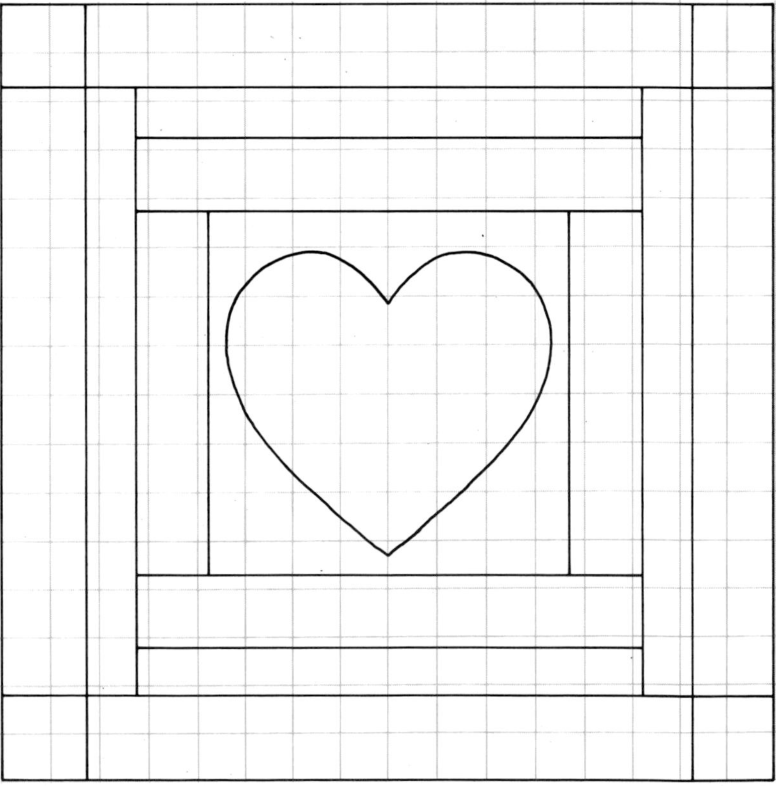

1 Square = 1 Inch

together, right sides facing, and sew on three sides. Clip the corners and turn the pillow cover right side out. Press lightly.

Insert a foam pillow form through the opening in the cover. Fold under the raw edges of the opening, pin closed, and sew edges together with neat slipstitches.

School House Pillow

To create a project that has great effect for a minimum of effort, make this attractive design. This famous patchwork-appliqué pattern is twice as easy if you machine appliqué the design to the pillow top.

Start by enlarging the pattern below. Cut out a paper pattern and lay it on the appliqué fabric. Then trace around the pattern on the right side of the fabric. When cutting appliqué, be sure to include a ¼-inch turn-under allowance on all edges.

Cut the background fabric to the desired size and center the appliqué design on the pillow top. Pin and baste securely. Complete instructions for machine appliqué are given on page 76. Follow them to complete the appliqué of the schoolhouse.

To make the ruffle, cut a strip of fabric twice the width of the finished ruffle and add ½ inch for seams. The fabric strip should be twice as long as the total of the four sides of the pillow.

Fold the strip in half lengthwise, wrong sides together. Then, follow the instructions given on page 47; gather and join the strip. Pin the ruffle to the pillow top so the raw edges of the ruffle line up with the raw edges of the pillow top. Sew in place.

Cut the pillow back the same size as the top. Lay on top of the pillow cover and the ruffle, right sides together, and sew on three sides only. Make sure the ruffle is inside and doesn't get caught in the seam. Clip the corners and turn the cover right side out. Insert a foam pillow form and stitch opening closed.

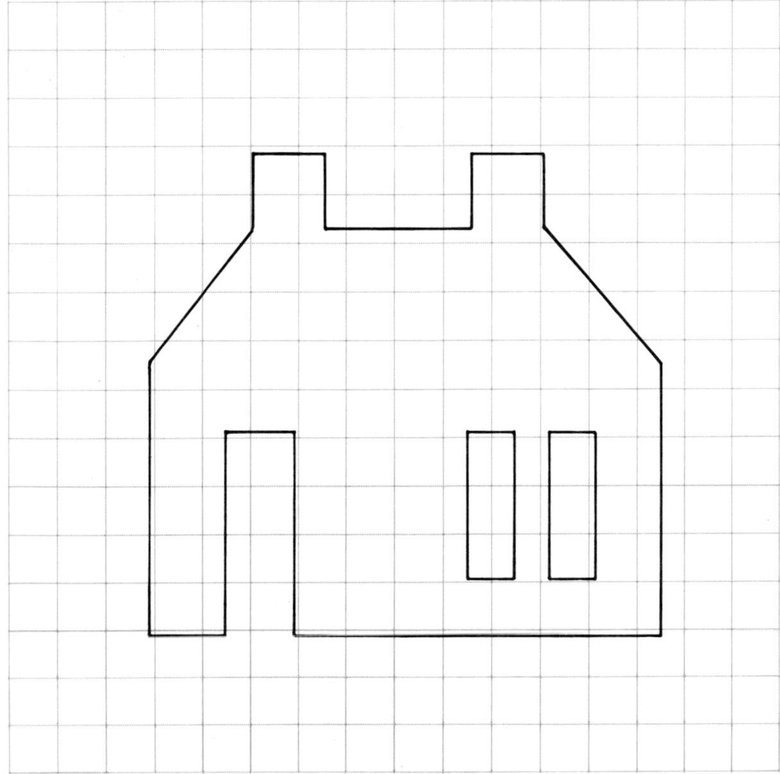

1 Square=1 Inch

Patchwork Place Mats

Place mats can be as simple or as complex as you want to make them. For openers, keep the patchwork easy. One of the mats shown on pages 8 and 9 is nothing more than two rectangular strips of print fabric sewn together in an L-shape and appliquéd to a floral print place mat.

The second of the place mats features several more rectangular strips joined in "log cabin" fashion. Though it looks complicated, it doesn't have to be.

Start with a center square or rectangle. Add pieces to the sides, top and bottom. Continue this procedure until your patchwork has reached the size you desire.

If you find your patchwork is square and you want to create a rectangular place mat, simply add vertical strips to either side to change the shape from square to rectangular.

When sewing place mats, remember they should be lined. Any patchwork project that will be washed repeatedly should have a backing fabric to keep the raw edges from raveling. You might also want to pad your place mats with a layer of batting or fleece.

Napkins can add still more color to your patchwork place mats. If you piece them, be sure to line them, too. Or, you may simply hem squares of print fabric coordinated with the place mats.

Quick and Easy Patchwork Place Mats

Patchwork place mats are a great way to use up odd scraps of fabrics left over from sewing. Since mats usually measure 12x18 or 20 inches, each piece can be quite small, giving you the chance to make use of even the tiniest bits of fabric. Combine a variety of prints and the mats will fit nicely into any table decorating scheme.

Materials

Pattern paper
Fabric for patches
1 yard 45-inch-wide cotton (lining for four mats)
1 yard polyester fleece (optional padding)

Directions

Cut a piece of paper 12x18 inches and mark it into six or eight large rectangles. Use a heavy wax pencil or a felt marker so the lines are bold. Then, within each rectangle, break the space up into smaller rectangles of different sizes. Number each small shape. On a second piece of the same size paper, make a tracing of the pattern to use as a guide while you are assembling the mat.

Cut the original pattern apart and use each piece as a cutting guide. Remember to add ¼-inch seam allowances to all sides of the pieces as you cut them. When all the pieces from one of the larger areas have been cut out, sew them together into a block. Press the seams and set the block aside. Repeat the same procedure for each of the other large blocks, referring to your pattern tracing whenever necessary. Then join the blocks together to form the finished top.

Cut a piece of lining fabric the same size as the pieced top. Stitch the lining to the top, right sides together, in a ¼-inch seam. Leave six inches open along one side for turning. For a padded mat, add a layer of fleece on top of the lining before sewing lining and top together. Then stitch as for an unpadded mat. Clip the corners of the mat, turn it right side out, and press. Slip-stitch the opening closed.

If you've padded the mat, you might want to machine stitch along the seams between the blocks to quilt it. This takes a little extra effort, but the result is a firmer place mat.

Quick and Easy Patchwork Tablecloth

If you can sew a straight seam, you can create this charming patchwork tablecloth. Four-inch squares come together in a hodgepodge of patterns in this practical and pretty bit of patchwork for your table. Add a demi-ruffle of eyelet for a touch of country elegance, then just see how well this table cover fits into any easygoing eating area.

Materials
Lightweight cardboard
Fabric for patches
Ruffled eyelet trim
Lining fabric

Directions
Make this patchwork tablecloth any desired size. First, decide on the finished size, then divide the width by four to determine how many squares wide your patchwork will be. Likewise, divide the length by four to find how many rows of squares you'll need. If necessary, add or subtract a few inches on length and width to make even multiples of four. Then make a cardboard template for cutting the squares.

Since the finished squares are 4x4 inches and you'll have to allow a ¼-inch seam allowance, cut a piece of cardboard 4½x4½ inches. If your cloth is large and requires a great number of squares, cut several templates. Then you can replace worn templates and avoid cutting blocks that aren't perfectly square. Place your fabric wrong side up, then lay on the template and trace around it. Cut along the penciled lines. If you're cutting squares from large lengths of fabric, you can avoid drawing every square by cutting a long 4½-inch-wide strip, then dividing the strip into 4½-inch squares.

Sew squares together to form rows, then sew the rows together to create the completed table cover. Pin ruffled eyelet to the edges, right sides together, and machine stitch ⅛ inch in from edge. Cut lining fabric to the finished size of the tablecloth. Place the lining and patchwork together, right sides facing and with the ruffle inside. Sew ¼ inch in all around the edges, leaving an opening on one side. Turn, press, and slip-stitch the opening closed.

Quick and Easy Patchwork Lounging Mat

A soft and sittable lounge mat like this one is as much at home indoors as it is out on the sun deck or patio. And it's a natural for children's summertime slumber parties too—comfortable, but lightweight and easy to tote almost anywhere.

Materials

1½ yards each of two solid colors and two complementary print fabrics
2 twin-size polyester quilt batts

Directions

Cut the fabric into thirty-four 6x36-inch strips. Sew pairs of strips together to form open-ended tubes. To do this, place two strips of fabric right sides together and pin securely. Sew up the long sides in ½-inch seams, but leave the short ends open. When you have completed 17 tubes, turn and press them and arrange them in an appealing sequence. Then overlap the adjoining long edges about ½ inch and topstitch them together. For a strong mat, sew two rows of stitches, each close to the folded edge, so the tubes are joined in what looks like a flat-fell seam.

Cut pieces of polyester batting 15x36 inches, and fold each one in thirds lengthwise. Pull a roll of batting through each tube to stuff the mat. Then machine baste across the ends of the tubes, being sure to catch the batting in the stitching. Trim the fabric and the batting close to the basting stitches.

Make long ties to hold the mat when it's rolled up. First, cut four strips of fabric approximately 6x50 inches. Then sew pairs of strips together, right sides facing, and make a diagonal seam across one end. Leave the other end open. Turn and press.

Open the long seam five inches in the center of one of the end tubes of the mat. Insert the raw edges of the ties and topstitch the seam closed. Bind the edges of the mat with 2½-inch-wide strips of one of the fabrics used for the tubes.

Quick and Easy Patchwork Chair Pad

For a room with several pretty prints, why not create a patchwork chair pad to bring them all together in a delightful medley of patterns? For the contemporary rocker featured at left, blue and white print fabrics combine nicely to provide the chair with a custom cover that's easy to stitch—and economical, too. This same style patching can work wonders in rejuvenating a favorite antique chair as well.

Materials
Assorted prints for patchwork
Solid color fabric for backing
Heavy canvas
Polyester quilt batting
or fleece

Directions
To start your chair pad, determine the size of the sling. Then cut a piece of heavy canvas to this size, adding five extra inches on each end for fitting over the frame and tacking down.

Plan your patchwork top so it will be the same length but one inch wider than the canvas. Decide on the size of your squares and make a template for them, adding ¼-inch seam allowance if you wish. Cut squares of print fabrics and sew them together into rows. Then stitch the rows together to form the cover.

Cut a piece of backing fabric the same size as the finished patchwork. Cut a layer of polyester fleece or quilt batting the same size as the canvas. For more padding, cut several layers.

Place the backing fabric on the floor, wrong side up. Lay the canvas on top of it, and the padding over the canvas. Then add the top, right side up. Baste all layers together. Quilt or tie the layers together. For quilting, machine stitch along the seams between the squares. Use a heavy needle and stitch slowly so as not to break or bend the needle. For tying, use pearl cotton threaded into a needle. Take a small stitch through all layers in the corners of the squares. Knot the threads and cut off the excess.

To finish the edges, fold the top over the canvas, then fold under the edge of the backing. Slip-stitch the side edges closed. Machine stitch along the edges, and attach cover to the frame.

Quick and Easy Patchwork Quilt and Shams

There's nothing more traditional-looking than a patchwork quilt made of squares and triangles. And the very nicest part of the quilt shown here is that it's not nearly as difficult as it may seem. The secret is to sew four triangles to each square, forming a large block. Once the blocks are sewn, the quilt top is pieced exactly as if you were working with single squares. It's the arrangement of colors and prints that makes a quilt like this so spectacular.

Materials

3 yards 45-inch-wide black print fabric
3½ yards 45-inch-wide green fabric
4¼ yards 45-inch-wide white fabric
7 yards backing fabric
Yellow knitting worsted
Polyester batting

Directions

To create the quilt you see here, cut 29 10-inch squares of black print fabric. Cut six 10-inch squares of green fabric. From white fabric, cut 72 triangles measuring 7x7x10 inches. Cut 68 triangles of the same size from green fabric. The measurements given above do not include seam allowances, so cut ¼ inch extra on all edges.

Sew triangles on each side of a square to form blocks. You'll need 17 blocks with black print squares and green triangles; 12 blocks with black print squares and white triangles; and six blocks with green squares and white triangles.

Sew four separate rows of five blocks alternating black and white blocks with black and green blocks. Start and end with black and white blocks. Sew three rows of five blocks alternating black and green blocks with green and white blocks. Start and end these rows with black and green blocks.

Sew rows in alternate color schemes together to form the completed quilt top. Piece backing fabric to the right size and assemble the top, batting, and backing according to the instructions on page 43. With yellow washable knitting worsted, tie the layers together where the green and white triangles meet.

To make pillow shams or covers, decrease the size of the squares and triangles. For a snug-fitting cover, cut squares 4¼x4¼ inches (add seam allowances) and triangles 3x3x4¼ inches. For a loose-fitting cover, cut squares 5x5 inches, and triangles 3½x3½x5 inches.

Cut 12 squares and 48 triangles. Make each cover with three rows of four blocks each. Assemble the covers in the same way as the quilt. Use backing fabric for backs of covers.

Quick and Easy Patchwork Comforter

One of the easiest ways to create the soft, inviting look of a puffy comforter is to make the quilt of separate little pillows, each stuffed to give you the degree of "puff" you're after. The quilt on this page shows you a foolproof method of making a pre-stuffed cover.

Materials

Fabric patches in sufficient quantity for desired size quilt
Pillow stuffing or batting

Directions

When determining quilt size, be sure the dimensions are divisible by a number that gives you a comfortable size pillow to work with. For example, the length and width of your quilt should be divisible by four if you want a quilt made of four-inch pillows.

To make each pillow, cut fabric the same width and twice the length of the planned pillow, plus the ¼-inch seam allowances. So, for a 4-inch pillow, cut fabric 4½x8½ inches. Fold the fabric in half, right sides together. Sew two sides and part of the third. Clip the corners and turn. Make sure corners are fully pushed out and square.

Stuff pillows with pillow stuffing or one or more layers of quilt batting cut to size. Then turn under the raw edges and slipstitch the opening closed. Make as many pillows as you need for your quilt.

Assemble the quilt first by laying the pillows on the floor in an attractive arrangement. Then make a squared diagram on paper, assigning numbers to each square to represent a pillow. Pin numbered pieces of paper to the pillows and store them in a convenient place as you work. When you're ready for a pillow, find the one with the right number and sew it in its assigned place.

Join pillows by slip-stitching. Overlap the edges of two pillows ⅜-inch and stitch across the top surface, then turn the pillows over and sew across the back. Two rows of stitching are needed to make the quilt strong and durable.

Once the quilt begins to take shape, decide which surface will be the top so the stitching is consistent—first across the top, then the back. When all the pillows are sewn together, the quilt is finished.

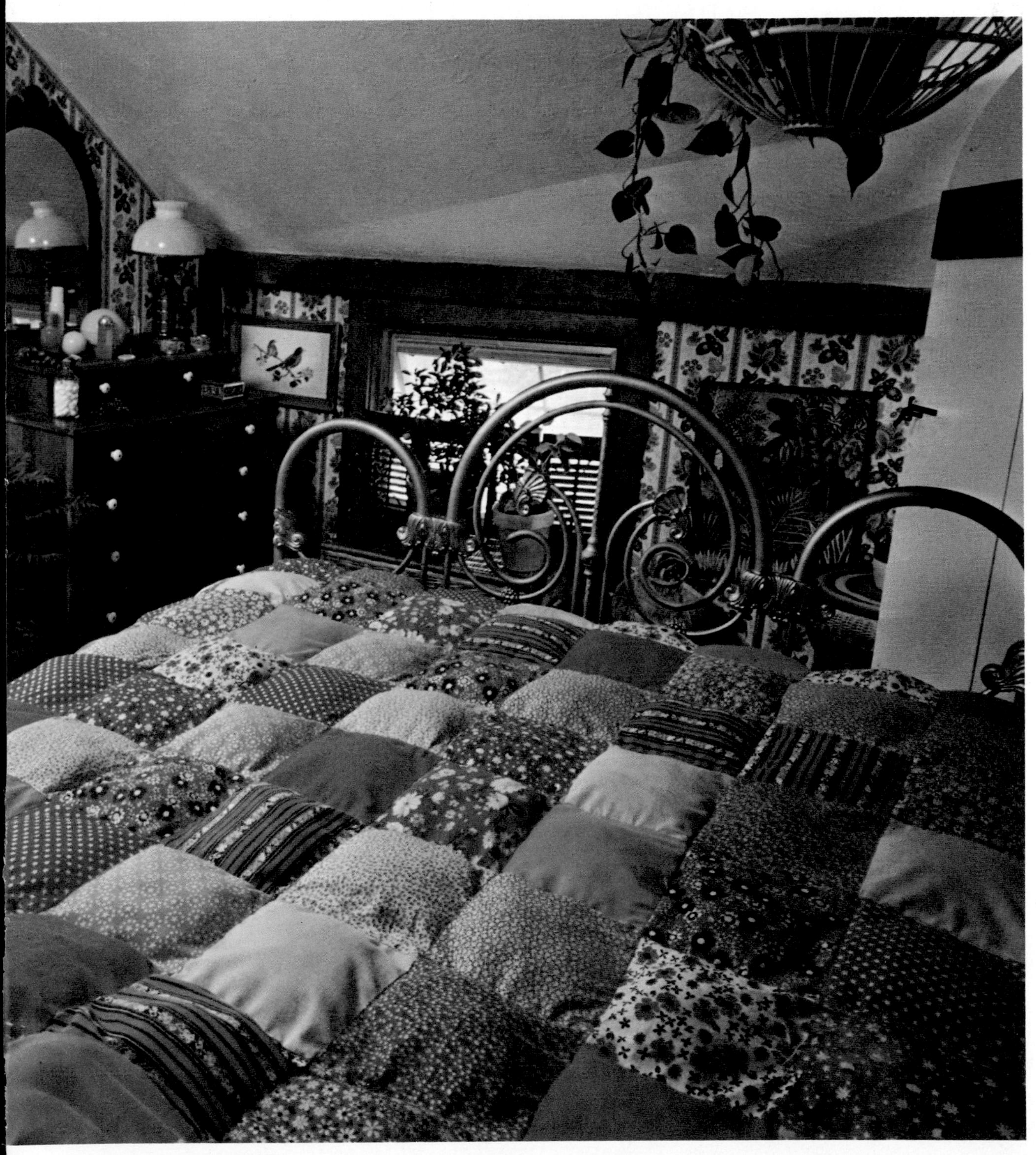

Pieced Patchwork—

A Kaleidoscope of Patterns

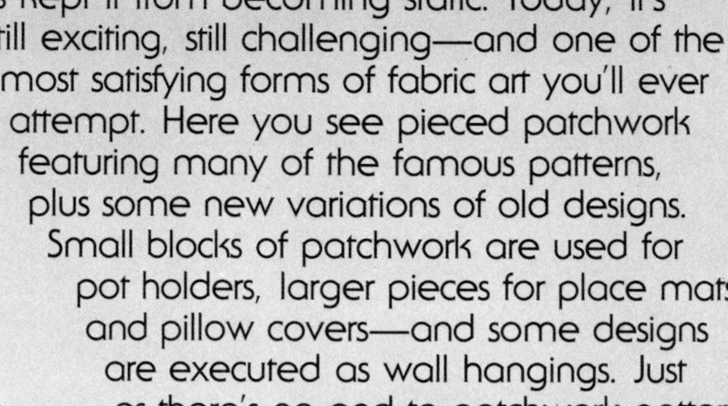

For several hundred years now, quilters have been putting together bits of fabric to come up with new and different patterns each time they "pieced." One small change in the arrangement of the pieces—or in the color relationship of the pieces—and a brand-new design emerged. And it's this chameleon-like quality about patchwork that has kept it from becoming static. Today, it's still exciting, still challenging—and one of the most satisfying forms of fabric art you'll ever attempt. Here you see pieced patchwork featuring many of the famous patterns, plus some new variations of old designs. Small blocks of patchwork are used for pot holders, larger pieces for place mats and pillow covers—and some designs are executed as wall hangings. Just as there's no end to patchwork patterns, there's no end to what you can do with the pieced patchwork you make. Complete instructions for all projects shown on these two pages begin on page 26.

SINGER

A Kaleidoscope of Patterns—Attic Windows

Attic Windows is a versatile and easy-to-piece pattern that adapts beautifully to a variety of projects. The scale and repeat of the pattern are suitable for small projects like pillows and place mats, but are equally effective on larger projects such as curtains and quilts. The handsome framed wall hanging shown on page 25 and detailed in the diagram at right is composed of 20 four-inch-square Attic Window blocks arranged in five rows of four blocks each.

Materials

¼ yard 45-inch-wide fabric in colors A, B, and C
16x20-inch double-weight poster board
Fabric glue
16x20-inch picture frame

Attic Windows

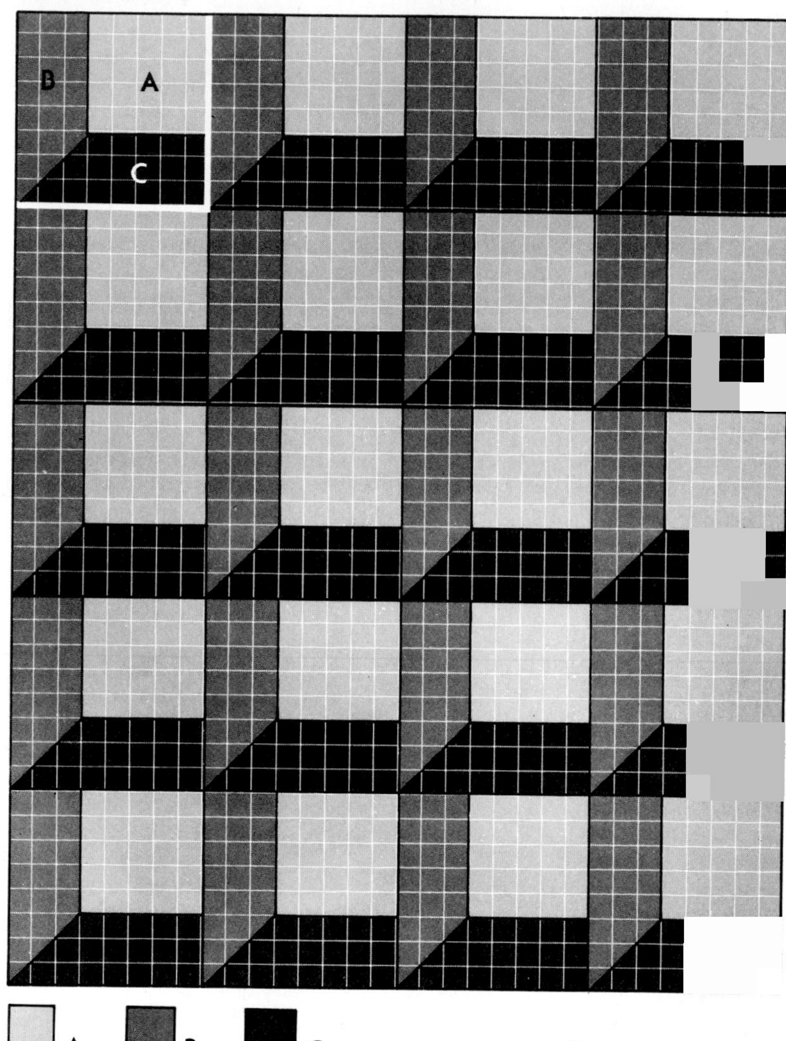

Directions

Enlarge the above pattern to size, and cut 20 squares from fabric A. Cut 20 pieces each of fabrics B and C. Be sure to add a ¼-inch seam allowance around all pattern pieces.

Construct 20 blocks by sewing color B along one side of the square of fabric A. Then add the C piece to form a four-inch square. Press seams open. Join four squares together in a row. Make five rows and join them together to form the completed hanging. Apply fabric glue to the outer ¼-inch edges of the poster board and to the seam allowances where the blocks are joined. With the patchwork face down on a hard, clean, smooth surface, center the glued side of the board and press it in place. Insert the patchwork-covered board in the 16x20-inch frame and hang.

Joseph's Coat

Joseph's Coat

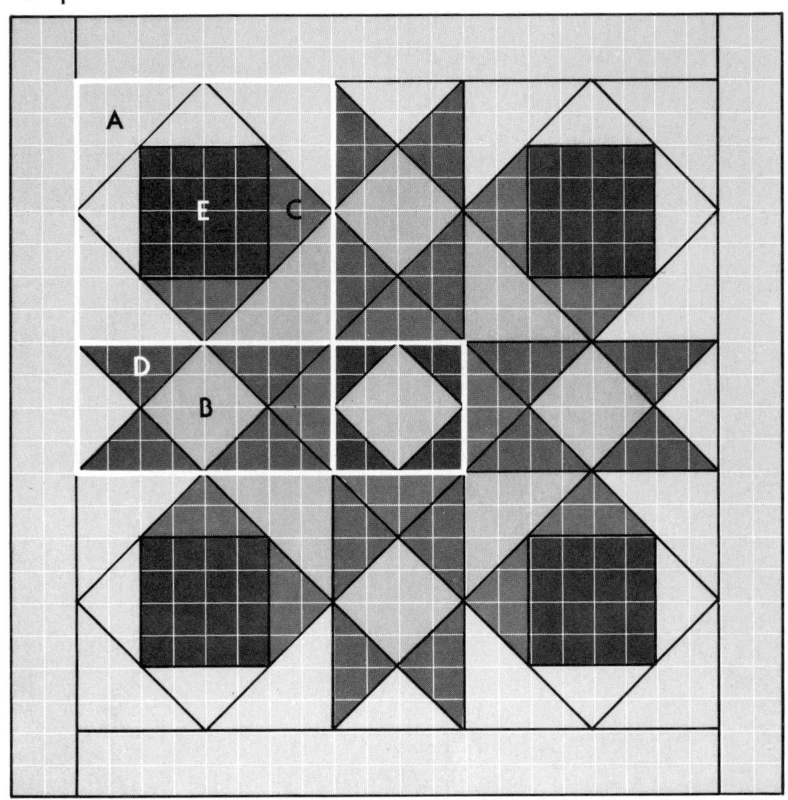

1 Square=1 Inch

Joseph's Coat is a striking pattern composed entirely of triangles and squares. The piecing of one 20-inch-square block of this pattern is intricate and requires precision stitching, but even a single completed block has great impact when mounted on the front of a 24-inch-square pillow (shown at far left on page 24).

Materials
1½ yards 45-inch fabric in color A
Scraps of fabrics B, C, D, E
24-inch pillow form
Quilt batting

Directions
Enlarge and follow the above diagram for pattern pieces and color placement. Cut all pieces with ¼-inch seam allowances. Start assembling pillow top by sewing two small A triangles and two C triangles to each of the four E squares, making larger squares. To each of these, sew three large A triangles and one B triangle. (Check diagram for placement.) To one B square, add the four E triangles and set aside. Next, piece four rectangular blocks consisting of six triangles and one B square. Join all the assembled blocks to form the "Joseph's coat" pattern shown here. To opposite sides of the finished square, add the shorter border strips, then add the longer ones.

Pin the completed top to a 21x21-inch piece of batting and quilt according to instructions beginning on page 43. Padding is smaller than the pillow top, so center it carefully. Outline quilt on all of the color B pieces and the color E squares. Cut a piece of backing 25x25 inches from fabric A. Attach the backing to the pillow top, right sides together. Leave an 18-inch opening on one side for turning. Do not clip corners. Instead, make a box seam two inches deep at each corner. Turn the pillow right side out and insert a 24-inch pillow form. Blindstitch the opening closed.

A Kaleidoscope of Patterns—Lisa's Choice

(continued)

Lisa's Choice is the traditional pattern used in the 16-inch-square wall hanging shown in the upper left-hand corner of page 25. Worked predominantly in two shades of one color (greens, in our sample), the star portion of the pattern takes on a strong dimensional effect. The basic pieced unit may be repeated any number of times to make a pillow, a tablecloth, or a quilt. For example, 20 of these 16-inch-square blocks will yield a quilt approximately 64x80 inches (four units wide by five units long).

Materials

Scraps of fabric in five colors
½ yard fabric for backing and hanging loops
Quilt batting

Lisa's Choice

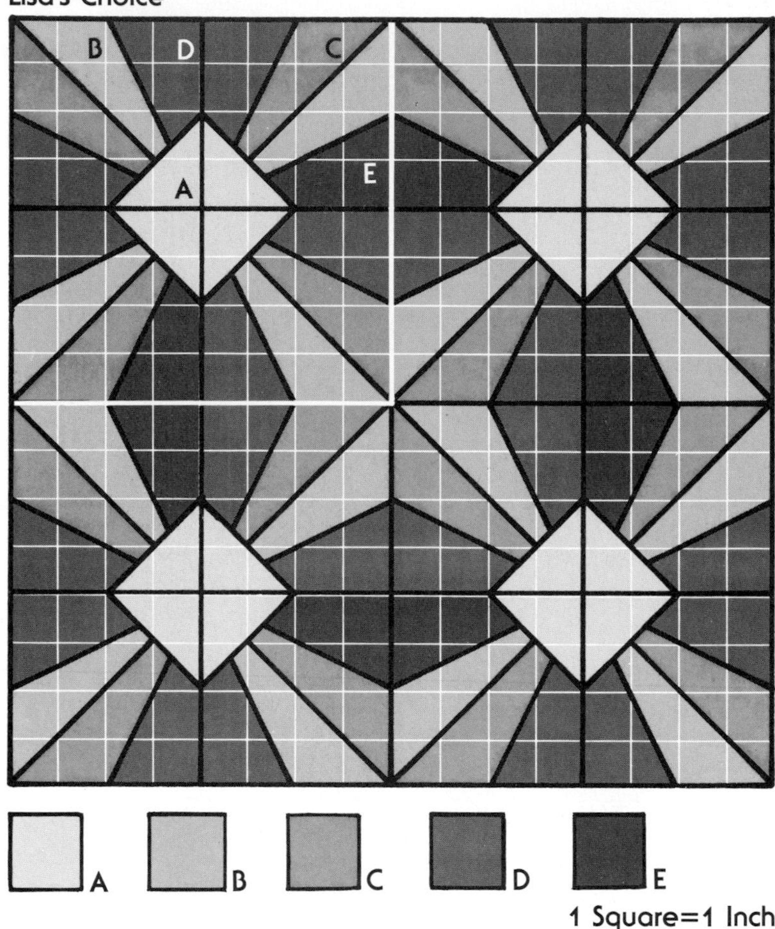

Directions

Enlarge the drawing to size and make a template for each shape. Add seam allowances. Cut 16 triangles in color A and 16 pieces each in B and C. Cut 24 D pieces. Cut four E pieces, then reverse the pattern and cut four more E pieces so you have four right-side and four left-side shapes. To piece Lisa's Choice, join B and C pieces along the long side. To eight of these pairs, add D to both the B and C sides. To four, add a D piece to the C side and an E to the B side. To four, add a D to the B side and an E to the C side. Now add an A triangle to each group to form four-inch squares. Arrange the blocks according to the diagram and piece four squares together into a row. Make four rows, then join the four rows to complete the basic block.

To make the block into a wall hanging, cut a piece of batting 17x17 inches and a piece of backing fabric the same size. Cut three hanging loops twice the desired width and length of the finished folded loop, plus seam allowances. Fold in half lengthwise. Stitch and turn. Press and position loops on patchwork face. Join pieced top, batting, and backing according to instructions beginning on page 43.

Galaxy

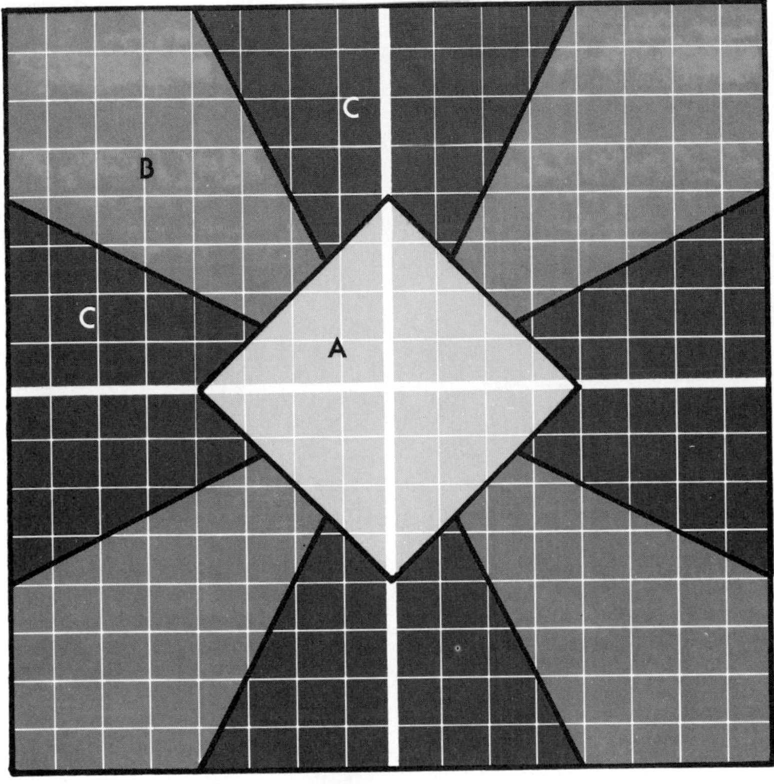

A B C

1 Square=1/2 Inch

The Galaxy pattern shown at left is another traditional quilt pattern that is equally handsome when used as a single block, or repeated across the length and breadth of a whole quilt. The pattern may be executed in solids (as illustrated in the rust, brown and green pot holder shown in the lower left-hand corner on page 24), but would look particularly striking pieced in a combination of prints and solids.

Materials

Scraps of fabric in three colors of your choice
¼ yard fabric for backing and loop
Quilt batting or polyester fleece

Directions

Enlarge the diagram to size and transfer the pattern pieces to paper or lightweight cardboard. Cut four triangles of color A and four pattern pieces of B. Cut eight pieces of C, four on the right side of the fabric, then reverse the pattern and cut four more so you have right-side and left-side pieces. Cut all pieces with a ¼-inch seam allowance.

Join the pieces by sewing a left- and a right-hand piece in color C to each side of the four pieces of color B. To these add a triangle, A, forming a four-inch square. Join the four squares according to the above diagram to form one block of the Galaxy pattern.

To make the block into a pot holder, cut 9x9-inch squares of fleece or quilt batting and of backing fabric. Baste patchwork to batting or fleece. Cut a 1x4-inch fabric strip for a loop. Fold it lengthwise, right sides together, and stitch. Turn the loop and pin it to a corner on the right side of the top. Stitch top to backing fabric, right sides together. Leave an opening for turning. Trim padding close to the seam line. Turn the pot holder and slip-stitch the opening closed. Quilt the pot holder following the instructions beginning on page 43.

A Kaleidoscope of Patterns—Seven Old Favorites

(continued)

Magic Cubes 1 Square=1 Inch

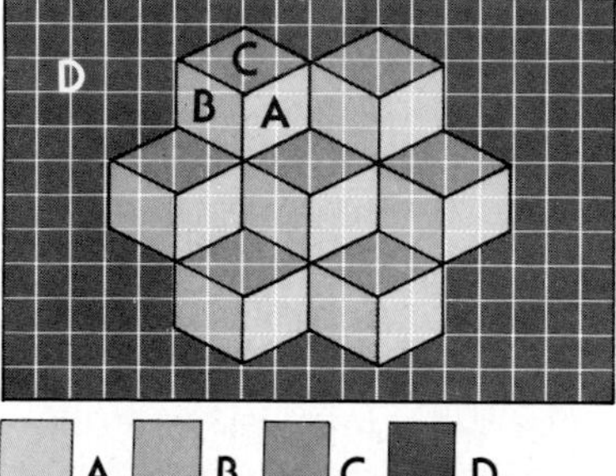

King's Cross 1 Square=3/4 Inch

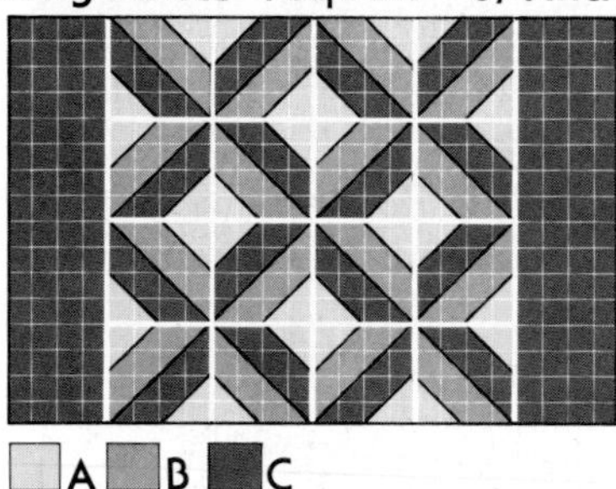

Sister's Choice 1 Square = 1 Inch

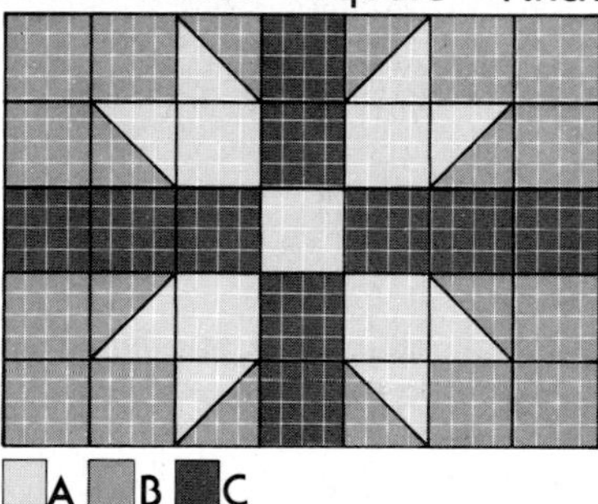

Rivoli Cross 1 Square=3/4 Inch

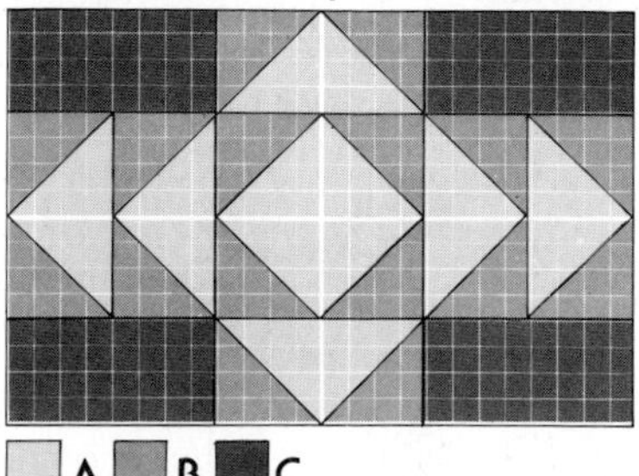

Here's an assortment of popular pieced patterns to add to your patchwork repertoire.

Magic Cubes

This pattern is a natural as an appliqué for a place mat (as shown on page 24) or for many other interesting projects. Enlarge the diagram and cut the pieces from colors of your choice. Be sure to add ¼-inch seam allowances.

Start by sewing the color A diamonds to the color B diamonds. Add the C diamonds to form seven hexagons. Then join the hexagons to form one large "magic cube" patch: Starting with a center hexagon, add the others clockwise.

Cut two pieces of D background fabric 14x20 inches. Cut batting to match. Center the patchwork on one piece of background fabric and machine-appliqué according to instructions on page 76. Baste the appliquéd top and batting together. Then sew backing to top, right sides together, leaving an opening for turning. Trim batting, turn, and press. Slip-stitch the opening closed and quilt following the instructions on pages 43 and 44.

King's Cross

For a striking place mat (shown on page 24), enlarge the diagram at left and cut 32 triangles of color A and 16 trapezoids each of B and C. Cut two 3¾x12¾-inch pieces of fabric C. Cut backing and batting 13x19 inches.

First join the B and C trapezoids along their long bases. Add an A triangle to the top of each trapezoid, forming a three-inch square. Arrange the squares in rows of four, so B and C trapezoids touch, then piece rows to form a 12-inch square. Add C strips to two sides, completing the top. Baste top and batting, and then stitch top to back, right sides together, leaving an opening for turning. Trim batting, turn, and slip-stitch closed. Machine-quilt according to instructions on page 44.

Sister's Choice

To make the patchwork bath mat shown on page 25, first enlarge the pattern at left. Then cut eight triangles each of colors A and B, five squares of A, 12 of B, and 10 of C. Cut batting and backing 21x29 inches.

Join pieces by sewing A triangles to B triangles to form squares. Follow the diagram and piece seven rows of five squares each. Join rows to complete the bath mat top. Press seams open.

Baste the completed top to the batting. Place the backing fabric on the bath mat top, right sides together, and stitch around the edges, leaving an opening. Trim batting close to stitching. Turn and slip-stitch opening closed.

Following instructions on page 44, outline-quilt the five areas of color A and the four rectangles of color C.

Rivoli Cross

A single unit of this pattern also makes a lovely place mat (see page 24). Enlarge the diagram at lower left and cut pattern pieces, adding seam allowances. Cut backing and batting to 13x19 inches.

Join the long side of each B triangle to the short sides of each A triangle to form rectangles, then sew two pairs of these into 6-inch squares. To each square, attach the C rectangles to make the ends of the mat. Then sew two rectangles along the long sides of the A triangles to form the center of the mat. Add remaining rectangles to each side of the center. Join side sections to center. Attach backing as for other place mats.

Hexagon Flower

While this pattern makes an interesting quilt, a single hexagon flower is charming as a pot holder. To make one, enlarge the diagram at upper right and make patterns for the pieces, adding ¼-inch seam allowances.

Cut six hexagons in color A and one in color B. Cut six diamonds in color C. Use one of the three colors for backing and cut this piece and batting approximately 9x10 inches.

Piece the six color A hexagons to the B hexagon, one at a time, working in a clockwise direction. Add the six C diamonds to complete the top. Make a hanging loop of the fabric you've chosen for the backing.

Pin and baste together the pieced top and the batting. Place the loop on the right side of the pot holder with the raw edges of the loop lined up with the raw edges of the top. Then place the backing fabric on the patchwork, right sides together. Sew around the edges, leaving an opening for turning. Trim batting close to seam line, turn, and slip-stitch the opening.

Machine-quilt along the outlines of the pieces, following the instructions on page 44.

Hexagon Star

To make the pillow shown on page 25, enlarge the drawing at center right and make patterns for the pieces. Cut six triangles of color A, six of B, and 12 of C. Cut 12 trapezoids of color A, six of B, and six of C. Cut with ¼-inch seam allowances. Cut batting and backing fabric to 20x 21 inches.

Piece the triangles to the shorter base of the trapezoids as follows: B triangles to C trapezoids; C triangles to A trapezoids; A triangles to B trapezoids. Join the resulting triangles in rows following the diagram, then join the rows together to complete the top.

Baste the completed top to a piece of batting and quilt the two layers. Follow the basic quilting instructions beginning on page 42. The pillow shown has concentric rows of quilting ³/₈-inch apart to fill the two central hexagonal areas. After quilting, complete the pillow by joining the backing fabric to the front. Place the two right sides together, and stitch around the edges, leaving an opening for turning; turn. Stuff with pillow stuffing. Stitch the opening closed.

Rolling Star

To make a pillow top of this popular pattern (like the one shown on page 25), enlarge the diagram at lower right. Make templates for the pattern pieces using ¼-inch seam allowances.

Cut eight diamonds from striped fabric and eight diamonds of color A. Cut eight squares and four triangles of color B. Cut two pieces of B 2¼x14 inches. Cut two pieces of A 2¼x14 inches, and two pieces 2¼x15½ inches. Cut pieces of muslin lining and backing fabric 16 inches square.

Piece the striped diamonds together to form an eight-pointed star. Add the color B squares as shown. Next, add color A diamonds, then add the triangles to form a large square. Sew the border pieces of color B to the outside edges. Repeat with color A border pieces to complete pillow top.

Pin the top right side up, to a piece of muslin, and round the corners. If desired, sew piping to the right side of the top. Place backing fabric on pillow top, right sides together. Sew around edges, leaving an opening for turning. Clip corners, turn, and press. Stuff with polyester fiberfill and stitch opening closed.

Flower **1 Square=1 Inch**

A B C

Hexagon Star 1 Square=1 Inch

A B C

Rolling Star 1 Square = 1 Inch

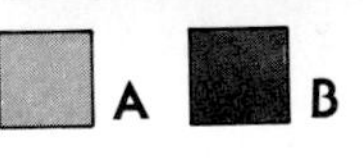

Star Pattern Curtains and Pillow

Want a big-impact project for your home? Then patch a star, like our saw-tooth pattern or classic eight-point design at right. Curtains give you plenty of patchwork charm, without being as time-consuming to make as a quilt or tablecloth. Better yet for a quickie project–try a dazzling star pillow like the one featured at right.

Materials

Cafe Curtains (See *Note.*)
3 yards orange border print
1 yard dark green print
1¾ yards yellow fabric
1 yard striped fabric
1 yard light green print
3½ yards lightweight white cotton (lining)

Pillow
¼ yard striped fabric
¼ yard dark green print
¼ yard light green print
¾ yard orange print
¼ yard yellow fabric
1 14- or 16-inch pillow form

Directions

Saw-tooth Star Curtains

Note: Yardage given is for four 30x30-inch panels. To change measurements, adjust the width of the border strips, add blocks of patchwork, or reduce the size of the pieces within a block.

Enlarge the diagram below and cut square and triangular templates for fabric patches. Preshrink the fabric before cutting. Using the diagram as a cutting and placement guide, cut out fabric pieces. Be sure to add ¼-inch seam allowances to edges before cutting.

Sew triangles together to form squares, then stitch squares together into rows as in the diagram. Press. Stitch rows together into a block, matching crosswise seams. For each panel, join four blocks, using 2½-inch-wide strips of border fabric to separate them. Join the blocks two at a time with a 12½-inch-long strip, then join the two sets of blocks with a 26½-inch-long strip.

Cut a piece of lining fabric the same size as the four-block section and baste it to the blocks. Then, cut two strips of border fabric 4½x26½ inches and stitch them to two opposite sides of the panel. Then cut two 4½x30½-inch strips and sew them to the remaining sides. Fold the border over the raw edges of the panel, turn under ¼ inch, and slip-stitch to the back of the panel.

Eight-point Star Pillow

Enlarge the diagram below and cut square and triangular templates for fabric patches. Using the diagram as a cutting and placement guide, cut out fabric pieces. For the border of a 16-inch pillow, cut two pieces 2½x16½ inches and two pieces 2½x12½ inches. To make a 14-inch pillow, cut strips 1½ inches wide instead.

Sew triangles together into squares. Press. Then lay out all the squares in rows to form the design shown in the drawing. Stitch pieces together one row at a time and press. Then join rows together, matching crosswise seams. Press. Stitch border pieces to block as indicated in the diagram. Back completed pillow top with yellow fabric, insert the pillow, and slip-stitch the cover closed.

Saw-tooth Star

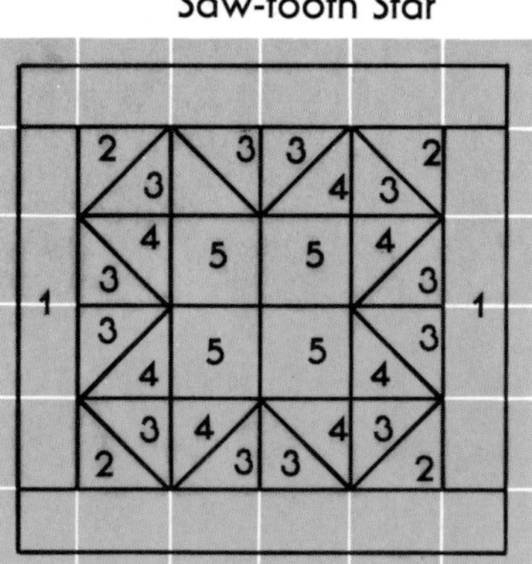

KEY **1 Square = 3 Inches**
1 = Border Print 4 = Stripe
2 = Dk Green Print 5 = Lt Green Print
3 = Yellow

Eight-point Star

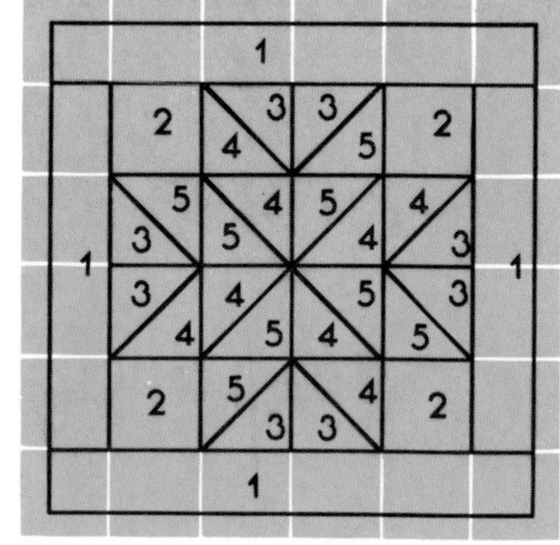

KEY **1 Square = 3 Inches**
1 = Border Stripe 4 = Orange Print
2 = Dk Green Print 5 = Yellow
3 = Lt Green Print

Right: Saw-tooth Star pattern
Far Right: Eight-point Star pattern

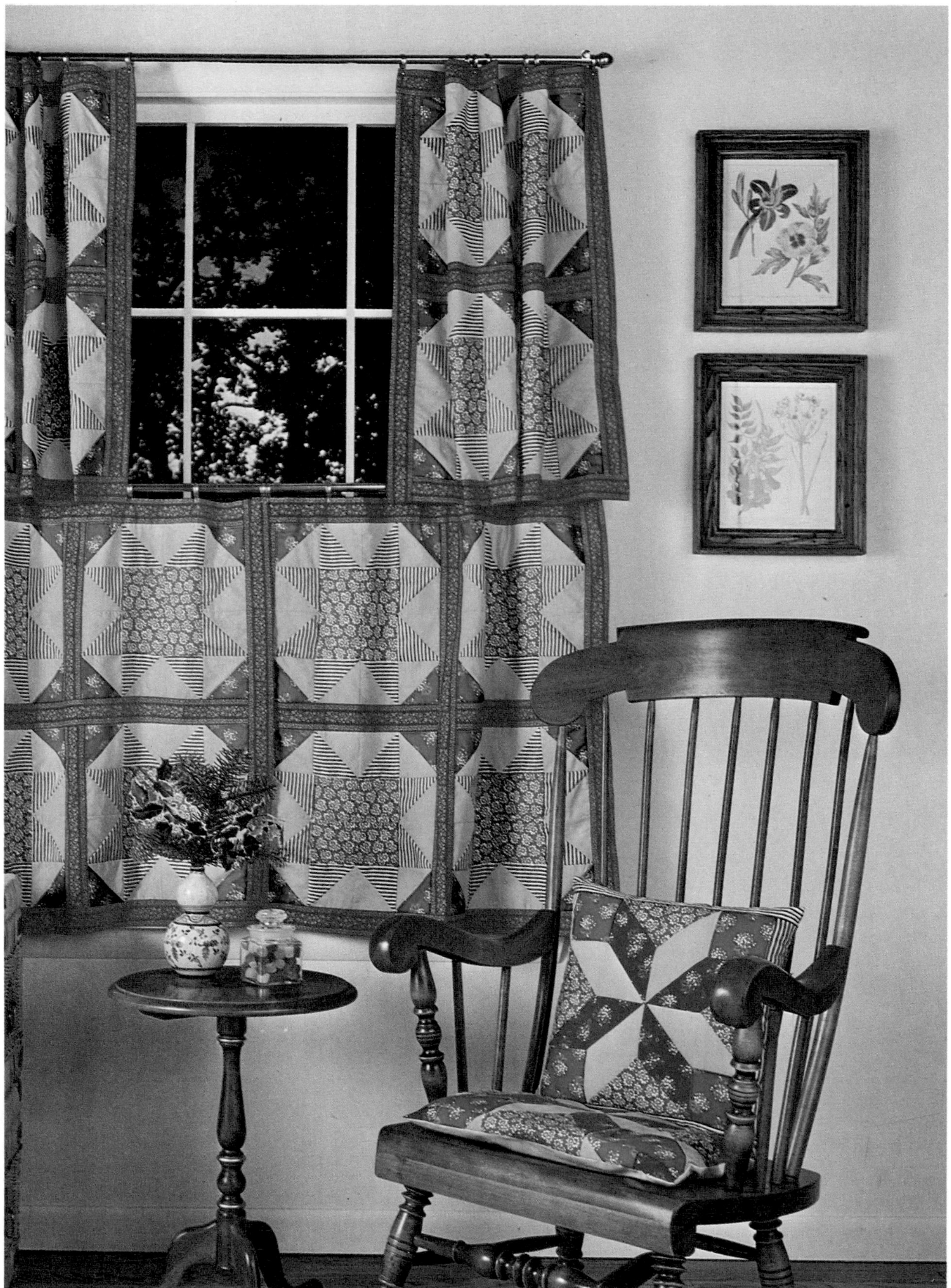

Star Pattern Quilt and Pillow Sham

Parading the colors has never been done more effectively than in this red, white, and blue star pattern quilt with matching pillow shams. Its finished size is about 80x96 inches.

Materials

Quilt

3 yards 36-inch red fabric
4 yards 36-inch white fabric
1¼ yards 45-inch small red and white polka dot fabric
1¼ yards 45-inch small blue and white polka dot fabric
¾ yard 45-inch large blue and white polka dot fabric
6 yards 45-inch backing fabric
Full-size quilt batting
Red, white, or blue embroidery floss (optional)

Pillow Sham

(Directions are on page 39.)
12x15 inches red fabric
¾ yard white fabric
9x14 inches small red and white polka dot fabric
9x14 inches small blue and white polka dot fabric
13x22 inches large blue and white polka dot fabric
⅔ yard red, white, or blue backing fabric

Directions

Star Pattern Quilt

Draw the patterns shown below on sandpaper or lightweight cardboard and cut out to use as templates for the quilt pattern pieces. The ¼-inch seam allowance is included in the dimensions given for the pieces.

Preshrink and press your fabric before you begin measuring and cutting. Straighten the grain of the fabric and be sure lengthwise and crosswise threads are at right angles to each other. When marking fabric for cutting, line up the sides of the squares and the right-angle sides of the triangles with the straight grain of the fabric. On the diamonds, the grain lines should run straight between the points.

Cut 120 diamonds of blue polka dot fabric and 120 of red polka dot fabric. From the white fabric, cut 120 triangles and 120 squares.

To sew your quilt by machine, use mercerized cotton thread and 10 to 12 stitches per inch. To sew by hand, use mercerized cotton thread and sew a running stitch about eight to 10 stitches per inch with a back stitch every two or three inches. Use ¼-inch seam allowances.

continued

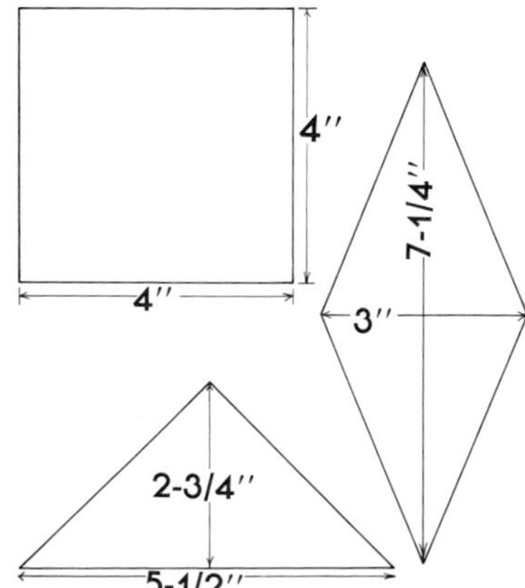

Right: Star-block pattern pieces

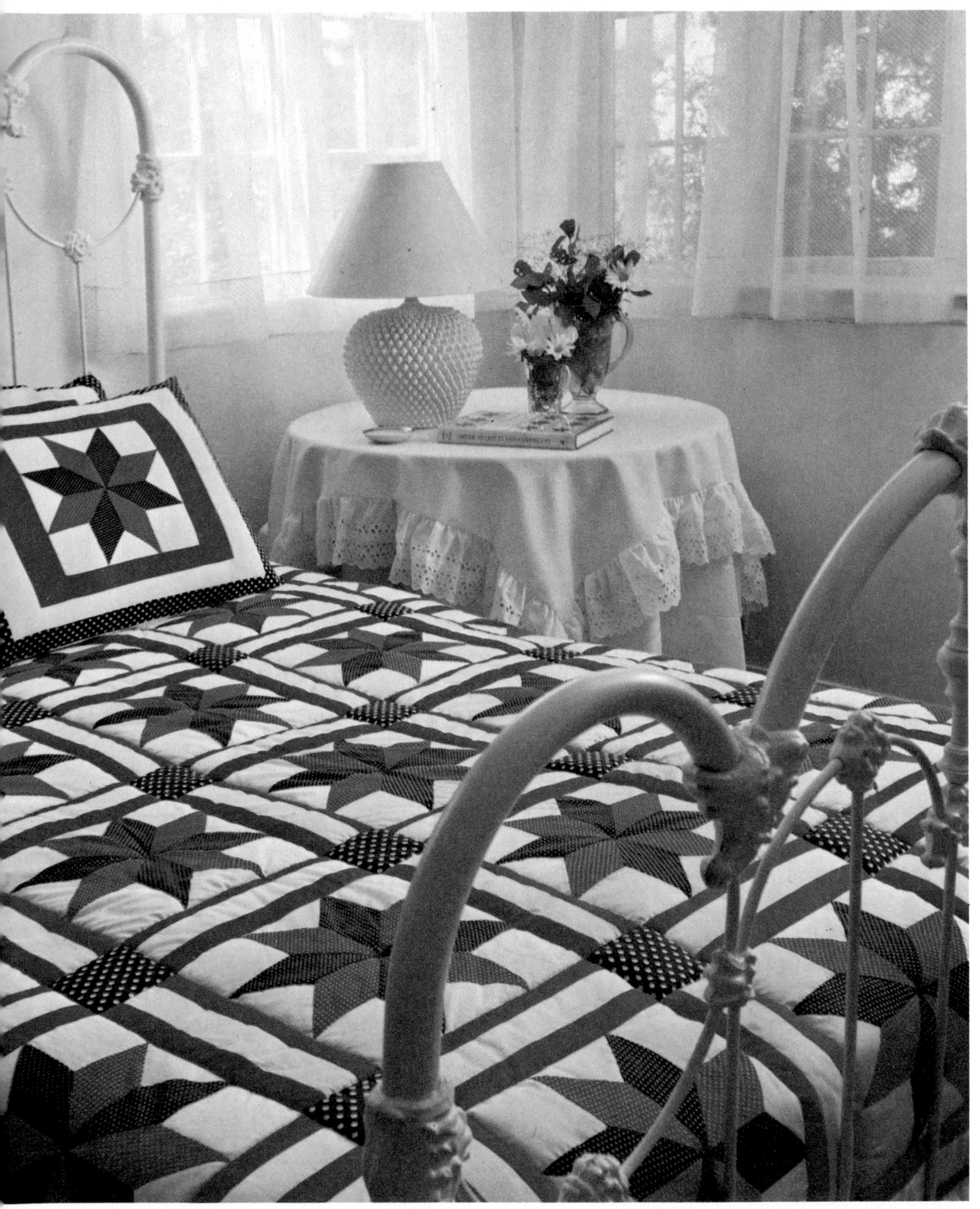

Star Pattern Quilt and Pillow Sham *(continued)*

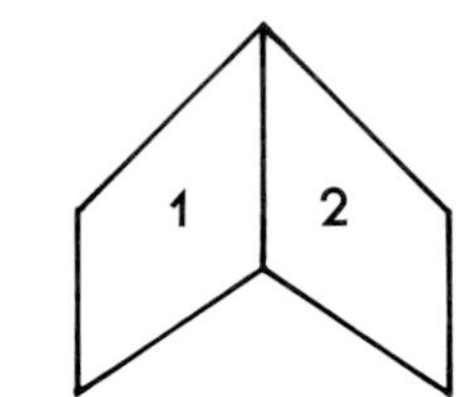

Stitch diamonds together

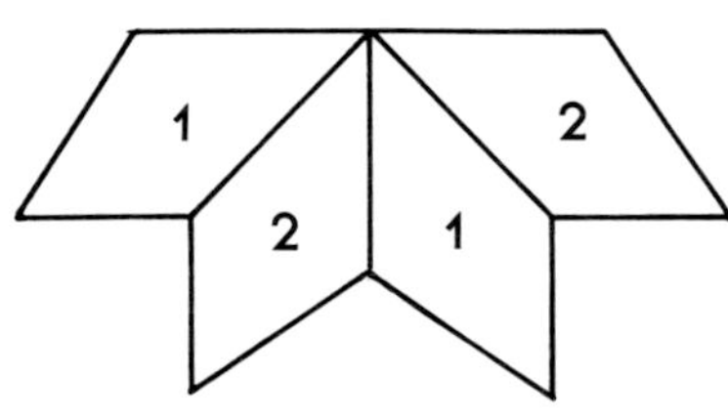

Stitch pairs together

Press all seams to one side, preferably toward the darker color. For instance, press the seams toward the blue or red fabric rather than toward the white fabric.

The construction of this diamond star block requires careful work. If you've never pieced a similar quilt block before, do a little practicing. Use the pattern templates, and cut pieces of scrap fabric. Then assemble a complete practice block from start to finish according to the instructions on the following pages.

For each design block you'll need four blue diamonds, four red diamonds, four white triangles, and four white squares. Separate all your cut pieces into 30 design-block units. You will find it helpful to pin or tack each unit together until you're ready to work on it. See instructions for tacking on page 11.

You may want to piece the star blocks before you cut the separating strips and blocks. Or you may want to do all the cutting at one time. In that case, you'll find cutting diagrams and information on page 38.

Assembling the Blocks

Make the stars first. Begin by sewing a red (1) and blue (2) diamond together (see top left diagram). Sew from one end to the other. Open the diamonds and press the seam allowances flat toward the dark (blue) side. Make three more diamond pairs combining one red and one blue section. As you stitch, always have the same color diamond on top, so you establish a definite right and left side of the unit, keeping the same color on the same side each time. Any deviation from this sequence will destroy the alternating diamond pattern of the finished star.

Next, sew two diamond pairs together as shown in the bottom drawing at the left. Make sure the colors are alternating. When these two diamond pairs are sewn together, you will have completed half the star. Sew two more diamond pairs together to make the second half of the star. Press seams. With right sides together, sew the two halves of the star together along the long straight edge. You should now have one complete eight-pointed star. Open the long seam and press it flat.

Insert the white triangles and squares next, when the star is completely assembled. This step requires patience, accuracy, and a little practice on spare scraps of fabric if you've never done it before. When you set your squares and triangles into the diamond star, remember you are joining pieces cut on the bias (the diamonds) with pieces cut on the straight grain of the fabric (the squares and short sides of the triangles). Because the bias diamond sides tend to stretch more than the sides cut on the straight grain, be extra careful with your piecing at this point. After setting the squares and triangles, you'll find that a good pressing will take care of any minor stretching or puckering problems.

To insert squares into the diamond star, mark one corner of each square with a dot (A) showing where the seams will meet (¼-inch in from two sides). See the top drawing on page 37. On the right side of the fabric, mark the diamond star ¼-inch in from the V on the seam line (B). See the second drawing from the top, on page 37. Use a white or yellow pencil for best results.

With the right sides of a white square and one diamond together, place the dot of the square (dot side up) on top of the dot of the diamond (A on top of B). It will help to stick a straight pin through the two dots to get them accurately lined up. Be sure the edges are straight. When the two points are correctly aligned the diamond point will extend beyond the edge of the square slightly.

With the square on top, sew from the end of the diamond to dot A. Stop with the needle in the fabric. (See drawing third from top.) Lift up the presser foot, leaving the needle in place. Rotate the diamond so the V and dot A are directly in front of you. Now, carefully lift up the white square and, with sharp scissors, clip from the edge of the diamond to the needle—but no further. This will ease the fabric so you can turn it, lay it flat, and stitch again.

Follow the bottom drawing and rotate the square on the needle so that the square side C-D lines up with the diamond side E. Pin in place. Put down your presser foot and continue sewing to the outer edge. Practice this technique once or twice and you'll see how simple it is to get pucker-free corners. Piece the other white squares and triangles into the diamond star using the same method. Be careful to place the squares and triangles in the correct position. Turn seams back toward the star and press down. Make 30 star blocks following these instructions. Then, if you haven't already cut the separating strips, now's the time to do it.

Piecing the Quilt Top

Cut and sew separating strips first. Straighten and press the fabric. From the red fabric, cut two border strips (A) 2x87 inches; two border strips (B) 2x103 inches; 14 strips (C) 1¾x106 inches; and 16 strips (D) 1¾x11¾ inches. From white fabric, cut two border strips (E) 2x87 inches; two strips (F) 2x103 inches; five strips (G) 2¼x106 inches; and eight strips (H) 2¼x11¾ inches. From the blue and white polka dot fabric, cut 42 4¾-inch squares. Mark cutting lines on the red and white fabrics with a pencil as shown in the diagrams on the following page. Use a yardstick to help you measure and draw straight lines. Cut the strips carefully along the marked lines.

With right sides together, sew two red lattice strips (C) to either side of one white lattice strip (G). Press. Sew six more (total seven) long strips like this. Now, cut one of these long strips into nine lattice-strip units, each 11¾-inches long. Repeat with the remaining long strips, giving you a total of 63 lattice-strip units.

Sew two short red strips (D) to either side of one short white strip (H). Sew a total of eight lattice-strip units like this. You now have a total of 71 lattice-strip units for your quilt top.

Assemble long separating strips by grouping six blue-dot squares and five lattice-strip units. Sew a blue-dot square to one end of a lattice-strip unit, add another square, then another lattice-strip unit, and so forth, as shown in the "Strip A" drawing on the following page. Press all seams toward the polka dot squares. Make six more long strips like this for a total of seven. Set these strips aside while you assemble the rows of blocks.

Assemble each row of blocks with six lattice-strip units and five star-design blocks. Sew a strip unit to one side of a star block, then sew another strip unit to the opposite side. Continue building up as shown in the "Strip B" diagram on page 38. Press all seams toward the red strips. Make five more long strips like this for a total of six.

continued

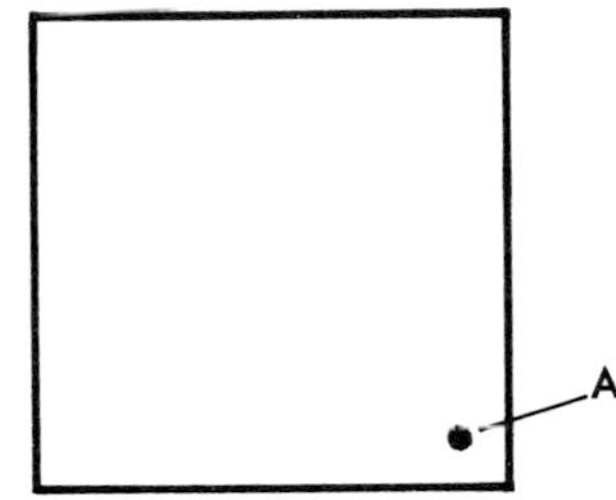

Mark the square

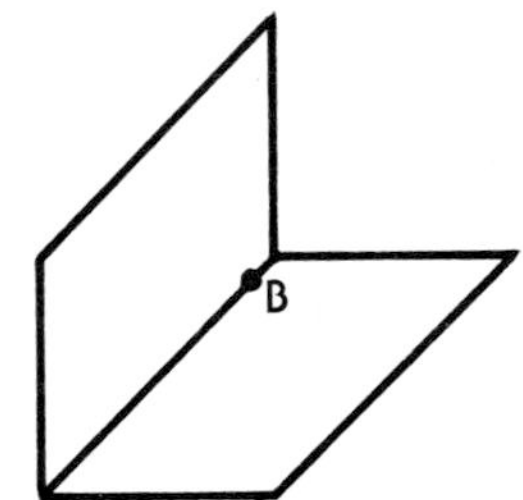

Mark the star

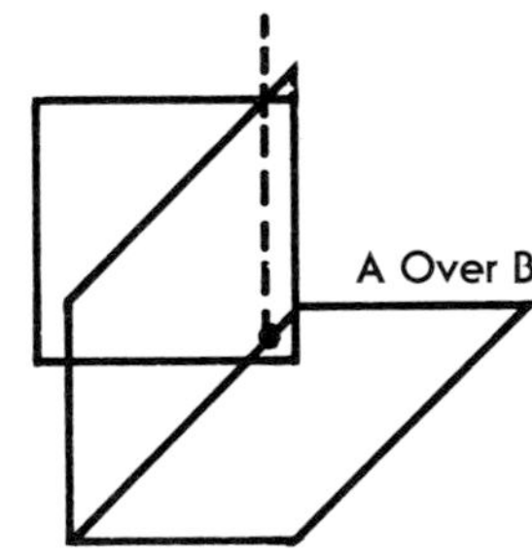

Match dots on square and star

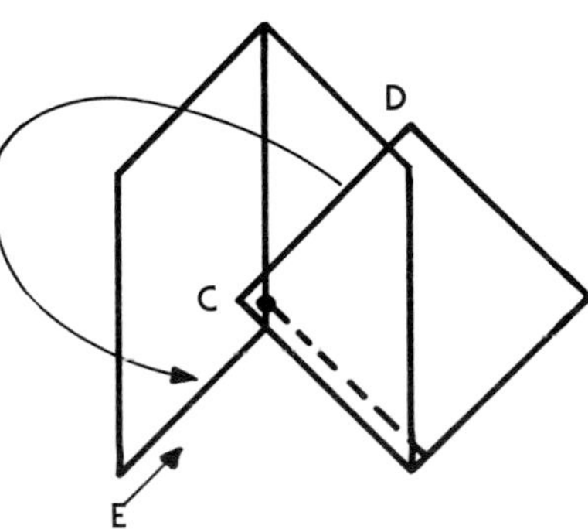

Rotate the square

Star Pattern Quilt and Sham *(continued)*

Cutting Diagram for Red and White Fabric

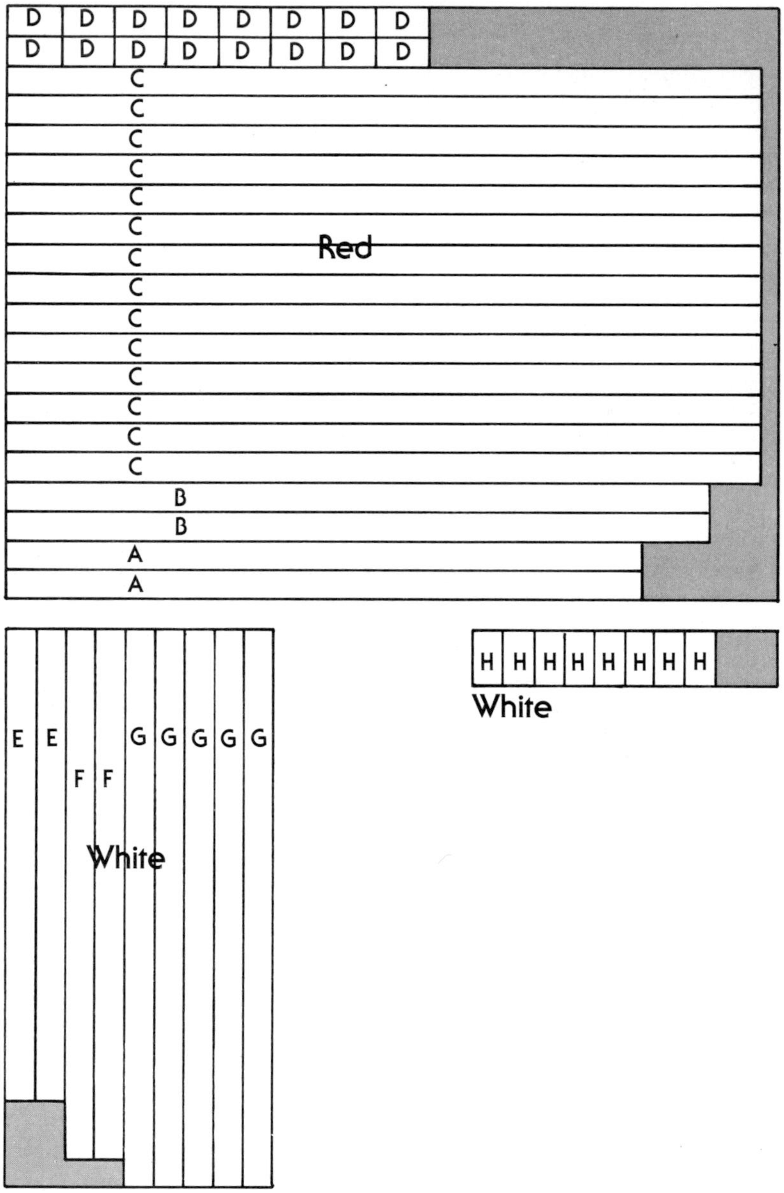

Strip A

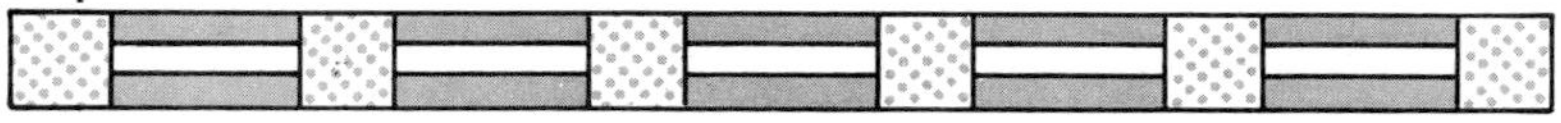

Strip B

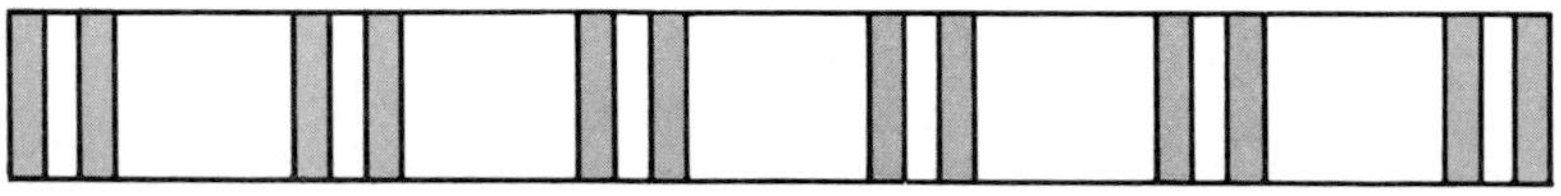

Join the rows by sewing a long strip A to the top of a long strip B. Then sew a long strip A to the lower edge of strip B, and continue, alternating A and B strips as shown in the illustration opposite. Be careful to pin the points where strip units and blue squares meet before you sew the long strips together.

Sew shorter white border strips (E) to the bottom and top of the quilt. Sew the longer white border strips (F) to the sides of the quilt. Trim if necessary. Sew the shorter red border strips (A) to the top and bottom of the quilt and the longer border strips (B) to the sides. Trim if necessary. Press all seams back away from the white border strip and toward the dark colors.

Assembling the Quilt

You're now ready to fill the quilt. For a traditional quilted effect, use one layer of high quality polyester quilt batting. For a puffier, comforter effect, use two or three layers of batting.

To create backing for your quilt, cut the six yards of fabric into two three-yard lengths. Sew them together vertically. Press seams.

For a finished edge, place pressed patchwork on top of the batting, right side up. Trim the batting to match your patchwork quilt top. Next, place the backing on top of the patchwork, wrong side up. (Right sides of the patchwork top and the quilt backing are now facing each other.) Trim the backing to match the top and batting, if necessary. Baste all three layers together around the edges, using long running stitches. Baste several rows vertically and horizontally to prevent shifting. Or baste from top to bottom, side to side, and diagonally from corner to corner. Stitch and loosen the machine tension. The fabric side should be on top and the batting underneath as you sew. It's helpful to have a card table or similar support to your left on which to rest the quilt so its weight doesn't pull on the seam while you sew.

Trim the corners of the quilt and excess batting if necessary. Remove basting stitches and turn the quilt right side out through the opening on one side. Straighten corners after the quilt is turned, but don't use a pointed object. Instead, use the eraser end of a pencil. Slip-stitch the opening closed by hand.

Place the quilt on the floor, and straighten the fabric with your hands. Pin all layers together in the center of each block and along the wide borders.

To tie your quilt, secure the three layers with a double thickness of floss (12 strands) and make a tie at least every four inches. In this design, it's best to tie at the end of each point in the star, in the middle of each star, and at the four corners of each design block. For tying instructions, see page 45.

If you prefer quilting to tying, see basic instructions beginning on page 42. Choose a quilting pattern to hand- or machine-stitch. This particular design could be machine quilted easily and effectively by stitching along the horizontal and vertical lines of the pieced quilt top.

Star-patterned Sham

Cut four small blue polka dot diamonds, four red polka dot diamonds, four white triangles, and four squares for each sham.

Follow the instructions given on page 36 to complete the star block. It's made in the same way as the block for the quilt.

Cut and sew the border strips next. Start by straightening and pressing the fabric. Mark cutting lines with a pencil, using a yardstick to help you measure and draw straight lines.

From the red fabric, carefully cut two pieces 2x12 inches and two pieces 3x15 inches. From white fabric, cut two pieces 2x16 inches and two pieces 3x18 inches. Using the blue polka dot fabric, cut two pieces 2x21 inches and two pieces 3x31 inches.

With right sides together, sew the shorter red strips to the top and bottom of the star block. The seam allowance is ¼ inch. Trim excess. Sew longer red strips to the sides. Press. In the same way sew the white strips to the top and bottom, then to the sides. Finish the border by sewing on the blue dot strips, using the same procedure. Press completely.

For the pillow backing, cut one piece 10½x26½ inches and one piece 13½x26½ inches. Turn under ¼-inch hem on a long side of each piece. First pin narrower piece of backing to pillow top, right sides together. Next, pin on the larger piece. Wider pieces will overlap the narrower pieces slightly. Stitch around all four sides. Clip corners, and reverse pillow sham through the opening in the back. Press.

Traditional-American Quilts and Quilting

Patchwork quilts are truly one of the most expressive forms of American folk art, as the vintage, one-of-a-kind Log Cabin quilt displayed here so beautifully demonstrates. Log Cabin, with its strip-pieced blocks, is just one of the many quilt patterns that have been handed down to us over the years. Like many others, it has changed with the times, and on pages 48 and 49 you'll find an exciting contemporary version of this classic pattern. In this section, you can begin your love affair with the American patchwork quilt. On the following pages you'll discover quilting basics—the old techniques and the new. Then, you'll find step-by-step how-to instructions for treasured American patterns like Windmill, Storm at Sea, and the ever-popular Star of Bethlehem.

Quilting Basics

It's what you do with your quilt after you've pieced or appliquéd the top that makes it a work of art—and a potential heirloom. Whether you're going to stage a neighborhood quilting bee or go it alone with your quilt and a sewing machine, here's a step-by-step guide to what you should know about quilting.

Quilting Patterns

Once your quilt top is completed, the next step is choosing a quilting design that will enhance the patchwork or appliqué of the top. For a pleasing appearance, it's important that the quilting design is compatible with the design of the quilt top. To make sure, draw a portion of your quilting design on tracing paper, or any other transparent paper, and lay it on top of the quilt. Study it and make sure the quilting stitches will augment rather than detract from the beauty of the quilt.

There are three common ways of quilting, and a variety of designs are available as patterns from craft and quilting shops. Or you can design your own quilting pattern.

Outline quilting is probably the most popular form of quilting. Here, the pieced patchwork is delineated by running stitches taken ⅛ to ¼ inch on either side of the seam lines, so each patch is outlined. This not only secures the layers of the quilt to each other, but also gives your quilt a dimensional quality.

In diagonal quilting, another popular pattern, diagonal lines are stitched at regularly spaced intervals across a quilt top. Stitching in the opposite direction results in a diamond quilting pattern.

Quilting in a curved line or scallop is also common. This is often called a shell pattern.

Transferring Your Pattern

No matter which quilting pattern you use, you'll find the following guidelines helpful when transferring it to your quilt top.

A mark that's too dark or indelible can detract from the beauty of the quilt, yet a line that's too light is difficult to stitch. To avoid these pitfalls, use dressmaker's chalk or a chalk pencil. If you use a soft lead pencil, make a dotted rather than a solid line, and cover the dots with your stitches.

Masking tape, in any width you choose, is also handy for marking straight lines. Stick the tape down and stitch slightly beyond both edges. Do not leave the tape on for any length of time, however, or it will make your quilt top gummy. And don't substitute adhesive or cellophane tape.

A template is essential for marking quilting lines for a scalloped or shell pattern. To make one, trace a row of half-circles of the desired size on a strip of cardboard. Then, cut them out along the traced line. Lay the pattern flat on the quilt top and mark the first row along the scalloped edge. To mark the second row, position the scallops so the low point on the curves of the second row is over the high point of the curves in the first row. Mark this row. Continue, alternating the position of the scallops, until the area to be quilted is filled.

A pan lid or plate also makes a good template for a scallop. Attach small pieces of masking tape to the sides of the lid or plate to mark the area to be traced, and in the middle of the curve to help mark alternate rows of scallops.

Designs traced on paper can be transferred with dressmaker's carbon and a tracing wheel, or by punching holes along the lines with a sharp pencil. Test the washability of carbon before using it.

To make a perforated pattern, trace the pattern onto brown wrapping paper. Then, with the sewing machine unthreaded, stitch along the lines. Lay the pattern on the quilt and mark the fabric by rubbing stamping powder or paste through the holes.

Combining Patterns

When choosing a quilting pattern, keep in mind that several different patterns often look great when combined in one quilt. Sometimes the pieced blocks are quilted along the seam lines; the plain blocks are quilted with a stitched design, such as a wreath or star; and the border is worked in diamonds or scallops.

Assembling the Quilt

When your quilt top is finished and marked for quilting, assemble the materials you need to put the quilt together: the quilt top (pressed and wrinkle free), the backing, the quilt batting, and pins or needle and thread.

For the back of your quilt, select a fabric of the same type and weight as the top. Often you can use a sheet. Or join together the number of lengths of fabric necessary to achieve the proper width. Backing may be plain white or neutral; however, you may also use prints or colors if they coordinate with the quilt top. You may use matching or contrasting fabric to bind the edges of the quilt.

Several types of quilt batting are available. Cotton batting is relatively flat and easy to stitch through when hand quilting. Polyester batting is thicker and makes a puffier quilt. Use several layers of polyester batting for the extra puffy, comforter look. For quilting small items, such as hot pads or place mats, you can also use polyester fleece—a firm, flat but soft padding used in tailoring.

Lay the backing on the floor, face down, and smooth it out until it is perfectly flat. Be sure the grain is straight and the corners square. Then place the batting on top of the backing and smooth it out until there are no wrinkles or lumps.

If you plan to quilt without a quilting frame, pin the batting and backing together and baste. (This gives added stability to the interlining and keeps it from shifting while you quilt.) If you plan to use a quilting frame, skip this step.

Place the pressed and marked quilt top over the batting. Smooth it out and square the corners. Pin through all three layers, starting in the center and going in all directions. Space pins about eight inches apart. Be sure to smooth out any lumps and wrinkles ahead of you as you go along, and take long (one inch), even stitches.

Baste the three layers together (see sketch at right). Using a running stitch, baste on the lengthwise and crosswise grain through the center of the quilt. Then baste diagonally from corner to corner and around the outside edges of the quilt.

Hand Quilting

Hand quilting can be done on a floor frame, on a quilting hoop, or on your lap without a hoop.

A floor frame is essential if quilting is to be a social function, for it allows several people to work on the quilt at the same time. This type of frame consists of two long poles to which the quilt is attached and stretched between the two side braces. The frame is supported by a table-height stand.

To use a floor frame, attach the quilt to the poles and roll it to one side, until the exposed area is tightly stretched. Make sure corners are square. Begin quilting about 12 inches from the edge and quilt toward yourself. When you complete the quilting in one area, roll the quilt under and expose a section of the unstitched top. Stretch the new area tight before quilting.

continued

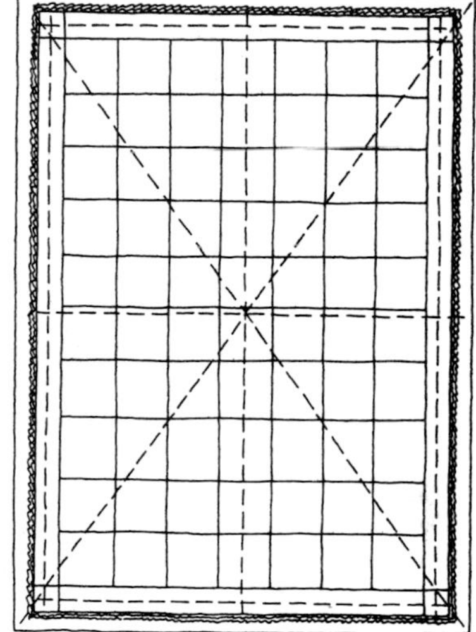

Basting layers together

Quilting Basics *(continued)*

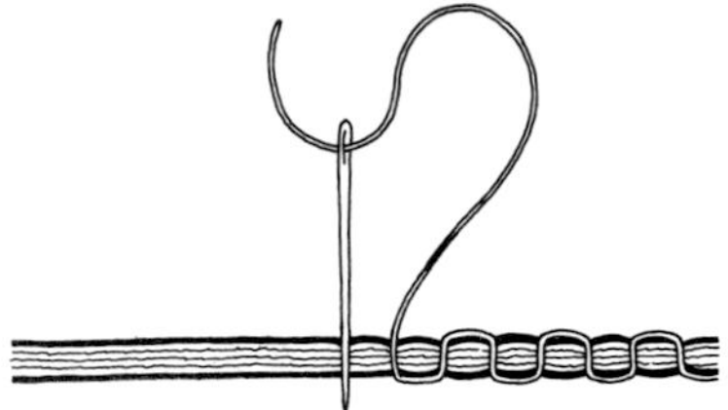

Two-hand quilting stitches

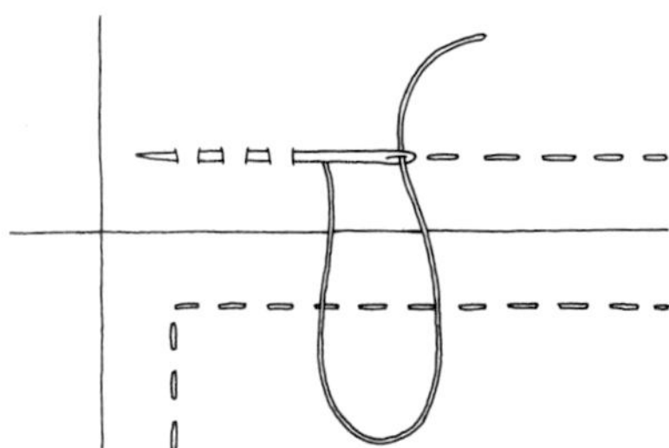

One-hand quilting stitches

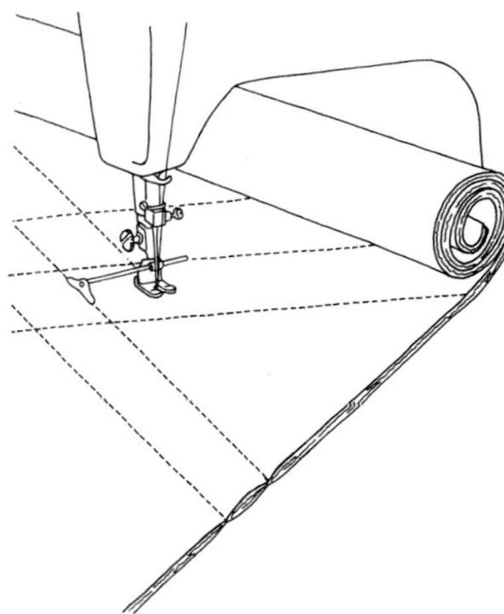

Machine quilting

The quilting hoop resembles an embroidery hoop, but is somewhat larger. It's used in the same way, however; the inner hoop fits under the quilt and the outer hoop on top, holding it tight. Thumbscrews on the hoops adjust to accommodate any thickness of quilt.

When using a hoop, start quilting in the center of the quilt and work toward the edges. As you complete a section, release the hoop and move it to an unstitched area.

Lap quilting requires no equipment. As in quilting with a hoop, you should start at the center of the quilt and work toward the edges. Hold the quilt firmly to keep layers from slipping.

Use waxed quilting thread for hand stitching and either a #8 or #9 sharp needle. Work with a single thread, about 20 inches long. Make sure the thread you choose is similar in color to the quilt fabric. Light-colored quilts usually are stitched in white; dark-colored quilts in blue, brown, or black.

Make short, even stitches. The secret of good quilting is to make sure each stitch goes through all three layers of the quilt. A dull or rough needle will make stitching difficult, so discard blunted needles. A thimble is often helpful when piercing the three layers of a quilt.

Start quilting by knotting the end of the thread and bringing the needle up through all layers of the quilt. Pull the knot through the backing until it's concealed in the batting.

There are two common methods of making a quilting stitch. With a little experimentation, you'll find the one that's most comfortable for you.

One method employs the left hand above the quilt and the right hand below it. Push the needle down through all thicknesses with the left hand, then push it up with the right hand, very close to the first stitch. The stitches should be the same length on both sides. (See the top drawing at left.) If you're left-handed, work with the left hand below the quilt and the right hand above it.

The other method is to take two or three running stitches at a time before pulling the thread through. (See the middle drawing at the left.)

When all the quilting is done, release the quilt from the frame and remove the basting threads. Be careful not to pull out any of the quilting stitches.

Machine Quilting

You can machine-quilt most quilting patterns, provided they are not extremely intricate. If you choose to machine-quilt, do the entire quilt with this method. Do not combine machine- and hand-quilting in the same quilt.

To machine-quilt, assemble the backing, batting, and top the same as for hand-quilting. However, you'll need additional basting to machine-quilt. (This helps keep the layers from slipping under the needle on the machine.) Baste horizontal and vertical rows, about four inches apart, over thc entire quilt using a fairly short basting stitch.

A quilting foot, while not essential, simplifies the stitching of straight patterns. Place the space bar of the quilting foot to either the right or left of the needle to ensure uniformly spaced lines in the quilting design (see the bottom drawing on the left).

If you're using a portable sewing machine, set it on a large table to support the quilt and keep it off the floor. Extend cabinet models by placing card tables adjacent to the machine.

Use regular mercerized sew-

ing thread and set the machine at six to eight stitches per inch. Loosen the tension and pressure a bit and make a quilt sample with top, batting, and back layers to test stitch tension. Upper and lower threads should lock in the middle of the layers.

Roll the quilt crosswise to the center and place the roll under the arm of the sewing machine. Work, row by row, from the center to the edge. Don't pull the quilt. Guide it gently and stitch at a slow, even pace.

When you've stitched half the quilt, remove it from the machine, roll the completed area, and unroll the unquilted portion. Again, slide the rolled half under the arm of the machine and quilt from the center toward the edge. When you're finished, remove the basting stitches.

Tying Your Quilt

This is a faster means of securing the three layers of a quilt together than quilting; however, it's not as decorative. If producing a work of fabric art is your goal, you will probably want to quilt the finished top. This usually takes anywhere from a couple of weeks to several months. But if time is limited, you may want to speed the process by tying your quilt, which you can do in an afternoon.

To tie a quilt, assemble as for quilting, with the backing, batting, and top laid out smooth and wrinkle-free. Pin and baste the layers together just as you would for quilting. Then place the quilt in a quilting frame if you have one, or work the quilt on the dining room table.

Mark the quilt at three- to eight-inch intervals, across and down. If the quilt is made of blocks, you can tailor your tying to the design and tie at the ends of star points, or at the four corners and center of a block.

Use an embroidery needle and string, yarn, or embroidery floss that either matches or contrasts with the quilt top. Use a single or double strand, depending on the desired effect.

Start at the center of the quilt and work to the edges. Push the needle through the layers and out the back, then reenter from the back, going through the layers and coming up ⅛ inch from the point of entry. Allow two inches of thread at either end of the stitch and cut. Tie the threads in a square knot and then trim the ends.

If you don't want the ties to show on the front of the quilt, reverse the procedure and tie the threads on the back side.

Finishing Your Quilt

There are a number of ways to finish the edges of the quilt. You can make borders by using bias tape or the same fabric you used for the quilt top, or by bringing the backing fabric around the edge to the front to form the binding. Or you can skip the binding altogether and stitch the top of your quilt to the back.

Finishing the edges without binding is possible on quilts with bands of fabric bordering a central design. The borders themselves enclose the design in the same way that an applied band or bias tape does. So you can sew the quilt top to the backing and batting without a separate binding strip. Use this method only when tying a quilt.

To finish a quilt this way, make sure the batting and backing are basted together firmly. Then lay the batting and backing down on the floor, with the right side of the backing fabric up and smooth out all wrinkles. Lay the right side of the quilt top down on the backing fabric, and pin all the way around.

continued

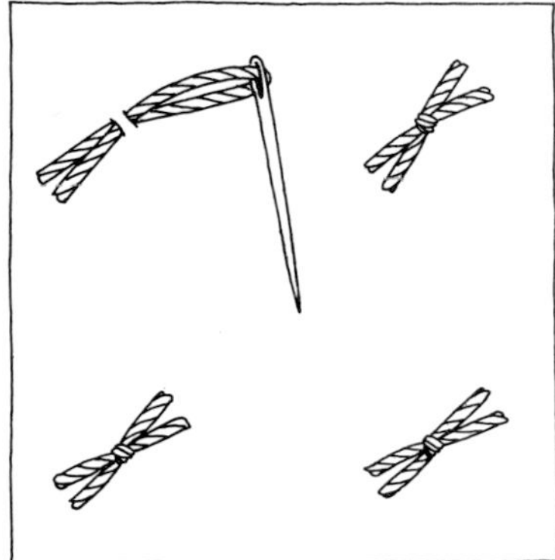

Tying the quilt

Quilting Basics *(continued)*

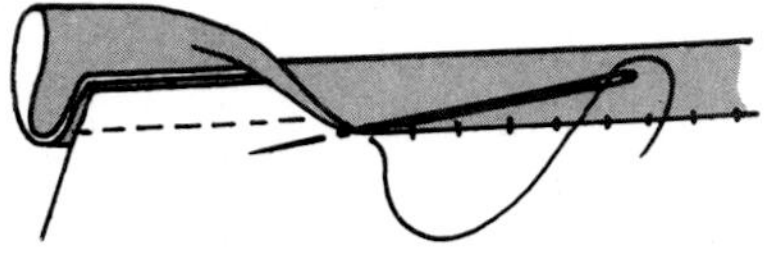

French binding

Machine-stitch around all four sides, leaving a section of one side open for turning the quilt. Turn the quilt through the opening and push out the corners, using the eraser end of a pencil. Slip-stitch the opening closed.

If you're using a commercial bias tape, pin the tape to the quilt top, right sides together, starting in the middle of a side. Then sew around all the edges of the quilt to secure the tape. Using the sewing machine will give you a stronger stitch, but be careful to keep the corners neat and square. Trim away the excess fabric and fold the tape to the back. Pin the tape in place and blindstitch by hand.

To make fabric binding, cut strips two inches wide and join them into a strip long enough to go completely around the quilt. Cut either with the grain or on the bias. If the quilt edge is scalloped or shaped, cut the binding on the bias. Attach the same way as bias tape.

To make bias binding, cut strips at a 45-degree angle across the grain of the fabric. To find the bias, fold the lower edge of the fabric up along the selvage edge. With your thumb, press the fold gently to form a light crease. Using this crease as a guide, cut strips twice the width of the finished binding, plus ¼ inch for each seam allowance.

To join lengths of bias, put the short ends of two strips together, right sides facing, and stitch with the grain (not the bias) in a ¼-inch seam. The seam will look diagonal on the binding. Tack both ends of the seam with a backstitch. Open up the seam and press it flat.

If you're buying bias binding, you may have to join several packages together. If you do, use the joining method given above to reach the proper length.

French binding is a means of finishing off your quilt edges with bias binding when durability and strength are important. To use this method, cut the bias strips four times as wide as the finished width, plus ¼ inch for each seam allowance. Fold the strips in half lengthwise, with wrong sides together, and press down. This will give you a double bias strip with two raw edges on one side and a fold on the other. Apply this double binding the same as regular bias binding. Be sure the two raw edges of the bias strip are placed next to the raw edge of the quilt. Stitch the binding down securely, then turn the folded edge to the reverse side of the quilt and stitch it down with a blindstitch. (See drawing at left.)

The backing fabric can also be used to bind the raw edges. When backing is used, the band is usually rather narrow—½ to two inches wide. If you plan to bind the edges this way, make allowances for the band when you're assembling the quilt for quilting. The backing fabric will have to be larger than the quilt top and batting. Plan for the backing to extend beyond the quilt top by double the width of the band, plus ½ inch to turn under as a seam allowance.

Extend the batting beyond the quilt top to the width of the finished band, less ¼ inch. For example, if you want a two-inch band, extend the backing 4½ inches beyond the quilt top, and trim the batting to extend 1¾ inches beyond the top. Since the three layers are staggered in size, plan to pin the margin of the backing over the batting to protect it during the quilting process. After quilting, remove all the pins and lay the quilt out flat.

Following the drawings at the right, fold the raw edges of the backing forward ½ inch all the way around the quilt. Press down lightly. Measuring in ½ inch diagonally, clip off the point of each corner. (See the drawing at top right.)

Next fold the corner of the backing over the batting, but do not fold the batting itself. Pin the corner to the quilt top, ¼ inch from the edge. (See drawing at center right.) Press.

Fold the sides of the backing over the batting. Place the folded edge of the backing ¼ inch in from the edge of the quilt top. The corners miter themselves. (See drawing at lower right.)

Baste this band down all around the quilt. Machine- or hand-sew ⅛ inch from the folded edge. Pivot at the corners. Slip-stitch the mitered corner.

You can use this same method of binding with the front of the quilt (the quilt top) overlapping the backing. Just reverse the procedure outlined above.

Adding Ruffles and Flounces

Ruffles and flounces also are used to edge quilts, particularly those with appliquéd and tied tops. The method of application is the same for both, the difference between them being that a flounce is deeper than a ruffle and often extends to the floor.

To add a ruffle to your quilting project, first measure all four sides. Plan to ruffle a strip of fabric twice this length. Next determine how wide you want your ruffle and cut fabric strips twice this width adding ½ inch for seam allowances. Join the strips together to form one long strip. Then join the two ends of the strip to form a circle.

Next, fold this strip in half lengthwise with the right side of the fabric out. Press down. Using a long gathering stitch on the machine, sew two lines of stitching ¼ to ½ inch in from the raw edges. Carefully pull the bobbin threads to create the ruffle. Gather a small section at a time to make sure the ruffling isn't too tight or too loose. For instance, mark off a 36-inch section with pins, then gather it until it measures 18 inches. That way, you will know your ruffle will come close to fitting around your quilt with only minor adjustments.

When the ruffle is gathered, start pinning it to the quilt top. Place the ruffle on top of the quilt face, with the raw edges of the quilt and the ruffle even. Baste the ruffle in place. Machine-stitch ¼ inch in from the raw edges.

To join the quilt top to the back and batting, lay the back down on the floor, wrong side up, and place the batting over it. Pin and baste the batting to the quilt backing, following the instructions on page 43. When the two layers are secured, turn them over so the batting is on the floor and the right side of the backing fabric is up. Carefully place the quilt top and ruffle on top of the backing fabric, right sides together. Make sure the ruffle is tucked inside and smoothed out so its bottom edge won't get caught in the seam. Pin all layers and baste.

Machine-stitch all around the edges of the quilt, leaving an opening on one side for turning the quilt. Sew with the quilt top up so you can see the stitching line securing the ruffle to the top. Be sure you sew inside this seam; otherwise, it will show when the quilt is turned.

Turn the quilt through the opening and straighten the corners, using the eraser end of a pencil. Slip-stitch the opening closed. Smooth the quilt out and tie to hold the three layers together. Remove all basting and gathering threads.

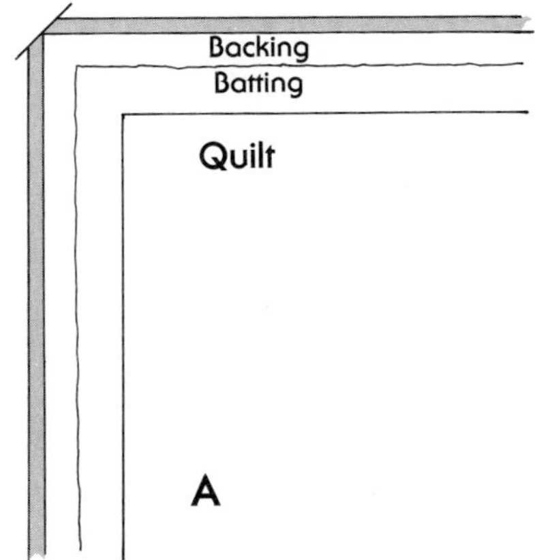

Turning under backing seam allowance

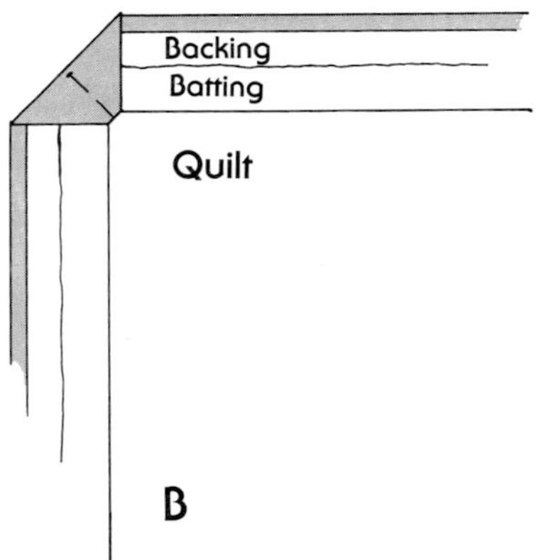

Folding corner over batting

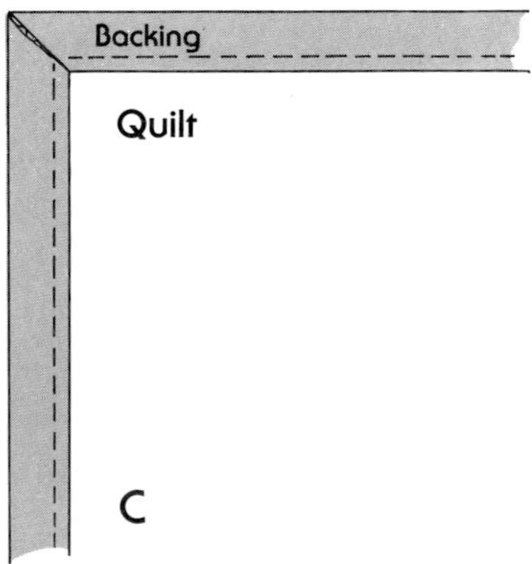

Folding band over batting and stitching to quilt top

New-fashioned Log Cabin Quilt

A traditional Log Cabin quilt, like the one shown on pages 40 and 41, is made of increasingly longer rectangles pieced together, L-shaped fashion, to form a block. But today, even the Log Cabin has gone prefab. This updated version of the famous quilt is made of strips of fabric sewn together diagonally across a square. When the squares are put together, they create the Log Cabin look.

Materials

Assorted colored fabric for strips
2¾ yards 45-inch-wide white fabric for center strips
6 yards 45-inch-wide medium blue fabric for backing
Quilt batting

Directions

The placement diagram below contains four blocks of this contemporary Log Cabin quilt. Enlarge ¼ of the diagram (1 block), and then make templates of the pattern pieces. Cut the center strip in each block from white fabric, or from some other light or bright color of your choice. (It's the consistent color of the center strip that creates the square effect in the quilt top.) Cut remaining strips from fabric in assorted colors and patterns. Be sure to add ¼-inch seam allowances to all sides of the pieces.

Sew the strips in each block together. For a full-size quilt, make 90 blocks. If you're making a larger or smaller quilt, adjust the number of blocks. Press all the seams flat.

When all the blocks are completed, lay them out on the floor and arrange them in a pleasant color pattern according to the placement diagram. You'll need nine rows of 10 blocks each. Be sure to position the blocks so the direction of the strips alternates, forming diamond shapes with the white center strips. Sew all the blocks in each row together. Then sew the rows together and press open the seams.

The edges of this quilt are bound by a border of backing fabric turned over the quilt top. See instructions on page 46 for assembling a quilt in this manner. (General directions for either hand or machine quilting begin on page 43.) The quilt shown here is hand-stitched around each square and on each side of the center strip.

Log Cabin

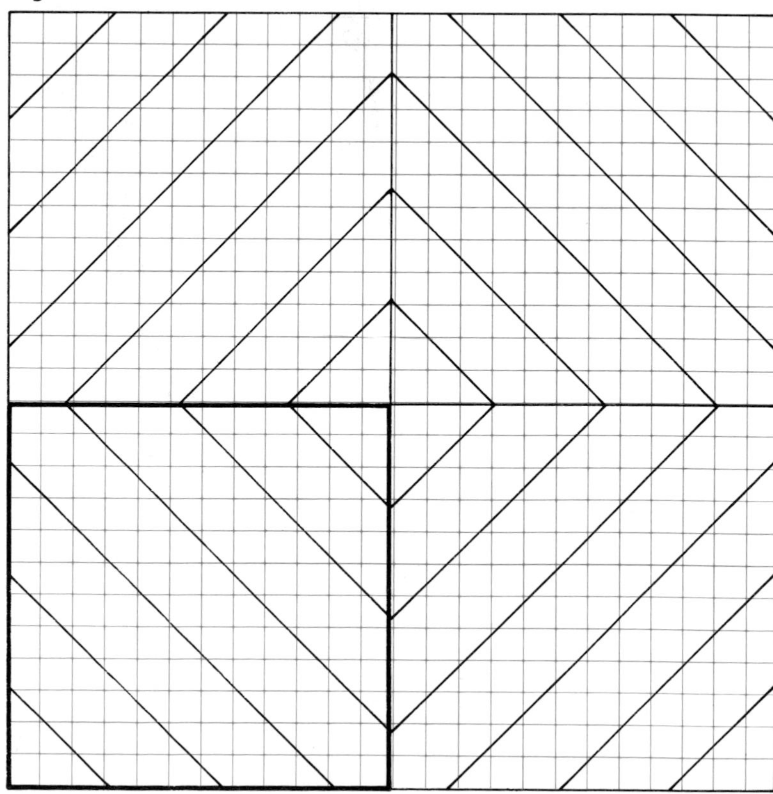

1 Square=3/4 Inch

Classic Star of Bethlehem Quilt

Even this adaptation, left, of the Star of Bethlehem quilt, opposite, is a quilting challenge.

Materials

7¾ yards 45-inch-wide yellow fabric
1¼ yards 45-inch-wide green fabric
1½ yards 45-inch-wide print fabric
1 sheet of 8½ yards fabric for backing
Quilt batting

Star-point assembly diagram

P
G G
Y Y Y
P P P P
G G G G G
Y Y Y Y Y Y
P P P P P P P
G G G G G G
Y Y Y Y Y
P P P P
G G G
Y Y
P

Directions

Read all instructions carefully before you begin. For a 94-inch-diameter star, first make a diamond pattern by drawing a line 6¾ inches long. Bisect this line at the midpoint with a second line $2\frac{13}{16}$ inches long drawn at right angles to the first line. Connect the end points of these two lines to make a diamond whose sides are each $3\frac{5}{8}$ inches long. Adding ¼-inch seam allowances to all pieces, cut 136 print diamonds (P), 128 green (G), and 128 yellow (Y). Cut four yellow triangles 37x26¼x26¼ inches and four yellow 26¼-inch squares. Following the diagram at right, sew diamonds into rows, then join rows into a large, diamond-shaped section. Make eight sections, and piece them together into an eight-pointed star.

Stitch large yellow squares and triangles in place. Next cut and sew 4-inch-wide strips of print fabric to the top and bottom edges of the quilt top. Then cut two 3-inch-wide green strips and sew one to each of the print strips. Cut two 4-inch-wide yellow strips and sew them to the green strips. Next cut and sew a 1½-inch-wide print strip to each of the side edges. Cut two 4-inch-wide yellow strips and sew one to each of the side print strips. Press seams open.

Assemble the quilt following instructions on page 43. Quilt along seams and extend stitching across the large squares and triangles. To finish, turn excess top fabric to back in a band.

Storm at Sea Quilt

Diamonds, squares, and triangles are all rigid geometric shapes, yet by piecing them together in the intricate pattern diagramed below, you can create the curves and rhythms of waves. Storm at Sea is one of the oldest and most popular patchwork patterns in America, and a real test of the quilter's piecing skill.

Materials

Light blue, dark blue, and white fabric totaling approximately 7 yards

5¾ yards blue backing fabric

Quilt batting

Color Key

A, C, F = Light Blue
B, E, G = White
D, H = Dark Blue

Directions

Enlarge the diagram below and make templates of cardboard or sandpaper for each of the different shapes.

For a 76x88-inch quilt, cut sufficient pieces, in the appropriate colors, to make up 42 large squares (pattern pieces A, B, C), 97 rectangles (pieces D, E), and 56 small squares (pieces F, G, H). Be sure to add ¼-inch seam allowances to all the pieces as you cut. First piece all the large squares, the small squares, and the rectangles separately. Press all the seams flat and away from the white areas and toward the dark colors.

When all the units are pieced, sew together into a long strip six large squares and seven rectangles (as in the right two-thirds of the diagram). Start and end with a rectangle. Make seven of these strips.

Then sew together into strips six rectangles and seven small squares (as in the left third of the diagram). Start and end with a small square. Make eight of these strips. Now sew the strips together alternating narrow and wide strips, and starting and ending with a narrow strip. Press the quilt top flat.

Cut and piece the blue backing fabric. Since the raw edges of the quilt will be bound with backing fabric, you'll need to cut the backing larger than the top. Assemble the quilt according to instructions beginning on page 43. Outline-quilt around the shapes in the quilt top. Finally, follow the instructions for making a border of backing fabric on page 46.

Storm At Sea

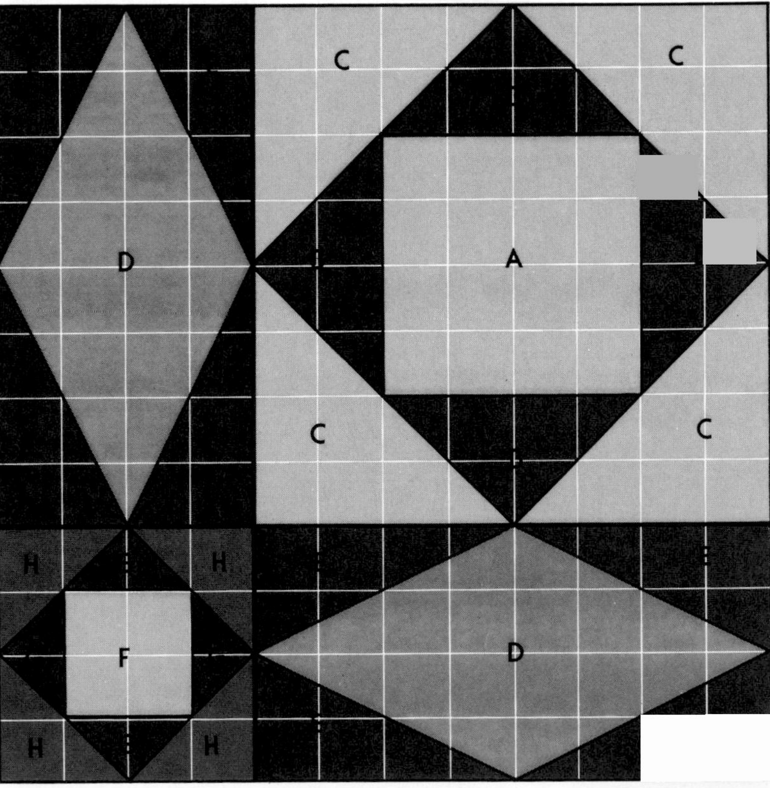

1 Square = 1 Inch

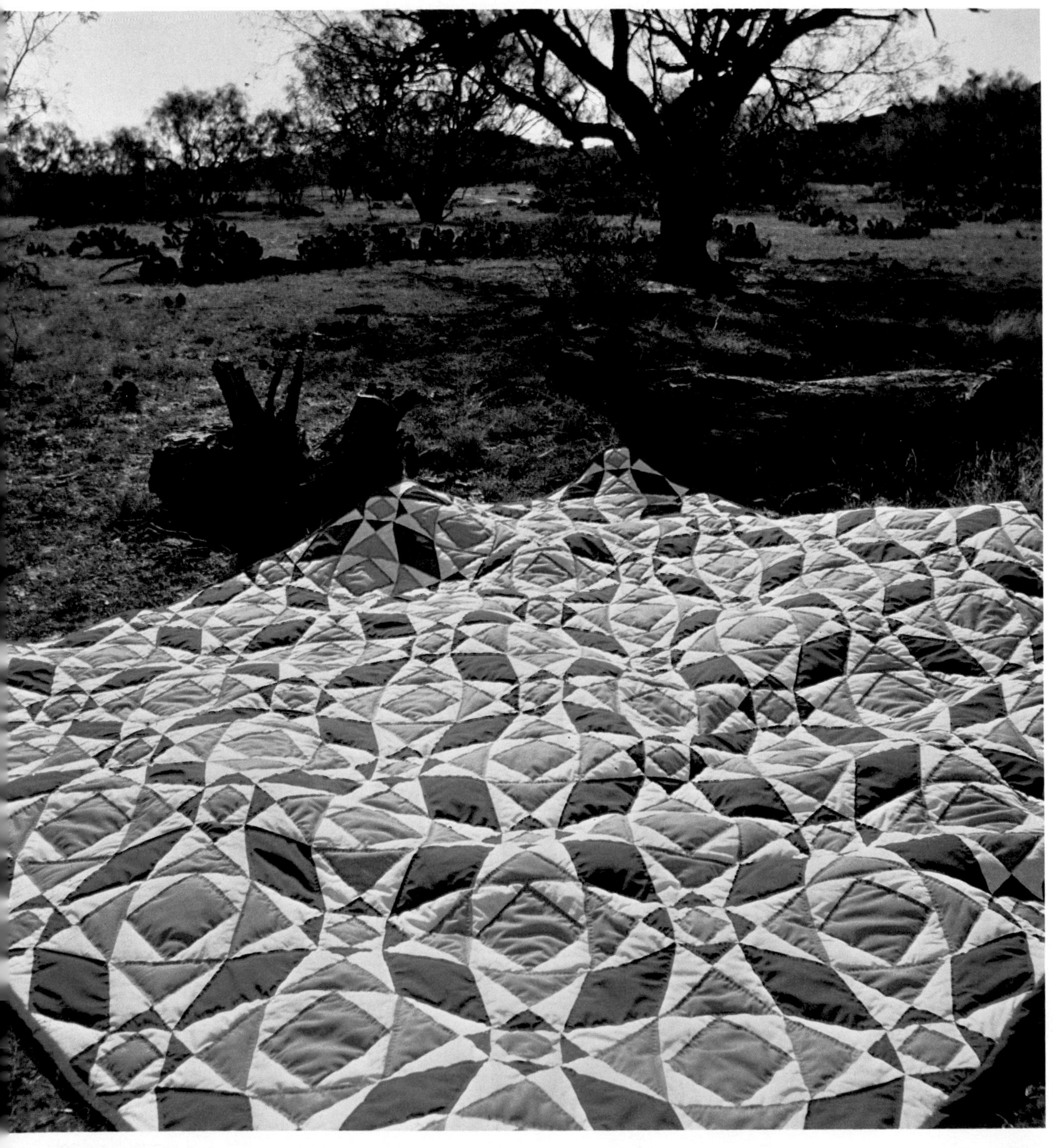

Easy-to-Stitch Windmill Quilt

Every quilt is a one-of-a-kind work of art, deriving its individuality from the colors and prints of selected fabrics, as well as from the quilter's unique interpretation of a given design. The quilt shown here, for instance, illustrates an ingenious way of piecing blocks of the ever-popular windmill pattern into a most unusual quilt top.

The basic windmill block is composed of nine squares. The center square and four corner squares of each block are cut from the same fabric, while the four slashed squares (composed of two triangles each) are cut and pieced from two contrasting fabrics, suggesting the vanes of the windmill. On some blocks the vanes are pieced in one direction, but in the opposite direction on others. The choice of colors and alternation in piecing gives the completed quilt top a pinwheeling sense of motion.

Materials

Assorted print, gingham, and solid color fabrics for the windmill pattern blocks

4 yards 45-inch-wide green fabric for background piecing

6 yards 45-inch-wide backing fabric

Quilt batting

Directions

The following instructions are for making an 85x102-inch quilt. Each finished block is 12 inches square. Enlarge the diagram below, and make templates for the square and triangular pattern pieces. Next draw a 12-inch square and cut it in half along the diagonal to make two 12x12x17-inch right-angle triangles. Cut one of these triangles in half again to make a 12x8½x8½-inch right-angle triangle. These two triangles (one large and one small) will be your templates for cutting the green background pieces of the quilt top.

From the assorted print, gingham, and solid fabrics, cut enough small squares and triangles to make 28 full windmill blocks and four diagonal half-blocks (for half-blocks, see dotted line on diagram). From the green fabric, cut 54 large triangles and 12 small triangles. Remember to add ¼-inch seam allowances to *all* pattern pieces. Piece blocks according to diagram (remembering to alternate the direction of the vanes on half the blocks). Next, set blocks together into strips with triangles between each block, as in the photo. Three strips of blocks will have five complete windmill blocks, pieced together with ten large green triangles and four smaller triangles (two each at either end of the strip). Two rows will have five complete pattern blocks, and a half-block at either end, pieced together with 12 large green triangles. Sew all five strips together to complete the top. Assemble the finished quilt top, batting, and backing, and complete according to quilting instructions on pages 42 through 47.

Windmill

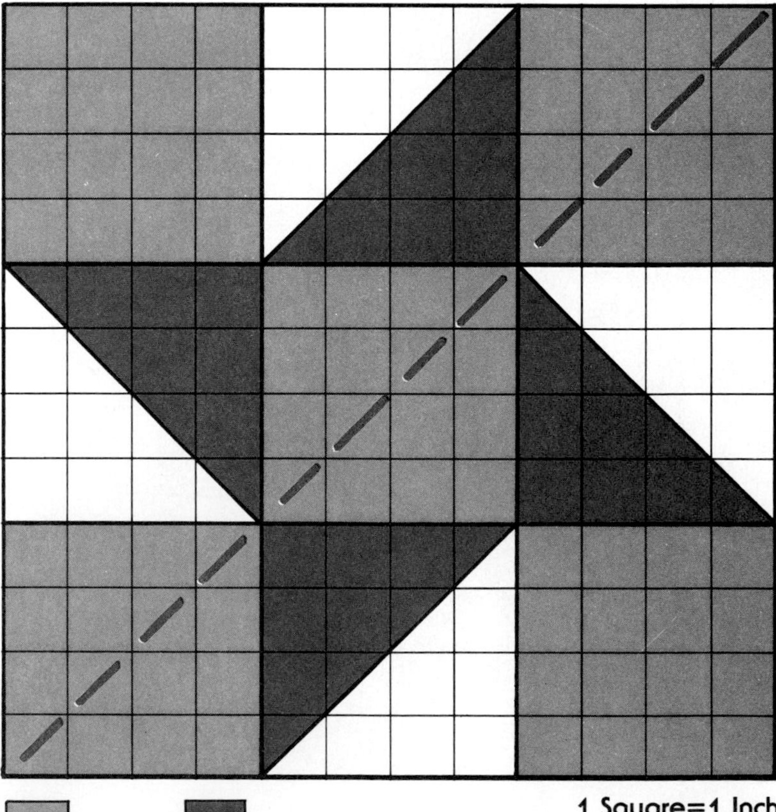

1 Square=1 Inch

Patchwork Plus-

Novelty Projects

Before anyone starts to think that the world of patchwork takes itself too seriously, we'd like to show you the lighter side of the craft. In this section, we feature novelty projects that take patchwork, quilting, and appliqué out of their traditional roles and give them a chance to have a little fun. You'll see appliqué for the bedroom, but this time as a headboard, not a quilt. Complete diagrams and instructions are given for a veritable album of quilting. And, on the next pages, you'll learn how to turn the kids loose with a box of fabric crayons to create the fun-loving quilt shown here. With a little imagination, there's no telling what you can do with patchwork, quilting, and appliqué.

TOMMY

A Child-Art Crayon Quilt

A crayon quilt can keep the whole family busy. On sheets of drawing paper, measure 12-inch squares and outline them lightly in pencil. Quilt artists should confine their drawings to this area, since the pencil lines represent the quilt block seams and anything beyond these lines will be lost on the finished squares.

Materials

1 set of Crayola brand fabric crayons
Medium-weight drawing paper
17 13-inch squares of white synthetic fabric
18 13-inch squares of bright-color fabric
2¾ yards border fabric
1 sheet or 6 yards of backing fabric
Polyester quilt batting

Directions

Before starting work on your quilt drawings, make a color test to see how well the fabric you've selected will take the crayon dye. This test will also show your artists how the colors will look when transferred to fabric. You'll find colors appear much more intense on fabric than on drawing paper. To make the color test, simply fill in small squares of each color on drawing paper and transfer the "test sheet" to a leftover piece of the fabric to be used for the quilt squares.

In planning designs for the quilt, keep in mind that drawings will transfer backwards. In the case of drawings with written captions, write the caption on a separate piece of paper, then trace it in reverse with crayon onto the main design.

To transfer crayon drawings to quilt squares, follow crayon package directions. Start by placing on the ironing board several folded sheets of newspaper, topped with a sheet of clean white paper. Place a square of white fabric on top of this ironing "pad." Using a stiff-bristled brush, brush all stray specks of crayon wax off the design paper before you place it on the fabric so they won't transfer. Lay the clean crayon design face down on the fabric, making sure the design is centered on the square. Finally, place another clean sheet of white paper between the transfer and the iron to avoid soiling the iron.

Turn the iron to the cotton setting to provide enough heat for transferring the crayon design effectively. Press with a steady, strong pressure over the entire design until the color becomes slightly visible through the top sheet of paper. Check frequently by carefully lifting a corner of the design to make sure the fabric is not scorching and the color is transferring evenly. Be careful not to shift the drawing on the fabric or you will blur the color and outline on the print. Once transferred to synthetic fabric, the crayon colors are permanent and completely washable. When transferred to all-cotton fabric, the crayon colors are softer and less color-fast.

To assemble the quilt, arrange the quilt blocks in seven rows of five squares each, alternating solid color and crayon squares. Arrange quilt so that four strips start and end with solid color blocks, and three strips start and end with crayon blocks. Join blocks into strips and then join strips into the completed quilt top, using ½-inch seam allowances. Press all seams toward solid color blocks.

Lay quilt backing out on the floor, wrong side up. Lay quilt batting on top of backing, followed by the quilt front, face up. Follow instructions given on page 43 for pinning and basting all layers together, then machine-stitch along all vertical and horizontal seam lines. Bind the quilt with seven-inch-wide strips of solid color fabric, folded in half lengthwise over three-inch-wide strips of batting to give a soft, puffy edging. To attach the binding, stitch the fabric strip to the topside of the quilt, right sides together. Miter corners and turn the edging to the back of the quilt. Blindstitch the edging in place. The finished quilt measures approximately 66x90 inches.

It's easy to make a crayon quilt to fit any size bed by simply changing the total number of 12-inch finished squares used. A twin-size quilt (54x90 inches) would require 14 solid color squares and 14 crayon squares arranged four squares wide and seven squares long. For a queen-size quilt (78x102 inches), use 24 squares of each (solid color and crayon) arranged six squares wide by eight squares long. A king-size quilt (90x102 inches) requires 28 squares of each type arranged seven squares wide and eight squares long.

With a little family cooperation, you can design and stitch a colorful crayon quilt in no time at all. While the youngsters are busy creating the art (above, left), Mom transfers their finished drawings onto fabric squares using a hot iron. The pictures must be pressed with strong, steady pressure to transfer completely (bottom, left). Crayon squares reproduced on synthetic fabrics are more brilliant and less likely to fade than on all-cotton material (above).

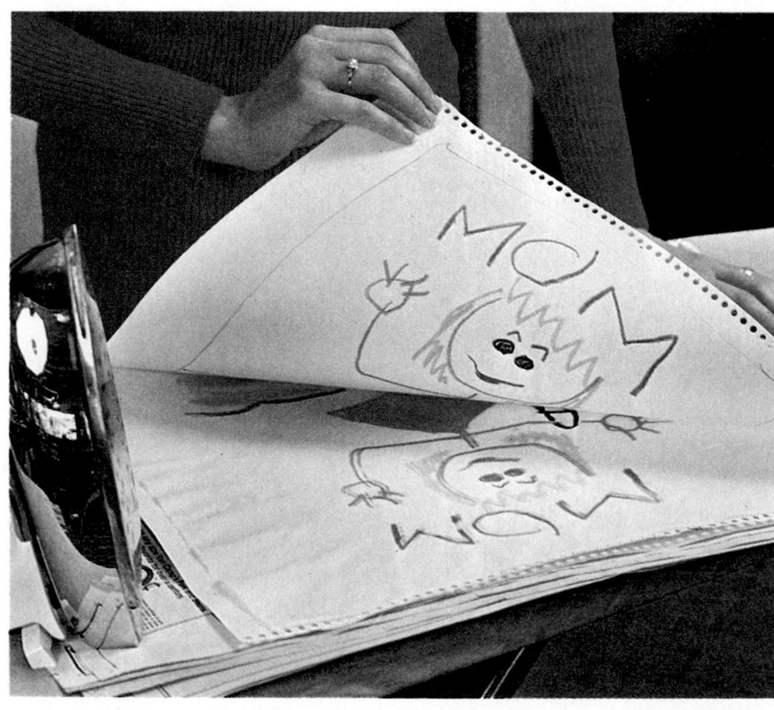

Appliquéd Headboard

Appliqué goes to the head of the bed with this classic, padded satin headboard. Our flowering vine design is worked in soft shades of green and dusty rose, but this delicate, stylized look can be adapted to whatever color scheme complements your bedroom.

Materials

1½ yards of 54-inch-wide eggshell satin (for twin-size headboard)
Scraps of satin in dark green, light green, dusty rose, and light pink
1 quilt bat
¼-inch plywood
3 yards muslin or inexpensive backing fabric
Staple gun or tacks
Fusible webbing

Directions

Start by enlarging the pattern below. Using the outline of the headboard pattern as a general guide, cut a piece of ¼-inch plywood that's 43 inches wide and 36 inches high at the peak of the headboard. Slope the contour of the top to conform to the pattern. These measurements are for a single or twin-size bed. To adapt the headboard to a full- or oversize bed, enlarge the drawing accordingly.

When the drawing is enlarged to the desired size, cut patterns for the flower, leaves, and stems using lightweight cardboard. Place each cardboard template on the wrong side of the appropriate color satin fabric, trace around edges, and cut out; do *not* add seam allowances. (Color key for diagram: D = dark green, L = light green, R = dusty rose, P = pink, E = eggshell.) Once the flowering vine and pink border strips are cut, arrange them in the proper place on the eggshell satin beginning nine inches from the top edge and six inches from each outer edge. Excess fabric will be folded and stapled to the plywood backing.

Cut pieces of fusible webbing using your cardboard templates as guides. Position the cut webbing under each satin piece and fuse them to the eggshell satin background fabric with a steam iron. Be sure that no webbing shows outside the edges of the satin. Fusing the appliqué pieces to the satin background fabric keeps them from slipping as you sew them in place. Cut and add border strips last.

Cut a piece of muslin and quilt batting that are the same dimensions as the eggshell satin. Sandwich the batting between the muslin backing and the satin, and baste all three layers together. Machine-appliqué around each fused design using ¼-inch satin stitches. Work slowly and carefully so that the stitching goes through all three layers. Hand-embroider the center of the flower in pink satin stitches.

Once the design is appliquéd, position the eggshell satin front on the plywood headboard. Smooth out the satin, turning the excess fabric to the back of the plywood, and staple or tack the fabric in place. Trim off the excess satin close to the staples.

To conceal the raw edges, cut a piece of backing fabric to fit the plywood headboard. Turn under the edges one inch and machine-hem. Place the backing against the plywood, then whipstitch it to the satin.

To adapt this project to a rectangular padded headboard, enlarge the design and turn it upside down so the straight edge is at the top. Then customize the border to conform to this rectangular shape.

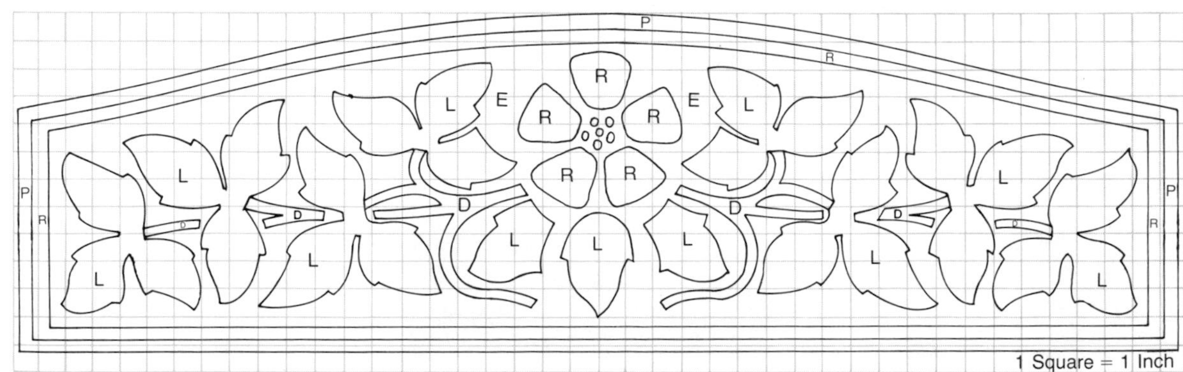

Contemporary Grandmother's Flower Garden Quilt

Traditionally, the Grandmother's Flower Garden quilt is a patchwork project that requires lots of intricate piecing. This contemporary version is done in sewing machine appliqué, allowing you to "grow" your quilt a whole flower at a time, instead of petal by petal. Flamboyant flowers in three different sizes and a startling variety of textures and fabrics combine in a striking way, making this quilt ideal for modern decorating. Remember, though, that a quilt combining fabrics of varying fiber content—such as double knits, cottons, and satins—should be dry-cleaned to keep it in the best condition.

Materials

8 yards muslin
8 yards of print or solid color backing fabric 45 inches wide
Assorted print fabric for flowers and centers
1½ yards print fabric for borders
Polyester batting

Directions

To make your own version of this quilt, first piece the muslin to the desired size for your bed, lay it on the floor, and place a single layer of quilt batting on top of it.

Next, using the patterns below, cut out as many of each of the three sizes of flowers as are necessary to cover the quilt top, starting at one corner and overlapping blossoms. Vary the sizes, colors, textures, and patterns of the flowers as much as possible. Do not add seam allowances to pattern pieces. Cut contrasting circles for each flower, center them on the flowers and pin in place. Baste all pieces in place through muslin and batting.

Using a ¼-inch satin stitch, machine-appliqué each flower and center in place, stitching through the fabric, batting, and muslin backing. See page 76 for complete instructions on machine appliquéing.

When the quilt top is finished, piece the print fabric to make a backing sheet as large as the quilt. Next cut and piece a 2½-inch-wide strip of binding fabric to go all around the quilt. Fold it in half lengthwise and press. Sew it to the quilt top, right sides together, using a ¼-inch seam allowance. Lay the quilt top on the floor face side down; place the backing fabric on top of it, right side up; turn the binding over the backing; and slip-stitch in place. For a thicker quilt, add extra layers of batting between the muslin and backing fabric. Tack backing fabric to quilt top at 12-inch intervals to keep it from shifting.

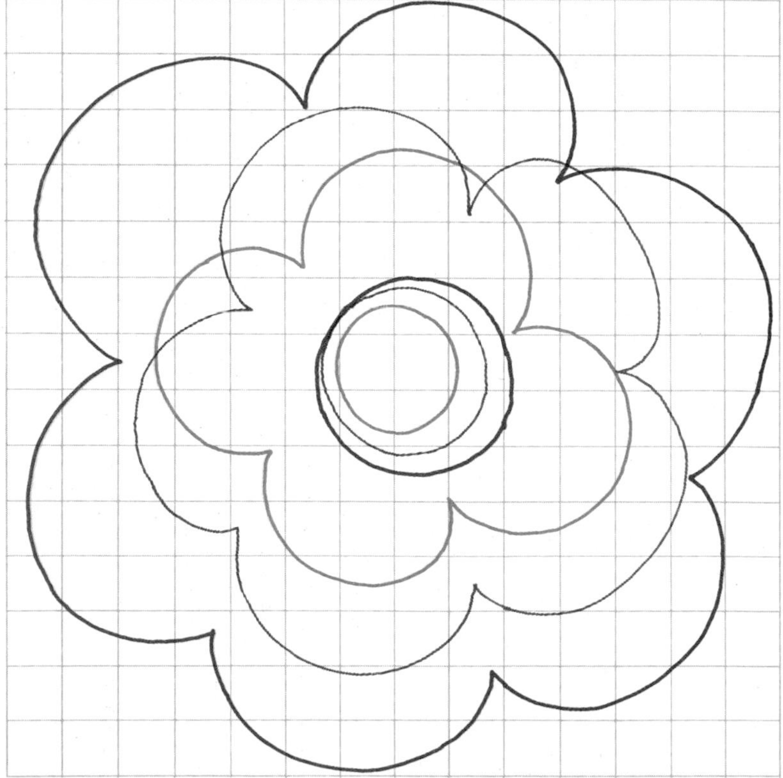

1 Square = 1 Inch

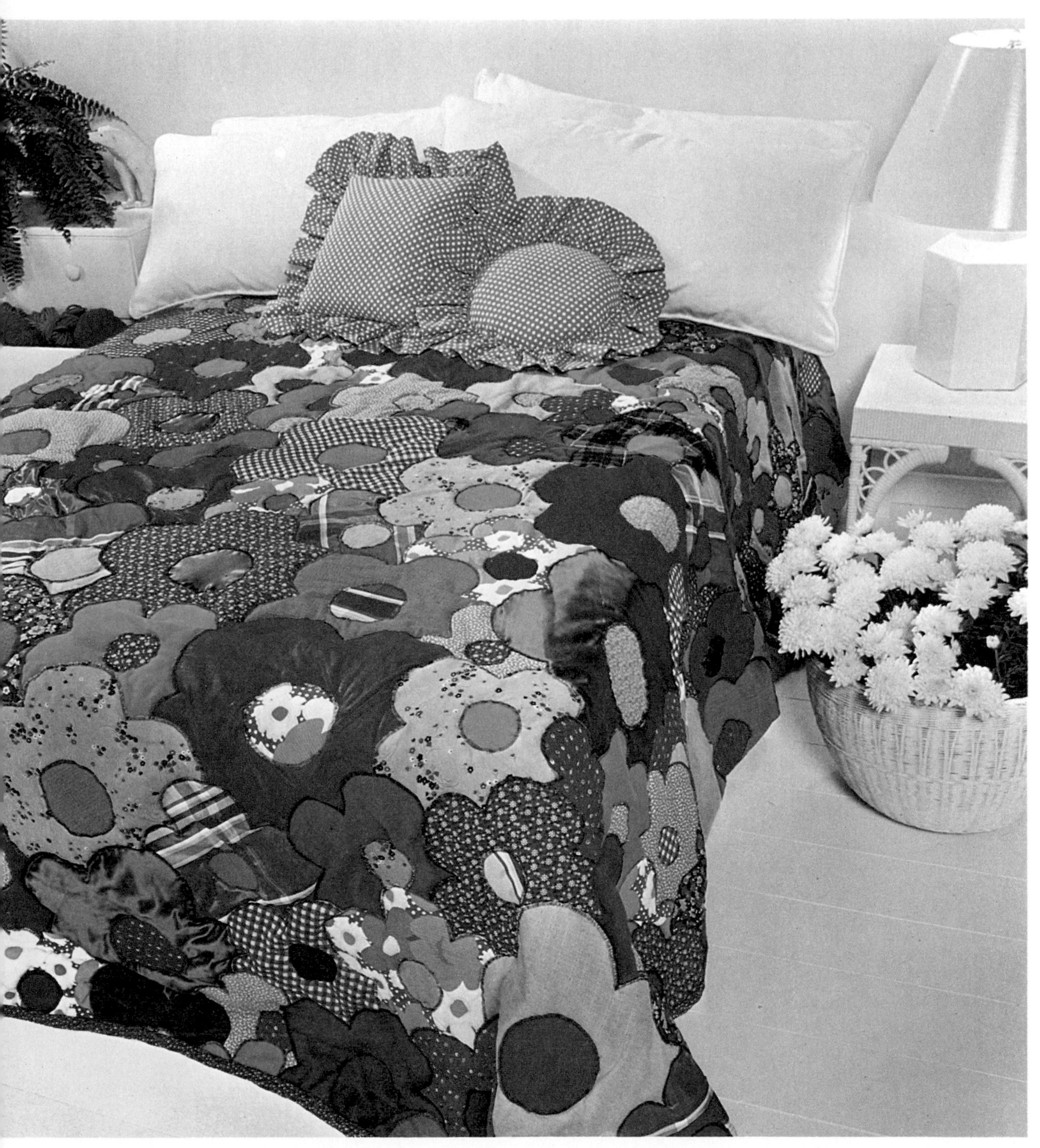

A Quilter's Quilt

If, in the course of this section, you've come to love quilts and quilting, then here's a project made to order for you. In this one quilt you'll be able to use all the techniques you've learned and in a most imaginative way. What is a quilt? In this case it's a spectacular 15-block storybook of quilting.

Materials

2 yards 45-inch blue fabric for borders
Fifteen 12-inch squares of fabric for block backgrounds
Assorted scraps of print and colored fabrics
Iron-on bonding fabric
White fabric paint
White sheet for backing
Polyester batting

Directions

To make this 48x76-inch quilt, collect all needed materials and enlarge the designs on the following pages (66 and 67). Make two copies of each block on tracing paper. You'll need one to cut into individual pattern pieces and one to lay over each block as a placement guide when you appliqué.

Press background fabrics smooth and cut out 12-inch-square blocks. Though blocks are finished to 10 inches, they're cut large to allow for take-up of fabric during the appliqué process. If a block is composed of several background pieces, machine-sew all pieces together and press the seams to one side.

Cut the larger appliqué pieces by laying the tracing paper pattern on the right side of the fabric and adding ¼-inch seam allowances to all edges. To simplify appliquéing the letters and small pieces, use iron-on bonding fabric. Draw exactly around the edge of pattern pieces on the shiny (bonding) surface of the iron-on fabric. Cut the pieces out and bond to the back of the print fabric to be appliquéd. Then cut the piece out of the print, adding ¼-inch seam allowance. To appliqué, turn under the seam allowance and slip-stitch each piece to the background. When appliquéing, refer to the photo of our quilt, since some pieces are behind others and must be sewn on first. As you pin and sew on each piece, lay the tracing paper pattern of the whole block over the work to check the placement of the pieces. Appliqué all blocks before quilting.

Each block is made up of different design elements and needlework techniques. Some require special treatment, so study each square carefully as you work. Here are some tips that may help with the individual blocks:

The *Color* block features a fabric rainbow. You need not stitch down the bottom edge of each strip because the next one overlaps it. Stitch down the bottom of only the yellow strip. Add the letters and hand, and embroider the hand details.

On the *Love* block, the "L" and "V" are one applique piece. The "E" and heart are separate.

The *Soft/Snoozy* square actually contains a block within a block. Appliqué the "Z's" on a separate piece of fabric, then appliqué that fabric to the main block. Appliqué sheeps' heads, bodies, then ears. Eyes and legs are embroidered in simple outline stitches.

The *Patchwork* block should be treated as two pieces. Add the letters to red fabric, then add a piece composed of two rows of patchwork squares. Appliqué the patchwork cat to a rectangle of red fabric, and embroider the details. Stitch that block to the lower right corner of the patchwork on the main block.

To work the *Appliquéd* block, stitch on design elements in the following order: basket handle, basket, flowers, then the letters (the basket texture will be quilted later).

The *Warm* block is worked in this sequence: Appliqué the sun and rings by themselves, then pin onto the background. Slip points of the sun behind outer ring and stitch points down. Now stitch the sun and rings down. Attach letters to the hill, and appliqué hill overlapping the sun. Add flowers and embroider stems and sun.

For the *Gentle Hands* block, appliqué the blue skirt, bodice, quilt, arms, hands, collar, face, hair, and glasses in that order. Add letters and embroidery.

continued

WHAT IS A QUILT? A QUILT IS....
COLOR
LOVE
SNOOZY
SOFT
ZZZZ
PATCHWORK
APPLIQUED
WARM
GENTLE HANDS
CRAZY
PUFFY
COZY
A GOOD NITE
PATTERNS
A TEXTILE SANDWICH
!
MODERN
EMBROIDERED DESIGNS THAT MAKE THE QUILT GAY
ARE PLEASURES AND DUTIES WE FIND ON OUR WAY
HOPE, LOVE AND KISSES ARE STITCHES SO BRIGHT
WHICH DECORATE LIFE WITH GLEAMS OF DELIGHT
WHILE SYMPATHY SWEET IS THE LINING TO HOLD
THE ODD SCRAPS OF FATE WHICH WE CANNOT CONTROL.
WE ARE BETTER THAN PATCHWORK BECAUSE OF THE SOUL.
OLD
FOUND EMBROIDERED ON BACK OF 1890 QUILT.

A Quilter's Quilt *(continued)*

1 Square = 1 Inch

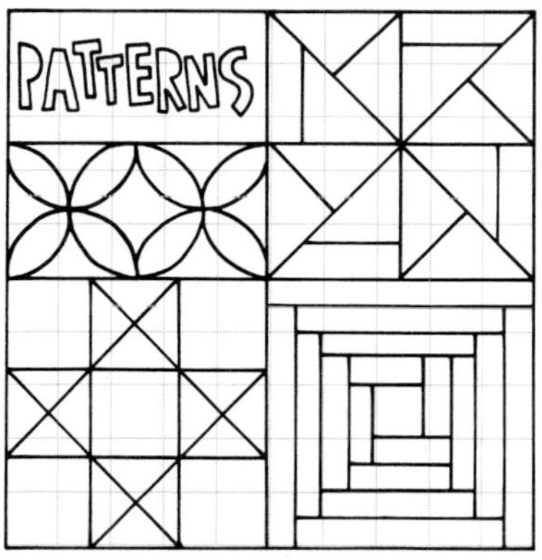

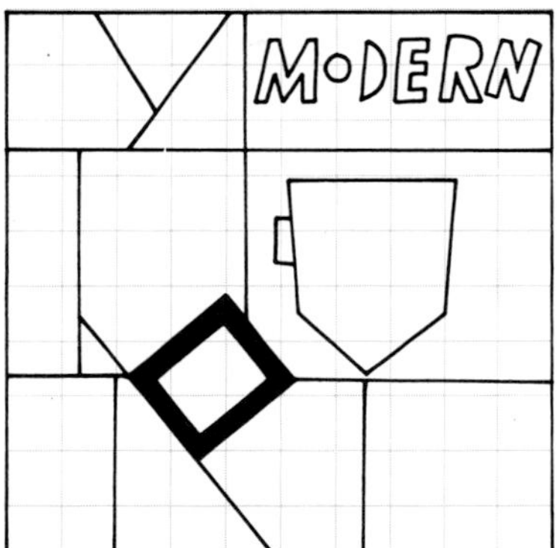

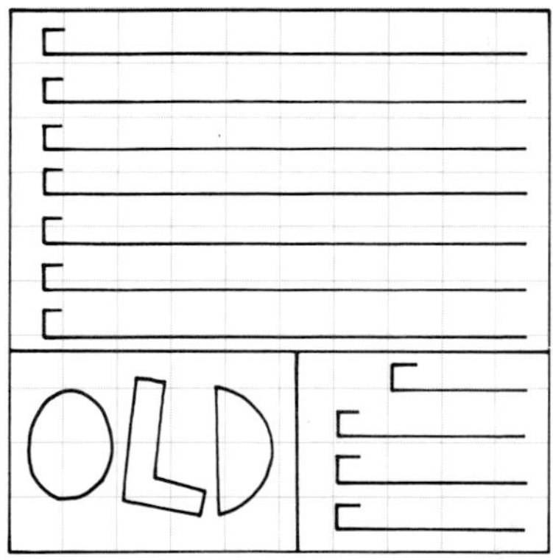

1 Square = 1 Inch

EMBROIDERED DESIGNS THAT MAKE THE QUILT GAY
ARE PLEASURES AND DUTIES WE FIND ON OUR WAY
HOPE, LOVE AND KISSES ARE STITCHES SO BRIGHT
WHICH DECORATE LIFE WITH GLEAMS OF DELIGHT
WHILE SYMPATHY SWEET IS THE LINING TO HOLD
THE ODD SCRAPS OF FATE WHICH WE CANNOT CONTROL
WE ARE BETTER THAN PATCHWORK BECAUSE OF THE SOUL.

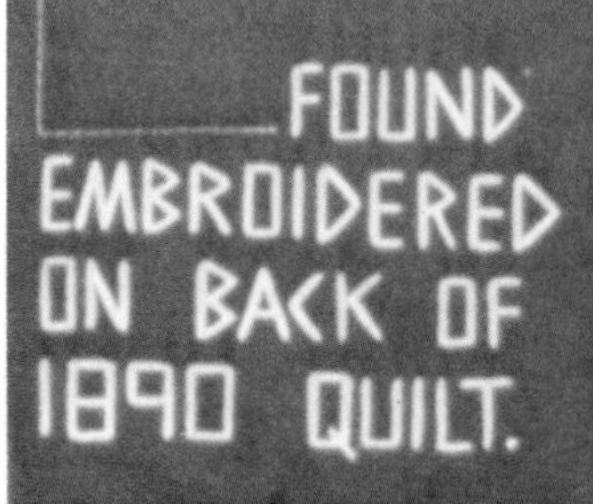

continued

A Quilter's Quilt *(continued)*

The *Crazy* quilt block is pieced on the sewing machine. Add letters. The zigzag edging on the pieces is added at the time of quilting.

The *Puffy* block is appliquéd with the letters, mouse, ears and tail. Embroider details. Tie this block; don't quilt it.

The *Cozy* square is easier if you piece the bird and leaves on the machine before you cut them out. Appliqué pieces in this order: nest, branches, leaves, eggs, bird, and letters. Embroider details.

Appliqué *A Good Nite* block. Add cheek last. Embroider eye and smile.

The *Patterns* block is treated as four separate pieces. Make the first piece and appliqué the letters. Make "Cathedral Window" rectangle, then attach to the letters block. Do sections in "Pinwheel," "Star," and "Log Cabin" designs. Join all sections together.

To make *A Textile Sandwich*, appliqué the letters to red fabric; the exclamation point to green, pieced to pink. Appliqué sandwich "fixin's," add embroidery details, and join the two pieces together.

The *Modern* square is treated as three strips. Appliqué letters and piece the rest of the top horizontal strip. Piece the center strip, attaching the pocket with machine-stitching outline. Piece the bottom strip, then join all three and appliqué the off-center red square onto the block.

To print the letters on the *Old* square, first print the poem in block letters on tracing paper. Lay carbon paper and the pattern on the fabric and tape the corners down. Trace over letters carefully with a dry ballpoint. Remove carbon and pattern and paint letters with fabric paint, laying on the paint in even strokes. When dry, paint a second coat. After that coat has dried, join the appliquéd lettered piece and the two painted pieces to form the complete block.

To complete quilt, layer 12-inch squares of sheet and polyester batting under each block. Baste all layers together. Machine quilt according to instructions given on page 44, using about eight stitches to the inch. Use white thread in the bobbin and change the top thread to match the face fabric. Stitch around all letters and designs, making sure no area larger than three or four inches is left unquilted.

Cut a 10-inch square of cardboard, lay it on the quilted blocks, and trace around, leaving a ¼-inch seam allowance. Stitch edges carefully, then trim off excess fabric.

Cut the following panels from both the blue fabric and sheet backing (these measurements include a ½-inch seam allowance): Ten panels 5x11 inches to use between three-block groups across the quilt; four panels 5x39 inches to use between the five rows of blocks vertically; two panels 6x67 inches for the two long sides of the quilt; and two panels 6x49 inches for the top and bottom edges. Cut matching batting pieces and baste to front fabric.

Make five strips of three blocks each, then join these five strips with the four panels to form the body of the quilt. Machine-sew both front panel edges. Machine-sew one backing panel edge, then hand-sew the other one in place. Add the side panels, leaving the outside edges open. Appliqué letters to the top strip, then add the top and bottom strips to the quilt. To finish the quilt, turn the front panel edges back over the backing and slip-stitch the face fabric to the backing.

Quilting Tips

Before you begin your next quilting project, keep these tips in mind. They're worth remembering because they can help you get a more professional finished look.

- Unsuitable quilting fabrics are those that are tightly woven (canvas or duck) or those that stretch and fray excessively (burlap or jersey). No matter what type of fabric you choose, always preshrink your fabric before you begin cutting the pattern pieces.
- Before buying materials for an entire project, buy just ¼ yard of each fabric and make a sample block. Then it's easy to detect and correct a weak color scheme or an inaccurate pattern.
- Polyester and cotton quilt batting are usually cut to standard sizes and are sold in several thicknesses. Quality varies, so experiment with different brands.
- Although cardboard patterns or templates are fine for small projects, plastic works better for quilt-size projects because it holds its edge longer than cardboard. You can buy plastic templates at most craft stores or you can make your own from plastic coffee can lids.

Appliquéd and Quilted Window Wall Hanging

For a room without a view, create one . . . with soft fabric fields and enchanting calico mountains.

Materials

Medium brown fabric for quilt background and bias binding
Fabric scraps for appliqué
Polyester batting

Directions

Enlarge the drawing below and trace onto the brown background fabric. Cut out all appliqué pieces in your choice of fabrics, adding seam allowances.

Baste and press under the seam allowance on each piece. Position the appliqué pieces according to the diagram; stitch in place (see pages 74 to 77).

Make slits in the background fabric behind each appliquéd area, lightly stuff with batting, then whipstitch openings closed. Assemble according to directions on page 43. Quilt as desired and finish edges with bias binding.

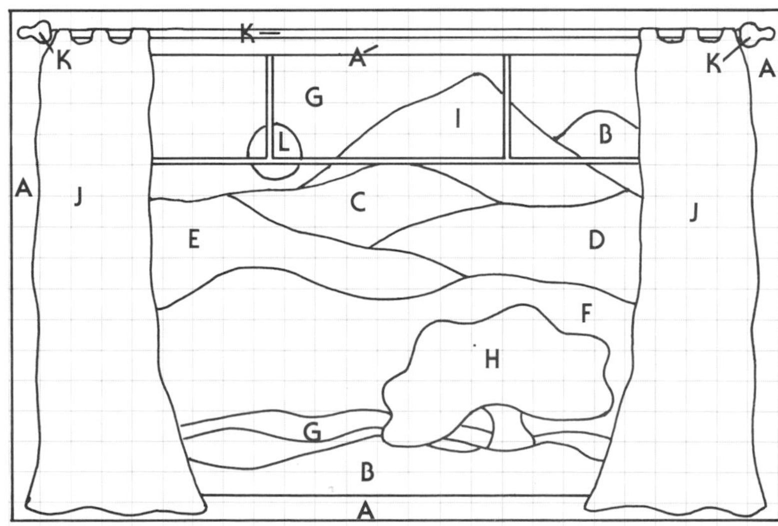

1 Square=2 Inches

COLOR KEY

A Medium Brown
B Black
C Green Print
D Polka Dot
E Medium Green
F Dark Green
G Blue
H Light Green
I Beige
J Floral Print
K Brass
L Sun Yellow

APPLIQUÉ

Learning to Appliqué

Because appliqué is such a versatile, exciting technique, you will find it fun and rewarding right from the start. To make sure you enjoy learning to appliqué, we have included step-by-step instructions for a variety of fabulous projects. Even a beginner can create the vibrant, attractive floral pillows shown here. Once you have mastered appliqué basics, you are on your way to self-expression in many fabric designs. Lots of quick-and-easy, sure-fire-success projects start you off, and after that, you will be able to combine different patterns and techniques to come up with some great stitchery possibilities. Complete how-to for these machine-appliquéd wildflower pillows starts on page 78.

Appliqué Basics

Appliqué can be as simple as a paper collage or as complicated as a thousand-piece jigsaw puzzle. But however complex the design, all appliqué involves the same procedure—applying one fabric to another. To help you get started on this exciting and challenging craft, here is some basic information on fabrics, cutting and sewing appliqués by hand or machine, and combining appliqué with other needlework techniques such as quilting and embroidery. Use these tips to add a personal touch to the "material" things in your life.

The first step in appliqué is to select a design. Unless you are already skilled in appliqué techniques, this may be the hardest step of all. So choose with care at first, for some designs are easier to stitch than others.

If you are a beginner, select a design with straight lines or gradual curves, and one with a relatively small number of large or medium-sized pieces rather than a trainload of tiny ones.

Next, decide on the technique you will use to secure the appliqué to the background fabric. While it is possible to glue fabrics or fuse them with iron-on webbings, sewing by hand or machine is more secure and, in most cases, more practical.

Then choose fabrics that are easy to sew, and you will have made a good start.

Selecting and Preparing Fabrics

A leisurely trip through a fabric store will unearth a wealth of fabrics for appliqué. Make your selection on the basis of the technique you will use (hand or machine appliqué), care requirements of the article you are making (will it be washed?), and compatibility of the fabrics you want to use together.

Felt is a wonderful fabric for appliqué. It works well with either hand or machine stitching, and because it is non-woven, it will not ravel. So you never need to turn under the edges. It does fade, however, and most felt has to be dry-cleaned.

For hand-appliqué—where you will turn under the edges of the pattern pieces before stitching—choose light- to medium-weight, supple fabrics that are easy to manipulate. One hundred percent cottons (or cotton blends) such as broadcloth, gingham, denim, and sailcloth and lightweight wools are all suitable. Some knits work well, but if a knit is very stretchy, back it with a scrap of cotton or iron-on interfacing to stabilize it.

For machine-appliqué, you can select from most weights, including upholstery fabrics. Some lightweight fabrics have enough body to sew well. Others, however, need interfacing to stitch well by machine.

Depending on the effect you are seeking, you will find interesting textures for machine work in velveteen, corduroy, homespun, peau de soie, and even vinyl, real leather, and felt.

The basic test for appliqué fabric is this: how easily does a needle slip through the fabric? Wool, cotton broadcloth, and wool felt all sew easily. The fine percales, such as those found in sheets, however, are sometimes difficult to stitch because they are closely woven, with a high number of threads per inch.

Next, how easily does a fabric ravel? Loosely woven fabrics ravel easily, making them hard to stitch by hand. One hundred percent cottons tend to ravel less than blends, making them favorites among quilters.

Evaluate each fabric by itself and in combination with others. For most projects, you will want to use fabrics of about the same weight, care requirements, and durability. For hanging panels, however, the sky is the limit. Mix textures, prints, and colors to get the effect you want.

When buying fabrics, start with the background color. It is easier to develop a whole scheme once you have selected the major color.

Mixing fabrics and patterns is a matter of personal taste. If you are comfortable with a potpourri of prints, use them.

Before cutting pattern pieces, straighten the grain of the fabrics and preshrink them.

Making Appliqué Patterns

After choosing a design, enlarge it following directions for enlarging and transferring designs on pages 272 and 273. This is your master pattern.

Make a second pattern to cut apart for the individual design elements. To keep track of the pieces, number or letter corresponding shapes on the cutting pattern and the master pattern. On large projects, jot down the total number of pieces to cut for each shape on the master.

For each shape to be used often in the overall design, make a sandpaper, cardboard, or plastic template that can be traced around many times. For other pieces, make heavy paper patterns. Do not add seam allowances to pattern pieces.

When shapes overlap on the overall design, cut each pattern piece as though it were uninterrupted. For example, if one leaf partially covers another leaf, cut two full leaf patterns, as shown on the diagram at right.

Cutting Pattern Pieces

When laying out patterns for cutting, position large appliqués so the straight grain of the fabric runs the same direction on both the appliqué and the background fabric. This prevents puckering and stretching of the appliqué during stitching or after washing. (The lengthwise grain runs parallel to the selvage of the fabric; the crosswise grain runs at right angles to the selvage.)

With fabric face up, lay out pattern pieces, leaving *at least* ½ to 1 inch between them to allow for seams (see diagram at right).

Trace patterns with a sharp pencil. *The pencil line represents the stitching or folding line, not the cutting line.* Unless directions for your project specify otherwise, cut pieces ¼ inch beyond the penciled outline.

If raw edges of appliqué pieces begin to ravel, touch the edges with a dot of white glue. When dry, the glue will be clear and the edge will hold securely.

Sometimes you will need to interface a piece. For machine appliqué, use iron-on interfacing on lightweight fabrics to prevent puckering. Also, if one piece of a pattern will partially cover another and the lower fabric is visible through the upper one, interface the top piece to hide the shadow or cut away the lower fabric after stitching.

For hand appliqué, cut interfacing without seam allowances. For machine appliqué, cut it the same size as the pattern piece.

Appliquéing by Hand

Hand and machine stitching are both "correct" approaches to appliqué. Choose between them on the basis of your project, its intended use, and the fabrics you have selected.

The first step in hand appliqué is to turn under seam allowances on pattern pieces. If desired, machine-stitch along the seam line (¼ inch from raw edges). Clip the seam allowance to the stay-stitching on curves and corners so turned edges lie flat and smooth. Next, baste along the fold of each piece (see lower diagram at right). Or, turn raw edges under as you stitch them to the background.

Sometimes two or more shapes are layered together onto the background; a flower petal, for instance, may overlap a stem. Do not turn under the seam allowance on the lower shape where it will be covered by the upper shape. Instead, clip the seam allowance and tuck the raw edge under the overlap.

Pin and baste the appliqués in place on the background fabric. Then you are ready to stitch.

continued

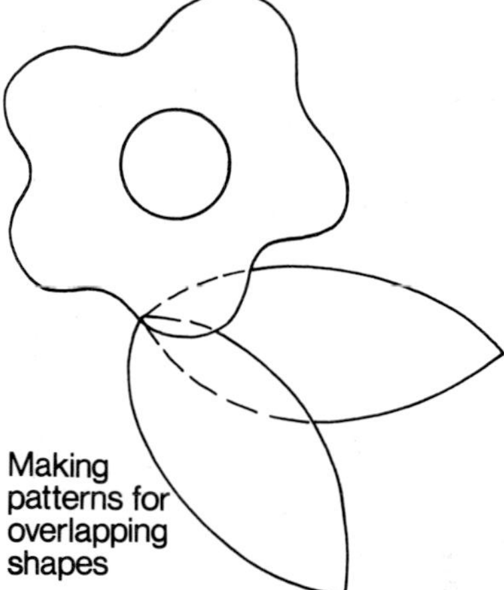
Making patterns for overlapping shapes

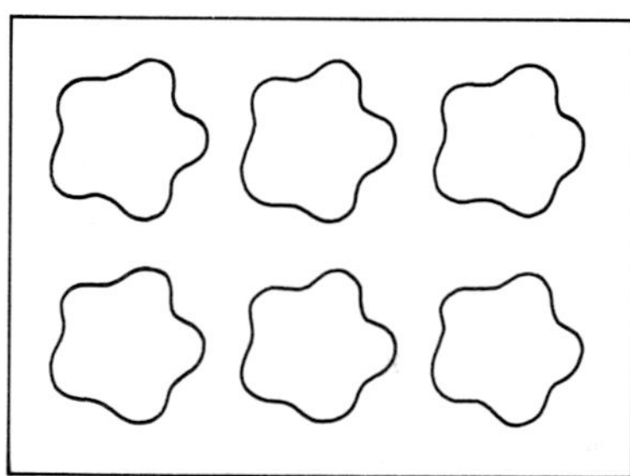
Leaving seam allowances between pattern pieces

Basting seam allowances

Appliqué Basics *(continued)*

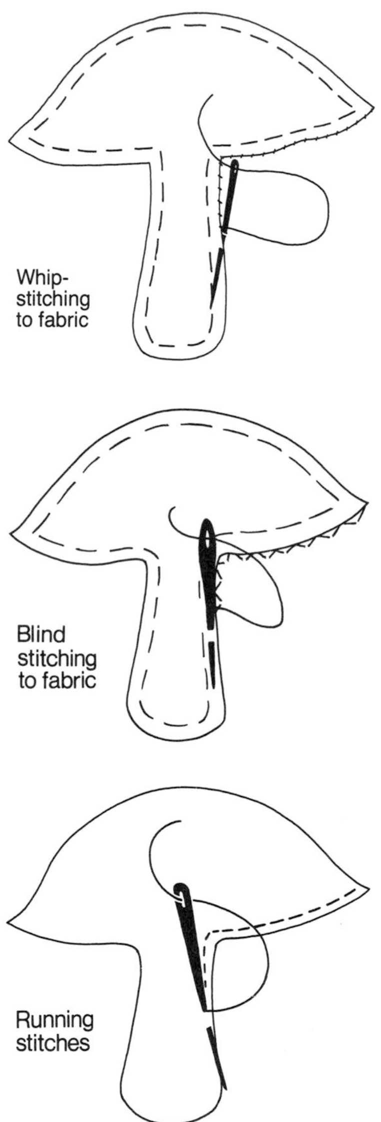

Most hand appliqué is based on a variation of a running stitch. The traditional appliqué stitch is the *whipstitch* (see top diagram at left). For this stitch, bring the needle up through the appliqué ⅛ to $\frac{1}{16}$ inch from the edge, and reinsert it into the background at the edge of the appliqué, making a small diagonal stitch. Bring the needle up again through the background and the appliqué and continue stitching.

With whipstitching, the edge of the appliqué will be held flat against the background fabric. It is a very secure stitch.

The *backstitch* is similar to the whipstitch in that it makes a flat edge and is very secure.

With the *blind stitch*, stitches are almost invisible in the appliqué piece (see the diagram at left). Bring the needle through the fold of the seam allowance and pick up a thread or two of background fabric at that point. Then pick up a thread or two along the fold of the appliqué. Repeat around the appliqué shape, making stitches about ¼ inch apart. This stitch is also secure, but it gives the edge of the appliqué a soft, puffy look.

The running stitch is often used in hand appliqué. Weave the needle in and out close to the folded edge of the appliqué, taking tiny stitches (see lower diagram at left). When worked in embroidery thread, this stitch is very decorative.

Much appliqué stitching will be along straight edges or curves and will present no problems. *On inside curves and corners*, however, snip the seam allowance so it can be turned smoothly. Then stitch as you would a straight edge, taking a tiny whipstitch where needed to prevent fraying.

To make an outside corner, first stitch one edge up to the hem allowance. Then, using the needle, turn the hem of the second edge under and continue stitching, as shown in the diagram opposite.

To make a pointed edge, stitch one edge first. Then, using the needle, turn under the second edge. Make a tiny whipstitch at the tip to keep the corner from fraying (see diagram opposite). Then stitch along the second edge.

Machine Appliqué

Most machine appliqué is done on a zigzag machine, although successful projects also can be completed on a straight-stitching machine (see the Rainbow Quilt on pages 90 to 93, for example).

For a straight-stitch machine, cut appliqué pieces with a ¼-inch seam allowance. Stitch along the seam line and clip curves as needed. Press seam allowance under and pin the appliqué piece to the background fabric. Machine-stitch around all edges ⅛ inch from fold.

To make the almost "traditional" machine satin stitch, cut all pieces, allowing at least ½ inch for seams on all sides. Pin appliqué pieces in position on background fabric and hand-baste if desired.

Next, machine-baste. With a short, straight stitch and matching thread, machine-stitch on marked lines. Or set the machine for medium-wide, medium-long zigzag stitches (10 to 12 stitches per inch) and zigzag-baste the appliqué in place. Trim excess fabric beyond the stitching with small, sharp scissors. To finish, set the machine for a zigzag satin stitch and zigzag over the basting on the appliqué pieces, covering the raw edges.

To get the best results, use even hand tension on the fabric. Guide, do not push or pull, fabric—to do so will make the work uneven. If the appliqué puckers, loosen tension.

When the design requires stitching a sharp corner, zigzag up to the corner and leave the needle in the fabric at the outside of the line of stitches. Then lift the presser foot and pivot the fabric. Lower the presser foot and start your stitching so the first stitch goes toward the inside of the design, overlapping the stitch just made. Then continue stitching.

To finish, pull threads to back side and tie off.

If the fabrics you are working with are lightweight and tend to draw during machine-stitching, support them with iron-on interfacing or a piece of organdy under the appliqué.

On highly textured fabrics that do not take a pattern well, work from the back of the background fabric. Do not mark stitching lines on individual pieces, but do mark the overall pattern on the *back* of the background fabric. Next, pin the appliqué in position on the front of the fabric and straight-stitch it in place from the back. Turn the fabric right side up, trim the margin beyond the stitch line, and machine satin-stitch on the front to cover the raw edges of the appliqué.

If your machine has a variety of decorative stitch settings, this is a perfect time to use them. You can richly embellish appliqué with several rows of fancy stitches in matching or contrasting colors. Also try using double needles with different colors of top thread—even metallics—for special effects.

Tools that Help

Good, sharp shears are a must for cutting out appliqués and for keeping fabric edges from fraying. Embroidery scissors are handy for cutting small shapes and for clipping seam allowances along curves.

Also have a supply of sharp, stainless steel pins and needles available. For hand appliqué, generally the heavier the fabric, the larger the needle you will need. For machine work, keep needles in various sizes on hand. Change needles regularly—dull ones are hard to stitch with.

Cotton or polyester thread works well for hand- or machine-stitching. Also try threads made for machine stitchery. Or use silk thread for a shiny, rich appearance.

Fusible webbings are valuable too, for a bit of webbing can hold a small appliqué piece in place better than a pin.

Appliqué Plus

There are numerous ways to embellish appliqué work, but the most commonly used ones are quilting and embroidery.

For traditional quilting, add batting and backing fabric to your appliqué and then hand- or machine-quilt in outlines around the appliqués, in blank areas between them, or within the appliqués themselves. Add dimension to individual appliquéd shapes with trapunto quilting—open the background fabric and add padding between the background and the appliqué. Many of the projects in this book call for quilting, since it is an integral part of much appliqué work.

If you want to use embroidery in combination with appliqué, try buttonhole stitches worked around the edge of the appliqué. They are not only decorative, but can be used in place of whipstitches to anchor the appliqué to the background fabric.

For textural interest, try French knots or a variety of raised stitches on the surface of your appliqué. Do not hesitate to experiment freely with embroidery stitches—they will make all of your appliqué projects uniquely your own.

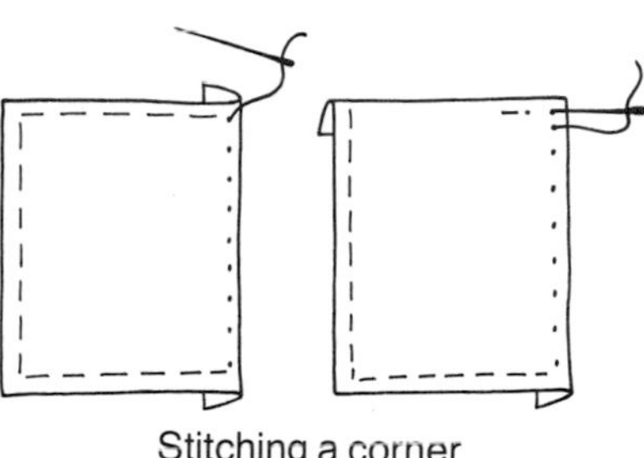
Stitching a corner

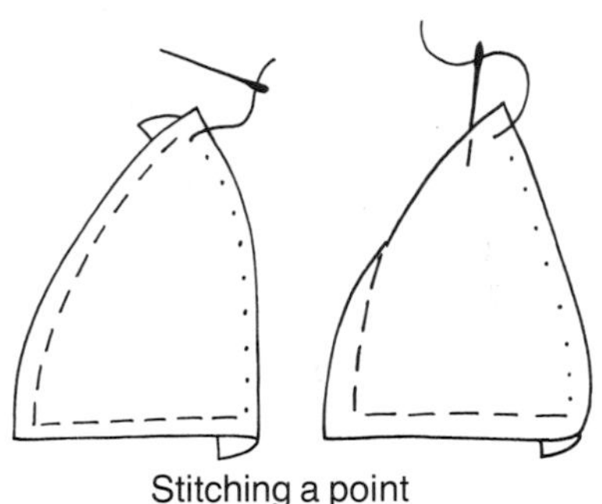
Stitching a point

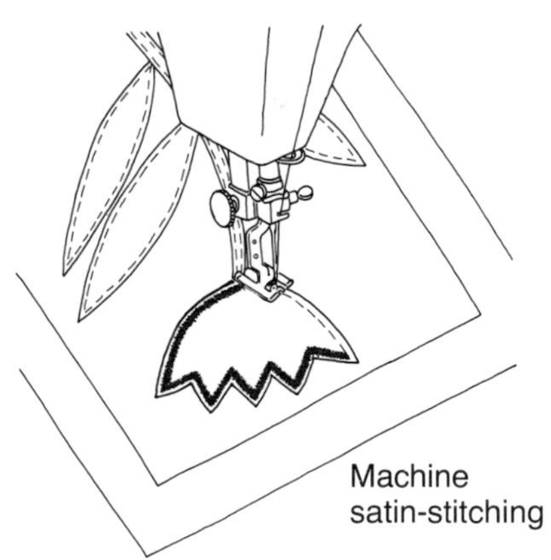
Machine satin-stitching

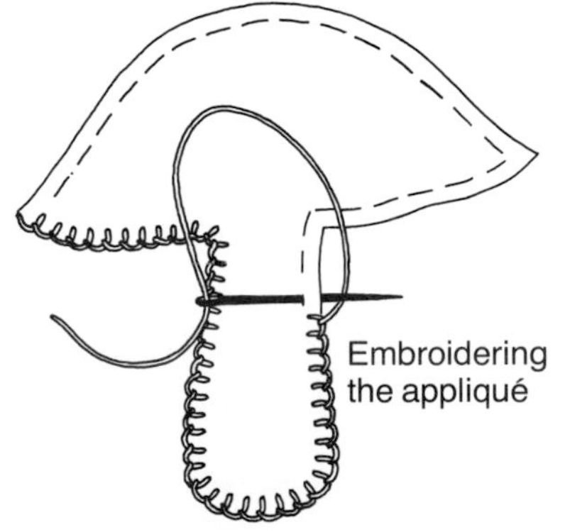
Embroidering the appliqué

Quick-and-Easy Wildflower Pillows *(shown on pages 72 and 73)*

For a bright splash of color in your living room make just one or all eight of our wildflower designs shown on pages 72 and 73. Machine-appliqué the basic shapes to a slightly textured background fabric, add machine-embroidered details, and stitch and stuff the covers into large (20-inch-square), dramatic pillows.

If leisurely hand-appliqué is more your style, you can still stitch up these beautiful pillows—we tell you how on the next page.

You also can use the patterns shown here to stitch the wildflower coverlet shown on pages 146 and 147.

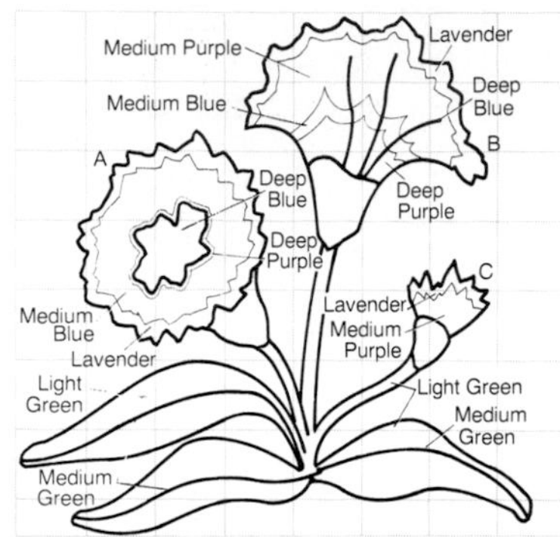

Bachelor's-button

Yellow
Deep Orange
B
Yellow
A
Medium Green
Medium Green
Deep Green
Deep Green

Dandelion

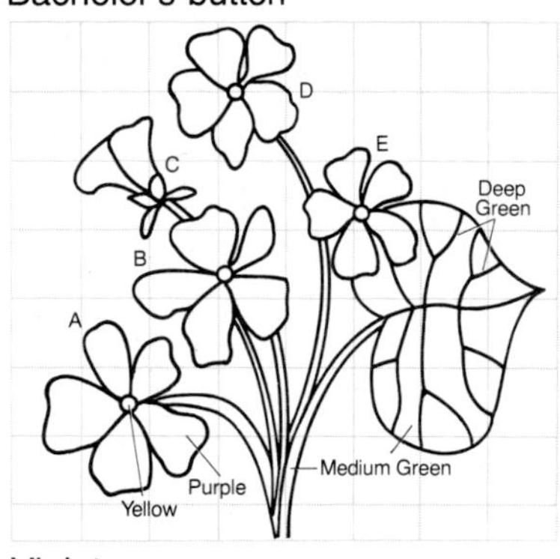

Violet

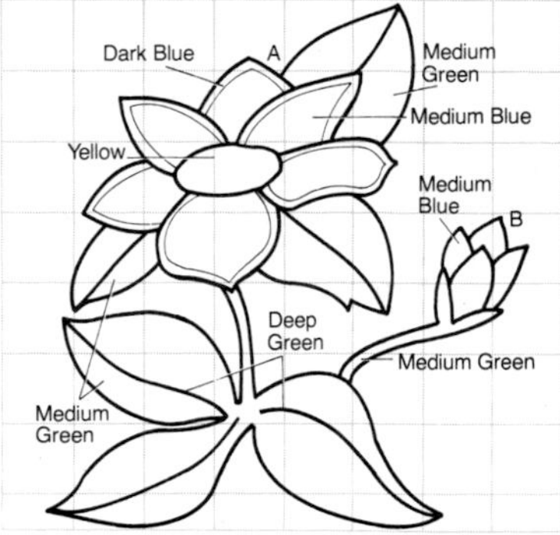

Hepatica 1 Square = 2 Inches

Materials
(for each pillow)
- ⅔ yard 44-inch-wide white Haitian cotton or any similar closely woven, medium-weight fabric
- Scraps of fabric in colors suggested in color key
- Thread to match fabrics
- Iron-on interfacing
- Polyester fiberfill or 20-inch pillow form
- 90 inches cotton cable cord

Directions
Enlarge patterns above and opposite. To add body to the fabrics and to help prevent puckering when they are stitched, fuse iron-on interfacing to wrong side of fabric scraps before cutting. Cut pattern pieces following the color guide, opposite. Add ½-inch seam allowances if you are appliquéing by machine.

Machine-appliqué in place small detail pieces such as flower centers before appliquéing flowers to pillow fronts.

For machine appliqué, follow these steps: Pin the piece to be appliquéd in position. With the sewing machine set for a medium-wide, medium-long (10 to 12 stitches per inch) zigzag stitch, baste around the edges of the appliqué with matching thread. Trim excess fabric beyond the stitching line. Reset the machine for wide, closely-spaced zigzag stitches and stitch around edges again, covering basting and raw edges with a neat line of machine satin stitches.

If fabric puckers or bobbin threads show on the surface of the fabric, adjust tension on spool and bobbin threads.

Arrange flowers on 22-inch squares of white fabric, positioning the appliqués so the lengthwise grain of the background fabric will run the same direction on all the pillows. Pin the flowers in place. Next, pin leaves and stems in place, tucking raw edges under flower petals, if necessary. When everything is in place, machine-baste (zigzag stitch) the pieces to the pillow and remove the pins.

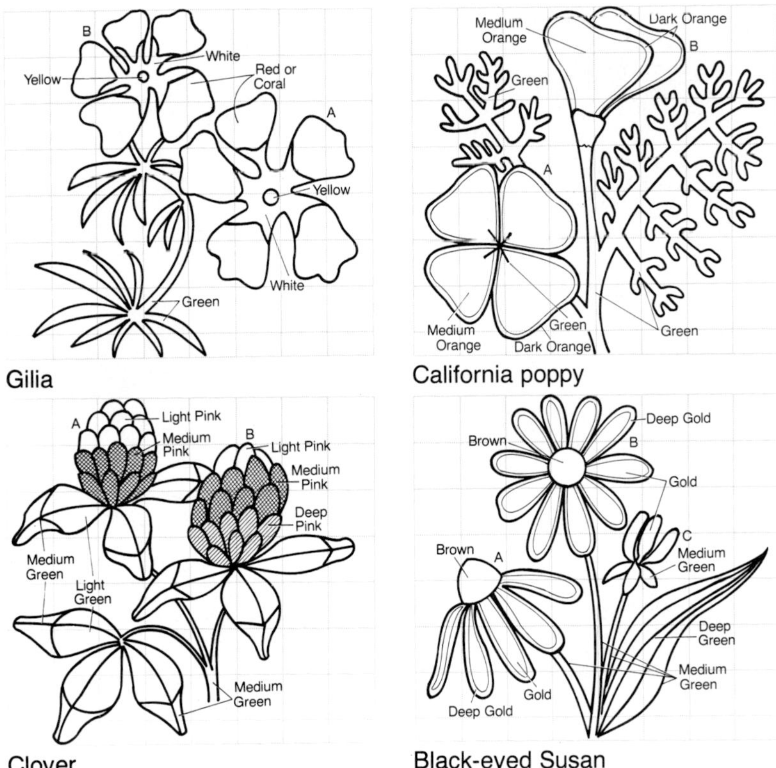

Gilia

California poppy

Clover

Black-eyed Susan

Sketch interior design details onto the fabric shapes with chalk and machine-embroider over the chalk lines using the same wide satin stitch used for the appliqués. Press the fabric.

Cut and piece 1½-inch-wide bias strips of green fabric. For each pillow, cover 90 inches of cotton cable cord with the bias strips using a zipper foot and matching thread. Pin and sew the cording to the front of the pillow 1 inch from the raw edges. Round the corners. Where ends of cording meet, fold under raw edge of cording fabric to form a clean edge.

Cut a 22-inch square of white fabric for the pillow back, making sure grain line runs the same direction as on the front. With right sides together, sew the front and back pieces together in a 1-inch seam. Leave an opening for turning. Trim seams and clip corners; turn right side out and press. Stuff the cover with polyester fiberfill or a pillow form and slip-stitch the opening closed.

To hand-appliqué the wildflower designs on the pillows, enlarge the patterns, adding ¼-inch seam allowances to all pieces. Cut stems on the bias so they can be curved easily. Cut pieces from fabric, turn under the seam allowance on each, and baste along the fold. Hand-appliqué small shapes to flowers before stitching flowers to pillow fronts, as above. Then hand-appliqué flowers, stems, and leaves to pillow fronts. Hand-embroider interior design details.

Assemble the pillow covers following directions above.

Color and Cutting Guide

Bachelor's-button: Flowers A and B are blue; flower C and center of flower A are lavender appliqués. Work details in purple thread. Cut and appliqué leaves and stems as a single piece.

Dandelion: Flower A is a solid yellow with deep yellow stitching; flower B is yellow with an orange appliqué center and deep yellow stitching. Cut and appliqué leaves and stems as a single piece with deep green stitching and veins.

Violet: Appliqué each flower as a single unit with yellow appliquéd center. Cut and appliqué leaf and stems as a single piece; outline veins and details of petals in satin stitches.

Hepatica: Cut and appliqué flower and bud as single pieces; appliqué leaves and stems individually. Use matching thread for details on flowers and leaves.

Gilia: Cut and appliqué flowers, yellow centers, and stem and leaf sections as single pieces; outline white portion of each petal with white thread.

California poppy: Cut and appliqué flowers A and B, stems, and leaf sections as single pieces; outline individual petals on flowers in satin stitches.

Clover: Lower half of each flower is deep pink, upper half is medium pink. Work appliqué and details in deep pink thread. Cut and appliqué stems and leaves individually; work details in deeper green thread.

Black-eyed Susan: Petals and centers of flowers A and B are cut and appliquéd individually and outlined with a deeper shade of thread. Flower C and leaf/stem unit are each cut as single pieces and details are outlined with satin stitching.

Quick-and-Easy Heart Pillow

Our simple heart pillow has just one shape hand-appliquéd onto the background fabric four times. With gradual curves and both an inside and an outside corner on each heart, this pillow is a great project for a beginner. And hand-quilting gives this pillow old-fashioned charm.

Materials

⅓ yard white or off-white cotton fabric
¼ yard red print fabric
¼ yard green print fabric
12-inch square of lining
12-inch square of quilt batting
White or off-white quilting thread
Polyester fiberfill

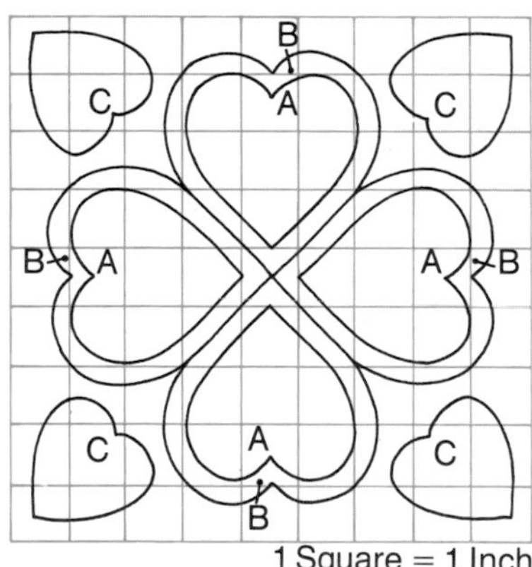

1 Square = 1 Inch

Directions

Note: Finished size is 11½ inches square.

Cut a 9¾-inch square from the white fabric. Cut 4 hearts (A) from the red print fabric and appliqué them to the white square as shown on the pattern, turning the raw edges under ¼ inch. Use whipstitches for a flat edge on the appliqué or blind stitches for a rounded edge.

Cut four 1⅝x11¾-inch strips from the green fabric. With right sides together, sew 1 strip to each side of the square, using ¼-inch seams. Miter the corners and clip excess material. Press seams to one side.

Cut a piece of lining and a piece of quilt batting to match the pillow top. Baste the three layers together, from the center to the edges, with the batting in the middle. Quilt around the appliquéd hearts, staying as close to the edge as possible. Take tiny running stitches and go through all three layers.

Using a hard lead pencil, *very* lightly draw around each appliquéd heart, using heart B as a pattern. Lightly draw around heart C four times, placing 1 heart in each corner, as shown on the pattern. Be sure to mark lightly, since the lines may not wash out completely. Quilt around each of these traced designs. Remove basting.

Cut a piece of white fabric to match the front, and with right sides together, sew the front to the back using a ¼-inch seam. Leave an 8-inch opening in one side for turning. Turn right side out and stuff. Slip-stitch the opening closed.

Quick-and-Easy Bird Pillow

This pillow design also is worked in gradual curves, but here you will get a chance to work with several layers of appliqués, fitting them together to form a graceful bird. A pieced patchwork border accents the appliquéd motif.

Materials

12½-inch square of dusty rose fabric
9¾-inch circle of white fabric
½ yard navy fabric
Fabric scraps in shades of green, purple, rust, coral, pink, and orange
Polyester fiberfill

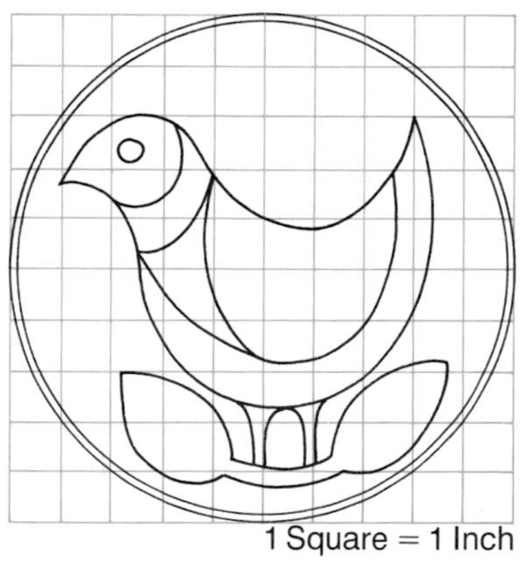

1 Square = 1 Inch

Directions

Enlarge the pattern and cut out pieces, referring to the photograph for colors. Fit smaller pieces onto large body piece of bird; turn under raw edges and appliqué in the following order: neck band, breast, wing, and eye. The edges of the throat, breast, and wing pieces should overlap so they barely touch when appliquéd.

Pin the bird, the bird's feet, and the leaves in place on the white circle. Tuck the feet under the body and leaf stem so that when edges are turned under, they will not expose raw edges of feet. Appliqué the bird's body onto the white circle.

Center the circle on the 12½-inch square and appliqué it in place. Edge the square with a border of 1-inch-wide navy blue strips, using a ¼-inch seam. Also using a ¼-inch seam, cut and piece random fabric scraps to make four 1½-inch-wide strips, referring to the photograph for color ideas. Piece the strips until they're long enough to go around the blue border. Press seams to one side. With right sides together, sew these strips to the navy strips in a ¼-inch seam. Finish the pillow front with navy strips sewn to the multi-colored strips. Cut these navy strips any width (1-inch-wide strips make a 15-inch pillow) and sew them to the striped border.

Cut a piece of navy fabric to match the pillow front, and with right sides together, sew the back to the front, leaving a 12-inch opening in one side. Turn, stuff, and slip-stitch the opening.

Quick-and-Easy Wall Hanging and Pillow

To create these contemporary views of nature, use simple shapes, bold colors, and trapunto quilting in combination with machine appliqué.

Materials

Scraps of velveteen, brushed corduroy, and broadcloth in rust, copen blue, brick red, orange, gold, white, and medium and light shades of gray-brown, red-brown, and green
Two 20x16½-inch pieces of navy blue broadcloth (pillow)
20x18 inches plum-colored cotton (wall hanging front)
20x18 inches printed flannel (wall hanging back)
½ yard iron-on interfacing
Pillow stuffing
Blue and red thread
Curtain rings

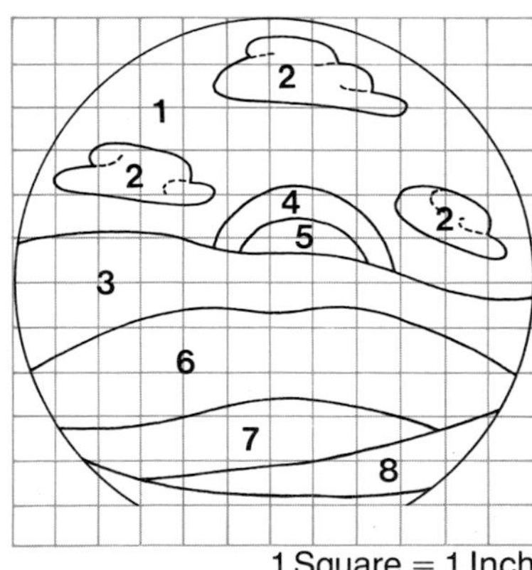

1 Square = 1 Inch

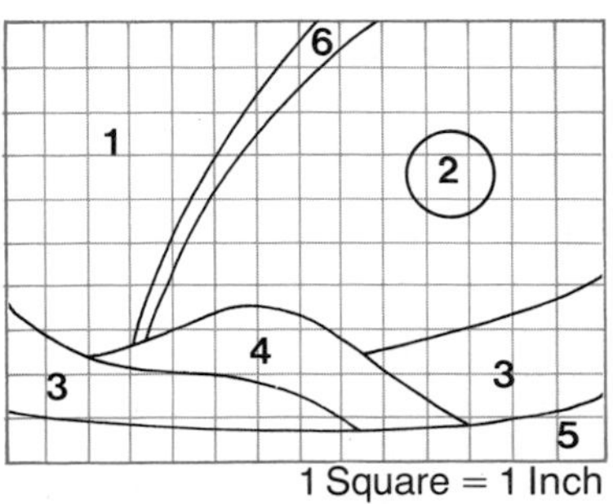

1 Square = 1 Inch

Directions

Wall Hanging

Enlarge the pattern at left, following directions on pages 272 and 273. Cut individual pattern pieces from fabric, referring to the photograph for colors. Cut the top half of the circle as a single brick red shape and appliqué clouds and sun pieces onto it. Add a ½-inch margin to pieces after lightly marking the seam line with pencil or dressmaker's carbon paper.

Cut matching shapes from iron-on interfacing and fuse interfacing to the wrong side of each piece. The interfacing should give the fabric enough body to keep it from puckering when it is stitched. If it does pucker, adjust thread tension on the sewing machine. Trace a 12-inch circle in the center of the plum-colored fabric.

Appliqué the shapes in the circle as follows: Pin a shape in position, following the numerical sequence on the pattern. Next, machine-baste on the seam line of the appliqué with a narrow-width, medium-length zigzag stitch (10 to 12 stitches per inch). Use red thread. (The bobbin thread should not be visible on the face of the fabric; if it is, adjust tension.) With sharp scissors, trim excess fabric beyond the stitching line.

Reset sewing machine for wide, closely spaced zigzag stitches (machine satin stitches); sew again over outlines of each appliqué, covering raw edges. Pin and machine-baste all pieces in place before doing any of the final stitching. Then satin-stitch all outlines at the same time—*except the outline of the circle*, which is satin-stitched later. Add wisps on clouds with felt pen.

To quilt the shapes in the appliquéd scene, turn the fabric wrong side up and make small slits in the background fabric behind each shape except the clouds. Be careful not to cut into the appliqué itself. Lightly stuff the shapes, using an orange stick to tuck stuffing into tight corners. Then slip-stitch the slits closed.

To assemble the wall hanging, cut two 4x4-inch squares. Cut each one in half across the diagonal and machine-baste one triangle to each of the corners of the plum-colored fabric as shown in the photograph. Do not satin-stitch yet. Next, with right sides together, stitch the back of the wall hanging to the front, leaving an opening for turning. Turn right side out and stuff lightly. Slip-stitch the opening. Then machine satin-stitch along the diagonals of the corner triangles and around the circle. Sew curtain rings to upper corners for hanging.

Pillow

Enlarge the pattern at left and cut out the pattern pieces, referring to the photograph for colors. Cut the green velveteen as a single piece and appliqué the arc and circle onto it. Fuse iron-on interfacing to backs of pieces. Mark a 10½x14-inch rectangle in the center of one of the pieces of navy fabric, and appliqué the shapes onto it in numerical order, following directions for the wall hanging. After machine-basting, satin-stitch all edges, including the outline of the large rectangle.

Quilt all of the shapes on the pillow except the copen blue arc (piece #6), following directions above.

To assemble the pillow, baste and then stitch the pillow front to the back, right sides together. Leave an opening for turning. Turn, stuff the pillow, and slip-stitch the opening closed.

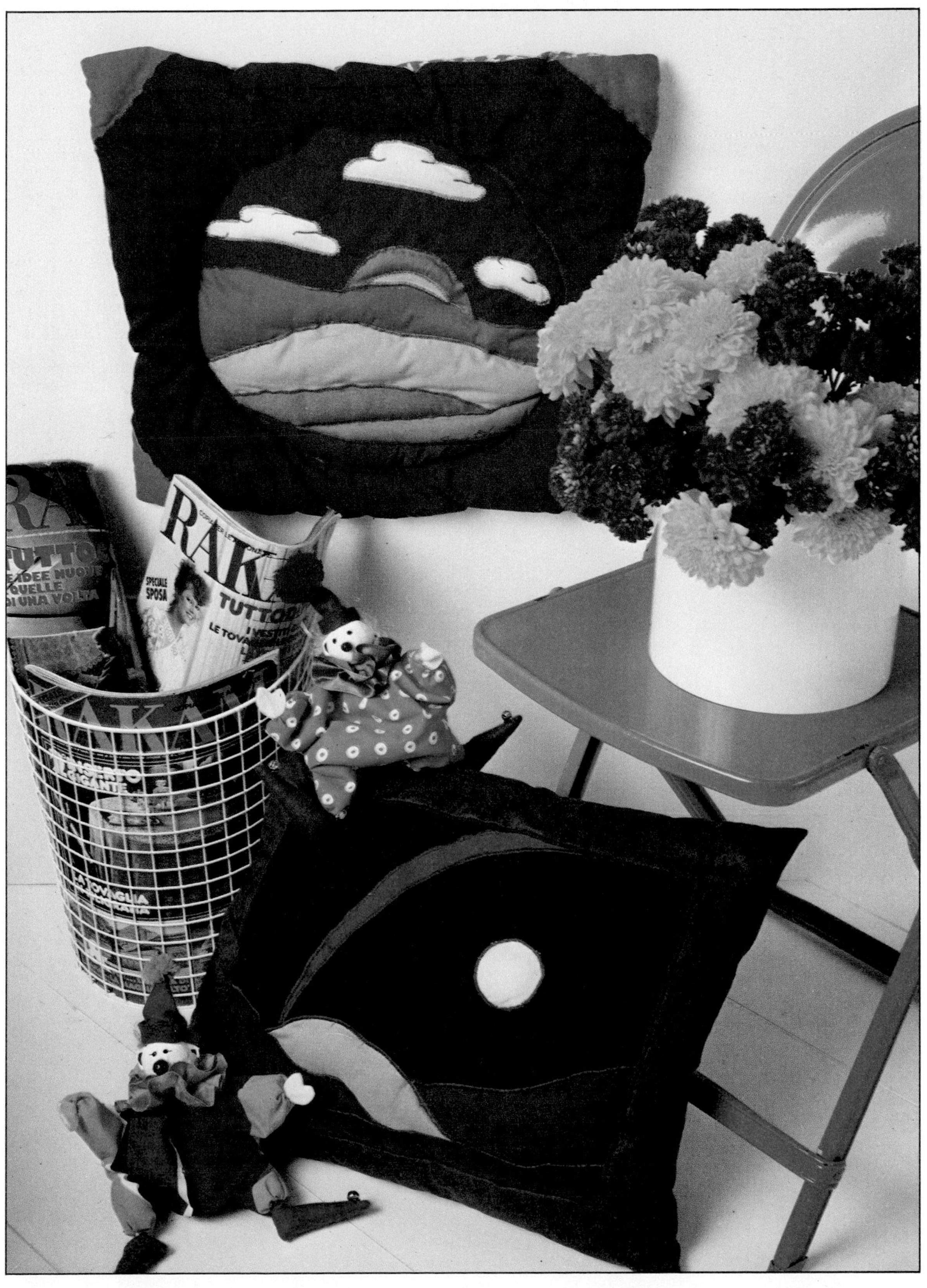
SPECIALE
SPOSA
GIGANTE
LA TOVAGLIA

Quick-and-Easy Baby Quilt

Here's a delightful way to use fabric scraps—machine-appliqué this 44x58-inch crib-size quilt. Preshrink the fabrics before you begin. Then appliqué the blocks and set them together with gingham strips. Tie the top to a layer of padding and backing for a speedy, economical, and practical gift for baby.

Materials

1½ yards 44-inch-wide white cotton
3 yards 44-inch-wide yellow and white gingham
¼ yard yellow cotton
1 crib-size package of quilt batting
Scraps of small cotton prints, ginghams, and solids in bright colors
Yellow yarn
#5 black pearl cotton
White quilting thread

Directions

Enlarge patterns and cut pieces from fabric, using the photograph opposite as a color guide. Appliqué design details onto each animal. Then cut twelve 12½-inch white squares. Center one animal on each square and appliqué in place with machine satin-stitching. Embroider small details with black pearl cotton.

To assemble the quilt, cut nine 2½x12½-inch gingham strips. Using ¼-inch seams, sew three strips between four blocks to make each row. Cut four 2½-inch strips the length of the rows; sew between rows and at sides of quilt. Cut and sew strips to top and bottom.

Cut batting and backing to match quilt top. Sandwich batting between top and backing, pin and baste the layers together, and quilt around the animals with white thread, if desired. Bind edges of the quilt with 1½-inch-wide yellow bias strips. Tie yarn through all layers and at intervals along gingham strips.

Quick-and-Easy Animal Toys

These enchanting appliquéd pillow toys trace their ancestry to the pottery of the Mimbres Indians of the Southwest. This ancient tribe was renowned for its early development of ceramics and its use of mythical and exaggerated figures—much like our fanciful interpretations of the antelope, quail, turtle, and insect.

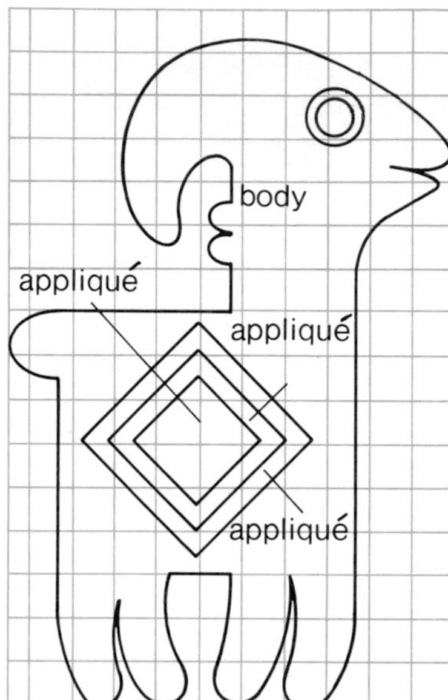

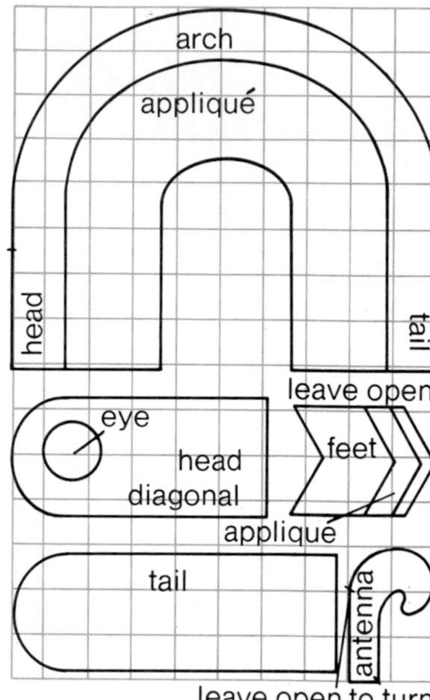

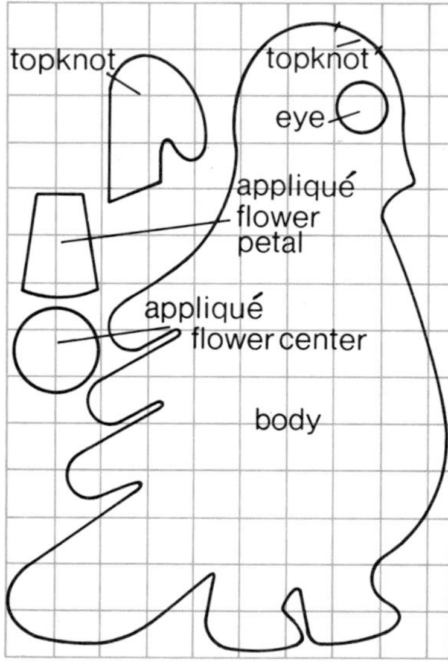

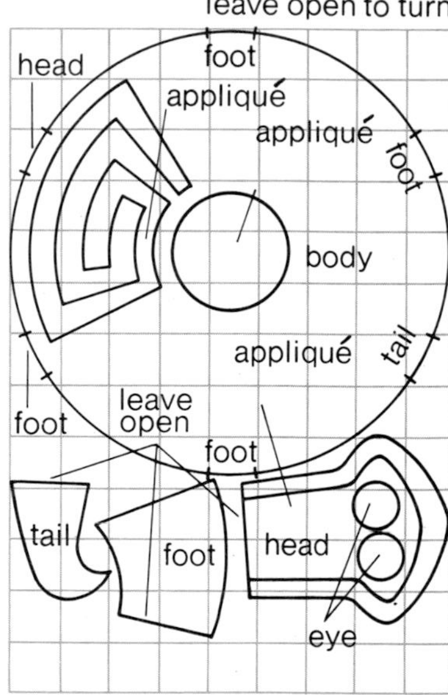

1 Square = 1 Inch

Materials

Polyester fiberfill

Turtle
$1/4$ yard dark green suede cloth
$1/8$ yard light green suede cloth
Dark green crewel yarn

Insect
$1/4$ yard purple corduroy
$1/4$ yard striped cotton fabric
Gray and blue-gray crewel yarn
Light brown suede cloth

Quail
$1/3$ yard beige crinkle cloth or other cotton fabric
$1/8$ yard chocolate brown suede cloth
Beige crewel yarn

Antelope
$1/3$ yard coral suede cloth
Light brown, medium brown, and pumpkin suede cloth
Medium brown crewel yarn

Directions

Enlarge pattern pieces and cut them from fabric, using the photograph as a color guide. Turn under raw edges of design details $1/4$ inch and appliqué in place. Embroider eyes with yarn French knots. With right sides together, sew small body pieces—head, tail, or feet—using a $1/4$-inch seam, leaving an opening. Turn right side out and stuff moderately. Machine-stitch the small body pieces to the front of the animal, then sew front to back body pieces, leaving an opening. Turn, stuff lightly, and slip-stitch.

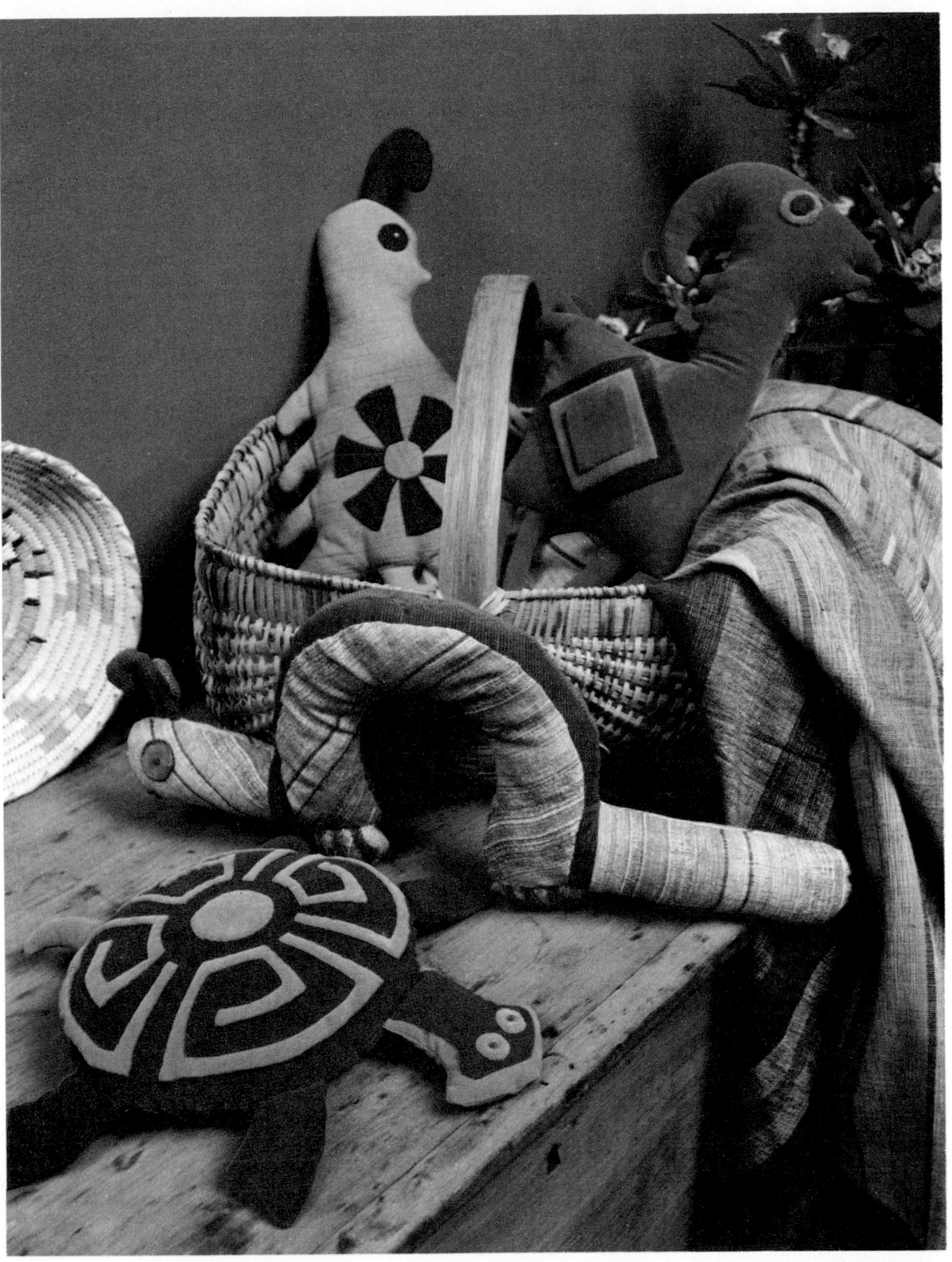

Quick-and-Easy Coverlet and Pillowcases

Chic and contemporary, this soft supergraphic comforter is also a snap to stitch. Made from only four pieces of fabric, it's a dream of a machine-appliqué project. And if you machine-quilt it too, you can make this coverlet in just one day.

Adapt the motif to fit a pair of pillowcases for a bedroom full of pizzazz.

Materials

2 yards each of white, black, and brown cotton (44-inch-wide)
4 yards white fabric (backing)
Quilt batting
Brown and white quilting thread
Black thread
Purchased pillowcases
3/8 yard each of black and brown fabric (pillowcases)
Scrap of rust-colored cotton

Directions

Enlarge the pattern below and cut the central motif from black fabric, adding 1/4-inch seam allowances. Machine stay-stitch on the seam line of the black circle and strip. Then press under the seam allowance, clipping the curves so edges are smooth.

Lay the white fabric flat. Pin the black strip over one long edge so the center of the inside rim of the black semicircle is 1/4 inch above the raw edge of the white fabric. Baste. Center the black circle 1 inch inside the semicircle; pin and baste. Appliqué the circle and strip to white fabric.

Lay out brown fabric, and position lower edge of black strip along one edge. Pin, baste, and appliqué in place.

Cut backing fabric in half and sew together along one long edge, making a piece 89x72 inches. Assemble the coverlet, following directions on page 43. Outline-quilt by hand or machine in rows 1 1/2 inches apart. Stop quilting 1 inch from the raw edge of the coverlet.

Turn raw edges to the inside 1/2 inch; slip-stitch.

For the pillowcases, repeat the quilt motif on one case. On the other, appliqué a rust-colored circle to a black and white pillowcase, as shown opposite.

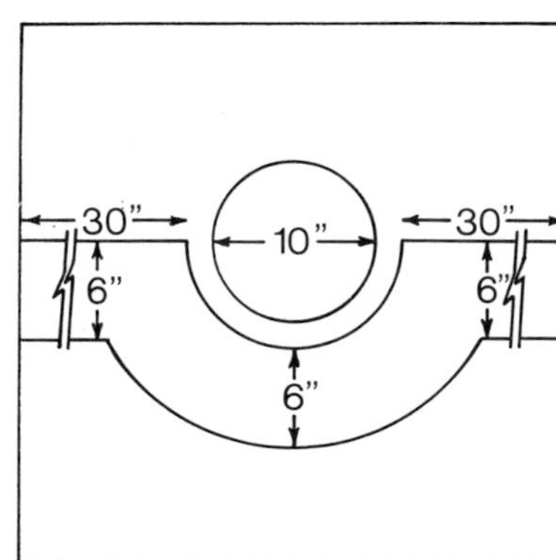

ABITARE
tray

Displaying your Skills

To show off your appliqué skills, here is a big, splashy, easy-to-stitch rainbow quilt that any stitcher would be proud of. In this section, you will find lots of colorful, big-impact projects designed to illustrate just how flexible appliqué can be. For instructions for making this quilt, stitched entirely by machine, please turn the page.

Rainbow Quilt *(shown on pages 90 and 91)*

Bursting with color, this rainbow quilt is made with fabric shapes that are machine-appliquéd into separate blocks. Each block is then quilted individually and sewn to an adjoining block with yellow binding to hide all raw edges.

Materials

Note: All fabric is 45 inches wide.
1¼ yards blue fabric
3⅔ yards yellow fabric
3½ yards red fabric
10 yards green fabric
Quilt batting (80x90-inch size)
Thread

Directions

Construct each block of the quilt separately, beginning with the largest one (top left in the diagram opposite) so you can use excess material for smaller blocks. After the tops of the blocks are appliquéd, assemble each one (with batting and backing fabric) and quilt it. Sew blocks together into three large pieces and sew large pieces together to make the complete quilt.

Enlarge the pattern opposite onto newsprint or brown paper.

When cutting pieces from fabric, add a ¾-inch seam allowance to all four sides of the blocks (background pieces) and a ¼-inch seam allowance to the outer, curved edges of the semicircular pieces. Read instructions below before cutting out any pattern pieces.

For each block, cut a square for the back from green fabric; set it aside. Cut quilt batting to size; set aside. Using the same pattern and following the color key, cut a square for the quilt front. Then cut semicircles from the appropriate-colored fabrics. *Do not cut the centers from the semicircles.*

Press under ¼ inch along the curved edge of all semicircles. Position the largest semicircle on the front piece. Topstitch it along the curved edge close to the fold using matching thread.

After stitching, trim excess fabric from *underneath* the curved edge of the appliquéd semicircle for use in other blocks. Topstitch the next largest semicircle in place in the same way. Continue appliquéing semicircles until the block is completed. *Trim away excess fabric from beneath semicircles only after the next piece has been topstitched in place.*

When all the blocks are appliquéd, assemble the green backing fabric, batting and appliquéd front for each one. Sandwich the batting between the front and back pieces of each block and pin the layers together about every 3 inches along the semicircular shapes. Machine-quilt just outside each semicircle using thread that matches the color of the fabric.

To assemble the quilt, cut yellow fabric down the length in five 1½-inch-wide strips (18 yards total). Stitch blocks together as explained below and in the numerical order indicated on the pattern. Join blocks into three large pieces as shown on the pattern, then stitch these large sections together in the same way.

To join two blocks, first cut a yellow strip the length of the seam (measure the actual blocks before cutting). Lay two quilt blocks together with the green sides (backs) facing. Place the yellow strip on top, with all raw edges even. Stitch together in a ½-inch seam and trim the seam allowance to ¼ inch.

Pull the blocks open; lay them flat. *Gently* press yellow strip toward seam, covering raw edges (too much heat or pressure will flatten batting). Topstitch strip along the fold. Turn under ½ inch on remaining edge and topstitch to adjoining block.

Finish the edges of the quilt by binding them with yellow fabric: Cut three strips down the length of the fabric, each 2¼ inches wide (to equal 9⅔ yards). With raw edges even, sew yellow strips to the back of the quilt in a ½-inch seam. Press binding to the outside and topstitch close to the edge on the quilt back. Then bring the strip to the front, turn under ½ inch on the remaining raw edge, and topstitch to the front, making sure the fold on the front hides the first two seams along the edge. Turn under the ends of the yellow strips at the corners of the quilt or stitch them together into a mitered corner.

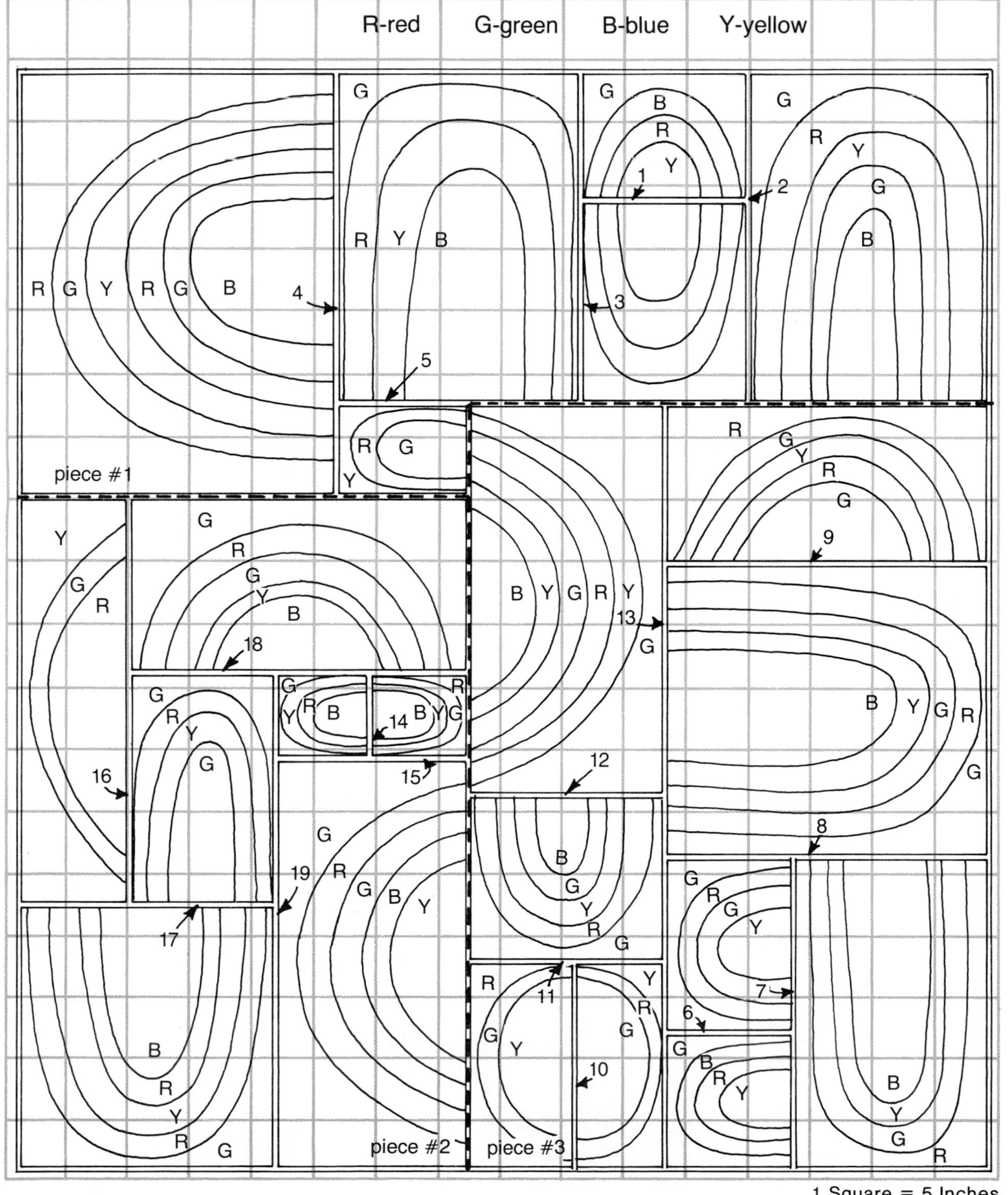
R-red
G-green
B-blue
Y-yellow
piece #1
piece #2
piece #3
1 Square = 5 Inches

Appliquéd Garden Scene

Create our "enchanted garden" wall hanging with only snippets of delicate floral fabrics. To make this delightful project, appliqué your pretty prints onto a floral background. Then add embroidery details to give the scene a rich, lively appearance. The quilted picture, which measures 14x19 inches, is a charming way to display your stitchery.

1 Square = 1 Inch

Materials

6x20 inches blue and white floral print (sky)
8x20 inches green and white floral print (ground)
½ yard print fabric (backing and border)
8x10 inches muslin (house)
Scraps of floral prints, with motifs that are ¾ inch to 1 inch in diameter (shrubs, flowers)
Green, red, orange, blue, lavender, yellow, and brown embroidery floss
White cotton thread
Dressmaker's carbon
Three 18x20-inch pieces of quilt batting
¼x14x19-inch piece of plywood

Directions

Turn under the seam allowance (¼ inch) on one long edge of the ground fabric and topstitch it to one long edge of the sky fabric, making the background for the scene. Appliqué or embroider the remaining design details onto this main piece.

Enlarge the pattern and transfer outlines to the background. Use outlines as placement guides for individual motifs.

Cut backing same as front. Sandwich batting between front and back pieces and baste layers together. Using two strands of white thread, quilt the ground in horizontal rows and the sky in semicircles, spacing rows and stitches ½ inch apart.

Cut muslin for house 1 inch wider and 3 inches higher than pattern. For clapboard siding, sew ¼-inch tucks in the fabric. Press raw edges under ¼ inch; appliqué in place. Cut roof and shutters, adding seam allowance. Fold under raw edges; appliqué. Cut and sew muslin squares over shutters (windows). Using two strands of blue floss, embroider windowpanes. Add a muslin chimney.

Embroider the evergreens in vertical rows of green satin stitches.

Cut shrubs and flowers from floral prints, adding seam allowances. Turn under edges and arrange them on the front, referring to the photograph opposite if necessary. Appliqué green floral shrubs along the horizon and around the house. Position clusters of flowers in front of the shrubs. For sunflowers (upper right), appliqué a ½-inch-circle (add seam allowances) of brown print fabric to the background. Then satin-stitch yellow triangular petals around the center; add embroidered green stems and leaves.

Embroider a monarch butterfly hovering near the sunflowers. Add embroidered flowers among the appliquéd flowers, and embroidered stems and leaves on some appliquéd blossoms.

Frame the picture with a 2½-inch border of floral fabric slipstitched to the sides. Mount on plywood, as shown.

Appliquéd Staircase Scene

A companion piece to the garden scene on page 95, this quaint appliquéd interior scene is also accented with quilting and embroidery. If you are thrifty with your fabric scraps—saving small pieces from previous projects—you'll probably have on hand everything you need to make this charming panel.

Materials

5x20 inches rust print (floor)
10x20 inches rust and beige print (wall)
½ yard print (backing and border)
¾ yard unbleached muslin
Scraps of brown fabric
Scraps of floral prints in green, blue, brown, and tan
Three 15x20-inch pieces of quilt batting
Brown, green, gray, and yellow embroidery floss
White quilting thread
15x19-inch piece of ⅜-inch plywood

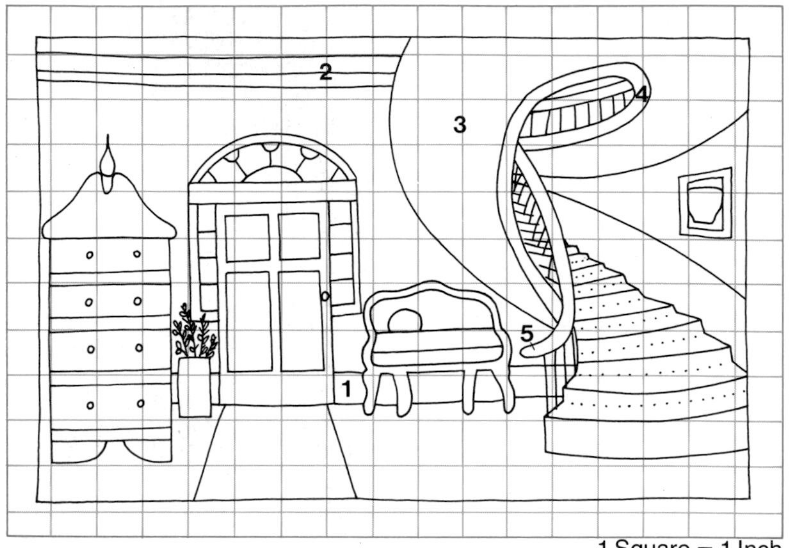

1 Square = 1 Inch

Directions

Turn under ¼ inch on long edge of the floor piece and stitch it to the wall piece, making the background. Cut backing to match, and sandwich batting between front and back. Baste layers together and quilt, spacing rows and stitches ½ inch apart.

Enlarge the pattern to use as a cutting and positioning guide. When cutting pieces for appliqué, add a ¼-inch seam allowance.

First, appliqué the molding strips (1 and 2 on the pattern). Cut base molding (1) from muslin, turn under raw edges, and appliqué along seam between floor and wall. Cut ceiling molding 3 inches deeper than the molding on the pattern and take two tucks in it before appliquéing it along the top of the wall.

Cut staircase (3) from a double layer of muslin. Turn under seam allowance, appliqué, and quilt. Add muslin trim (4) to edge of staircase. Appliqué brown print banisters (5). Embroider stairs in outline and running stitches. Add gray floss posts.

To make the bureau, appliqué a brown rectangle in place. Add the feet of the bureau, then the top and drawer struts. Finish with satin-stitched finial (at center top) and drawer pulls.

For the window and door, cut window arch and sides from muslin (in one piece) and appliqué. Add blue print windows. Over this, stitch door, a narrow strip for the lintel over the door, and door panels. Add white embroidered windowpanes and a black doorknob.

Cut out, appliqué, and quilt the runner in front of the door.

For the sofa, appliqué green print "upholstery" first, then embroider legs and edging in brown satin stitches. Add green embroidered outline stitches to mark the front and back of the seat on the sofa. Appliqué a tiny round pillow to the back.

Appliqué a fabric vase and fill it with embroidered yellow flowers. Finish with an appliquéd picture on the wall: sew down a brown patch, then a muslin patch, and finally, an appliquéd flower.

Edge the scene with a 1½-inch border of printed fabric and a 3-inch muslin border. Mount on plywood.

Swan Pillow and Curtains

Our beautiful black swan is appliquéd onto a pillow and then enlarged and adapted for a curtain panel. Each piece of the design is sewn down with running stitches worked in pearl cotton—an unusual and attractive appliqué technique.

Materials

Pillow

15-inch circular pillow form with 2-inch boxing
28-inch circle of black cotton
13-inch circle of white cotton
1x41 inches green bias strip
10-inch circle of heavy dacron quilt batting
Scraps of light blue, dark green, rust, brown, and coral cotton
#5 pearl cotton in colors to match fabric

Curtains

8 yards 45-inch-wide black cotton (see note at right)
4 yards white cotton
½ yard dark green cotton
½ yard light blue cotton
¼ yard brown cotton
Scraps of coral cotton
#5 pearl cotton in colors to match fabrics

1 Square = 1 Inch

Directions

Pillow

Enlarge the pattern below and cut out pieces, referring to the photograph for colors. Add ¼-inch seam allowances to all pieces.

Turn under seam allowances on all pieces; baste. Pin and baste pieces to white circle. Using pearl cotton to match fabrics, appliqué pieces with small running stitches along the edges. Turn under and baste a ½-inch hem in the white circle.

Fold green bias strip in half lengthwise and pin behind white circle, letting ¼ inch of the folded edge show along the front. Join ends of the strip and baste in position.

Using black pearl cotton, sew basting stitches ½ inch from edge of black circle; gather the circle. Slip pillow form inside circle, centering it. Draw fabric up around pillow form, spacing gathers evenly. Place batting over empty space inside black fabric. Center and pin appliquéd white circle over batting. Appliqué the edge of the white circle to black fabric; sewing through all layers. Finish by embroidering the eye of the swan with black pearl cotton.

Curtains

Note: Fabric requirements are for two 36x58-inch curtains, each lined and interlined to minimize fading. To make curtains of a different size or without interlinings, adjust fabric amounts.

First make a drawing of the curtain (it need not be full-size). For each curtain, draw a rectangle and mark it 36 inches wide and 58 inches long. On the inside and lower edges of each curtain, mark a 5-inch-wide black border. In the upper outside corner, mark a black rectangle 19 inches wide by 41 inches long. The white, appliquéd panel is an L-shaped piece 12 inches wide that fits between the outer border and the inner black rectangle (see photograph). On the diagram, mark the vertical length of the white panel (53 inches on the outer edge; 41 inches on the inside) and its horizontal dimensions (31 inches on the lower edge; 19 inches on the upper, inside edge).

Add ½-inch seam allowances to all dimensions and cut out pieces. Cut the L-shaped white panel double so black lining and interlining will not show through. Instead of cutting it as an L-shaped piece, cut the outer 5-inch border (black) in a single strip and miter the lower inside corner.

Enlarge the swan motif to 1½ times the size for the pillow, adding extra leaves and a fourth cattail to the design and extending the stems on the cattails and the blue waves, as shown in the photograph. Reverse the swan motif for the second curtain.

Cut out pattern pieces and appliqué them to the white panel, following instructions for the pillow. Embroider the swans' eyes.

To assemble the curtain fronts, baste inside hems in black strips (along edges that will be joined to white panels). Appliqué them to white panels, matching seam lines.

For hanging loops, cut five 32½x5-inch pieces of black for each curtain. With right sides facing, stitch long edges together in a ¼-inch seam. Turn right side out and press. Fold tabs in half and space them evenly across top of curtain front with raw edges even. Baste.

Cut black lining and interlining to match fronts. Layer interlining, lining, and curtain front (wrong side up). Pin and stitch layers together, catching tabs in seam. Leave bottom edge open. Turn, press, and slipstitch lower edge, turning in seam allowance.

Machine Appliquéd Crèche Banner

Appliquéd by machine and featuring touches of machine embroidery, our contemporary Christmas crèche measures 30x50 inches. Make yours to fit any wall space you choose.

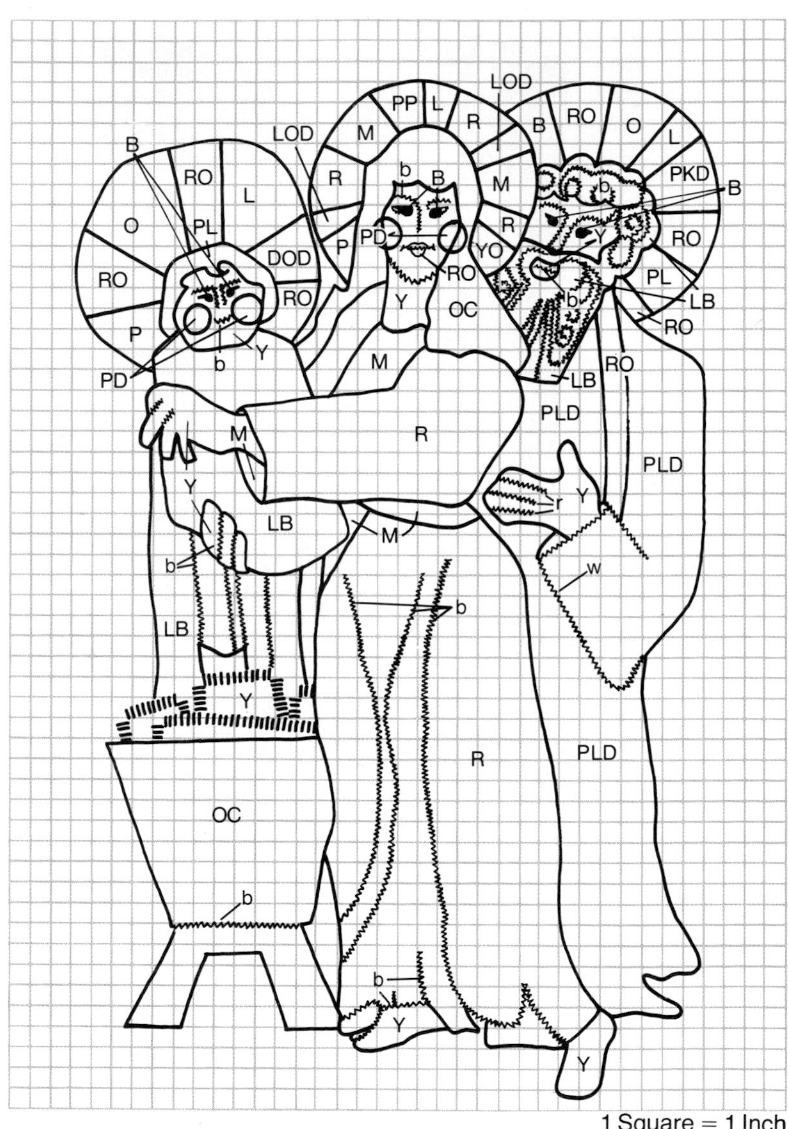

1 Square = 1 Inch

Materials

2¼ yards drapery-weight muslin
2¼ yards polyester quilt batting
1½ yards fusible webbing
1½ yards red fabric
½ yard yellow fabric
½ yard white fabric
½ yard red calico fabric
1 yard purple polka dot fabric
Scraps of pink, purple, red, orange, and blue fabric
Red and black sewing thread
1 skein black embroidery floss
8 yards red hem tape
Tissue paper
Brown wrapping paper

Color Key

Pink	P
Red-orange	RO
Orange	O
Purple	PL
Dark orange dot	DOD
Light orange dot	LOD
Red	R
Maroon	M
Pink-purple	PP
Yellow-orange	YO
Orange calico	OC
Lavender	L
Pink dot	PK
Purple dot	PLD
Light beige	LB
Yellow	Y
Black	B
~~ = stitching colors	
Black	b
Red	r
White	w

Directions

Enlarge the pattern and transfer to paper. Cut pieces without seam allowances—they will fit together flush, like a puzzle.

From white fabric, cut the infant (including head, halo, and Mary's hands). From red, cut Mary (including head, halo, and arm). From purple, cut Joseph. Using fusible webbing to hold pieces, appliqué smaller shapes to main pieces. Lightly pencil-in facial features and drapery lines. Zigzag-stitch design details, following the pattern. Appliqué finished pieces to the background. Add the manger. Fray pieces of yellow fabric (straw) and fuse in place. Baste quilt batting to the back and quilt. Bind edges with red hem tape, and stitch tape to back top for hanging rod.

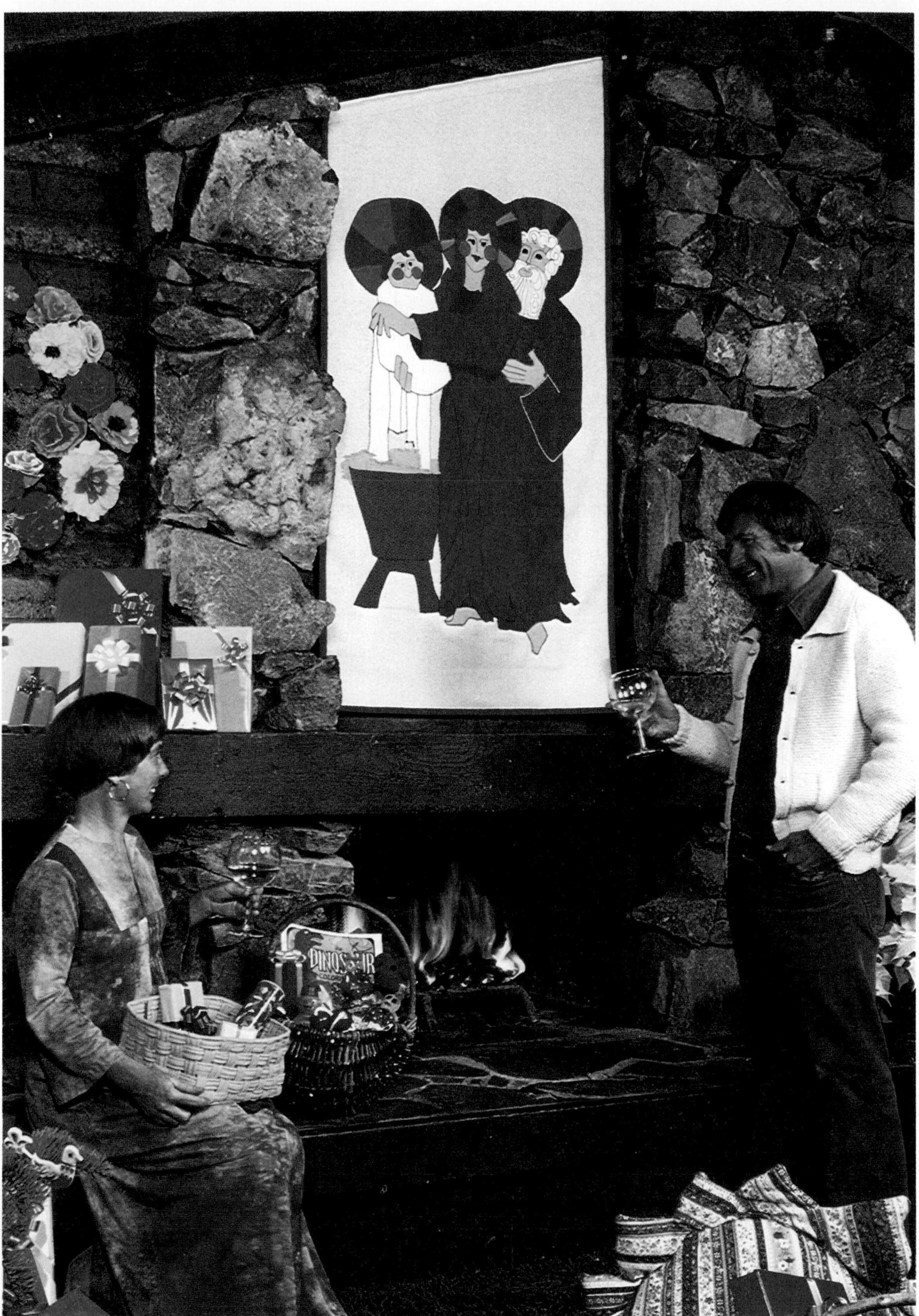

Festive Rejoice Banner

You'll feel like rejoicing when you hang this colorful appliquéd banner. The mood it evokes is especially suited to Christmastime, but the exuberant message is a welcome sight all year.

To simplify construction, iron the letters to the muslin with fusible webbing to hold them in place for machine satin-stitching.

Materials

2½ yards natural-colored drapery fabric or medium-weight muslin for background
2½ yards white lining fabric
Pieces of broadcloth in various colors and prints for vertical stripes and letters
3 packages 2-inch-wide red hem tape
Fusible webbing
Matching thread and embroidery floss
Curtain rod

Directions

Note: The finished size of the banner is 84x30 inches.

Cut drapery fabric or muslin background piece to measure 84x32 inches. Also cut a matching lining piece.

Enlarge the pattern below. Cut the vertical stripes from broadcloth and pin them to the background material. Machine- or hand-appliqué around the edges. Turn a ¼-inch hem if you appliqué by hand; trim the raw edges if you machine-appliqué.

Cut the seven letters from broadcloth, referring to the photograph for color suggestions. Arrange the letters on the stripes and baste them in place. Appliqué with tiny whipstitches if you are sewing by hand.

Or, iron the letters in place with fusible webbing and stitch them down with machine zigzag stitching or another decorative machine embroidery stitch.

Gently press the finished banner front on the wrong side.

Machine-stitch a length of hem tape to the top of the lining piece, ½ inch from the raw edge. Then stitch the remaining long edge of the tape to the lining to make a casing. Do not stitch ends.

Sew the lining to the back of the muslin, using a ½-inch seam.

Pin hem tape around edges, folding it in half to cover the edges, and slip-stitch in place. Insert a curtain rod for hanging.

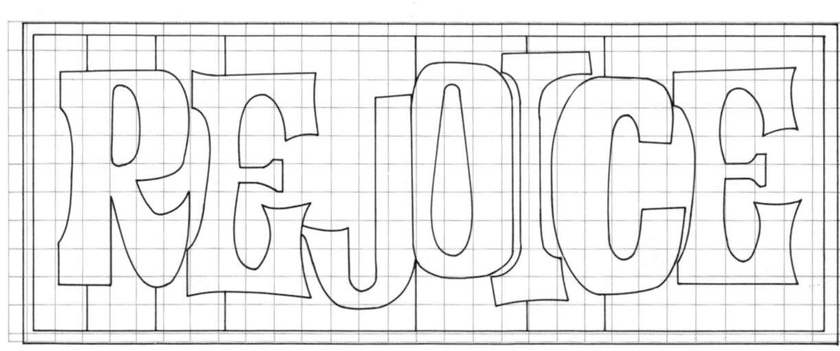

1 Square = 3 Inches

JOICE

Appliquéd Bird Quilt and Pillows

The striking appliquéd comforter and pillows shown here are the natural habitat for a rare flock of fantastical birds. Though you may never see this group of fine feathered friends gathered together in an honest-to-goodness tree, for the appliqué artist, anything is possible.

This lively contemporary quilt and the matching pillows can be either machine- or hand-stitched.

Materials

Note: All measurements refer to 44- or 45-inch-wide cotton broadcloth

5 yards brown for tree trunk, branches, and border strips
2½ yards beige for border strips
1⅔ yards dark green for leaves and ground
2 yards medium green for leaves and ground
2 yards white with brown polka dot
¼ yard black
¼ yard rust
⅛ yard each of red, purple, navy, gold, pink, off-white, gray, and medium blue
5 yards matching or contrasting fabric for backing
2 packages 96x96-inch quilt batting
#5 pearl cotton in the following colors: gold, rust, black, purple, navy, red, blue, gray, pink, medium green, dark green, brown, and white
Basting thread
Graph paper
Transfer pencil or dressmaker's carbon
Quilting hoop or frame

Directions

Note: The quilt shown above and opposite is 86 inches square. The center appliquéd square (without borders) is 58x58 inches. Change the size of the quilt by varying the size of the borders.

Directions for the four appliquéd pillows shown with the quilt, opposite, are on pages 106 and 107.

Preshrink all the fabric. Enlarge the pattern on page 106 for the appliquéd center panel and transfer it to a large sheet of brown paper. This will be the master pattern.

Trace each separate shape on the quilt (birds, tree trunk, and branches) onto a separate sheet of paper and cut out all paper pattern pieces. Select a single complete leaf shape and make one leaf pattern for all 76 leaves. Number all pattern pieces to correspond to the shapes on the master pattern.

To construct the basic background for the quilt top, lightly trace the outlines of the top half of the background onto the polka dot fabric and cut out, adding ½-inch seam allowances all around. Next, trace off the dark green ground piece and cut out, adding ½-inch seam allowances. Baste under the seam allowance along the top edge of the green ground piece; pin and baste to the bottom of the polka dot piece, overlapping seam allowances. Repeat for the medium-green ground piece.

continued

Appliquéd Bird Quilt and Pillows *(continued)*

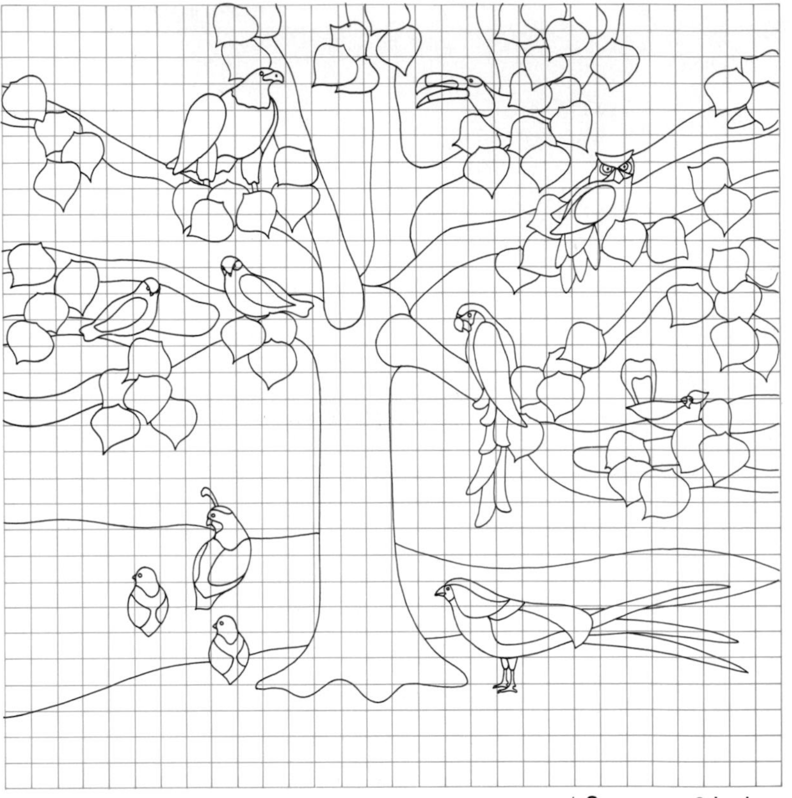

1 Square = 2 Inches

Place your master pattern on top of the pieced background fabric and lightly trace outlines of the tree shape, birds, and leaf placement onto the background. Use a transfer pencil or dressmaker's carbon paper.

Next, cut out all the trunk and branch shapes from brown fabric, adding ¼-inch seam allowances to each piece. Carefully turn under all seam allowances and baste. Then pin and baste trunk and branches in place on the background fabric.

Cut 33 dark green and 43 medium green leaves, adding ¼-inch seam allowances. Turn under seam allowances, baste, and press. Arrange leaves on tree trunk and branches following the master pattern. Trim excess fabric where leaves overlap; pin all leaves in place.

Finally, cut out and assemble pieces for each bird, working on one bird at a time. Place all bird and leaf pieces in position before sewing to ensure that raw edges are properly covered. Trim away excess fabric where necessary.

When all pieces of the quilt have been pinned or basted in position, appliqué around the edges of each one, taking small running stitches in matching pearl cotton ⅛ inch from all folded-under edges. (Or, slipstitch appliqué pieces in place with matching sewing thread.)

Where indicated on the pattern, embroider beaks, eyes, and talons in satin stitches, using gold, black, or rust pearl cotton.

To assemble the quilt, cut two 4-inch-wide strips of brown fabric and machine-stitch to the top and bottom of the appliquéd panel with ½-inch seams. Repeat with two 4-inch-wide brown strips along the sides of the panel, squaring the corners.

Next, add 11-inch-wide strips of beige fabric to the top and bottom of the quilt panel, and then to each side of the panel (again using ½-inch seams). Press all seams toward outside edges of the quilt.

Piece backing to size from a sheet, muslin, or from matching or contrasting fabric.

Cut two layers of batting to size. Lay the backing fabric wrong side up on the floor, spread two layers of batting on top, then add the quilt top, face up, on top of batting.

Align all the edges, then pin and baste through all layers; use long stitches running diagonally from corner to corner and through horizontal and vertical centers. Mount on a quilting hoop or frame, if desired.

Stitching through all layers, use white pearl cotton to outline-quilt around all shapes on the polka dot background. Then use dark and medium green thread on the ground areas, following all seam lines and quilting around the base of the tree trunk. Next, quilt around each bird on the ground. Finally, quilt along the inner and outer edges of the dark brown border.

Trim the backing and batting so the outside edges are even with the edges of the top. Cut four long pieces of 2-inch-wide brown fabric; sew one strip to each edge of backing fabric (½-inch seams).

Turn under raw edges of brown fabric, press, and fold this binding strip to the front of quilt. Baste to quilt top, then sew through all layers with dark brown pearl cotton, securing binding to the quilt top.

1 Square = 1 Inch

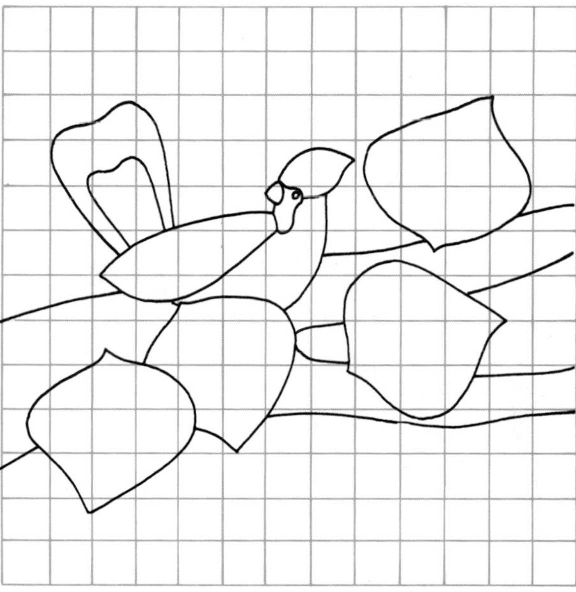

1 Square = 1 Inch

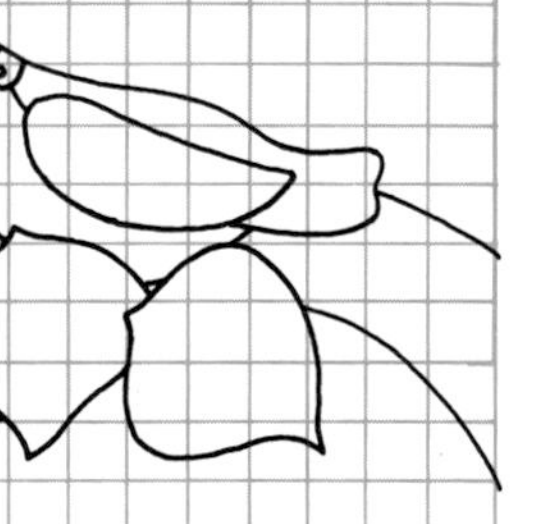

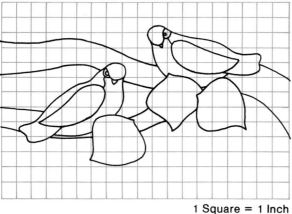

1 Square = 1 Inch

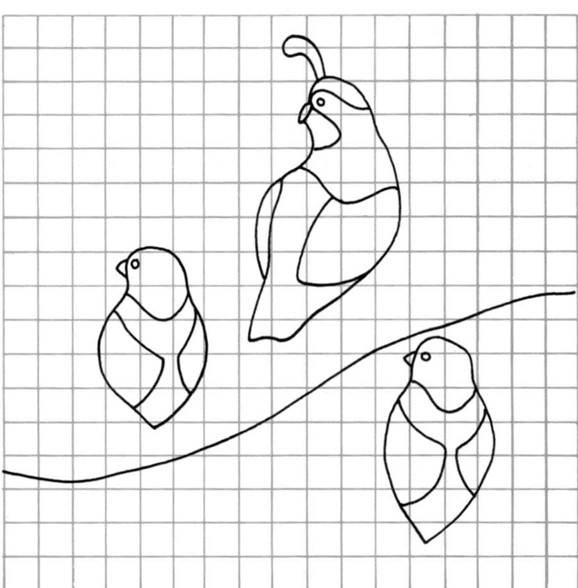

1 Square = 1 Inch

Pillows

Enlarge the patterns on this page. Cut out and appliqué the pieces onto circular or rectangular pillow fronts, following the instructions for sewing the quilt top. To enhance the designs, trapunto-quilt individual shapes on the birds, following directions on page 112.

To complete each pillow, cut backing fabric to size. Stitch it to the pillow front, right sides together, leaving an opening for turning. Turn the cover right side out, stuff, and slip-stitch.

Special Appliqué Techniques

In this section, you will find appliqué projects "with a difference." Each one has some unusual feature to help you discover new ways of working with fabrics. Our tablecloth, for instance, is worked in shadow appliqué—a technique for using sheers. Here also are designs for hand- or machine-stitching in padded, shaped, or embroidered appliqué, lacework, and reverse appliqué—all exciting techniques. For tablecloth how-to, turn the page.

Shadow Appliqué—Tablecloth and Napkins

(shown on pages 108 and 109)

Shadow appliqué is the creative art of stitching with sheers. For this technique, one sheer fabric is appliquéd atop another, or a heavier fabric is appliquéd to the underside of a sheer or between two layers of transparent fabric. The look is soft and delicate—like a shadow.

The organdy tablecloth shown on pages 108 and 109 is appliquéd by hand in the traditional pin stitch—a pulled-thread embroidery technique. It creates a decorative line of holes similar to hemstitching—but unlike hemstitching, this stitch works beautifully on curves.

If you are a fan of old-fashioned needlework, you will want to add this technique to your repertoire.

Materials

- 44x44 inches soft, sheer, white cotton organdy or lawn
- 1 yard soft, sheer, beige cotton organdy or lawn
- ¼ yard each of lightweight cotton broadcloth in pale pink, pale yellow, and pale green
- ¾ yard white batiste or fine handkerchief linen (4 napkins)
- Gray cotton embroidery floss
- Small tapestry needles
- Black felt-tip pen
- Tissue or brown paper

Directions

Enlarge the patterns for the border and the central motif, opposite. Tape together enough tissue or brown paper to make a piece 44 inches square. Then transfer to the paper the patterns for the central motif and border and go over the outlines with a felt-tip pen. This is your master pattern. Lay the sheer fabric over it to be sure appliqués are in position.

Transfer the outlines of each shape to the fabrics indicated on the pattern by laying the pressed fabric over the master pattern and lightly marking the outlines with a hard pencil. Cut out the appliqués, adding ¼-inch seam allowances. Except on the beige border that extends around the cloth, turn under the seam allowance on each shape, baste close to the folded edge, and press. Then trim the seam margin to about ⅛ inch. On the border piece, turn under and baste only the seam allowance on the curved (inside) edge. The straight (outside) edges will be sewn to the edges of the white organdy piece later, after smaller pieces have been appliquéd.

Lay the white organdy over the master pattern and pin and baste the appliqués in position on the right side of the fabric. Where appliqués meet, lap flower petals over stems and leaves (except at the bases of the flowers, where the stems should overlap the flowers slightly). To overlap, remove the basting on the piece to go underneath along the area of the overlap. Clip into the seam allowance with scissors and pull it out flat. Then lap the top piece over it.

Appliqué pieces in position with tiny pin stitches, pulling the thread tight with each stitch to make a line of decorative holes around each appliquéd shape.

To make pin stitches, use a single strand of embroidery floss in a small, blunt tapestry needle. Work with the fabric firmly in hand so you can pull on the thread. Slide the thread end under the appliqué (out of sight). Bring it up at A in the background fabric right next to the appliqué (see the stitch diagram, opposite). Take a tiny backstitch (1/16 inch or smaller), and bring the needle up again at A. Pull the thread tight to create a tiny hole in the fabric, and take a second backstitch. Bring the needle up again in the appliqué fabric directly above A; pull the thread tight. Reinsert the needle at A and bring it up again at B, 1/16 inch or less ahead. Repeat this double backstitching and catch-stitching around the appliquéd shape, securing it to the fabric.

When all parts of the central motif have been appliquéd with pin stitching, add embroidery to the design. Use tiny backstitches for the dotted lines on the pattern, and satin stitching and French knots or seed stitches in the centers of the green flowers, as shown in the photograph on pages 108 and 109.

Work the border by first stitching the beige border appliqué to the background fabric (right sides together) around the outside (straight) edges. Use a ¼-inch seam. Press the appliqué to the front of the white organdy and pin and appliqué the curved edges, leaves, and flowers in position.

To make the napkins, cut fabric into four 15-inch squares. One-half inch from the edges of the fabric, mark curves as shown in the photograph on pages 108 and 109. Machine satin-stitch along design lines and trim excess fabric beyond the stitching. Using part of the motif from the center of the cloth, appliqué a flower, leaves, and stem in one corner of the napkin. Follow directions above for pin-stitching.

1 Square = 1 Inch

Color Key

Y Yellow
P Pink
G Green
W White
B Beige

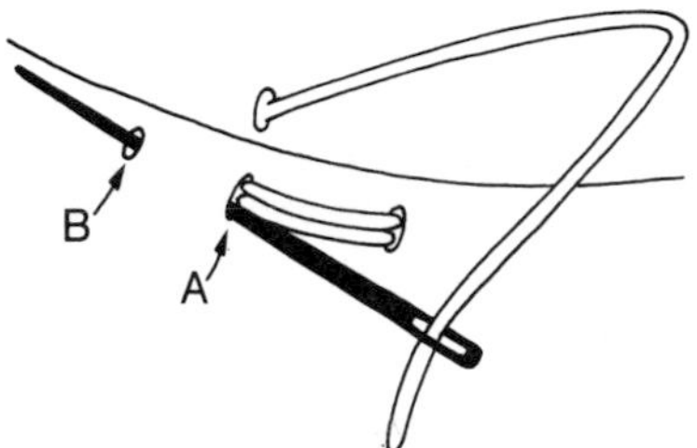

Pin stitch for shadow appliqué

1 Square = 1 Inch

Quilted Appliqué—A Soft Brass Headboard

Quilted appliqué—called trapunto quilting—is the technique of sewing two pieces of fabric together, cutting the back piece open, and stuffing the appliquéd shape to give it dimension. It is often used in conjunction with regular quilting (padding with batting between top and bottom layers of fabric) for a look that is soft and plush, but with areas of high relief.

The trapunto quilted brass headboard shown here is a simple project to get you started on this easy and exciting aspect of appliqué. On the next two pages is a quilted appliqué wall hanging as well.

Materials

1⅔ yards 45-inch-wide print fabric (background and binding)
1⅓ yards solid-color fabric
1¼ yards gold fabric
Dacron quilt batting
#5 pearl cotton in gold
#5 pearl cotton to match background fabric
Dressmaker's carbon

Directions

Cut a 12x44-inch piece from the print fabric and set it aside. Enlarge the pattern below and transfer it, centered, to the remaining printed fabric. Then trace pattern pieces onto a separate sheet of paper and cut them from the gold fabric. Follow the straight grain of the material and add a ⅜-inch seam allowance.

Turn under seam allowances and pin pieces to the background.

Using gold pearl cotton, appliqué the pieces to the background with small, even running stitches close to the folded edges of the appliqué pieces. Overlap all raw edges.

For trapunto-quilting, cut slits in the *background fabric only* behind each appliquéd piece (do not cut into the gold fabric). Using scraps of batting, lightly stuff the appliquéd pieces. If necessary, use an orange stick to push stuffing into small spaces. Whip-stitch the slits closed.

Cut solid-color backing fabric and quilt batting to size and pin them to the back of the front piece, with batting in the middle. Pin the layers together and quilt around the appliqué, using pearl cotton to match background fabric.

Cut and piece 90 inches of 1½-inch-wide bias binding from the extra print fabric. Fold the long edges under ¼ inch and sew to the raw edges with pearl cotton.

Sew a 2-inch-wide strip just below the top of the quilt in back. Insert an adjustable curtain rod and hang from wall hooks.

1 Square = 6 Inches

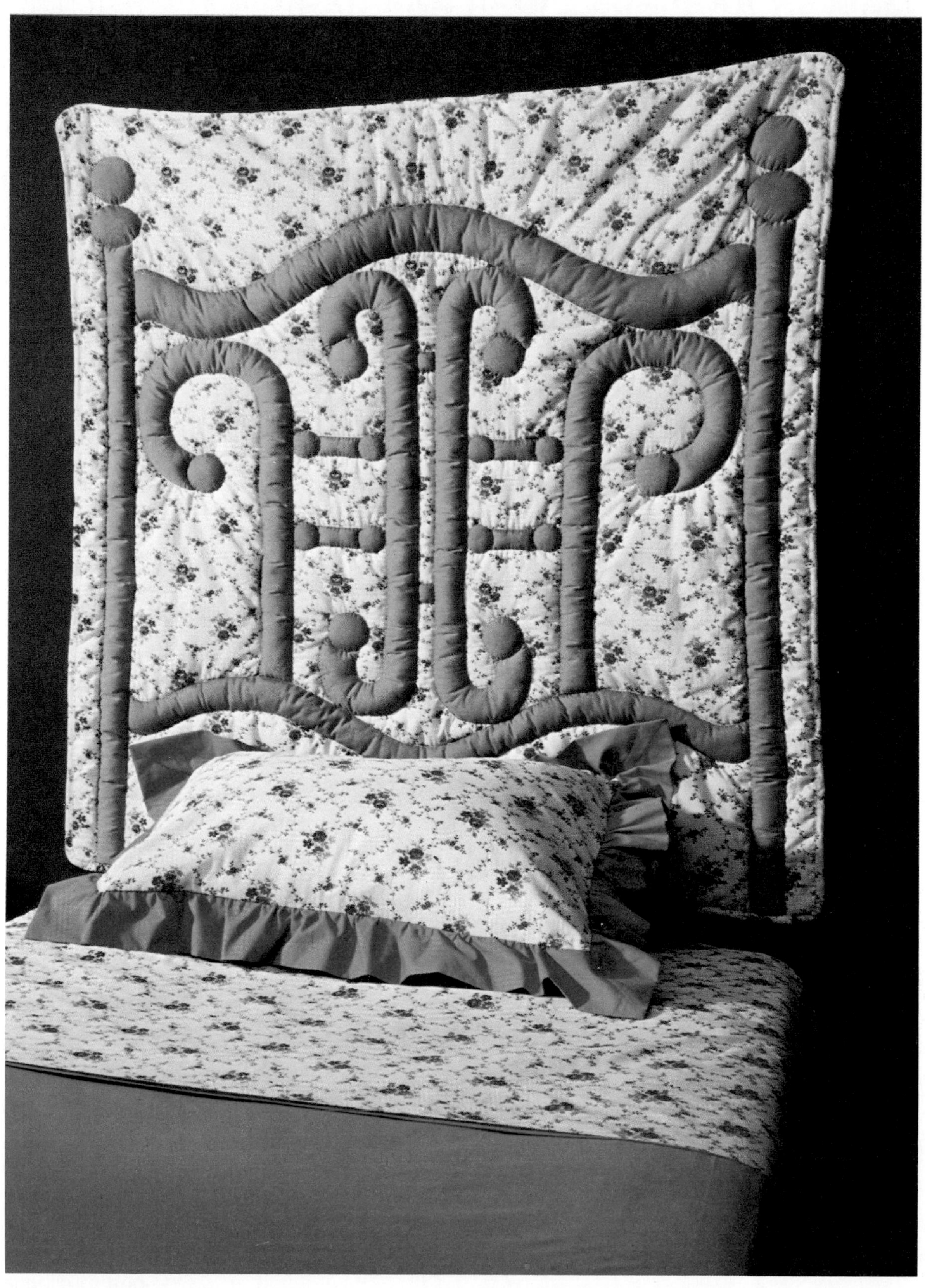

Quilted Appliqué—Wall Hanging

Our silhouette in white is an introspective study of a farm wife at work. To make this wall hanging, sew appliqué pieces in place from the wrong side of the background fabric and then trim excess fabric away from each of the body shapes. Finish with machine satin stitching and hand-embroidered accents.

Materials

White or off-white fabrics in 5 or 6 different weights and textures, such as upholstery fabrics and loosely woven linen:
- 1¼ yards (A) (see diagram)
- ¾ yard (B)
- ½ yard (C)
- ½ yard (D)
- ¼ yard (E)

1 yard quilt batting
Matching thread
Natural-colored or ecru silk buttonhole twist
Four 34-inch artist's stretcher strips
Stapler and staples
Dressmaker's carbon or transfer pencil

Directions

Enlarge the pattern and transfer it (centered) to the *wrong* side of a 40x40-inch piece of background fabric (A). Be sure to reverse the design when you transfer it so it will be right side up on the face of the fabric.

Appliqué each pattern piece to the front of the background in the following order: left arm, spoon handle, right arm, face, head covering, bodice, bowls, and fingers.

Do not cut out pattern pieces before appliquéing them. Instead, pin each piece to the face of the fabric, matching grain lines. Turn the fabric over (wrong side up) and straight-stitch along the pattern line for that piece. Then trim excess appliqué fabric close to the stitched line. Stitch and trim each piece before proceeding to the next one.

Using buttonhole twist, machine satin-stitch around each appliquéd piece, covering raw edges. Satin-stitch dotted lines on the bodice also.

For quilting, cut a slit in only the background fabric behind each appliquéd piece. Cut batting to fit inside each piece and insert between the two layers. Whipstitch the slit closed.

Assemble stretcher strips and staple the fabric to the frame. Using buttonhole twist, embellish the neckline, upper arms, bodice front, and thumb with hand-embroidered outline stitching. Embroider through the appliqué only—not through batting or backing.

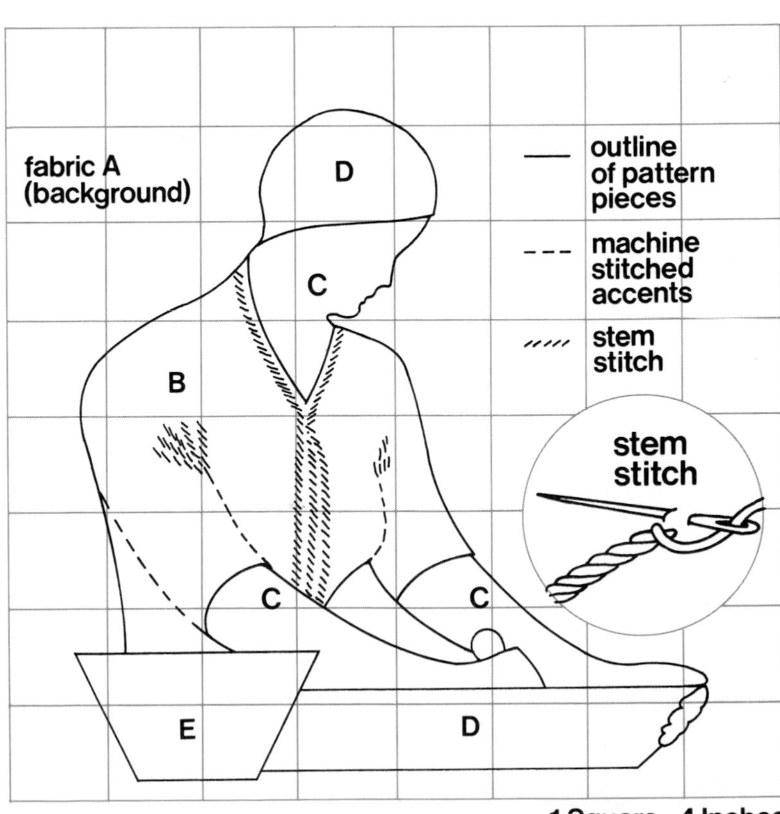

1 Square = 4 Inches

Shaped Appliqué—Floral Pillows

Here is another way to add dimension to your appliqué work in addition to quilting: shape the appliqué as it is sewn to the background fabric, gathering and pleating it into soft folds. The floral pillows opposite are appliquéd in just this way. For each one, cut small pieces of ribbon (the "petals" on our flowers), gather the edges, and shape the petals as you stitch.

This is truly individualized appliqué—for every flower you make, like every flower in nature, will be unique.

Materials (for each pillow)
1 yard light yellow velveteen
1½ yards cotton cable cord
1 skein each of #3 pearl cotton embroidery thread in light, medium, and dark green
Embroidery needles
Polyester fiberfill

Pansy Pillow
½ yard 2-inch-wide dark purple velvet ribbon
¼ yard 1½-inch-wide light purple velvet ribbon
¼ yard 2-inch-wide dark magenta velvet ribbon
1 skein each of velvet or cotton embroidery thread in light and dark yellow
Thread to match ribbons

Hydrangea Pillow
1 yard 2-inch-wide light blue grosgrain ribbon
½ yard 2-inch-wide medium blue grosgrain ribbon
Thread to match ribbons

Directions
Cut two 16-inch circles of velveteen for each pillow. From the remaining fabric, cut and piece bias strips to cover the cording for the edge of the pillow front.

Enlarge the patterns opposite and transfer them to tissue paper. Trace each one onto the front of one of the circles of fabric, using dressmaker's carbon paper and a tracing wheel or pencil.

Cut the ribbon into 2-inch lengths. For each petal, turn under the raw (cut) edges of the ribbon ¼ inch and press lightly on the wrong side. Be careful not to crush the nap on the velvet ribbon. Do not turn under the finished edges of the ribbon.

Using thread to match ribbons, sew tiny running stitches along one finished (unfolded) edge of the ribbon. Pull up the gathers but do not tie them off.

Begin making flower petals by whipstitching the *ungathered finished* edge of the ribbon to the outside edge of a petal outline marked on the pattern. Whipstitches should be close together to hold the appliqué firmly in place.

Next, pull the folded edges of the ribbon around to follow the outlines for the sides of the petal and whipstitch them in place. Remember that petal outlines are round or triangular and ribbons are not. Also, ribbon pieces are larger than petal shapes. So, while stitching each ribbon in place, shape it to fit into the outlines of the petal by gathering and folding all but the top edge, which will have been whipstitched along the outside of the shape. Lift up each ribbon in the middle of the petal shape to get it out of the way while stitching the side (folded) edges in place.

To finish each petal, arrange the gathered edge of the ribbon along the lower (inside) edge of the petal shape and whipstitch in place. The ribbon will be bunched and folded in the middle of the petal. Tuck a few tiny stitches (that go through the background fabric) underneath the folds in the ribbon to anchor them.

Follow directions below for the order of stitching for each pillow.

To complete each pillow, baste the covered cording to the pillow front 1 inch from the raw edge. With right sides together, sew the pillow front to back, leaving an opening for turning. Clip the curves, turn the pillow cover right side out, and stuff. Then slip-stitch the opening.

Pansy Pillow
Begin by appliquéing the #1 petals to each flower, referring to the photograph for colors. After stitching the top and sides of each petal, pull the gathered edge of the ribbon snug and anchor it in the center of the flower with a few stitches. Add the side petals (#2 and #3) and then the light-colored petal (#4) in the same way. Complete the petals by adding a few small stitches inside of each one to hold the folds and tucks in the ribbon.

Add straight-stitched accents to the petals with light and dark yellow thread radiating from the center of the flower. Cover the raw edges of the ribbon in the center of the flower with three or four large French knots, wrapping the thread around the needle five or six times for each one.

Using light, medium, and dark shades of green pearl cotton, embroider the stems in satin stitches and the leaves in close herringbone stitches. Then complete the pillow, following directions above.

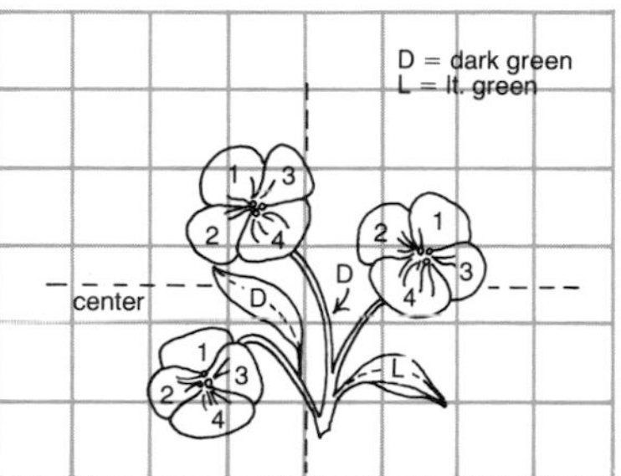

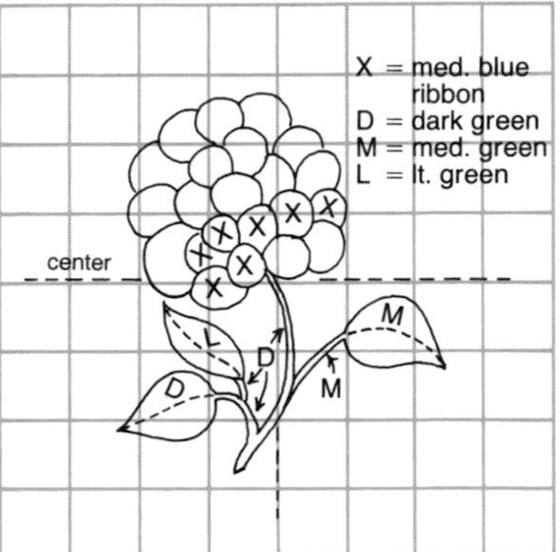

Hydrangea Pillow

To work this flower, appliqué the light blue petals around the outside of the flower head first, following the general instructions. While stitching, arrange each ribbon so the gathered edge falls toward the inside of the flower. Then add center flower petals, stitching center ribbons so that their folds overlap the gathered edges of ribbons that form the outside petals. Add medium blue petals last. Anchor folds with tiny stitches tucked underneath.

When the ribbon flower is completed, embroider the stem in satin stitches and the leaves in close herringbone stitches, following color directions on the pattern. Finish the pillow by following the general instructions opposite.

Coat both of these shaped appliqué pillows with soil-retardant spray, if desired. To clean, vacuum lightly around ribbons.

Appliqué and Stitchery—Wall Hanging

Every contemporary appliqué artist understands and appreciates the contributions of this amazing little machine to the craft.

To stitch up your own tribute to the sewing machine, make our wall hanging using a variety of appliqué and embroidery techniques. Begin with regular appliqué, add trapunto quilting, then tuck and fold other appliqués to give your machine real-life dimension. Finish with simple embroidery stitches to enhance the design.

Materials

16x22 inches black fabric
⅔ yard gray fabric
1 yard white fabric
6x20 inches orange fabric
5x5 inches tan fabric
1 yard unbleached muslin
6x12 inches black, orange, and tan print fabric
10x16 inches black and gray print fabric
15x15 inches black and silver metallic fabric
12 inches black middy braid
Black and tan embroidery floss
Silver metallic thread
Black sewing thread
Polyester fiberfill
Dressmaker's carbon
20-inch and 25-inch pairs of artist's stretcher strips
Staple gun
Wire for hanging
Picture frame (optional)

Directions

Cut a 28x33-inch rectangle from the white fabric and a 24x29-inch rectangle from the muslin. Center the muslin on the wrong side of the white fabric, leaving a 2-inch border on all sides. Machine-baste the two pieces together along the sides in a ½-inch seam. Turn and baste a ½-inch hem in the white fabric. Press.

Enlarge the pattern and center it face up on the right side of the white fabric. Lightly trace the pattern onto the fabric using dressmaker's carbon and a tracing wheel or pencil.

Cut out the pattern pieces adding a ¼-inch seam allowance and following the fabric color guide. Do not cut the white fabric for the background panels, the metallic shape on the left end of the sewing machine, or the gray and black fabric shape at the center bottom.

Using two strands of tan floss, embroider the details on the black sewing machine, following the stitch guide. Using random straight stitches, appliqué the tan, oval stitch-length indicator to the right end of the sewing machine with black sewing thread. Work all the black embroidery on the tan oval except the couching stitches down the center of the oval.

Turn and press seam allowances on gray (B), orange (C), and black/orange/tan print (E) pieces. Position the pieces on the white background and appliqué in place using black sewing thread.

Appliqué the black and silver metallic piece (H) to the left side of the machine using tiny stitches and black thread.

Cut a 5x6-inch piece of black and silver fabric. Turn the edges under ¼ inch and press. Machine-stitch ⅛-inch tucks down the long side, spacing them ½ inch apart. Appliqué the piece to the background using a neat slip stitch. Match the shape's left and lower edges to the outline shown in diagram. Trim fabric ¼ inch beyond outlines at

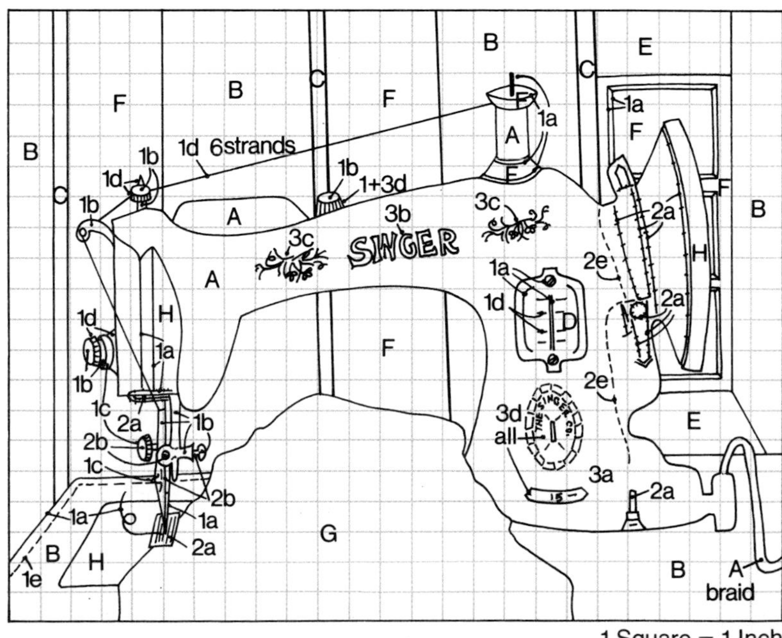

1 Square = 1 Inch

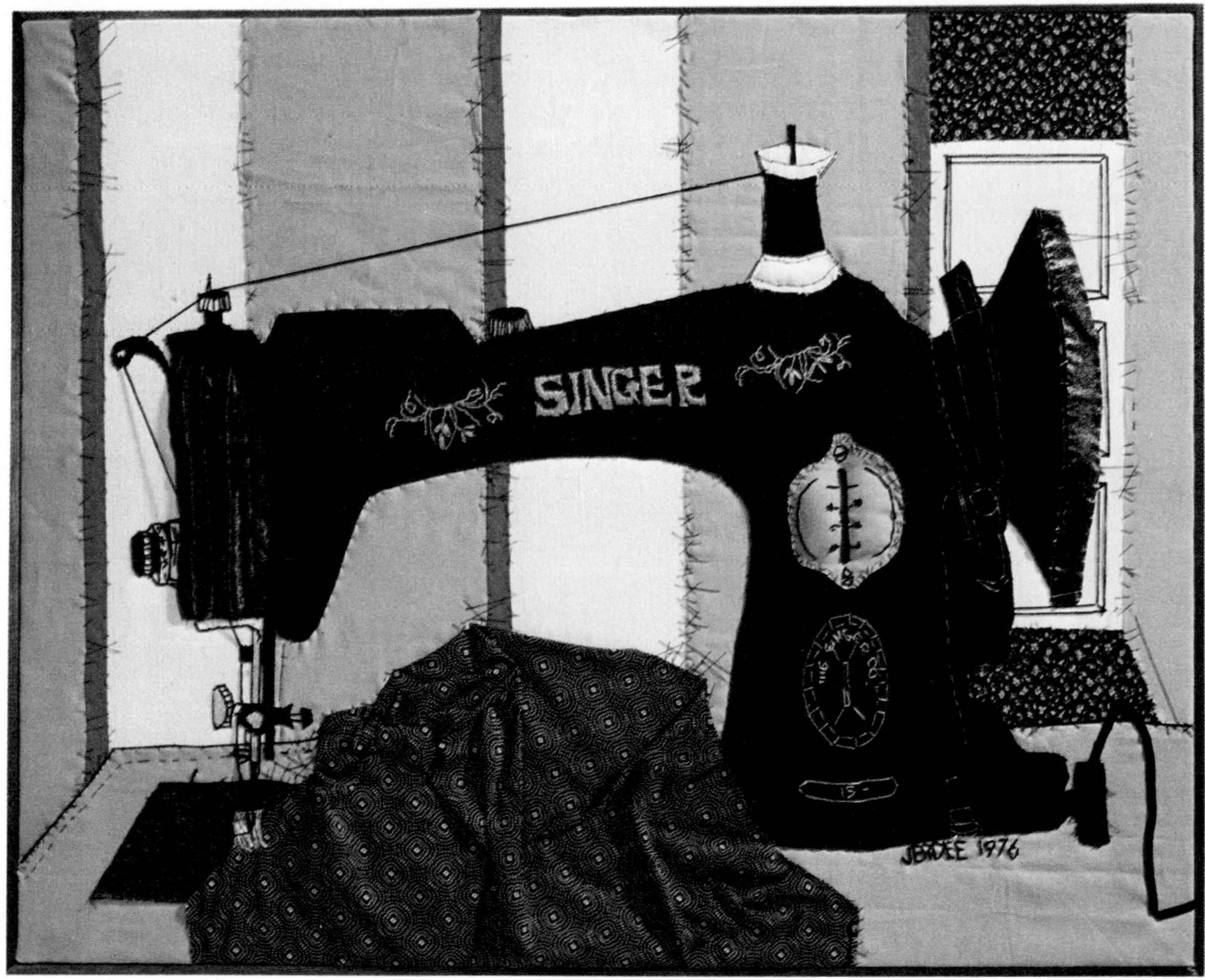

upper edge and right side of shape. Slip-stitch fabric to the background along the edges.

Appliqué the sewing machine and remaining shapes to the background. To make gray and black print "fabric" under the machine's needle, slip-stitch around edges of the shape, then crumple or pleat excess fabric in center to make "folds." Slip-stitch folds in place so the fabric looks gathered.

Add dimension to the machine by trapunto-quilting some sections. Turn the hanging over to the muslin side. Cut slits through muslin beneath the sewing machine and stuff with padding until shape is gently rounded. Use an orange stick to work stuffing into small spaces, if necessary. Slip-stitch the opening.

Using two strands of floss, embroider the rest of the design, following the stitch guide, but use six strands for the thread between spool and needle. Use one strand of silver where called for.

To further contour the machine, pull the following couching stitches from the right side through the padding to the back of the hanging with tight overcast stitches: tan oval, both ends of the machine, and the silver running stitches on the right end.

Assemble stretcher strips into a frame. With right side down, center the hanging inside the frame. Beginning in the center of each side, staple the hanging to the back of the frame. Mount in a purchased frame, if desired.

Fabric Key
A Black
B Gray
C Orange
D Tan
E Black/orange/tan print
F White
G Black/gray print
H Black and silver metallic

Thread Key
1 Black floss
2 Silver metallic
3 Tan floss

Stitch Key
a Couching stitch
b Satin stitch
c Stem stitch
d Straight stitch
e Running stitch

Reverse Appliqué—Wall Hanging

This wall hanging is a challenging project indeed—and probably not one for beginners. But if you are ready for a major undertaking, we think you will find it exciting.

Inspired by an ancient Peruvian monument built by the Incas, this "Gateway to the Sun" wall hanging is worked entirely in reverse appliqué. For this technique, pieces of fabric are stacked together and the top layers are then cut away to reveal the colors beneath. Careful planning, cutting, and stitching are essential for this work—but the unusual results are worth it.

The pattern (on page 124) is divided into five sections. Cut and stitch each one separately before assembling this 30x45-inch hanging.

Materials

Note: All fabrics are 45-inch-wide cotton broadcloth
3½ yards dark blue fabric
2¼ yards purple fabric
1¾ yards gold fabric
1 yard each of dark red, light green, orange, and forest green fabric
⅚ yard cherry red fabric
½ yard pink fabric
⅓ yard brown fabric
Thread to match fabrics
Dressmaker's carbon paper
Pattern-tracing fabric
Sharp embroidery scissors (or other small scissors)

Directions

Enlarge the pattern on page 124, following directions on pages 272 and 273. Note that there are five sections in the design. Make a separate pattern for each one by transferring each section to a rectangle of pattern-tracing fabric the same size as the fabric layers in that section (see specific directions below). Then construct each section individually before stitching it to the adjoining section. Trace the pattern lines onto the fabric layers with dressmaker's carbon. Do not cut into the pattern itself; keep it in one piece.

Work the design for each section as follows: Layer the fabrics in the order given in the specific directions that follow for each pattern. Transfer design lines to the top layer of the fabric. *Adding ¼-inch seam allowances, cut along design lines to—but not through—the color indicated on the pattern.* Start cuts with sharp-pointed embroidery scissors; do not start them at corners. When adding seam allowances, bear in mind that you will be cutting into the top layer or layers to reveal the fabric beneath, so *add seam allowances to the top layer or layers above the color indicated on the pattern.* For example, if you cut through gold and purple to blue, add seam allowances to gold and purple layers.

After cutting along outlines, pin shapes in position and set aside top layers that are completely cut away.

Appliqué shapes with thread to match the color of the fabric being sewn down. Use a regular appliqué stitch, and if necessary, trim away underlayers of fabric to reduce bulk in hems as pieces are stitched. When sewing, appliqué from the bottom layer up, stitching the topmost layer in place last.

Pattern #1 (border): Layer 1⅓ yards each of gold (top), purple, and navy blue fabric. Pin together every 6 inches along the edges.

Pin the border pattern on top of the fabric and transfer design lines with dressmaker's carbon. Add ½-inch seam allowances to outer edge and cut it through all layers. Ignoring the purple triangles in the outer border for the moment, trace and cut the inner and outer edges of gold to the color indicated on the pattern. Add ½-inch seam allowances. Trace and cut inner edge of border through purple and blue layers, this time adding ¼-inch seam allowances. Set aside inner rectangles for cutting out smaller pieces.

Trace squares on gold, add seam allowances, and cut out to purple layer only (do not cut *into* purple fabric). With a ruler and chalk or pencil, mark an "X" on each purple square between diagonal corners. Cut along the "X" to blue, extending cuts ½ inch under gold layers at corners (see the how-to diagram on page 122). This completes the triangle shapes that accent the squares.

Starting with the bottom left square, fold under the two horizontal purple triangles, extending the one at the outer gold edge ⅝ inch into the blue margin, as shown in the photograph (the base of the triangle will be under the gold fabric). Turn under the seam allowance and pin. Fold under triangles in remaining squares as indicated on the pattern, extending one triangle into the blue border on alternate squares. Pin. To sew, clip ¼ inch into gold corners, turn under seam allowance on triangles, and stitch, starting ¼ inch under the gold edge. Next, turn under gold hems and stitch. Turn under seam allowance on inner edge of border and baste.

continued

Reverse Appliqué—Wall Hanging *(continued)*

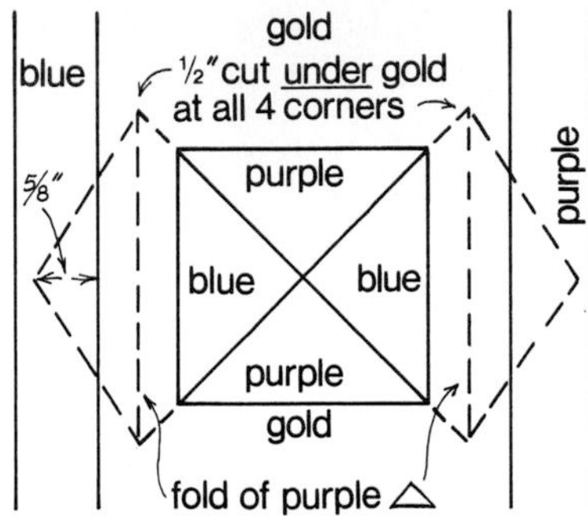

Cutting border triangles

Pattern #2: Cut the following nine colors into 18x22-inch pieces and layer in the order listed: brown (top), dark red, pink, light green, orange, navy blue, forest green, purple, and cherry red. Lay the pattern over the fabric and pin along the top edge.

Trace the lines of the *lower half* of the design, including the line in the center along the top of the brown area. Cut to dark red along this center horizontal line, adding the seam allowance to the brown fabric. Make remaining cuts in lower half of the pattern by working from left to right: make vertical cuts between sections first, then lift the strip of fabric between cuts and make horizontal cuts. For example, cut the slanted lines at the lower left of the pattern *to—but not through*—the navy fabric. Lift the wedge of fabric, revealing the navy blue beneath, and trim it along the horizontal *(top)*, leaving the seam allowance on the brown fabric.

After cutting and pinning the lower half of the design, replace the pattern over the lower half and pin across lower edge. Unpin the top. Fold the pattern down and remove the upper half of the brown fabric—above the center horizontal line that was cut first. Pin the brown fabric in position. To make remaining cuts, pin pattern over fabric, trace the line to be cut, fold the pattern down and cut to the color indicated. Remove the fabric above the line and pin the shape. Do not cut triangles yet.

In triangular area, cut horizontal lines first, starting in the middle of the design above first row of triangles. For example, with pattern over fabric, trace line at top of lowest row of triangles. Fold down pattern and cut along this line to orange (add seam allowance). Remove dark red fabric above orange; replace pattern and trace the next horizontal line. Continue as above.

After tracing and cutting horizontal lines, cut curved line at top of pattern, adding ¼ inch seam allowance. Then replace pattern, trace vertical lines separating center section of triangles, and trace triangles onto color strips. Cut through vertical lines to purple, extending cuts ½ inch under brown layer. Pin together all layers of the cut segment (in the center) and cut to purple along the bottom of the center segment ½ inch under the brown layer. Remove the pinned, cut segment (purple shows through).

Turn the cut segment upside down and pin it back into its original place. The top edge of the segment (dark red) should be even with the top edge (forest green) of the color strips at each side. To make hemming easier, remove from the cut segment the pink and light green layers that are directly under the dark red layer. Pin dark red back in its original place.

Turn under seam allowances on all pieces, baste, and appliqué, starting at the top of the design and working toward the center. Trim underlayers to remove bulk as necessary. On the bottom half of the design, appliqué shapes in place from left to right.

Pattern #3: Cut the following into 12x22-inch pieces and layer in the order indicated: cherry red (top), purple, light green, forest green, pink, navy blue, and orange. Pin layers together on short sides. Pin top edge of pattern to top layer.

Trace outlines of cherry red arches, adding seam allowances to cherry red. Pin along arches and cut away fabric to purple. Discard cherry red fabric except where pinned. To cut remaining shapes from the pattern, work from the top of the design to the bottom.

Starting with purple, cut each successive layer as follows: Trace the V-shaped outline of the triangle in the upper arch onto the fabric. Cut the *top layer of fabric only* along the outline, adding seam allowances and extending the cut ½ inch *under* the cherry red arches. Pin the triangle in place. Next, trim away the top layer, except for the pinned triangles, between the upper and middle arches.

To cut the multicolored center arch, trace the outline of the shape and pin the shape in position. Add seam allowances and cut away the remaining top layer, extending the cut ½ inch under the cherry red bands. Discard excess fabric. Repeat this procedure for the multicolored arch at the bottom of the pattern.

Work through all three arches with one color at a time, starting with purple and working to the bottom layer (orange). Then, turn under all seam allowances, clipping corners and curves. Appliqué all shapes in place with thread to match fabrics. Stitch the bottom layer (orange) first, then work toward the top layer (red). When hemming colors whose cut edges extend ½ inch under cherry red bands, continue the sewing line under the bands for ½ inch.

Appliqué pattern #2 to #3 as indicated on the pattern.

Pattern #4: Cut the following colors into 12x22-inch pieces and layer in the order indicated: forest green (top), gold, light green, dark red, brown, navy blue, and purple. Pin the top edge of pattern #4 to the layered fabrics. Work from left to right.

Mark outline of forest green mountain (including circles) and cut to layer beneath (gold). Trace around larger circle onto a separate scrap of pink fabric, adding ½ inch all around. Cut out pink and tuck into circular cutout as shown. Then trace outlines on remaining mountains on the left and cut top layers as indicated.

For mountains on the right, fold layers already cut (dark green to dark red) out of the way. Then cut brown, blue, and purple layers. Pin layers as they are cut. Appliqué all layers in place, starting on the right and working toward the left. Appliqué design #3 to design #4 along lines indicated on pattern.

Pattern #5: Cut the following colors in 12x22-inch pieces and layer in order indicated: light green (top), orange, forest green, navy blue, dark red, gold, and purple. Pin the pattern along the left edge of the fabric layers.

Trace outline of light green ray onto fabric. Pin and cut. Discard remaining top layer. Mark and cut successive right-hand rays in the same way. When they are pinned and cut, unpin pattern from left edge; repin along top edge of layers of fabric.

Trace outlines, pin, and cut rays on left of pattern starting with orange layer at bottom. After all are cut, appliqué in place beginning with left-hand rays. Appliqué pattern #4 to #5.

To assemble the hanging, appliqué the border to the center of the design. Turn the hanging over and trim excess fabric beneath each pattern area, leaving ¼-inch seam margins. Cut blue backing to size and stitch to front, right sides together, leaving an opening. Turn, press, and hand-quilt along border as shown in the diagram at right. Sew curtain rings to upper back for hanging.

continued

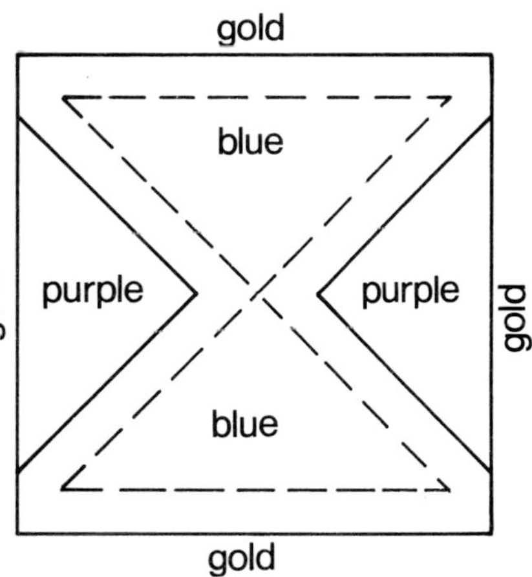

Quilting border triangles

Color Key (for pattern on page 124):

G	Gold
PL	Purple
N	Navy blue
B	Brown
O	Orange
LG	Light green
P	Pink
FG	Forest green
DR	Dark red
CR	Cherry red

Reverse Appliqué—Wall Hanging *(continued)*

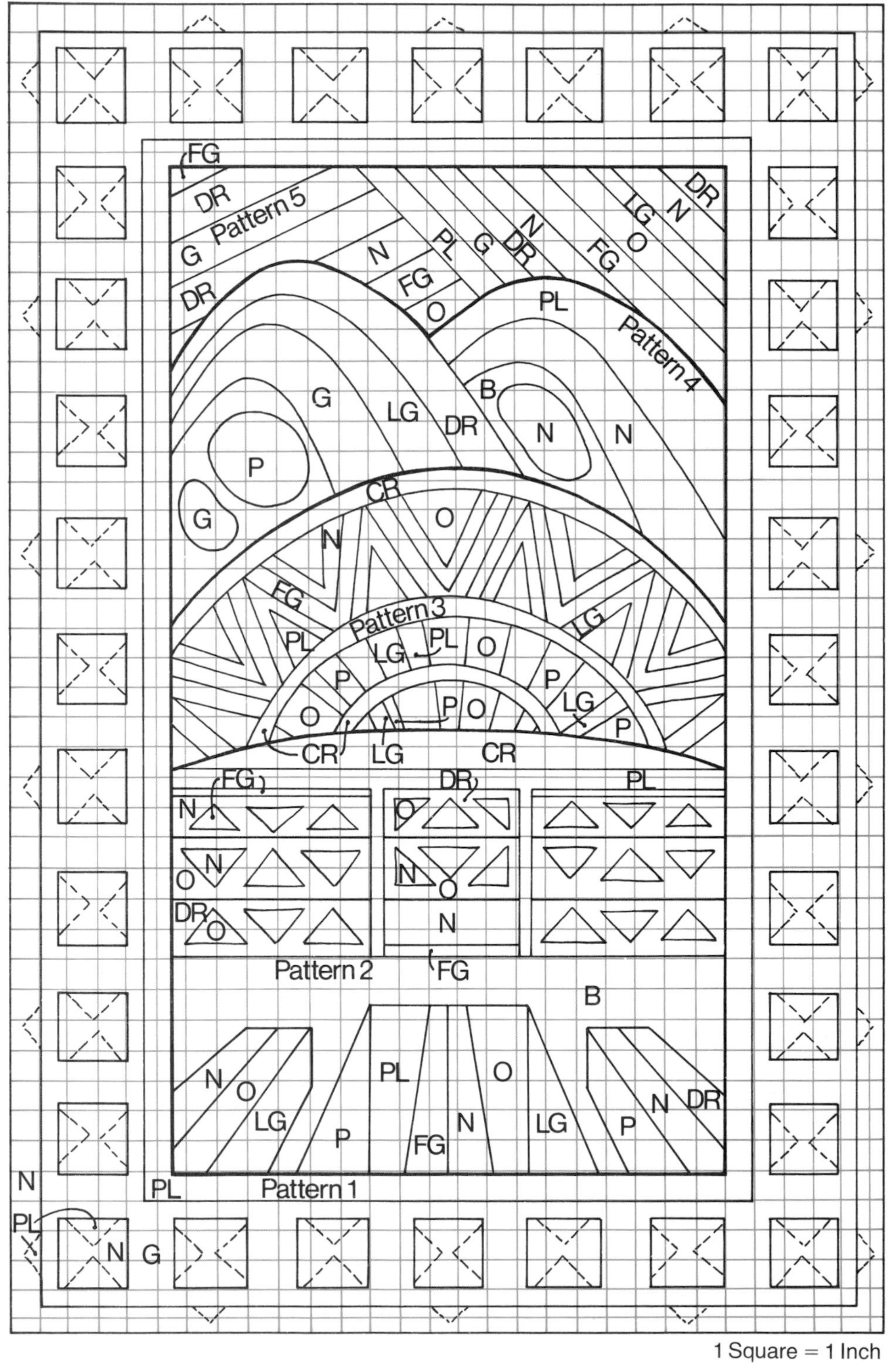

1 Square = 1 Inch

Lace Appliqué—Gift Box

New life for old lace—that's the secret to these next two projects. The satin gift box shown here, for example, is embellished with small pieces of fine antique lace cut from doilies and a tablecloth. Each design is appliquéd with tiny backstitches tucked into the lace itself to completely hide them from view.

Materials

⅔ yard satin or cotton sateen (or any medium-weight fabric with a close weave)
⅔ yard lining fabric
Cardboard for pattern
Mat board
Quilt batting
Lace, ribbon, or other decorative trims
Beeswax

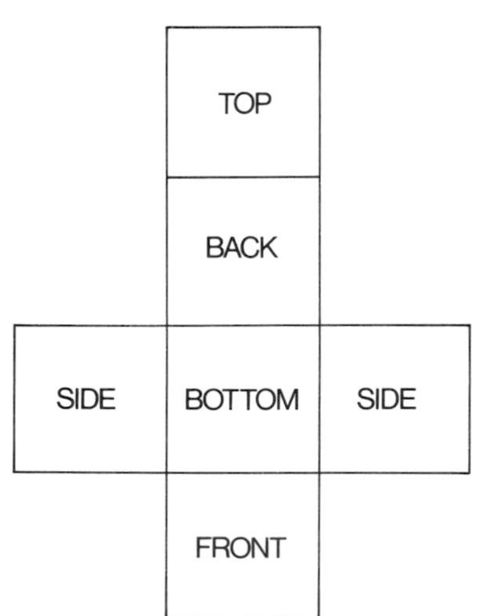

7-Inch-Square Box Pattern

Directions

For a 7-inch-square box, cut a 7-inch cardboard square (template). Trace six template patterns onto wrong side of lining fabric, leaving space between squares for ½-inch seams. Cut out squares, adding seam allowances. (Change box size by changing template size.)

Sew lining squares together, as shown at left. Cut out satin squares and stitch together. Press all seams open.

Appliqué lace or other trims to the satin. Use a thread that matches the lace, and sew with tiny back- or running stitches that anchor the lace snugly to the background fabric.

With right sides together, sew lining to satin, leaving open the bottom of the front square. Turn; press carefully.

Cut ¼ inch off two adjacent sides of the cardboard template. Using this as a pattern, cut six squares from mat board. Slip a square into the open end of the front piece; slide to top of box. Stuff small pieces of batting between mat board and fabric. Stuff corners firmly.

Using a zipper foot, stitch seam line between top and back.

Slide a mat board square into the back piece and repeat the stuffing procedure, then stitch. Do the same with each section until all the squares are stuffed. Slip-stitch opening closed.

Pin corners of side sections to the front and back sections to form a box. Pull thread through beeswax and slip-stitch the box together along its four corners.

Lace Appliqué—Quilt

If you have a collection of beautiful lace doilies, dresser scarves, antimacassars, or even place mats, you will find our lace appliqué quilt a wonderful way to display them creatively. Appliqué each piece to a square of cotton broadcloth that can be assembled into a 22-inch square. Next, stitch squares together into a quilt large enough for a queen-size bed. To finish this elegant but practical sampler of treasured handiwork, add a wide lace border (ours came from the edge of an old tablecloth) and decorative hand embroidery.

Materials

4 yards 44-inch-wide cotton/polyester fabric in assorted colors
5½ yards matching or contrasting fabric for backing and border
2 large sheets quilt batting
Twelve 14- to 16-inch round or square lace or crocheted doilies or antimacassars, or any combination of large and small doilies (as shown in the photograph)
10 yards 4-inch-wide old or new lace edging
#5 pearl cotton in white and ecru

Directions

Note: Finished size is about 78x100 inches. Seams are ½ inch.

Wash and preshrink all fabric. Repair old lace with matching thread and wash in cold water and mild soap (no bleach). Do not use delicate or very old pieces of lace since they wear quickly.

Arrange lace pieces to your satisfaction in four rows of three pieces (or groups of pieces) each. Then select backing fabric to complement each grouping of lace. Cut fabrics into squares and rectangles that can be joined into 22-inch squares. (Add seam allowances to all pieces.) After appliquéing lace to fabric, stitch three squares together into a row; then join four rows to make the top. When cutting the fabric squares, keep in mind arrangement of colors.

Begin by centering lace on squares. To make sure the lace lies flat on the fabric squares, press it lightly, then carefully pin it in place. Then stretch the fabric in an embroidery hoop and appliqué.

Appliqué lace in place with matching thread. Take tiny whipstitches or running stitches so the appliqué blends with the design of the lace. Appliqué in just enough places to hold the lace securely.

If your lace pieces and doilies are too small or too plain for the fabric squares, try adding a bit of embroidery—such as French knots, open chain stitches, or straight stitches—to help make the lace look larger or more decorative.

When all lace is appliquéd, assemble the quilt top by sewing squares together. Press seams to one side. Featherstitch over seam lines using pearl cotton thread.

Add 8-inch-wide border strips around the perimeter of the quilt and appliqué lace edging to the border. Cut the backing material and quilt batting 1½ inches narrower than the quilt top on all sides. Center the layers beneath the quilt top and tuft through the layers at the corners of each 22-inch square, using pearl cotton.

Fold raw edges of the border to the back side, turn raw edges under, and slip-stitch to backing.

Caring for Lace

Handmade lace, old or new, requires special attention in order to preserve its beauty and keep it in good condition. Here are some tips to help keep lace as fresh as the day it was made.

Make any needed repairs before washing the lace, stitching carefully and always inserting the needle *between* the threads, not into them. Using a small, blunt tapestry needle will help prevent split threads. To repair holes, weave horizontal threads as for darning; then, weave in and out of these threads to duplicate the design.

Gently wash the repaired lace in sudsy water, being careful not to rub or squeeze. Rinse the lace and wrap it in a towel, then block it on a fabric-covered board until dry, (at least overnight). When blocking, use stainless steel pins to avoid rust.

If stubborn stains persist, treat with diluted lemon juice or hydrogen peroxide, or have the stains treated professionally.

Avoid molding and yellowing by storing lace in a cool, dry, dark place. Lay pieces flat with a layer of tissue paper between.

Patterns from Quilts

Because appliquéd quilts have been popular in America for generations, we have included a collection of traditional patterns for you to make. Some, like this tulip design, combine appliqué with pieced patchwork, while others are entirely appliquéd. And some patterns are easy to stitch while others are more complex. So whatever your level of skill, we think you will find a design to challenge your creativity. Directions for our tulip quilt begin on the next page.

Tulip Basket Quilt

(shown on pages 128 and 129)

This traditional tulip basket pattern is a combination of pieced patchwork and appliqué. First make the baskets by piecing triangles of red and green fabric and filling them with appliquéd flowers.

Appliqué the motifs onto the blocks on the diagonal. Then set blocks together with white triangles around them and add a graceful appliquéd border. Our finished quilt measures 72x90 inches.

Materials

15 yards white cotton (front and backing)
3¼ yards green cotton
1⅜ yards red cotton
½ yard yellow cotton
Quilt batting
Thread to match fabrics

Directions

Enlarge the pattern and cut out pieces, adding ¼-inch seam allowances and referring to photograph for colors. Cut stems on the bias. Turn and baste seams on stems, leaves, and flower pieces.

Cut eighteen 14½-inch white squares; appliqué 12, leaving 6 plain. For outside edges of top, cut ten 14½-inch right triangles, with longest edge on straight grain of fabric. For corners, cut four 14½-inch triangles with one short edge on the straight grain.

Piece together triangles in the tulip basket first, pressing seams to one side. Turn and baste seam allowance around basket; position it on white block so square becomes a diamond. Baste. Turn under seam allowance on basket handles and baste to block.

Pin stems in place, add leaves, and position flowers. Assemble each flower individually, starting with the bottom layer (green) and working out (yellow, red, green). Baste and appliqué.

To assemble the top, set white squares between appliquéd ones, using ¼-inch seams. Edge with white triangles, following directions above. Stitch an 8½-inch-wide white border to the top. Appliqué stem, leaves, and tulips to border, as shown. Assemble quilt with backing and batting, following directions on page 43. Quilt, and then bind edges with 2½-inch-wide red bias strips.

Caring for Handmade Quilts

Whether your handmade quilt is a collector's item or simply a treasured family keepsake, it deserves special handling and care. Here are some tips for cleaning and storing all types of handmade quilts.

Identifying Quilt Fabrics

If your quilt needs cleaning, first identify its fabrics. Cotton and linen, derived from plant fibers, require different handling than wool and silk, made from animal fibers.

Most antique quilts are cotton, wool, or a combination of cotton and wool. You can usually identify fabric by its feel; or, use the "burn test." Snip a thread of cloth from the quilt and light the thread in an ashtray. Cotton burns quickly and smells like charred paper; wool smolders and gives off a strong odor.

The cotton/wool test won't work for crazy quilts because they're made from a combination of silk, velvet, and wool, which makes them difficult to clean. For advice on the care of crazy quilts, ask a textile expert.

Cleaning Wool Quilts

Quilts that contain any wool fabric must be cleaned as if they were made entirely of wool. Although old wool quilts can be washed safely, a careful dry cleaning may be easier and safer.

Use a reputable cleaner who does his/her own work. Ask that a fresh supply of dry cleaning solvent be used, and emphasize that the quilt is *not* to be pressed after dry cleaning.

Cleaning Cotton Quilts

Before cleaning a cotton quilt, test the dyed areas of the fabric for color-fastness. Mix one teaspoon of fine-washable cold-water detergent in a quart of soft water. Place two or three drops of this solution onto a patch of cloth. Wait about five seconds, then press the moist area between several white tissues and check for traces of dye. Rinse the fabric with clear water and blot with a clean towel.

If each quilt fabric is color-fast, it's safe to wash the quilt; if one color bleeds, consult a textile expert before washing.

For extra protection during washing, make a "bag" of white nylon net that's eight to nine inches wider and longer than your quilt. Leave one end open and insert the quilt. Stitch the end closed and sew a large X through all three layers. If your quilt is dusty, vacuum it through the nylon bag before washing.

Rub lukewarm water into a clean bathtub to hand-wash your cotton quilt. If the water is hard, add 1½ tablespoons of water softener for every three gallons of water. Soak the quilt for about one hour, then drain.

Refill the tub, adding 1½ tablespoons of fine-washable cold-water detergent per gallon of softened water. Soak the quilt for about 30 minutes, gently moving the fabric up and down. Drain and repeat two or three times until the water is clear.

Gently rinse the quilt in lukewarm, softened water and drain. Repeat this procedure until all of the soap is removed. For the final rinse, omit the water softener and rinse in clear water.

Press the water from the quilt without wringing or squeezing. Blot the quilt with towels until all excess moisture is removed.

To dry, hang your quilt in the shade over three or four parallel clotheslines on a dry, slightly breezy day, using clothespins without metal hinges. When the quilt is dry, remove it from its nylon bag; do not iron.

If your quilt is new, sturdy, or not very valuable, you might try machine washing. (Never use a washing machine for an old or valued quilt.) Sew the quilt into a white nylon mesh bag and fill the machine tub with lukewarm, softened water. Add 1½ teaspoons of fine-washable cold-water detergent per gallon of water. Let the quilt soak for 30 to 40 minutes, then set the machine on a gentle cycle and let the quilt agitate for about three minutes. Drain and repeat until the dirt is removed. Rinse the quilt in cool water, then machine-dry on a gentle cycle or hang it on the line.

Removing Stains

If your quilt has spots or stains, ask an expert for advice on removing them. They may need special treatment, since untreated stains on cloth undergo chemical changes. If you use home remedies, you might remove the delicate fabric along with the stain. It may be better to live with the spot than to risk damaging your quilt.

Storing Quilts

To avoid creases and dust, cover a wooden dowel or cardboard mailing tube that's five inches longer than the quilt with clear plastic. Roll the quilt loosely onto the dowel or tube. Hang the quilt in a dark, well-ventilated storage area, avoiding extreme dampness or heat. Cover the quilt with plastic.

If roll storage is impractical, folding and bagging the quilt is the alternative. Air and refold your quilt four times a year, padding the folds with tissue paper. Place the quilt in a roomy plastic bag, and unless the fabric is wool, don't seal the end. If the quilt contains wool, add one cup of moth crystals and seal tightly.

Aunt Mary's Rose Quilt

Simplicity of design adds much to the charm of old quilts—especially when they are beautifully and expertly quilted in a variety of patterns that enhance the motif. Aunt Mary's Rose Quilt—a variation of the Rose of Sharon motif—is just such a design. Each of the nine blocks is appliquéd with a large rose and four graceful buds. The blocks are then set together with pink and white borders to make a quilt 79 inches square.

Materials

Note: All fabrics are 44 or 45 inches wide
9½ yards white or off-white polished cotton
⅝ yard green cotton
½ yard medium pink cotton
1¾ yards light pink cotton
Thread to match fabrics
Quilt batting

1 Square = 1 Inch

Directions

Enlarge the pattern below at left and cut cardboard, sandpaper, or plastic templates for each of the pieces. Transfer the patterns to fabric and cut out, adding ¼-inch seam allowances.

Turn under the raw edges on the pattern pieces, clipping curves and corners. Baste.

From the white fabric, cut nine 17x17-inch blocks. Fold them in half vertically and press. Fold in half horizontally and press. Position appliqués on the blocks, centering the rosebuds and centers of the petals on the large flower on folds of the blocks. Pin and baste appliqués in position. Then, with thread to match fabrics, appliqué pieces in place.

When all blocks are appliquéd, cut six 3½x17-inch pink strips. Using ¼-inch seams, sew two strips between three blocks to make a row. Press seams to one side. Assemble three rows.

Cut four pink strips 3½x56 inches (measure rows to verify dimensions). Stitch two strips between three rows and one each at the top and bottom of the quilt. Cut two pink strips 3½x61 inches (measure to verify dimensions) and sew one to each side of the top. Press seams to one side.

For the border, cut two white strips 9x62 inches (approximately) and sew to the top and bottom. Cut two white strips 9x79 inches (approximately) and sew to the sides of the quilt. Press seams to one side.

Cut batting and backing fabric to size, and assemble the entire quilt, following directions on page 43. Baste the layers together and quilt, referring to the photograph for suggestions or using a design of your own.

After quilting, bind the raw edges with 1½-inch-wide bias strips cut and pieced from the remaining white fabric.

Rose Wreath Quilt

Made in Ohio in 1868 by Sarah Elliott, this beautiful quilt features the rose—one of the most dearly loved of appliqué motifs. Here it is worked into a wreath and accented with leaves. And the wide strips of plain fabric that separate the appliqué blocks have been heavily embellished with elaborate quilting.

The elegant handiwork in this quilt is a true inspiration to contemporary quilters.

Materials

9½ yards 44-inch-wide white cotton fabric
1 yard red cotton fabric
5½ yards green cotton fabric
¼ yard orange cotton fabric
White quilting thread
Quilting needle
Quilt batting
Quilting frame (optional)
Cardboard
Tissue paper
Hard lead pencil
Artist's knife

Directions

This 78-inch-square quilt is made of nine 14-inch-square appliquéd blocks separated by 7-inch-wide plain strips. A narrow green border and a wide white one, appliquéd with blossoms and buds, frame the central design. To make the quilt a different size, alter the size or number of the blocks, or the width of the border strips.

Enlarge the patterns for the block and border, opposite, to size. Transfer the pattern pieces to cardboard, sandpaper, or plastic templates. Cut pieces as indicated on the chart, turn under the seam allowances, and baste. Stitch orange centers to the red blossoms. For the vines, cut and piece 1-inch-wide bias strips. *Add ¼-inch seam allowances around all pattern pieces as you cut them out.*

For each block, cut a 14½x14½-inch white square. Fold the square in quarters and press. Mark a circle 10 inches in diameter in the center of the block for the green ring.

Position four flowers on the folds, then cut green bias strips to fit between them along the circle. Tuck the raw edges of the strips under the blossoms, and pin leaves in place as shown on the pattern. Baste all the pieces and then appliqué the entire design in place using small appliqué stitches. Complete 9 blocks.

When appliquéing bias strips in curves, sew down the inner edge of the curve first, then stretch the outer edge a bit as you appliqué it in place, so the curved piece will lie flat, without puckering.

To assemble the quilt top, cut six 7½x14½-inch white strips. Sew a strip to each side of an appliquéd block, then sew an appliquéd block to the second side of each strip, making a row of three blocks with two white strips between them. Assemble three rows.

Next, cut two white strips 7½x56½ inches (measure the length of the rows you've sewn together to verify dimensions). Sew a strip to each side of an appliquéd row, then sew the other appliquéd rows to the strips, for a top about 56 inches square.

Cut two green strips 2½x56½ inches (approximately) and sew them to opposite sides of the square. Then cut two strips 2½x60½ inches (approximately) and sew to top and bottom. Or, cut all strips about 60 inches long, sew to the central square, and miter corners.

Cut two white border strips 9½x60½ inches and sew them to the opposite sides of the green border. Finish with two 9½x78½-inch strips sewn to the top and bottom. Or, cut four 78½-inch strips, sew them to the green strips, and miter the corners.

Appliqué the border design as shown in the photograph, above. Baste the vine in place first, then position and baste the stems, leaves, blossoms, and buds. Appliqué everything in place.

Press the finished quilt top on the wrong side over a padded board so you don't flatten the appliquéd pieces. Then assemble the entire quilt, following instructions on page 43. After quilting, bind the edges with narrow strips of the remaining green fabric.

Blue Grove Quilt

One way of making a pattern for appliqué is to cut it from folded fabric–the same way children cut snowflake designs from folded paper. This technique is characteristic of Hawaiian quilts and gives them their distinctive look.

This quilt, however, was made in Ohio in 1861 by Mary Grove. And since we do not know if Mary set out to make a typically Hawaiian quilt (although her motif looks much like a pineapple), we give you the complete pattern instead of just a segment. But you may still try folding the fabric to create your own "Hawaiian snowflake," following directions on page 162.

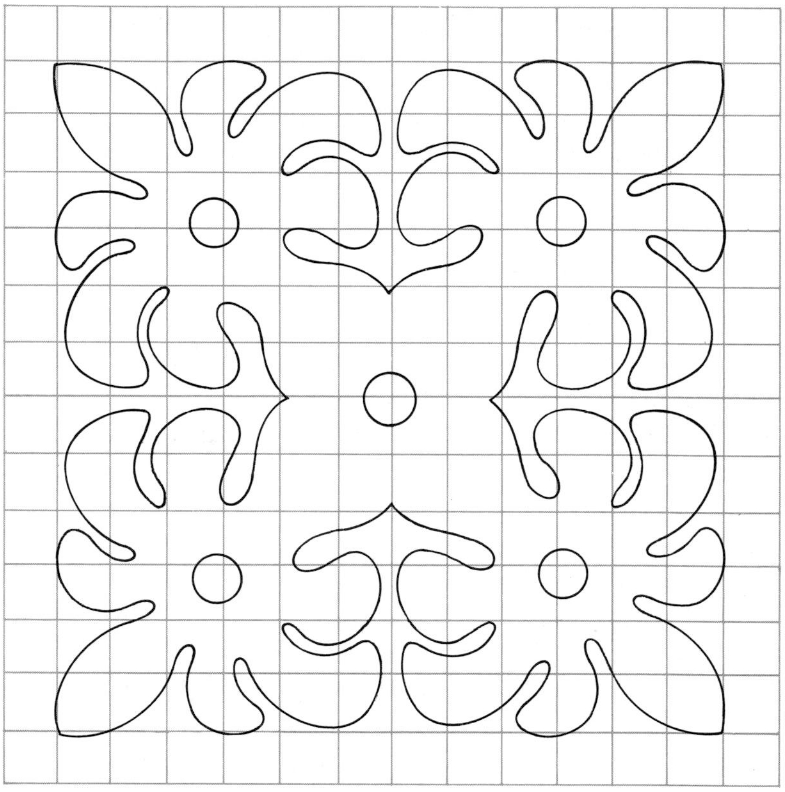

1 Square = 1 Inch

Materials

9½ yards white fabric
5¾ yards blue print fabric
Quilting thread
Quilt batting
Cardboard or sandpaper

Directions

Enlarge the pattern and transfer it to a cardboard or sandpaper template. Cut 16 designs from blue fabric, adding ¼-inch seam allowances. Turn under seam allowances, clipping curves as necessary. Baste. For inner circles on pattern, snip fabric inside the circle and trim excess to within ¼ inch of design line. Clip curves, turn under the seam margin, and baste.

Cut sixteen 14½-inch squares of white fabric. Fold fabric in quarters and crease. Center a blue pineapple motif on each square, baste diagonally from corner to corner, and appliqué in place.

Assemble blocks into rows by cutting twenty 2½x14½-inch strips of blue fabric. Stitch strips between four blocks and to ends of each row (making four blocks and five strips on each row). Cut five strips the length of each row (about 66 inches) and 2½ inches wide. Set four rows together with five strips between and at the ends.

For the border, cut two white strips 3½x66½ inches (approximately) and sew to top and bottom of quilt top. Cut two white strips 3½x72½ inches (approximately) and sew to sides of top. Cut and piece ⅞-inch-wide bias strips for the border. Turn under the seam allowances and appliqué to the white strip in a cable design.

Complete the final assembly of the quilt, following directions on page 43. Quilt either in diagonal rows, as shown, or follow the outline of the motifs. Bind edges with remaining blue fabric.

Rose of Sharon Quilt

Rose motifs are a popular appliqué design. And this one–the beautiful Rose of Sharon pattern–is an especially attractive although somewhat elaborate rendition. To make a quilt like the one pictured here (about 82 inches square), you need nine 28-inch blocks. If you're not up to making an entire quilt, stitch just one square to make a dramatic pillow or wall hanging.

Because of this pattern's size and number of pieces, it is easier to stitch together the appliqués that make up the roses first, before pinning anything to the background fabric. You may use a blind stitch instead of the regular appliqué stitch to give your appliquéd roses an attractive puffed look.

Materials

13 yards 36-inch-wide white cotton
3¼ yards green cotton
2 yards red cotton
1¾ yards pink cotton print
½ yard yellow cotton print
Thread to match fabrics
Quilt batting

Directions

Enlarge the pattern, opposite, and transfer it to tissue paper to make the master pattern. Then, using carbon paper and a pencil, transfer the pattern to cardboard and cut out a template for each pattern piece. Do not add seam allowances to cardboard templates.

Referring to the photograph for colors, trace around the cardboard templates onto the fabrics with a hard lead pencil, outlining the number of pieces needed for a complete block: four large leaves, eight small leaves, and petals and centers for one large flower and eight small flowers. If the edges of the templates become worn, cut new ones. Cut bias strips of green fabric for stems; they curve easily without puckering when appliquéd. Add ¼-inch seam allowances to all pieces when cutting.

Turn under and baste a ¼-inch hem in the yellow print flower centers and in each of the petal pieces that make up the roses; clip curves as necessary.

Make the large flower first. Pin and baste the center of the flower to the smallest petal piece. Then pin and baste the remaining petal pieces together, taking them in order of size and color. When the entire flower is formed, appliqué the pieces together and remove the basting stitches. Repeat this stacking and basting procedure for each of the small flowers; then appliqué each layer. Use a blind stitch for the appliqué work.

1 Square = 1 Inch

Cut a 28-inch square of white fabric for each block. Fold it in quarters and press, making sure creases are visible when the square is opened. Position the large rose over the center of the square; baste. Next, pin the four longer stems along the creases, curving them as indicated on the pattern. Add large leaves around the central flower, tucking the raw edges of the leaves and stems under the flower. Check the position of all the pieces against the master pattern by laying the tissue paper over the fabric block; make any necessary adjustments in their location. Pin and baste the pieces in position, using the master pattern as a guide.

Next, pin and baste the remaining short stems, leaves, and small flowers. Check their position against the master pattern. Then appliqué everything in place. Complete eight more appliquéd blocks (for a total of nine).

To assemble the quilt top, sew three large blocks together into a row, using ¼-inch seams. Press seams to one side. Then stitch three rows together into the finished top.

Assemble the quilt with a layer of batting and backing cut to size, following the directions on page 43. Quilt in the pattern of your choice. To finish, cut and piece 1½-inch-wide green bias strips to go around the quilt. With right sides together, stitch bias binding to quilt top in a ¼-inch seam. Turn under ¼ inch on remaining raw edge, and whipstitch to back of quilt.

Dresden Plate Quilt

Quilt lovers everywhere will recognize this classic Dresden plate pattern—a favorite among quilters for years.

To make this design, first piece sections of the plate, and then appliqué the entire motif to the background fabric. Careful cutting and stitching are important to make the appliqué lie flat and smooth. We recommend that you make a sample block before cutting the pieces for the entire quilt.

Materials

12 yards 45-inch-wide white or off-white fabric
Assorted fabric scraps (see note at right)
Queen-size (81x97 inches) quilt batting
Thread

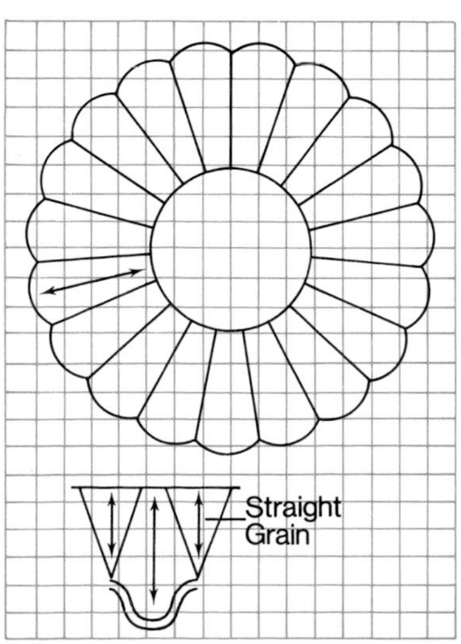

1 Square = 1 Inch

Directions

Note: Our 79x97-inch quilt is composed of twenty 17-inch-square appliquéd blocks. The plate design has 19 wedges in it. To determine the amount of fabric needed for wedges, plan to cut 18 plate wedges from ¼ yard of fabric, or 36 wedges from ⅓ yard of fabric. Cut 14 border wedges from ¼ yard of fabric, or 28 wedges from ⅓ yard of fabric. To make a quilt the same size as ours (with 20 blocks), cut 380 plate wedges and 117 print border wedges.

Enlarge the pattern below and transfer it to tissue paper. This is the master pattern. Without adding seam allowances, trace the wedge pattern onto cardboard, sandpaper, or a plastic lid and cut it out with an artist's knife or razor blade, keeping edges straight.

Make a sample block first. Cut 19 wedges from different fabrics. Trace the pattern onto the fabric for each wedge, leaving sufficient margins to allow for ¼-inch seams. Be sure to trace and cut pieces with the straight grain of the fabric running down the center of the wedge, as indicated on the pattern. When the edges of the template become worn, make a new one.

Piece the wedges by hand or machine as shown on the pattern, using ¼-inch seams. *But leave ¼ inch unsewn* at each end of each wedge so the inner and outer edges of the plate can be turned easily when the design is appliquéd to the square. Gently press all seams to one side, being careful not to stretch the fabric.

When the plate design is assembled, pin and baste a ¼-inch hem in the inner and outer edges of the circle. This makes it easier to appliqué the plate patterns to the white blocks.

Cut a 17½-inch-square background block from white fabric and center the plate motif on it, checking its position against the master pattern. Pin and baste the design in place.

To appliqué, whipstitch the inside edge first, then the outside edge, making sure the pattern lies flat and smooth. If it does not sit correctly on the block, make adjustments in the seams between the pieces and, if necessary, in the pattern for the wedge. If the block is satisfactory, cut wedges for the remaining 19 blocks and piece and appliqué them to the background blocks, following directions for the sample block. Cut the wedges carefully so they are all the same size.

To assemble the quilt top, stitch four blocks together into a row, using ¼-inch seams. Make five rows, then stitch the rows together. Press all seams to one side.

To make the border, cut 109 white triangles and 117 print border wedges, making sure the straight grain of the fabric runs down the middle of each piece. Except for the corners of the quilt, piece the wedges and triangles alternately, as shown in the photograph at right. For the corners, piece three border wedges together. With right sides together, sew the border to the edge of the quilt in a ¼-inch seam. Press the seam to one side. Cut and piece 1-inch-wide white bias strips until they measure 13 yards. Set aside.

Cut backing fabric and batting to size and assemble the entire quilt, following directions on page 43. After basting, quilt in the patterns shown in the photograph at right, or in a design of your own. After quilting is finished, bind the edges of the quilt with the bias strips. With right sides together, baste and then stitch the binding strip to the front of the quilt in a ¼-inch seam. Clip curves and corners, then fold strip in half. Turn under ¼ inch on remaining raw edge and slip-stitch to the back of the quilt.

Appliqué-Designs From Nature

The appliqué projects shown here and on the following pages forever capture beautiful moments in nature through the use of fabric and thread and some easy-to-learn appliqué stitchery. Once you master basic appliqué techniques, you'll never be at a loss for design ideas if you consider the world of nature, just as we did. Our pictorial designs, which adorn quilt tops and coverlets, were inspired by scenes from nature and range from graceful butterflies to delicate wildflowers.

Directions for the appliquéd quilt top shown here begin on the following pages.

Appliquéd Butterflies and Blossoms (shown on pages 142 and 143)

Butterflies and flowers are both popular designs for appliqué, and in this delightful quilt top, they combine in bold, colorful blocks. Although old-style quilts often used these same motifs, their scale and dynamic color give this quilt an exciting modern appearance.

Materials

4 yards muslin
1½ yards orange check, 45-inch fabric
1½ yards solid orange, 45-inch fabric
Assorted prints and solids for appliqué pieces
1 sheet or 6 yards fabric for backing
Polyester batting

Directions

Instructions are for a 64x76-inch quilt.

Enlarge the drawing at right to fit a 13-inch finished block, and make a tracing paper pattern. With carbon paper, trace the outline of each appliqué piece on cardboard and cut out templates. *(Note:* left and right wings, body, leaves, and flower motif are each cut as single shapes. Details are embroidered on after shapes have been appliquéd in place.) Save the tracing paper pattern to use as a placement guide for the appliqué pieces.

Cut 30 butterflies and 30 blossoms. Bodies of butterflies and leaves of flowers should be cut of dark fabric; butterfly wings and flower petals should be cut from assorted prints and solids. Remember when transferring patterns to your fabric to trace with the fabric right side up and to add ¼-inch seam allowances to all pieces before cutting.

Cut 30 13½-inch squares of muslin, 49 strips of orange checked fabric 3x13½ inches long, and 20 three-inch squares of solid orange. Cut four solid orange strips 3x91 inches long and four strips 3x75 ½ inches long. Piece strips if necessary. Cut eight three-inch squares of orange check. (Measurements for strips and squares include ¼-inch seam allowances.)

Position the leaves on the muslin block using the tracing paper pattern as a guide. Follow general instructions on the preceding pages and appliqué. Place the flower petals over the leaves and appliqué. Position butterfly wings and appliqué, then top them with the body sections. Appliqué. Embroider petal details on the flowers and antennae on butterflies. Add decorative stitches to the appliqué. If you're working by hand, use a buttonhole or blanket stitch on the outer edges of wings and petals, and an outline stitch to separate the flower petals and centers. If machine appliquéing, use a narrow satin stitch. Make 30 appliquéd blocks.

Make rows of blocks by alternating butterfly squares and orange checked strips, starting and ending with blocks. Use five blocks and four checked strips for each row, and be sure that all butterflies are facing the same direction.

Make four joining strips by alternating checked strips and solid squares, starting and ending with checked strips. Use six strips and five squares for each joining strip. Sew one row of blocks to one joining strip, making sure the solid square is positioned directly over the checked strip separating the blocks. Sew another row of blocks to the other side of the joining strip. Continue alternating block rows and joining strips until the quilt top is completed.

Sew one check square to each end of the four 75½-inch-long solid orange strips. Sew one of these border strips to the top of the quilt and one to the bottom. Set the other two aside. Sew one 91-inch-long solid orange border strip to each long side of the quilt. Set the other two strips aside. Sew ends of the long border strips to the checked corner squares, and press all seams in the completed quilt top.

Assemble the quilt top, batting, and backing, and quilt following the instructions starting on page 43. Outline-quilt appliqué pieces and quilt along seams that join blocks and strips.

Join the four remaining border pieces to form a large "frame." Pin frame in place on the face of the completed quilt, right sides together, and sew around all four sides of the quilt. Clip corners, turn, and press. Turn under raw edges and stitch this fabric frame to the backing fabric to finish the quilt.

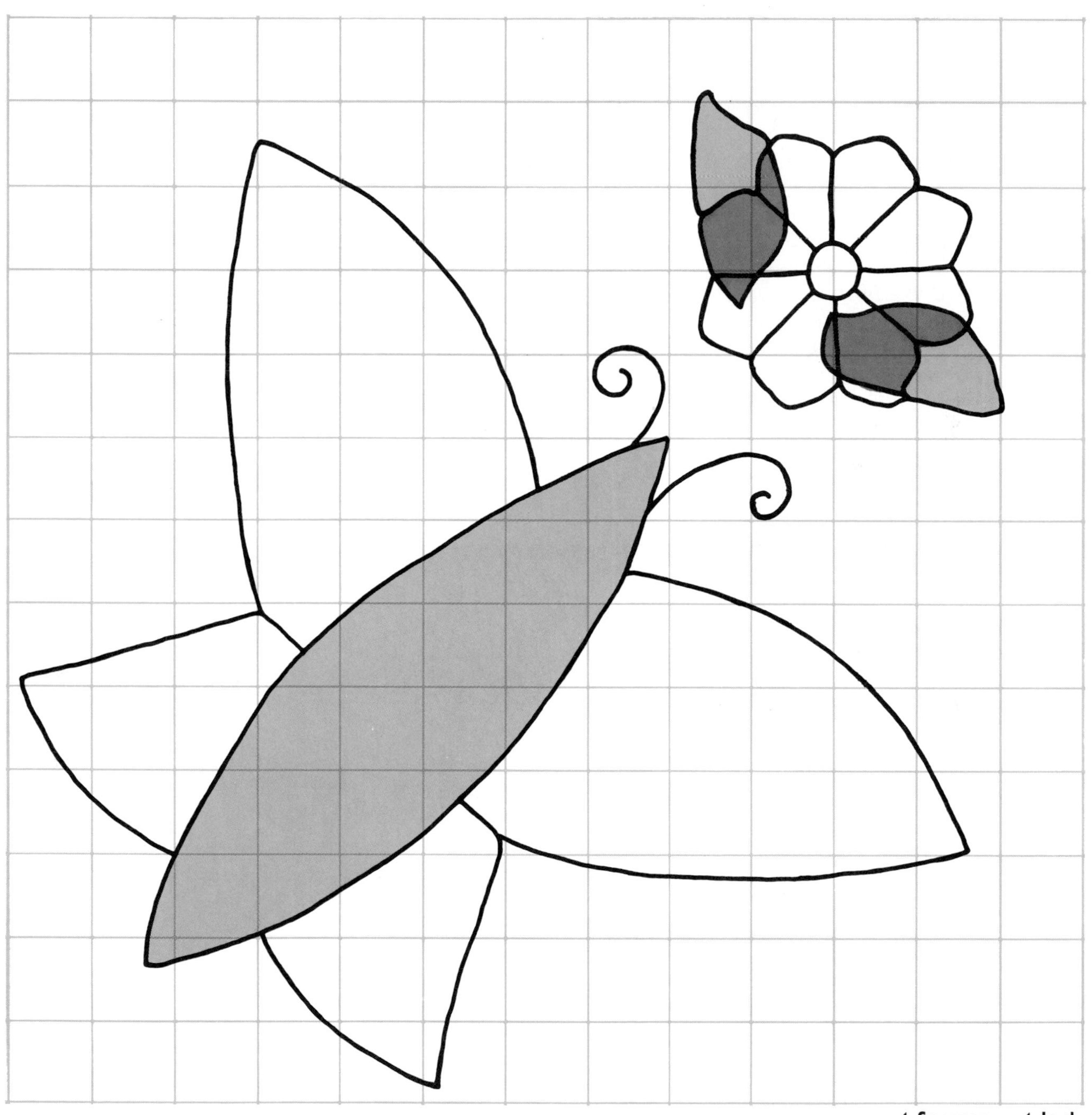

1 Square = 1 Inch

Appliquéd and Embroidered Wildflower Coverlet

The eight simple wildflower designs pictured on the opposite page can be artfully combined in any size quilt you desire to make. Our directions are for the quilt shown—a 40x52-inch crib-size coverlet. Each of the floral motifs in the quilt is hand appliquéd and given added emphasis by touches of hand embroidery. By enlarging any of these designs, you can use them in lots of different projects—as our machine-appliquéd pillow illustrates. For patterns, see pages 78 and 79.

Materials

2¾ yards white 45-inch cotton blend fabric
1½ yards green 45-inch fabric
Scraps of fabric in colors for flowers
Pearl cotton embroidery thread
Polyester batting

Directions

To make this wildflower coverlet, cut 12 11-inch-square blocks of white fabric. Next enlarge the designs shown on pages 78 and 79, using a scale of 1 square = 1¼ inches. Make a properly sized pattern on tracing paper, then use it to make cutting patterns for each appliqué piece. With carbon paper, trace the appliqué shapes from the tracing paper to heavy paper or lightweight cardboard. Keep the tracing paper pattern intact to use as a placement guide.

Use the photo opposite as a color guide, and cut appliqué pieces of the fabric colors shown. Add ¼-inch seam allowances to each appliqué shape, and work one block at a time. Follow the instructions on pages 75 and 76 for hand appliquéing. When the appliqué pieces have been hand-stitched in place, embroider leaves, stems, and details on each flower as indicated on the pattern. For our 12-block quilt, three of the eight flower patterns are repeated twice, and we included a personal block with embroidered name and birth date in the lower right-hand corner.

When all blocks have been appliquéd and embroidered, press them gently to remove all wrinkles. Make a 10½-inch square of cardboard and place on the appliquéd block. Be sure the flower is positioned the way you want it, then mark around the cardboard square and trim excess fabric away so you have a 10½-inch square block. Finished quilt blocks are 10 inches. Sew with ¼-inch seam allowances.

Cut nine green strips 2½x10½ inches. Lay appliquéd blocks on the floor in the desired arrangement. Using ¼-inch seam allowances, sew together four blocks with three green strips between. Strips should be sewn between the top of one block and the bottom of the next. Make three vertical rows of blocks. Cut two strips of green fabric 2½x46½ inches. Using ¼-inch seam allowances, sew these two strips between the three rows of blocks to form the completed block section of the quilt.

Cut the border strips of green fabric. You'll need two strips 3½x46½ inches, two strips 3½x34½ inches, and four squares 3½x3½ inches.

Sew the two 46½-inch-long strips to the outside side edges of the block section. Next sew a 3½-inch square at each end of the two 3½ x 34½-inch strips. Pin these two pieced strips at the top and bottom of the block section. Make sure the seams match so the small corner square lines up with the border strip that joins it. Sew with a ¼-inch seam allowance.

Press all seams away from the white blocks and toward the green strips that surround them. Following the instructions beginning on page 43, assemble the completed quilt top, batting, and backing. Cut the backing from the remainder of the white fabric. Machine- or hand-quilt along the seam lines of the blocks and green strips. Finish the edges as desired.

To make a companion pillow, as shown, enlarge a single flower block to any size you choose—from 12 to 18 inches. Machine-appliqué the pillow top using techniques outlined in general appliqué instructions (pages 74 through 77). Make or buy covered cording to edge the pillow. Sew the cording to the finished pillow top with the raw edges of the cording placed along the raw edges of the right side of the pillow. Cut the pillow back to the appropriate size and sew to the front, right sides together. Leave one side open, turn, and insert pillow form. Stitch closed.

FOR CATHERINE

Colorful, Contemporary Butterfly Quilt

If there's a bedroom in your home that needs livening up, nothing will do it faster than this appliquéd quilt, all abloom with butterflies and stylized posies.

Materials

(All fabrics listed are 44-45 inches wide)
¼ yard yellow
2 yards gold
2 yards orange
1¾ yards rust
1 yard scarlet
¼ yard burgundy
⅛ yard magenta
1½ yards hot pink
6 yards apple green
¼ yard kelly green
⅛ yard white
1 skein white embroidery floss
1 skein burgundy embroidery floss
Polyester batting

Directions

The dimensions given here will produce a quilt approximately 67x92 inches, suitable for a twin bed with dust ruffle. Instructions for enlarging the quilt are on page 155, so you can customize your quilt to the size of your bed.

Start by preshrinking and pressing all fabrics. Make the apple green backing sheet first by cutting the six yards of fabric into three equal lengths. These will measure about 72 inches long. Cut a 15-inch-wide strip from the length of one of these so it measures 15x72 inches. Sew this narrow strip between the two other uncut pieces using ½-inch seam allowances. This will give you a 72x103-inch sheet to use as backing for your quilt. Press the seams open. Use the rest of the green fabric for cutting appliqué pieces.

Each quilt block is keyed with a number. Study the block placement diagram on page 150 to familiarize yourself with the sections of the quilt. Colors for each appliqué piece are indicated by the letter symbols given in the color guide on page 154.

Using the graph drawings on pages 151 through 154 as size guides, start by cutting out all the background blocks. Cut blocks 7, 12, 14, 18, and 20 from gold fabric. Cut blocks 1, 8, 10, 15, and 21 from orange. From the rust fabric cut blocks 3, 9, 13, and 17. Use the scarlet fabric for blocks 4, 6, and 19. Cut blocks 2, 5, 11, and 16 from the hot pink fabric.

The dotted line on the drawings indicates the seam line; the solid line is the cutting line. Cut the blocks ¼ inch outside the indicated cutting line to compensate for any drawing-up that occurs while appliquéing the blocks. Excess fabric will be trimmed later.

Enlarge each block to its actual size using tracing paper. With carbon paper, trace the outline of each appliqué piece onto lightweight cardboard or heavy paper. Since each pattern piece will be used only once, making a durable template isn't essential. Keep the tracing paper pattern intact to use as a placement guide.

This quilt is a combination of reverse appliqué and regular appliqué techniques, but if you prefer, the entire quilt may be appliquéd the usual way. The following blocks are worked in regular appliqué: 2, 4, 7, 10, 11, 12, 13, 14, 16, 17, 18, and 19. The following are done in reverse appliqué: 1, 3, 5, 6, 8, 9, 15, 20, and 21.

The diagram in the upper left corner of page 150 shows you how reverse appliqué is done. Instead of sewing a shape to the background fabric, the shape is cut out of the background fabric, leaving a ¼-inch allowance on the inside, to be turned under and sewn to an under-fabric which shows through the cutout shape. The under-fabric has to be cut large enough so that the background fabric can be pinned to it as you sew. The inner details are done afterward in the same way. Because of this, you need not trace inner details of the butterfly when you trace the outer outline on reverse appliqué blocks, since the inner part will be cut out and removed. Trace inner details as each layer is completed. (In both reverse and regular appliqué, the body of each butterfly is appliquéd on top of the wings after the butterfly wings have been appliquéd.) When turning under the edges for reverse appliqué, curved edges and corners should be clipped. Cut only a few inches at a time to help keep the piece in position. It's best to cut a small portion, sew it, then repeat clipping and stitching until the shape is completely appliquéd.

continued

Colorful, Contemporary Butterfly Quilt *(continued)*

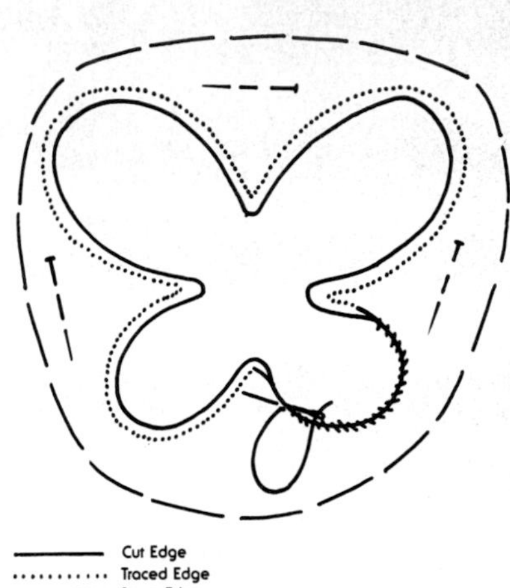

Reverse appliqué technique (for blocks 1, 3, 5, 6, 8, 9, 15, 20, and 21)

Quilt block placement diagram

1 2 3 4
5 6 7
9 10 11
8 12
13 14 16
15 17
18 19 20 21

Pin the appropriate tracing paper patterns to the matching cut fabric backing blocks, centering the appliqué pattern carefully. Use dressmaker's carbon and a tracing wheel to trace just enough marks to indicate the position of the appliqué shapes. If you reverse appliqué the blocks so indicated (see diagram, above left), trace the entire appliqué outline on the blocks rather than just placement markings.

Next, working one block at a time, trace the appliqué shapes onto the appropriate color fabrics. (Refer to the color symbol key on page 154.) Trace around each appliqué piece on the right side of the fabric and cut out leaving a ¼-inch seam allowance on all edges. This will be clipped and turned under in the appliquéing.

continued

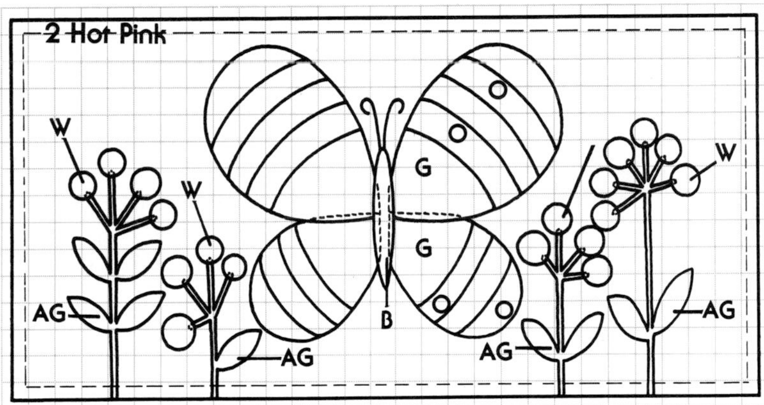

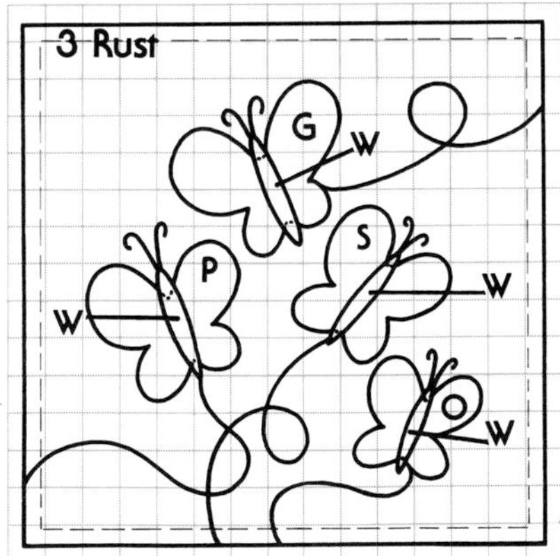

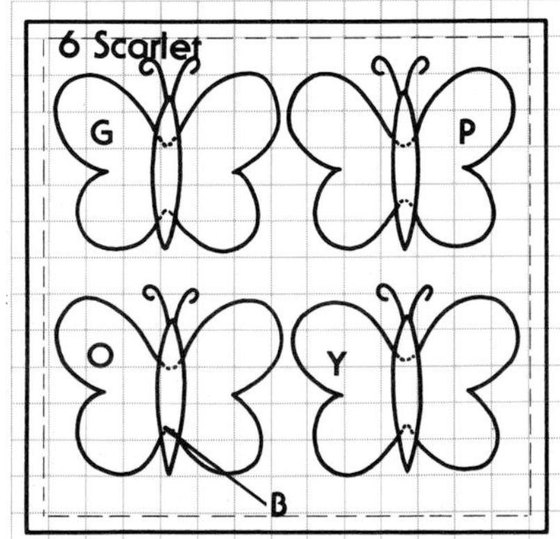

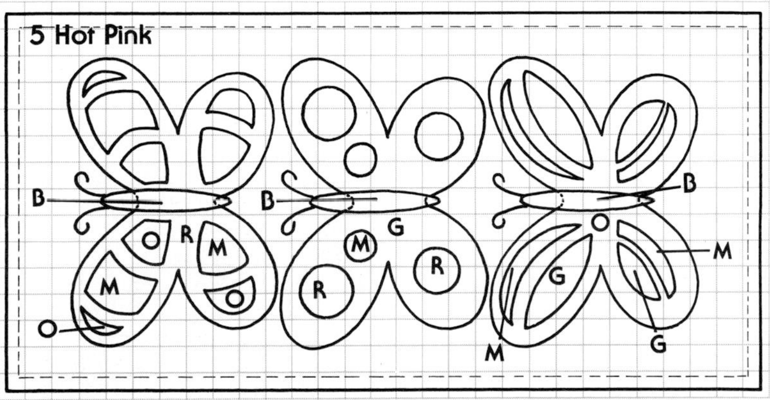

1 Square=1 Inch

Colorful, Contemporary Butterfly Quilt *(continued)*

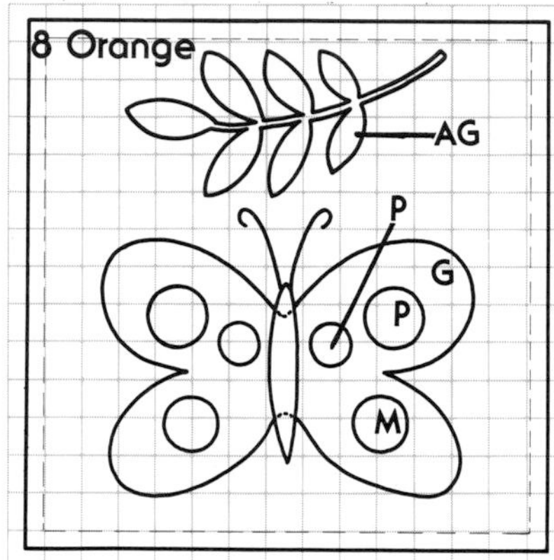

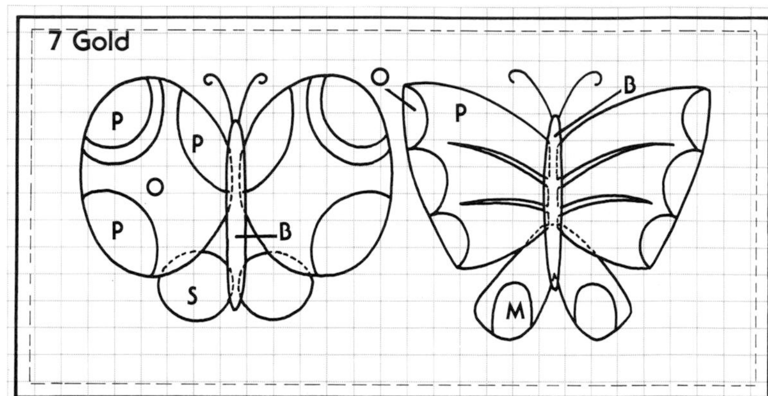

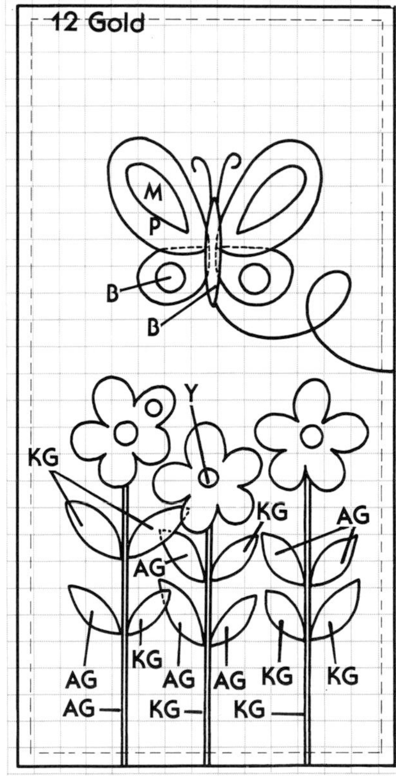

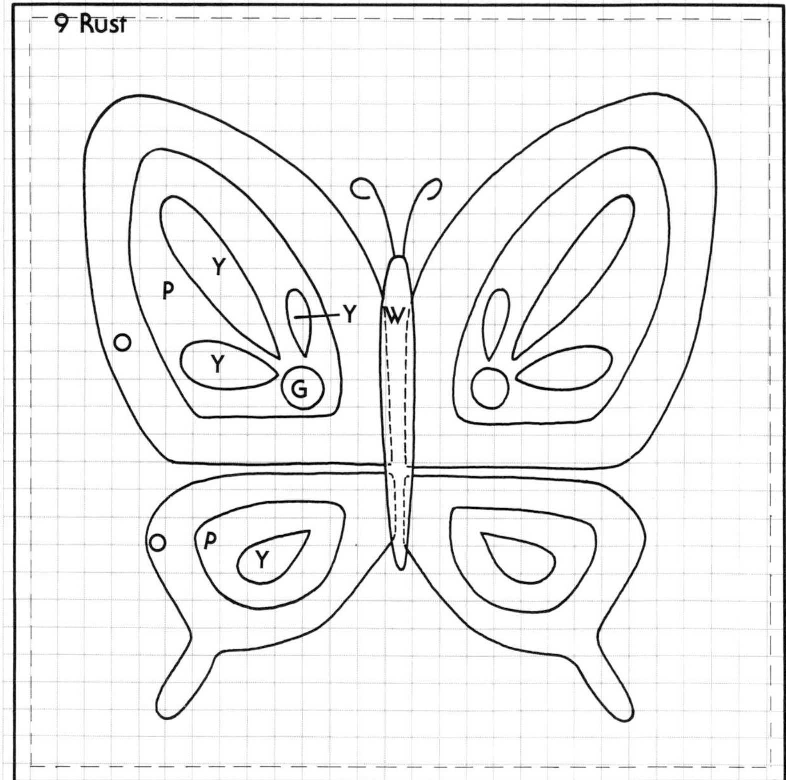

1 Square = 1 Inch

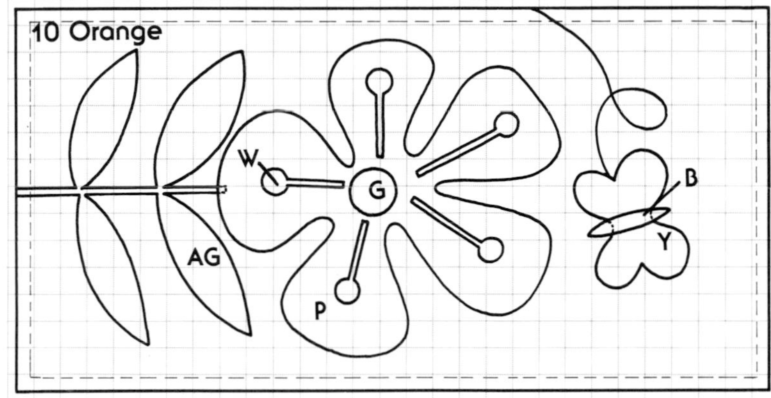

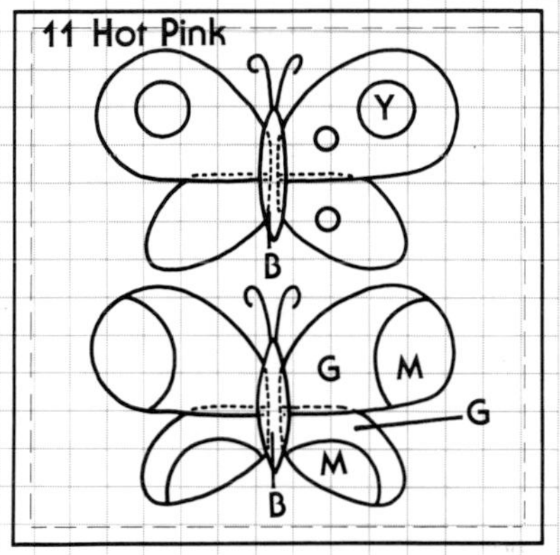

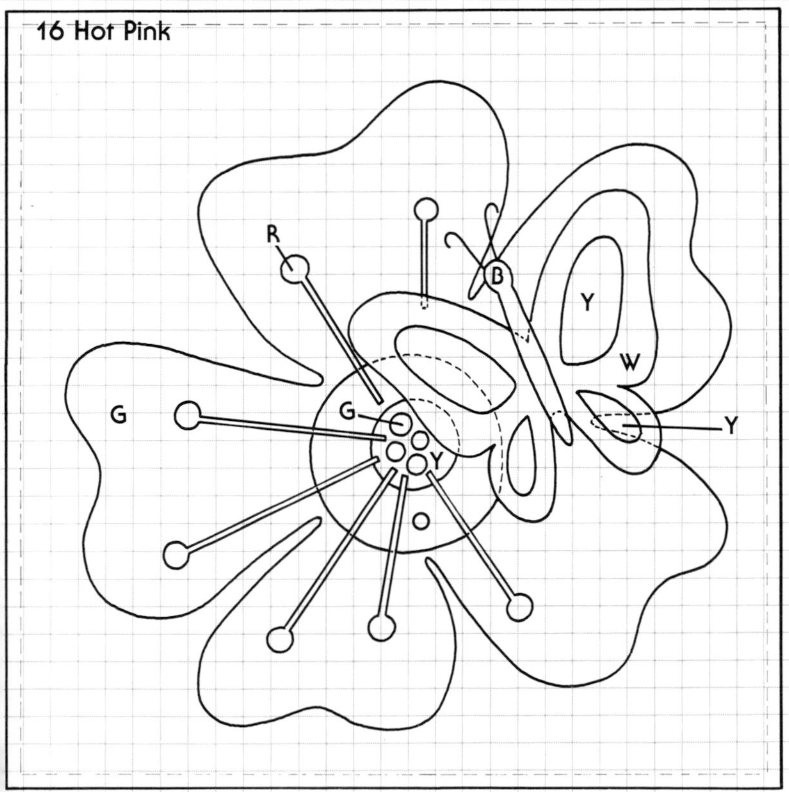

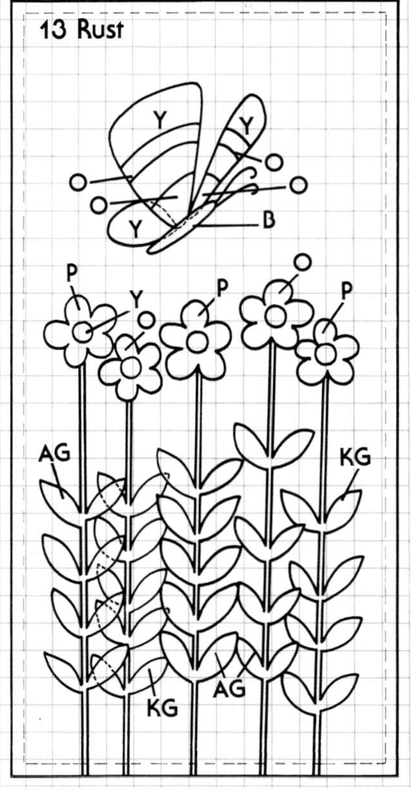

1 Square=1 Inch

continued

Colorful, Contemporary Butterfly Quilt *(continued)*

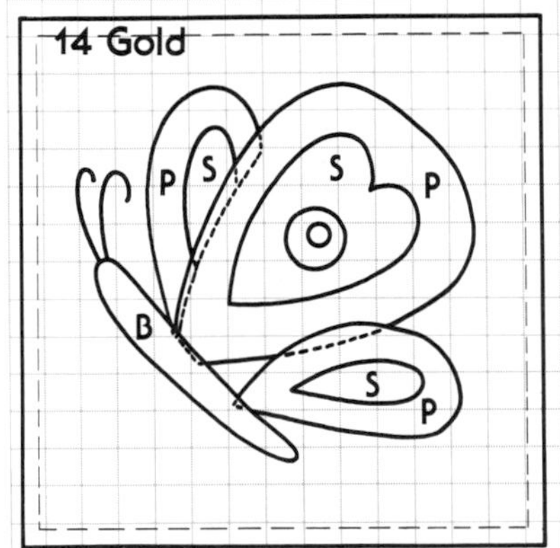

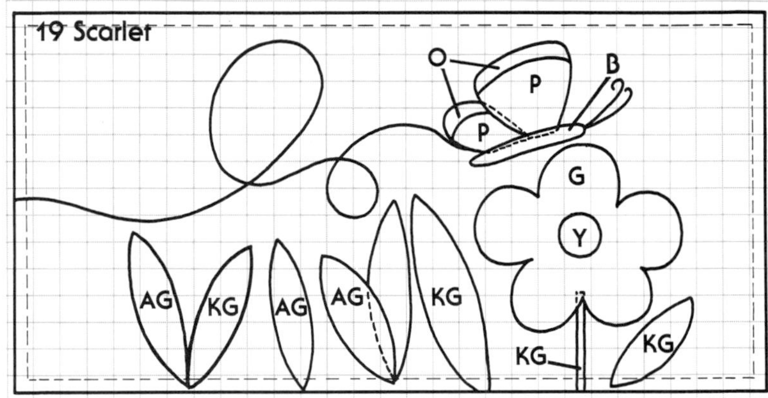

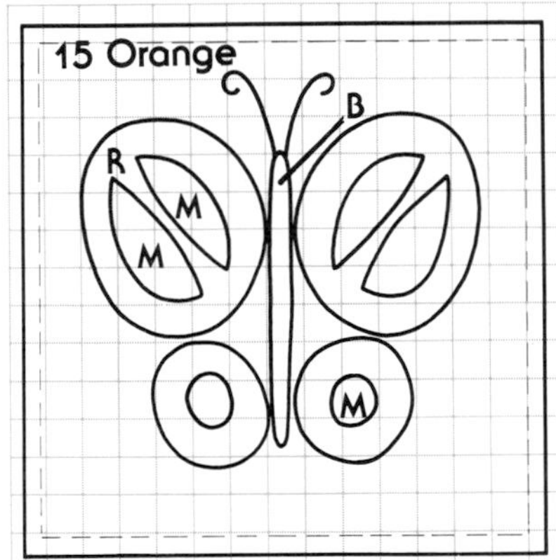

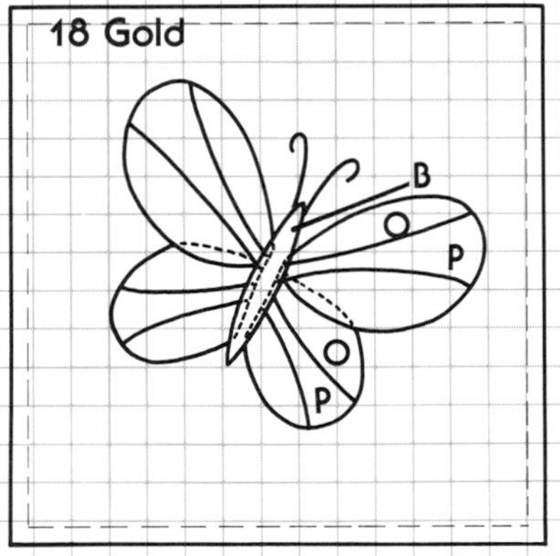

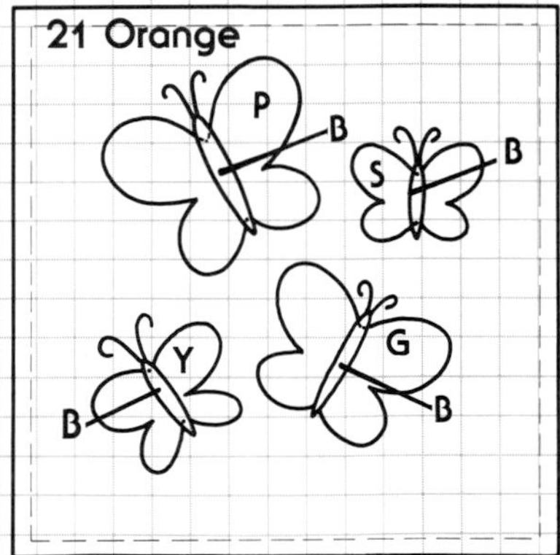

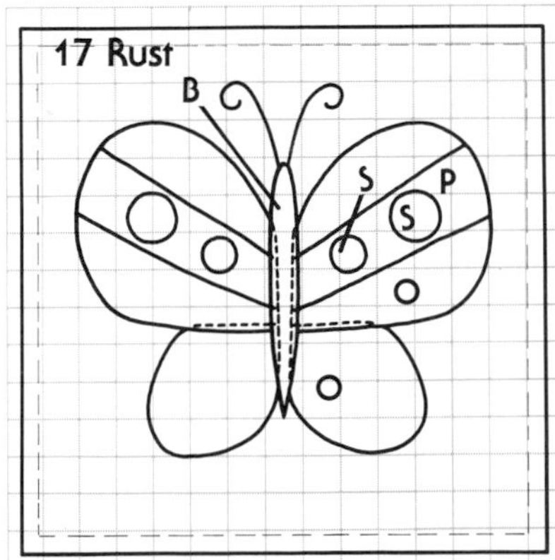

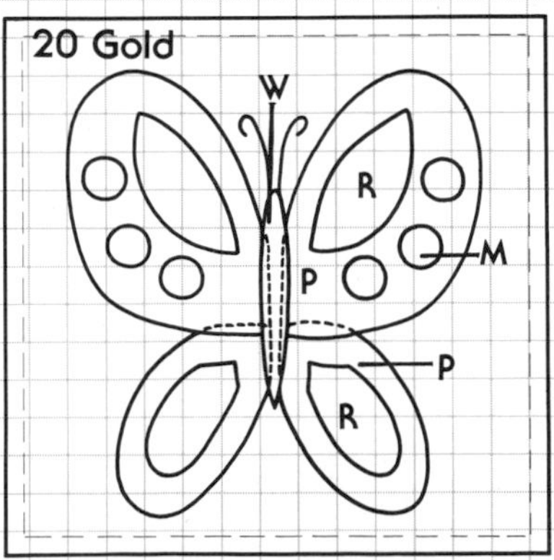

COLOR KEY

Y Yellow
G Gold
O Orange
R Rust
S Scarlet
B Burgundy
M Magenta
P Hot Pink
AG Apple Green
KG Kelly Green
W White

1 Square = 1 Inch

Appliquéing the pieces to each block will be easier if you machine-stitch along the traced outline of each appliqué piece, then clip and turn under the ¼-inch allowance. Using the placement marks on the block, position each appliqué piece, then pin down and baste to hold it in place while you slip-stitch. See pages 74 to 77 for complete appliqué instructions. Continue making all blocks until completed. Finish the reverse appliqué designs as explained on page 148, if you decide to use that technique.

With embroidery floss to match the bodies, embroider the antennae on each butterfly using an outline stitch. Use a running stitch to embroider the flight patterns on those blocks where indicated.

When blocks are finished, pin the patterns to each and trim on the cutting line to ensure that the blocks are accurately sized and perfectly square.

Arrange completed blocks on the floor, using the diagram on page 150 for placement. Sew all blocks together on the sewing machine, using ½-inch seam allowances. Press each seam flat as you sew it. Don't press the seams open, but press them all in the same direction. Continue until all blocks are sewed together to form the quilt top.

Baste together the top, backing, and batting to prepare for the quilting. First place the backing on the floor with open seams up and stretch taut by taping the corners to the floor. Place tape around all edges so the fabric is stretched flat. Unroll the batting and center it on top of the backing. Place the top, right side up, over the batting, centering it as much as possible, and leaving equal portions of the backing fabric showing all around. Make sure all three layers are smooth and flat.

With a long length of quilting thread, start at the center of the quilt and baste diagonally out to each corner, keeping the quilt "sandwich" as flat as possible. Baste horizontally and vertically in the same way. Remove the tape from around the edges of your quilt.

You are now ready to quilt by whichever means you choose. See pages 43 and 44 for instructions on quilting with a floor-standing frame, a quilting hoop, or by the lap method. Machine-quilt if you choose. You'll find those instructions given, too.

Quilt around each appliqué shape and around the edges of each block.

When the quilting is completed, lay the quilt flat and trim the batting to 1½ inches from the edge of the quilt top. Trim the green backing to 2½ inches from the edge of the quilt top.

Fold the backing edge over to the top of the quilt, turning under ½ inch. Pin or baste all the way around so the quilt is bound by the backing. You will have a 1-inch-wide border all around the quilt. Beginning on page 45, you'll find complete instructions for forming a binding of the backing fabric and mitering the corners for a finished look.

Machine-stitch the border or slip-stitch by hand.

If you would like to make this quilt for any bed larger than a twin-size, there are several ways of enlarging the design. Here's how to go about it:

For a slight increase in size, simply increase the length and width of the batting sheet to the desired size and increase the length and width of the backing sheet by twice the number of inches you want to add. For example, to change our 67x92-inch design to a 70x95-inch quilt, cut the batting exactly to size, piecing if necessary, and piece the backing to measure 73x98. When the backing is folded over, this will give you a full 4-inch-wide border on all sides instead of the 1-inch border shown in our quilt.

The size of the quilt can also be increased by adding narrow strips of apple green fabric between the squares to match the quilt's backing and border. Cut long strips of green 2 inches wide and sew them between all blocks, using ½-inch seams. The only exception is between blocks 14 and 15, which should be sewn together to make a single rectangular block. This procedure will add 3 inches to the width and 4 inches to the length of the quilt. For a greater increase, make the strips wider.

If you want to make a substantial increase in the size of the quilt, you'll have to take other measures. One possibility is to duplicate either side strip of five blocks on the opposite side of the quilt. For example, you could repeat blocks 1, 5, 8, 13, and 18 on the right-hand side of the quilt, or repeat blocks 4, 11, 12, 17, and 21 on the left-hand side of the quilt.

To lengthen the quilt, repeat the bottom row of blocks (18, 19, 20, and 21) at the top. If you choose to enlarge the quilt this way, remember to enlarge the backing and batting accordingly, and to purchase additional fabric for the extra squares.

By repeating the top and bottom or side rows of blocks, you can customize your quilt to whatever bed size you want.

For a king-size bed, you may want to double the entire quilt and make two of each block. Sew the blocks together following the diagram on page 150, then sew the two separate quilt tops together. Simply double the fabric requirements to make a king-size quilt.

Creative Appliqué

As you have seen, appliqué is much more than an exciting challenge—it also is a creative craft. Even basic appliqué allows you to fabricate unique patterns and designs. And as the projects in this section demonstrate, you can combine appliqué with a variety of other needlework techniques to achieve dramatic results. Now it is time to apply all the skills you have learned and demonstrate your mastery of the stitcher's art with projects like this king-size zoo bag, which combines appliqué with regular and trapunto quilting (for how-to, please turn the page). For a beautifully unique appliqué project, create the lace butterfly on page 167, with its lovely use of antique doilies. Or turn to page 160 for all the instructions for making an appliquéd portrait of your child. The sampler quilt on pages 162 to 166 of this section is an album of appliqué motifs from American quilts—a legacy from the past to inspire your handiwork today.

64
Crayola
CRAYONS
BUILT-IN SHARPENER

Appliquéd Zoo Sleeping Bag and Monkey Tote

(shown on pages 156 and 157)

If your children are fond of animals, they are sure to love this cozy sleeping bag, machine-appliquéd with all their favorites from the zoo. Cut the animals from the fabrics used for the border strips, assemble them and add trapunto quilting, then appliqué them to the bag.

After the bag is fully assembled with padding and lining, hand-quilt around the animals and along each border. The finished bag measures about 50x67 inches.

To make the tote bag, appliqué a monkey to fabric and stitch it onto a satchel.

Materials

3½ yards bright blue fabric
2½ yards orange fabric
2½ yards yellow fabric
3 yards green fabric
Scraps white and red fabric
6 yards 36-inch-wide fabric for lining
4 yards nonwoven interfacing
2 king-size quilt batts
108-inch zipper
½ pound polyester fiberfill
Thread to match fabrics
Blue quilting thread
Brown wrapping paper

Cut fabric as follows:

2 pieces blue, 38½x56 inches
4 pieces yellow, 2½x50 inches
4 pieces yellow, 2½x68 inches
4 pieces orange, 3x50 inches
4 pieces orange, 3x68 inches
4 pieces green, 3½x50 inches
4 pieces green, 3½x68 inches

Directions

On brown paper, enlarge designs at right. Connect ½-inch marks at edges of diagram to make a grid: 1 square equals 2¾ inches. Cut appliqués from remnants, using the photograph on pages 156 and 157 as a guide. Cut basic shape from one color, then cut detail pieces to appliqué (for example, cut tiger from orange, then cut stripes from blue fabric scraps).

Pin detail pieces to animal shapes, then pin each animal to interfacing. Lightly mark non-appliquéd detail lines with pencil. (Each animal is stitched and padded before it is applied to the bag.)

Set the sewing machine on medium-width zigzag and medium-length stitch. Stitch around all appliqué details, leaving a small opening for stuffing. Next, stuff details lightly and baste openings closed. Set the machine on satin stitch (widest zigzag, closest stitch) and stitch over all basting lines.

Zigzag-baste along detail lines and again around outside edges of animal shapes, leaving an opening. Stuff lightly and baste opening closed. Then satin-stitch along all detail lines. Trim any excess interfacing from edges of animals.

Pin or baste animals in position on piece of blue fabric; machine-zigzag in place, then satin-stitch around all outside edges of each animal. Remove basting threads.

Cut out "My Zoo" and pin or glue in place. Satin-stitch.

Next, stitch yellow, orange, and green strips together, using ½-inch seams, to make bands for sleeping bag front and back. Make four 50-inch strips and four 68-inch strips. Press seams open.

With right sides together, pin strips to outer edges of blue center sections. Stitch, starting ½ inch from each corner. Next, miter all corners; stitch. Trim excess fabric from the mitered seams.

Place right sides of front and back pieces together, and stitch along one long side. Press open.

Cut lining fabric into three pieces, each measuring 34x68 inches. Stitch all three pieces together, making one piece that is 68x100 inches long. Press seams open.

With right sides facing, pin the lining and sleeping bag cover together along the top and sides. Stitch across the top and down 10 inches from the top on both sides. Turn to the right side and press.

To pad the bag: Slip two layers of batting into the bag and pin them to the wrong side of the lining. Trim the batting so it is ¼ inch narrower than the lining. Baste the batting to the lining, and then pin the bag cover to the lining and batting.

Press outer seam allowances on the cover and lining to the inside. Open the zipper. Place the bottom of the zipper at the bottom of the bag's center seam. Pin the zipper in place between the lining and the cover. Baste and then stitch the zipper in place, catching both the cover and the lining with a row of stitching. Or, apply nylon fastening tape along the same opening.

To quilt the bag: Using quilting thread and medium-length straight stitches, hand-quilt around all animals and bands. Start quilting in the center of the bag and work toward the outside edges. When quilting is finished, remove all basting.

For the tote bag: Appliqué a monkey motif onto one half of an 18x35-inch piece of orange fabric. Fold fabric in half (18x17½ inches) and stitch sides. Add a yellow lining and orange handles at the top, as shown in the photograph on page 157.

MY ZOO

Appliquéd Portrait

Here is your chance to "paint" with fabric! Creating an appliquéd portrait of your child like the one shown here is one way to make appliqué a very personal medium. Use our pattern below, or make your own from a photographic slide following our instructions.

Materials

35x46 inches unbleached muslin, or a sufficient quantity for your portrait
½ yard small-print fabric (wallpaper) (see note below)
½ to ⅓ yard each of a variety of solid-color velvets (quilt)
½ yard brown print velvet (quilt and headboard)
½ yard unbleached muslin (pillow, arm, face)
Scrap of print fabric (nightgown)
Scraps of quilt batting
Brown sewing thread
Brown and black floss
Brown and black yarn
31- and 42-inch stretcher strips

Directions

Note: The fabrics suggested are for the portrait shown; to estimate the amount of fabric needed for your own portrait, see below.

Enlarge our pattern below or make a pattern of your own by taking a slide snapshot of your child and working from the slide. The photograph for the portrait shown was taken while the child was in bed with her favorite quilt. In your picture, you may wish to include a toy, blanket, or some other dearly loved possession of your child. Take several slides and poses of the child so you can select the composition you like best.

Insert the slide into a slide projector and project the image onto a wall covered with a sheet of white paper the same size as the finished portrait (ours is 31x42 inches). Tape the paper to the wall with masking tape so it does not shift, and work in a darkened room so you can easily see the lines in the photograph.

With a soft lead pencil or felt-tip pen, draw the lines of the composition onto the paper (be sure the pen does not bleed through onto the wall). Trace the outlines of the basic shapes, such as the head, bedstead, and blanket, and then add as many detail lines as necessary to fill out the image without making it overly complicated. This is your master pattern. Copy it onto tissue paper, mark corresponding shapes on both patterns, and cut the tissue apart into the separate shapes and pattern pieces.

To determine fabric amounts, trace pattern pieces onto an 18x44-inch piece of paper (equivalent to ½ yard of fabric) and purchase fabric accordingly.

To make the portrait, transfer the outlines of the shapes to the muslin background fabric, allowing a 2-inch margin of fabric around the design. Cut shapes to be appliquéd from the various fabrics. Do not add seam allowances. Instead, fit pieces together like a jigsaw puzzle. Pin them in place and machine zigzag-stitch to the background for a crisp, contemporary look. Then cover outlines between appliquéd shapes (on the quilt, for instance) with lengths of yarn or embroidery floss couched with machine zigzag stitches.

If you are making the portrait shown, complete all the quilt in this way, but do not stitch along the top of the quilt. Then appliqué the "wallpaper" to the upper portion of the background. Tuck the "wallpaper" down inside the loose quilt edge, then stitch. If you are working a design of your own, complete the large areas of the pattern in the same way.

Next, assemble stretcher strips into a frame and stretch the fabric over it. Add the remaining shapes—the headboard, pillow, and nightgown—by cutting out pattern pieces and hand-stitching them in place with straight stitches worked in a zigzag pattern. Vary the length of the stitches for interest. While appliquéing the pillow in place, pad it with a small amount of quilt batting.

Cut the entire head from muslin. Then cut out hair shapes from assorted pieces of lightweight cotton, and fuse them in place with fusible webbing. When the head is complete, back it with a thin layer of batting and hand-stitch it to the composition. Finish facial features and details on head with couching and satin stitches worked in embroidery floss.

Cut out arm piece, adding ¼-inch seam allowances. Turn under raw edges and stitch in place. Tuck a small amount of padding into the arm as you stitch. Add couched floss along lines of fingers.

Appliquéd Sampler Quilt

An appliquer's album of patterns, the quilt at right is a wonderful way to display your stitchery. Any of these 25 patterns (see pages 164 to 166) would make a beautiful quilt, pillow top, or wall hanging. All together, they present a stunning sampler of appliqué art.

This quilt is 108 inches square, but you can adjust the size to fit your own bed with our directions.

Materials

7½ yards 44-inch-wide white fabric (front)
10 yards 44-inch-wide fabric (backing)
4 yards print fabric (strips between blocks)
2½ yards green fabric (leaves and stems)
1½ to 2 yards each of 4 different fabrics for appliqués
Scraps of 2 or 3 additional fabrics in accent colors
Four 18½x18½-inch squares of print fabric for Hawaiian quilt blocks
1 yard fabric (binding)
One 120-inch-square quilt batting

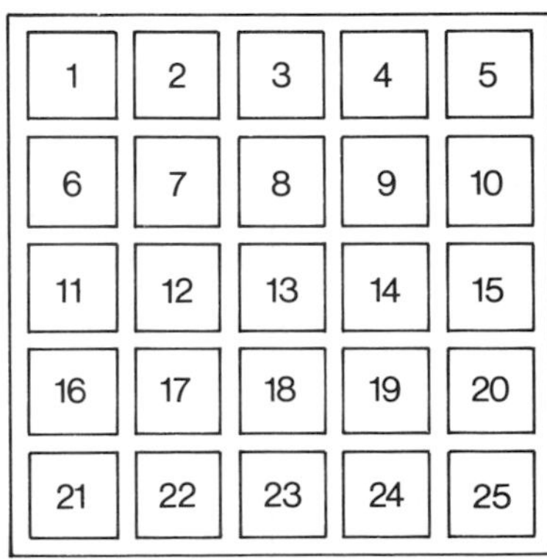

Sampler Quilt

Directions

Our sampler quilt is made of twenty-five 18-inch-square blocks separated by 3-inch-wide borders. The blocks are set into five rows of five blocks each. To make a smaller quilt, reduce the size of the blocks. For example, 12-inch blocks separated by 3-inch borders will make a quilt approximately 78 inches square, while 14-inch blocks with 3-inch borders will assemble into an 88-inch square.

Decide on the size of your quilt and enlarge the patterns for the blocks on the pages that follow, referring to the directions for enlarging designs on page 272. The scale given with the patterns is for the king-size quilt. In addition to the master pattern for each block, make a second pattern to cut apart for pattern pieces.

Preshrink all the fabric and press it smooth. Then cut twenty-five 18½x18½-inch white squares for background blocks.

For all the blocks except the four Hawaiian cutouts in the corners of the quilt, cut appliqués from fabrics, referring to the photograph for colors. Add ¼-inch seam allowances to all pieces. Cut bias strips of green fabric to use for stems. Turn under the seam allowances on all pieces, clipping curves as necessary, and baste.

Pin the appliqués for each block in place, checking their position against the master pattern. Baste and then whipstitch each appliqué to the background fabric.

Make the Hawaiian cutouts in the corners of the quilt in one of two ways. Transfer the design as it is shown in the patterns on the following pages to the fabric with dressmaker's carbon and a tracing wheel. Do not add seam allowances to the patterns. Cut the fabric along the pattern outlines, turn under raw edges ¼ inch, and baste. Or, cut out the motif the same way you would cut a paper snowflake. Fold the print fabric in half vertically and press; fold it in half horizontally and press again. Fold it diagonally (into a triangle); press all folds. Then mark the pattern, drawing a line through the vertical center of the design. Next draw a line from the center into one corner, segmenting ⅛ of the motif. Lay the segment of the motif over the folded fabric, matching the straight grain of the fabric to the vertical center of the pattern, and the bias fold of the fabric to the diagonal on the pattern. With sharp scissors, cut around the design through all layers of fabric. Open up the cutout motif, turn raw edges under ¼ inch, and baste along the fold. Center the motif on the white block, pin, baste in position, and appliqué.

When all the blocks are assembled, arrange them according to the placement diagram at left for stitching into rows. For each row, cut four 3½x18½-inch strips and sew them between five blocks using ¼-inch seams. Press seams to one side. Assemble five rows with five appliquéd blocks each.

To assemble rows into the quilt top, cut six 3½x102½-inch strips (measure the length of the rows to verify dimensions). Sew a strip between each row and one each at the top and bottom of the quilt. Finish by stitching one 3½x108½-inch strip (approximately) to each side of the quilt. Press seams to one side.

To make the back of the quilt, sew together three lengths of 44-inch-wide fabric. Press the seams open and trim off the selvages, as they are hard to quilt through. Assemble and complete the quilt, following directions on page 43. After quilting or tying, bind the raw edges of the quilt in the color of your choice.

continued

Appliquéd Sampler Quilt *(continued)*

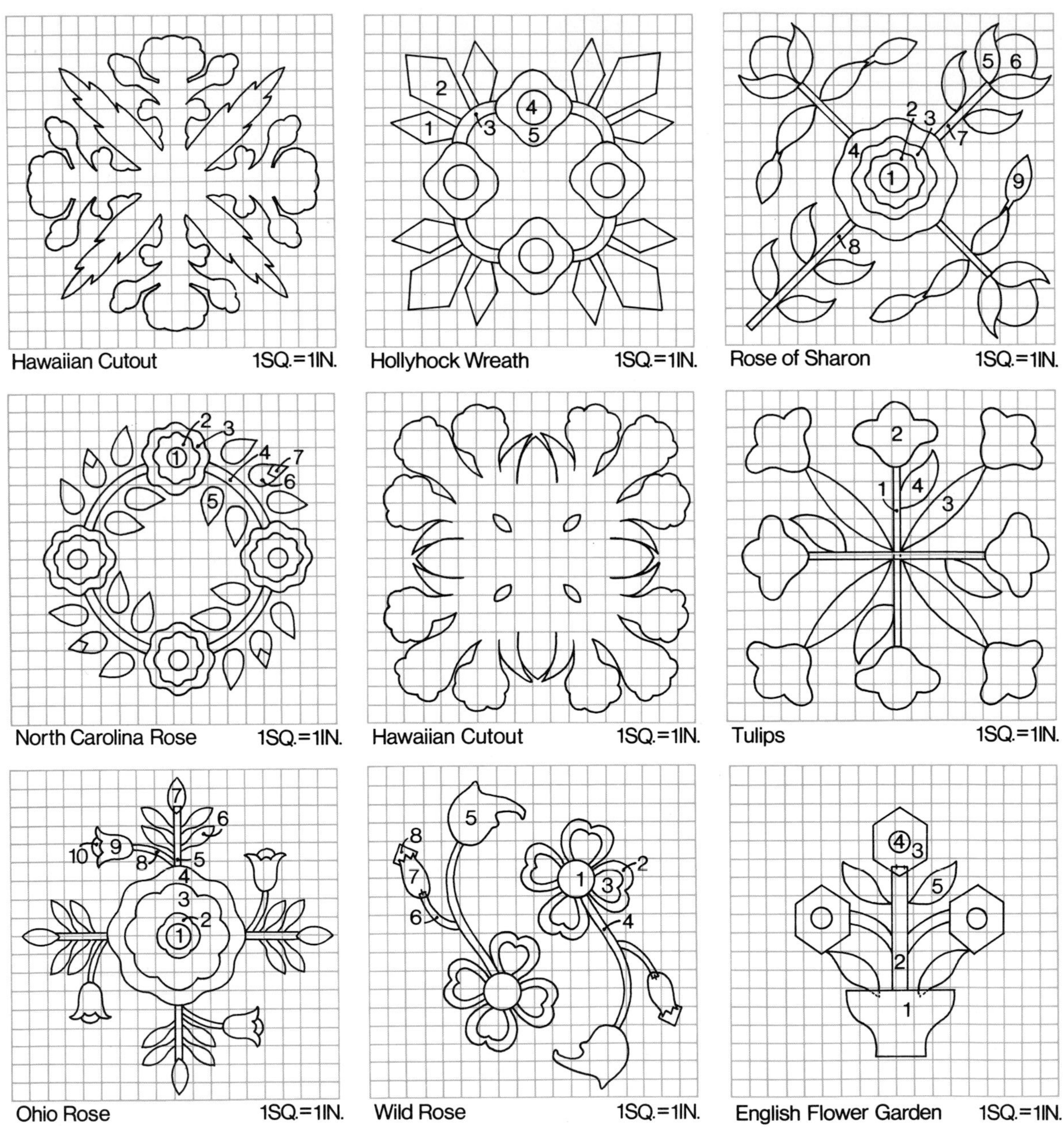

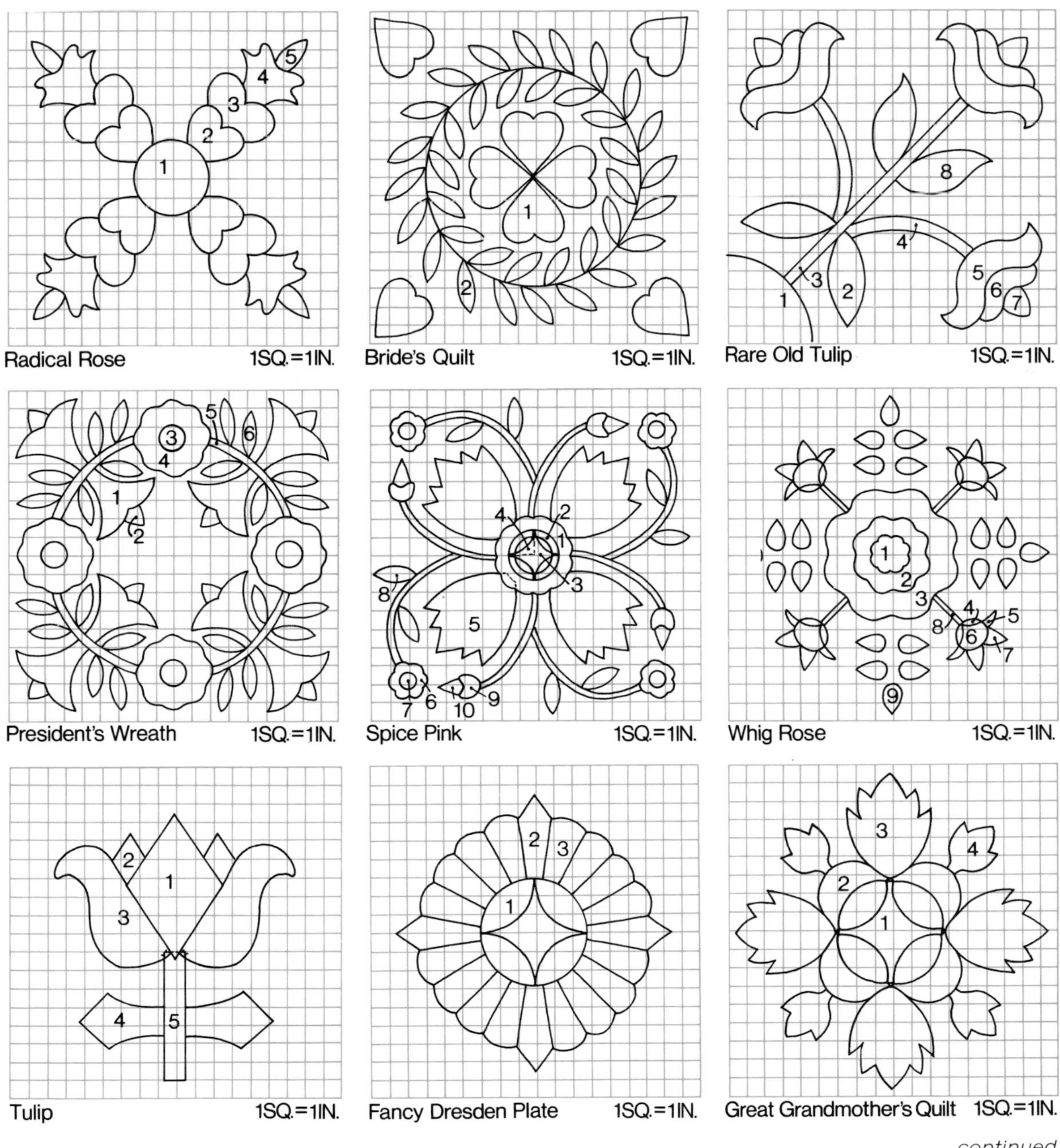

1
2
3
4
5
Radical Rose
1SQ.=1IN.
1
2
Bride's Quilt
1SQ.=1IN.
1
2
3
4
5
6
7
8
Rare Old Tulip
1SQ.=1IN.
1
2
3
4
5
6
President's Wreath
1SQ.=1IN.
1
2
3
4
5
6
7
8
9
10
Spice Pink
1SQ.=1IN.
1
2
3
4
5
6
7
8
9
Whig Rose
1SQ.=1IN.
1
2
3
4
5
Tulip
1SQ.=1IN.
1
2
3
Fancy Dresden Plate
1SQ.=1IN.
1
2
3
4
Great Grandmother's Quilt
1SQ.=1IN.

continued

Appliquéd Sampler Quilt *(continued)*

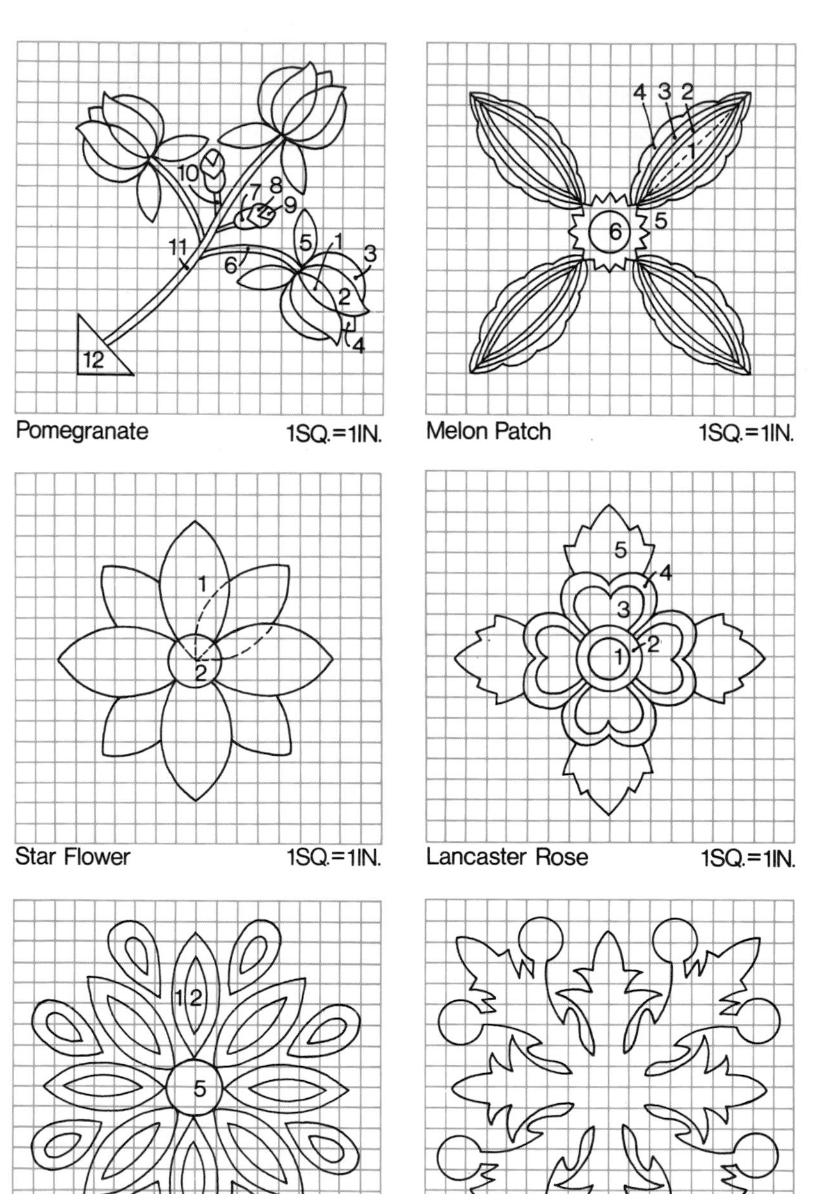

Pomegranate 1SQ.=1IN.

Melon Patch 1SQ.=1IN.

Star Flower 1SQ.=1IN.

Lancaster Rose 1SQ.=1IN.

Daddy Hex 1SQ.=1IN.

Hawaiian Cutout 1SQ.=1IN.

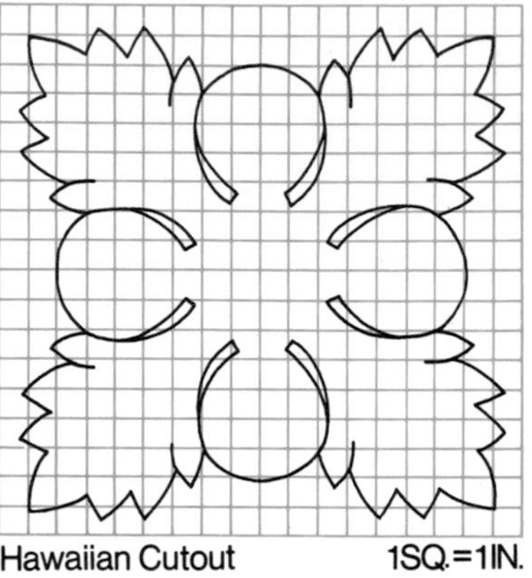

Hawaiian Cutout 1SQ.=1IN.

Transferring Designs

To transfer designs, dressmaker's carbon paper and a tracing wheel are especially easy to use. (The carbon paper should be as close to the color of the fabric as possible, yet still visible.) Place the carbon face-down between the fabric and pattern and trace the design, using enough pressure to transfer it to fabric.

A hot transfer pencil is also easy to use. (Keep the pencil sharp to prevent the lines from blurring.) Trace the design on the back of the pattern and iron the transfer in place, being careful not to scorch the fabric.

A blue lead pencil works well on light-colored, lightweight fabrics. Tape the pattern to a window and place the fabric over it, using dotted lines to trace the design.

Basting is an effective way of transferring a design to dark, soft, textured, stretchy, or sheer fabrics. Draw the pattern on tissue paper and pin it to the fabric. Baste around the design, then tear away the paper. Remove basting stitches when the project is finished.

Appliquéd Butterfly Wall Panel

Organdy and lace combine beautifully in this butterfly wall panel. For an off-white tint, soak the lace pieces in strong black coffee for thirty minutes before you begin.

Materials

1 square yard white cotton organdy
Two 10½-inch-diameter lace doilies for upper wings
Two 7-inch-diameter lace doilies for lower wings
9 assorted lace circles or ovals for body, antennae, and lower wing tips (see note below)
#3 and #5 ecru pearl cotton
Four 33-inch artist's stretcher strips
Graph paper
Tracing paper
Ecru sewing thread

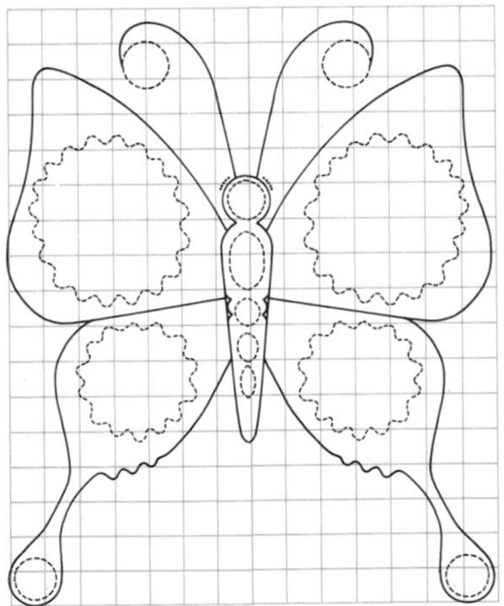

1 Square = 2 Inches

Directions

Enlarge the pattern, reversing it to complete the design. Tape the pattern to a table and center organdy over it.

For upper and lower wings, pin four large doilies to the fabric (indicated by dotted lines on pattern). Pin lace to the fabric for body, antennae, and wing tips. Using ecru thread, baste around outlines of wings and bodies. Using small, hidden stitches, sew lace to fabric around the *outer* edges.

Turn the fabric over and carefully cut an opening behind the large doilies and the wing tips to within ½ inch of the lace edge. Turn fabric under ¼ inch and sew edges to the lace. Do not cut the fabric behind the body and antennae appliqués.

Using #3 pearl cotton, outline wings with couching: lay the thread along the outline and overcast with ecru sewing thread. Then stem-stitch along outer edge of couching with #5 pearl cotton.

Using #3 pearl cotton, outline body and head with long-armed featherstitches, filling inner edge of outline with longer "spokes."

Embroider antennae in open chain stitches with #5 pearl cotton.

For butterfly eyes, work a line of five French knots following the curve of the head (see pattern diagram). Add three short straight stitches to the lower body, as shown in the photograph.

Cover organdy with a press cloth and iron with low heat. Turn up a ¼-inch hem on raw edges, and frame on stretcher strips.

CROCHETING & KNITTING

Afghans

Crocheting and knitting are both needle arts that enable you to create warm, wonderful things for your home. In this section, you will find many such projects, just waiting for you to make and begin enjoying for years to come. Top on the list of popular projects for knitters and crocheters alike are afghans. And no wonder, when you realize how a brightly colored afghan can cozy and personalize a room just by being there. The afghan spread out before you here is in the popular granny tradition, and this particular one is a sampler of the many different types of granny squares. You may crochet an afghan similar to this one (see page 172 for complete instructions), or you can make a complete afghan from any one of the squares—as you'll see illustrated on pages 178 and 179 with the star motif afghan.

Granny Square Sampler Afghan

(shown on pages 170 and 171, and page 174)

This unique piece of crochet is an inspiration to granny square devotees. Make one similar to ours, based on variations of several patterns, or use just one motif throughout.

These instructions are meant to be used chiefly as guidelines to get you started on your own original sampler. You'll find ample opportunity here to give free reign to your creative talents.

Materials

Knitting worsted, 4 ply acrylic, 4 oz. skeins
- 2 navy blue
- An assortment of the same type of yarn in different colors

Size H crochet hook

Finished size

46x55 inches (approximate size)

Note: If, when assembling, motifs do not fit as desired, simply add on another row of crochet where needed. Some border colors are charted. Work from diagram on page 175 and use bright colors throughout.

Directions

Granny square motif (A)—Make 6.

A-1 (1 granny square with 7 rnds): With first color ch 4; join with sl st to form ring.

Rnd 1: Ch 3 (counts as 1 dc), 2 dc in center of ring, * ch 3, 3 dc in center of ring, rep from * 2 more times, end with ch 3; join with sl st to top of beg ch 3. End off.

Rnd 2: With second color, in ch 3 sp of previous rnd work (ch 3, 2 dc, ch 3, 3 dc) (corner), * in next ch 3 sp work (3 dc, ch 3, 3 dc), rep from * twice, join with sl st to top of ch 3. End off.

Rnd 3: With third color, (ch 3, 2 dc, ch 3, 3 dc) in ch 3 at corner sp, then work 3 dc between each 3 dc group on sides and (3 dc, ch 3, 3 dc) in each corner; join with sl st. End off.

Rnds 4, 5, 6, 7: Using a different color for each row, rep instructions for rnd 3.

A-2 (4 granny squares with 3 rnds each): Follow instructions for the first three rnds above. Whipstitch the four squares together to form one square.

Border—With navy work 3 dc between each group of dc along edges, and (3 dc, ch 3, 3 dc) in each corner; join with sl st. End off.

A-3 (2 granny squares with 3 rnds each): Follow instructions for the first three rnds above. Whipstitch the two squares together to form a rectangle.With brown, work border as in pattern A-2. Along one long border edge only, work 1 dc in each st. End off.

A-4 (1 granny square with 7 rnds): Follow instructions for A-1 granny square. *Note:* Use navy for seventh rnd.

A-5 (2 granny squares with 4 rnds each): Follow instructions for the first four rnds above. *Note:* On last rnd of one square use navy. Whipstitch squares tog to form rectangle.

A-6 (2 granny squares with 5 rnds each): Follow instructions for the first five rnds above. *Note:* On last rnd of one square use navy. Whipstitch squares tog to form rectangle.

Star motif (B)—Make 5.

B-1 (1 star motif with 9 rnds): Work each motif in different colors.

Basic star square: Ch 3, sl st to 1st ch to form ring, ch 1.

Rnd 1: * 1 sc in center of ring, ch 4, 1 sc in 2nd ch from hook, 1 sc in each of next 2 ch sts, rep from * 4 more times (5 spoke center); join with sl st to beg sc. End off.

Rnd 2: Attach new color in center top st of any spoke, ch 1 sc in same sp, * sk next 3 sc, (1 trc, 1 dc, 1 trc) in next sc, sl st to top of next spoke, rep from * around; join with sl st to beg sc. *Do not end off.*

Rnd 3: * sk next st, (1 hdc, 1 dc, 1 trc, ch 1, 1 trc, 1 dc, 1 hdc) in top of next st, sk next st, sl st in top of next st, rep from * around; join with sl st to beg st. End off.

Rnd 4: Attach another color in ch 1 back loop st at any point, * sk next 3 sts, (1 trc, 3 dc, 1 trc) in next st, sk next 3 sts, sl st in back loop of ch 1 point, rep from * around; join with sl st to beg st. End off.

Rnd 5: Attach second color in any st, (work through both loops), 2 sc in each st around (60 sc); join with sl st to beg sc. End off.

Rnd 6: *Note:* Work on right side in top back loops only. With star point at top, count clockwise 8 sc from point (this will be in sc above 3rd dc in rnd 4). Attach same color as rnd 2, work ch 6, 1 trc in next sc, * 1 dc in next sc, 1 hdc in each of next 2 sc, 1 sc in each of next 7 sc, 1 hdc in each of next 2 sc, 1 dc in next sc, 1 trc in next sc, ch 2, 1 trc in next sc, rep from * around; join with sl st to top of 4th ch of beg ch 6. End off.

Rnd 7: Attach same color as rnd 4 in ch 2 corner sp, ch 3, 1 sc in same sp, * 1 sc each in next 15 sts, 1 sc in next ch 2 sp, rep from * around; join with sl st to beg sc. End off.

Rnd 8: Attach same color used in rnd 4 in ch 2 corner, rep rnd 7 (17 sc on each side).

Rnd 9: Attach same color as rnd 5 in any corner sp, (ch 2, 1 hdc, ch 3, 2 hdc) in same sp, * sk next sc, 2 hdc in next sc, rep from * across to next corner, * work

(2 hdc, ch 3, 2 hdc) in same corner sp, rep from * around; join with sl st to top of beg ch 2. End off.

Rnd 10: With new color work 2 hdc between groups of hdc along all edges, and (2 hdc, ch 3, 2 hdc) in each corner. End off.

B-2 (1 star motif with 4 rnds): Follow instructions for first 4 rnds above.

Rnd 5: Attach fifth color in top of 3rd dc of previous rnd, (ch 4, 2 trc, ch 3, 3 trc), in same sp, * 2 dc in next st, 1 hdc in next st, 2 sc in next st, 1 hdc in next st, 2 dc in next st*, ** (3 trc, ch 3, 3 trc), in next st, rep from * through **, 2 more times, and from * to *, 1 more time; join with sl st to beg trc. End off.

Rnd 6: Attach sixth color and work 1 sc in each st along edges, and (2 sc, ch 3, 2 sc), in each corner. End off.

Rnd 7: With navy, work * (3 dc, ch 3, 3 dc), in each corner, and sk next 2 sc, 3 dc in next sc, sk next 2 sc along edges; join with sl st to beg dc. End off.

B-3 (1 star motif with 9 rnds): Follow same directions as for pattern B-1, using a different color combination and working last rnd with navy.

B-4 (1 star motif with 9 rnds): Follow same directions as for pattern B-3.

B-5 (1 star motif with 4 rnds): Follow directions for pattern B-2, with the exception of using a different color for rnd 7.

Diamond square motif (C)—Make 5.

Note: Work all rnds in different colors.

C-1 (1 diamond square motif): Starting at center with first color, ch 4, sl st to first ch to form ring, ch 1.

Rnd 1: Work 6 sc in center of ring, join with sl st to beg sc. Do not end off.

Rnd 2: Ch 2 (counts as 1 hdc), 1 hdc in same sp, 2 hdc in top of each sc around (12 hdc); join with sl st to beg ch 2. End off.

Rnd 3: Attach second color, ch 1, 1 sc in top of next st. * ch 1, sc in next st, rep from * around; join with sl st to beg st. End off.

Rnd 4: Attach third color in any ch 1 sp, ch 3 (counts as 1 dc), 2 dc in same sp, * 3 dc in next ch 1 sp, rep from * around (12 groups of 3 dc); join with sl st to beg dc. End off.

Rnd 5: Attach fourth color in any dc. Ch 3 (counts as 1 dc), 2 dc in same dc, ch 2, 3 dc in next dc (corner), * 1 hdc in next dc, 1 sc each in next 5 dc, 1 hdc in next dc *, ** (3 dc in next dc, ch 2, 3 dc in next dc), rep from * through ** two more times and from * to * one more time; join with sl st to beg dc. End off.

Rnd 6: Attach fifth color in ch 2 corner sp. Work 2 sc in same sp, * 2 sc in next dc, 1 sc each in next 11 sts, 2 sc in next dc, 2 sc in corner sp, rep from * 3 more times; join with sl st to beg sc. End off.

Corners—Attach yarn to second sc before 2 sc corner, work 1 sc in same sp, and in each of next 12 sts, ch 1, turn, * decrease 1 sc, 1 sc in each st across, (decreasing 1 sc on last st), ch 1, turn, rep from * 6 more times. End off. Work three other colored corners the same way.

Border—With navy work 1 dc in each st along all of the edges, and (2 dc, ch 2, 2 dc), in each corner; join with sl st to beg dc. End off.

C-2 (1 diamond square motif): Work the same as for pattern C-1, except for different colors.

C-3 (1 diamond square motif): Work the same as for pattern C-1, except for different colors.

C-4 (1 diamond square motif): With first color ch 5, sl st to first ch to form ring.

Rnd 1: Ch 3 (counts as 1 dc), 1 dc, ch 1, 2 dc, in center of ring, * ch 3, (2 dc, ch 1, 2 dc), in center of ring, rep from * 2 more times; ch 3, join with sl st to beg dc. End off.

Rnd 2: Attach second color to ch 3 corner sp, (ch 3, 2 dc, ch 3, 3 dc) in same sp, * ch 4, 1 long sc in center of ring, covering ch 1 sp of previous rnd, ch 4 *, ** (3 dc, ch 3, 3 dc), in next ch 3 sp, rep from * through **, 2 more times, and from * to * 1 more time; join with sl st to beg dc. End off.

Rnd 3: Attach third color to ch 3 corner sp. Work (2 sc, ch 2, 2 sc), in same sp, * 1 sc each in next 3 dc, ch 1, 1 trc in sc st in previous rnd, ch 1, 1 sc each in next 3 dc *, ** (2 sc, ch 2, 2 sc), (corner), rep from * through ** 2 more times, and from * to * 1 more time, sl st in first sc. End off.

Rnd 4: Rep directions as given for rnd 6 in C-1 substituting sc for dc, and having 9 sc instead of 11.

Corners—Rep directions as given for corners in C-1.

C-5 (1 diamond square motif): Rnds 1, 2, 3, 4: Rep directions as given for C-1.

Rnds 5, 6, 7: Work each rnd in a different color with 1 sc in each sc along all edges, and (2 sc, ch 2, 2 sc), in each corner.

Rnd 8: With navy work * (3 dc, ch 2, 3 dc), in each corner, and along each edge work sk 1 sc, 3 dc in next sc, sk 1 sc, rep from * around. End off.

Simple square motif (D)—Make 5.

D-1 (1 simple square motif): With first color, ch 11.

Row 1: 1 sc in second ch from hook, and in each ch st across (10 sc), ch 1, turn.

Row 2: 1 sc in each sc across, ch 1, turn.

Rows 3 through 15: Work as for row 2, omit ch 1 on end of row 15. End off.

Border—Rnd 1: With second color ch 3, work 1 dc in each st

continued

Granny Square Sampler Afghan *(continued)*

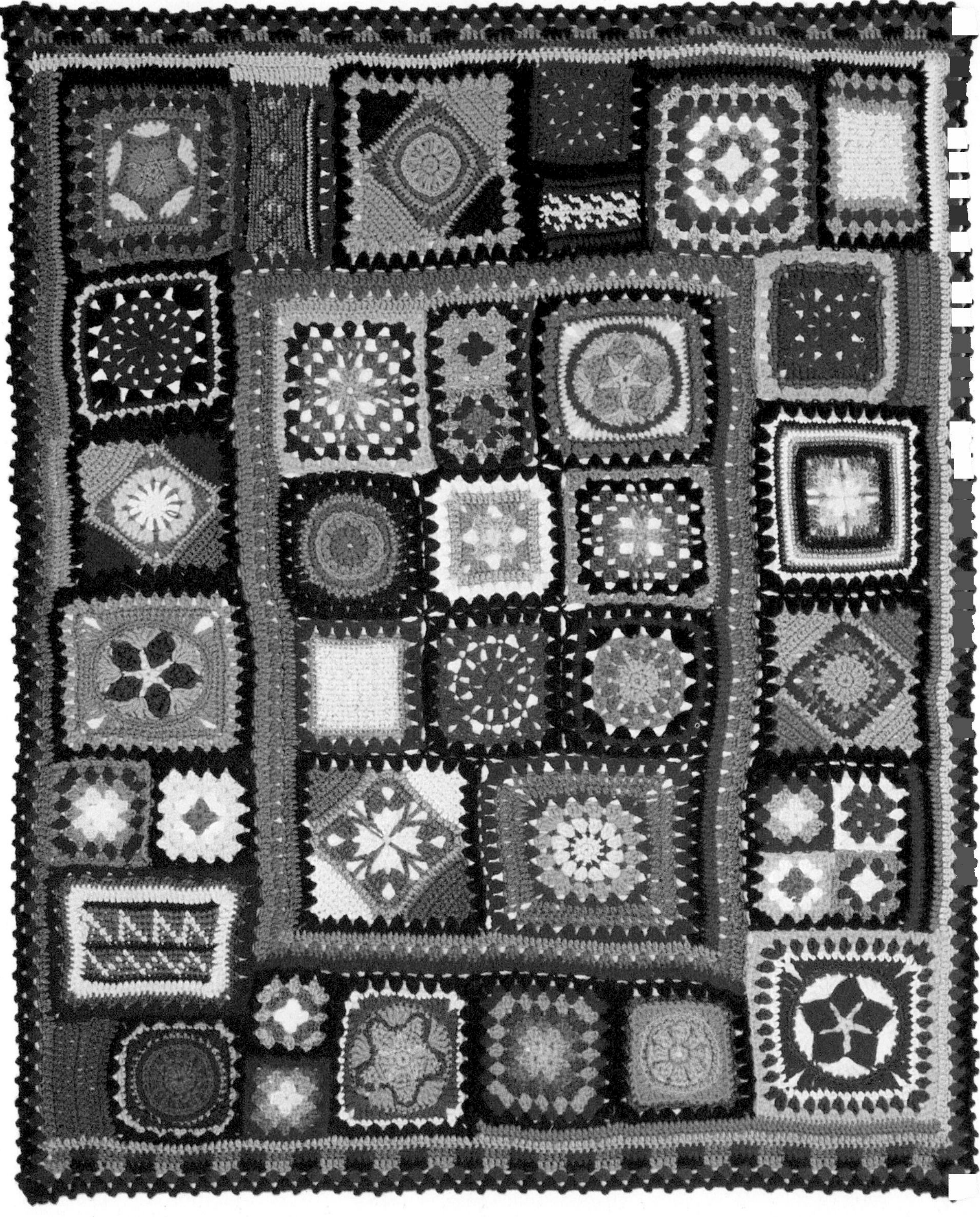

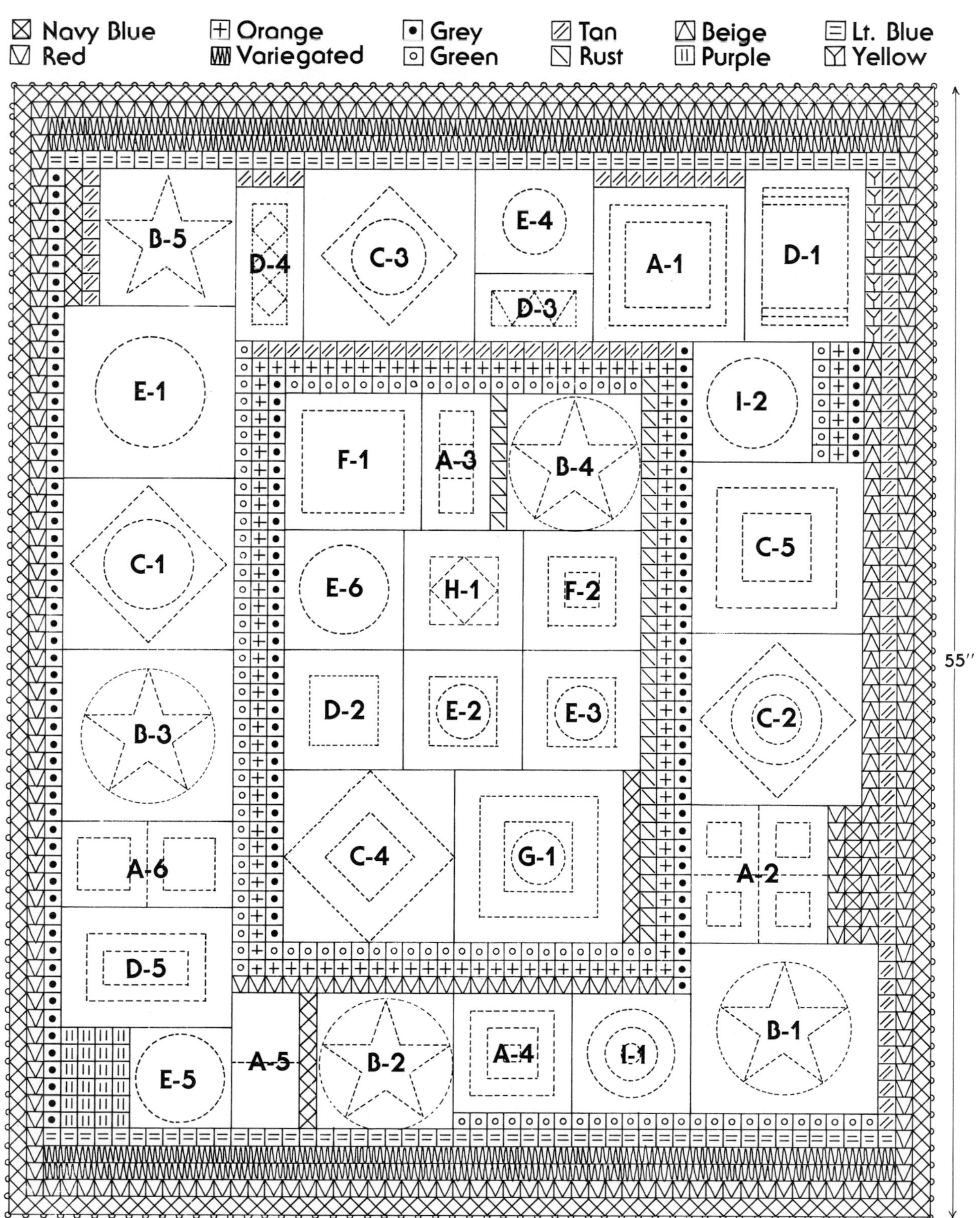
Navy Blue
Red
Orange
Variegated
Grey
Green
Tan
Rust
Beige
Purple
Lt. Blue
Yellow
B-5
D-4
C-3
E-4
D-3
A-1
D-1
E-1
F-1
A-3
B-4
I-2
C-1
E-6
H-1
F-2
C-5
B-3
D-2
E-2
E-3
C-2
A-6
C-4
G-1
A-2
D-5
E-5
A-5
B-2
A-4
I-1
B-1
55″
46″

continued

Granny Square Sampler Afghan *(continued)*

around edges, and (2 dc, ch 2, 2 dc) in each corner.

Rnds 2 and 3: On each 10 sc edge, work 2 rows of 1 dc in each dc. Make each row a different color.

Rnd 4: Attach navy in corner, and work (3 dc, ch 2, 3 dc), in each corner, and 3 dc in every third st along all edges. End off.

D-2 (1 simple square motif): With first color, ch 16.

Row 1: 1 sc in second ch from hook and in each ch st across (15 sc), ch 1, turn.

Row 2: 1 sc in each sc across (15 sc), ch 1, turn.

Rows 3 through 15: Rep row 2. End off.

Border—Rnd 1: With second color work 1 sc in each st along edges, and (2 sc, ch 2, 2 sc) in each corner. End off.

Rnd 2: Rep rnd 1 with a new color.

Rnd 3: Work (3 dc, ch 2, 3 dc), in each corner, and 3 dc in every third st along all edges. End off.

D-3 (1 simple square motif): With first color, ch 16.

Row 1: With first color make sc in ea of the first 2 sts, * change color, sc in ea of next 2 sts, change to first color, make 2 sc in ea of next 2 sts, rep from * across chain.

Row 2: Sc in ea sc across, having second color over first color. Repeat rows 1 and 2 for total of 5 rows.

Borders—Rep rnds 1, 2, 3 as given in D-2 border directions.

D-4 (1 simple square motif): Rows 1 through 20: Rep directions as given for D-1, but extend rows to the count of 20.

Border—Rep rnds 1, 2, 3 as given in D-2 for borders.

Design—With another color, work embroidery in cross-stitch in diamond shape across center of sc panel.

D-5 (1 simple square motif): Rep directions given for D-4 for 20 rnds and including 1, 2, 3 border rnds.

Rnd 4: Work (3 dc, ch 2, 3 dc) in each corner, and 3 dc between each dc group along edges. End off.

Design—Work embroidery in cross-stitch in zigzag pattern across center of sc panel.

Circle motif (E)—Make 6.

E-1 (1 circle motif): With first color ch 4, sl st in 1st ch to form ring.

Rnd 1: Ch 1, work 12 sc in center of ring; join with sl st to beg sc, do not end off.

Rnd 2: *Note:* Work in both loops. Ch 3 (counts as 1 dc), 2 dc in same sp, ch 1 * sk next sc, 3 dc in next sc, ch 1, rep from * around (6 groups of 3 dc); join with sl st to beg dc. Do not end off.

Rnd 3: Work 1 sl st in top of next dc, ch 3, 1 dc in same sp, * ch 1, sk next dc, 2 dc in next ch 1 sp, ch 1, sk next dc, 2 dc in next dc, rep from * around (12 groups of 2 dc), ch 1, join with sl st to beg dc. End off.

Rnd 4: Attach second color in ch 1 sp. Ch 3 (counts as first dc). Work * (3 dc, ch 3, 3 dc), in same sp (corner), 3 dc bet next group of 2 dc, 2 times, rep from * 3 more times; join with sl st to beg dc. End off.

Rnd 5: Attach third color. Work 1 sc in each st and between groups of dc, and in each corner work 1 sc, ch 3, 1 sc; join with sl st to beg sc. End off.

Rnd 6: Attach navy in ch 3 corner. Ch 3 (counts as first dc). Work * (2 dc in same sp, ch 3, 3 dc), in corner sp *, ** sk next 2 sts, 3 dc in next st, rep from along edge to next corner, rep from * through ** around; join with sl st to beg dc. End off.

E-2 (1 circle motif): Work in solid color as in directions for E-1 for 5 rnds. Work sixth rnd in navy.

E-3 (1 circle motif): Work 5 rnds as in directions for E-1, except work each rnd in a different color.

6th rnd: Work in navy.

E-4 (1 circle motif): Work in solid color for 3 rnds only as given in directions for E-1.

Rnd 4: Attach second color in ch 1 sp. Ch 3 (counts as first dc), make * (3 dc, ch 2, 3 dc), in same sp (corner), work ** 3 dc bet next group of dc in previous rnd, 2 times, rep from * through ** 3 more times. End off.

Rnd 5: With navy work 1 dc in each st along each edge, and (2 dc, ch 2, 2 dc) in each corner. End off.

E-5 (1 circle motif): Work same motif as in directions E-3.

E-6 (1 circle motif): Work same motif as in directions E-3.

Variation motif (F)—Make 2.

F-1 (1 variation motif): With first color ch 4, sl st in 1st ch to form ring.

Rnd 1: Ch 3 (counts as 1 dc), 4 dc in center of ring, * ch 5, 4 dc in ring, rep from * 2 more times, ch 5; join with sl st to beg dc. End off.

Rnd 2: Attach second color in ch 5 sp. Work * (3 dc, ch 3, 3 dc) (corner sp), ch 1, sk next 2 dc, (1 dc, ch 1, 1 dc), between second and third dc, rep from * 3 more times; join with sl st to beg dc. End off.

Rnd 3: Attach third color in ch 3 corner sp. Work * (3 dc, ch 3, 3 dc) in same sp, ch 2, 1 dc in ch 1 sp, ch 1, 3 dc in next sc sp, ch 1, 1 dc in next ch 1 sp, ch 2, rep from * 3 more times; join with sl st to beg dc. End off.

Rnd 4: Attach fourth color in ch 2 corner sp. Work * (3 dc, ch 3, 3 dc), in same sp, 3 dc in next ch 2 sp, ch 2, 2 dc in top of center dc of 3 dc group of previous rnd, ch 1, 3 dc in next ch 2 sp, rep from * 3 more times; join with sl st to beg dc. End off.

Rnd 5: Attach fifth color to ch 3 corner sp, work * (3 dc, ch 3, 3 dc) in same corner sp, sk next

2 dc, 3 dc in top of next dc, sk next dc, 3 dc in top of next dc, sk next dc, 3 dc in top of next dc, sk next dc, 3 dc in top of next dc, sk next 2 dc, rep from * 3 more times. End off.

F-2 (1 variation motif): Rep directions as for F-1.

Big Square Motif (G)—Make 1.

Starting at center with first color ch 4, sl st to first ch to form ring, ch 1.

Rnd 1: Work 6 sc in center of ring, join with sl st to beg sc. Do not end off.

Rnd 2: Ch 2 (counts as 1 hdc), 1 hdc in same sp, 2 hdc in top of each sc around (12 hdc); join with sl st to beg ch 2. End off.

Rnd 3: Attach second color, ch 1, 1 sc in top of next st, * ch 1, sc in next st, rep from * around; join with sl st to beg st. End off.

Rnd 4: Attach third color in any ch 1 sp, ch 3 (counts as 1 dc), 2 dc in same sp, * 3 dc in next ch 1 sp, rep from * around (12 groups of 3 dc); join with sl st to beg dc. End off.

Rnd 5: Attach fourth color between any dc group, * ch 3, 1 sc between next group of dc, rep from * around; join with sl st to beg st. End off.

Rnd 6: Attach fifth color in any ch 3 sp, (ch 3, 2 dc, ch 3, 3 dc), in same sp (corner), * 3 dc in next 2 ch 3 sps, (3 dc, ch 3, 3 dc), in next ch 3 sp, rep from * around. End off.

Rnd 7: Attach sixth color in ch 3 corner. Work (3 dc, ch 3, 3 dc) in each ch 3 corner and 3 dc between each dc group along all edges. End off.

Rnds 8 and 9: Attach seventh color, work 1 dc in top of each st along edges and (1 dc, ch 3, 1 dc), in each corner. End off.

Rnd 10: Attach eighth color and rep directions as for rnd 7.

Violet Motif (H)—Make 1.

Start at center with yellow, ch 4, sl st to beg ch to form ring.

Rnd 1: * 1 sc in center of ring, ch 4, rep from * 3 more times; join with sl st to beg sc. End off.

Rnd 2: Attach lavender in sc st, 1 sl st in same sp, * (1 sc, 1 hdc, 1 dc, 1 hdc, 1 sc), in next ch 4 sp, 1 sl st in next sc (petal), rep from * 3 more times; join with sl st to beg sl st. End off.

Rnd 3: Attach green to back loop of sc in any petal, ch 3 (counts as 1 dc), 1 dc, ch 3, 2 dc, in same sp, 2 dc in back loop of next hdc in previous rnd, * ch 1, sk next 3 sts in previous rnd, 2 dc in back loop of next hdc, (2 dc, ch 3, 2 dc), in back loop of dc, 2 dc in back loop of next hdc, rep from * 2 more times; join with sl st to top of beg dc. End off.

Rnd 4: Attach lavender and work 1 hdc in each st along all edges and (2 hdc, ch 3, 2 hdc) in each ch 3 corner. End off.

Rnd 5: Attach white in ch 3 corner, (ch 3, 1 dc, ch 3, 2 dc), in same sp, * sk next hdc sp, 2 dc in next hdc, rep from * along all edges and (2 dc, ch 3, 2 dc), in each ch 3 corner. End off.

Rnd 6: Attach navy, work 3 dc between each dc group along all edges with (3 dc, ch 3, 3 dc), in each ch 3 corner; join with sl st to beg dc. End off.

Rose motif (I)—Make 2.

I-1 (1 rose motif): With first color ch 4, sl st to first ch to form ring.

Rnd 1: Work 8 sc in center of ring; join with sl st to beg sc.

Rnd 2: Ch 3 (counts as 1 dc), 4 dc in same sc sp, drop loop from hook, * insert hook from front to back of work in first dc of the 5 dc group, draw dropped loop through, ch 1 to fasten, (petal made), ch 3, 5 dc in next sc, rep from * 6 more times (8 petals), ch 3; join with sl st to beg dc. End off.

Rnd 3: Attach second color in ch 3 sp, (ch 3, 2 dc), in same sp, * dc in next ch 1 sp, 3 dc in next ch 3 sp, rep from * around (32 dc); join with sl st to beg dc. End off.

Rnd 4: *Note:* Work in top back loop only. Attach third color in dc back loop, (ch 3, 1 dc, ch 1, 2 dc), in same sp, * 1 dc in next dc, 1 hdc in each of next 2 dc, 1 sc in next dc, 1 hdc in each of next 2 dc, 1 dc in next dc, ** (2 dc, ch 1, 2 dc) in next dc, rep from * through ** 2 more times, and from * to * one more time; join with sl st to beg dc. End off.

Rnd 5: Attach fourth color, work 1 sc in each st along edges, and (1 sc, ch 2, 1 sc), in each corner ch 1 sp; join with sl st to beg sc. End off.

Rnd 6: Attach navy in ch 2 corner, (ch 3, 2 dc, ch 3, 3 dc), in same sp, * sk next sc, 3 dc in next sc *, rep from * to next corner, ** (3 dc, ch 3, 3 dc), in same sp, rep from * through ** 2 more times, and from * to * 1 more time; join with sl st to beg dc. End off.

I-2 (1 rose motif): Work motif same as I-1, but work rnd 6 with bright color. Add 3 rows of dc in bright colors to one side of motif to finish.

Afghan assembly—Following photo and diagram on pages 174 and 175, whipstitch center motifs together first. *Note:* If squares do not fit as desired, simply add another row of dc.

Borders—Rnds 1, 2, 3: Make each border rnd a different color. Work 3 dc in every third st along all edges, and (3 dc, ch 3, 3 dc) in each corner.

Whipstitch the rest of squares according to diagram in same manner. Add as many borders as desired to edge afghan, by working in same manner as described for borders around center motif squares.

On last border of afghan, work a picot st between each 3 dc group to finish. Work 1 sc, * ch 3, sl st in top of sc just made (picot st), sc in next 3 sts, picot, rep from * around border.

Crocheted Star Motif Afghan

With just one motif–this patriotic star from the granny square afghan on the preceding pages–you can make a spectacular afghan like the one pictured at right. Size is 40x54 inches, less fringe.

Materials

4 ply acrylic knitting worsted, 4 oz. skeins
1 yellow
2 blue
2 red
5 white
Size H aluminum crochet hook

Directions

Note: Afghan is made of 35 squares: 18 blue stars with alternating red and blue borders, and 17 red stars with alternating blue and red borders. Each star motif is 8 inches square. Stars have yellow centers (Rnd. 1); Rnds. 4, 7, and 9 are all white.

Basic star square – Starting with yellow, ch 3, sl st to 1st ch to form ring, ch 1. Rnd 1: * 1 sc in center of ring, ch 4, 1 sc in 2nd chain from hook, 1 sc in each of next 2 ch sts, rep from * 4 more times (5 spoke star center); join with sl st to beg sc. End off.

Rnd 2: Attach mc in center top st of any spoke, ch 1, sc in same sp, * sk next 3 sc, (1 trc, 1 dc, 1 trc) in next sc, sl st to top of next spoke, rep from * around; join with sl st to beg sc. *Do not end off.*

Rnd 3: * sk next st, (1 hdc, 1 dc, 1 trc, ch 1, 1 trc, 1 dc, 1 hdc) in top of next st, sk next st, sl st in top of next st, rep from * around; join with sl st to beg st. End off.

Rnd 4: Attach white in ch 1 back loop st of any point, * sk next 3 sts, (1 trc, 3 dc, 1 trc) in next st, sk next 3 sts, sl st in back loop of ch 1 point, rep from * around; join with sl st to beg st. End off.

Rnd 5: Attach 2nd color in any st, (work through both loops), 2 sc in each st around (60 sc); join with sl st to beg sc. End off.

Rnd 6: (*Note:* Work on right side in top back loops only.) With star point at top, count clockwise 8 sc sts from point (this will be in sc above 3rd dc in rnd 4). Attach mc, work ch 6, 1 trc in next sc, * 1 dc in next sc, 1 hdc in each of next 2 sc, 1 sc in each of next 7 sc, 1 hdc in each of next 2 sc, 1 dc in next sc, 1 trc in next sc, ch 2, 1 trc in next sc, rep from * around; join with sl st to top of 4th ch of beg ch 6. End off.

Rnd 7: Attach white in ch 2 corner sp, ch 3, 1 sc in same sp, * 1 sc each in next 15 sts, 1 sc in next ch 2 sp, rep from * around; join with sl st to beg sc. End off.

Rnd 8: Attach 2nd color in ch 2 corner, rep rnd 7 (17 sc on each side).

Rnd 9: Attach white in any corner sp, (ch 2, 1 hdc, ch 3, 2 hdc) in same sp, * sk next sc, 2 hdc in next sc, rep from * across to next corner, * work (2 hdc, ch 3, 2 hdc) in same corner sp, rep from * around; join with sl st to top of beg ch 2. End off.

Assembling – Alternate blue and red squares. Attach rows together on right side with white, working with sl st.

Border – (*Note:* Alternate rows of white, red, and white.)

Rows 1, 2, and 3: Work 2 hdc bet groups of hdc along all edges, and (2 hdc, ch 3, 2 hdc) in each corner.

Fringe – Use double strands of 9-inch-long white yarn. Fold in half, and with crochet hook, knot around edges of afghan between each hdc group.

Grandmother's Flower Garden Afghan

This familiar patchwork quilt pattern can also be made into a most attractive crocheted afghan. Worked up in springtime colors, the afghan brings a flower garden atmosphere to your home all year 'round. Use any colors you fancy to whip up this quick and easy crochet–a perfect pick-up-and-go project worked one "petal" motif at a time. Another plus for the Grandmother's Flower Garden pattern–it provides an ideal way to use leftover yarn pieces.

The finished measurements for our afghan are 48x60 inches.

Materials

Knitting worsted, 4 oz. skeins
- 9 green (G)
- 1 yellow (Y)
- 1 flame
- 1 blue (variegated)
- 1 coral
- 1 gold
- 1 rust (variegated)
- 1 pale yellow
- 1 med. blue
- 1 pink
- 1 lt. blue
- 1 multicolor (variegated)

Size F crochet hook

Gauge

Each motif measures 3½ inches point to point.

Directions

Note: Crochet 145 green motifs for the background, 18 motifs in yellow for flower centers, and 6 motifs (all one color) for each of the 18 flowers.

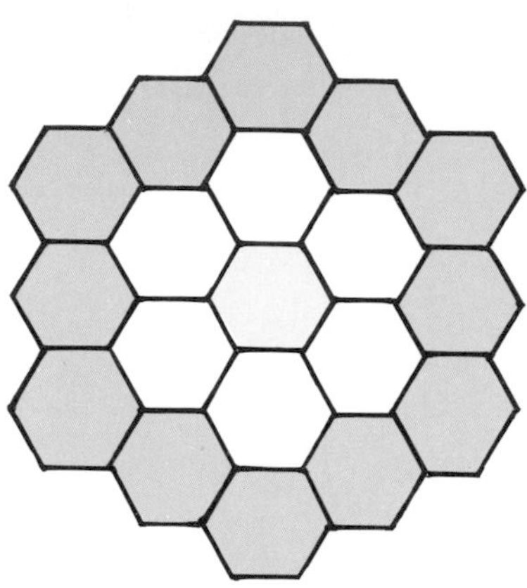

Pattern stitch—To make cluster, yo hook and draw up loop, yo and draw up another loop, (five strands on hook), yo and draw through all loops on hook, ch 1. One cluster made.

Hexagonal motif—Ch 6, join with sl st to form ring, ch 1. Rnd. 1: Work 6 cluster sts in ring; join in top of first cluster with sl st, ch 1.

Rnd. 2: In first sp between clusters of previous row, make 2 cluster sts. Proceeding around, make 2 clusters in each sp. (There should be 6 *double* clusters.) Join with sl st, ch 1.

Rnd. 3: Make one cluster in space between double clusters of previous row. Proceeding around, make double clusters over previous doubles, and a single cluster in the space between. (There should be 6 double alternating with 6 single clusters.)

Rnd. 4: Keeping double clusters over previous double clusters, and single clusters in the spaces between, continue around. Join with sl st, break off yarn and weave in loose end.

Finishing—Whipstitch all the motifs together with the green background color, following the diagram for placement. Finish the edge with 2 rows of sc in green all around.

Classic Americana Pattern

This lovely old design is equally as beautiful in today's homes as it was in the stately residences of days gone by. Crochet it as an afghan for your sofa, or as a coverlet for a twin-size or double bed. Directions are given first for a 48x62-inch afghan, with 66x102-inch twin bed and 76x102-inch double bed sizes in parentheses. (These sizes do not include the fringe, which adds several inches.)

Materials

Bernat Berella, "4," 4 oz. balls 18 (21-27) off-white
Size G crochet hook

Gauge

4 dc = 1 inch
Note: Entire afghan is worked in back loop only.

Directions

Pattern stitch for shell—Row 1: 1 dc in 4th ch from hook, 1 dc in same st, skip next 2 sts, 1 sc in next st, skip next 2 sts, * 5 dc in next st (shell), skip next 2 sts, 1 sc in next st, skip next 2 sts, repeat from * across row, ending 3 dc in last st (half shell)—29 (40-45) shells and 2 half shells.

Row 2: Ch 1, turn, working in back loop only, 1 shell in next sc, * 1 sc in 3rd dc of next shell, 1 shell in next sc, repeat from *, ending 1 sc in top of turning ch—30 (41-46) shells. Row 3: Ch 3, turn, 2 dc in first st, * 1 sc in 3rd dc of next shell, 1 shell in next sc, repeat from *, ending 3 dc in top of turning ch—29 (40-45) shells and 2 half shells. (Always count ch 3 as first dc.) Repeat rows 2 and 3 for pattern stitch.

Pattern stitch for dc—Row 1: Ch 3, turn, working in back loop only, 1 dc in each st across row—181 (247-277) sts. Repeat row 1 for pattern stitch.

Pattern stitch for bobble—Row 1: Ch 3, turn, working in back loop only, 1 dc in each of next 4 dc, * 5 dc in next st, remove hook from st, insert hook in back loop of first st of 5 dc just made and draw loop of last st through loop on hook (back loop bobble), 1 dc in each of next 5 dc, repeat from *, ending back loop bobble in next st, 1 dc in turning ch—30 (41-46) bobbles.

Row 2: Ch 3, turn, 1 dc in each of next 3 sts, * 5 dc in next st, remove hook from st, insert hook in front loop of first st of 5 dc just made and draw loop of last st through loop on hook (front loop bobble), 1 dc in each of next 5 sts, repeat from *, ending front loop bobble in next st, 1 dc in next st, 1 dc in turning ch. Bobbles will be on right side.

Repeat rows 1 and 2 for pattern st. Ch 184 (250-280) sts. Work in pattern st as follows: 8 rows shell pattern. 8 rows dc pattern. 8 rows bobble pattern. 8 rows dc pattern.

Repeat these 32 rows 3 times more for small size afghan only. Do not fasten off. For medium and large size coverlets only, repeat these 32 rows 4 times more, ending 8 rows shell pattern, 9 rows dc pattern. Do not fasten off.

Edging—For all sizes: With right side facing you, * 5 dc in turning ch of next row (shell), 1 sc in last st of next row, skip 1 row, repeat from * to first corner, working 1 shell in corner st. Work same edging on remaining lower and side edges. Fasten off. Fringe—Cut strands of yarn 10 inches long, knot 10 strands in space between 2nd and 3rd st of shell st on 3 sides of afghan. Trim ends. Steam lightly.

CARING FOR KNITS

All yarns are now labeled with laundering recommendations—including information as to whether they can be machine-washed, must be laundered by hand, or must be dry-cleaned.

■ *For machine-washing, use a mild soap or detergent. Machine-dry at the regular setting. (Be sure the article is thoroughly dried so that it will return to its original size and shape.)*

■ *For items that require hand-washing, use lukewarm water and a mild soap or detergent. Note: If you use a washing compound that calls for cold water, follow the manufacturer's instructions.*

Rinse well. Squeeze to eliminate excess water. Roll article in Turkish towel, squeezing again. Remove from towel, and lay it flat until it is dry.

■ *To block a knitted or crocheted article, pin it to the ironing board with wrong side up. Using rust-proof pins, pin it in place, stretching to desired measurements.*

Steam lightly—one way only—with a moderately hot iron over a damp cloth, taking care not to let the weight of the iron rest in any one spot. Steam press the seams. Leave the garment pinned to the board until it dries.

■ *Do not block acrylic yarns in the same manner as outlined above. First, pin the garment to a padded surface, stretching and pinning according to blocking measurements. Then, lay a damp cloth over entire garment and allow it to remain there until article is thoroughly dry.*

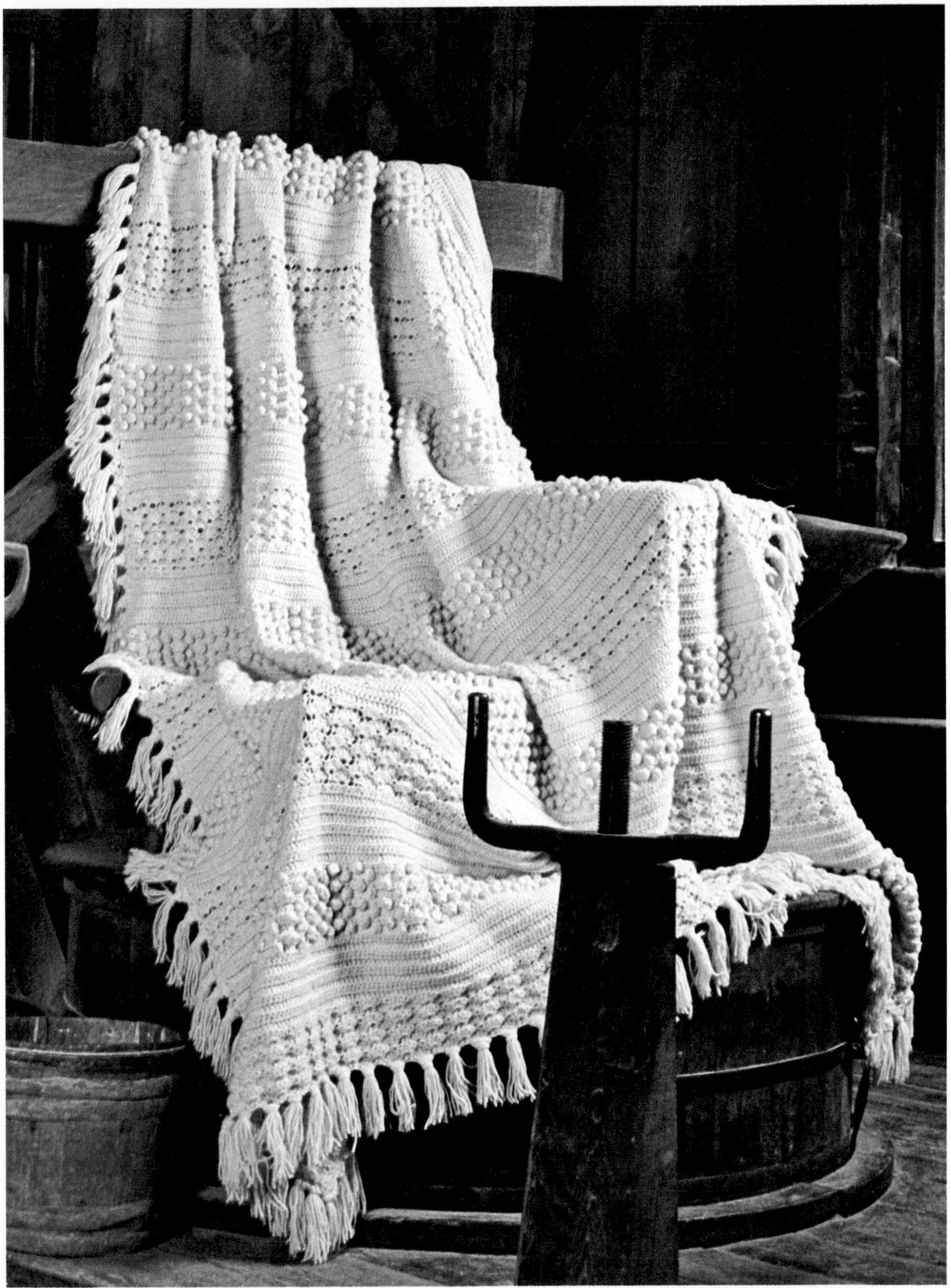

Brilliant Flower Patch Afghan

Using the afghan stitch–an easy crocheting technique–you can create this stunning afghan a square at a time. After each square is completed, you simply embroider on a whopping big flower in bright sunshine shades (see chart on page 186 for floral motifs). Finished size is about 44x76 inches.

Materials

Bernat Sesame, "4," 4 oz. balls
12 white main color (MC)
3 lt. olive (color A)
3 dk. olive (color B)
1 goldenrod (color C)
1 orange (color D)
or
Bernat Berella Germantown, 4 oz. balls
12 white main color (MC)
3 lt. olive (color A)
3 dk. olive (color B)
1 honey color (color C)
1 orange (color D)
Size H afghan hook
Size E crochet hook

Gauge

9 sts = 2 inches, 4 rows = 1 inch

Directions

Afghan stitch—Row 1: Draw up a loop in each st of ch, leaving all loops on hook (Fig. 1); take off loops as follows. Yo hook, draw through 1 loop, * yo draw through 2 loops, repeat from * across row (Fig. 2); the loop remaining on hook counts as first loop of next row (Fig. 3).

Row 2: Skip first upright bar (Fig. 3). Draw up a loop in next and each remaining upright bar (Fig. 4), leaving all loops on hook; take off loops in same manner as row 1. Repeat row 2 only for specified length.

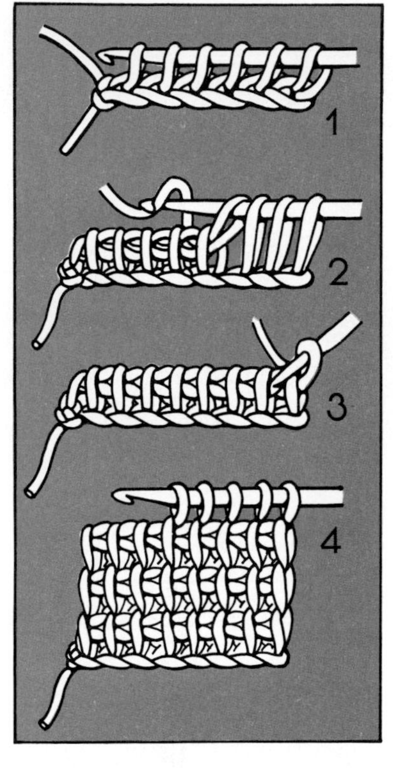

Squares—Make 15. Using MC and afghan hook, ch 63 sts. Work even in afghan st for 51 rows. Work 1 sl st in each upright bar. Fasten off.

Border—Using crochet hook, join color A at top right-hand corner, ch 1, 2 sc in same st, * 1 sc in each of next 61 sts, 3 sc in corner st, 1 sc in each row (50 sc), 3 sc in corner st, repeat from * around, join with sl st to top of ch 1.

Rnd. 2: Ch 1, turn, * 1 sc in each st to corner, 3 sc in corner st, ** 1 sc in each of next 5 sts, sk 1 st, rep from ** to next corner st, 3 sc in corner st, rep from * around, join—54 sts on each side. Rnds. 3 and 4: Ch 1, turn, 1 sc in each st and 3 sc in each corner st. Rnd. 5: Fasten off color A, pull color B through loop on hook and work 1 sc in each st and 3 sc in each corner st. Fasten off.

Cross stitch design—Following chart, work cross stitch designs on afghan stitch squares in the following manner.

Each upright bar across row of afghan st is counted as 1 st. Following the chart, count the upright bars. You will note that there are two holes formed by afghan st after each upright bar.

Working from left to right, join color on wrong side at lower hole and work across next upright bar to upper hole. Then bring needle through lower hole directly below (Fig 5). Continue on number of sts for color being used. Then work from right to left to form cross (Fig. 6). Be careful not to pull too tightly.

Make 8 squares with color C flowers and 7 in color D, alternating colors.

Finishing—Make 5 strips. Using color B, overcast 3 squares tog. Then overcast the 5 strips tog. Using color B, work in sc, working 3 sc in each corner st. Fasten off.

Fringe—Cut strands of color B 15 inches long. Knot 1 strand in each st across each short end of afghan. Trim ends. Steam lightly.

continued

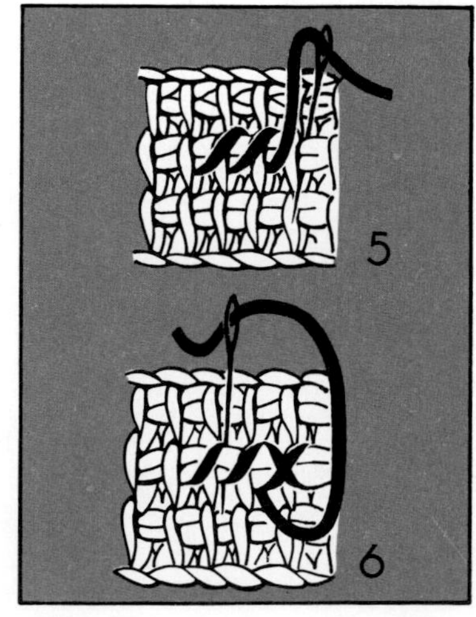

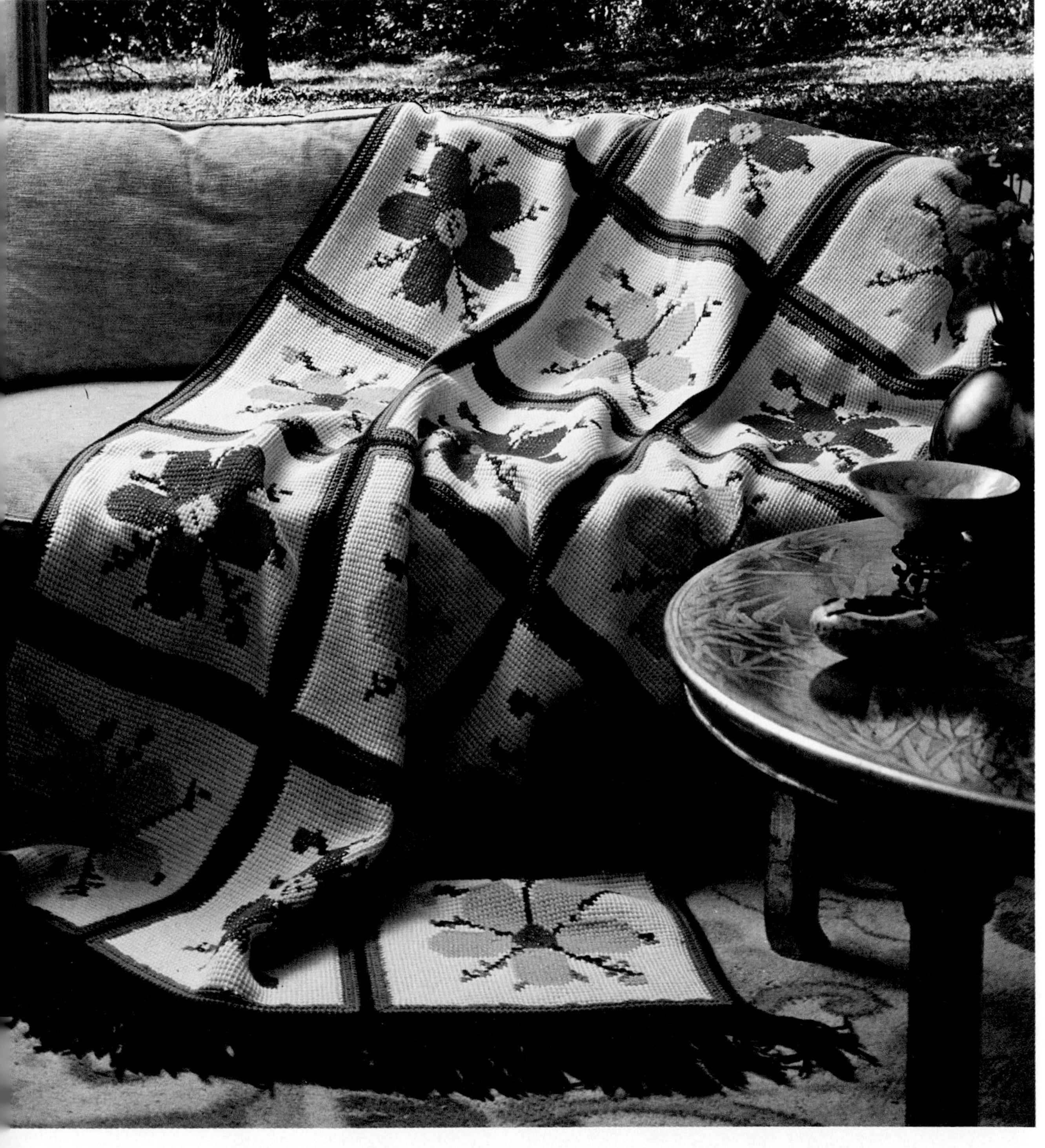

Brilliant Flower Patch Afghan *(continued)*

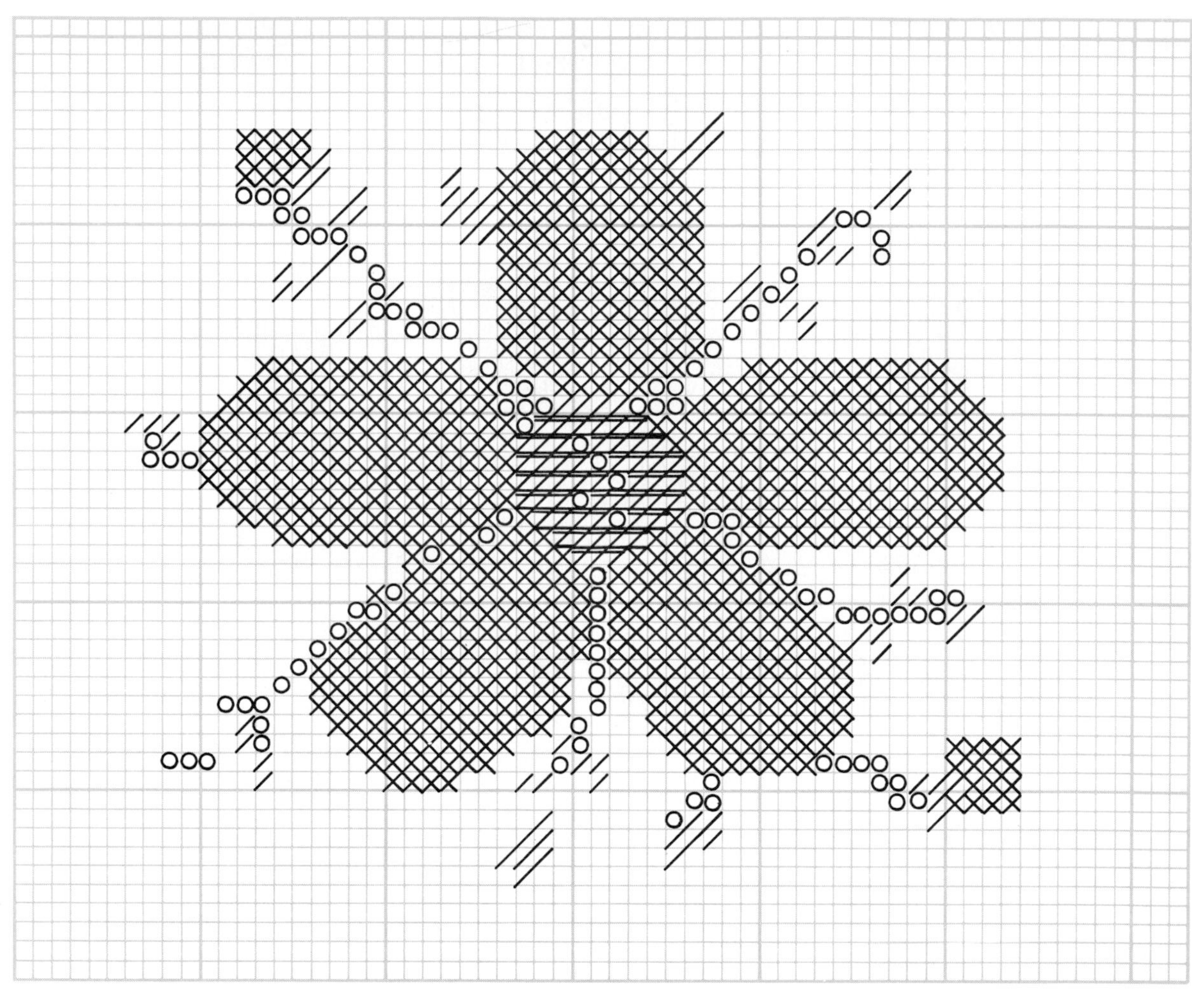

□ = White Main Color (MC)

/ = Lt. Olive (Color A)

O = Dk. Olive (Color B)

X = Goldenrod (Color C)

Z = Orange (Color D)

Cozy Quilt-Patterned Throw

Here's a fabulous way to use leftover yarn. For this easy-to-knit afghan, collect sport-weight yarn in a variety of colors. As you knit each triangle (using garter stitch), combine your yarn with ecru knitting worsted. The results of your efforts produce this lovely variegated crayon effect.

Materials

Knitting worsted, 4 oz. skeins
- 10 ecru
- 10 colors sport-weight yarn

Size 10½ knitting needles

Gauge

Each square measures 6½ inches

Directions

The entire afghan is worked in garter st, k every row.

Working with two strands of yarn, ecru plus one of the colors of yarn, cast on 2 sts.

Row 1: Inc 1 st, k across row. Rep 13 times; break off color and add a second color. Rep row 1 four more times. Bind off rem 20 sts.

Work 256 triangles in same manner. Whipstitch four triangles tog to form squares. Join eight squares in each strip. Join the eight strips together. See picture insert for finished design.

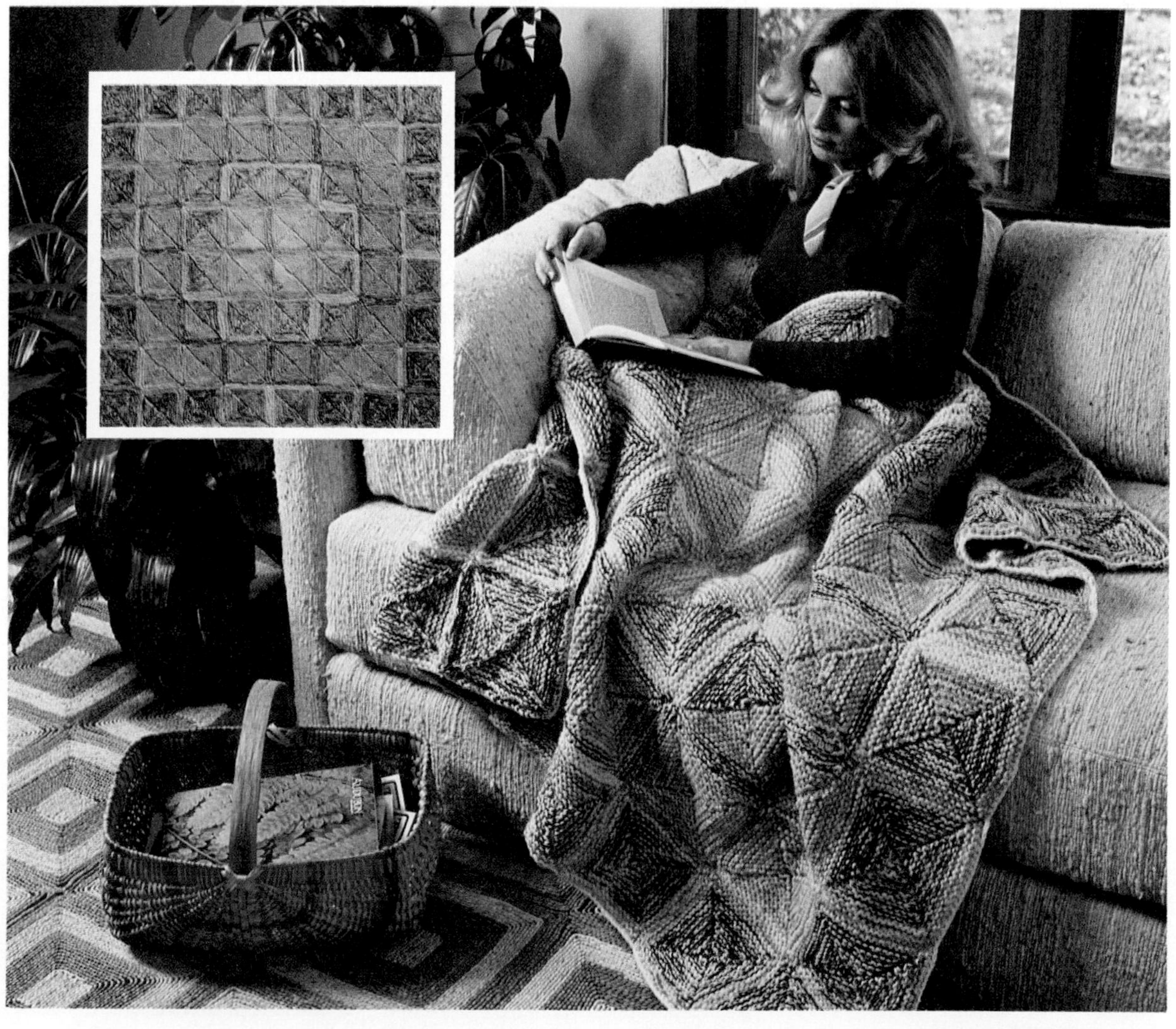

Quick Knit Patchwork Afghan

This afghan, with its simple garter stitch squares in bold and vibrant colors, is completely contemporary. So if you're looking for a work-up-fast project in tune with today's casual life-style, you'll want to try this one. It's virtually a no-fail design, even for beginners. Smashing striped squares add just enough challenge and interest to keep any knitter going great guns. This afghan measures approximately 47x47 inches.

Materials

Unger's Nanette, 1 3/4 oz. ball
- 3 red (A)
- 3 green (B)
- 3 orange (C)
- 3 blue (D)
- 6 off-white (E)

Size 10 knitting needles

Gauge

4 sts = 1 inch. Each block to measure 5 inches square

Directions

Pattern St—Garter st (k every row).

Solid squares—With size 10 needles, cast on 20 sts. Work even in garter st for 5 inches. Bind off. Make 11 squares in each of the 5 colors A, B, C, D and E—55 squares.

Striped squares—With size 10 needles and any contrasting color (A, B, C or D), cast on 20 sts. K 5 rows. Fasten off. * Attach E and k 6 rows with E; attach contrast color and k 6 rows with the contrasting color; rep from * until there are 8 stripes in all. Break yarn after each color change. Attach contrast color and k 5 rows. Bind off. Make 11 striped squares in each of colors A, B, C and D combined with E—44 squares.

Short bands—Make 2. With size 10 needles and E, cast on 180 sts. Work garter st for 3/4 inch. Bind off.

Long bands—Make 2. With size 10 needles and E, cast on 228 sts. Work garter st for 3/4 inch. Bind off.

Finishing—Arrange squares as shown or as desired. Alternate striped squares, using some with stripe in a horizontal position and others with stripe in a vertical position. Alternate solid squares with garter st in a horizontal position and others in a vertical position. Arrange colors to suit your individual taste. Sew squares tog on wrong side, taking in a small amount on the seam. Sew 9 squares across for width and 11 squares for length. Sew bands in place, matching corners. Steam lightly on wrong side. Do not press.

KNITTING TIPS

- *When you are joining a new ball of yarn, always join at the outer edge. With the new strand, make a slipknot around the strand you are knitting with. Then move the slipknot up to the edge of your work and continue knitting with the newly attached strand. (Knot will thus be concealed in a seam instead of in the body of your garment where it might show.)*
- *When you are working with more than one color, always pick up the color you are about to use from underneath the dropped strand. This prevents holes as you are changing colors.*

Old-Fashioned "Windowpane" Knitted Afghan

This puff stitch afghan has much of the beauty of stained window glass, because of the fascinating way bits of brilliant yarn colors are used. In fact, colors that would not ordinarily look well next to each other become harmonious because of the black yarn similar to the leading in stained glass that separates the colorful "panes" and forms the puffs at the same time.

This afghan measures about 46x70 inches.

Materials

Knitting Worsted, 4 oz. skeins
2 black
An assortment of colors that totals approximately 18 ounces
Size 10½ 29-inch circular knitting needle
Size F crochet hook

Gauge

4 sts = 1 inch, 6 rows = 1 inch

Directions

With black yarn, cast on 128 sts. Work 4 rows in st st (k 1 row, p 1 row). Tie in the first color and work 6 rows in st st.

Tie in black, k 4, * ravel or drop the next color st 6 rows down to the black. Put the right needle through the black loop from the front of work, then insert tip of right needle under horizontal rows of dropped sts, yo, pull under the horizontal rows and back through black loop to front of work again; place st last made on left needle and k 1 st. K 5 more sts, and rep from *. Follow pattern across row, then p back with black.

Tie on another color and follow the instructions above.

Continue in this manner until the afghan is 60 inches long. End with 4 rows of black st st.

Crocheted edging—Work 1 row of sc around entire afghan, working 3 sc at each corner. (Total number should be a multiple of 10 plus 2.)

Pattern row—Sl st in first sc, * 1 sc in next sc, 1 hdc in next sc, 1 dc in next sc, 1 tr in next sc, 5 dtr in next sc, 1 tr in next sc, 1 dc in next sc, 1 hdc in next sc, 1 sc in next sc, sl st in next sc; rep from * to end. Fasten off.

KNITTING KNOW-HOW

■ *Always buy enough yarn to complete your project, making sure the dye lot of each skein is the same. (Dye lots can vary.)*

■ *Always bind off stitches in the pattern of your garment or project, and work loosely to ensure "give" in the bound-off edge.*

■ *To pick up stitches, always work from the right side of your project. Using one needle only and a strand of yarn, insert the point of the needle through the knitting a short distance from the edge. Next wrap the yarn around the needle as if to knit, and draw the loop through the piece. Continue in this manner, spacing your stitches evenly.*

■ *If you drop a stitch, use a crochet hook to pick it up. In stockinette stitch, insert the hook through the loop of the dropped stitch from the front of the work to the back, with the hook facing upward. Pull the horizontal thread of the row above through the loop; repeat to the top and place dropped stitch on needle. If you are using a pattern stitch, pick up the stitch in the pattern.*

THE CIVI

Honeycomb Throw and Basket Stitch Pillow

Combine a solid color with a contrasting variegated yarn, add a little fancy stitchery, and you've got this unique throw and companion pillow. The throw measures about 48x58 inches, without fringe; the pillow is 14 inches square.

Knit Throw

Materials

American Thread Co., Sayelle, 3½ oz. skeins
- 5 burnt orange (A)
- 6 blue variegated (B)

2 markers
Size 9 circular knitting needle
Size 4 crochet hook

Gauge

4½ sts = 1 inch. 6 rows = 1 inch

Directions

Note: Hexagon pattern has a multiple of 8 sts plus 6 (edge sts not counted in multiple).

Cast on 214 sts of color B. K 20 rows of garter st. (Separate 4 sts at each end by markers since they are always garter st and not included in directions.)

Row 1 hexagon pattern: Change to color A and k 6. * sl 2 as if to p, k 6 *, rep from * to * across row, end k 6.

Row 2: P 6, * hold yarn in front, sl 2 as if to p, p 6 *, rep from * to * across row, end p 6.

Rows 3 and 5: Same as row 1. Rows 4 and 6 same as row 2.

Rows 7, 8, 9, 10: Change to color B and k all sts, including sl sts in previous rows.

Row 11: Change to color A and k 2, * sl 2 as if to p, k 6 *, rep from * to *, end sl 2 as if to p, k 2.

Row 12: P 2, * sl 2 as if to p, p 6 *, rep from * to *, end sl 2 as if to p, k 2.

Rows 13 and 15: Same as row 11. Rows 14 and 16 same as row 12. Rows 17, 18, 19, 20: Same as rows 7, 8, 9, 10.

Rep from row 1 through 20 until you have 19 pat repeats; rep rows 7 through 16. Change to color B and k 19 rows of garter st and cast off.

Finishing—At each end work one row of sc (cast on and cast off rows). Dampen throw in water to which fabric softener has been added (to avoid static electricity). Roll in towels to remove moisture, block to size.

Fringe—Cut 12-inch lengths of both color A and B for fringe. Use three strands for each unit. Leave about 1½ inches of space between each group of three strands. Trim fringe to an even length.

Note: Carry color of yarn not in use up right side by looping yarn in use around it so there isn't a long float of unused yarn.

Knitted Pillow

Materials

American Thread Co., Sayelle, 3½ oz. skeins
- 1 burnt orange (A)
- 1 blue variegated (B)

Size 9 knitting needles
14-inch-square pillow form

Gauge

5½ sts = 1 inch

Directions

Plaited basket st pat—uneven number of sts.

Row 1: K 2 * sk one st, k 2nd st, k 1st st, remove both sts from left needle *, rep from * to *, end k 1.

Row 2: P 2, * sk 1st st, p 2nd st, p 1st st, remove both sts from left needle *, rep from * to *, end p 1.

Cast on 77 sts of color B, p 1 row. * Work 4 rows of plaited basket st pat (rows 1, 2, 1, 2). Change to color A, work 4 rows in same pat (rows 1, 2, 1, 2) *. Rep from * to * 8 times, work 4 more rows in color B, cast off.

Work another piece, following the same instructions.

Finishing—Placing right sides tog, whipstitch around three sides, turn to right side, insert pillow, and whipstitch fourth side closed. *Note:* When sewing back and front tog, alternate ends so cast-on end is joined to cast-off end.

STITCH GAUGE

■ *When you see the word "gauge" at the beginning of a knit or crochet instruction, this is what it means. Gauge specifies how many stitches per inch you should have using a specified crochet hook or knitting needle. Since the sizing of any article is dependent upon this gauge, you must adjust your work to the given gauge or your finished article will not be the size indicated in the instructions.*

■ *Since everyone does not knit or crochet with the same tension, it is important to check your gauge before you start a project. Cast on or chain about 20 sts, using recommended yarn and needles or hook, and work about 4 inches in specified pattern. Bind or fasten off. Block swatch, then measure to see if rows and stitches correspond to required gauge.*

■ *If your stitch gauge is less than one given in instructions, try next size smaller needles or hook, and again check your gauge. If your stitch gauge is greater (more stitches per inch), try next size larger needle.*

For Your Table

Would you like to dress your table in an elegant downpour of lace, like the exquisite antique Victorian crocheted tablecloth pictured here? Or perhaps you'd rather go country with patterns that suggest heavy pottery, checks, and pretty prints? Well, whatever your style and your preference, you'll find beautiful, doable patterns to knit and crochet for your table in this section crammed with very special projects. For example, crocheters will delight in our jute place mats that are so easy even a beginner will be able to whip up one or more in just one sitting. And for experienced knitters, we present a challenge—knitted lace—an old art that is becoming very popular once again. The tablecloth shown on pages 198 and 199 features the lovely and popular apple blossom pattern. You may vary the size of any of our patterns to fit your own individual requirements. For complete instructions for the tablecloth at left, please turn the page.

Crochet Pattern from the Past *(shown on pages 194 and 195)* Crocheted Lace Tablecloth

To re-create this fragile-looking Victorian lace tablecloth, you will need to crochet 210 round motifs and 182 joining motifs for a 5x5-foot tablecloth like the one shown in the photo on the preceding page.

Materials
Size 20 crochet thread
13 balls ecru
Size 11 steel crochet hook

Directions
Ch 8, join with sl st to form a ring. Row 1: Ch 3 (counts as first dc), 23 dc in ring, sl st in top of first dc.

Row 2: * Ch 5, sk 1 dc, sl st once in each of next 2 dc *, rep from * 7 more times (there should be 8 loops on this round). End with a sl st in 1st st.

Row 3: Sl st to 3rd st of ch, ch 7, dc in same st * ch 4, dc in center st of next loop, ch 4, dc in same st (this makes a shell), rep from * 6 times, join with a sl st in top of first dc (there should be 16 sp on this rnd).

Row 4: Ch 1, 4 sc in next loop, sc in next dc, 4 sc in next loop, sc in next dc, rep around ending with a sl st in first sc.

Row 5: Ch 1, sc in next sc, sc in next sc, continue around ending with a sl st in first sc.

Rows 6, 7, and 8: Rep row 5.

Row 9: Ch 4, dc in next sc, ch 1, dc in next sc, ch 1, dc in next sc, rep around (there should be 78 dc on this round).

Row 10: Sl st in 1st sc, * ch 5, sk 2 sps, sl st in each of next 2 sps *, rep from * around. Join (there should be 20 loops on this rnd).

Row 11: Sl st to 3rd st of ch, ch 6, dc in same st, * ch 3, dc in center st of next loop, ch 3, dc in same st *. Rep from * around in pattern, ending with ch 3 and sl st in 3rd ch.

Row 12: Sl st into sp, ch 5, dc in same sp, ch 3, sc in next sp, ch 3, in next sp make dc, ch 3, dc (shell), ch 3, sc in next sp, ch 3; make shell in next sp. Rep in pattern, ending with a sl st in top of first dc.

Row 13: Rep row 12, making ch 4, sc in center sc, ch 4, bet shells. Break thread.

Joining—Join two motifs tog while working the last rnd. At any shell, make a dc on the second motif, ch 1, sl st in shell on first motif. Ch 1, dc in same sp as last dc on second motif, ch 3, dc in shell sp on second motif, ch 1, sl st in shell sp on first motif, ch 1, dc in shell on second motif, ch 3, dc in next shell. Ch 1, sl st in shell on first motif, ch 1, dc in shell on second motif.

Motifs for joining round medallions—Ch 5, join with sl st to form ring. Ch 15, sc bet 1st and 2nd motif, ch 15, sc in ring. Ch 10, sc in point on 2nd motif, ch 10, sc in ring. Ch 10, sc in point on 2nd motif, ch 10, sc in ring. Ch 15, sc bet 2nd and 3rd motif, ch 15, sc in ring.

Ch 10, sc in 3rd motif, ch 10, sc in ring. Ch 10, sc in 3rd motif, ch 10, sc in ring. Ch 15, sc bet 3rd and 4th motif, ch 15, sc in ring. Ch 10, sc in 4th motif, ch 10, sc in ring. Ch 10, sc in 4th motif, ch 10, sc in ring. Ch 15, sc bet 4th and 1st motif, ch 15, sc in ring. Ch 10, sc on 1st motif, ch 10, sc in ring. Ch 10, sc on 1st motif, ch 10, sc in ring. Break off thread.

Begin a tablecloth with a pattern of large and small medallions—like the ones pictured opposite—and crochet until you cover your table with these fresh, white "snowflakes." Directions given below are for a 5½-foot square, but you can make any size you wish. In fact, this pattern has wonderful possibilities for bed-spreads, table runners, pillow tops, and even elegant lace curtains. And despite its intricate appearance, you'll be able to turn out many motifs in a single evening.

Materials
Bedspread cotton thread, 4 cord, 650 yd. balls
7 white
Size 5 steel crochet hook

Directions
For a 5½-foot square, you will need 121 large medallions and 100 small medallions.

Large medallion—Ch 5, sl st in first ch to form ring.

Rnd 1: (Ch 10, sc in ring) 6 times.

Rnd 2: Sl st in ea of first 5 chs of ch 10 to bring thread into position. *Ch 8, sc in center st of next loop. Rep from * around, ending sl st in last sl st before first ch 8 (makes 6 spaces).

Rnd 3: Sl st in next ch. (Ch 3, 2 dc, ch 2, 3 dc) in first sp. *Ch 3, (3 dc, ch 2, 3 dc) in next sp. Rep from * around, ending ch 3; sl st to top of first ch 3.

Rnd 4: Sl st in ea of next 2 dc

and in first ch of ch 2. *Ch 8, sc in next ch 3 sp, ch 8, sc in next ch 2 sp. Rep from * around, ending sl st in base of first ch 8 (12 spaces).

Rnd 5: Ch 1, *(sc, hdc, dc, 3 trc, dc, hdc, sc) in first ch 8 sp. Sc in sc between loops. Rep around from *, ending sl st in sl st of rnd 4.

Rnd 6: Sl st in ea of next 5 sts. Sc in same sp as last sl st. *Ch 8, sc in center trc of next group. Rep from * around, ending sl st in first sc of rnd.

Rnd 7: Ch 1, *(sc, hdc, 7 dc, hdc, sc) in first ch 8 sp. Sc in sc between loops. Rep from * around ending sl st in sl st of rnd 6.

Rnd 8: Ch 6, sk 2 sts, dc in next st. *Ch 3, sk 2 sts, dc in next st. Rep from * around, ending ch 3, sl st in 3rd ch of ch 6 (48 spaces).

Rnd 9: Ch 6, dc in next dc, ch 3, dc in next dc, ch 3, dc in next dc. Ch 3, sl st in top of dc just made. Ch 5, sl st in same st. Ch 3, sl st in same st. (Triple picot). *Ch 3, dc in next dc, ch 3, dc in next dc, ch 3, dc in next dc, triple picot in top of last dc. Rep from * around ending with sl st in 3rd ch of ch 6 and triple picot in same st. End off (16 triple picots).

Joining large medallions—Make one large medallion as described. Make 2nd large medallion except attach it to first large medallion as follows: When making triple picot, ch 3, sl st to top of dc. Ch 2, sc thru long part of a picot of first medallion, ch 2, sl st in same sp with first ch 3. Ch 3, sl st in same sp. (The two medallions are connected by their triple picots.) Join the two medallions in the same way by their next picots. Continue around as described for the first medallion. Join the other large medallions in the same way according to the diagram. When 4 large medallions have been connected in a square, insert a small medallion in the center.

Small medallion—Ch 5, sl st to first ch to form ring.

Rnds 1 and 2: Same as rnds 1 and 2 of large medallion.

Rnd 3: Sl st in ea of first 2 chs of ch 8. Ch 8, sk 3 ch, dc in next ch. Ch 5, dc in second ch of next ch 8. Rep around with dcs in 2nd and 6th chs of ea ch 8, and ch 5 between dcs. End sl st to 3rd ch of ch 6 (12 spaces).

Rnd 4: Ch 3, 2 dc in first sp. Triple picot in top of 2nd dc, 3 dc in same sp. Ch 1, 3 dc in next sp. Connect with large medallion by sc thru large part of picot. 3 dc in same sp. Ch 1, 3 dc in next sp, sc thru large part of next picot of large medallion, 3 dc in same ch 5 sp. Ch 1, (3 dc, triple picot, 3 dc) in next sp. Continue around connecting small medallion with all 4 large medallions and making a triple picot between the large medallions. End sl st to top of ch-3. End off.

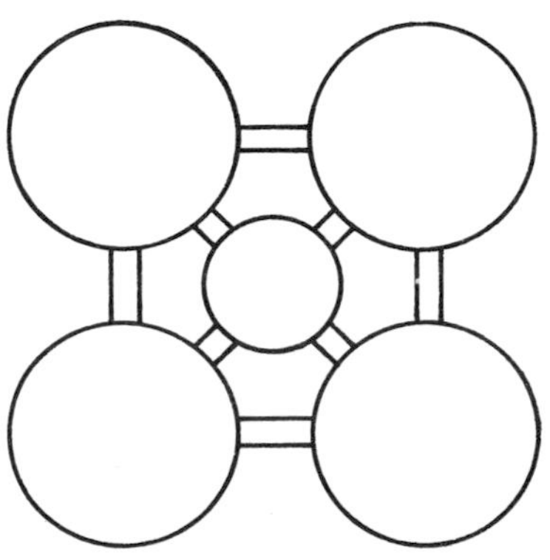

Knitted Lace Tablecloth

If you're an experienced knitter with a desire to do something different, try this challenging project. The pattern we feature here is the beautiful apple blossom design worked in ecru thread.

Materials

Knit-Cro-Sheen Thread, 550 yd. balls
3 ecru
Size 2 double-pointed knitting needles (set of 5)
Size 4 16-inch circular knitting needle (for rows 25-59)
Size 6 29-inch circular knitting needle (for rows 60-191)
Size 4 crochet hook
Note: In order to simplify and abbreviate the basic knitting terms, the following abbreviations are used in this design:
O means yarn over
(O)2 means thread over twice
Skb means slip 1, knit 1, pass slip stitch over
N means narrow (knit 2 tog)
Snb means slip 1, knit 2 tog, pass slip stitch over
V 2 means to increase by knitting in front and in back of stitch
K1b means to knit in back of stitch
V 3 means to increase by knitting in front, in back, and in front of stitch

Directions

With crochet hook, ch 5. Join. Sc 8 sts in circle. Hook through both loops, draw up and place on knitting needles, 2 sts on each of 4 double-pointed needles. *Note:* K plain all rows that are not numbered. Insert a marker so you can tell where each rnd begins. Repeat the directions for each row around entire row.

Row 1: K. Row 3: K. Row 5: K 1, o. Row 7: k 1, o, k 1, o.

Row 9: (k 1, o) 4 times.

Rows: 11, 12, 13, 14: P. Row 15: K. Row 16: (k 1, o) 8 times.

Row 18: K 16, o. Row 20: K 4, (o, skb) 4 times, k 3, n.

Row 22: K 16, o. Row 24: K 2 (o, skb) 6 times, k 1, n.

Row 26: K 16, o. Row 28: K 4 (o, skb) 4 times, k 3, n.

Row 30: K 16, o. Row 32: K 6 (o, skb) twice, k 5, n.

Row 34: K 3, o, k 10, o, k 3, o.

Row 36: K 19. Row 38: K 10, o, k 9, o.

Row 40: K 21. Row 42: K 5, o, k 11, o, k 5, o. Row 44: K 24.

Row 46: K 12, o, k 12, o.

Row 48: K 26 (o) twice. Row 50: K 26, o, k 2, o. Row 52: K 26, o, k 4, o. Row 54: K 26, o, k 1, n (o) twice, skb, k 1, o. Row 56: K 26, o, n, (o) twice, skb, n, (o) twice, skb, o.

Row 58: Skb, k 22, n, o, k 3, n (o) twice, skb, k 3, o.

Row 60: O, skb, [n (o) twice, skb] 8 times, n, o.

Row 62: O, n, o, (o, skb, n, o) three times, skb, n, o, (o, skb, n, o) four times, o, skb (There is only one yarn over after the first group of three).

Row 64: O, k 1, o, k 2, [n (o) twice, skb] three times, k 1, n, o, k 1, o, skb, k 1, [n (o) twice, n] three times, k 2.

Row 66: O, k 3, o, [n (o) twice, skb] four times.

Row 68: O, k 5, o, k 2, [n (o) twice, skb] three times, k 2.

Row 70: O, k 7, o, skb, k 2, [n (o) twice, skb] twice, k 2, n. Row 72: O, k 9, o, skb, k 3, n, (o) twice, skb, k 3, n.

Row 74: O, k 11, o, k 2 [n (o) twice, skb] twice, k 2.

Row 76: K 13, o, [n (o) twice, skb] three times, o.

Row 78: K 5, snb, k 5, o, k 3 [n (o) twice, skb] twice, k 3, o.

Row 80: K 4, snb, k 4, o, k 2, [n (o) twice, skb] three times, k 2, o. Row 82: K 3, snb, k 3, o, k 1, [n (o) twice, n], four times, k 1, o.

Row 84: K 2, snb, k 2, o, [n (o) twice, skb] five times, o.

Row 86: K 1, snb, k 1, o, k 3, [n (o) twice, skb] four times, k 3, o. Row 88: Snb, o, k 2, [n (o) twice, skb] five times, k 2, o. Row 90: K1b, k 1, [n (o) twice, n] six times, k 1, o.

Row 92: [n (o) twice, n] seven times. Row 94: O, skb, [n (o) twice, skb] six times, n, o.

Row 96: [n (o) twice, n] seven times.

Row 98: O, skb, [n (o) twice, skb] six times, n, o. Row 100: O, k 6, o, k 2, [n (o) twice, n] three times, k 2, o, k 6.

Row 102: O, k 1, o, k 7, o, [n (o) twice, skb] four times, o, k 7. Row 104: O, k 3, o, skb, k 6, o, skb, [n (o) twice, skb] three times, n, o, k 6, n.

Row 106: O, n, o, k 1, (o, skb) twice, k 6, o, skb, k 1, [n (o) twice, skb] twice, k 1, n, o, k 6, n.

Row 108: O, k 2, o, snb, o, k 2, o, skb, k 6, o, skb, k 2, n, (o) twice, skb, k 2, n, o, k 6, n. Row 110: O, k 3, o, snb, o, k 3, o, skb, k 6, o, skb, k 6, n, o, k 6, n. Row 112: O, k 4, o, snb, o, k 4, o skb, k 6, o, skb, n, o, skb, n, o, k 6, n.

Row 114: O, k 5, o, snb, o, k 5, o, skb, k 6, o, skb, k 1, n, o, k 6, n. Row 116: O, k 6, o, snb, o, k 6, o, skb, k 6, o, snb, o, k 6, n. Row 118: O, k 5, n, o, k 3, o, skb, k 5, o, skb, k 13, n. Row 120: O, k 5, n, o, k 5, o, skb, k 5, o, skb, k 11, n.

Row 122: O, k 5, n, o, k 7, o, skb, k 5, o, skb, k 9, n.

Row 124: O, k 7, o, k 3, snb, k 3, o, k 7, o, skb, k 7, n.

Row 126: O, k 8, o, k 3, snb, k 3, o, k 8, o, skb, k 5, n.

Row 128: O, k 9, o, k 3, snb, k 3, o, k 9, o, skb, k 3, n.

Row 130: O, k 8, n, o, k 9, o, skb, k 8, o, skb, k 1, n.

Row 132: K 8, n, o, k 11, o, skb, k 8, o, snb, o. Row 134: k 4, n, k 3, o, k 2, o, skb, k 9, o, k 3, skb, k 4, o, k 3, o.

Row 136: K 3, n, skb, k 2, o, k 3, o, skb, k 8, o, k 2, n, skb, k 3,

o, n, o, k 1, o, skb, o. Row 138: K 2, n, skb, k 2, o, k 4, o, skb, k 7, o, k 2, n, skb, k 2, o, n, o, k 3, o, skb, o. Row 140: K 1, n, skb, k 2, o, k 5, o, skb, k 6, o, k 2, n, skb, k 1, (o, n) twice, o, k 1, (o, skb) twice, o.

Row 142: N, skb, k 2, o, k 6, o, skb, k 5, o, k 2, n, skb, o, (n, o) 2 times, k 3, (o, skb) twice, o, (36 sts in every pattern). Row 144: Snb, k 2, o, k 7, o, skb, k 4, o, k 2, snb, (o, n) three times, o, k 1, (o, skb) three times, o.

Row 146: Snb, k 1, o, k 8, o, skb, k 3, o, k 1, snb (o, n) three times, o, k 3, (o, skb) three times, o. Row 148: Snb, o, k 9, o, skb, k 2, o, snb, (o, n) four times, o, k 1, (o, skb) four times, o.

Row 150: Skb, o, k 4, n, o, k 1, o, skb, k 4 (o, n) five times, o, k 3, (o, skb) four times, o.

Row 152: K1b, o, k 1, o, skb, k 1, n, o, k 3, o, skb, k 1, n, o, k 1, o, k1b, (o, n) five times, o, k 1, (o, skb) five times, o.

Row 154: (skb, o) twice, snb, o, n, o, k 1, o, skb, o, snb, (o, n) seven times, o, k 3, (o, skb) five times, o.

Row 156: O, skb, o, (skb, o) twice, skb, k 1, (n, o) twice, k 1, o, (skb, o) three times, skb, k 1, (n, o) twice, k 1, o, snb, o, k 1, (o, skb) twice, k 1, (n, o) twice, K 1.

Row 158: O, k 3, o (skb, o) twice, snb, (o, n) twice, o, k 3, (o, skb) twice, o, snb, (o, n) twice, o, k 3, (o, skb) twice, o, snb, (o, n) twice.

Row 160: O, k 5, o, skb, o, skb, k 1, n, o, n. Row 162: O, k 7, o, skb, o, snb, o, n.

Row 164: O, k 9, o, skb, k 1, n. Row 166: O, k 11, o, snb.

Row 168: K 13, o, k 1, o.

Row 170: K 5, snb, k 5, o, k 3, o. Row 172: K 4, snb, k 4, o, k 5, o. Row 174: K 3, snb, k 3, o, k 7, o. Row 176: K 2, snb, k 2, o, k 9, o.

Row 178: K 1, snb, k 1, o, k 11, o. Row 180: O, snb, o, k 13.

Row 182: O, k 3, o, k 5, snb, k 5. Row 184: O, n, o, v 3, o, skb, o, k 4, snb, k 4.

Row 186: (O, n) twice, o, v 3, (o, skb) twice, o, k 3, snb, k 3.

Row 188: (o, n) twice, o, k 5, (o, skb) twice, o, k 2, snb, k 2.

Row 190: (o, n) twice, o, k 7, (o, skb) twice, o, k 1, snb, k 1.

Row 191: K.

Cast off using a crochet hook. Cast off 4 sts at one time, ch 12, cast off 5 sts at one time, ch 12, cast off 4 sts at one time, ch 12, cast off 4 sts at one time, ch 12, cast off 3 sts at one time, ch 12. Continue all around edge. Finished cloth is about 66 inches in diameter.

Place Mats and Napkin Rings

Jute and linen place mats, coasters, and napkin rings add the natural look that is so popular for today's casual dining.

Round Jute Place Mat

Materials
90 yds. 3 ply natural jute
Size K crochet hook

Directions
Ch 6, join with sl st to form a ring.

Rnd 1: Ch 1, make 6 sc in ring, join with sl st to first sc. Rnd 2: Ch 1, 2 sc in each sc around, join. Rnd 3: Ch 1, 2 sc in first sc, 1 sc in next sc, * 2 sc in next sc, 1 sc in next sc. Rep from * around, join.

Rnd 4: Ch 1, * 1 sc in first sc, 1 sc in next sc, 2 sc in next sc. Rep from * around, join. Rnd 5: Same as rnd 3.

Rnd 6: Same as rnd 4. Rnd 7: Ch 1, 1 sc in each of first 4 sc, 2 sc in fifth sc, * 1 sc in each of next 4 sc, 2 sc in fifth sc. Repeat from * around, join. Rnd 8: Ch 1, 1 sc in each sc around, join. Rnd 9: Same as rnd 8. Rnd 10: Same as rnd 7.

Rnd 11: Same as rnd 8. Rnd 12: Same as rnd 8. Rnd 13: Ch 1, 1 sc in each of first 5 sc, 2 sc in sixth sc, * 1 sc in each of next 5 sc, 2 sc in sixth sc. Repeat from * around, join. Rnd 14: Ch 1, 1 sc in each of first 6 sc, 2 sc in 7th sc, * 1 sc in each of next 6 sc, 2 sc in 7th sc. Repeat from * around, join.

Rnd 15 and 16: Same as rnd 8. Fasten off.

Matching Napkin Rings

Materials
6 yds. 3 ply natural jute
Size K crochet hook

continued

Contemporary Place Mats and Napkin Rings *(continued)*

Directions

Ch 10, join with sl st to form a ring.

Rnd 1: Ch 1, 1 sc in each ch st, join. Rnd 2: Ch 1, 1 sc in each sc, join. Rnd 3: Same as rnd 2. Fasten off.

Rectangular Jute Place Mat

Materials

60 yds. 3 ply natural jute
40 yds. 3 ply coral jute
Size K crochet hook

Directions

With natural jute, ch 31.

Row 1: 1 sc in second ch from hook and in each ch to end. Ch 1, turn. Row 2: 1 sc in first and each sc to end. Ch 1, turn. Repeat row 2 for next 24 rows. Fasten off.

Coral Trim—Row 1: 1 sc in each sc starting at right, top edge. 2 sc in same sc at corner and continue down side working 1 sc in between each row. Continue working bottom and other side in same way, ending with sl st to first sc of this row. Row 2: Ch 1, 1 sc in each sc around all four sides, ending with sl st to first sc of this row.

Row 3: * Ch 4, skip 2 sc, 1 sc in next sc. Repeat from * until scalloped on all 4 sides, ending with sl st to first sc of this row. Fasten off. (Skip only 1 sc at corners or wherever needed to make scallops look even.)

Matching Napkin Rings

Materials

6 yds. 3 ply coral jute
Size K crochet hook

Directions

Ch 10, join with sl st to form a ring. Rnd 1: Ch 1, 1 sc in each ch, join with sl st to first sc. Rnd 2: Ch 1, 1 sc in each sc, join. Rnd 3: * Ch 3, sk 1 sc, 1 sc in next sc.

Rep from * until scalloped all the way around, ending ch 3, sk 1 sc, join with sl st to first st in first scallop. Fasten off and turn inside out.

Scallop on other edge same way, keeping scallops directly across from each other.

Coral Coaster

Materials

14 yds. 3 ply coral jute
Size I crochet hook

Directions

Ch 4, join with sl st to form ring. Rnd 1: Ch 1, make 6 sc in ring. Join with sl st to first sc. Rnd 2: Ch 1, 2 sc in each sc around, join. Rnd 3: Ch 1, 2 sc in first sc, 1 sc in next sc, * 2 sc in next sc, 1 sc in next sc, rep from * around, join.

Rnd 4: Ch 1, * 1 sc in first sc, 1 sc in next sc, 2 sc in next sc, repeat from * around, join. Rnd 5: Same as rnd 3. Rnd 6: * Ch 3, skip 2 sc, 1 sc in next sc, repeat from * around, join. Fasten off.

Linen Openwork Place Mat

Materials

½-pound tube, F. J. Fawcett natural (10/2) linen yarn (for two place mats)
Size 8 knitting needles

Gauge

Seed st, 4 sts = 1 inch (blocked)

Directions

In addition to the basic k and p sts, you will need to know how to ksb, which means to k into the st below.

Pattern sts: (10 seed sts used for border not given in directions after pattern begins).

Seed st (even number)—Row 1: K 1, p 1. Row 2: P 1, k 1.

Seed st borders (1st 5 sts and last 5 sts)—Row 1: K 1, p 1, k 1, p 1, k 1, pattern sts, end p 1, k 1, p 1, k 1, p 1. Row 2: K 1, p 1, k 1, p 1, k 1, pattern sts, end p 1, k 1, p 1, k 1, p 1.

Ladder st—Multiple of 5 sts plus 1.

Row 1: * Ksb, k 2 tog, yo, k 2 tog *, rep * to * 13 times, end ksb.

Row 2: * P 2, (k 1, p 1, into yo), p 1 *, rep from * to * 13 times, end p 1.

Cast on 76 sts (after 5 sts put on marker and before last 5 sts. These sts are always seed sts and not included in directions for place mat).

Row 1, 2, 3, 4, 5, 6, 7: Seed st.

Row 8: P the 66 sts bet markers.

Row 9: Begin pat rows 1 and 2, rep 25 times.

Row 59: K across row between markers, being sure to ksb as in previous rows.

Rep 7 rows of seed st. Cast off in pat (this means to con in seed st in cast off row).

Blocking—Dampen mat in medium strength starch and block to size.

Napkin Ring for Linen Place Mat

Materials

Leftover linen from place mats
Size 8 knitting needles

Directions

Cast on 10 sts.

Row 1: K. Row 2: P.

Row 3: * K 2, ksb, k 2 tog, yo, k 2 tog, ksb, k 2.

Row 4: K 2, p 2, k 1, p 1, into yo, p 2, k 2. Rep rows 3 and 4 four times. K 4 rows *. Rep from * to * 3 times. *Note:* Always ksb on 3rd and 8th sts.

Cast off and sew two ends tog.

Blocking—Dip napking ring in full strength starch and slip it onto any bottle that measures six inches in circumference. Dry, then remove napkin ring.

Spiral Crocheted Table Toppers

Once you've mastered this basic pattern, you can make lots of different-size mats for your table. An entire luncheon set of this tasteful design will go well with several different-style table settings. Here, you see a touch of the old fashioned combined with a natural contemporary look. You may also use this tasteful pattern for much more elegant dining. Or if you like, make a single doily or a set of small coasters as a charming gift.

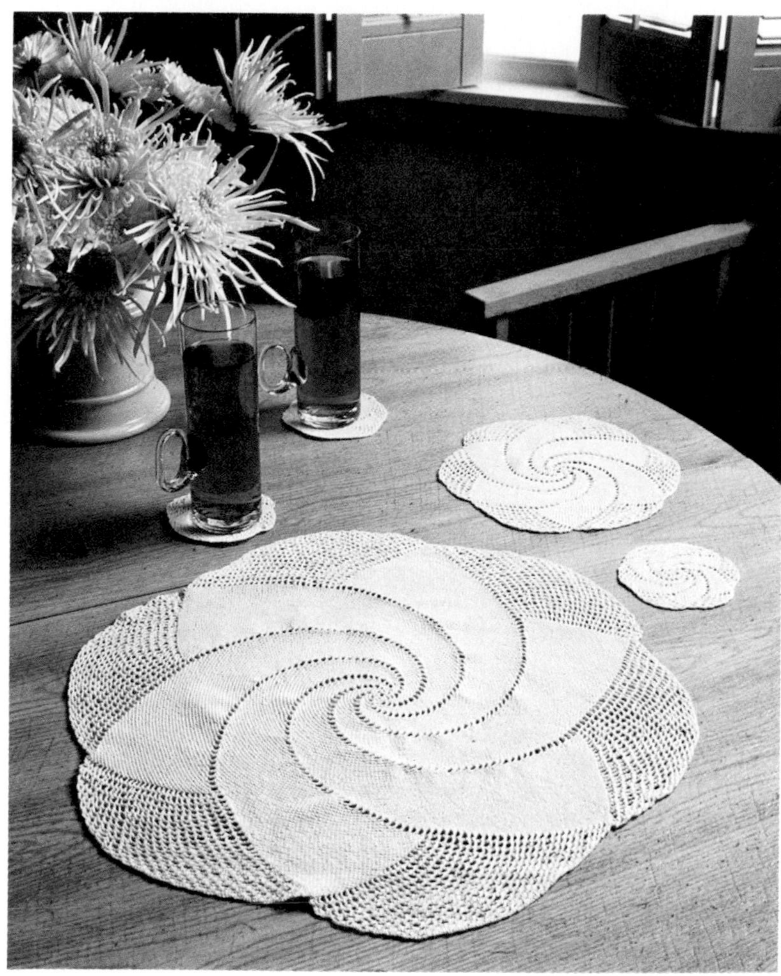

Materials

J. & P. Coats "Knit-Cro-Sheen"
Amount determined by size and number of doilies
Size 7 steel crochet hook

Directions

Note: Place mat measures 17¼ inches in diameter; next size, 7½ inches in diameter; next size, 4¾ inches in diameter; smallest size, 4¼ inches in diameter.

Ch 5, join with sl st to form a ring.

Rnd 1: * ch 4, sc in ring, rep from * 5 more times (6 loops on this rnd). Hereafter, do not join rnds.

Rnd 2: * ch 4, 2 sc in loop, rep from * around.

Rnd 3: * ch 4, 2 sc in loop, sc in next sc, rep from * around.

Rep rnd 3 until desired size, then * ch 4, sc in loop, ch 4, sk first sc, sc in each sc skipping the last sc, rep from * around.

Continue in this manner, having 2 less sc in each sc group and 1 loop more bet sc groups in each rnd, until 1 sc remains in each sc group. End last rnd with ch 2, dc in first sc to form last loop.

If the piece seems to need extra sts to allow it to lie flat, increase the amount of sts in the ch between the sc groups.

Continue as described until the doily has attained the desired size.

When groups of loops meet, fasten off thread. Steam press doily to block.

MEASURING WORK

Spread your knit or crochet articles out on a flat surface without stretching them. Measure down the center.

When you are measuring the length, always place a marker, such as a safety pin or piece of colored thread, in the center of the row so that the measurement from that point will be accurate.

Country-Style Crocheted Place Mats

For a quick and easy crochet project that's bound to attract rave notices, try these flower place mats. Made of washable rug yarn, they're no problem when it's time to launder them.

Materials

Coats & Clark's Craft and Rug Yarn, 140 yd. pull-out skeins
- 3 cocoa brown
- 2 ivory
- 2 dk. brown

Size I crochet hook

Note: The above material will make 5 mats, each 17 inches in diameter.

Directions

First flower—Starting at center with cocoa brown, ch 8. Join with sl st to form ring. Rnd 1: Ch 1, * sc in ring, ch 3, then, holding back on hook the last loop of each tr, make 2 tr in same ring, yo hook and draw through all 3 lps on hook—cluster made; ch 3. Rep from * 5 times. Join with sl st to first sc—6 petals. Fasten off. Mark first flower as center flower.

Second flower—With cocoa brown, ch 8. Join to form ring. Rnd 1: Ch 1, in ring make sc, ch 3 and cluster, with wrong side of first flower facing, join with sl st to top of any petal on first flower, ch 3. Rep from * on first rnd of first flower. Fasten off.

Third flower—With cocoa brown, ch 8. Join. Rnd 1: Ch 1, in ring make sc, ch 3 and cluster, with wrong side facing, join to top of next free petal on first flower to the right of previous joining of petals; ch 3, in same ring make sc, ch 3 and cluster, join to top of next free petal on second flower, ch 3 and complete flower as before. Make and join 3 more flowers as third flower was joined to first and second flowers.

Seventh flower—Work as before until first and second petals have been joined; work 3 more petals; then make another petal joining it to corresponding petals on first and second flowers.

Border—Attach ivory to any joining sl st between petals on outer edge of center. Rnd 1: Ch 1, sc in same place where yarn was attached, * (ch 5, sc in top of next cluster) 3 times; ch 5, sc in joining sl st between next 2 petals. Rep from * around. Join last ch 5 to first sc—24 lps. Rnd 2: Ch 1, 5 sc in each lp around. Join to first sc. Fasten off.

Attach dark brown to center sc on any lp. Rnd 3: Ch 1, sc in same place where yarn was attached, * ch 5, sc in center sc on next loop. Rep from * around. Join. Rnd 4: Ch 1, sc in same place as sl st, * 5 sc in next lp, sc in next sc. Rep from * around. Join.

Rnd 5: Sl st in next 2 sc, ch 1, sc in next sc, * ch 6, sk next 5 sc, sc in next sc. Rep from * around. Join. Rnd 6: Ch 5, in same place as sl st make tr, ch 1 and tr, * ch 1, tr in next lp, ch 1, in next sc make (tr, ch 1) twice and tr. Rep from * around. Join to fourth ch of ch 5. Fasten off.

Attach ivory to center tr of any 3 tr group. Rnd 7: Ch 1, sc where yarn was attached, * ch 3, sk next tr, sc in next tr, ch 3, sc in center tr of next 3 tr group. Rep from * around. Join. Rnd 8: Ch 1, 3 sc in each lp around. Join. Ch 1, turn and work sl st loosely in each sc. Join to first sl st. Fasten off.

With rust-proof pins, pin mat out to measurement and steam lightly through damp cloth. Allow to dry thoroughly before removing pins so it will retain blocked measurement.

For Your Bedroom

What could add more beauty and character to a bedroom than a handmade crocheted or knitted bedspread, an assortment of pillows, or even a coverlet for a baby's bassinet or crib? Comfort and an air of relaxation are of prime importance in furnishing and decorating bedrooms, and these lovely patterns convey that message. You will find traditional, contemporary, and country styles. And by adding or deleting a few stitches, you can adapt them to fit any bed size. Instructions for the bed cover and pillows shown here are given on pages 208 and 209.

Knitted Bed Cover and Pillows *(shown on pages 206 and 207)*

Our beautifully patterned bed cover snugs a mattress like a contour sheet. It measures 39x75x7½ inches thick and fits a single bed mattress.

Key pillows to drawings. Ssk means slip 2 sts knitwise, and k the two tog.

Knitted Bed Cover

Materials

Coats & Clark "Speed-Cro-Sheen"
35 balls brown
Size 5 36-inch-long circular knitting needle
4 yds. ¼-inch-wide elastic

Gauge

19 sts = 4 inches, 13 rows = 2 inches

Directions

Top—Starting at the lower edge, cast on 185 sts; do not join. Turn. Starting with a p row, work 4 rows in stockinette stitch (p 1 row, k 1 row).

Work pat as follows—Row 1: (wrong side) p across.

Row 2: K 3, * yo, with yarn in back sl 1 as if to p, k 1, psso, k 7, k 2 tog, yo, k 1. Rep from * across, end last rep with yo, k 3. Row 3 and all wrong-side rows: p across.

Row 4: K 4, * yo, sl 1, k 1, psso, k 5, k 2 tog, yo, k 3. Rep from * across, end last rep with yo, k 4. Row 6: K 3, * (yo, sl 1, k 1, psso) twice; k 3, (k 2 tog, yo) twice; k 1. Rep from * across, end last rep with k 3. Row 8: K 4, * (yo, sl 1, k 1, psso) twice; k 1, (k 2 tog, yo) twice; k 3.

Rep from * across, end last rep with k 4. Row 10: K 3, * (yo, sl 1, k 1, psso) twice; yo, sl 1, k 2 tog, psso, yo, (k 2 tog, yo) twice; k 1. Rep from * across, end last rep with k 3.

Row 12: Rep row 8. Row 14: K 5, * yo, sl 1, k 1, psso, yo, sl 1, k 2 tog, psso, yo, k 2 tog, yo, k 5. Rep from * across. Row 16: K 6, * yo, sl 1, k 1, psso, k 1, k 2 tog, yo, k 7. Rep from * across, end last rep with k 6. Row 18: K 7, * yo, sl 1, k 2 tog, psso, yo, k 9. Rep from * across, end last rep with yo, k 7. Rows 20, 22, and 24: K across. Row 25: P across.

Rep these 24 rows (rows 2 through 25) for pattern until total length is about 72 inches, ending with row 23. Bind off.

Note: Two or three inches are allowed for stretching when blocking.

Side—Cast on 42 sts. Row 1: K 2 for casing, sl 1 as if to k for turning ridge of casing; k 39. Row 2: P across. Rep these two rows alternately until total length is about 216 inches, without stretching. Bind off. Stretch side to measure about 225 inches when blocking.

Finishing—Block to measurements. Sew short edges of side piece tog. Turn casing to wrong side at turning ridge and stitch in place, leaving a 1-inch opening for elastic. Sew opposite long edge of side to outer edge of top with seam at a corner, and easing in outer edge of top to fit. Slip elastic through casing; pull to desired length and cut elastic, allowing 1 inch for sewing. Sew ends of elastic together; sew across opening.

Small Ecru Pillow (No. 1)

Materials

Cotton parcel post twine
300 yds.
Size 6 knitting needles
½ yd. lining fabric
Thread
1 lb. Dacron/polyester stuffing

Gauge

9 sts = 2 inches, 7 rows = 1 inch

Directions

Pillow front—Cast on 52 sts.

Row 1: (wrong side) p.

Row 2: K 2, * yo, k 2 tog, k 4, ssk, yo, k 2; rep from *. *Note:* Ssk, means to slip 2 stitches knitwise, then knit the 2 sts tog. Rep rows 1 and 2 (pat) until 12 inches from beginning. Bind off all sts. Make back same as front.

Finishing—Block each piece to a 12-inch square (string will stretch slightly when pillow is stuffed): Sew three sides together. Cut two pieces of fabric 13½ inches square and with right sides together, stitch on three sides (½-inch seams). Turn lining right side out, press, stuff, and slip-stitch fourth side closed. Insert pillow in knitted cover; stitch fourth side of cover closed.

Natural Jute Pillow (No. 2)

Materials

4 ply jute
2 balls natural
Size 10½ knitting needles
½ yd. lining fabric
Thread
Dacron/polyester pillow stuffing

Gauge

3 sts = 1 inch, 3 rows = 1 inch

Directions

Pillow front—Cast on 42 sts. Follow pat (rows 1 and 2) given for small ecru pillow above. Continue pat until 14 inches from beg. Bind off. Make back same as front.

Finishing—Block both pieces to measure 14x17 inches. Sew three sides together. Cut two pieces of fabric 15½x18½ inches for lining. Stitch together on three sides, turn to right side, press, and stuff. Stitch fourth side closed. Insert lining in pillow cover; stitch fourth side of cover closed.

Natural String Pillow (No. 3)

Materials

Parcel post twine, 160 yd. balls
4 balls
Size 10 knitting needles
½ yd. lining fabric
Thread
Dacron/polyester pillow stuffing
Sewing needle

Gauge

3 sts = 1 inch, 4 rows = 1 inch

Directions

Pillow front—Working with two strands of string together, cast on 48 sts. Rows 1 and 2: P.

Row 3 (wrong side): K.

Row 4: * k 1, (yo, ssk) 3 times, k 1; rep from *.

Rows 5, 7, 9, 11: P.

Rows 6, 10: * k 2, (yo, ssk) 2 times, k 2; rep from *.

Row 8: * k 3, yo, ssk, k 3; repeat from *.

Row 12: Rep row 4.

For pat, rep rows 1 to 12 four more times. Rep rows 1 to 3 once. Bind off. Make back the same.

Finishing—Block pieces to measure 14x16 inches. Stitch tog on three sides. Cut two pieces of fabric 15½x17½ inches. Stitch together on three sides, turn, press, stuff, and stitch fourth side closed. Insert pillow form; stitch fourth side closed.

Spice-Colored Pillow (No. 4)

Materials

Coats & Clark "Speed-Cro-Sheen"
4 balls spice
Size 8 knitting needles
½ yd. lining fabric
Thread
Dacron/polyester pillow stuffing

Gauge

4 sts = 1 inch, 6 rows = 1 inch

Directions

Front and back—Working with two strands together, cast on 40 sts. Then, follow instructions for working front and back of natural string pillow (No. 3) above.

Finishing—Block both pieces to 12x11 inches. Stitch three sides together. Cut two pieces of fabric 13½x14½, stitch together on three sides. Turn, press, stuff, and stitch fourth side closed. Insert pillow form in cover; sew fourth side of pillow closed.

Filet-Patterned Bed Coverlet (or Tablecloth)

This old and treasured pattern has just as much appeal today as it ever did. To crochet a spread this size, you need twenty 10½-inch-square blocks. Or alter the dimensions to fit any bed (or table).

Materials
Bedspread Crochet Cotton, 650 yd. balls
8 balls white
Size 5 steel crochet hook

Gauge
Each square approximately 10½ x10½ inches without edging

Directions
Ch 8, join with sl st to form a ring.

Row 1: Ch 3 (counts as first dc), make 3 more dc in ring, * ch 5, 4 dc in ring, rep from * around twice more, ending with ch 5, sl st in top of first dc.

Row 2: Ch 3 (counts as first dc), dc in next 3 dc (3 dc in next sp, ch 5, 3 dc in same sp)—makes corner sp—dc in next 4 dc, 3 dc in next sp, ch 5, 3 dc in same sp, dc in next 4 dc, 3 dc in next sp, ch 5, 3 dc in same sp, dc in next 4 dc, 3 dc in next sp, ch 5, 3 dc in same sp, sl st in top of first dc.

Row 3: Ch 5, sk 2 dc, dc in next dc, ch 2, sk 2 dc, dc in next dc, * ch 2, dc in center st of next ch 5 sp, ch 5, dc in same sp, ch 2, dc in next dc, ch 2, sk 2 dc, dc in next dc, ch 2, sk 2 dc, dc in next dc, ch 2, sk 2 dc, dc in next dc, rep from * twice more. End with ch 2; join with sl st in third st of starting ch.

Row 4: Ch 5, dc in next dc, ch 2, dc in next dc, 2 dc in next sp, dc in next dc, 3 dc in next sp, ch 5, 3 dc in same sp, dc in next dc, * 2 dc in next sp, dc in next dc, (ch 2, dc in next dc) 3 times, 2 dc in next sp, dc in next dc (3 dc, ch 5, 3 dc) in corner sp, rep from * twice more. Then dc in next dc, 2 dc in next sp, ch 2, sl st in third st of starting ch.

Row 5: Ch 5, dc in next dc, 2 dc in next sp, dc in next 7 dc * (3 dc, ch 5, 3 dc) in next sp, dc in next 7 dc, 2 dc in next sp, dc in next dc, ch 2, dc in next dc, 2 dc in next sp, dc in next 7 dc, rep from * twice more, ending with 2 dc in next sp, sl st in top of first dc.

Row 6: Ch 5, dc in next dc (ch 2, sk 2 dc, dc in next dc) 4 times, * ch 2, dc in center st of next sp, ch 5, dc in same sp as last dc, ch 2, dc in next dc (ch 2, sk 2 dc, dc in next dc) 4 times, ch 2, dc in next dc (ch 2, sk 2 dc, dc in next dc) 4 times, rep from * once more, ending with ch 2, sl st in third st of starting ch.

Row 7: Ch 5, dc in next dc (ch 2, dc in next dc) 3 times, (2 dc in next sp, dc in next dc) 2 times, 3 dc, ch 5, 3 dc in next sp (corner sp), * dc in next dc (2 dc in next sp, dc in next dc) twice, (ch 2, dc in next dc) 7 times, (2 dc in next sp, dc in next dc) twice, (3 dc, ch 5, 3 dc) in next sp, rep from * twice more. Then (dc in next dc, 2 dc in next sp) twice, dc in next dc, ch 2, dc in next dc, ch 2, dc in next dc, ch 2, sl st in third st of starting ch.

Row 8: Ch 5, dc in next dc (ch 2, dc in next dc) twice, 2 dc in next sp, dc in next 10 dc's, (3 dc, ch 5, 3 dc), corner sp, * dc in next 10 dc, 2 dc in next sp, dc in next dc (ch 2, dc in next dc) 5 times, 2 dc in next sp, dc in next 10 dc's, (3 dc, ch 5, 3 dc), corner sp, rep

continued

Filet-Patterned Bedspread *(continued)*

from * twice more, ending with dc in next 10 dc, 2 dc in next sp, dc in next dc, ch 2, dc in next dc, ch 2, sl st in third st of starting ch.

Row 9: Ch 5, dc in next dc (ch 2, dc in next dc) twice, (ch 2, sk 2 dc, dc in next dc) 5 times, ch 2, dc in third st of corner ch, ch 5, dc in same sp as last dc, ch 2, dc in next dc, * (ch 2, sk 2 dc, dc in next dc) 5 times, (ch 2, dc in next dc) 5 times, (ch 2, sk 2 dc, dc in next dc) 5 times, ch 2, dc in third st of corner ch, ch 5, dc in same sp as last dc, ch 2, dc in next dc, rep from * twice more, ending with (ch 2, sk 2 dc, dc in next dc) 5 times, ch 2, dc in next dc, ch 2, sl st in third st of ch.

Row 10: Ch 5, dc in next dc, (ch 2, dc in next sp) 5 times * (2 dc in next sp, dc in next dc) 3 times, in corner sp make 3 dc, ch 5, 3 dc, dc in next dc, (2 dc in next sp, dc in next dc) 3 times, (ch 2, dc in next dc) 11 times, rep from * 3 more times ending with (ch 2, dc in next dc) 4 times, ch 2, sl st in third st of starting ch.

Row 11: Ch 5, dc in next dc (ch 2, dc in next dc) 4 times, 2 dc in next sp, dc in next 13 dc, in corner sp make 3 dc, ch 5, 3 dc, * dc in next 13 dc, 2 dc in next sp, dc in next dc (ch 2, dc in next dc) 9 times, 2 dc in next sp, dc in next 13 dc, in corner sp make 3 dc, ch 5, 3 dc, rep from * three more times, ending with dc in next 13 dc, 2 dc in next sp, dc in next dc, (ch 2, dc in next dc) 3 times, ch 2, sl st in third st of ch.

Row 12: Ch 5, dc in next dc, (ch 2, sk 2 dc, dc in next dc) 6 times, * ch 2, dc in third st of corner sp, ch 5, dc in same sp as last dc, ch 2, dc in next dc, (ch 2, sk next 2 dc, dc in next dc) 6 times, (ch 2, dc in next dc) 9 times, (ch 2, sk next 2 dc, dc in next dc) 6 times, rep from * twice more, ending with (ch 2, dc in next dc) 3 times, ch 2, sl st in third st of starting ch.

Row 13: Ch 3, 2 dc in next sp, dc in next dc, (ch 2, dc in next dc) 7 times, * 2 dc in next sp, (dc in next dc) 4 times, in corner sp make 3 dc, ch 5, 3 dc, (dc in next dc, 2 dc in next sp) 4 times, (ch 2, dc in next dc) 7 times, 2 dc in next sp, dc in next dc, (ch 2, dc in next dc) 7 times, rep from * three more times, (dc in next dc, 2 dc in next sp) 4 times, (ch 2, dc in next dc) 6 times, ending with ch 2, sl st in top of first dc.

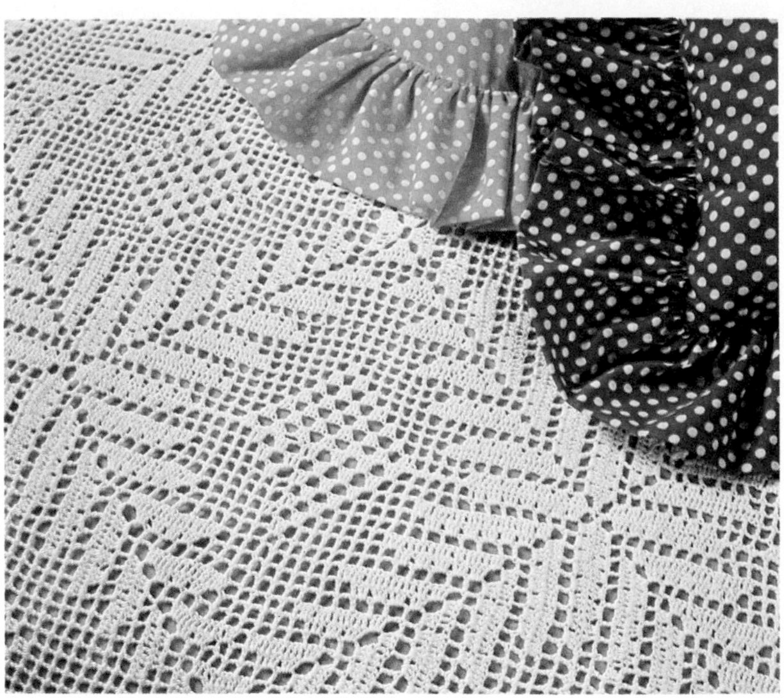

Row 14: Ch 5, sk next 2 dc, dc in next dc, 2 dc in next sp, dc in next dc (ch 2, dc in next dc) 5 times, * 2 dc in next sp, dc in next 16 dc, in corner sp make 3 dc, ch 5, 3 dc, dc in next 16 dc, 2 dc in next sp, dc in next dc, (ch 2, dc in next dc) 5 times, 2 dc in next sp, dc in next dc, ch 2, sk 2 dc, dc in next dc, 2 dc in next sp, dc in next dc, (ch 2, dc in next dc) 5 times, rep from * twice more, ending with 2 dc in next sp, dc in next 16 dc, in corner sp make 3 dc, ch 5, 3 dc, dc in next 16 dc, 2 dc in next sp, dc in next dc (ch 2, dc in next dc) 5 times, ch 2, sl st in third st of ch.

Row 15: Ch 3, 2 dc in next sp, dc in next dc, ch 2, sk next 2 dc, dc in next dc, 2 dc in next sp, dc in next dc (ch 2, dc in next dc) 4 times, (ch 2, sk 2 dc, dc in next dc) 7 times, ch 2, dc in center st of next sp, ch 5, dc in same sp, ch 2, dc in next dc, * (ch 2, sk next 2 dc, dc in next dc) 7 times, (ch 2, dc in next dc) 4 times, 2 dc in next sp, dc in next dc, ch 2, sk next 2 dc, dc in next dc, 2 dc in next sp, dc in next dc, ch 2, sk 2 dc, dc in next dc, 2 dc in next sp, dc in next dc, (ch 2, dc in next dc) 4 times, (ch 2, sk 2 dc, dc in next dc) 7 times, ch 2, dc in center st of next sp, ch 5, dc in same st, ch 2, dc in next dc, rep from * twice more, ending with (ch 2, sk 2 dc, dc in next dc) 7 times, (ch 2, dc in next dc) 4 times, 2 dc in next sp, dc in next dc, ch 2, sl st in top of first dc.

Row 16: Ch 5, sk 2 dc, dc in next dc, 2 dc in next sp, dc in next dc, ch 2, sk 2 dc, dc in next dc, 2 dc in next sp, dc in next dc, (ch 2, dc in next dc) 6 times, (2 dc in next sp, dc in next dc) 5 times, in corner sp make 3 dc, ch 5, 3 dc, dc in next dc, * (2 dc in next sp, dc in next dc) 5 times, (ch 2, dc in next dc) 6 times, 2 dc in next sp, dc in next dc, ch 2, sk 2 dc, dc in next dc, 2 dc in next sp, dc in next dc, ch 2, sk 2 dc, dc in next dc, 2 dc in next sp, dc in next dc, (ch 2, dc in next dc) 6 times, (2 dc in next sp, dc in next dc) 5 times, in corner sp make 3 dc, ch 5, 3 dc, dc in next dc, rep from * twice more, ending with (2 dc in next sp, dc in next dc) 5 times, (ch 2, dc in next dc) 6 times, 2 dc in next sp, dc in next dc, ch 2, sk 2 dc, dc in next dc, 2 dc in next sp, sl st in top of first dc.

Row 17: Ch 3 (counts as first dc), 2 dc in next sp, dc in next dc, ch 2, sk 2 dc, dc in next dc, 2 dc in next sp, dc in next dc, ch 2, sk 2 dc, dc in next dc, 2 dc in next sp, dc in next dc (ch 2, dc in next dc) 4 times, dc in next dc, 2 dc in next sp, dc in next 19 dc, in corner sp make 3 dc, ch 5, * dc in next 19 dc, 2 dc in next sp, dc in next dc, (ch 2, dc in next dc) 4 times, (2 dc in next sp, dc in next dc, ch 2, sk next 2 dc, dc in next dc) 4 times, 2 dc in next sp, dc in next dc, sk 2 dc, dc in next dc, 2 dc in next sp, dc in next dc, sk 2 dc, dc in next dc, 2 dc in next sp, dc in next dc, sk 2 dc, dc in next dc, 2 dc in next sp, dc in next dc, (ch 2, dc in next dc) 4 times, 2 dc in next sp, dc in next 19 dc, in corner sp make 3 dc, ch 5, 3 dc, rep from * twice more, ending with dc in next 19 dc, 2 dc in next sp, dc in next dc (ch 2, dc in next dc) 4 times, 2 dc in next sp, dc in next dc, ch 2, sk 2 dc, dc in next dc, 2 dc in next sp, dc in next dc, ch 2, sl st in top of first dc.

Row 18: Ch 5, dc in next dc, 2 dc in next sp, dc in next dc, ch 2, sk 2 dc, dc in next dc, 2 dc in next sp, dc in next dc, ch 2, sk 2 dc, dc in next dc, 2 dc in next sp, dc in next dc, ch 2, sk 2 dc, dc in next dc, 2 dc in next sp, dc in next dc (ch 2, dc in next dc) 3 times, (ch 2, sk 2 dc, dc in next dc) 8 times, ch 2, dc in center st of corner, ch 5, dc in same st, ch 2, dc in next dc, * (ch 2, sk 2 dc, dc in next dc) 8 times, (ch 2, dc in next dc) 3 times, (2 dc in next sp, dc in next dc, sk next 2 dc, dc in next dc) 5 times, 2 dc in next sp, dc in next dc (ch 2, dc in next dc) 3 times, (ch 2, sk 2 dc, dc in next dc) 8 times, ch 2, dc in center st of corner sp, ch 5, dc in same st, rep from * twice more, ending with (ch 2, sk 2 dc, dc in next dc) 8 times, (ch 2, dc in next dc) 3 times, 2 dc in next sp, dc in next dc, ch 2, sk 2 dc, dc in next dc, 2 dc in next sp, dc in next dc, ch 2, sk 2 dc, dc in next dc, 2 dc in next sp, sl st in third st of ch.

Row 19: Ch 3, 2 dc in next sp, dc in next dc (ch 2, sk 2 dc, dc in next dc, 2 dc in next sp, dc in next dc) 3 times, (ch 2, dc in next dc) 5 times, (2 dc in next sp, dc in next dc) 6 times, in corner sp make 3 dc, ch 5, 3 dc, * dc in next dc, (2 dc in next sp, dc in next dc) 6 times, (ch 2, dc in next dc) 5 times, (2 dc in next sp, dc in next dc, ch 2, sk 2 dc, dc in next dc) 6 times, 2 dc in next sp, dc in next dc, (ch 2, dc in next dc) 5 times, (2 dc in next sp, dc in next dc) 6 times, in corner sp make 3 dc, ch 5, 3 dc, rep from * twice more, ending with (2 dc in next sp, dc in next dc) 6 times, (ch 2, dc in next dc) 5 times, 2 dc in next sp, dc in next dc, ch 2, sk 2 dc, dc in next dc, 2 dc in next sp, dc in next dc, ch 2, sl st in top of first dc.

Joining blocks—Sew all blocks together with a whipstitch, being careful to match stitches. See photo at the left.

Edging—Row 1: Attach thread in any corner sp, ch 3 (counts as first dc), dc in same sp, ch 2, sk 2 dc, dc in next 2 dc, ch 2, sk 2 dc, dc in next 2 dc. Con in this manner, evenly spacing 2 dc around. In the corners make 2 dc, ch 5, 2 dc. End rnd by making 1 dc, ch 5 in beg corner, make sl st in top of first dc.

Row 2: Ch 3 (counts as first dc), dc in same sp, ch 3, 2 dc in next sp, ch 3, 2 dc in next sp. Continue in this manner until corner sp, then make 2 dc, ch 5, 2 dc, in next sp make 2 dc, ch 3, 2 dc. Continue on around work ending with ch 5, sl st in top of first dc.

Row 3: Rep row 2.

Row 4: Ch 3 (counts as first dc), ch 1, dc in same sp, ch 1, dc in same sp, ch 1, dc in same sp, ch 1, dc in same sp (this makes 5 dc with ch 1 sp bet) in corner sp, then ch 3, sk next 3 sp, in next ch 3 sp make (dc, ch 1) 5 times. Continue in pattern. In each corner sp, make (dc, ch 1) 5 times. End rnd with sl st in top of first dc.

Row 5: Sl st to first sp bet dc's, ch 5, sl st in first st of ch making a picot, sc in next sp, ch 5, picot, sc in next sp, ch 5, picot, sc in next sp, ch 3, sc in next sp, ch 3, sc in sp bet dc's, ch 5, picot. Continue on in pattern, ending with ch 3, sl st in first st.

Crocheted Bed Canopy or Valance

Remember when your favorite linen hankies were trimmed with dainty hand-crocheted edgings? If so, you'll be amazed to know that this bold bed canopy was made from just such an old-fashioned edging pattern. Executed in natural jute, it makes a world of difference.

Why not experiment with expanding the scope of old crochet patterns in new ways like this? Besides using this pattern for a bed canopy, use it also to make dramatic valances to add the finishing touch to simple window treatments.

Materials

4 ply jute (amount determined by length of valance)
Size J crochet hook
Note: Scallops are 20 inches deep and 16 inches across. Experiment with various weights of cord, string, or jute, and with different sizes of crochet hooks to get a valance that is in scale with your particular needs.

Directions

Ch 17. Row 1: Dc in fourth ch from hook, 1 dc in next ch, in next ch make cluster, ch 2, cluster, (to make cluster: make 3 dc in same sp, holding back last loop of each, thread over and through all loops at once), ch 2, sk 2 ch, cluster in next ch, ch 2, dc in last ch.

Row 2: Ch 3, turn; make cluster with the turning ch counting as first dc and 2 dc in next sp, ch 2, cluster in next sp, ch 2, (cluster, ch 2, cluster) in ch 2 sp between previous clusters, dc in next dc, ch 3, dc in each of next 3 dc, dc in turning ch.

Row 3: Ch 3, turn; dc in each of next 3 dc, ch 3, dc in next dc, (cluster, ch 2, cluster) in center of previous double cluster, ch 2, cluster in next sp, ch 2, cluster in next sp, ch 2, cluster in turning ch.

Row 4: Ch 3, turn; sk first sp, cluster in next sp, ch 2, cluster in next sp, ch 2 (cluster, ch 2, cluster) in center of previous double cluster, dc in next dc, ch 3, dc in each of next 3 dc and in turning ch.

Row 5: Ch 3, turn; dc in each of next 3 dc, ch 3, dc in next dc, (cluster, ch 2, cluster) in center sp of previous double clusters, ch 2, cluster in next sp, dc in top of next cluster.

Row 6: Ch 3, turn; sk first sp, in center of previous double clusters make (cluster, ch 2, cluster), dc in next dc, ch 3, dc in each of next 3 dc, dc in turning ch.

Row 7: Ch 3, turn; dc in each of next 3 dc, ch 3, dc in next dc, in center of previous double clusters make (cluster, ch 2, cluster) ch 2, cluster in next sp, ch 2, dc in turning ch of previous row.

Ch 3, turn; go back and rep from row 2 for pat, until reaching desired length. End work with row 2.

Edging—(Do not cut jute) Ch 5, turn, sc in top of fourth dc, ch 5, sc in next sp, ch 5, sc in next sp, ch 5, sc in next sp, etc. Continue on in this manner having ch 5 loops around bottom of work. When you get to the end, ch 1, turn work around, make 8 sc in each loop around. At end, sl st in last sc and cut jute.

Crib Coverlets

A handmade coverlet for a baby's crib, carriage, or bassinet is surely a labor of love. Whether it's for your own baby—or a gift for someone else's—you'll delight in trying these easy-to-stitch patterns.

Coverlet on Chair

Materials

Columbia-Minerva Nantuk Bulky, 2 oz. skeins
- 2 green (A)
- 2 lt. green (B)
- 2 yellow (C)
- 2 orange (D)
- 2 peach (E)
- 2 pink (F)

Size K crochet hook

Gauge

1 pat (13 sts) = 4½ inches; 1 row = 1 inch

Directions

With A, ch 87 to measure approximately 32 inches.

Row 1: Dc in 3rd ch from hook (ch 2 always counts as first dc), dc in each of next 2 ch, (sk 1 ch, dc in each of next 5 ch, 3 dc in next ch, dc in each of next 5 ch, sk 1 ch) 6 times, dc in each of last 3 ch, working off last 2 loops of last dc with B, cut A. Ch 2, turn.

Row 2: Sk first dc, through *back loops* only dc in each of next 2 dc, (sk 1 dc, dc in each of next 5 dc, 3 dc in next dc, dc in next 5 dc, sk 1 dc) 6 times, dc in each of last 3 dc, working off last 2 loops of last dc with C, cut B. Ch 2, turn.

Row 3: Working through *front loops* only rep row 2, working off last 2 loops of last dc with D, cut C, ch 2, turn.

Row 4: Rep row 2, working off last 2 loops of last dc with E, cut D, ch 2, turn.

Row 5: Rep row 3, working off last 2 loops of last dc with F, cut E, ch 2, turn.

Row 6: Rep row 2, working off last 2 loops of last dc with A.

Continue in color sequence and pat (ridge is always on same side) until there is a total of 37 color stripes, ending with A stripe. Do not fasten off. Secure all ends, matching color stripes.

Edging—Rnd 1: Ch 1, turn. Through *back loops* only, work sl st loosely in each dc to corner, 2 sc in each row to lower edge, sl st in each ch (base of dc) to corner, 2 sc in each row to top edge. Join and fasten off. Join A in first sc on side edge. From same side as first rnd, work sl st loosely in each sc on edge. Join and fasten off. Work sl st in same way on other side. Steam lightly.

Coverlet on Bassinet

Materials

Coats & Clark Craft and Rug Yarn, 4 oz. skeins
- 2 white
- 2 lime green
- 3 yellow

Size H aluminum crochet hook

Gauge

Each square measures 3¾ inches

Directions

Make 15 squares, using lime for the 1st rnd, yellow for 2nd rnd, and white for 3rd rnd. Make 20 squares, using white for the 1st rnd, lime for 2nd rnd, and yellow for 3rd rnd.

Basic square—With 1st color ch 4; join with sl st to form a ring. Rnd 1: Ch 3 (counts as 1 dc) 2 dc in center of ring, * ch 3, 3 dc in center of ring, rep from * 2 more times, end with ch 3; join with sl st to top of ch 3. End off.

Rnd 2: With 2nd color, in ch 3 sp of previous rnd work (ch 3, 2 dc, ch 3, 3 dc) corner, * in next ch 3 sp work (3 dc, ch 3, 3 dc), rep from * twice, join with sl st to top of ch 3. End off.

Rnd 3: With 3rd color, (ch 3, 2 dc, ch 3, 3 dc) in ch 3 at corner sp, then work 3 dc between each 3 dc group on sides and (3 dc, ch 3, 3 dc) in each corner; join with sl st. End off.

Assembling—Arrange the blocks with the 15 blocks that have lime for the 1st rnd in three rows with five blocks in each row. Use the 20 squares that have white for the 1st rnd to make a border rectangular center section. Whipstitch together on wrong side, picking up top back loops only.

Border—Row 1: With yellow work 3 dc between groups of dc along all edges, and (3 dc, ch 3, 3 dc) in each corner. End off.

Rows 2, 3, 4, and 5: Repeat as for row 1, alternating with lime and white rows.

Note: To make picot, ch 3, sl st in first ch. Row 6: Attach yellow to ch 3 corner, (ch 3, 2 dc, ch 3, picot, 3 dc) in same sp, * picot, 3 dc between next group of dc, repeat from * along all edges, and (3 dc, picot, 3 dc) in each corner; join with sl st to top of ch 3. End off.

LEFTOVER YARN

■ *You can use leftover yarns for many projects. Just be sure that it's all the same weight and fiber.*

■ *You can also use fine yarns, if you combine two or more strands with heavier yarns, such as knitting worsted. (Work a small sample to see exactly how many strands produce the same weight.)*

■ *Test the yarn for color fastness before combining it with other colors. Wash a small amount, and if the water becomes discolored, don't mix it with other yarns.*

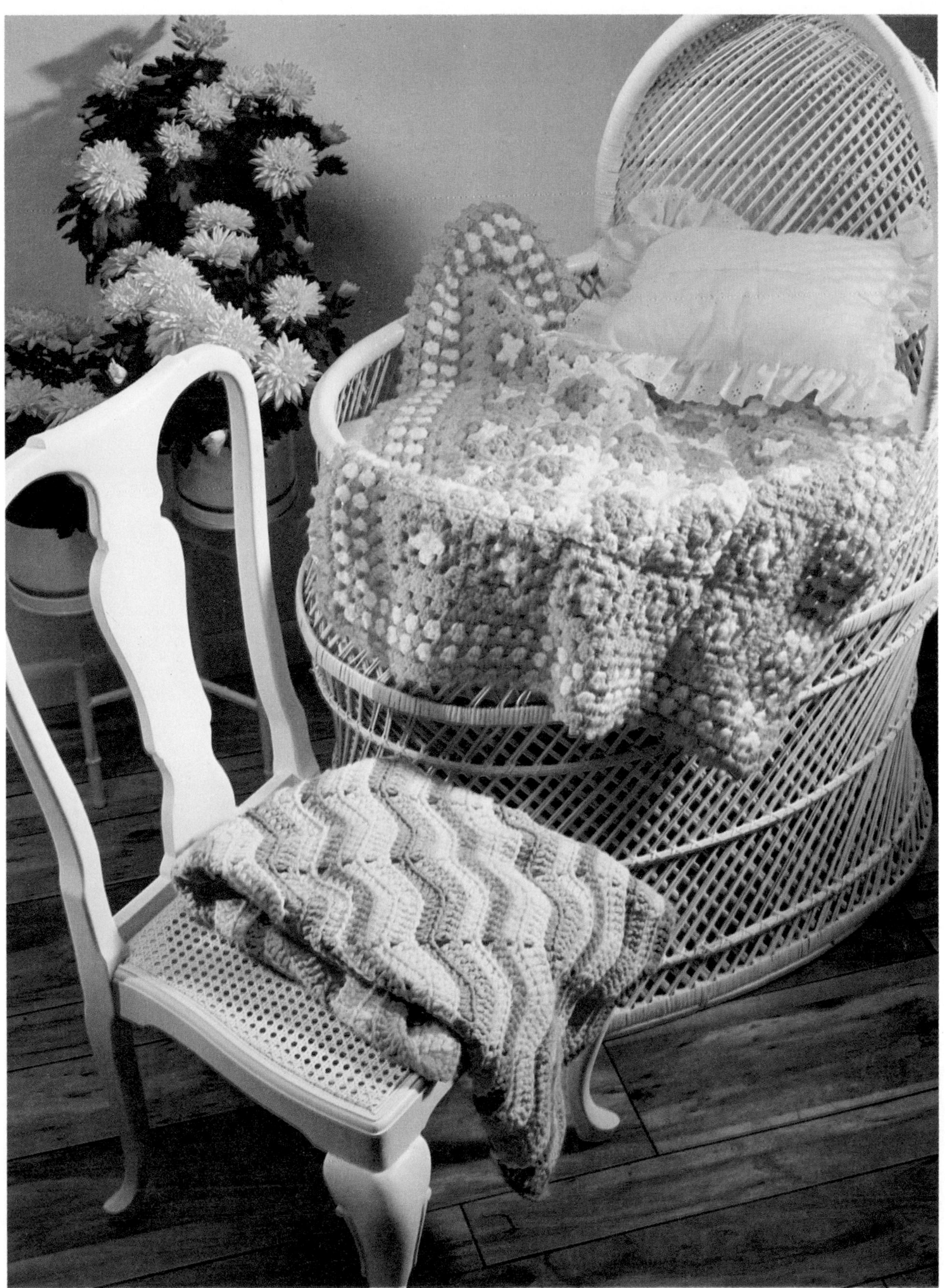

Embroidered Knitted Throw

This white throw, with sprigs of wildflowers embroidered on large triangles, adds a lift to either an adult's or a child's room.

Knit of alternate triangles of garter stitch and stockinette stitch, it measures 38x50 inches.

Materials

Knitting worsted, 4 oz. skeins
- 5 white

Persian or Persian-type yarn, 3 ply, 1 oz. skeins
- 4 bright yellow
- 1 lt. yellow
- 5 lavender-pink
- 5 bright green
- 1 lt. green
- 5 medium blue

Size 8 knitting needles
Size K crochet hook
Blunt-end tapestry needle

Gauge

4 sts = 1 inch

Note: Make six 12x18-inch st st triangles, six 12x18-inch garter st triangles, four 12x9-inch st st triangles, and four 12x9-inch garter st triangles (see page 220).

Directions

12x18-inch st st triangles—cast on 72 sts. Row 1: p. Row 2: k 2 tog, k to last 2 sts, k 2 tog. Rep rows 1 and 2 until 1 st remains. Break yarn and draw end through rem st.

12x18-inch garter st triangles—cast on 72 sts. Row 1: k. Row 2: k 2 tog, k to last 2 sts, k 2 tog. Rep rows 1 and 2 until 1 st remains. Break yarn and draw end through rem st.

12x9-inch st st triangles—cast on 36 sts. Row 1: p. Row 2: k 2 tog, k to end of row (no dec at end of row). Rep rows 1 and 2 until 1 st remains. Break yarn and draw the end of the yarn through rem st. Make two triangles like this, two with the dec at the end of the k rows instead of at the beginning.

12x9-inch garter st triangles—cast on 36 sts. Row 1: k. Row 2: k 2 tog, k to end of row (no dec at end of row). Rep rows 1 and 2 until 1 st remains. Break yarn and draw end of yarn through rem st. Make two triangles like this, 2 with the dec at the end of the dec row instead of at the beg.

Press triangles lightly with steam iron, and embroider floral motifs on the six large st st triangles. Arrange triangles (see drawing) and whipstitch all of the sections together.

Crochet border—Row 1: Sc all around afghan. Row 2: Sc 2 sts, dc 4 sts in 1st st, * skip 2 sts, dc 5 sts in 3rd st. Rep from * around row. Fasten off.

Embroidery—*Note:* Work the flowers, stems, and leaves freehand on the blanket, following a basic pattern. Use a double strand of yarn throughout. Work thread ends into the back to avoid knots.

Step 1: First, embroider circular flowers in Pekinese stitch (see diagrams) in each of the 12x18-inch st st triangles. For this stitch, work a framework of straight stitches and then lace yarn through the framework to form flower "petals." Don't pull the yarn too tightly as you work; it should stand slightly above the surface of the knitting. Each triangle has a large flower and a small one.

On one end of the blanket, work the larger flower in yellow and the smaller one in pink; then reverse the colors for the opposite end. Work light green French knots in the center of the yellow flowers and light yellow French knots in the center of the pink flowers.

Step 2: Add gently curving stems in stem stitch to the yellow and pink flowers. Work leaf stems in stem stitch and leaves in individual chain stitches.

Step 3: Finally, add a sprinkling of four or five blue forget-me-nots with bright yellow centers to each triangle to balance the larger flowers and stems. Make the forget-me-nots with five petals in individual chain stitches around a French knot.

Pekinese stitch

1. Work a foundation of small running stitches from A to B in a spiral shape:

2. Then, starting at B, work running stitches back along the spiral, filling in the blank spaces left the first time. Bring the thread up again at A.

3. From here on out, the needle does not enter the knit background. Slip the needle from the bottom up under stitch number 2 and pull thread through.

4. Bring the needle back and under the first stitch, from the top down. Carry the needle *over* the working thread and pull it through.

5. Begin the next stitch by carrying the needle under stitch number 3, from the bottom up.

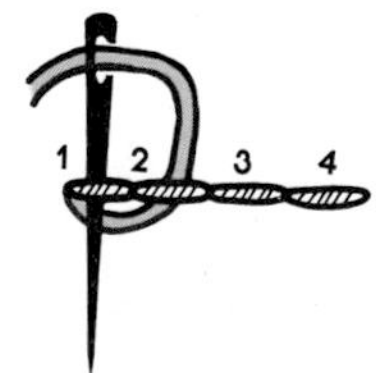

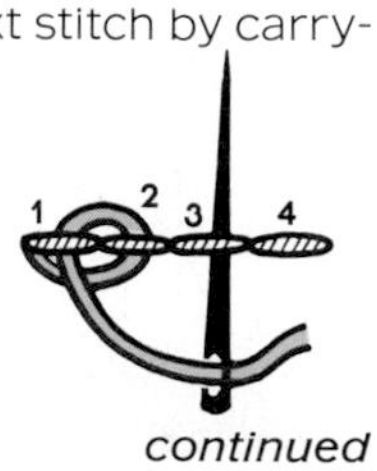

continued

Embroidered Knitted Throw *(continued)*

6. Pull thread through and insert the needle under stitch number 2, from the top down, and over the working thread.

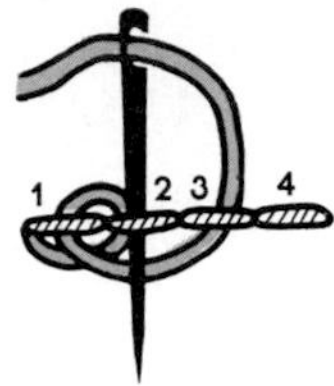

7. Continue working this way, as in steps 5 and 6, to the end of the line.

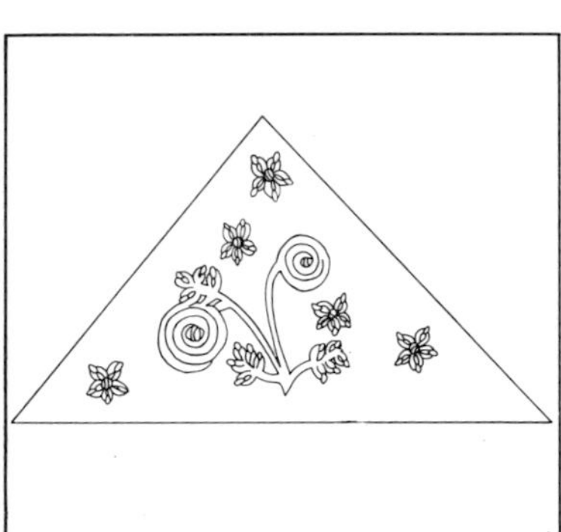

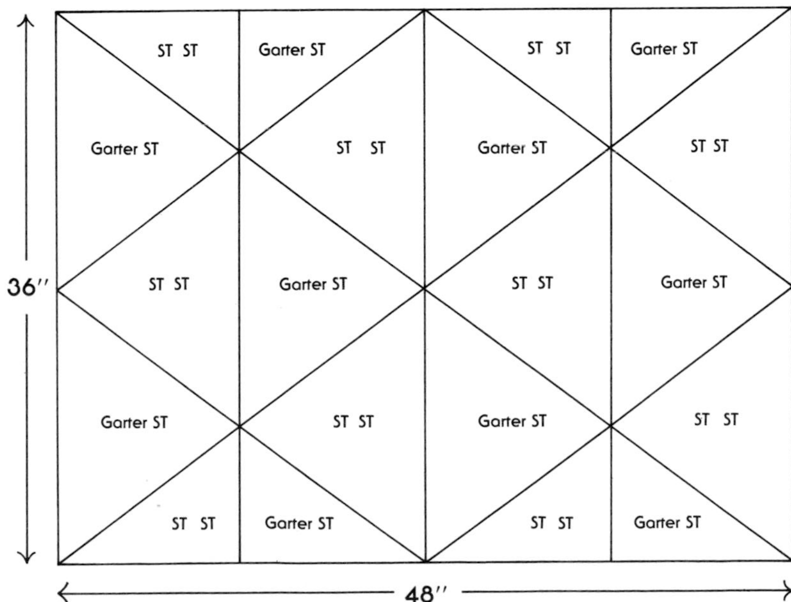

SUPPLIES AND TOOLS

You'll enjoy working on crocheted and knitted projects—and make them easier to accomplish—if you acquire a supply of useful items that ensure accuracy. Keep them handy, along with your yarn.

- *Always have handy a yardstick or a tape measure (the non-stretch variety).*
- *Add different sizes of crochet hooks and knitting needles (both straight and circular) until you have a good assortment.*
- *Keep a needle gauge stored with your needles.*
- *Have a pair of small scissors with sharp points tucked in with your knitting or crocheting.*
- *Keep a supply of markers (small plastic rings) for marking beginnings of rows or patterns.*
- *One or more stitch holders always come in handy. (These look like large safety pins and are invaluable for holding stitches.)*
- *Large-eyed needles are a must.*

Crocheted Bed Throw

For something out of the ordinary, use this crocheted throw to top a patchwork quilt, and let the bright colors peek through the cobweb-like designs of the coverlet.

Materials

4 ply sportweight yarn, 2 oz. skeins, ivory or eggshell
61 (for twin-size bed)
83 (for queen-size bed)
Size F crochet hook

Gauge

Each finished square should measure about 5¼ inches across. *Note:* Make 27 squares for twin-size bed, 33 for queen-size bed.

Directions

To begin: Ch 10 and join into ring with sl st.

Rnd 1: Ch 3, (counts as first dc); make 31 dc in ring; join with a sl st to first dc of rnd.

Rnd 2: Ch 3; dc bet each dc of preceding rnd (inserting hook under all 3 yarns bet each st of preceding rnd); join with a sl st to first ch 3 of rnd.

Rnd 3: Ch 3; * crochet 1 dc bet each dc of preceding rnd; 7 times (making first of these 7 dc just after sl st at end of preceding rnd, and again being sure to insert hook under all 3 yarns); crochet 2 dc in next st (first corner) *; rep from * to * 2 more times. Finish rnd with 8 dc; join with a sl st.

Rnd 4: Ch 3; * crochet 8 dc, then 1 dc in first corner st of preceding rnd (inserting hook under all 3 yarns in middle of dc); 1 ch, 1 dc in second corner st. * Repeat 2 more times from * to *, beg in sp bet corner dc and following dc. Finish fourth side with 8 dc, 1 dc in corner dc, ch 1, and join with a sl st.

Rnd 5: Ch 3; * 9 dc, then crochet 1 dc in first dc of corner, ch 3, 1 dc in other corner dc *. Rep 2 more times from * to *. Finish rnd with 9 dc, 1 dc in corner dc, ch 3, join with a sl st.

Rnd 6: Ch 3; * dc 10, crochet 1 dc in first dc of corner, ch 5, dc 1 in other corner dc *. Rep 2 more times from * to *. Finish rnd with 10 dc, 1 dc in corner dc, ch 5; join with sl st.

Rnd 7: Ch 3: * dc 11, dc 1 in corner dc, ch 7, dc 1 in other corner dc *. Rep from * to * 2 more times. Finish rnd with 11 dc, 1 dc in corner dc, ch 7, and join with a sl st.

Rnd 8: Ch 3; * dc 12, dc 1 in first dc of corner, ch 9, dc 1 in other corner dc *. Rep 2 more times from * to *. Finish off square with 12 dc, 1 dc in first dc of corner, ch 9, 1 sl st; break yarn and pull through last st, being sure to leave about 24 inches of yarn with which to join squares.

Joining—To join first 27 (33) squares: Iron squares on wrong side, using damp cloth. Arrange in "L" shape with 17 squares on long side, and 10 on shorter side (19 and 15 for queen-size bed).

Note: Now is the time to measure your bed to see if you'll need additional squares for length or width. With squares still arranged in an L-shape, join dc sides (not ch sts) using sl st on wrong side.

Finishing—To complete the spread: Now make 160 (252) squares as follows: For each of the next 160 (252) squares, follow directions for the first 7 rnds. On the 8th rnd, join each square to the L-framework as follows: Proceed with first three sides of eighth rnd as above, but finish the fourth side with 12 dc, 1 dc in corner dc, ch 7, then 1 sl st in the middle of ch 9 of the square directly above, ch 3, 1 sl st in the middle of ch 9 of square directly to left, ch 3, 1 sl st in 4th ch st of square you are finishing up, ch 3, and then 1 sl st to close the square. Now join dc sides of new square to the dc sides of adjacent squares, using sl st on the wrong side (as for joining initial squares into L-shape above).

Continue to join squares, as each is completed, to the framework of original squares, using the L-framework as top and side edges of the spread.

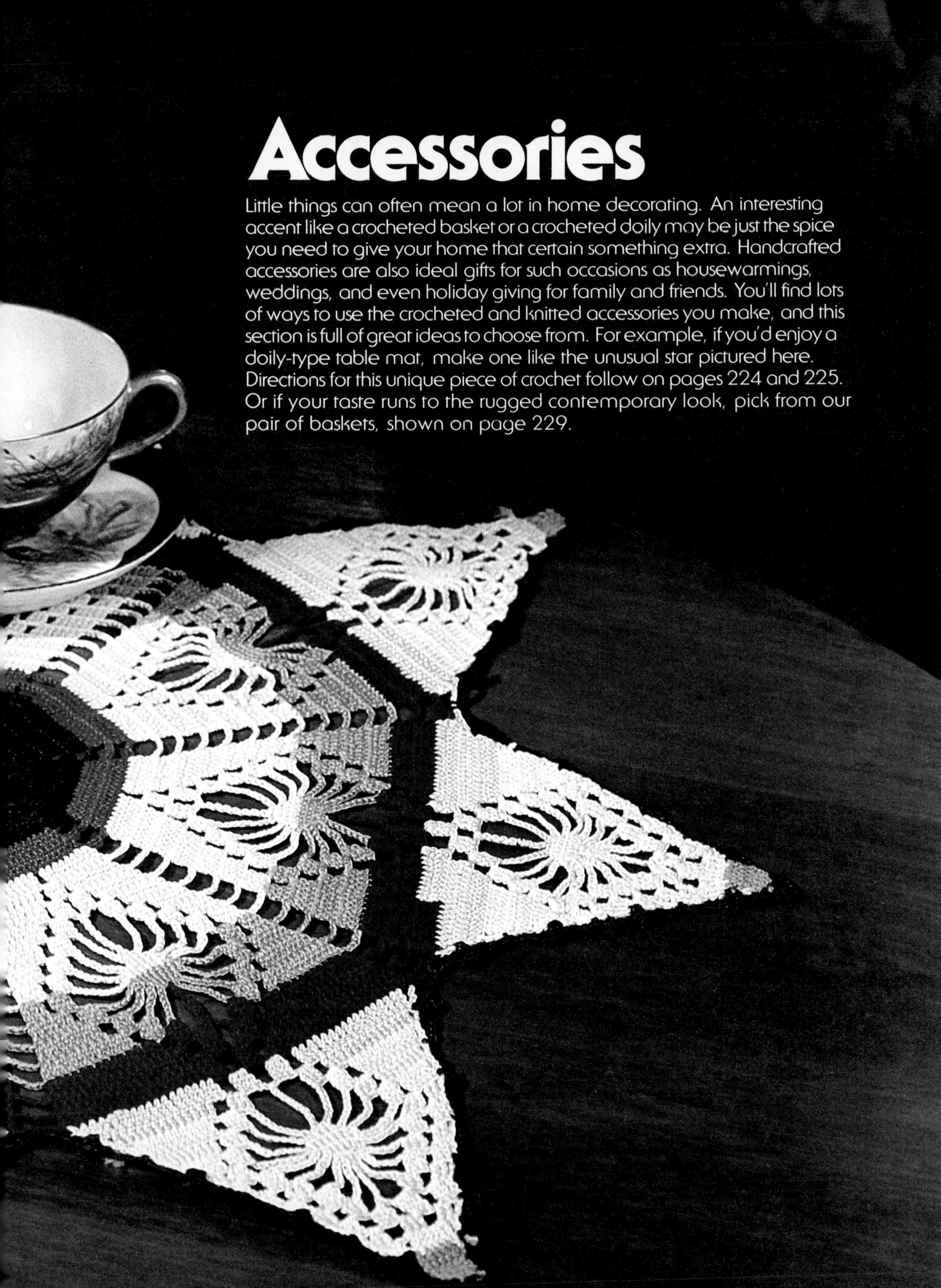

Accessories

Little things can often mean a lot in home decorating. An interesting accent like a crocheted basket or a crocheted doily may be just the spice you need to give your home that certain something extra. Handcrafted accessories are also ideal gifts for such occasions as housewarmings, weddings, and even holiday giving for family and friends. You'll find lots of ways to use the crocheted and knitted accessories you make, and this section is full of great ideas to choose from. For example, if you'd enjoy a doily-type table mat, make one like the unusual star pictured here. Directions for this unique piece of crochet follow on pages 224 and 225. Or if your taste runs to the rugged contemporary look, pick from our pair of baskets, shown on page 229.

Star Doily or Table Mat *(shown on pages 222 and 223)*

The eight-pointed star-shaped doily pictured on the previous pages measures 20½ inches in diameter. For the crocheting enthusiast, this project offers a great opportunity to use small amounts of leftover crochet thread from former projects.

Make it up in a combination of your favorite colors, or in a solid color, such as white or ecru.

Materials

J&P Coats
Knit Cro-Sheen
- 1 black
- 1 rust
- 1 lt. green
- 1 blue
- 1 dk. red
- 1 tan
- 1 orange

Size 10 steel crochet hook

Directions

At center with first color, ch 6. Join with sl to form ring. Rnd 1: Ch 3 (to count as one dc), 23 dc in ring. Join with sl st to top of ch-3.

Rnd 2: Ch 3, dc in same place as sl st, dc in next dc, 2 dc in next dc, ch 1, * 2 dc in next dc, dc in next dc, 2 dc in next dc, ch 1. Rpt from * around. Join last ch 1 to top of ch-3 — 8 groups.

Rnd 3: Ch 3, dc in same place as sl st, * dc in 3 dc, 2 dc in next dc, ch 2, 2 dc in next dc. Rpt from * around joining last ch 2 to top of ch-3.

Rnd 4: Ch 3, dc in same place, * dc in each dc to last dc of this group; 2 dc in last dc, ch 3, 2 dc in next dc. Rpt from * around. Join.

Rnds 5 and 6: Work as for rnd 3 having ch 4 bet groups on rnd 5; ch 5 bet groups on rnd 6 — 13 dc in each group. Fasten off at end of rnd 6. Attach 2nd color to last joining.

Rnds 7 and 8: Work as for rnd 3 having ch 6 bet groups on each rnd — 17 dc in each group. Fasten off. Attach 3rd color as before.

Rnd 9: Ch 3, dc in same place, * dc in 7 dc, ch 2, sk next dc, dc in next 7 dc, 2 dc in last dc, ch 6, 2 dc in next dc. Rpt from * around. Join.

Rnd 10: Ch 3, dc in next 7 dc, * ch 2, 3 dc in sp, ch 2, sk next dc, dc in 8 dc, ch 6, dc in next 8 dc. Rpt from * around. Join.

Rnd 11: Ch 3, dc in same place, * dc in next 6 dc (ch 2, 3 dc in sp) twice; ch 2, sk next dc, dc in 6 dc, 2 dc in next dc, ch 6, 2 dc in next dc. Rpt from * around. Join.

Rnd 12: Ch 3, dc in next 6 dc, * ch 2, 3 dc in sp, ch 8, thread over hook 6 times, insert hook in center sp and pull through — 8 lps on hook; (thread over and draw through 2 lps) 7 times — long st made; ch 8, 3 dc in next sp, ch 2, sk next dc, dc in 7 dc, ch 6, dc in next 7 dc. Rpt from * around. Join.

Rnd 13: Ch 3, dc in next 5 dc, * ch 2, 3 dc in sp, ch 8, sc in top of ch 1p, sc in long st, sc in top of ch 1p, ch 8, 3 dc in next sp, ch 2, sk next dc, dc in 6 dc, ch 6, dc in next 6 dc. Rpt from *. Join.

Rnd 14: Ch 3, dc in next 4 dc, * ch 2, 3 dc in sp, ch 8, sc in top of ch, sc in 3 sc, sc in top of ch, ch 8, 3 dc in sp, ch 2, sk next dc, dc in 5 dc, ch 6, dc in 5 dc. Rpt from * around. Join.

Rnd 15: Ch 3, dc in next 3 dc, * ch 2, 3 dc in sp, ch 8, sc in ch, sc in 5 sc, sc in ch, ch 8, 3 dc in next sp, ch 2, sk next dc, dc in 4 dc, ch 6, dc in 4 dc. Rpt from * around. Join; fasten off. Attach 4th color as before.

Rnd 16: Ch 3, dc in next 2 dc. *Ch 2, 3 dc in sp, ch 8, sc in 7 sc, ch 8, 3 dc in sp, ch 2, sk next dc, dc in 3 dc, ch 6, dc in 3 dc. Rpt from * around. Join.

Rnd 17: Ch 3, dc in next 2 dc, * 3 dc in sp, ch 2, 3 dc in ch lp, ch 8, sc in 7 sc, ch 8, 3 dc in ch lp, ch 2, 3 dc in sp, dc in 3 dc, ch 6, dc in 3 dc. Rpt from * around. Join.

Rnd 18: Ch 3, dc in next 5 dc, * 3 dc in sp, ch 2, 3 dc in ch lp, ch 8, sk next sc, sc in 5 sc, ch 8, 3 dc in ch lp, ch 2, 3 dc in sp, dc in 6 dc, ch 6, dc in 6 dc. Rpt from * around. Join.

Rnd 19: Ch 3, dc in next 8 dc, * 3 dc in sp, ch 2, 3 dc in ch lp, ch 8, sk next sc, sc in 3 sc, ch 8, 3 dc in ch lp, ch 2, 3 dc in sp, dc in 9 dc, ch 6, dc in 9 dc. Rpt from * around. Join; fasten off. Attach 5th color as before.

Rnd 20: Ch 3, dc in next 11 dc, * 3 dc in sp, ch 2, 3 dc in ch lp, ch 5, thread over hook 4 times; pull up a lp in center sc — 6 lps on hook; (thread over hook and draw through 2 lps) 5 times — a long st made; ch 5, 3 dc in ch lp, ch 2, 3 dc in sp, dc in 12 dc, ch 6, dc in 12 dc. Rpt from * around. Join.

Rnd 21: Ch 3, dc in 14 dc, * 3 dc in sp, ch 2, 3 dc in lp, ch 3, sk long st, 3 dc in lp, ch 2, 3 dc in sp, dc in 15 dc, ch 6, dc in 15 dc. Rpt from * around. Join.

Rnd 22: Ch 3, dc in same place as sl st, * dc in 17 dc, 3 dc in sp, (ch 2, 3 dc in next sp) twice; dc in 17 dc, 2 dc in next dc, ch 6, 2 dc in next dc. Rpt from * around. Join; fasten off. Attach 6th color as before.

First point — Row 1: Ch 3, sk first dc, draw up a lp in each of next 2 dc, (thread over and draw through 2 lps) twice — dec made; dc in 17 dc, (ch 2, 3 dc in sp) twice; ch 2, sk 2 dc, dc in 19 dc. Ch 3, turn.

Row 2: Sk first dc, make a dec, dc in 14 dc, ch 2, 3 dc in sp, ch 6, dtr in next sp, ch 6, 3 dc in sp, ch 2, sk 2 dc, dc in 16 dc. Ch 3, turn.

Row 3: Sk first dc, make a dec, dc in 11 dc, ch 2, 3 dc in sp, ch 6, sc in ch lp, sc in dtr, sc in ch lp, ch

6, 3 dc in sp, ch 2, sk 2 dc, dc in 13 dc. Fasten off. Attach 3rd color to last dc made, ch 3 turn.

Row 4: Sk first dc, make a dec, dc in 8 dc, ch 2, 3 dc in sp, ch 6, sc in ch lp, sc in 3 sc, sc in ch lp, ch 6, 3 dc in sp, ch 2, sk 2 dc, dc in 10 dc. Ch 3, turn.

Row 5: Sk first dc, make a dec, dc in 5 dc, ch 2, 3 dc in sp, ch 6, sc in ch lp, sc in 5 sc, sc in ch lp, ch 6, 3 dc in sp, ch 2, sk 2 dc, dc in 7 dc. Ch 3, turn.

Row 6: Sk first dc, make a dec, dc in 2 dc, 3 dc in sp, ch 8, sc in 7 sc, ch 8, 3 dc in sp, sk 2 dc, dc in 4 dc. Ch 3, turn.

Row 7: Sk first dc, make a dec, dc in next dc, ch 3, 3 dc in ch lp, ch 8, sk next sc, sc in 5 sc, ch 8, 3 dc in ch 1p, ch 3, sk 3 dc, dc in next 3 dc. Ch 4, turn.

Row 8: 3 dc in sp, ch 3, 3 dc in lp, ch 8, sk next sc, sc in 3 sc, ch 8, 3 dc in lp, ch 3, 3 dc in sp, tr in last dc. Ch 4, turn.

Row 9: 3 dc in sp, ch 3, 3 dc in lp, ch 8, sc in center sc, ch 8, 3 dc in lp, ch 3, 3 dc in sp, tr in last dc. Ch 4, turn.

Row 10: 3 dc in sp, ch 3, 3 dc in lp, ch 4, dtr in sc, ch 4, 3 dc in lp, ch 3, 3 dc in sp, tr in last dc. Ch 3, turn.

Row 11: 3 dc in space, (ch 3, 3 dc in lp) twice; ch 3, 3 dc in sp, tr in last dc. Ch 4, turn.

Row 12: 3 dc in sp, (ch 3, 3 dc in sp) twice; tr in last dc. Ch 4, turn.

Row 13: 3 dc in sp, dc in 3 dc, 3 dc in sp, tr in last dc. Fasten off. Attach 7th color to last tr made; ch 3, turn.

Row 14: Sk tr and dc, make a dec, dc in 4 dc, make a dec. Ch 3, turn.

Row 15: Sk dc, make a dec, dc in 3 dc. Ch 3, turn.

Row 16: Sk dc, makes 2 decs. Fasten off. *Sk next ch-6 on doily, attach 6th color to next dc. Rpt rows 1 through 16 of first point. Rpt from * around.

Border: Attach first color to a ch-6 bet points, ch 1, 2 sc in same chain, ** ch 6, * sk next row, in end of next row make dc, ch 3, sc in 3rd ch from hook—picot made and dc; ch 4, sk next row, sc in end of next row, ch 4. Rpt from * along entire edge of this point, ch 6, 2 sc in next ch-6 bet points. Rep from ** around. Join; fasten off.

To block, stretch and pin doily to a padded surface. Cover with a wet cloth so doily feels damp, and allow to dry before removing pins. Or gently steam press with a warm iron. Hand wash in mild soap and warm water.

CROCHET HOOK SIZES

You can refer to the chart below to convert conventional crochet hook sizes to their nearest equivalent metric size.

LETTER EQUIVALENT	*MILLIMETERS (MM)*
B	*2.00*
C	*2.50*
D	*3.00*
E	*3.50*
F	*4.00*
G	*4.50*
H	*5.00*
I	*5.50*
J	*6.00*
	6.50
K	*7.00*
	8.00
	9.00
P	*10.00*

Filet Crochet Chair Set

In our grandmother's day, fancy chair sets like the one shown on the following page were used to protect the backs and arms of fine parlor furniture. And since nothing ordinary would have been considered appropriate, these antimacassars —as they were called—were often beautiful and imaginative pieces of needlework.

With today's return to nostalgia in home decor, antimacassars are right back in style. And this one is especially delightful.

Materials

J & P Coats "Big Ball" Best Six Cord Mercerized Cotton, Art. 105, size 30 or
Clark's "Big Ball" Mercerized Cotton, Art. B. 34, size 30 or
Clark's "Big Ball" Mercerized Cotton, Art. B. 345, size 30
2 balls No. 1 white
Size 10 steel crochet hook

Gauge

5 blocks or spaces = 1 inch; 6 rows = 1 inch

Note: Be sure to check your gauge before starting item. Use any size hook that will obtain stitch gauge above.

Directions

Arm cover (make 2)—Starting at lower edge, ch 27.

Row 1 (right side): Dc in 4th ch from hook and in next 2 ch—starting block made; dc in next 3 ch—another block made; make 6 more blocks. Ch 11, turn.

Row 2: Make a starting block and 2 blocks, working last dc of

continued

Filet Crochet Chair Set *(continued)*

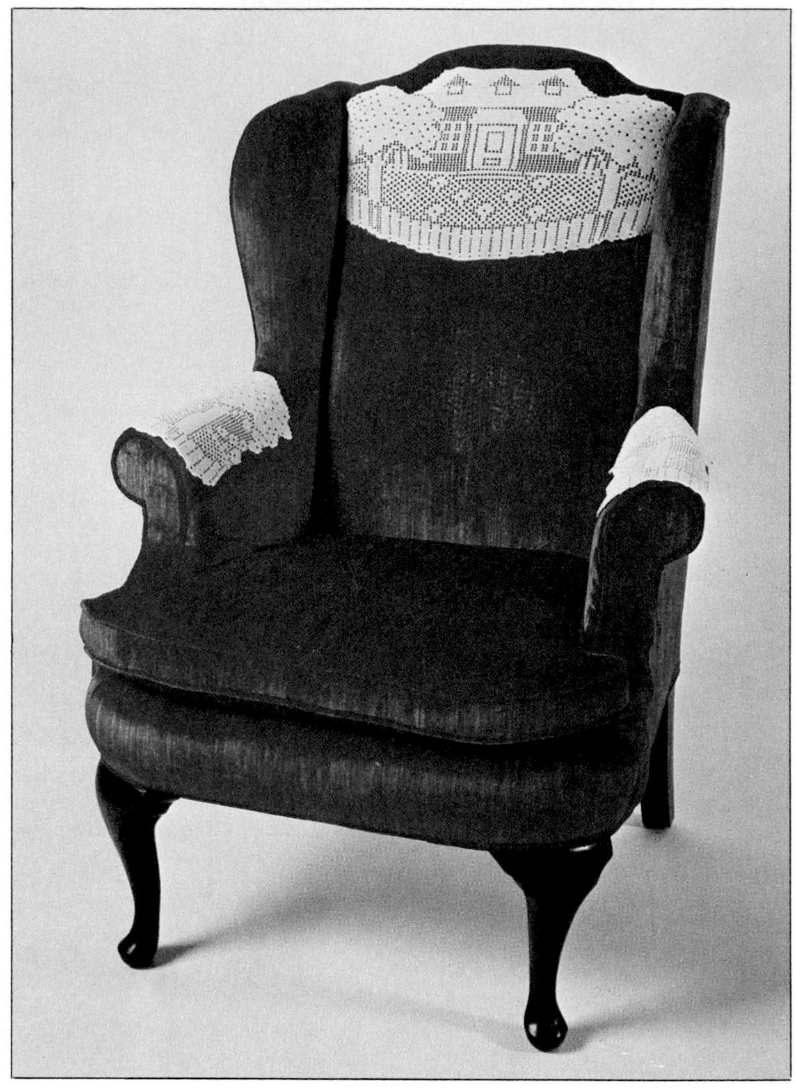

last block in first dc—3 blocks increased at beg of row; dc in next 3 dc—block over block made, make 1 more block, ch 2, sk 2 dc, dc in next dc—sp over block made, make 2 blocks, 1 sp and 1 block, dc in next 2 dc and in top of turning ch—block over block at end of row made, thread over, insert hook in same place as last dc and draw up a loop—3 loops on hook—thread over and draw through 1 loop—this makes a ch st and 3 loops remain on hook—(thread over and draw through 2 loops) twice—foundation dc made; thread over, insert hook in the ch st at base of previous foundation dc and draw up a loop, thread over and draw through 1 loop, (thread over and draw through 2 loops) twice—another foundation dc made; make another foundation dc to complete a block—1 block increased at end of row; inc 2 more blocks at end of row. Ch 11, turn.

Row 3: Inc 3 blocks at beg of row, make 2 more blocks, 1 sp, 2 blocks, 2 dc in ch 2 sp, dc in next dc—block over sp made, 5 blocks, 1 sp, 2 blocks, inc 3 blocks at end of row. Ch 11, turn.

Row 4: Inc 3 blocks at beg of row, make 2 blocks, 1 sp, 5 blocks, 1 sp, 2 blocks, 1 sp, 5 blocks, 1 sp, 2 blocks, inc 3 blocks at end of row. Ch 3, turn.

Row 5: Dc in next 3 dc—starting block over block made, make 1 block, 1 sp, 5 blocks, 1 sp, 3 blocks, 2 sps, (1 block, 1 sp) twice; 5 blocks, 1 sp, and 2 blocks. Ch 5, turn.

Row 6: Starting block at beg of row—1 block increased at beg of row; make 5 blocks, 1 sp, 2 blocks, (1 sp, 1 block) twice; 2 sps, 3 blocks, 1 sp, 2 blocks, 1 sp, 5 blocks, inc 1 block at end of row. Ch 8, turn.

Row 7: Starting block at beg of row, make 1 more block—2 blocks increased at beg of row; make (1 sp, 2 blocks) 3 times; 1 sp, 3 blocks, 2 sps, (1 block, 1 sp) twice; (2 blocks, 1 sp) 3 times, working the dc of last sp in top of ch 3; inc 2 blocks at end of row. Ch 5, turn.

Starting with row 8, follow chart, reading from right to left on all odd-numbered rows and from left to right on all even-numbered rows until 31 rows have been completed. Turn.

Row 32: Sl st in each of first 4 dc, ch 3—1 block decreased at beg of row; complete first block, make 1 block more, 1 sp, 2 blocks, 1 sp, 1 block, 7 sps, 3 blocks, 2 sps, 1 block, 1 sp, 1 block, 5 sps, 1 block, 1 sp, 2 blocks, 1 sp, 2 blocks, leave remaining 2 dc and turning ch unworked—1 block decreased at end of row. Turn.

Starting with row 33, complete arm cover. Follow chart.

Chair back—Starting at lower edge, ch 54.

Row 1 (right side): Make starting block and 17 more blocks. Ch 17, turn.

Row 2: Make starting block and 4 more blocks—5 blocks increased at beg of row; complete row following chart. Read from right to left, including *center*, then for other half of row omit *center*, and follow chart back again to right edge, increasing 5 blocks at end of row. Starting with row 2, complete remainder of chair back. Follow chart in same way.

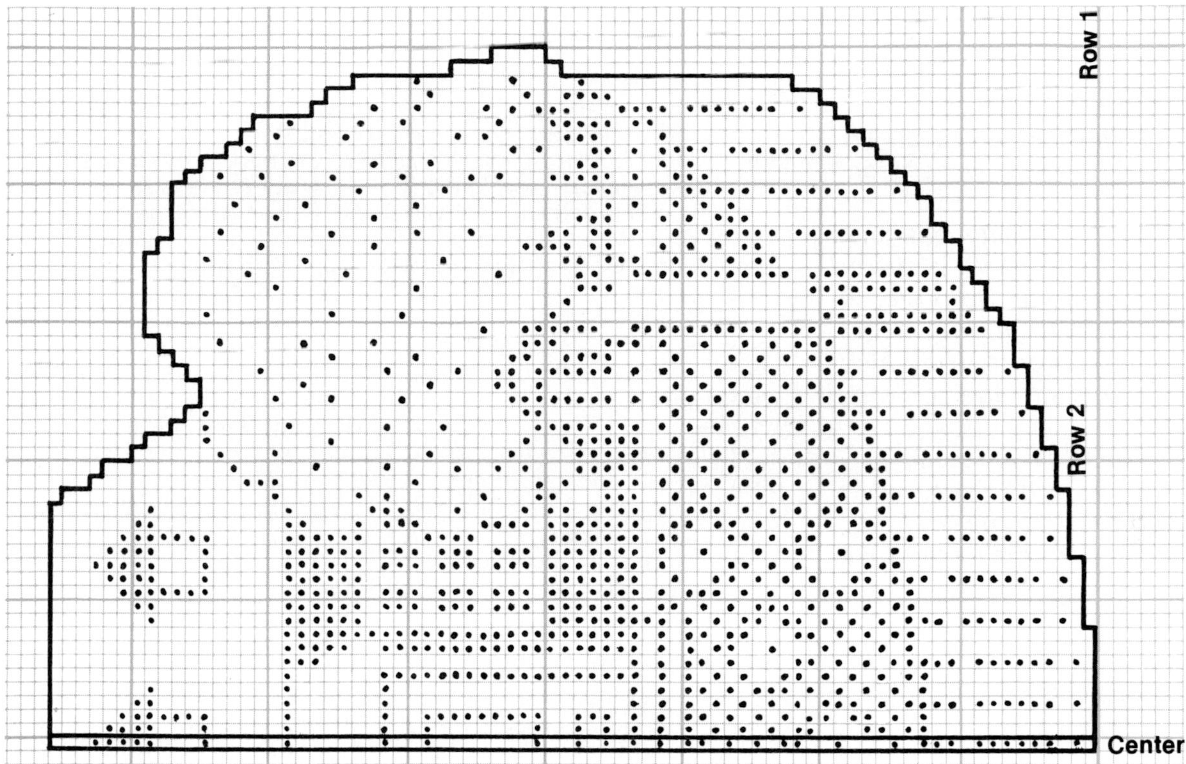

 = space

Chair Back

□ = block

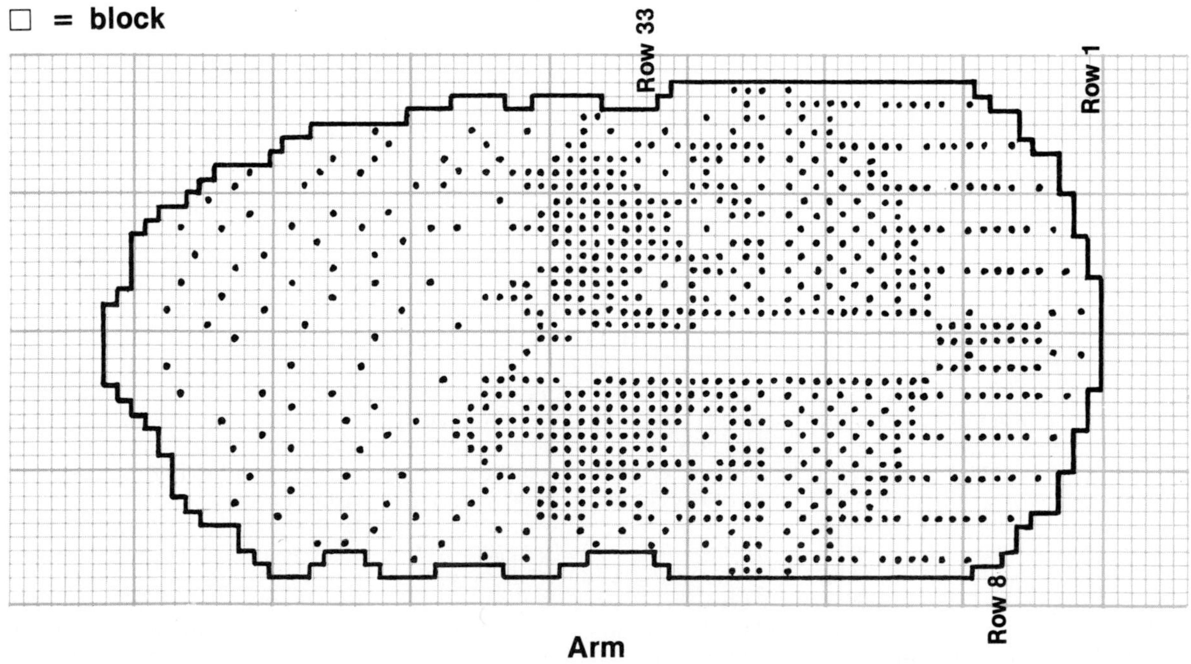

Arm

Crocheted Cord Baskets

Common, everyday cotton cord takes on an exciting new dimension when you use it to crochet novelty baskets, such as the two pictured on the opposite page. In addition to adding decorative accents, they also provide storage for many items.

These crocheted baskets are inexpensive and easy to make, and work up amazingly fast.

Round Basket (left in photo)

Materials

3 ply cotton cord
75 yds. (approximately)
Size K crochet hook

Finished size

Approximately 9 inches in diameter and 6 inches high

Directions

Bottom of basket—Ch 5: join with sl st to form ring. Ch 1 to begin second rnd.

Rnd 1: Inc by working 2 sc in every st of base ch.

Rnd 2: Repeat rnd 1.

Rnd 3: Continue to sc, increasing with 2 sc in every other sc of preceding rnd.

Rnd 4: Inc with 2 sc in every fourth sc of preceding rnd.

Rnd 5: Inc with 2 sc in every sixth sc of preceding rnd.

Rnd 6: Inc with 2 sc in every eighth sc of preceding rnd.

Sides of basket—Rnd 1: Ch 3 (counting as first dc), then dc around base in every st. Join last dc to first dc with a sl st, then ch 3 for beginning of second rnd.

Rnd 2 and 3: Continue to dc in every stitch in preceding rnds.

Rnd 4: Inc by crocheting 2 dc in every eighth st of preceding rnd (this is the last inc rnd).

Rnd 5: This will be the first row of scalloped edging. There are 3 ch sts per scallop. After attaching last dc of preceding rnd with a sl st, ch 3; sk two sts of preceding rnd and attach chain to third st of preceding rnd with a sc. Work 3 more ch sts, sk 2 sts of preceding rnd, and attach ch to third st with a sc. Repeat scallop pattern around entire rim of basket.

Rnd 6: Repeat rnd 5, joining each ch scallop from center top of one scallop on preceding rnd to center top of adjacent scallop.

Rnd 7: Repeat rnd 6, end off cord, and weave in loose ends with crochet hook.

Oval Basket (right in photo)

Materials

3 ply cotton cord
65 yds. (approximately)
Size K crochet hook

Finished Size

Approximately 5½ inches high, 9 inches wide, and 5½ inches deep

Directions

Bottom of basket—Ch 12.

Rnd 1: Ch 2 for beginning of rnd, then sc to end of base ch. Ch 2 (to ease around curve at end of base ch), then sc down other side of base ch. Mark end of ch so you can count rnds.

Rnds 2, 3, 4: Continue to sc up and down base ch, increasing with a ch st after every two sc sts at end of base ch (to ease curve). In all, there should be four rows of sc on either side of base ch.

Sides of basket—Rnd 1: Ch 3 for beginning of dc row. Dc around base in every stitch. Join last dc of this rnd to first dc with a ch st. Ch 3 for beginning of second rnd.

Rnd 2: Repeat dc pattern, but inc around curves at ends of the oval by crocheting two dc in every third st around the curve. No increase around sides.

Rnd 3: Every sixth st, dc two sts in one dc of preceding rnd. This will give a slightly flared shape to basket.

Rnd 4: This will be the first row of ch scallops. To make scallop edging, follow instructions for rnds 5-7 of sides of round basket given above. End off cord, and weave in loose ends with crochet hook.

CROCHET HOOKS

Although crochet hooks are available in a variety of materials and a broad range of sizes, they are all basically the same shape. The thickness of the shaft, or shank, determines the size of each stitch and the hook at the end catches the yarn.

- *The most widely used hooks are made of aluminum because it is lightweight, strong, and smooth. Also, they come in many sizes.*
- *Plastic hooks, except for the very large sizes which you would use only for very thick yarns, cords, or rope, are not advised. In the smaller sizes, they become brittle and break easily.*
- *Steel hooks come in the smaller sizes, usually have a sharper point, and are used for lace-type crocheting that requires fine crochet threads.*
- *You will also find some wooden hooks, but these are not as durable as the aluminum and steel hooks, except in the very large sizes.*
- *The hook size given with instructions is based on average tension. If you crochet tighter or looser than the average, use a larger or smaller hook to achieve the correct gauge.*

Basic Crochet Stitches

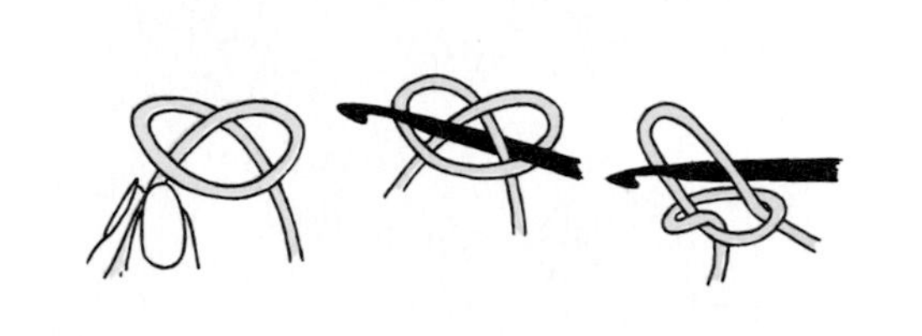

Start by making a slip knot on crochet hook about 6 inches from end of yarn. Pull one end of yarn to tighten knot.

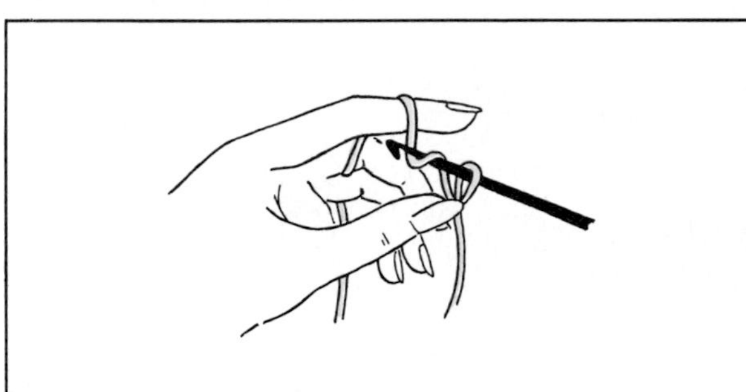

Hold the hook between right index finger and thumb, as you would a pencil. Wrap yarn over ring finger, under middle finger and over index finger, holding short end between thumb and index finger. If you need more tension, wrap yarn around little finger. Insert hook under and over strand of yarn.

Make the foundation chain by catching strand with hook and drawing it through loop. Make the chain as long as pattern calls for.

Crocheting Abbreviations

beg	begin(ning)
bet	between
ch	chain
dc	double crochet
dec	decrease
dtr	double treble
hdc	half double crochet
inc	increase
lp(s)	loop(s)
pat	pattern
rnd	round
sc	single crochet
sl st	slip stitch
sp	space
st(s)	stitch(es)
tog	together
yo	yarn over

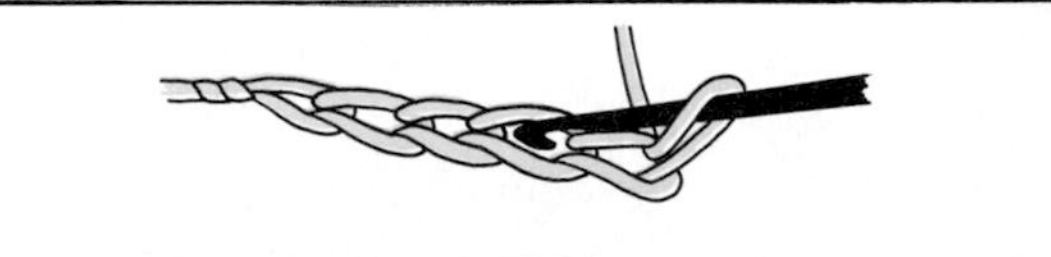

Single crochet: Insert the hook into the second chain from the hook, under two upper strands of yarn.

Draw up a loop.

Draw yarn over hook.

Pull yarn through the two loops, completing single crochet stitch. Insert hook into next stitch, and repeat last four steps.

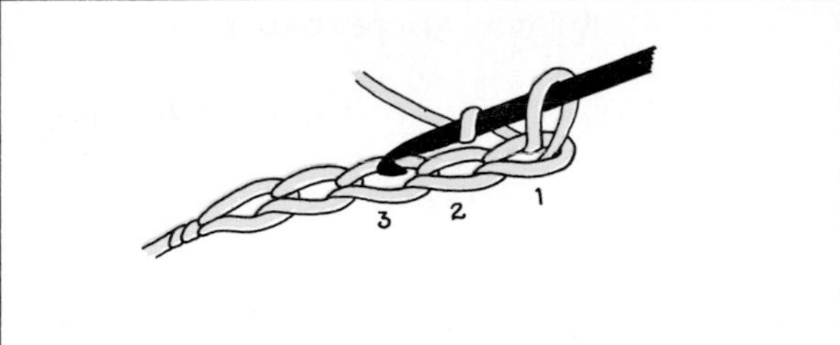

Half double crochet: With yarn over hook, insert hook into third chain, under the two upper strands of yarn.

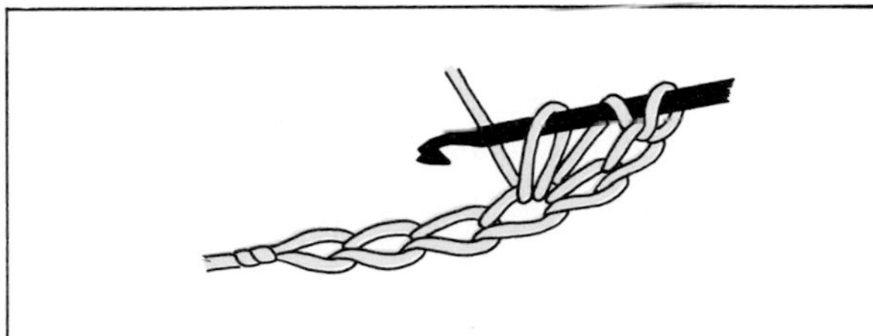

Draw up a loop.

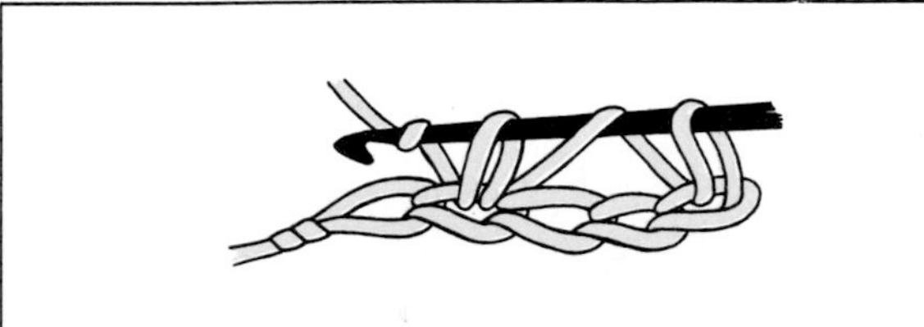

Draw yarn over the hook.

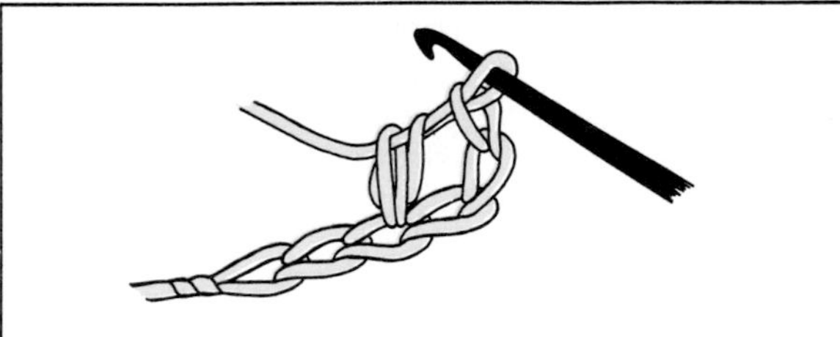

Pull through the 3 loops, completing the half double crochet.

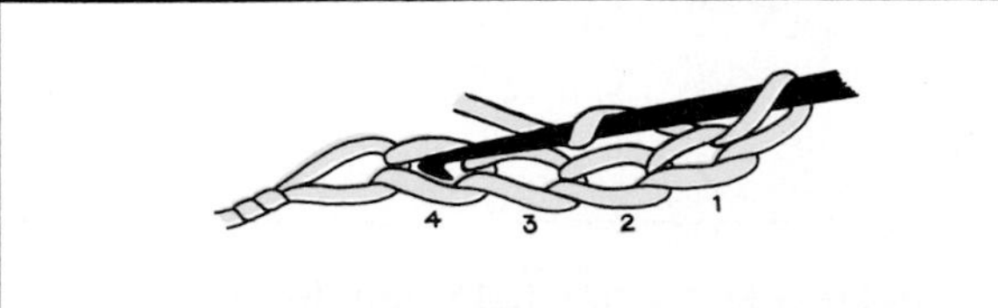

Double crochet: Holding yarn over hook, insert hook into fourth chain, under the two upper strands of yarn.

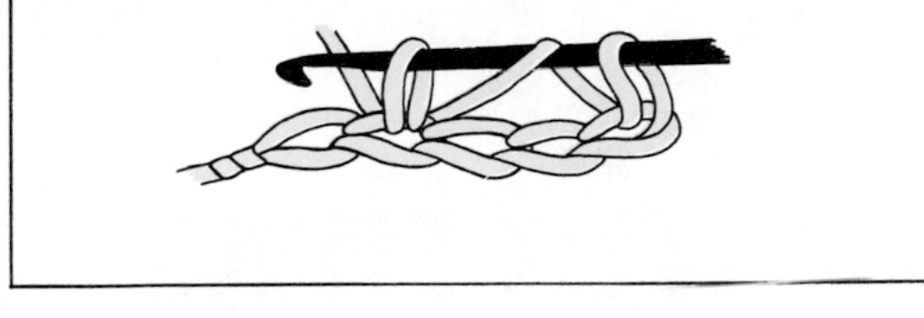

Draw up a loop.

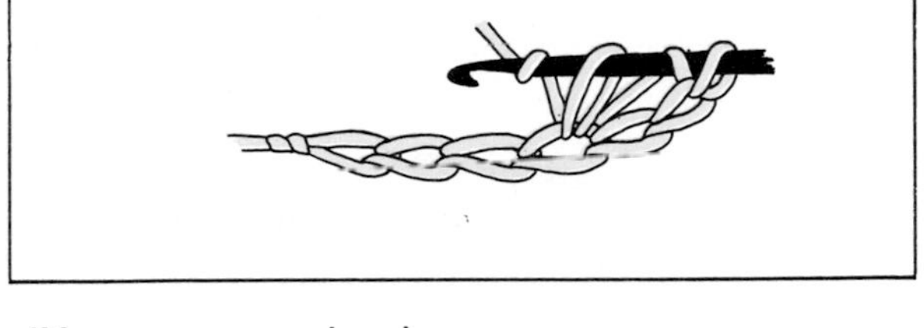

Wrap yarn over hook.

Draw yarn through two loops.

Yarn over again and through last two loops on hook. This completes double crochet.

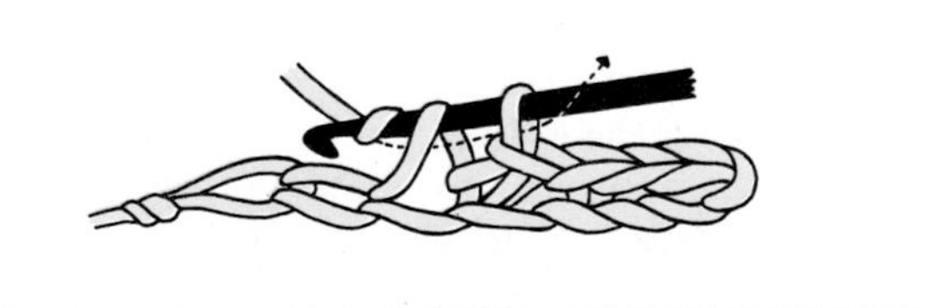

Slip stitch: After you've made the foundation chain, insert the crochet hook under the top strand of the second chain from the hook, and yarn over. With a single motion, pull the yarn through the stitch and loop on the hook. Insert the hook under the top strand of the next chain, then yarn over and draw the yarn through stitch and loop on hook. Repeat this procedure to the end of the chain.

Basic Knitting Stitches

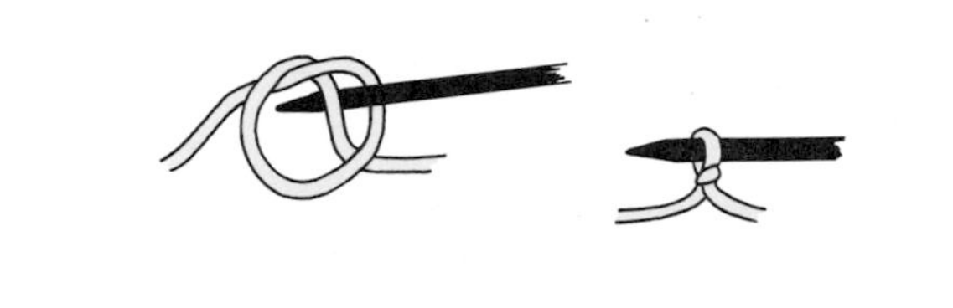

To cast on, make a slip knot around needle at a distance from yarn end that equals one inch for each stitch to be cast on.

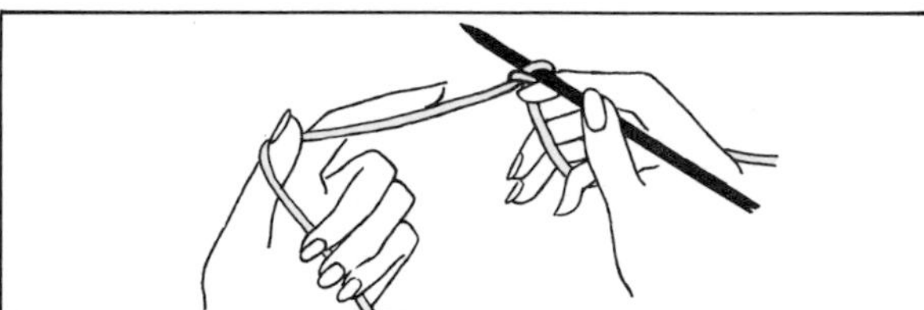

Hold needle that has slip knot in your right hand and make a loop of the short length of yarn around your left thumb.

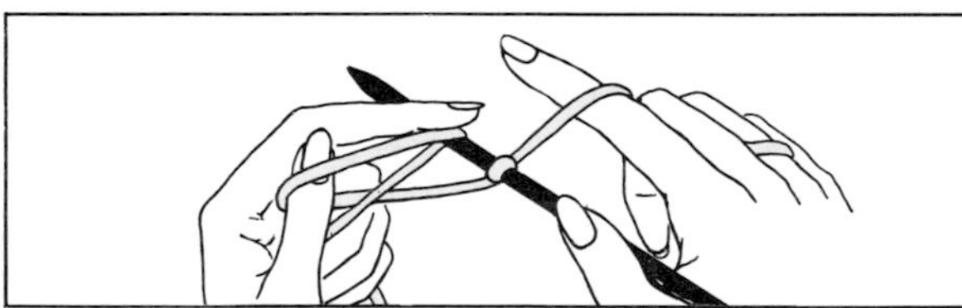

Insert point of needle in your right hand under loop on your left thumb. Loop yarn from ball over fingers of your right hand.

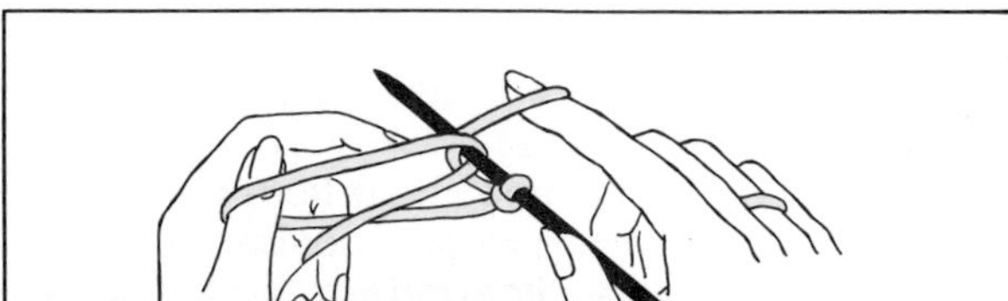

Wind yarn from ball under and over needle and draw it through loop, leaving the stitch on the needle.

Knitting Abbreviations

k	knit
p	purl
st(s)	stitch(es)
tog	together
pat	pattern
inc	increase
dec	decrease
beg	beginning
sp	space
rnd	round
yo	yarn over
rem	remaining
rep	repeat
sk	skip
st st	stockinette stitch
MC	main color
CC	contrasting color
sl st	slip stitch
psso	pass slip st over
dp	double-pointed

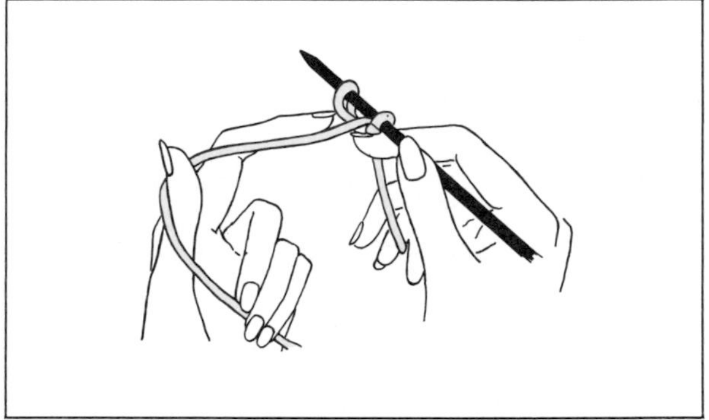

Tighten stitches on needle and bring yarn end around thumb so it is ready for next stitch. Repeat the last four steps until you have desired number of stitches. Switch needle with cast-on stitches to left hand.

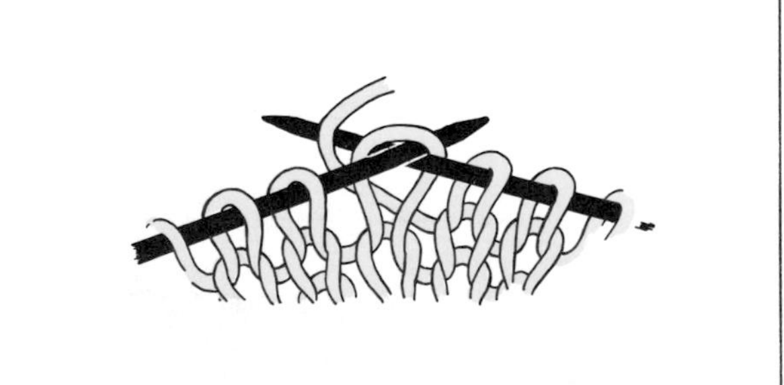

To make a knit stitch, hold needle with stitches in left hand and other needle in right hand. Insert right needle through stitch on left needle from front to back. Pass yarn around point of right needle to form loop.

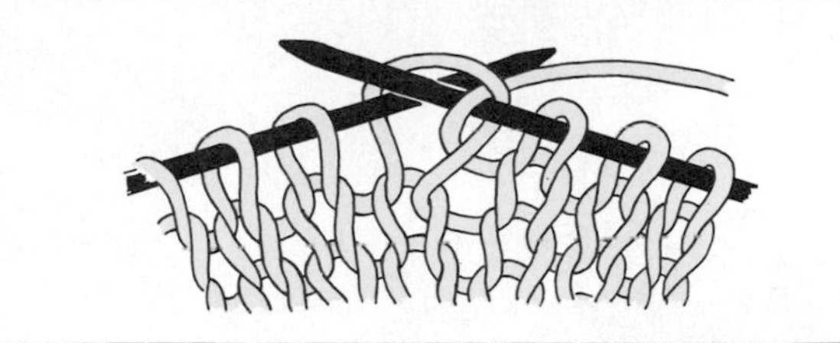

Pull this loop through stitch on left needle, and draw loop onto right needle.

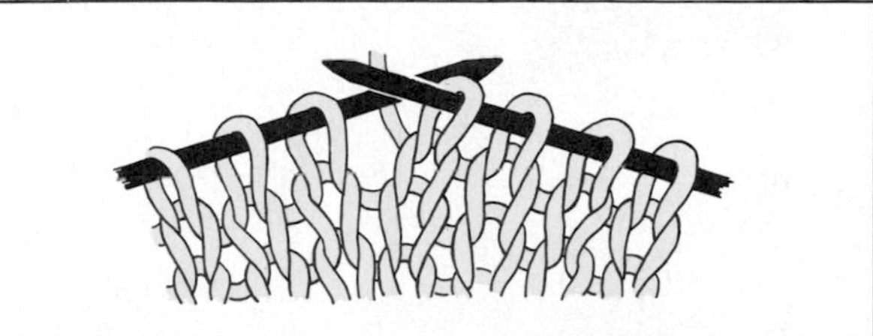

Now, slip the stitch completely off of the left needle. Repeat these steps until you have transferred all of the stitches from the left needle to the right needle. This completes one row of knitting. When you start working on the next row, move needle holding stitches to your left hand, and free the needle to your right hand.

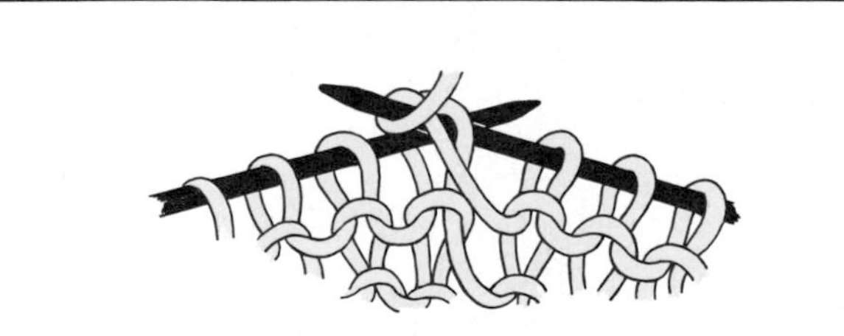

To make a purl stitch, hold the needle with the stitches in your left hand and the other needle in your right hand. Insert the right needle through the stitch on the left needle from back to front. Wind the yarn around the point of the right needle to form a loop.

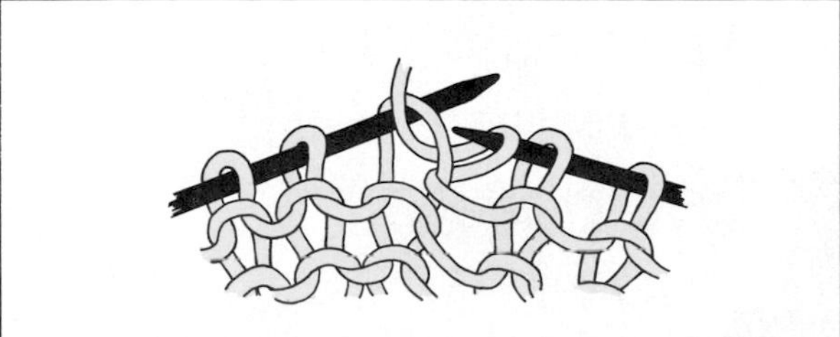

Draw a loop through the stitch on the needle in your left hand, and transfer it to the needle in your right hand.

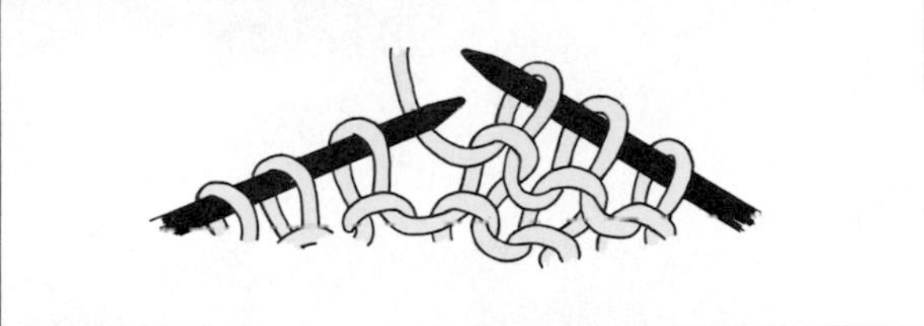

Slip stitch completely off left needle. Repeat these steps until all loops on left needle have been transferred to right needle. This completes one row of purling. Switch needles and work next row.

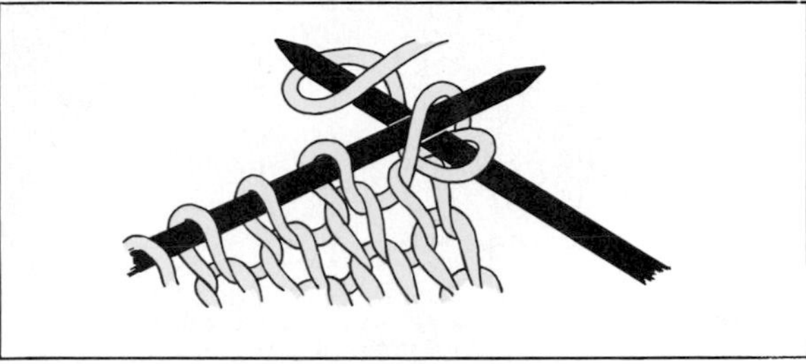

In order to increase a stitch, knit or purl as usual, but do not slip it off the left needle. Instead, insert right needle into back of stitch and knit or purl into stitch a second time. Slip both onto right needle, resulting in two stitches. To decrease, knit or purl two stitches together at the same time. To slip a stitch, insert the right needle as if to purl (unless directions read to do it as if to knit). Then slip stitch onto right needle without working; be careful not to twist stitch.

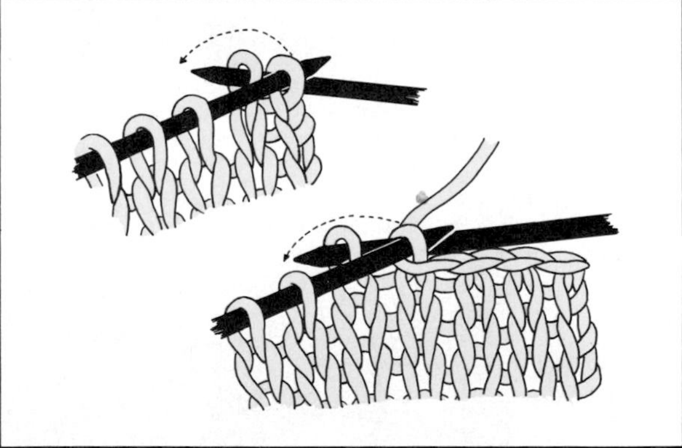

To bind off, work two stitches in pattern loosely. With left needle, lift first stitch over second stitch and off right needle. This binds off one stitch. Repeat this same technique for required number of stitches. If you are binding off an entire row, continue until one stitch remains; break yarn and draw end through the last stitch.

NEEDLEPOINT

Needlepoint

An Exciting and Elegant Craft

Needlepoint is one of our most popular needle arts. And no wonder—since this exciting and creative craft is not only easy to master, but also offers so many techniques and materials to inspire you. You can work everything from minute stitches on fine-mesh canvas to quick-and-easy quickpoint rugs; from smooth, flat stitches to magnificently textured ones; and from delicate pictorial designs to bold, splashy geometrics. And in this section, you'll find beautiful and imaginative projects that illustrate just how varied and rewarding needlepoint can be. For example, we include quickpoint and other simple-to-stitch projects like the rug and pillows shown here. For complete instructions, please turn to page 242.

Needlepoint Basics

Crafting beautiful fabric is what needlepoint is all about. Needlepoint is a form of embroidery on canvas in which the stitches cover the background fabric completely, creating an exciting new fabric from the basic materials of stitchery. And while design is important, an understanding of materials and techniques also is essential to successful completion of a needlepoint project.

Here's what you need to know to get started. When you're ready to begin stitching, please turn the page for stitchery tips.

Mono canvas

Needlepoint Canvas

Needlepoint canvas is a sturdy, open-weave fabric that is used as a framework for the stitches that are worked into it. It is available in several weaves and a large number of widths, and it is sized according to the number of vertical threads per inch; the larger the number of threads per inch, the smaller the actual stitches will be.

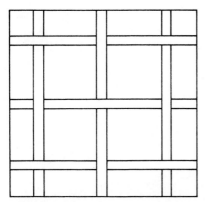

Mono canvas, shown at left, is made with single threads woven together in a plain over-and-under weave so each mesh, or space between threads, is the same size. It is available in #10-, #12-, #14-, #16-, #18-, #20-, and #24-count sizes (threads per inch).

Penelope canvas is made with *double* threads, as shown at right. It's a strong canvas that can be used for regular stitches that cover the double threads (gros point) or for fine stitches worked into the smaller spaces formed by the double threads (petit point).

The most widely used penelope canvas is #10/20-count; the first mesh number indicates threads per inch for gros point and the second indicates threads per inch for petit point. It can also be found in #11/22-count and #12/24-count sizes, and is available in #3½-, #4-, #5-, and #7-count sizes for rugs and other quickpoint projects.

Interlock canvas, shown at right, is a locked-weave canvas also made with double threads. Warp threads are twisted between each pair of weft threads, making this canvas resistant to raveling and distortion from the pull of the stitches.

Because of the way they're woven, the threads of interlock canvas cannot be separated for petit point, but they're easy to see through and paint. Interlock canvas is available in sizes ranging from less than three to more than 50 threads per inch.

While canvas is available in linen, nylon, or plastic, the most widely used form is cotton because it's strong and retains its starched body well (linen canvas tends to become limp). Nylon and plastic canvases are durable, but plastic is best for projects that need to be stiff and flat or that have pieces that are cut and pieced together. Nylon is similar to plastic but is more flexible.

Most canvases are white, but some ecru, tan, and peach shades also are available. And cotton and linen canvases are easily dyed.

Judging Quality in Canvas

For a genuinely beautiful and long-lasting piece of needlepoint, use the best materials you can afford. Here are a few pointers for judging quality.

First, be sure the canvas is woven of long, smooth threads. Spaces between threads should be clear rather than full of fuzz or hairs from warp and weft threads. Also look for canvas that is free of knots and weak-looking or broken threads.

The weave should be uniform, with an equal number of warp and weft threads per inch. Warp threads and selvages should be straight, crossing weft threads at right angles. If the weave is crooked to begin with, it's apt to be crooked even after blocking.

Yarns and Threads

The sky's the limit when choosing yarns and threads for needlepoint, as long as you can thread the fiber you've selected through the eye of a needle. Don't hesitate to use wool, cotton, linen, and silk yarns, as well as metallic threads, macrame cords, ribbons, and even fabric strips for special effects!

Wool is the most popular yarn for traditional needlepoint, however. Of the many types available, *Persian wool* is the most widely used because it wears well, is easy to work with, and is available in over 300 colors. Each strand of Persian wool is made of three plies loosely twisted together so they can be separated and used individually.

Nantucket wool, which comes in tightly twisted four-ply strands, is comparable to a two-ply strand of Persian wool. Long fibers give this yarn a texture similar to tapestry yarn.

Tapestry wool comes in four-ply strands. It's a strong, smooth yarn available in a wide variety of lot-dyed colors so you can be sure colors are consistent, which makes it an excellent yarn for stitching backgrounds.

Crewel wool, used for embroidery, is a fine yarn that's especially nice for petit point. It comes in one-, three-, and five-ply sizes.

When purchasing yarn, try to buy enough for the entire project so you can be sure colors match. Also, look for colorfast yarns so you don't ruin a beautiful piece of handwork in the blocking stage.

If yarns are not colorfast, rinse dye residues from them by soaking them in lukewarm water while they're still wrapped in skeins. Let them dry thoroughly before you begin stitching.

Needles and Other Tools

For stitching needlepoint, use tapestry needles with blunt tips and large, elongated eyes. They'll help you avoid splitting the yarns or threads of the canvas and won't put undue stress on the yarn in the needle. The needle should be large enough to hold the thread easily, but small enough to pass through the mesh on the canvas without distorting the threads.

Check the chart at right for the needle to fit your canvas.

Equipment needed in addition to needles includes scissors with sharp, narrow points for snipping out mistakes; an emery-stuffed pincushion for polishing needles; masking tape; and a yarn caddy, if desired.

Frames

Many needlepointers mount their canvases in a frame for working, freeing both hands for stitching (with one hand atop the canvas and the other beneath it). This often results in a more even tension, which minimizes distortion of the canvas during stitching and reduces the need for blocking. Also, large projects are frequently worked more easily on a frame than in your lap.

There are several types of frames available. A scroll or slate frame is the most commonly used type because it's adjustable and is available in several sizes. To use one, attach canvas to rollers at the top and bottom and lace it to the sides, as shown at right. (Make sure the grain of the canvas is straight as you attach it to the frame.) The rollers turn the canvas so you can work the design one section at a time.

Mount the frame on a floor stand or prop it against a table to free your hands for stitching.

To make your own frame, assemble artist's stretcher strips into a frame at least one inch larger on all sides than your project. Staple canvas to the frame with grain lines straight.

If you wish to work in your lap, roll the canvas rather than folding it to avoid breaking the sizing. Roll it around a cardboard tube (from paper towels) and secure the ends with paper clips.

continued

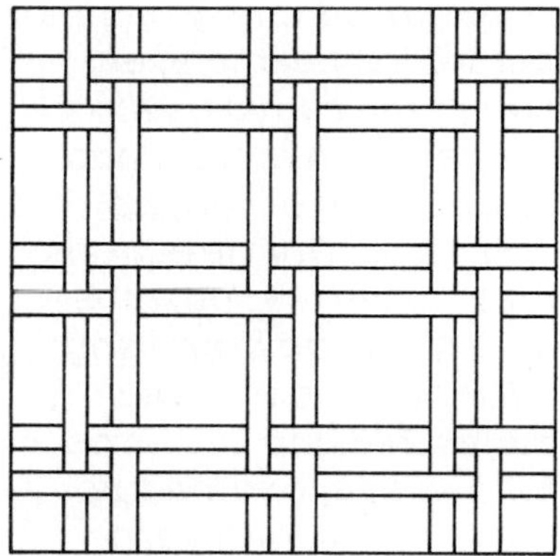
Penelope canvas

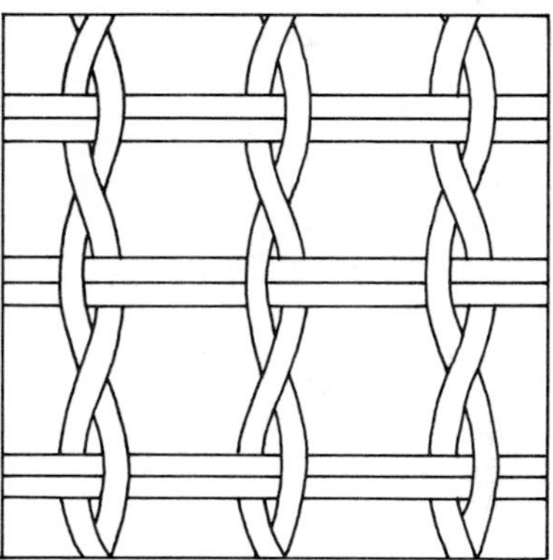
Interlock canvas

Canvas size	Needle size
#3½, #4, #5	#13
#7	#15
#10	#18
#12	#20
#14, #16	#22
#18, #20, #24	#22

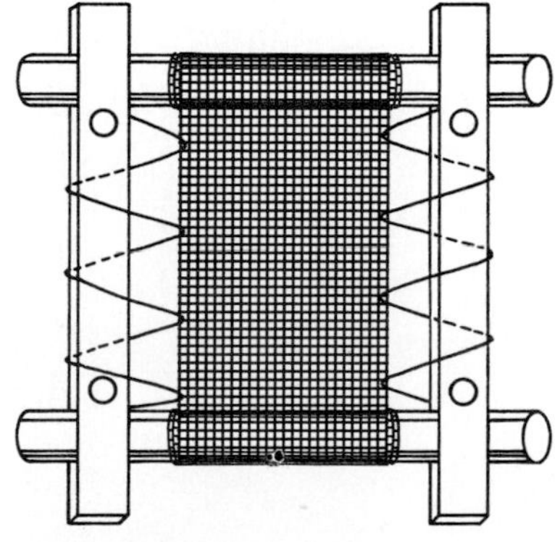
Mount canvas in a frame

Needlepoint Basics *(continued)*

Beautiful stitchery begins before the needle ever enters the canvas, with the careful handling and preparation of canvas and yarns. For directions for transferring designs to canvas and preparing it for needlepoint, see pages 248 and 272. And following are some tips for working with yarn and making the stitches that will start you off to successful stitching.

After completing your needlepoint, block it to restore the canvas to its original shape and to prepare it for final finishing.

Working with the Grain of the Yarn

Yarn, like fabric, has "grain." If you run a piece of wool through your fingers or across your cheek, you'll notice that it is smoother in one direction than the other. And when dividing strands of cotton embroidery floss, you'll find they separate fairly easily in one direction, but get hopelessly tangled in the other! If you thread the needle so you stitch "with the grain," working the thread in its smoother direction, the yarn will remain springy and attractive-looking longer than if you stitch "against the grain."

Cutting Yarn into Short Lengths

Cutting yarn into short lengths also prevents it from looking worn and tired from being pulled through the canvas too often. Cut floss or cotton pearl about 36 inches long and wool strands about 18 inches long. Silk and metallic threads should be cut to even shorter lengths.

Separating Strands into Plies

Next, separate strands into individual plies, if necessary. Then put plies back together again before threading the needle. This minimizes the amount of twist in the yarn so stitches cover the canvas better and are smoother and flatter.

While the number of plies used for a stitch depends on the size of the canvas, it's also influenced by the direction of the stitches. Diagonal stitches, such as tent stitches, lie directly over an intersection of threads. Straight stitches, such as bargello stitches, lie between threads and may require additional plies to cover the canvas adequately. So if necessary, plan to use one or more additional plies in the needle for straight stitches than for diagonal ones.

Stitching without Knots

Knots tied on the back of the canvas are apt to cause unsightly bumps. To avoid them, weave ends of yarn into the back of the work, or begin and end with waste knots. To make a waste knot, knot end of yarn and insert needle into canvas from front to back, so knot is on top. Then stitch over thread end, securing it. Clip knot and pull end of yarn to the back.

Working the Stitches

If you are a beginning needlepointer — or an experienced one learning a new stitch — keep scrap canvas handy to practice on. The time spent mastering a new stitch will be amply rewarded once you switch to your actual project canvas. The tension on the stitches will be more uniform once you've mastered the technique, and you'll spend less time picking out inaccurate or unattractive stitches.

To avoid splitting and damaging stitches already worked, whenever possible stitch "from empty to full": bring the needle up from the back of the canvas to the front, in an empty mesh; then take it down, from front to back, in a mesh that already has another stitch in it — a full one.

As you stitch, maintain even tension on the thread from stitch to stitch and with every motion needed to make a single stitch. If you pull the yarn too tight, it will not cover the canvas completely. When worked too loose, yarn tends to snag easily. With uniform tension, the stitches will look better and you'll be less apt to distort the canvas.

Finally, it's easiest to stitch a design with separate needles threaded with yarn in each color. When working with several needles, however, don't carry the yarn more than a few meshes across the back of the canvas.

Instead, weave thread through the backs of the stitches already worked. Or weave the thread end into the back, clip it, and start fresh in the new location.

Stitching with the Grain of the Canvas

Stitching with the grain of the canvas reduces tension on the threads and the degree of distortion of the canvas, which makes blocking easier. Stitches also cover canvas better than if they're worked against the grain.

This technique is particularly important on backgrounds, since they form a large part of most needlepoint designs. And the best background stitch, which distorts canvas the least, is probably the basket-weave stitch. To work it with the grain, you need to examine the canvas before you begin stitching. (For basic stitch how-to, see the Glossary on page 321.)

To determine whether the first row of basket-weave stitches should be worked from right to left or from left to right, observe the cross of canvas threads that the first stitch will cover. If the vertical (warp) thread is on top, work the needle vertically, point down, from the top left stitch in the row. The row will run downhill from upper left to lower right.

If the horizontal (weft) thread is on top, work the needle horizontally, with the point to the left, from the bottom right stitch in the row. The row will run uphill from right to left.

Blocking Needlepoint Canvas

After stitching your needlepoint, return the canvas to its original shape by blocking it on a firm, flat surface. A good blocking job eliminates the distortion that occurs from the tension and pull of the stitches.

If you've worked in basket-wcavc stitches, which greatly reduce distortion, you may need only to steam-press the back of the canvas to restore its shape.

A design worked entirely in continental stitches, however, may be very distorted and need two or three blockings before it returns to its original shape. Here is an explanation of the correct procedure for blocking your needlepoint canvases.

Sprinkle the canvas with water until the yarn feels damp (but not drenched) on both sides. Or, wet a clean towel, wring it out, and leave the canvas wrapped inside the damp towel for several hours or overnight.

Tack the damp needlepoint facedown to a blocking board made of clean, ½-inch plywood or pine boards. (Be sure to use rustproof thumbtacks or push pins.) Make sure the blocking board is larger than the needlepoint piece and has straight edges. To help line up the edges, cover the board with gingham fabric and use the checks as a guide for squaring canvas, or mark it with a 1-inch grid drawn with a *waterproof* marking pen.

When tacking the canvas to the board, start in corner A, as shown in the diagram at right, and gradually move down sides AB and AD, placing the tacks one inch apart. Make sure the canvas is flush with the blocking board so the edges are straight. Then continue along sides BC and CD, ending in corner C. Pull the canvas taut as you go, making sure the edges are straight and aligned with the gingham checks or the 1-inch grid.

Sprinkle canvas with water again and let it dry thoroughly — at least 24 hours — before removing from the board.

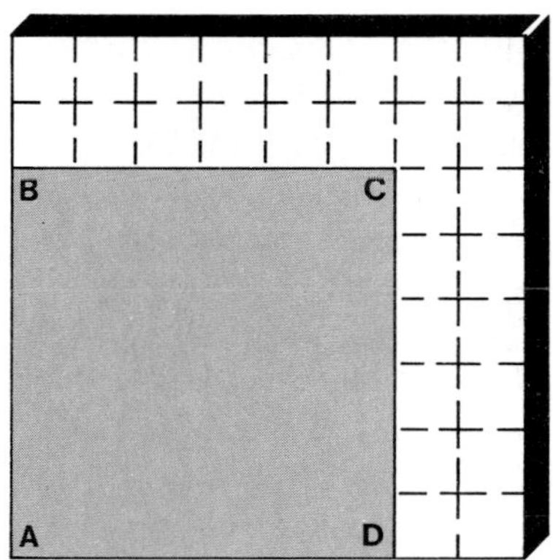

Mount canvas on a blocking board

Easy-to-Stitch Wildflower Designs *(shown on pages 236 and 237)*

Wildflowers make lovely needlepoint motifs, whether worked into pillows or a rug, as shown on pages 236 and 237, or into a mirror frame, as shown here. The natural beauty of their simple shapes and brilliant colors makes them easily adaptable to canvas.

Patterns for nine wildflower designs are on page 244. To make the pillows, rug, or frame, enlarge the patterns to different sizes and work them on a variety of canvases in easy-to-master continental and basket-weave stitches.

Pillows
Materials

For each pillow:
14x14 inches #10-count penelope canvas
4-ounce skein #505 green Paternayan 3-ply Persian yarn
Small amounts of Persian yarn in colors shown on patterns
#22 tapestry needle
Polyester fiberfill
14x14 inches backing fabric
Waterproof marking pen

Directions

Note: Finished pillows are ten inches square.

Enlarge the patterns on page 244, using a scale of "one square equals 1¼ inches." Trace each design (centered) onto canvas, using a waterproof marking pen and following the directions on page 248. Tape the edges of the canvas to prevent raveling. Mount canvas in a frame for stitching, if desired.

Begin by stitching the flowers, stems, and leaves in continental stitches, referring to the patterns for colors. Work the background in green basket-weave stitches. (Refer to the Glossary on pages 321 to 323 for stitch how-to, if necessary.) Block finished needlepoint following directions on page 241.

To assemble pillows, sew fronts to backs, right sides facing, stitching close to the last row of needlepoint. Leave an opening for turning. Trim seams to within ½ inch; turn right side out. Stuff the pillow and slip-stitch the opening.

continued

Easy-to-Stitch Wildflower Designs

Rug

Materials

2 yards 40-inch-wide #5-count penelope rug canvas
4-ounce skeins of Paternayan rug yarn, or a similar substitute, in the following amounts and colors: 15 #505 green; 10 #005 white; 2 each #545 and #589 green; 3 #569 green; 1 each of #580 and #527 green; #958, #968, #424, and #978 orange; #421 gold; #144 brown; #741 and #731 blue; #662 and #622 violet; #239, #259, and #279 pink; and #483 yellow
2 yards 36-inch-wide burlap
5½ yards rug binding
#13 tapestry needle
Waterproof marking pen
Masking tape
Staple gun and staples
Carpet thread

Directions

Note: The size of the finished rug is 36x62 inches.

Using a scale of "one square equals one inch," enlarge the patterns and trace them onto separate sheets of paper. Bind the edges of the canvas with tape.

Each motif is worked in a 10½-inch square. The white borders are six stitches wide (1¼ inches).

Beginning two inches below the top raw edge of the canvas, mark off the first six rows for the white border, using a waterproof marker. Measure down 10½ inches and mark another six rows. Continue until you've measured six bands (five blocks).

Next, working from the wide (selvage) edge of the canvas and starting 1½ inches from the edge, mark off a band six rows wide. Measure 10½ inches and mark another six rows. Continue until you have four bands. The canvas should be divided into five rows of three blocks each, with each block separated by a six-row border.

Trace one flower in the center of each square, varying the direction so the flowers either face toward or away from the center.

Work flowers first, using continental or basket-weave stitches. Then work white borders, increasing one stitch in each of the last five rows at the corner of each square to achieve the angled-corner effect shown in the photograph on pages 236 and 237. Fill background with dark green yarn, using basket-weave stitches.

To block the rug, follow directions on page 241. Press seam allowance under; tack to back of rug. Stitch rug binding to the raw edges of the canvas, then cut burlap to fit back of rug. Stitch burlap to binding on back.

Mirror Frame

(shown on page 242)

Materials

22x28 inches #10 mono or #10/20 penelope canvas
#18 tapestry needle
Paternayan 3-ply Persian yarn, or a similar substitute, in the following amounts and colors: 3 ounces each of #010 white and #505 green; 25 yards each of #G64, #545, and #589 green; and 5 yards each of colors indicated on patterns
Waterproof marking pen
½-inch plywood frame to fit finished canvas
14 feet of ½-inch half-round molding to fit edges of frame
Green paint to match background
Mirror to fit inside frame
Brackets
Staple gun and staples
White glue

Directions

Note: The finished size of the frame is 16½x23 inches.

Enlarge the patterns so each square equals ⅓ inch, and trace the patterns onto separate sheets of paper. Bind edges of canvas with masking tape.

Draw the frame on the canvas as follows. Two inches above the lower edge of the canvas, mark off three rows of threads for the first white border. Leaving a two-inch margin along the left side, mark a similar three-row-wide border. Beginning in the lower left corner of the frame, mark one 2¾-inch square and one three-row-wide border; continue across the bottom of canvas until there are five squares divided and bordered with six rows of three-row-wide borders.

Mark the top edge of the bottom frame border (see photograph on page 242). Then, working up the left side of the frame, mark seven 2¾-inch squares divided by borders. Repeat for right side and top.

Following the directions on page 248, trace one wildflower motif onto each square, centering the flowers. Vary the placement of the flowers as shown in the photograph. Work flowers first, using a half cross-stitch. Then fill borders and background with half cross-stitches or continental stitches. When working borders, increase one stitch in each of the last three rows at the corner of each square to achieve the angled-corner effect shown in the photograph.

Block the finished canvas, following the directions on page 241. Then cut a plywood frame to fit behind the needlepoint (cut out the center).

Trim unworked canvas so the edges can be turned under

Bachelor's-button

Dandelion

Violet

Gilia

California poppy

Hepatica

Clover

Black-eyed Susan

Queen Anne's Lace

and stapled to the back of the plywood. Apply a layer of glue to one side of the plywood frame and stretch the canvas in place on top of the glue. Staple the edges in back and let dry.

Cut half-round molding to fit the inside and outside edges of the frame, mitering the corners. Paint the molding green and glue the pieces in place on the frame. Attach mirror to back of frame with brackets.

Work wildflowers in colors indicated on patterns, *except* on the mirror frame eliminate flower C of the Black-eyed Susan design and work petals of violets in varying shades of purple with centers in yellow and gold.

Quickpoint WELCOME Rug

Large-mesh canvas makes this 27x42-inch WELCOME rug, with its Jacobean-style border, a quick and easy project to stitch. The completely graphed pattern is on page 246, but you may substitute your name or initials in the center of the rug by following the directions below.

Materials

1⅓ yards 36-inch-wide #5-count interlock rug canvas
Wool rug yarn in the following colors and amounts: white (250 yards), dark blue (200 yards), medium blue (50 yards), and light blue (50 yards)
Large tapestry needle
Masking tape
Waterproof marking pen
Graph paper
4 yards 1-inch-wide blue grosgrain ribbon (optional)
4 yards 4-inch-wide rug binding
11 feet 1x2-inch lumber (frame)
Wood glue and nails
Eye hooks and picture wire
Staple gun

Directions

Cut canvas to 31x46 inches to allow a 2-inch margin around the design. Bind the edges of the canvas with masking tape to keep yarn from tearing on them. Then mark the center of the canvas with a waterproof pen by locating the middle horizontal and vertical threads.

The pattern shown on page 246 is for the upper left quadrant of the border design. Work from the chart, or copy the entire design onto graph paper by flopping the pattern to reproduce the stitch sequence for each quarter of the border.

Center the design on the canvas and begin by working the outermost dark blue border in continental stitches. Work the second and third blue borders, the floral motif, and the WELCOME letters in continental stitches. Fill the background in the center of the rug with white basket-weave stitches. (For an explanation of the stitches, see the Glossary on pages 321 to 323.)

Block the completed rug, following the directions on page 241.

To finish the rug, whipstitch the edge of the rug binding securely to the edge of the needlepoint stitches around the edge of the rug. Assemble a 24x42-inch frame with the 1x2-inch lumber, glue, and nails. Then place the rug facedown on a table and center the frame over it. Starting in the middle of each side, pull the margin of the rug to the back of the frame and staple in place. Miter the corners. The edge of the outermost blue border in the design should fall along the front of the frame.

For an attractive finish on the edge of the frame, blindstitch 1-inch-wide blue ribbon in place over the rug binding along the side edges of the frame. Attach eye hooks and wire for hanging.

How to Stitch a Name or Monogram in the Center of the Rug

To stitch your name or monogram in the center of the rug, work the borders and floral motif following the directions above. Then find a suitable alphabet style by looking through needlepoint or embroidery books; transfer the letters to tracing paper. Or, sketch your letters freehand, making sure they will adapt well.

To plan the size of the letters, keep in mind that the center of the rug measures about 72x150 meshes. Allow a margin of four or five meshes at the sides of the letters so they don't run into the border, and about two meshes between letters. Then divide the number of letters in your name or monogram into 140 to determine the *average* number of meshes you'll need for each letter. Use this only as a guide, however, because some letters such as "I" or "i" require less space than others, such as "m" or "w."

Chart the letters on a sheet of five-squares-per-inch graph paper. This makes them full size so you can easily tell whether they'll need to be enlarged or reduced to fit the available space. When you've designed the letters on graph paper and are satisified that they'll fit attractively in the center of the rug, stitch them in place with continental stitches.

Quickpoint WELCOME Rug *(continued)*

(Actual dimensions of rug are 42 X 27 inches worked on five-squares-per-inch interlock canvas. Pattern is ¼ of border)

Color Key
- Dark Blue
- Medium Blue
- Light Blue

1 Square = 1 Stitch

Welcome

Quickpoint Rose Wreath

With needlepoint, you can enjoy the beauty of roses year 'round. This quickpoint wreath is worked in wool rug yarns, mounted on plywood, and framed. Because of the large-mesh canvas, progress is fast, especially since you use only two basic stitches – continental and basket-weave. Secure the canvas to a needlepoint frame while you work to prevent distortion.

The pattern and a closeup view of the wreath are on pages 250 and 251.

Materials

26x26 inches #5-count rug canvas
¾ pound white rug yarn (see note at right)
Approximately 15 yards rug yarn in each of the following colors: red, pink, and green (see note at right)
#13 tapestry needle
Masking tape
Needlepoint frame or four 26-inch artist's stretcher strips
Quilt batting
28x28x⅜-inch piece of plywood
10 feet of 1x3-inch pine
White paint

Directions

Note: We used Paternayan rug yarns for this wreath; the specific color numbers are noted on the chart on page 250. Other rug yarns of comparable weight and color may be substituted, however.

Bind the raw edges of the canvas with masking tape to prevent fraying. Then mount the canvas on a needlepoint frame or on artist's stretcher strips to prevent distortion as you work.

Because yarn sometimes contains color residue that runs when the needlework is blocked or cleaned, soak it for a few minutes in cool water. Then let it dry thoroughly before beginning to stitch.

Mark the center of the canvas and begin stitching there, following the chart on the next page. Work the roses first, and then the leaves, using continental stitches. Finally, work the background in the center of the wreath and around the roses until the square measures 23½x23½ inches. Use either continental stitches or basket-weave stitches for the background.

Cut two layers of quilt batting the exact size of the finished wreath. Center the batting and the canvas on the plywood board without cutting or turning the canvas; staple the canvas in place.

Notch *the edges* of the pine boards to the thickness of the plywood (about ⅜ inch), cut and miter the boards to fit the plywood, and glue and nail the frame together. Paint it white. Mount the plywood in the frame by tacking it in place with wire brads.

continued

Transferring a Design to Canvas

Enlarge or reduce your pattern to size on brown wrapping paper or white craft paper, following the directions on page 272. Then go over the outlines with a black marking pen so they are easy to see. Next, tape the pattern to a large, flat surface and cover it with a sheet of clear plastic or acetate to keep it clean, if desired. Center the canvas on top of the pattern and secure it with masking tape. Be sure to leave at least two inches of canvas on each side of the design for blocking and finishing.

Using a light-colored waterproof pen, transfer the pattern to the canvas. To be sure the pen is waterproof, test it by marking on a sample piece of canvas and sprinkling the canvas with water. If the lines don't run or bleed, the pen is safe to use. It is important to use a light-colored pen so the lines do not show through the stitching once you work the canvas. Transfer the entire design to the canvas by tracing over the pattern, following the lines carefully. This technique gives you a basic pattern outline that is adequate when working a simple design with easy-to-read lines and shapes.

If your pattern is more complicated or requires intricate shading, it's a good idea to paint your canvas with acrylic or oil paints, as explained on page 273. This assures you of getting all the details and shading shown on the original pattern. Another way to work a needlepoint pattern, especially when only a portion of it is given, is to chart the entire design on graph paper with symbols or colored pencils and work directly from the chart onto canvas.

Quickpoint Rose Wreath *(continued)*

1 Square = 1 Stitch

Color Key

Symbol	Color
■	# 818 dark red
◪	# 848 med. dark red
☒	# 858 med. red
◿	# 868 light red
⊡	# 878 pink
◙	# 505 dark green
◎	# 510 med. dark green
▪	# 555 med. light green
⊞	# 570 light green
□	# 010 white

Easy-to-Stitch Bargello Bench

Wonderfully quick, easy, and versatile, bargello is satin stitching on canvas. Traditionally, it is worked over four threads in a "dome-and-spires" or "flame-stitch" design. The pattern is established with the first line of stitches across the canvas, and all subsequent rows duplicate it exactly. And by varying yarns and colors, the effect can be dramatic, as in the bench cover opposite, or subtle, as in the pillow on page 293.

Materials

10 shades of 3-ply Persian yarn (see note at right)
21x31 inches #12-count interlock canvas, or sufficient canvas to fit your own bench (be sure to add 2-inch margins to each side)
#18 tapestry needle
Needlepoint frame (optional)
Masking tape
Quilt batting
⅜x15x23-inch plywood board, or size to fit your bench
Staple gun

Directions

Note: This bargello pattern uses five shades each in two different colors of yarn. Use four 32-inch strands of yarn of each shade (approximately 3½ yards) to make the 17x27-inch cover shown.

To adjust the yarn quantities to fit your bench, stitch one complete row of the design. Determine how much yarn you have used for the row and then determine how many rows you will need to complete the design. Do this by counting the number of meshes in the length of the finished design and dividing by four (since each stitch covers four threads of canvas).

If you need to adjust the width of the rows, work one row starting in the center of the row and working out to one side. Stop the design wherever necessary, or continue the design if the rows need to be longer. To continue the design, pick up a portion of the design from the pattern below and stitch that extra portion on both sides of the canvas (so the design remains symmetrical).

Tape the edges of the canvas to prevent raveling. With a waterproof pen, mark a 2-inch border on the canvas to be left unstitched. Attach the canvas to a scroll frame, if desired, to minimize distortion from the stitching and to reduce the need for blocking when the needlepoint is finished.

Begin stitching with the lightest shade of one color. Following the chart below, begin the first horizontal row on the left-hand side of the canvas and work to the center. Then, reverse the pattern shown in the chart below and complete the row by stitching to the right-hand side of the canvas.

Complete four more rows, one on top of the other, using each shade of the first color. Work the rows according to shade, going from light to dark. Then begin a sixth row, using the lightest shade of the second color. Complete the next four rows as for the first color, going from light to dark so each shade is used once.

These first ten rows make up the pattern repeat. Continue working this repeat until you reach 27 inches, or the desired length.

To finish the two ends, fill in the pattern between the peaks using the correct color sequence so rows are even across ends.

Block the canvas, following the directions on page 241. Cut three to five 15x23-inch pieces of quilt batting and layer them on top of the plywood. Cover the batting with the finished bargello and staple the 2-inch margins to the back of the board.

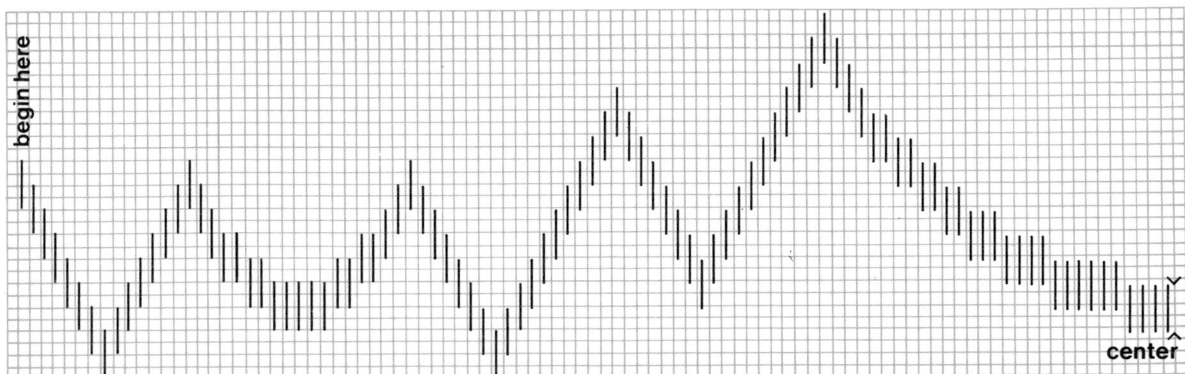

1 Square = 1 Mesh

Pillows

A Primer of Design and Pattern

Pillows are pretty, practical, and small enough to be a perfect showcase for needlepoint stitches and patterns. Begin with a pillow to master a new stitch or technique, then try a larger project. Among our pillows, you'll find a wealth of designs to perk up your stitchery repertoire, starting with the "woven" pillows shown here, in which the design is made by the stitches themselves (directions are on the next page). Following those are easy-to-stitch variegated-yarn pillows and some old favorites—patterns from quilts and a farmer's kerchief—as well as an elegant floral design and a sampler pillow. See page 258 for directions for assembling your pillow.

"Woven" Pillows *(shown on pages 254 and 255)*

The outstanding texture and pattern of some needlepoint stitches show to best advantage when the stitches are worked in simple box-and-border designs, as the pillows shown on pages 254 and 255 illustrate. Needlepoint these pillows in weaving, long-arm cross-, wheat-sheaf, and Scotch stitches.

Materials

For each pillow:
18x18 inches #5-count rug canvas
#13 tapestry needle
½ yard off-white brushed corduroy (backing)
Polyester fiberfill

White and Rust Pillow

70-yard skeins (2 ounces each) 3-ply Bucilla Multi-Craft Yarn, or a similar substitute, in the following amounts and colors: 2 off-white and 1 rust
1⅔ yards ⅞-inch-wide off-white grosgrain ribbon

White and Blue Pillow

Two 70-yard skeins (2 ounces each) 3-ply off-white Bucilla Multi-Craft Yarn
3½ yards blue 3-ply yarn
1¼ yards ⅝-inch-wide blue grosgrain ribbon
1⅔ yards ⅞-inch-wide blue grosgrain ribbon

White, Blue, and Green Pillow

70-yard skeins (2 ounces each) 3-ply Bucilla Multi-Craft Yarn, or a suitable substitute, in the following amounts and colors: 2 off-white, 1 blue, and 1 green

Directions

Bind the edges of the canvas with masking tape. Then mark the center horizontal and vertical threads and mount the canvas in a frame for working, if desired.

Following charts opposite, work pillows in stitches indicated. Note that each chart is for one portion of a pillow; reverse as necessary to complete the design. The weaving stitch, long-arm cross-stitch, and wheat-sheaf stitch are explained below. For an explanation of the remaining stitches, see pages 321 to 323. Complete each pillow front as indicated in the directions below, then assemble the pillows following directions on page 258.

White and Rust Pillow

To begin, count down six rows and over six rows from the center of the canvas. Begin stitching in the lower left corner of the center square, following the diagram opposite. In row 1, work a half cross-stitch in every other mesh across the canvas. For row 2, work back across the row from right to left, making a reversed continental stitch over two rows of canvas, with the lower edge of the stitch in the same mesh as the lower edge of the half cross-stitches (see pattern diagram). For row 3, start in the mesh that the second row passed over; work half cross-stitches over two rows of canvas. For row 4, start in the mesh that row 3 passed over; work reversed continental stitches over two rows of canvas. Continue until the last row, then repeat row 1. Finish with one fill-in stitch at the end of each line of the pattern.

To work the border of rust long-arm cross-stitches, begin at the left end of the row. First work a single cross-stitch over two threads of the canvas. Then bring the needle up again at the beginning of the cross-stitch, carry it across four threads and up two, and reinsert in the canvas as shown in the diagram opposite. Bring it straight down two threads and up again. Then carry it back four threads and across two; reinsert in the canvas at the first cross-stitch, making an elongated cross. Bring the needle across two threads (on the underside) and down two threads (on the underside) and to the front again. Repeat the steps above, making the next stitch. At the end of the row, work a cross-stitch over two rows as a filler stitch, turn the canvas, and continue.

Work the remainder of the pillow front in weaving and long-arm cross-stitches, as indicated on the pattern. Finish by working one row of white continental stitches around the last rust border.

Block the completed pillow, following directions on page 241. Then stitch grosgrain ribbon to the edge of the pillow front, between the last row of the border and the row of continental stitches.

White and Blue Pillow

Machine-stitch grosgrain ribbon to canvas between threads 21 and 24 (counted from the center), carefully mitering corners. Just inside the ribbon on the left side, work a row of wheat-sheaf stitches as shown opposite. For each stitch, work five upright Gobelin stitches over four rows of canvas. Then bring the needle up under the center (third) stitch but slide it under the two right-hand stitches and bring it out on the right side of the upright stitches. Carry yarn to the left, across the five stitches. Tuck the needle under the stitches and reinsert it in the canvas under the center (third) stitch, pulling snugly so upright stitches fan out. Each set of stitches shares a mesh with the

White and blue pillow 1 Square = 1 Stitch

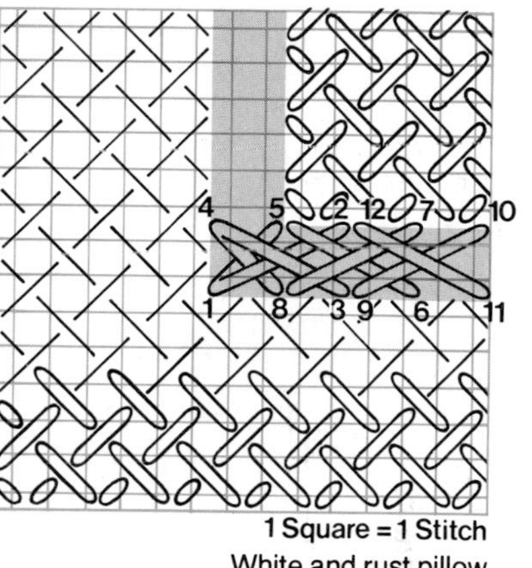

1 Square = 1 Stitch
White and rust pillow

adjoining set, as shown in the diagram. To finish, work an upright cross-stitch over two rows of canvas between each set of sheaf stitches. Then work a row of backstitches between the ribbon and the sheaf stitches to cover canvas threads.

Next, fill the center with weaving stitches. Work outer border in Scotch stitches, forming a checkerboard design as shown in the pattern diagram. After completing Scotch stitches, work a blue upright cross-stitch in the middle of each set of four squares and wrap yarn around the cross, forming a mock French knot.

Finish the outer border by working upright stitches as indicated on the pattern and covering them with cross-stitches as shown. Work one row of white continental stitches around the design. Block the completed pillow front, following directions on page 241. Then stitch blue grosgrain ribbon to the outer edge of the pillow, following directions for the rust and white pillow. Assemble following directions on page 258.

Weaving stitch–White
Long-arm cross-stitch–Rust

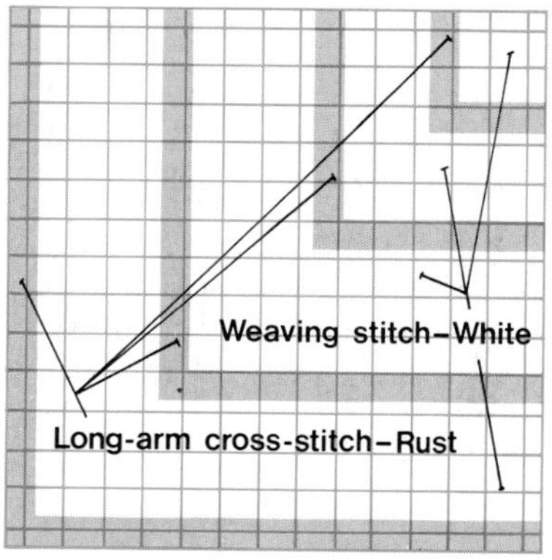

1 Square = 1 Inch
White and rust pillow

White, Blue, and Green Pillow

Work in weaving stitches and long-arm cross-stitches, following directions for the rust and white pillow. After the needlepoint is completed, block the pillow, following directions on page 241. Assemble the pillow, following directions on page 258.

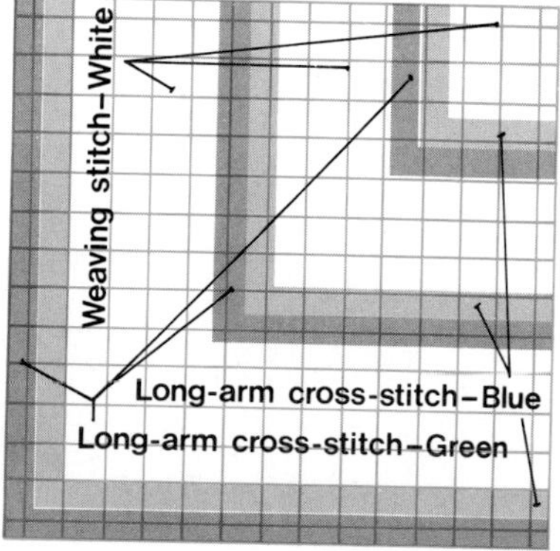

1 Square = 1 Inch
White, blue, and green pillow

Designs with Variegated Yarn

Variegated knitting yarn can add a new twist to traditional needlepoint! The changing colors form brilliant patterns in the two simple-to-stitch pillows, opposite.

The pillow on the left is worked entirely in basket-weave stitches for diagonal rows of color. The one in the chair is a combination of diagonal basket-weave stitches and horizontal continental stitches worked in boxes.

Materials

(For each pillow)
16x20 inches #10-count canvas
Two 3½-ounce skeins 4-ply Coats and Clark Mexicana variegated knitting yarn, or a similar substitute
#18 tapestry needle
Masking tape
Waterproof marking pen
½ yard navy or yellow backing fabric
Polyester fiberfill

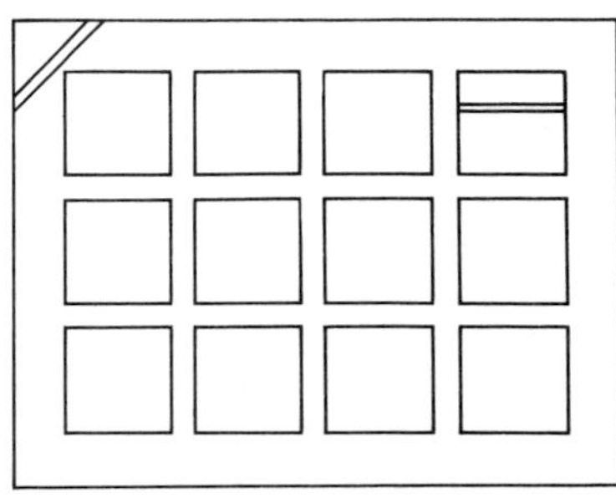

Directions

Plain Variegated Pillow

Using a waterproof marking pen, draw a 12x16-inch rectangle on the canvas, leaving a two-inch border around each side. Bind the edges of the canvas with masking tape to prevent raveling, and mount the canvas in a frame, if desired.

Begin working the design in either the lower left or upper right corner. Work the entire pillow in basket-weave stitches, referring to the Glossary on pages 321 to 323 for stitch how-to, if necessary.

The changing colors in the variegated yarn create the pattern. To vary the pattern, work small sections rather than entire rows. For example, stitch several inches of basket-weave stitches at a time. If the colors begin to run together and change too often so that the design begins to look busy, work the pillow in smaller sections, referring to the photograph for ideas. But work an entire row every so often to make colors look brighter and more distinct.

Vary the positions in which rows begin and end, making some rows longer than others.

Block the pillow, following the directions on page 241. Trim the canvas margins to within one inch of the needlepoint. Cut backing fabric to match the pillow front, and assemble the pillow following the directions below.

Variegated Pillow with Squares

Using a waterproof pen, draw an 11x14½-inch rectangle (centered) on the canvas. Bind the edges of the canvas with masking tape and mount the canvas in a frame for working, if desired.

Following the pattern below at left, mark twelve 2½-inch squares (25x25 threads) with a waterproof pen. Leave six threads between each square and twelve threads around the outside edges, as shown in the pattern.

Work the squares in horizontal rows using continental stitches. Then fill the background with basket-weave stitches worked on the diagonal. Because of the variegated yarn and the two different stitches, the squares will contrast with the background.

Block the pillow, following directions on page 241; trim the canvas to within one inch of the needlepoint. Cut backing fabric to match canvas, and assemble the pillow following directions below.

How to Assemble a Pillow

To assemble your pillow, cut backing fabric the same size as the pillow front. If desired, add welting as follows. Cut cable cord to go in seam of pillow front, plus two inches. Cut and piece 1½-inch-wide bias strips of fabric to cover cording. Using a zipper foot, machine-stitch fabric over cording. Baste cording to pillow front between the first and second rows of needlepoint.

With right sides facing, stitch pillow front to back on three sides, between first and second rows of needlepoint. Leave one side open for turning. Clip corners and trim the seam margin to ½ inch. Turn right side out, stuff, and slip-stitch the opening.

Quilt-Pattern Pillow—Attic Windows Design

Patterns from quilts make beautiful and charming motifs for creative stitchery. This attic windows design, for example, is a traditional pattern popular among our pioneer ancestors. To duplicate it, work a mini-quilt in needlepoint using tapestry wool on #14-count canvas, and finish it as a pillow.

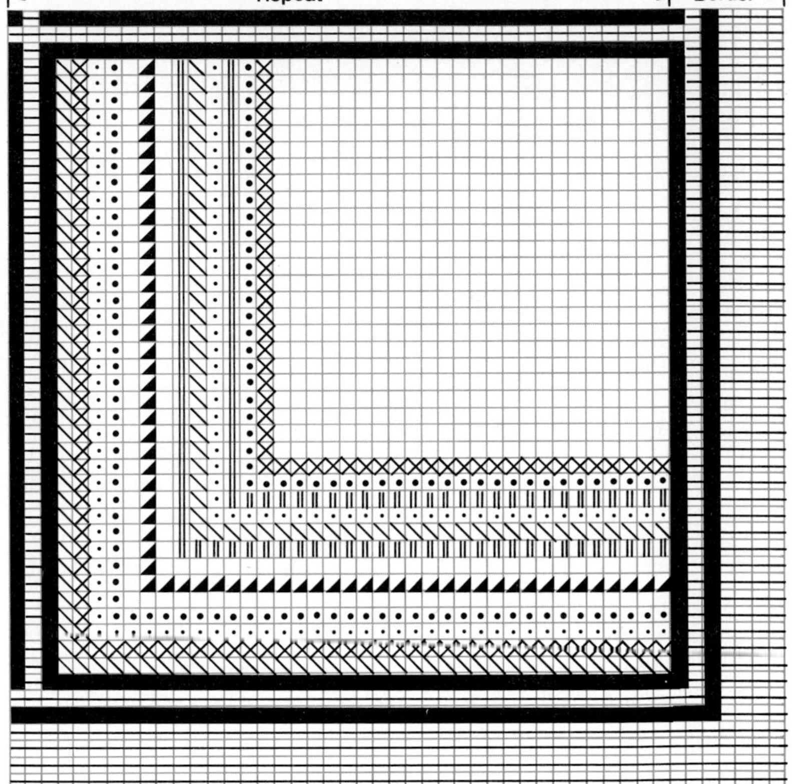

Materials

42 yards light blue tapestry yarn
16 yards dark rust tapestry yarn
32 yards tapestry yarn in each of the following colors: navy blue, light rust, medium rust, white, gold, and dark blue
58 yards gray tapestry yarn for border around pillow
17x17-inch piece #14-count canvas
#18 tapestry needle
Masking tape
Waterproof marking pen
½ yard gray backing fabric
Polyester fiberfill

Directions

The pattern above is for the square in the lower right corner of the pillow and the border design. Repeat it 16 times, in four rows of four squares each, to make the pillow 12½ inches square.

Using a waterproof pen, draw a 12½x12½-inch square in the center of the canvas. Bind the edges of the canvas with masking tape to prevent raveling, and if desired, mount the canvas in a frame to prevent distortion and minimize the need for blocking.

Use complete strands of tapestry yarn for stitching, and begin and end each strand with a waste knot to reduce bulk on the back of the canvas. Beginning in the lower right corner of the canvas, stitch the border design and square, following the color key. Work single rows of color in continental stitches, but work the upper right square in each block with basket-weave stitches, referring to the Glossary on pages 321 to 323 for stitch explanations, if necessary. Then stitch the remainder of the pillow as indicated above, following the "repeat" and "border" notations on the pattern.

Block the finished canvas, following the directions on page 241. Trim unworked canvas to within ½ inch of the needlepoint; cut backing fabric to match. Assemble the pillow following the directions on page 258.

THE
QUILTERS
Women and
Domestic
Art

Quilt-Pattern Pillow— Chrysanthemum Bargello Design

The "chrysanthemum" was a popular quilt motif a hundred years ago, and today it's still as appealing. To enjoy it even more, why not needlepoint this charming design?

Each "block" of the needlepoint mini-quilt, opposite, is worked in bargello and tent stitches, with a diamond-eye stitch in the center. Stitch nine flower motifs, then work the background in basket-weave stitches until the pillow is 15 inches square.

Materials

19x19 inches #12-count canvas
#18 tapestry needle
3-ply Persian yarn in the following colors: olive green, dark yellow, medium yellow, and brick red
½ yard green velveteen
1¾ yards cable cord (optional)
Graph paper (10 squares per inch)
Needlepoint frame (optional)

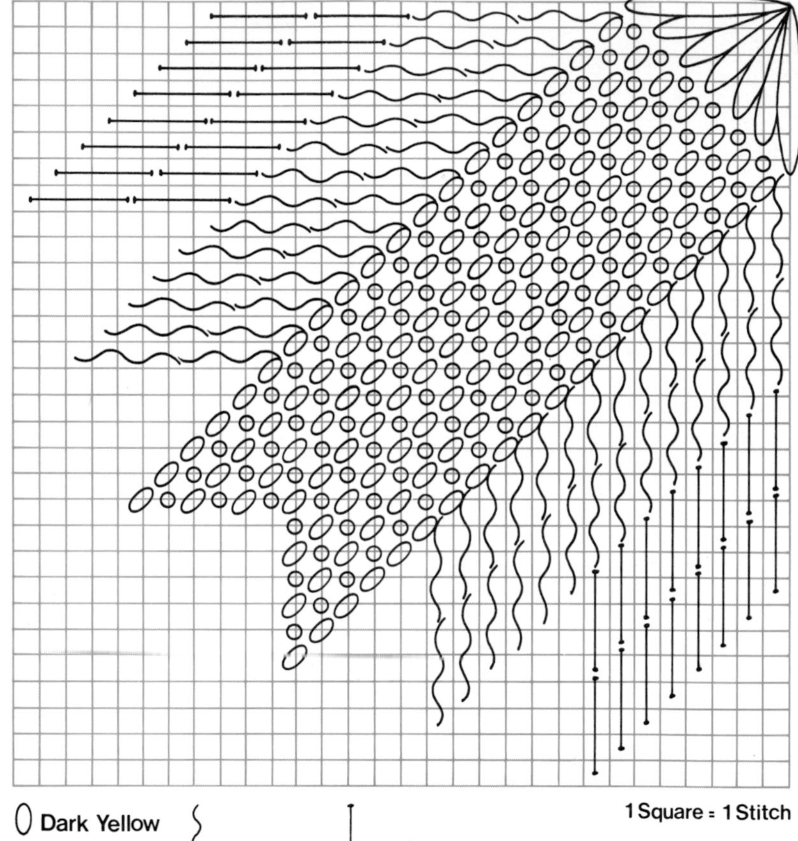

Directions

The pattern above is for one-fourth of one of the motifs in the pillow. Transfer it to graph paper, reversing as necessary to complete it. The center stitch, horizontally and vertically, is worked only once. The design is worked nine times on the pillow, in three rows of three motifs each, and the points on each star share a mesh with the points of the adjoining stars. You may transfer the entire pillow design to graph paper, or work from the chart.

Bind the edges of the canvas with masking tape, and mount the canvas in a frame, if desired. Begin stitching in one corner, leaving a 2-inch margin of unworked canvas. Using full, 3-ply strands of wool, stitch the arms of the motif in bargello and tent stitches, as indicated on the pattern. Work the center in a diamond-eye stitch. Finally, work the background in green basket-weave stitches, adding four additional rows around the edges of the motifs. For an explanation of the stitches, see the Glossary on pages 321 to 323.

Block the finished needlepoint following the directions on page 241. Then cut backing fabric to size and use remaining fabric to cover cording, if desired. Assemble the pillow following the directions on page 258.

Bandanna Design

Delightful pillow patterns sometimes come from unlikely places! The design opposite, for example, was inspired by a traditional red kerchief. While basket-weave stitches are used for the background, Smyrna stitches and cross-stitches also add textural interest to this old-fashioned and familiar design.

Materials

16x16 inches #10-count canvas
3-ply Paternayan Persian wool yarn, or a similar substitute, in the following amounts and colors: 95 yards #R69 red, 20 yards #105 dark brown, and 20 yards #005 white
#18 tapestry needle
Masking tape
Graph paper
Needlepoint frame (optional)
½ yard dark brown velveteen for backing
1½ yards cable cord
Polyester fiberfill

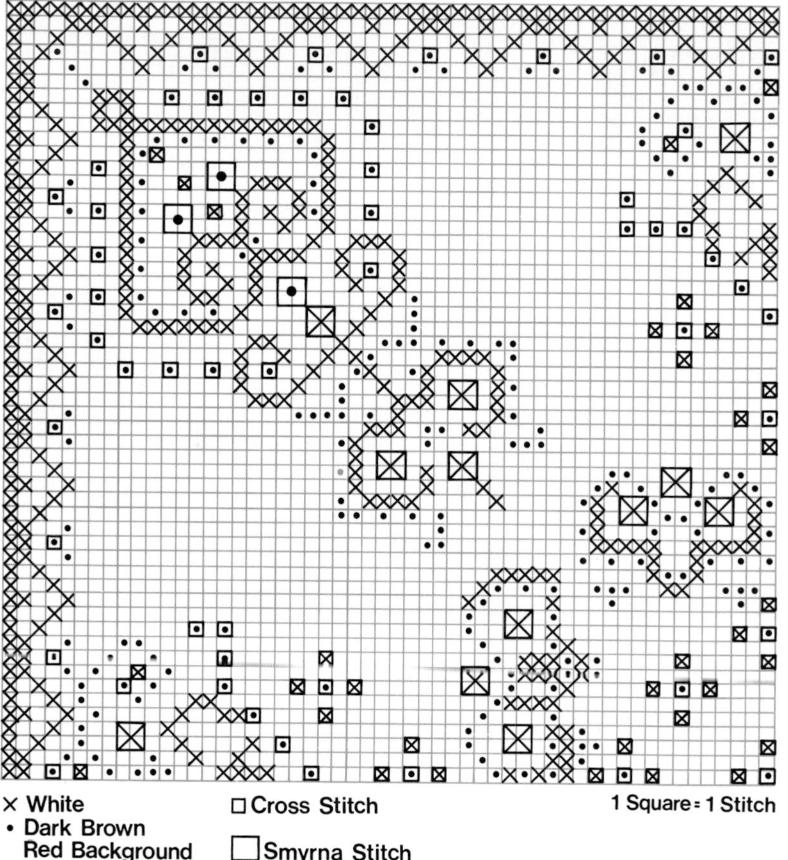

× White
• Dark Brown
Red Background
□ Cross Stitch
□ Smyrna Stitch
1 Square = 1 Stitch

Directions

The pattern above represents one quarter of this 12x12-inch pillow design. Transfer it to graph paper and complete the design by flopping the pattern three times to produce the entire pillow.

Bind the edges of the canvas with masking tape to prevent raveling, and label the top so you are careful not to turn or twist the canvas as you work. Mount the canvas in a frame to minimize distortion, if desired.

Begin working the design from the pattern, using full 3-ply strands of yarn and leaving a 2-inch margin for blocking around the edges. Work the brown and white designs in continental, Smyrna, and cross-stitches before filling in the red background in basket-weave stitches. Refer to the Glossary on pages 321 to 323 for an explanation of the stitches, if necessary.

When the pattern is complete, add five rows of red basket-weave stitches around the outside edges so none of the design is lost when the pillow is assembled.

Block the canvas, following the directions on page 241. Then trim the margin of the canvas, cover the cable cord, cut the velveteen backing, and assemble the pillow following directions on page 258.

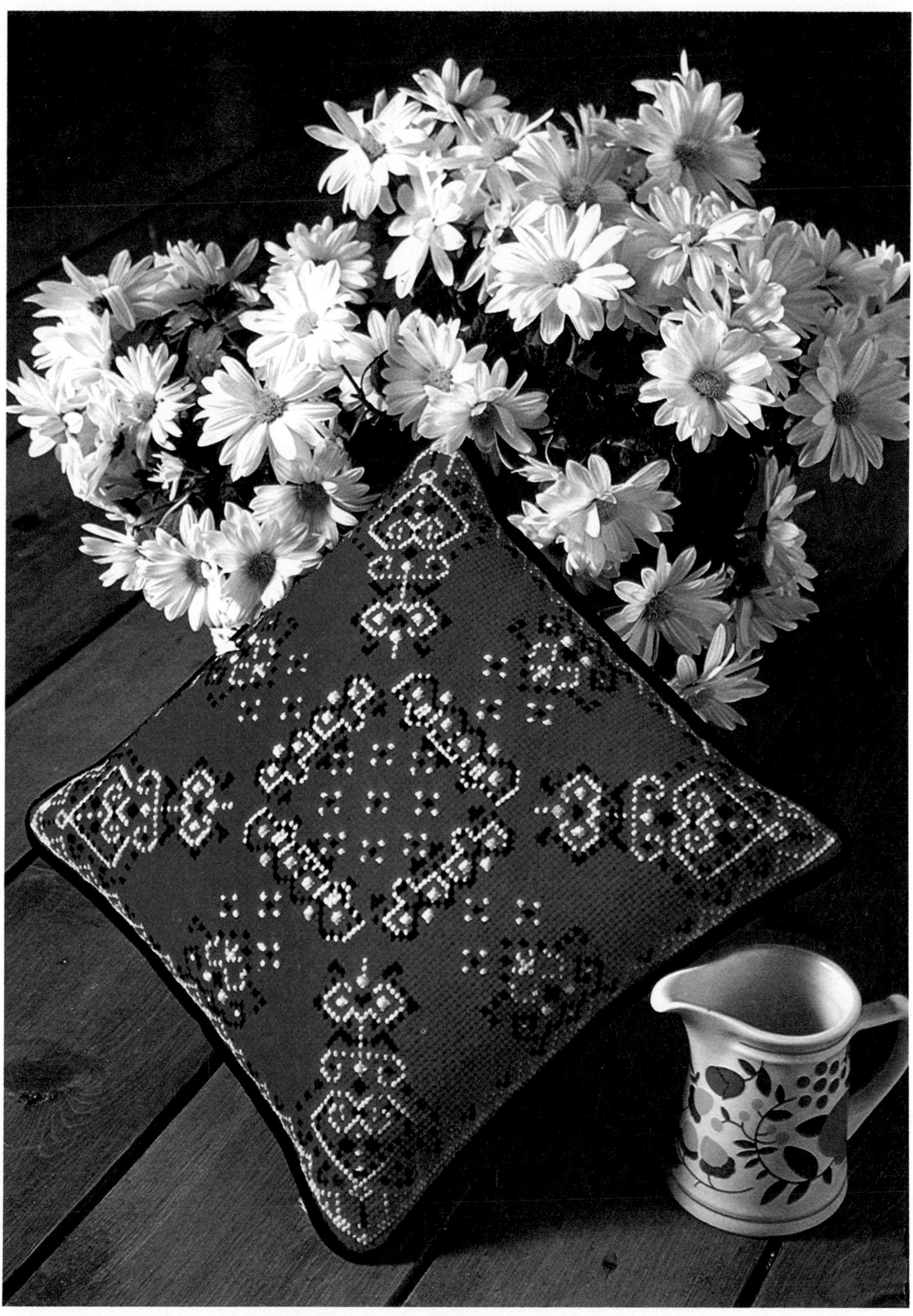

Wedding Ring Pillow

Special occasions call for special tributes, such as the lovely wedding ring pillow, opposite. To stitch up this romantic design, use cashmere and cross-stitches in the border, and basket-weave and continental stitches for the blocks of flowers. Between each block, work a stylized wedding ring in mosaic stitches. The finished pillow is 12 inches square.

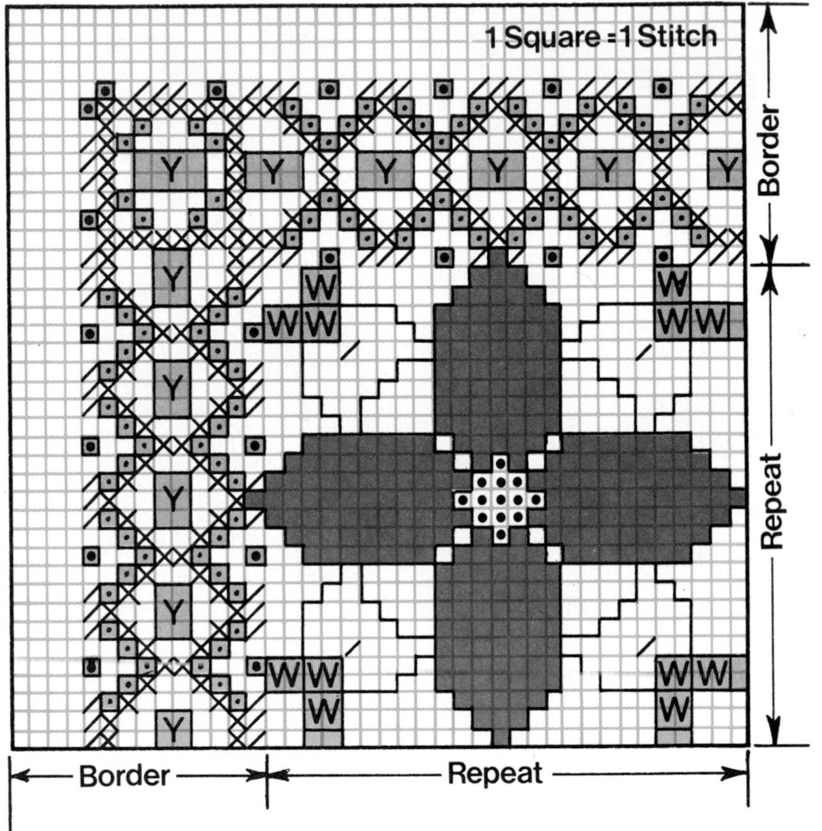

Materials

16x16 inches #14-count canvas
1 ounce (approximately 44 yards) #743 blue 3-ply Paternayan Persian wool yarn, or a similar substitute
½ ounce (approximately 22 yards) #590 green 3-ply Paternayan Persian wool yarn, or a similar substitute
40-yard skeins Elsa Williams wool tapestry yarn, or a similar substitute, in the following amounts and colors: 2 #N105 pink, 2 #N304 yellow, 2 #N805 off-white, 1 #N900 white, and 1 #N401 dark green
#19 tapestry needle
Masking tape
Graph paper
½ yard pale green velveteen
Polyester fiberfill
1½ yards cable cord

Color Key

- ● Dark Green Continental Stitch
- ● Dark Green Cross-Stitch
- W White Mosaic Stitch
- • Blue Cross-Stitch
- Y Yellow Cashmere Stitch
- □ White Continental Stitch
- ☒ Pink
- ◸ Green

Directions

The pattern above represents the upper left corner of the pillow. Transfer it to graph paper and continue charting the design until there are 25 flower motifs (five rows of five flowers each), following the repeats indicated on the pattern.

Bind the edges of the canvas with masking tape and mount the canvas in a frame, if desired. Begin working the design, leaving a 2-inch margin of unworked canvas around the edges. Use 2-ply strands of Persian wool yarn and full strands of tapestry yarn.

Work the pink, yellow, and blue flowers in basket-weave stitches; then work the pale green leaves and the dark green centers in continental stitches. Fill in the background in basket-weave stitches, and work the white squares in mosaic stitches. Work the border design one color at a time in the stitches indicated on the chart. For stitch how-to and diagrams, see the Glossary on pages 321 to 323.

Block the finished canvas following the directions on page 241. Trim the unworked canvas to within ½ inch of the needlepoint.

Cut green velveteen the same size as the needlepoint canvas. Then use remaining velveteen to cut and piece 1¼-inch bias strips to cover cording. Assemble the pillow following the directions on page 258.

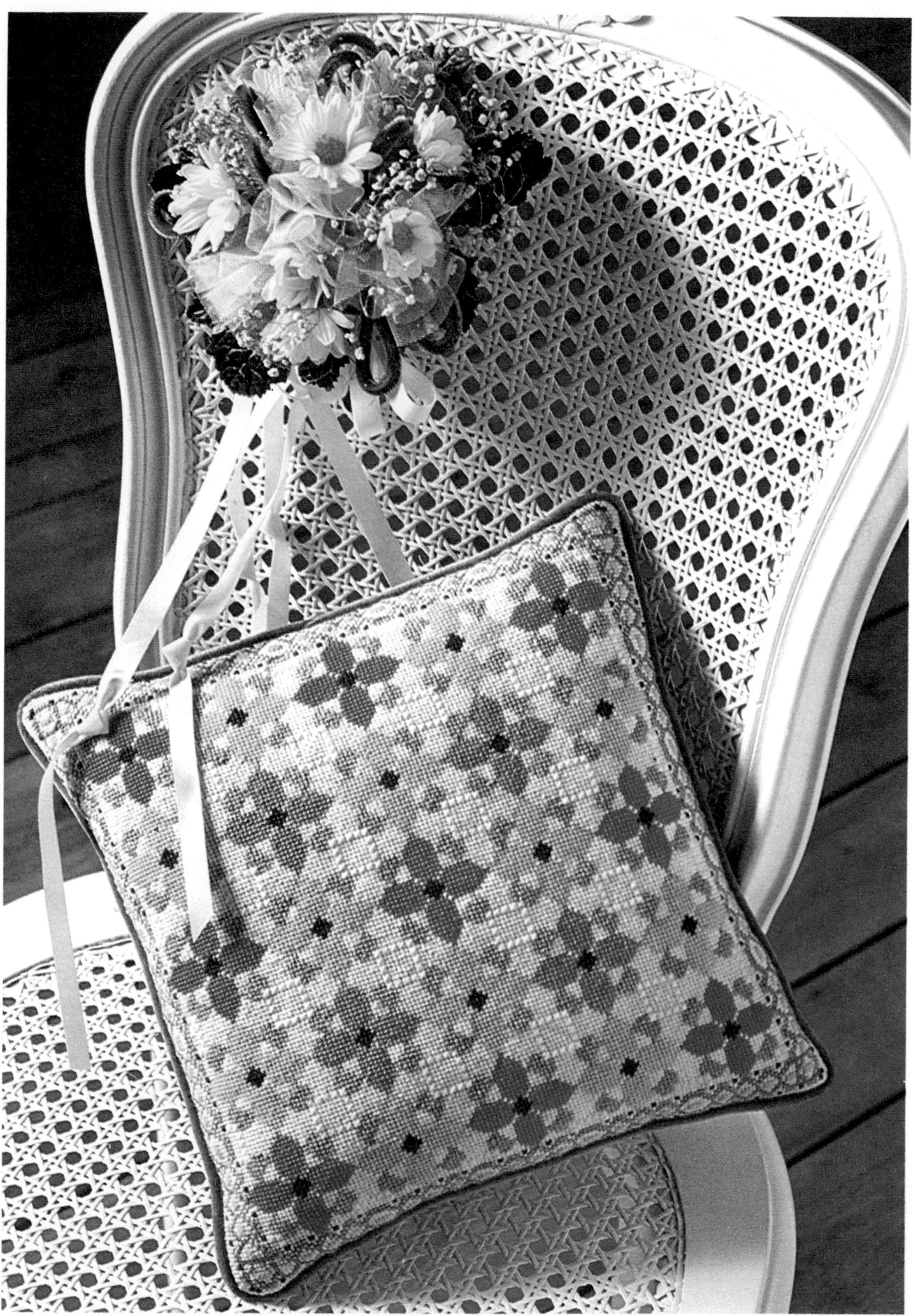

Paper-Doll Sampler Pillow

A variety of pleasing needlepoint patterns that combine different stitches and techniques are used in this sampler pillow. Although the dolls are worked in basket-weave stitches, the cream-colored background is worked in reverse basket-weave — a technique that leaves the "weaving" pattern on the finished side. The border is divided into sections so you can practice a number of stitches, working each design as explained at right.

Materials
16x16 inches #10-count canvas
3-ply strands of Persian wool yarn in cream, red, pink, light yellow, medium yellow, light turquoise, medium turquoise, medium green, dark green, medium orange, dark orange, light brown, and medium brown
#18 tapestry needle
Waterproof marking pen
Masking tape
1½ yards calico fabric
Polyester fiberfill

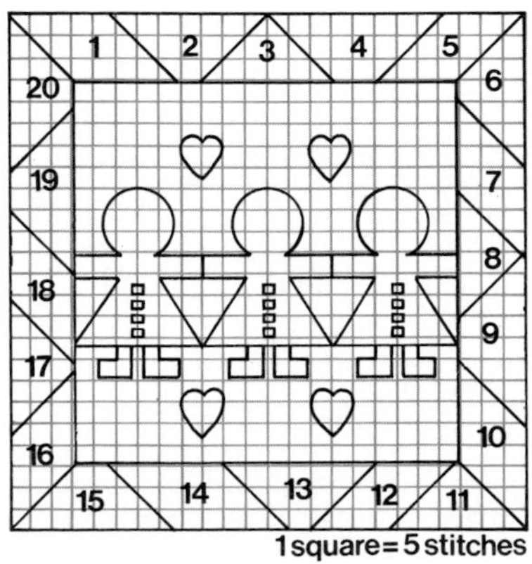

Directions
Tape the edges of the canvas and, using a waterproof pen, draw a 90x90-mesh square in the center. Then mark a border 16 meshes wide around the square. Enlarge the pattern and transfer it to canvas, following the directions on page 272. (Dolls are 30 stitches wide.)

Using full 3-ply strands of yarn, work light-colored background stitches first so darker colors do not show through. Refer to the Glossary on pages 321 to 323 for an explanation of stitches.

Work dolls and hearts in basket-weave stitches and buttons in Smyrna stitches, referring to the photograph for colors. Use reverse basket-weave stitches for the background. Work a row of brown continental stitches around the square and to divide the border into sections. Work each section following the specific directions below.

1 — Vertical orange stripes: Work dark orange rows in Smyrna stitches with two rows of continental stitches between (one in light orange and one in cream).

2 — Diagonal turquoise stripes: Work in continental stitches, making each diagonal line two stitches wide. Use any combination of light turquoise, dark turquoise, and cream.

3 — Yellow and cream checks: Work the cream-colored cross-stitches first, with one row of yellow continental stitches between.

4 and 14 — Gingham checks: Work in Scotch stitches, using the medium color in every row; then alternate dark and light colors.

5, 12, and 20 — Polka dots: Alternate a solid row of tent stitches with one leaving every fourth stitch blank. Fill with red, turquoise, or brown.

6 — Green and turquoise vertical stripes: Work the medium and dark turquoise rows in cashmere stitches with two rows of continental stitches (one in cream and one in green) between.

7 — Yellow checks: Work in yellow and cream mosaic stitches.

8 — Brown checkerboard: Work the vertical rows in upright Gobelin and continental stitches. Work the horizontal rows in slanting Gobelin and continental stitches. Fill with cream continental stitches.

9 — Tulips: Work flowers in pink and red tent stitches.

10 — Orange squares: Work cream-colored Scotch-stitch squares in opposite directions, with orange continental stitches between.

11 — Horizontal stripes: Work green and cream continental stitches.

13 — Yellow vertical stripes: Work cream rows in mosaic stitches, with light yellow Smyrna stitches between.

15 — Brown horizontal stripes: Dark brown stripes are slanting Gobelin stitches; work brown and cream cross-stitch tramé between.

16 — Oranges: Work in shades of orange and green as shown.

17 — Vertical turquoise stripes: Work two rows of tent stitches in light turquoise with cream-colored cross-stitches between.

18 — Green hearts: Work as shown in the photograph.

19 — Red and pink horizontal stripes: Work cream-colored stripes in upright Gobelin stitches. Work red and pink rows of continental stitches between. Alternate directions of stitches.

To finish the pillow, block the canvas following the directions on page 241. Cut a 4-inch-wide strip of calico fabric and fold it in half across the width. Baste the two long ends together and gently pull the stitches to gather the fabric. Baste the ruffle around the pillow so the ruffle lies against the right side of the canvas.

Trim the canvas margins to ½ inch and cut a piece of calico fabric to match. Assemble the pillow following the directions on page 258.

Andy 6
Andy 8

Adventures in Needlepoint

Unique Projects to Stitch

Needlepoint can be fresh and imaginative! To prove it, here's a section filled with adventurous stitchery. For example, why not work in the round —to create a scenic hassock—or make delightful bride and groom dolls? Or adapt motifs, such as our children's artwork, shown below. Directions are on the next page.

Adapting Designs for Needlepoint

Once you've learned your needlepoint stitches, you may wish to try your hand at designing your own piece of needlepoint. Then you'll be sure the finished product fits your needs exactly and you'll have the satisfaction of being your own designer.

Here are some pointers to get you started, as well as basic how-to for enlarging, reducing, and transferring designs – either your own or those in this book.

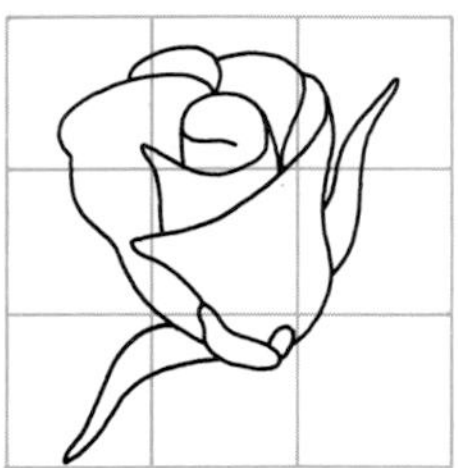

The original pattern

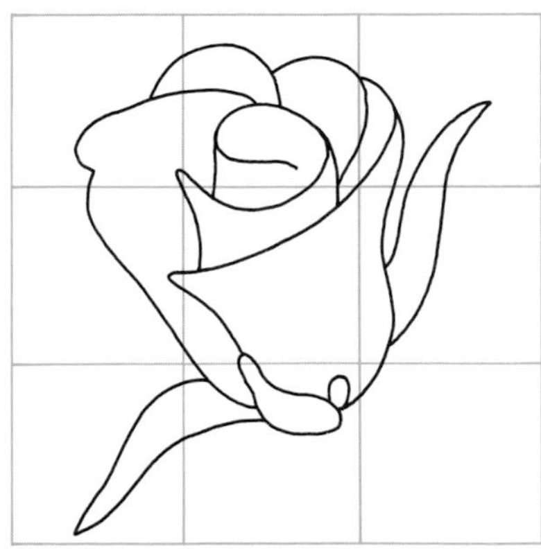

Enlarging on a grid

Before You Begin

First, decide what to stitch. Will it be a chair seat, a picture, a pillow? How large will it be? And where will it go? The room in which a stitchery will live can greatly influence its design.

On a piece of paper, draw an accurate outline, like an empty picture frame, around your proposed project. Do your drawing and sketching on tracing paper placed over this outline "frame" to be sure the finished design will be the right size and shape.

Designing Methods

There are as many ways to begin designing as there are needlework designers. Here are some of the more widely used techniques.

Try tracing shapes from existing designs and rearranging them within the outline frame. Pictures from magazines, books, greeting cards, and coloring books and motifs from printed textiles such as slipcovers are good sources. A photograph, a child's artwork, or a rubbing from a furniture carving can also be your starting point.

Choose a pattern appropriate to the area where it will be placed. If you use a motif from a room's carved woodwork to inspire a pillow border, the pillow will belong in that room. Look around the work's future home for designs. Then photograph, trace, rub, or sketch them.

Borrowing designs from nature is also exciting and challenging. Cut a melon or tomato in half and study its patterns. Look at shells, areas of tree bark, or wave lines on a beach. Sketch or photograph what you see. A camera reduces three-dimensional nature to two dimensions, making the designer's job easier. Eliminate nonessential details and you may have an exciting, totally original design.

For a more contemporary or even abstract design, work with paper shapes, following the directions on page 298.

Enlarging and Reducing Designs

Once you have a design, it may be the wrong size for your project. There are several ways to enlarge or reduce it.

Working With a Photostat

The easiest way to change the size of the design is to take it to a blueprint company. Ask for a "positive copy" of the design, specifying the dimensions you want. When the copy is ready, draw black outlines around the important shapes; omit unimportant details. Then draw your outline frame around the design and the pattern is complete.

Enlarging With a Grid

Some designs, such as many in this book, are marked with a grid — small squares laid over the design. With others, such as original designs of your own, you may wish to add a grid. To do so, tape the pattern to a table and secure a sheet of clear plastic over it. Using a fine-tip marking pen, rule the plastic into ½-inch squares, making a grid such as the one at left.

Next, enlarge or reduce the design by drawing a second grid on tissue or brown paper, following the scale indicated on the pattern, if there is one. If there is no scale, mark your outline frame with the same number of squares as are on the plastic sheet.

Next, number the horizontal and vertical rows of squares in the margin of the original pattern. Transfer these numbers to the corresponding rows on the new pattern.

Begin by finding a square on your grid that corresponds with a square on the original. Mark your grid wherever a design line intersects a line on the original. (Visually divide every line into fourths to gauge whether the design line cuts the grid line halfway or somewhere in between.)

Working one square at a time, mark each grid line where it is intersected by the design. After marking several squares, connect the dots, following the contours of the original as shown in the lower diagrams, opposite. Work in pencil so you can erase.

Patterns Without Grids
To enlarge or reduce a design without a grid, you need to know at least one of the dimensions of the final pattern. Draw a box around the original design. Then draw a diagonal line between two opposite corners.

On the pattern paper, draw a right angle and extend the bottom line to the length of the new pattern. Lay the original in the corner and, using a ruler, extend the diagonal. Then draw a perpendicular line between the diagonal and the end of the bottom line, as shown at right.

Divide the original and the new pattern into quarters, number the sections, and transfer the design as explained above (see diagrams at right).

Transferring Designs
To transfer your design to canvas, use waterproof marking pens, following the directions on page 248. Or, paint the canvas with artist's acrylic paints, following directions below.

Painting a Canvas
To paint a needlepoint canvas, you'll need some tools and equipment. Gather together artist's acrylic paints in the appropriate colors; a palette or palette paper; palette knife; small-, medium-, and large-pointed brushes; and a spray bottle of water. Acrylic paints are nice to use because they dry quickly, mix and clean up with water, and are waterproof when dry. They also come in a wide range of colors and are easy to mix.

Begin by taping your design to a flat surface. Cover it with a sheet of clear plastic if you wish to save it. Center the canvas over the picture, allowing at least two inches of canvas to extend beyond the design frame on all sides. (You'll need this margin around the needlepoint for blocking and finishing later.) Tape the canvas in place.

If you discover that your design is hard to see beneath the canvas, trace the predominant lines on the pattern with a fine-tip black marking pen.

Put a small daub of each of the colors you intend to use on your palette. When you're ready to use a color, spray a little water on it and mix the paint with the palette knife until it is smooth and the consistency of whipped cream. The paint should flow evenly onto the canvas, but not drip through it.

Use the small brush for fine details and outlining, the medium brush for slightly larger areas, and the large brush for the background. Start by outlining the main parts of the design. When this paint dries, add color in adjacent areas. Wash brushes in water before changing colors.

If paint covers the spaces in the canvas, use a toothpick to clear them. Allow the painted canvas to dry thoroughly.

To test the quality of the paint, sprinkle water over a sample of painted canvas. If the color runs slightly, spray the painted canvas *very lightly* with clear acrylic to keep colors from running and spoiling the stitchery when the piece is blocked.

Enlarging without a grid

Segmenting the original

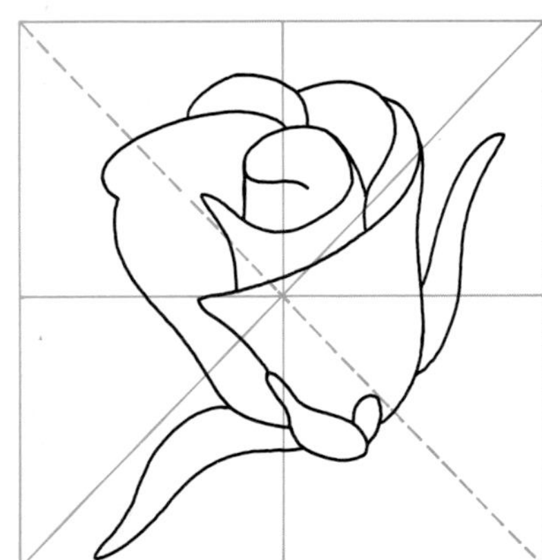

Transferring the design

Chinese Dollhouse Rug

Designed to resemble an antique Oriental rug, this elegant miniature is stitched small-scale on #18-count canvas. The tiny continental and basket-weave stitches give the design fine detail and make it perfect for dollhouses or miniature room displays.

Materials

11x14 inches #18-count canvas
3-ply Paternayan Persian yarn, or a similar substitute, in the following amounts and colors: 14 yards #266 dark rust, 22 yards #274 medium rust, 6 yards #287 light rust, 22 yards #005 white, 5 yards #314 dark blue, 10 yards #380 medium blue, 8 yards #381 medium-light blue, and 5 yards #382 light blue
40 yards fine linen macrame cord (fringe)
Waterproof marking pen
Masking tape
11x13 inches rust velveteen
#22 tapestry needle
Colored pencils (optional)
Graph paper (optional)
Needlepoint frame (optional)

Color Key
■ dark rust
■ medium rust
□ light rust
□ white
■ dark blue
◪ medium blue
■ medium light blue
□ light blue

Directions

The pattern below represents one quadrant of the finished rug. You may stitch from the chart, or transfer it to graph paper with colored pencils, reversing as necessary to complete the design.

Mark the center of the canvas with a waterproof pen, and bind the edges with masking tape to prevent raveling. If desired, mount the canvas in a needlepoint frame to minimize distortion.

Use one strand of yarn throughout, and begin stitching in the center of the design if you are working from the chart. Stitch small details in continental stitches and larger areas in basket-weave stitches (stitch directions are on pages 321 to 323).

Block the finished rug following the directions on page 241, and trim the unworked canvas to within ½ inch of the needlepoint. Cut a piece of backing fabric to match. With the right sides facing, sew pieces together, leaving one end open. Turn, press, and slip-stitch.

For the fringe, cut two 27-inch pieces of cord and approximately 155 pieces each 2½ inches long. Thread a long piece into a needle and tie it into a lark's head knot in the corner mesh in the last row of needlepoint at one end of the rug. Adjust the ends of the yarn so one end is about 1½ inches long. The longer, outside end will be the bearer cord for the knots that make the fringe. Tie remaining short cords into alternate spaces in the canvas along the last row of stitching, making sure ends are even. Tie all short cords into two rows of horizontal double half-hitch knots. Repeat for the other end of the rug. To finish, trim ends evenly.

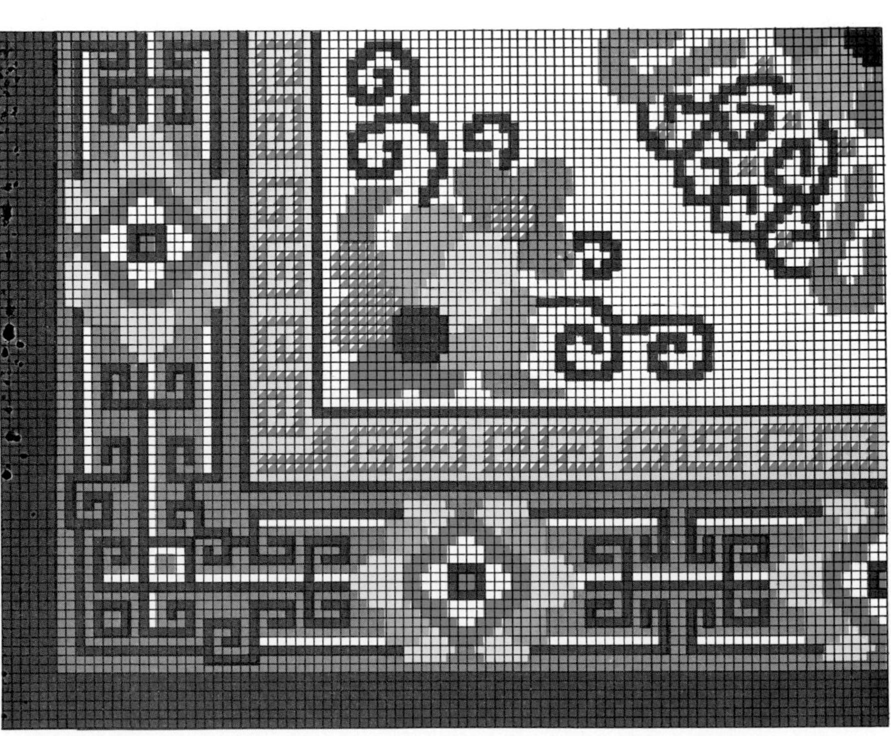

Needlepoint Flowers

Needlepoint petals keep these flowers beautiful year after year. Worked in basket-weave stitches, each petal is gracefully shaped with copper wire.

Materials

(For three 5-petal flowers — one large and two small)
1 yard #10-count penelope canvas
1 skein 3-ply Persian yarn in each of the following colors: dark, medium, and light pink and magenta (or four shades of purple), and white
¾ yard medium-weight fabric (for backing)
Small pearl or silver beads
1 spool copper bead wire
1 package green plastic tape or florist's tape
6½ yards medium-gauge copper wire
#17 tapestry needle
Waterproof marking pen

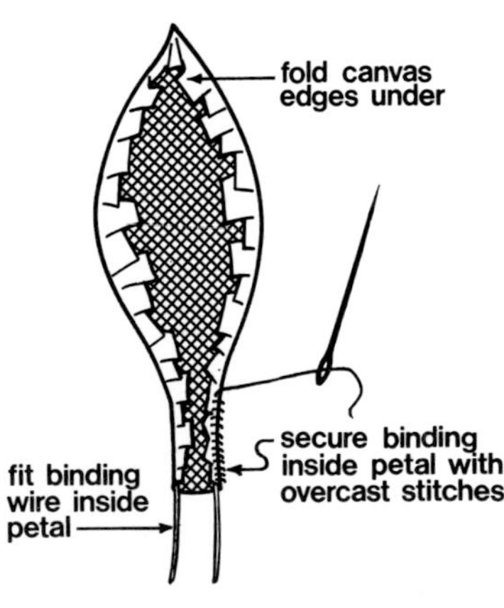

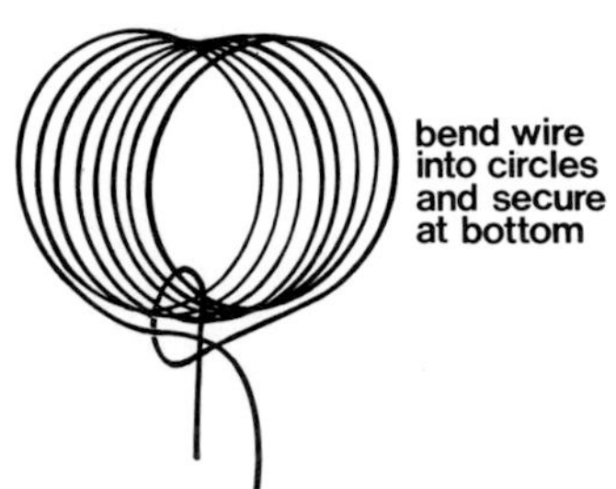

Directions

Note: Flowers are about six and ten inches across.

Cut ten 4x7-inch pieces of canvas for the small petals and five 5x8-inch pieces for the large petals. Using a waterproof pen, transfer the petal designs at right to the canvas.

Work each petal in basket-weave stitches, following the color key and substituting shades of lavender for the pink, if desired. Use full strands of yarn throughout. Work outer edges of each petal first. Then fill the center vein with magenta or dark purple and stitch remainder of petal.

After finishing a petal, cut around the needlepoint, leaving ½ inch of unworked canvas. Carefully fold under the canvas edges and steam-press.

Cut copper wire 14 inches long for small petals and 17 inches long for large petals. Bend the wire to fit the outer edge of each petal and slip it beneath the folded edges. Using yarn to match edge of petal, anchor wire in place with closely spaced overcast stitches, as shown at left.

Lay petal on the bias of the backing fabric and cut out backing, adding a ¼-inch seam allowance. Slip-stitch lining to needlepoint, turning in the seam allowance. Complete five petals for each flower.

For centers, cut one yard of bead wire. Tie a knot three inches from one end; string with beads to within four inches of the end. Knot wire again three inches from the end, leaving one inch free between beads and knot.

Loop wire into eight circles; anchor circles together at the bottom with a few twists of the wire ends, as shown at left.

To assemble each flower, grasp five petals in one hand with the ends pointing down. Arrange them so they fan gracefully. Insert free ends of the beaded cluster into the center, and anchor by twisting wires. Wrap additional wire around the bottom of the petals, then cover the wire with florist's tape. Shape the petals by bending the wires in them.

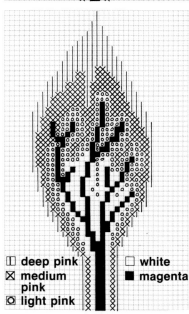

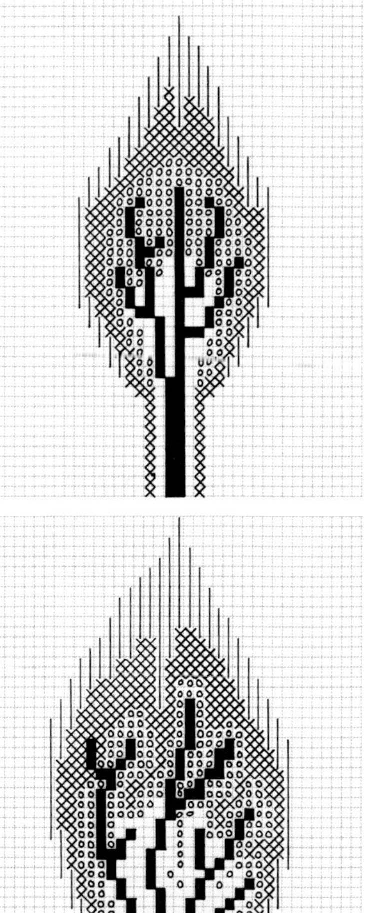

1 Square = 1 Stitch

Mosaic-Pattern Jewel Box

This lovely decorative box is an adventure in easy-to-master needlepoint stitches. The stitches, worked in both wool and cotton yarns, form two different patterns – one for the top of the box and the other for the sides. When the needlepoint is complete, each piece is backed with mat board and then padded and lined with red satin. The patterns at right represent one-fourth of the finished designs.

Materials

- 3-ply Paternayan yarn, or a suitable substitute, in the following amounts and colors: 45 yards #852 coral, 12 yards #242 red, and 18 yards #793 light blue
- 16-yard twists #3 DMC pearl cotton, or a suitable substitute, in the following amounts and colors: two #943 teal blue and one #907 chartreuse
- ¼ yard #12-count interlock canvas
- Two 4½x4½-inch pieces mat board
- Four 2½x4½-inch pieces mat board
- #18 tapestry needle
- ¼ yard red crepe-backed satin or lining fabric
- Red sewing thread
- #7 embroidery needle
- Quilt batting
- 6x6-inch piece red felt
- Craft knife
- Fabric glue
- Clothespins
- 3 cinnabar beads for trim

Directions

The finished box measures 4¾x4¾x2⅝ inches. Stitch the pieces separately and then sew them together. Cut each piece with about two extra inches of canvas on each side. Bind the canvas edges with masking tape.

Cut four side pieces (7x5 inches) and one top piece (7x7 inches) from canvas and stitch them as shown on the patterns at right. Slant the stitches toward the center. Refer to the Glossary on pages 321 to 323 for an explanation of the stitches.

Stitch one section of color at a time, beginning in the center of each design. Use one strand of pearl cotton and two strands of Persian wool throughout.

When each piece is complete, do one row of continental stitches around all four sides with red yarn. Block the canvas if necessary, following the directions on page 241.

To begin constructing the box, trim the canvas edges to within ½ inch of the stitching.

Glue the mat boards to the backs of the needlepoint pieces, using white glue sparingly. Fold the canvas edges around the boards, using clothespins to hold the edges down. Let dry. Cut and glue a piece of red felt to the sixth piece of mat board.

Cut six pieces of quilt batting to match the six pieces of mat board. Cut two 5½-inch squares and one 3½x20-inch rectangle from the red satin.

Align the four side pieces to make one long row. Match the quilt batting with the mat boards (with the needlepoint side face-down). Then, pin the satin to the batting along the edges, turning the raw edges under. Whipstitch the satin to the needlepoint. String three beads on red yarn and insert the end of the yarn into the top before stitching the satin.

Fold the long piece into four sides and whipstitch the seams. Attach the bottom piece, felt side down. Attach the top on one side (opposite bead handle) the same way you joined the side seams. Keep the stitching fairly loose so the lid lies flat and does not spring open.

Color Key

A Coral
B Red
C Teal blue
D Chartreuse
E Light blue

Stitch Key

1 Mosaic stitch
2 Double leviathan stitch
3 Continental stitch
4 Slanting Gobelin stitch
5 Half-cross-stitch
6 Smyrna stitch

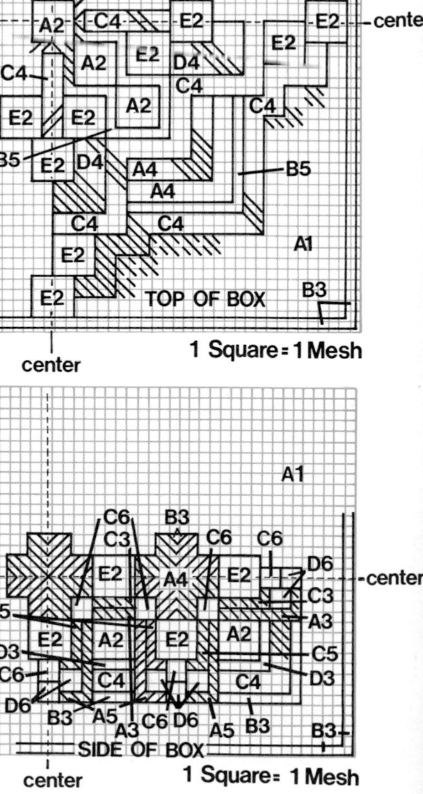

Bride and Groom Dolls

Adults as well as children will delight in the whimsy and charm of this demure bride and proper bridegroom.

The dolls, which are about 24 inches tall and 10 inches wide, are worked on #14-count canvas in continental and basket-weave stitches. They are good examples of shaped needle-point—pieces that are cut and made three-dimensional rather than left flat for framing or hanging. The patterns are on page 282.

Materials

1 yard #14-count canvas for each doll (see note)
3-ply Paternayan Persian wool yarn, or a similar substitute, in the colors indicated on the pattern on page 282 (see note at right)
#22 tapestry needle
Waterproof marking pen
Masking tape
¾ yard white velveteen (bride)
¾ yard gray velveteen (groom)
Polyester fiberfill

Directions

Note: Both dolls shown opposite were worked on #14-count canvas. They may, however, be worked on larger (or smaller) mesh canvas—or on Penelope canvas, if you wish. The finer the canvas used for the dolls, the more detail you will have in the finished designs.

The amount of yarn you use depends on how tightly you stitch. To judge your own yarn gauge, work one square inch of scrap canvas in basket-weave stitches; measure and note the amount of yarn used as you stitch. Then estimate the total number of square inches in each color in the design and multiply that number by the amount of yarn used to work one square inch. If you are unable to judge the amount of yarn required, enlarge and transfer the pattern to the canvas and work several sample rows. Take the sample with you to your needle-point shop and get help in estimating the amounts of yarn needed. Be sure to buy sufficient yarns in the same dye lots to complete the project so you don't have unattractive variations in the colors.

Following the directions on page 272, enlarge the patterns on page 282 onto a large sheet of paper. Transfer them to canvas as follows: tape the paper pattern to a table or flat surface, then tape canvas over the pattern, leaving at least a 2-inch margin of canvas completely around each pattern for blocking. Using a *light-colored, waterproof pen* (such as pale gray or blue), trace the outlines of the design onto the canvas. If the design is difficult to see under the canvas, trace over outlines with a fine-tip black marking pen. It is not necessary to color the canvas before you begin stitching. For correct placement of colors, simply refer to the numbered sections of the pattern and to the color key on page 282 as you work.

Press the canvas with a dry iron, and bind all the edges with masking tape to keep the canvas from raveling and to prevent yarns from catching in the rough edge of the canvas as you stitch. If desired, mount the canvas in a frame for stitching to minimize distortion as you work.

Using two strands of yarn throughout, outline all areas of the canvas first in a single row of continental stitches in the appropriate colors. Next, work small detail areas. Then work the larger, solid areas of each pattern, such as the bride's gown and veil and the groom's coat, in basket-weave stitches. (Refer to the Glossary on pages 321 to 323 for an explanation of the stitches, if necessary.) When each doll is completed, work an additional two rows of continental stitches completely around the outer edges so none of the design is lost when the doll is sewn together. (This extra margin will be taken up in the seam when you sew the needlepoint pieces to the velveteen backing fabrics.)

Block the finished needlepoint, following the directions on page 241.

To assemble the dolls, lay the needlepoint on the velveteen backing, right sides facing. Baste the pieces together to prevent shifting. Machine-stitch around the outlines of each doll, running the machine stitches inside the two extra rows of needlepoint stitches. Stitch again, ⅛ inch outside the first row of stitching. Leave the bottom of the doll open for turning and stuffing. Trim excess canvas and velveteen close to stitching. Carefully turn the doll right side out and press lightly. Stuff both dolls with polyester fiberfill and slip-stitch the bottom edges closed.

continued

Bride and Groom Dolls *(continued)*

1 Square = 1 Inch

Scenic Hassock *(continued on page 284)*

Scenic Hassock *(continued)*

If you're a needlepoint enthusiast who enjoys the challenge of a grand-scale project, you'll love the mural hassock shown on page 283 and closeup, opposite. And it can be stitched in record time, thanks to quickpoint canvas, heavy rug yarn, and a variety of fast-working stitches. For diagrams of the stitches, see pages 321 to 323.

Materials

- 3⅓ yards #5-count penelope canvas
- 70-yard skeins Aunt Lydia's rug yarn in the colors and amounts listed in color key
- #13 tapestry needle
- Masking tape
- Graph paper or brown wrapping paper
- Shredded foam, polystyrene pellets, or a similar substitute
- Waterproof marking pen
- Carpet thread
- Heavy muslin or lightweight canvas

Directions

Note: The finished hassock is 16 inches high, 26½ inches in diameter, and 86 inches around its circumference.

Enlarge the patterns opposite and below and transfer them to graph paper or brown wrapping paper. Tape the patterns to a flat surface; then tape canvas atop them, leaving a 2-inch margin around the edges of the design. Using a waterproof pen, lightly sketch the outlines of the design onto the canvas.

Using the appropriate color, outline each motif of the landscape with a single row of tent stitches. When one of the larger motifs, such as a hill, is to be stitched in a combination of colors, outline it in the darkest color to be used in that area. All of the smaller motifs are stitched in simple tent stitches; patterned stitches and combinations of colors are used only in larger areas. See the Glossary for pattern diagrams for the stitches.

The lakes, rivers, and meandering path are worked in a combination of colors for a textured effect. For the water, cut two equal lengths of light and dark turquoise, separate each length into three plies, and combine two light plies and one dark ply. Do the same for the path, using two plies of beige and one of dark brown. Outline both the water and path areas with one row of tent stitches in the darker shades.

When stitching the top of the hassock, outline the outer edge in medium blue tent stitches and the clouds in peach tent stitches. Fill clouds with white and cream and the sky with medium blue.

To assemble the hassock, trim the canvas to within one inch of the stitching. Fold the margins under and steam-press. Use carpet thread to whipstitch together the short ends of the long body strip, aligning motifs carefully. Reinforce the seam and cover the whipstitching with yarn to match motifs or sky.

Pin-fit the top to the body of the hassock. Whipstitch top to body and then cover whipstitching with a row of medium blue yarn. Turn the hassock upside down and stuff. For the base, cut a 28½-inch circle of muslin or canvas and pin-fit it to the bottom of the hassock. Whipstitch securely with a double strand of carpet thread.

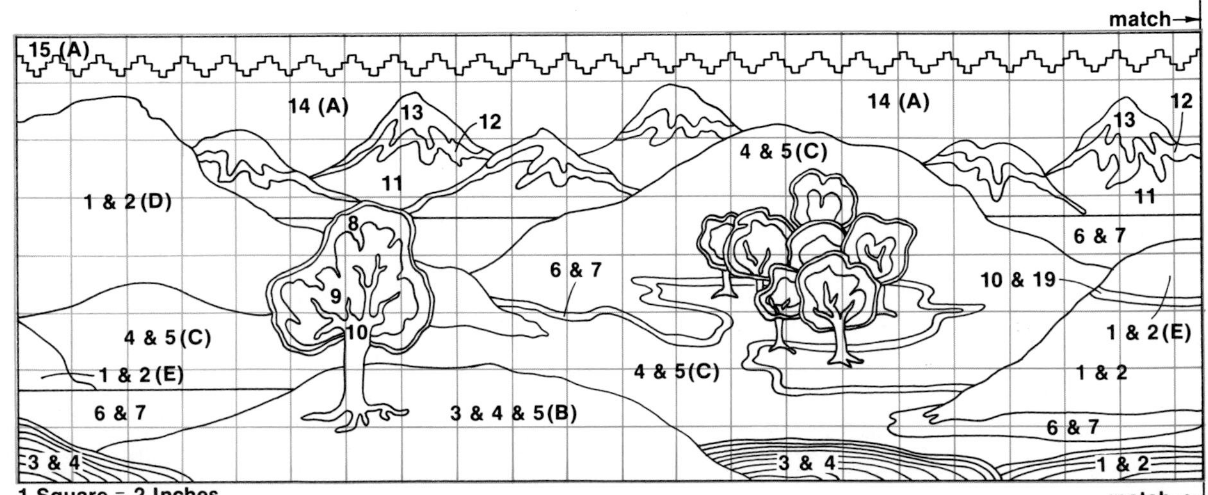

Color Key
1 Burnt orange (3 skeins)
2 Peach (3)
3 Evergreen (3)
4 Grass green (3)
5 Spring green (3)
6 Dark turquoise (2)
7 Light turquoise (2)
8 Emerald (1)
9 Jade (1)
10 Dark brown (1)
11 Purple (2)
12 Lavender (1)
13 Cream (2)
14 Light blue (4)
15 Medium blue (1)
16 White (1)
17 Dark yellow (1)
18 Light yellow (1)
19 Beige (1)

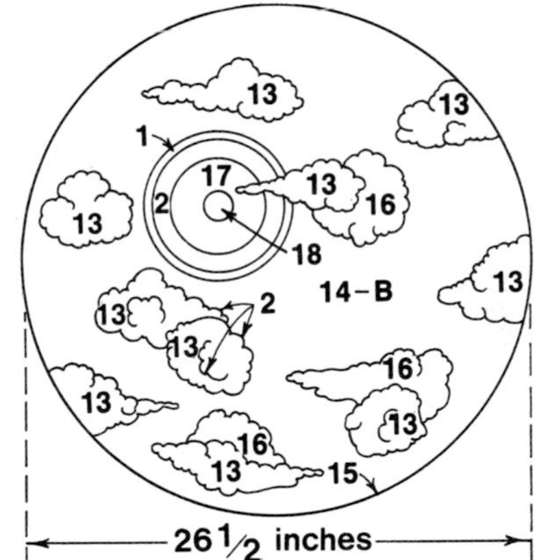

Stitch Guide
A Bargello flat stitch
B Mosaic or Scotch stitch
C Variation on mosaic stitch
D Bargello flat stitch variation
E Diagonal flat stitch with tent-stitch outline

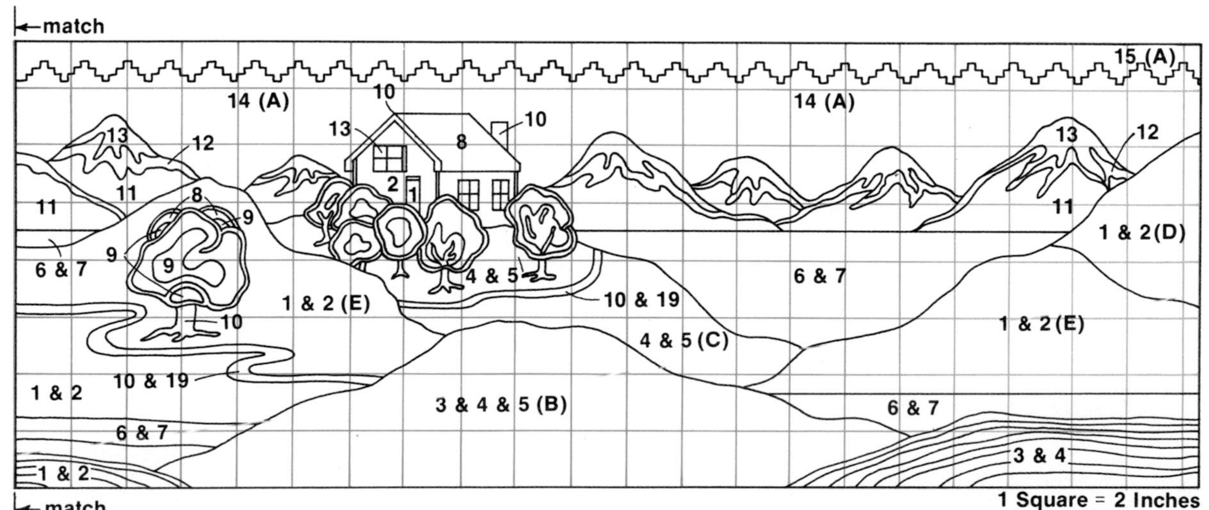

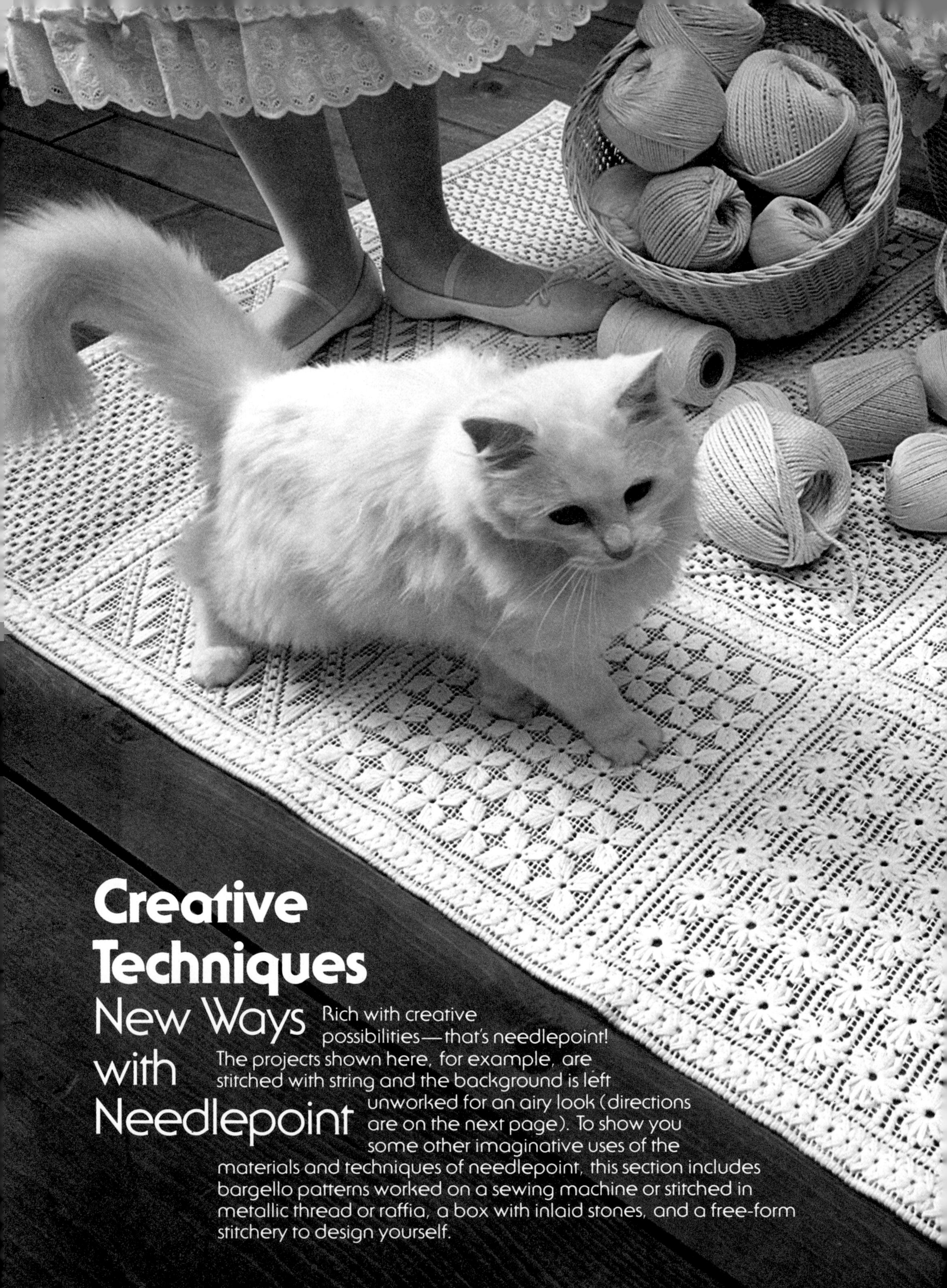

Creative Techniques

New Ways with Needlepoint

Rich with creative possibilities—that's needlepoint! The projects shown here, for example, are stitched with string and the background is left unworked for an airy look (directions are on the next page). To show you some other imaginative uses of the materials and techniques of needlepoint, this section includes bargello patterns worked on a sewing machine or stitched in metallic thread or raffia, a box with inlaid stones, and a free-form stitchery to design yourself.

String Needlepoint—Pillows and Rug *(shown on pages 286 and 287)*

The light and lacy look of the rug and pillows shown on pages 286 and 287 is actually exposed needlepoint canvas that lets the backing fabric shine through. And, the open canvas further sets off the cotton yarn used for stitching.

So if you think string is just for wrapping around packages and forgetful fingers–think again! It's a stunning material for needlepoint, too.

Materials

20x20 inches #5-count canvas for each pillow
49x76 inches #5-count canvas for rug with 15 squares
Lily "Sugar 'n Cream" cotton yarn (available in 125-yard balls) in the following amounts for each design: A — 142 yards: B — 136 yards; C — 206 yards; and D — 166 yards
#13 tapestry needle
5/8 yard colored backing fabric for each pillow
Polyester fiberfill
Needlepoint frame or two pairs of 20-inch artist's stretcher strips
Waterproof marking pen
White sewing thread
Staple gun (optional)

Directions

The finished size of each square in the rug and pillows is about 16x16 inches and includes a 12-inch center panel surrounded by a two-inch border. There are four designs in all, shown opposite as A, B, C, and D. The borders for each design are the same.

To make the pillows, bind the edges of the canvas with masking tape. Mount the canvas in a needlepoint frame or staple it to a frame assembled from artist's stretcher strips so you can pull the yarn firmly as you work. The tension applied during stitching creates the lacy, open look of this needlepoint.

Remember that there is a two-inch margin of unworked canvas around all four sides of the design. Each center panel actually measures 61 meshes square, and borders are 10 meshes wide.

Choose one of the four designs to needlepoint, making sure to center the design as it is worked on the canvas. Also allow for the border pattern and the two-inch margin of canvas for blocking and seam allowances or hem.

Cut the yarn into two-yard lengths for easier handling. Thread the needle with one of the lengths and knot the two ends to form a piece of yarn one yard long.

Unlike many needlepoint stitches and patterns, some of these designs are worked easiest from left to right. Follow the stitching sequence indicated by the numbers on each pattern, and draw the threads firmly with each stitch for a pulled-thread effect. Hold the yarn close to the canvas and pull it in the direction of the next stitch to help open the mesh. The doubled yarn will increase the pull on the canvas and produce more of an openwork look than a single thread would. Since you're using doubled lengths of yarn, it is important to keep the strands from twisting so stitches lie flat on the canvas. Every now and then, let the needle fall loosely away from the canvas as you work so the threads will untwist.

Follow the designs opposite, repeating the portion of the pattern shown to complete an entire square. After working the center panel, stitch the border pattern completely around the edge.

When the pillow front is finished, block the needlepoint following the directions on page 241.

To assemble the pillow, cut two pieces of backing fabric to match the size of the canvas. Baste one piece to the back of the canvas. Then, with right sides facing, sew the canvas to the other piece of fabric, leaving one side open for turning. Clip corners and trim the seam allowance to ½ inch. Turn, stuff, and slip-stitch the opening.

To make the rug, use a single piece of canvas; it will measure about 45x72 inches when finished. Draw 15 squares on the canvas using a waterproof pen. Leave a border between each square, and allow a two-inch border of unworked canvas around the edges. Remember that each square is 61 meshes wide and each border is 10 meshes wide. Follow the placement diagram, opposite, for the arrangement of squares and patterns.

Stitch each square, following the directions above. Finish one center panel before starting the next, leaving 10 meshes empty between each panel for the border. Work the border pattern last.

To finish the rug, fold the two-inch margin in half and then turn it to the back of the rug. Stitch it to the back side with double lengths of white sewing thread.

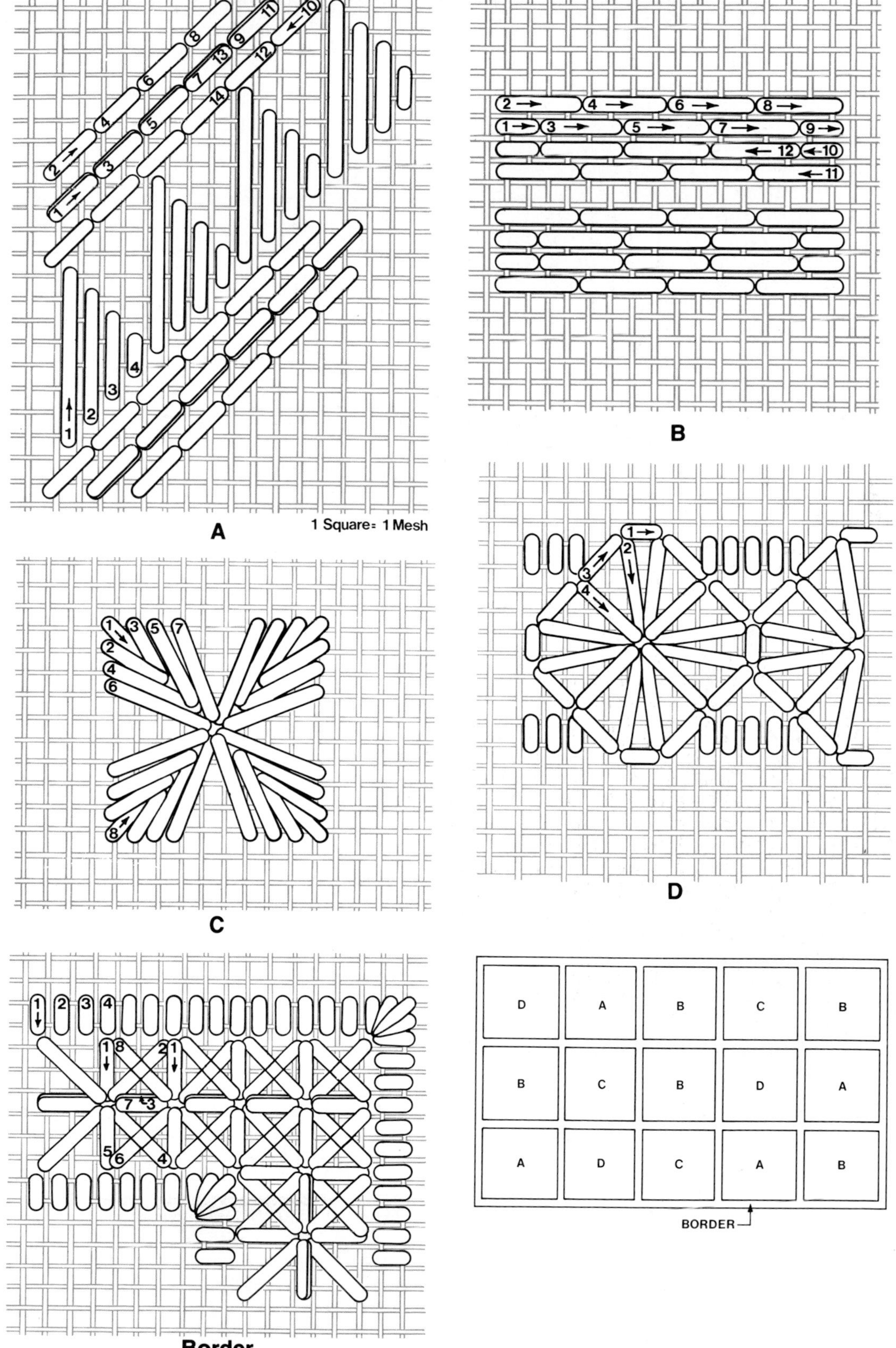
A
1 Square= 1 Mesh
B
C
D
Border
D A B C B
B C B D A
A D C A B
BORDER

Sewing-Machine Bargello—Chair Seat

Beautiful bargello patterns, like the one shown on this chair seat, can be stitched on a zigzag sewing machine as well as by hand. And with a little practice, you will see how easy and creative machine needlepoint can be.

This "domes-and-spires" pattern, done entirely by machine, is worked on #18-count canvas, covering four meshes with each stitch. Stitch each row the same as the first.

Materials

Zigzag sewing machine
22x22 inches #18-count mono canvas (or size to fit seat)
#20 cotton thread, or any similar substitute, in purple, dark blue, light blue, olive green, yellow, and gold
Sheet of polyester quilt batting
⅜-inch plywood board for seat
White sewing thread for bobbin
Masking tape
Waterproof marking pen
Staple gun or tacks
Soil-retardant spray

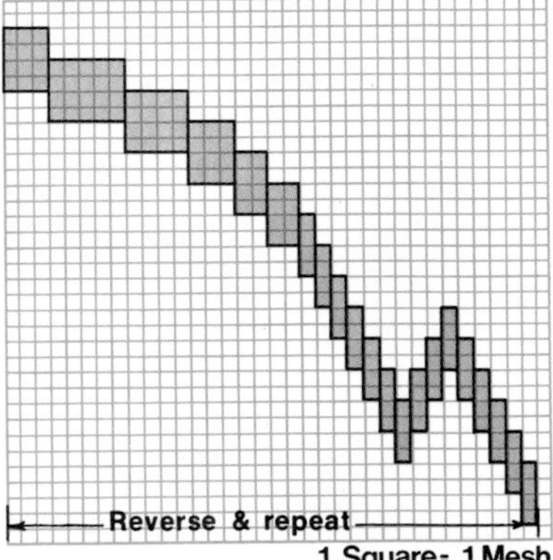

Directions

Bind the edges of the canvas with masking tape to prevent raveling. Mark the outlines of the chair seat on the canvas with a waterproof marking pen. When stitching the chair seat, extend the pattern at least ½ inch beyond these lines to allow some overlap when the edges are turned under.

Thread the sewing machine with purple thread on top and white in the bobbin. Set the machine for its widest zigzag stitch, remove the presser foot, and lower the machine's feed dogs. Using a sample piece of canvas, choose a starting point close to one edge. Place your right hand on the wheel of the machine, guide the needle into the first mesh, and bring the bobbin thread to the top of the canvas to prevent threads from jamming. Let the needle swing across to the fourth open mesh and back again. Hold the canvas stationary for several stitches, allowing threads to build up on its surface. This is called bar-tacking and gives the canvas a texture and dimension similar to bargello done by hand.

Once you have the feel of this technique and the tension of the stitches is adjusted correctly, practice the "domes-and-spires" pattern as shown on the chair seat. To make the second bar tack, place the needle into the next row *and two meshes away* from the first set of stitches. Continue bar-tacking, following the pattern to the end of the row. Place the zigzag setting on "0" and sew several up-and-down stitches along the side of the bar tacks to secure them to the canvas. Without this step, the line of stitching would unravel. You might want to try several more rows of practice stitching before moving on. To do this, change thread colors for each row. (Always use white thread in the bobbin.)

To begin working the chair seat, study the pattern at left and the sample piece you have just stitched. Using the pattern as a stitch guide and reference, count the canvas meshes so the peak of the bargello design (the highest point) falls along the top edge of the outline you have drawn on the canvas. Choose a starting point close to one edge of the canvas and start stitching at the widest end, always moving the needle from side to side, as shown in the close-up photographs, opposite.

Place the needle in the first mesh and move it across to the fourth mesh so the stitch covers three threads of canvas. (Every stitch in the design will be the same size.) Bar-tack across these four meshes to allow threads to build up on the canvas surface (as on your practice piece), going back and forth about five times so the canvas is completely covered.

For the next bar tack, carefully place your needle in the next row, *two meshes away from* the first set of bar tacks (as for the practice piece) and continue placing the needle and bar-tacking (following the pattern at left) until one row of bargello is complete. Be sure the stitching extends ½ inch beyond the actual size of the chair seat to allow a margin when turning the edges under.

At both ends of every row, place the zig-zag setting on "0" (for straight stitching) and sew several up-and-down stitches along the side of the bar tacks to help secure them (as you did for the practice piece). This is an important step since without it, your stitches will ravel and pull out.

The color sequence of the chair seat is: purple, dark blue, light blue, olive green, yellow, and gold. To begin the second row, change the

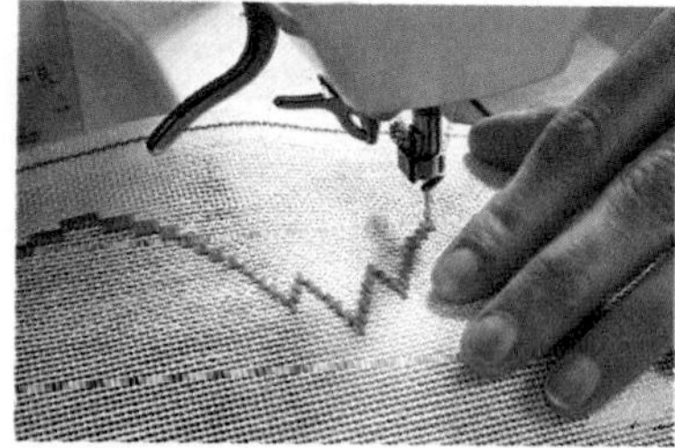

To form the pattern, bar-tack across four meshes on wide zigzag.

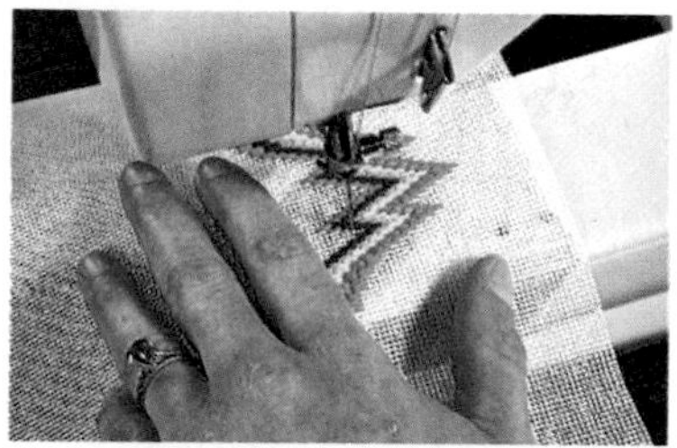

Change the color of the thread before beginning each new row.

Here's what you need to "needlepoint" with a zigzag sewing machine.

purple thread to dark blue and work row 2 as for row 1. Change colors each time you start a new row.

Continue in this way, stitching one row of color at a time, until the bargello is complete. If necessary, block the canvas following the directions on page 241.

Cut a ⅜-inch piece of plywood to fit the chair seat dimensions exactly and place a layer of quilt batting on top of the board. Place the finished canvas on top of the batting, right side up, and turn all three layers over. Secure the canvas to the backing board using a staple gun or tacks and pulling tightly along each side. Clip corners where necessary to make the canvas lie as flat as possible. Treat the bargello with a light coat of soil-retardant spray and have the piece dry-cleaned when necessary.

Metal Threads and Inlays: Bargello Pillow and Box

Needlepoint is more than just applying yarn to canvas; it can involve many different materials as well, like the metallic threads and decorative stones used in this project. The pillow and box shown at right use both of these creative materials to make two otherwise ordinary projects into something special.

The bargello pillow, backed with gold lamé, is worked in horizontal rows starting with a row of flame-shaped lozenges along the top. The box is worked in an abstract design using mother-of-pearl stones and gold and silver threads.

All of the stitches are listed in the Glossary on pages 321 to 323, and patterns are on pages 294 and 295.

Pillow
Materials

20x24 inches #18-count mono canvas
3-ply Paternayan Persian wool, or a suitable substitute, in the following colors and amounts (in yards): #010 eggshell (11), #168 light gray (6), #020 pink-beige (4), #464 peach (4), #592 pale green (2), #537 mint green (2), #B42 blue (2), #166 medium gray (3), #620 light lavender (3), and #017 light gray (1)
#3 DMC pearl cotton embroidery thread in the following colors and amounts (in yards): #3033 eggshell (6), #677 yellow (2), #3 snow white (6), #415 light gray (3), and #554 lavender (4)
6-strand DMC cotton embroidery floss in the following colors and amounts (in yards): #3023 gray-brown (2), #670 pale gold (2), #415 light gray (2), #301 light gray (2), and #318 dark gray (3)
10 yards gold cloisonné thread
14 yards silver cloisonné thread
#22 tapestry needle
Masking tape
20x24 inches gold lamé fabric
Waterproof pen
Pillow stuffing

Directions

Bind the edges of the canvas with masking tape to prevent raveling and mount the canvas in a needlepoint frame, if desired. With a waterproof marking pen, draw a two-inch border around the canvas.

Begin stitching the pillow by working the flame-shaped lozenges along the top of the pillow. The lower edge of the lozenge establishes the key line for the remainder of the pillow; all subsequent rows are worked in the same pattern using different colors.

The upper edge of the lozenge is a reverse of the key line; rows stitched above the lozenges to the top edge of the pillow (approximately one inch) follow the same pattern.

Starting at the marked line at the top right side of the pillow, count down 24 threads to begin stitching the top of the lozenge. Follow the diagram on page 294 and begin at the point marked "start." Each stitch should cover four threads on the canvas. Do not pull the yarn or thread too tightly because doing so will expose the canvas underneath and the yarn will not cover completely.

When working with wool, separate strands into individual plies; use two plies for stitching. When working with floss, use six strands. Cut wool into 18-inch lengths, and metallic threads into 10 to 12-inch lengths so they do not become worn-looking from being pulled through the canvas an excessive number of times.

When working with cloisonné thread, be careful strands do not tangle or knot. Apply beeswax to ends to keep them from unraveling. (If cloisonné twists or ravels, it will not cover canvas completely.)

Following the diagram, work the first row in gold cloisonné. Repeat the row seven more times across the canvas, for a total of eight flame-shaped lozenges. Be careful to work the center stitch only once between each of the lozenges.

After working the top of the lozenge, work the remainder of the motif inside the outlines, as indicated on the pattern. Fill centers of the lozenges with varying colors and threads, as indicated on the color key with the pattern (see page 294).

continued

Metal Threads and Inlays: Bargello Pillow and Box *(continued)*

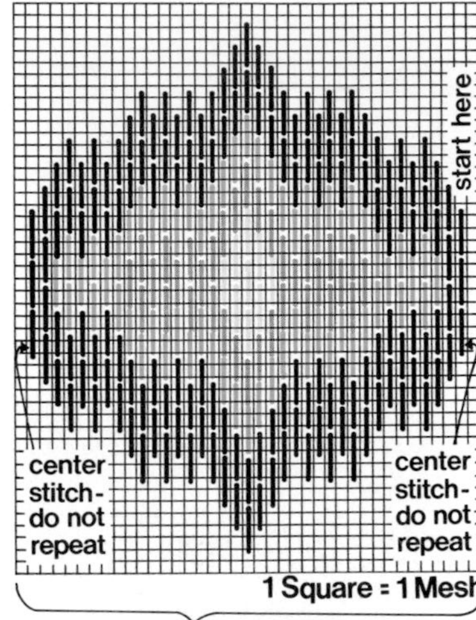

Color and Thread Key: Pillow

Except when indicated, stitch one row in each of the following colors and threads:

1. Eggshell pearl cotton
2. Eggshell wool
3. Lavender pearl cotton
4. Light lavender wool
5. Silver cloisonné
6. Dark gray floss
7. Light gray pearl cotton
8. Medium gray wool
9. Light gray wool
10. Silver cloisonné
11. Light gray floss
12. Blue wool
13. Snow white pearl cotton (two rows)
14. Eggshell wool
15. Snow white pearl cotton
16. Pink-beige wool
17. Light gray wool
18. Mint green wool
19. Pale green wool
20. Pale gold floss
21. Gold cloisonné
22. Yellow pearl cotton
23. Peach wool
24. Gray-brown floss
25. Pink-beige wool
26. Eggshell pearl cotton
27. Light gray wool
28. Gold cloisonné

To fill the canvas between the top of the lozenge and the top (straight) edge of the pillow, start with the row of stitches immediately above the lozenge and work one row with eggshell wool. Work the next row, above it, with eggshell pearl cotton. Work the row above that with light gray wool, and fill the remaining empty rows with silver cloisonné. As you near the top of the pillow, make stitches shorter to compensate for the straight edge (so the stitches end in a straight line).

Work the first row below the gold cloisonné key line in pink-beige wool, using two strands. Work all remaining rows below the key line following the color and yarn sequence listed in the chart at left. Work the sequence approximately 2½ times, or until the pillow is 20 inches long.

Block the finished pillow following the directions on page 241. Then trim the two-inch border of unworked canvas to ½ inch. Cut two pieces of muslin the same size as the trimmed canvas and stitch them into a pillow form. Stuff and slip-stitch the opening. Then cut a piece of gold lamé to size and finish the pillow, following the directions on page 258.

Accent the lower edge of the pillow with seven tassels made from leftover yarn. For each tassel, wrap eggshell and beige yarns and threads 20 times or more around a 2½-inch piece of cardboard. Tie strands tightly together, leaving the ends of the tying strand four inches long. Clip loops.

Wrap leftover colored threads around the top of the tassel to a depth of about ⅝ inch, and thread the ends of the wrapping thread through to the inside of the tassel. Add gold and silver accents, if desired. Stitch to the pillow as shown in the photograph.

Box Materials

- 3-ply Paternayan Persian wool yarn, or a similar substitute, in the following colors and amounts (in yards): #137 purple (9), #758 blue (2), #592 green (6), #464 peach (5), #014 off-white (5), and #015 pale yellow (6)
- 7 yards #3 white pearl cotton
- 8 yards gold cloisonné thread
- 8 yards silver cloisonné thread
- 11x13-inches #10-count canvas
- 1½x1⅞-inch mother-of-pearl shell
- 5 small pearl-like stones
- 3½x6x9-inch wooden box with 5¾x8¾-inch recessed top (see note below)
- #18 tapestry needle
- Masking tape
- Waterproof marking pen
- Quilt batting or mat board
- White glue

Directions

Note: The finished size of this design is 8¾x5¾ inches (to fit inside a recessed top the same size). If you need to adjust the finished size, extend the design lines or add a border to make the design larger. Or, use a smaller scale when enlarging the pattern to make the finished design smaller.

Tape edges of canvas. Enlarge the pattern opposite, following directions on page 272, and trace it onto canvas with a waterproof pen. Center the design so there are at least two inches of unworked canvas on all sides. The entire design is worked in basket-weave stitches except where otherwise noted. Use full three-ply strands of Persian wool yarn, and refer to the Glossary on pages 321 to 323 for how-to instructions.

Work all of the basket-weave areas, referring to the pattern for colors and to the Glossary for stitch how-to. When working

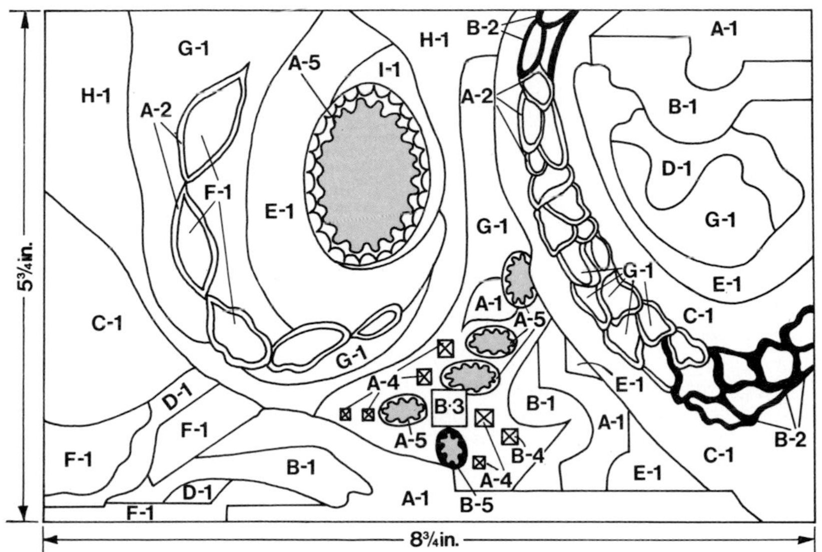

Color and Stitch Key: Box
Gold—A
Silver—B
Purple—C
Blue—D
Green—E
Peach—F
Off-white—G
Pale yellow—H
White pearl cotton—I

Basket-weave stitch—1
Chain stitch—2
Triple cross-stitch—3
Cross-stitch—4
Buttonhole stitch—5

with the cloisonné thread, cut short pieces so they are less likely to tangle or knot. Apply beeswax to the ends to keep the pieces from unraveling. Do not let the thread become twisted or it will not cover the canvas.

Next, fill remaining areas in chain, triple-cross-, and cross-stitches. (Refer to the Glossary for stitch how-to.) Do not work the canvas under the stones.

Glue each stone in place on the canvas, using white glue that dries transparent; let dry. Sew the stones in place (using gold or silver cloisonné) one at a time, using a buttonhole stitch around the edges, as shown in the diagram at right. Pull the loops tightly, adding another row of stitches inside the first row until the stones are secure.

Block as instructed on page 241 and trim the unworked canvas to within ½ inch of the finished edges. Turn under the unworked canvas and glue to the back. Cut a piece of quilt batting or mat board to fit under the needlepoint and glue the entire finished piece to the recessed area in the top of the box.

Securing Stones to Canvas

To secure the stones to the needlepoint, first glue them in place on the canvas; let glue dry thoroughly. Then, using either gold or silver cloisonné (as indicated on the color key) bring the needle up at 1 (see diagram). Go down at 2, leaving a small, fairly tight loop on top of the stone. Bring the needle up at 3 and down at 4. Repeat this procedure until you have made a complete circle around each stone.

Begin the second round by bringing the needle up and over the first loop (formed by stitch 1-2), making a detached buttonhole stitch. Then take the next stitch over the second loop (stitch 3-4); pull fairly tightly, drawing the stitches closer to the center of the stones. Continue around, making detached buttonhole stitches over the loops formed by the first round of stitches. End the thread on the back side of the canvas.

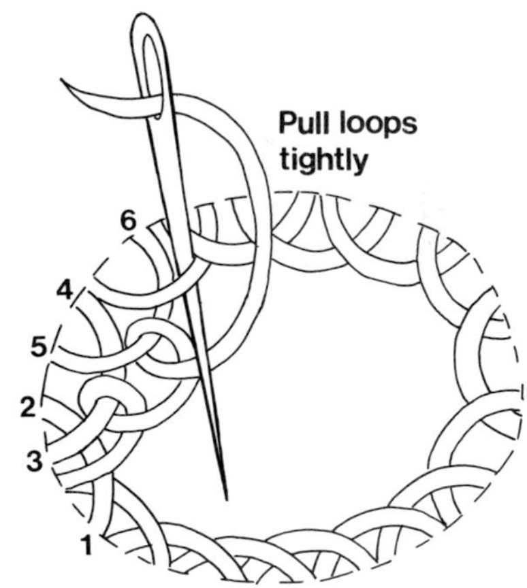

Raffia Stitchery—Bargello Baskets

Exciting new materials are available for needlepoint! These stunning contemporary baskets, for example, are bargello-stitched in sleek Swistraw ribbon on sturdy but flexible plastic canvas.

Materials

10½x13½-inch sheets Columbia Minerva plastic mesh
Tapestry needle
Waterproof marking pen

Cylinder
2 sheets plastic mesh
One 24-yard skein matte-finish Swistraw in each of the following colors: powder blue, purple, lemon yellow, medium blue, hot pink, and orange

Octagon
3 sheets plastic mesh
Two 24-yard skeins brilliant-finish Swistraw in each of the following colors: canary yellow, rose, vermilion, lime green, turquoise, and purple

Cube
3 sheets plastic mesh
One 24-yard skein brilliant-finish Swistraw in each of the following colors: lavender, medium blue, champagne, and salmon

General Directions

Cut plastic mesh, following the directons below. If measurement falls between meshes, extend it to the next solid line.

Cut 60-inch pieces of Swistraw; use doubled. Begin in lower left corner except for cube, which begins in the center.

On charts at right, each grid line equals a plastic filament; each square equals one mesh.

Join pieces by overcasting with matching Swistraw.

Cylinder: Cut two 4½-inch-wide mesh strips; join into a 4½x18-inch strip. (Overlap the two strips by four meshes; sew together with Swistraw.) Work the cylinder in rows of flame stitches across the width. Each stitch covers five "threads."

Hold the strip with a 4½-inch end closest to you and begin an inch above the edge. Stitch as shown in the photograph. Work each row the same as the first one. When one inch from the end, join the strip into a circle by overlapping the ends three meshes. Adjust stitch length.

For the base, cut a 5½-inch circle; join every third mesh.

Octagon: Cut eight 6¾x3½-inch rectangles; complete one panel using the chart at right. Work variations for the next seven panels, studying the photograph to see how color bars extend from panel to panel.

Take stitches over edges of meshes at top only; at other edges, leave one line of plastic unstitched. Join panels.

Cut an eight-sided figure, 3½ inches per side, and join it to the panels along the bottom.

Cube: Cut five squares of mesh, about 40 meshes each (six inches). Following the chart at right, stitch four sides. (The chart shows the upper right quarter of each side; repeat to complete each side.)

Begin by making a small cross-stitch in the center of the square and working out. Vary color combinations on each side. Take stitches over edge of meshes. Join the four sides. For the base, trim one line of plastic on two adjacent edges of the fifth square. Stitch base to sides and corners.

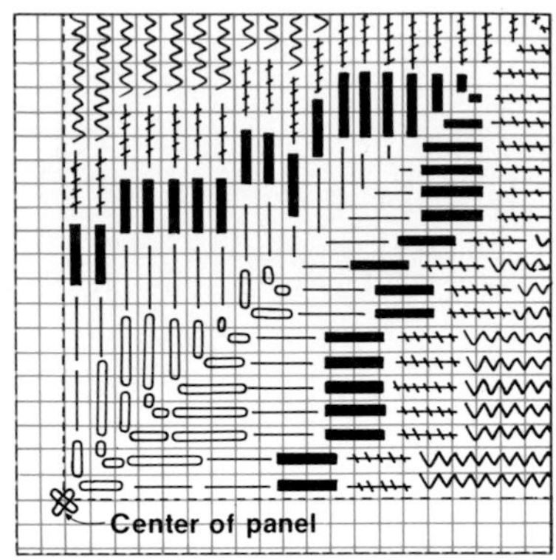

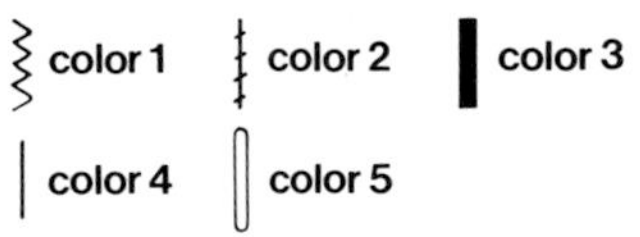

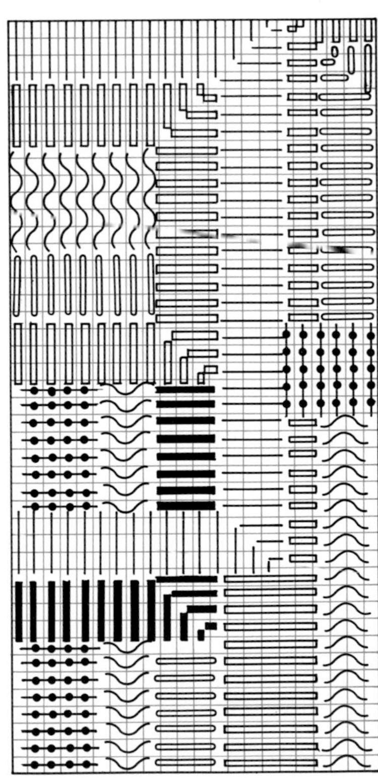

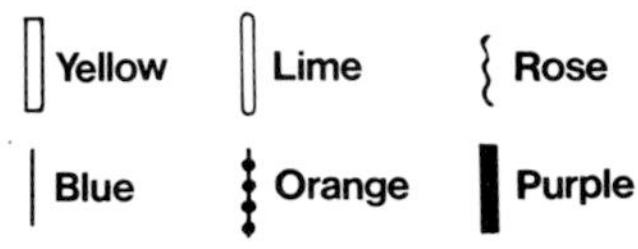

WIRE ART
Needlework Boutique

Free-Form Stitchery

Create your own free-form needlepoint piece and let your imagination guide you through a galaxy of ideas, colors, and stitches. If you clip and turn the edges of your canvas, you can achieve wonderful outlines and curves, as in our example at right.

If you're stuck for design ideas, just take a favorite object, make an abstract drawing of it, and transfer the drawing to canvas. Follow the general instructions at right, but use your imagination to come up with a truly unique needlepoint creation. No pattern is given, so colors and shapes are left entirely to you.

Materials

Needlepoint canvas
Scraps of yarn in assorted colors
Tapestry needle
Graph paper
Waterproof marking pen
Colored pencils

Directions

The abstract needlepoint piece shown opposite is meant to be a one-of-a-kind design. When planning and stitching your own free-form sampler, use our piece for ideas, but keep your design creative and original. Refer to the photograph for color and placement ideas, if desired, but draw an original pattern incorporating your own ideas and preferences into the design.

Our sampler is approximately 5x11 inches and is worked on a single piece of #12-count canvas. Feel free to make your design any size and to stitch it on the canvas of your choice. You can use purchased canvas, a scrap left from a previous project, or even several scraps in different sizes joined together as a ground for your creative stitchery.

Before you begin stitching, plan your design on paper. Here are several useful design techniques. The first could be called the "paper dolls" technique. Cut out various leaves, triangles, or other shapes that appeal to you. Arrange them on paper and then trace around them. Leave the outline of the design irregular, rather than placing the shapes in a box or frame. With this type of designing, the trick is to look not only at the shapes, but also at the background areas. These are called "negative spaces" and should be as pleasingly arranged as the objects themselves.

If abstractions appeal to you, try designing with cut or torn paper. Take a sheet of paper and cut or tear it into large and small fragments. Arrange these on the paper until both the shapes and the negative spaces please you. If the paper forms are cut from different colored tissue paper, their overlappings may suggest color schemes. Or, sketch an abstract shape by closing your eyes and "scribbling" with a pencil on a piece of paper. Open your eyes and evaluate your "design." If necessary, divide the shape into a number of smaller shapes.

Fill each section of your design with colored pencils, making a pleasant color arrangement. Or, using a pencil for shading, divide the design into light, medium, and dark areas. Plan to put your strongest colors in the heavily shaded areas and the palest colors in the lightly shaded areas. You may wish to leave some spaces open for needle weaving or drawn-thread work.

When you're pleased with the overall design, transfer the general outlines to canvas, following the directions on page 248. Work sections in a variety of colors and stitches, using the paper pattern as a guide. Combine cutwork and pulled-thread work to give your design see-through areas, as shown in the photograph.

When you're pleased with the overall design, transfer the general outlines to canvas, following the directions on page 10. Work sections in a variety of colors and stitches, using the paper pattern as a guide. Combine cutwork and pulled-thread work to give your design see-through areas, as shown in the photograph.

When the sampler is complete, block gently and trim the edges of the canvas to within ½ inch of the stitching. Turn under the ½-inch margin and press, clipping where necessary and tacking to hold in place. Back with a piece of fabric, if desired. (Be sure to cut holes in the backing fabric to allow light to show through the cut areas.)

Display your original free-form stitchery in a standing frame made with sheets of clear acrylic, if desired.

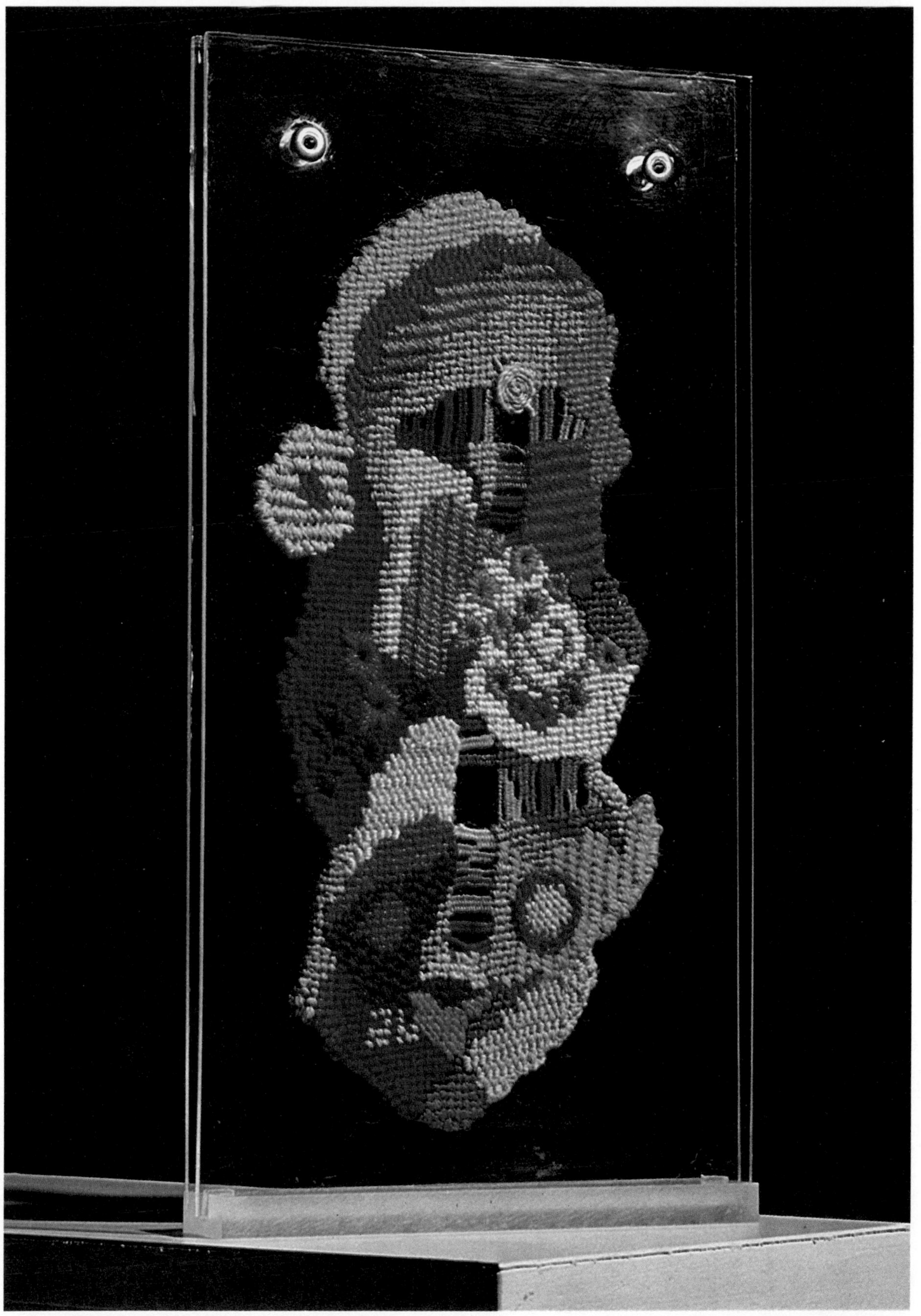

Spectacular Stitchery

Art from Your Needle

Using yarn on canvas the way an artist uses paint on canvas, you can create beautiful needlepoint designs like the fishpond rug shown here. The projects in this section are masterpieces of color and pattern. Although each one demands a good deal of time, the results are well worth the effort—needlepoint stitchery like this is a joy forever. To create this very special fishpond rug with intricate petit-point detailing, please turn the page.

Fishpond Rug *(shown on pages 300 and 301)*

This rug comes alive with subtly-shaded flora and petit-point fauna. Create special effects by blending contrasting colors of wool, and using cotton floss for shimmery highlights on the goldfish.

Refer to the outline pattern and closeup photographs on the following pages for color and shading details.

Materials

1½ yards (36-inch-wide) #10/20-count penelope canvas
3-ply Persian wool (see note)
Cotton embroidery floss (see note)
#18 tapestry needle
#24 tapestry needle
Four yards bias tape
Waterproof marking pen
Fabric for backing, if desired

Directions

Note: You will need 3-ply Persian yarn in white, black, gray, dark yellow, goldenrod, medium and dark bittersweet, light tangerine, light and dark salmon, orange, melon, light silver, light sand, pale russet, sapphire, pale blue, pale and light beige, lilac, and ice green. You will also need varying shades—from light to dark—of loden green, olive green, dark olive, spruce green, lime green, and bronze green. The background is worked in combinations of medium-olive and medium-bronze greens, and requires approximately 400 yards of each color. In addition, you will need cotton floss for the petit-point animals in colors shown in the photograph.

Enlarge the outline pattern on page 303 according to the directions on page 272. Transfer the pattern to the canvas with a waterproof marking pen, leaving a three-inch margin all around. If desired, mount the canvas in a frame to prevent warping.

Needlepoint the design, using the photographs, pattern, and these directions as a guide. Feel free to make changes or modifications in the colors to match your decorating scheme.

Lily Pads: The rounded lily pad shapes are worked in basket-weave stitches with three strands of Persian wool and a #18 tapestry needle. Referring to the pattern and photograph, work the lily pads in shades of green. Note that several pads are shaded on the pattern, indicating they are "below" the water's surface, or in shadow. Work these pads in the darkest shades of green, or in blends of green and another color, such as rust. (To blend a color, simply replace one strand of yarn with a contrasting strand.) Work the pads "floating" on the water in shades of bright light green, with accents of yellow or blue-green so they show up more clearly.

Water Lilies: Refer to the pattern for outline and positioning of water lilies, and to the closeup photo for color and shading. Work the flowers in continental stitches (see directions on pages 321 to 323). If desired, add French knots for flower centers.

Background: Begin filling background in upper right corner of rug with basket-weave stitches. To achieve the striated effect, blend olive and bronze greens as for shaded areas of lily pads, alternating the dominant color. Be sure to leave areas for the petit-point figures as shown in the outline pattern.

Goldfish, Frog, Butterfly: Work the figures in petit point (see directions on page 303) using a #24 tapestry needle. Refer to the closeup photograph on page 305 and to the chart to work the first goldfish. Work all other fish with similar shading, and other figures according to the photographs. Use floss to create shimmery areas on figures; use two or more shades of floss for shading.

Spider, Web, Butterfly Detail: For spider, embroider body and legs with short satin stitches using one strand of black wool. For web, combine two strands white floss and one strand green floss; lay on canvas in the position shown on the pattern. Couch floss to canvas with short stitches every ¼ inch. Couch each strand of the web; couch brown floss similarly for butterfly antennae.

To finish, block the rug (see directions on page 241). For edges, trim excess canvas from rug, leaving a ½-inch margin. Stitch bias tape to canvas edge and fold under. Tack other edge to canvas, tucking tape along curves so rug will lie flat. If desired, blindstitch a fabric backing to reverse side of rug for protection. Shake the rug to remove loose dirt particles. Dry-clean when necessary.

Petit Point

Petit point is a means of adding more detail to needlepoint projects, since it is worked on canvas that yields 18 or more stitches per inch. Mono canvas with 18, 20, or 22 stitches per inch (and finer) is suitable for small projects that are worked entirely in petit point. Penelope canvas, however, is recommended for projects with a combination of both petit point and larger needlepoint stitches, and it has a distinctive double-thread weave. To work petit point on penelope canvas, just separate the threads with the tip of your needle, and work four tiny stitches where just one larger needlepoint stitch would have been. Work petit point with one strand of Persian wool or several strands of embroidery floss. Whichever you use, make sure that the fiber is neither so thick that it distorts the canvas, nor so thin that the canvas threads show through.

continued

Fishpond Rug *(continued)*

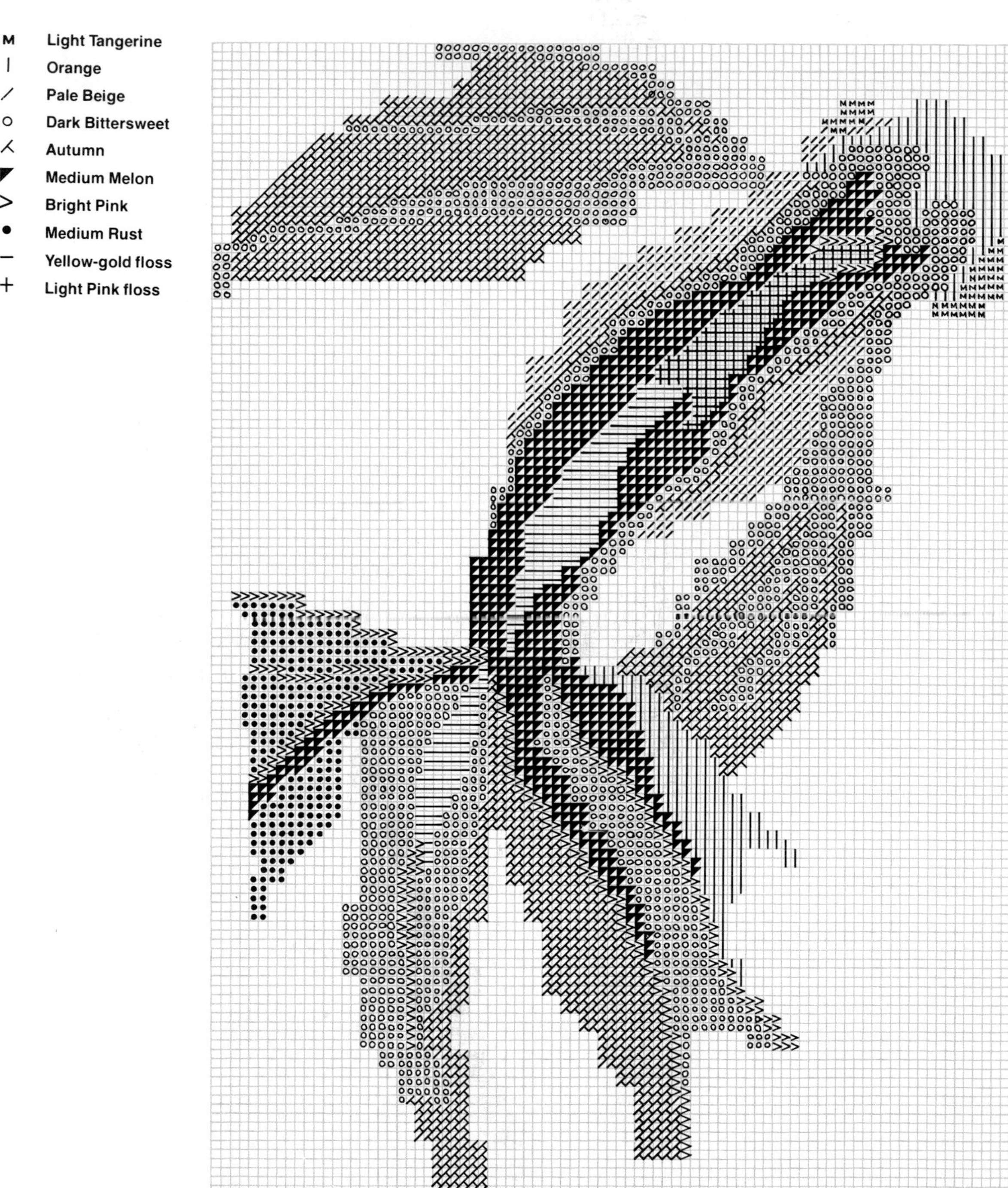

PETIT-POINT FISH

1 Square = 1 Stitch

Della Robbia Wreath

All the color and glory of a traditional Della Robbia wreath are captured in this beautiful needlepoint creation.

The wreath, stitched entirely in continental stitches, is worked one section of color at a time. Work directly from the pattern on pages 308 and 309, repeating the pattern four times to complete the wreath.

Mount the finished needlepoint on a plywood board, adding layers of quilt batting for dimension.

Materials

3-ply Paternayan yarn, or a similar substitute, in the amounts (32-inch strands) and colors on pages 308 and 309
24x24 inches #14-count canvas
Eight to twelve #19 tapestry needles
24x24 inches ⅜-inch plywood
Compass (for drawing circles)
Waterproof marking pen
Quilt batting
20x20 inches green felt
4-inch-wide red velvet ribbon
Masking tape
Staple gun

Directions

Bind the edges of the canvas with masking tape to prevent raveling, and draw an 18-inch circle in the middle of the canvas using a compass and waterproof pen. Divide the circle into fourths and draw a 7-inch circle in the center of the 18-inch circle. The small circle is the center of the wreath and will not be filled in. Wait until the needlepoint is complete before cutting out the center circle.

Count the squares from the inside edge to the outside of the wreath to make sure they equal the number on the graph (pages 308 and 309). Adjust the size of the circle so it corresponds to the number of squares on the graph, if necessary.

Add an extra ½ inch (about 7 spaces) to the inner and outer edges of the graph and the circle on the canvas. These spaces will be filled with additional white yarn to match the background so that when the wreath is cut and turned, none of the design will be lost.

Soak the yarn in cold water for three to five minutes to remove any color residue and to make sure the colors do not run. Gently squeeze out excess moisture and lay the yarn flat to dry. (Do not dry the yarn in direct sunlight.) Be sure the yarn dries thoroughly before you begin stitching.

Separate strands into individual plies, and use two plies for stitching. Begin stitching one quadrant of the wreath, following the graph on the following pages. The entire wreath is done in continental stitches (see the Glossary on pages 321 to 323). Work one section of color, carry the yarn to the back, and leave it long and threaded on the needle (rather than ending or cutting it) so that when you need the same color again, you will not have to re-thread a new strand. If the long yarns get in your way while stitching, pull them to one side and tape them to the canvas.

When you finish one quadrant, label one end of the pattern A and the other end B. To begin work in the second quadrant, match end B of the first quadrant to end A of the second and begin stitching. Continue in this way until all four sections are complete. Work the white background as you go, filling in the extra ½ inch along the inside and outside edges.

Block the wreath according to the directions on page 241. Since the entire wreath is done in continental stitches, it may be necessary to block the canvas twice. Cut around the wreath shape and the inside circle, leaving two inches of unworked canvas along both inside and outside edges.

Cut a 17¼-inch circle from the plywood board and sand the rough edges until they are smooth. Then, cut a 6½-inch circle from the center of the large plywood circle and sand the edges.

Cut three layers of quilt batting to match the size of the plywood. With the batting as padding, lay the wreath on top of the plywood and staple the canvas to the back of the board, pulling the edges tightly. Clip curves when necessary to make edges lie flat and to eliminate puckering.

Cut a piece of green felt to match the plywood and glue it (with a light, even coat of white glue) to the back of the wreath, covering the canvas edges. Let the glue dry thoroughly.

Tie a bow with 4-inch-wide red velvet ribbon and tack the bow in place at the bottom of the wreath, making sure it is secure. Trim the ends of the bow as desired.

continued

Della Robbia Wreath *(continued)*

Color	Symbol
R 70 Light holly (9 strands)	L
R 10 Dark holly (9 ")	/
010 White (45 ")	□
G 74 Pale green (11 ")	○
G 64 Light green (20 ")	M
G 54 Med. green (19 strands)	+
504 Dark green (35 ")	◤
865 Light golden red (6 ")	—
855 Light red (8 ")	•
845 Med. red (20 ")	▲
810 Dark red (24 ")	×

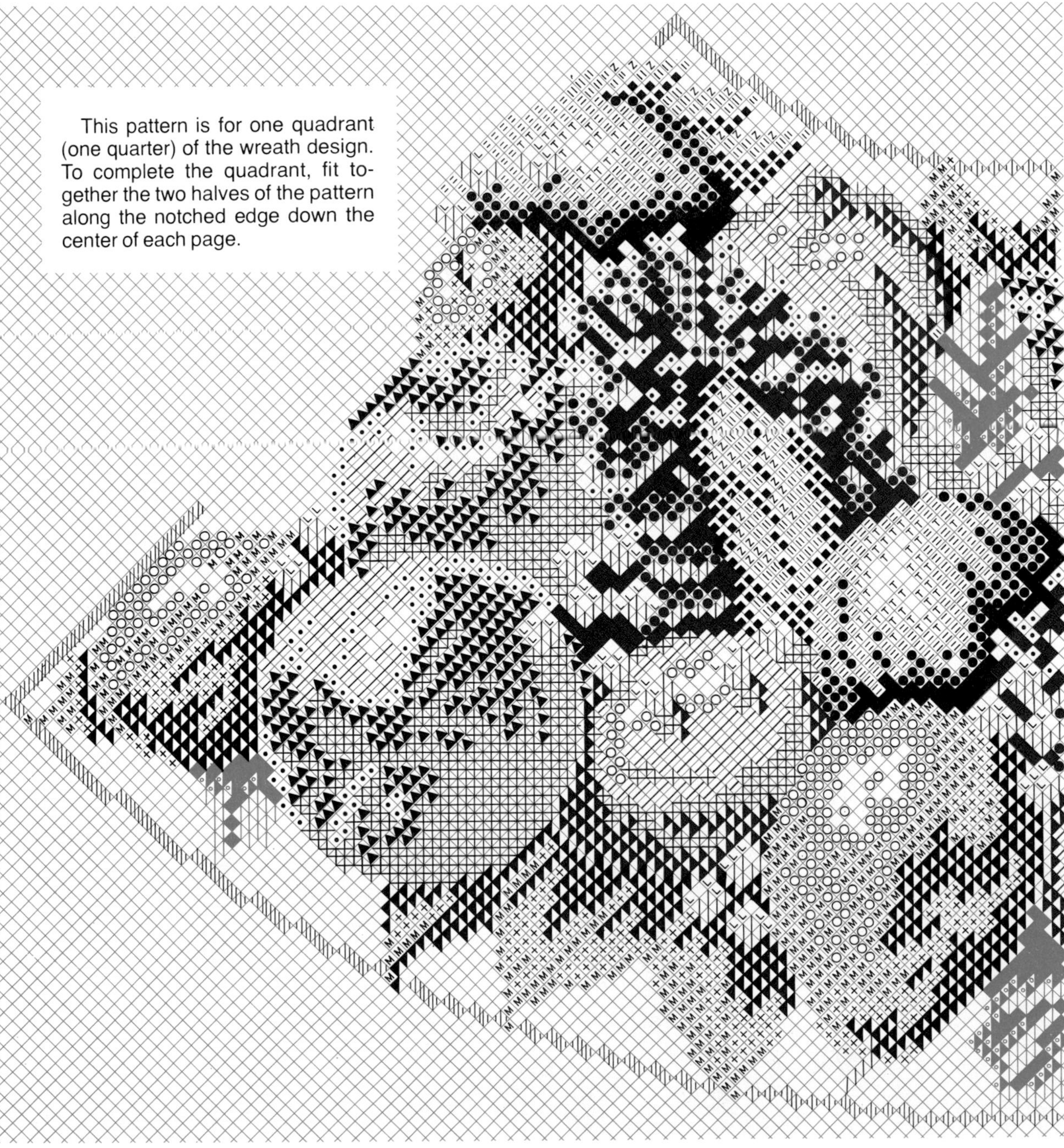

This pattern is for one quadrant (one quarter) of the wreath design. To complete the quadrant, fit together the two halves of the pattern along the notched edge down the center of each page.

975 Pale orange (5 strands)	T	535 Light blue green (4 strands)	z	427 Med. yellow (13 strands)	×
965 Light orange (10 ")	=	113 Dark brown (24 ")	■	441 Light lemon yellow (17 ")	—
960 Med. orange (7 ")	●	405 Med. brown (12 ")	●	437 Pale lemon yellow (17 ")	○
958 Dark orange (7 ")	■	420 Light brown (10 ")	/	590 Light olive green (11 ")	/
528 Dark blue green (6 ")	▪	430 Pale brown (12 ")	•	553 Med. olive green (8 ")	◢
532 Med. blue green (6 ")	‖	433 Dark yellow (gold) (12 ")	◢	540 Dark olive green (9 ")	■

One square equals one intersection of threads on the canvas.

Work in continental stitches, adding seven rows of stitches to the inner and outer edges marked on the pattern.

Needlepoint Crèche

Christmas manger scenes have spanned many centuries and cultures. Our stately crèche figures are a happy combination of old-world expressiveness and contemporary geometrics.

Although there are a variety of color combinations, the use of a single stitch—the continental stitch—keeps the project simple. Patterns for the figures are on pages 312 to 315.

Materials

3 ply Persian wool in the colors and amounts listed on the chart on page 312
1⅔ yards 36-inch mono canvas (12 or 14 meshes per inch) (See note)
#17 tapestry needle
9x12-inch felt pieces in the following amounts and colors: 1 orange, 1 yellow, 1 turquoise, and 2 navy blue
8½-inch piece of 1/16-inch-diameter brass wire for staff
24-inch piece of 1/32-inch-diameter aluminum wire for angel wings
Lightweight cardboard
White glue
Shredded foam or cotton batting for stuffing
Waterproof pen
1-inch masking tape

Directions

Note: To reduce warping and buckling of completed needlepoint, you may wish to substitute interlock for mono canvas. In addition, interlock won't ravel when trimmed, so you need not apply white glue to the edges of the completed needlepoint.

Enlarge the patterns on the following pages according to the directions on page 272. Cut the canvas pieces two inches larger on all sides than the patterns show, and bind raw edges with masking tape. Position canvas pieces over the enlarged patterns, leaving two inches of canvas all around and making sure that the horizontal and vertical threads of the canvas run square to the facial detail. Trace the outlines with a waterproof pen. As an alternative, do not cut the canvas pieces apart, but transfer up to four patterns to one large piece of canvas. Mount in a working frame, and stitch all the figures at once.

Using two strands of the three-ply wool and following color key on page 312, work the figures entirely in continental stitches. Begin and end threads with waste knots. Begin with facial details and work all areas of one color with the same length of yarn. For example, work Joseph's forehead, cheeks, eyelids, and chin in white before working other facial details. Then fill in hair and body areas. Go ahead and assemble this figure, or wait and assemble the entire crèche at once. Block if necessary.

To assemble, carefully apply a thin line of glue ⅛ inch from the edge of the completed needlepoint around all sides and allow to dry. This glue prevents raveling (if you are using interlock canvas, eliminate this gluing step). Trim around needlepoint ¼ inch from all outside edges, being careful not to cut into glue or stitches. To give the head its rounded shape, make a ⅜-inch-deep cut into each V at top of figure. Fold Vs inward (making a dart) and stitch together with one strand of the same color yarn as used in adjoining needlepoint. Close back seam similarly.

Turn figure upside down and stuff. For bottom, trace and cut cardboard oval to fit; cut felt oval also, adding ¼ inch margin to cardboard pattern. Glue cardboard, centered, to felt oval. Allow to dry. Position felt bottom on inverted figure (with cardboard to the inside), and tuck the extra felt to the inside. Using one strand of yarn, sew felt bottom to the edge of the figure, keeping raw edges of felt and canvas inside.

For halos, glue and trim around edges of needlepoint halos as for the figures. Fold under raw edges and glue. Cut matching halo from felt; glue lightly to back of needlepoint halos. If desired, place a stack of books or other heavy objects on halo to keep it flat until glue dries. Stitch together edges of felt and needlepoint. Using one strand of matching yarn, attach halo to head.

Glue and trim angel wings as for halos. Fold under raw edges of canvas. Before gluing them down permanently, cut aluminum wire to fit around outer edges of wings for stiffening. Bend wire to match outline of wings. Position shaped wire inside folded-under canvas edges; glue edges down. Cut felt to fit wings. Stitch together felt and needlepoint and attach wings to angel.

For shepherd's staff, cut an 8½-inch piece of brass wire, and bend into shape as shown on the pattern. Attach to hand section of shepherd with matching yarn.

continued

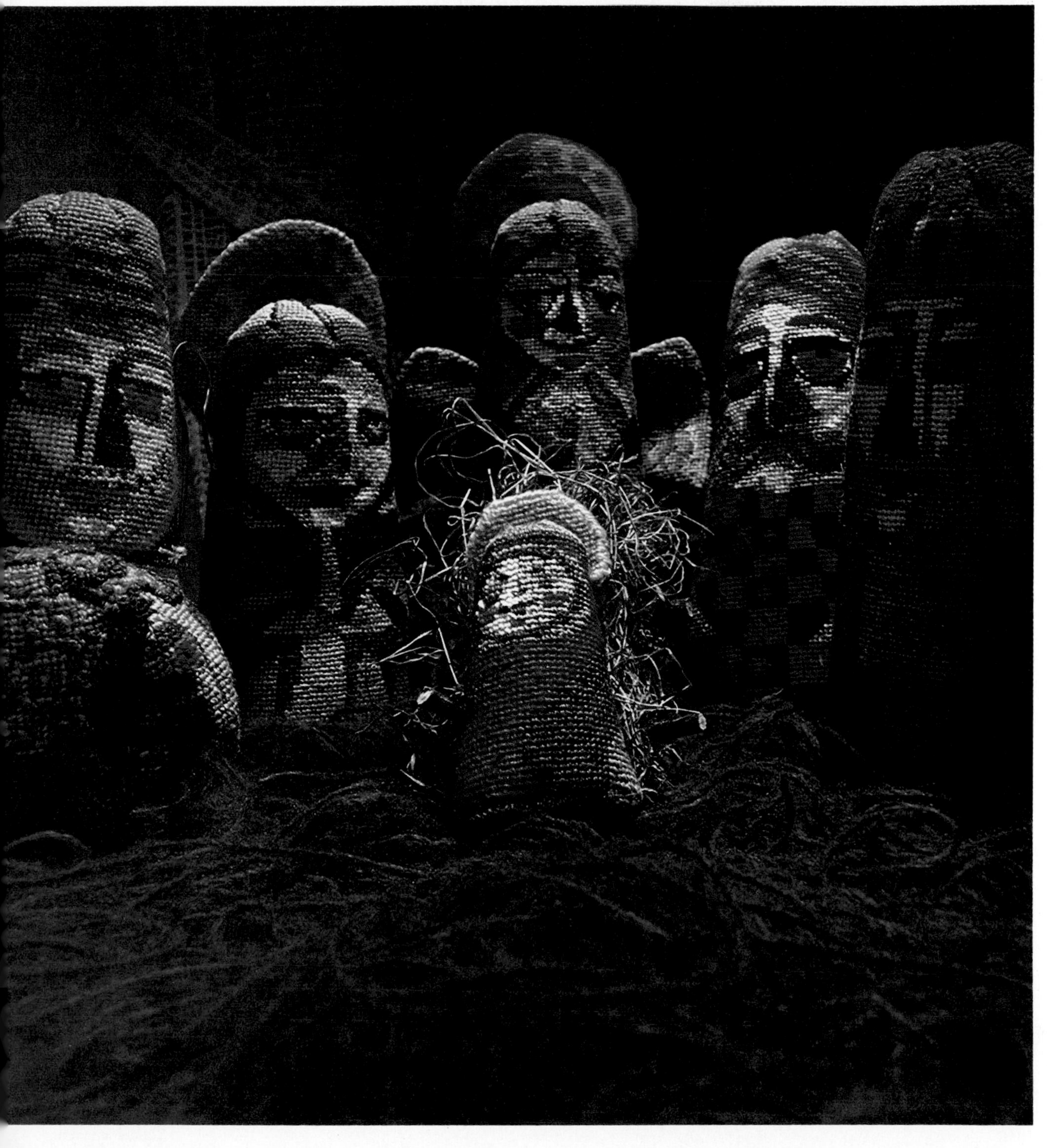

Needlepoint Crèche *(continued)*

Color Key

You may use yarn in the colors listed below, or see the note on page 315 for alternatives.

Color	Number	Yards
White	1	15
Pink	2	8
Light fuchsia	3	14
Magenta	4	5
Bright red	5	10
Deep red	6	4
Crimson red	7	6
Vermilion	8	4
Light orange	9	12
Orange	10	12
Burnt orange	11	30
Pale yellow	12	2
Light yellow	13	5
Yellow	14	6
Golden yellow	15	2
Yellow-gold	16	4
Gold	17	12
Yellow-ocher	18	26
Light olive	19	2
Olive	20	18
Light blue-green	21	12
Medium blue-green	22	15
Dark blue-green	23	10
Light blue	24	5
Sky blue	25	8
Light true blue	26	18
Medium blue	27	10
True blue	28	5
Royal blue	29	19
Heather blue	30	16
Dark heather blue	31	10
Navy blue	32	24
Dark navy blue	33	5
Pale lavender-blue	34	2
Light lavender-blue	35	12
Lavender-blue	36	26
Lavender	37	14
Red-violet	38	10
Dark purple	39	10
Light tan	40	2
Tan	41	12
Burnt sienna	42	13

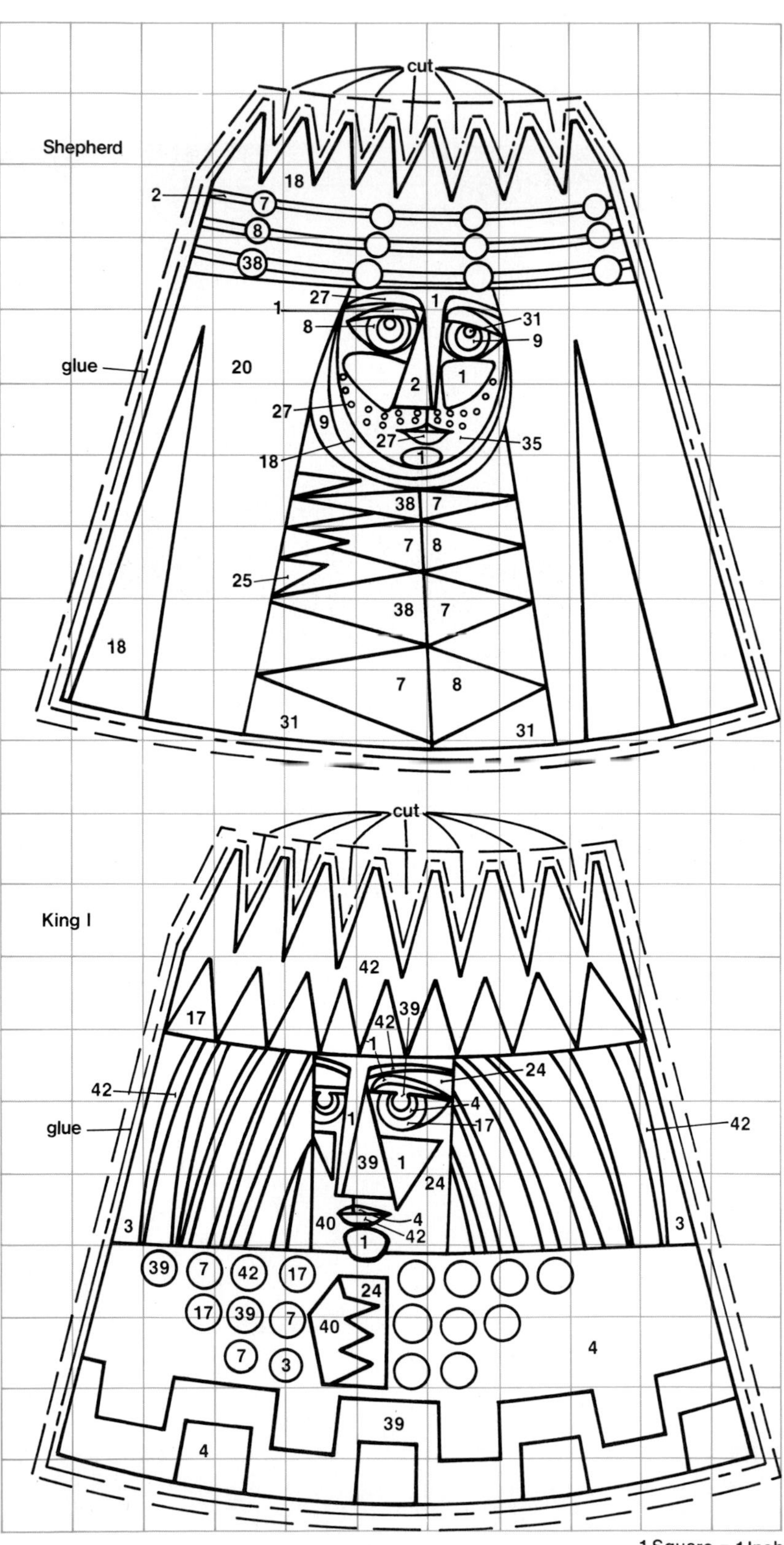

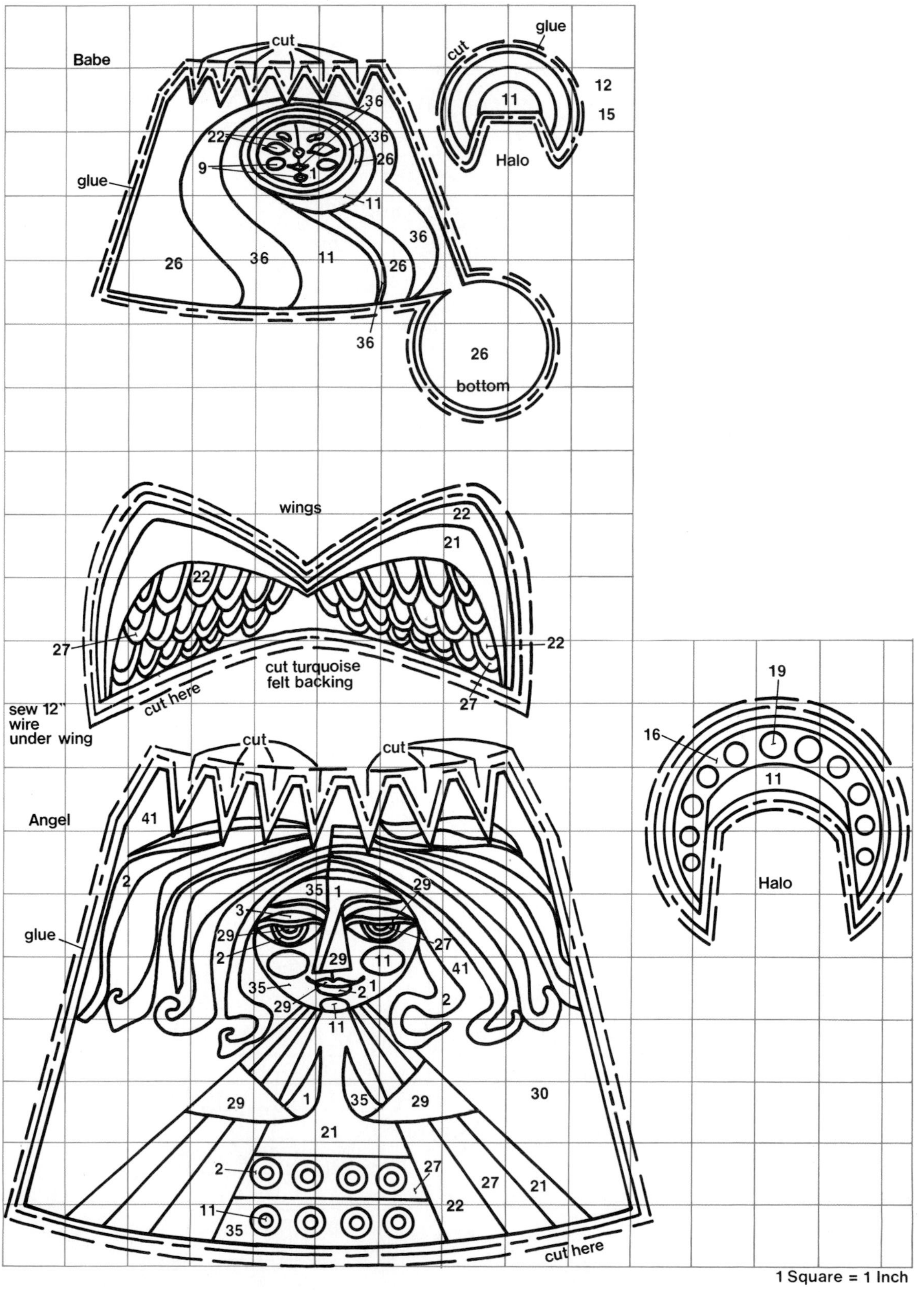

1 Square = 1 Inch

Needlepoint Crèche *(continued)*

1 Square = 1 Inch

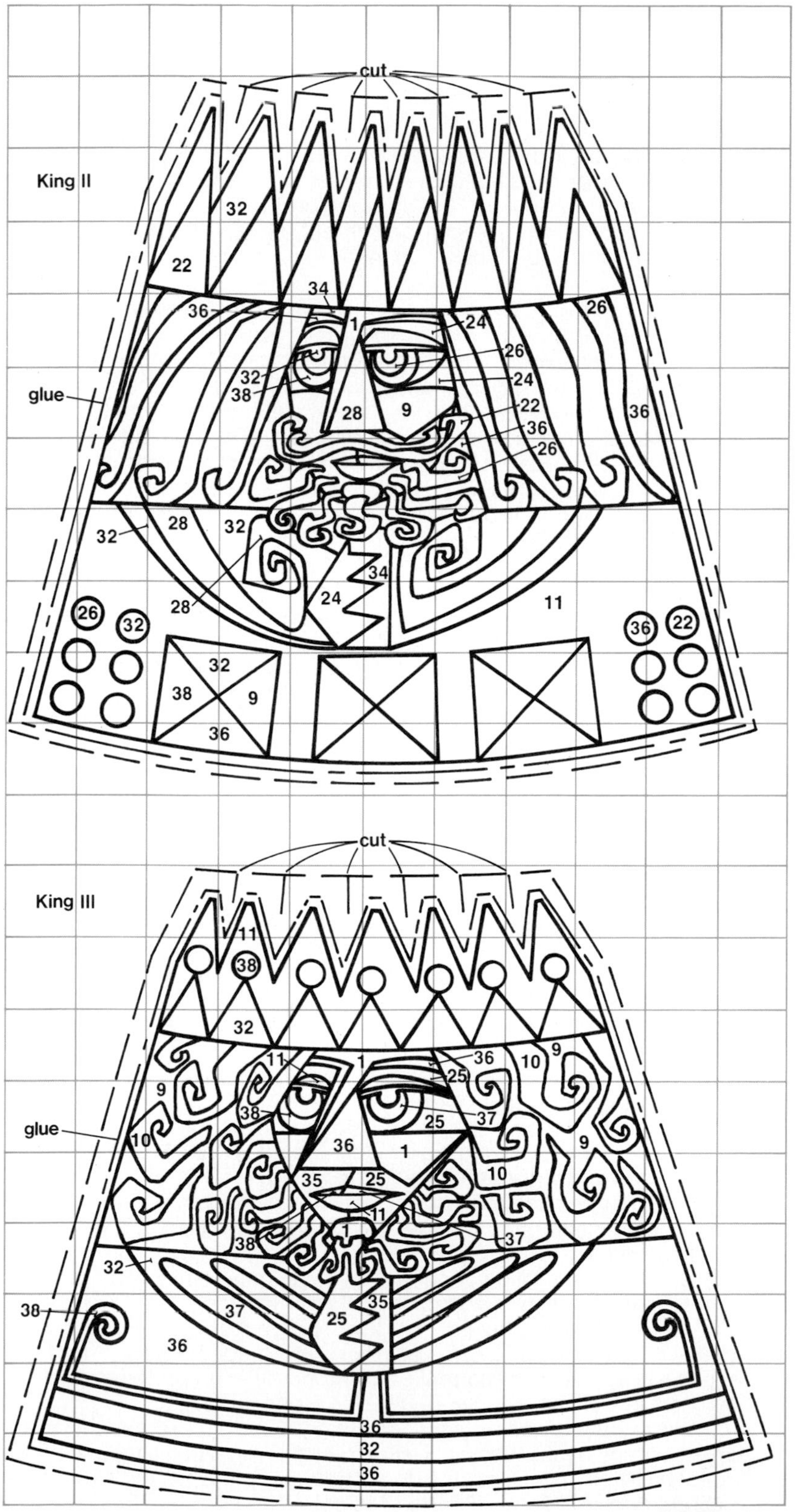

King II

King III

Creating Color Schemes

In this needlepoint project, rich hues and lustrous tonal values are achieved by using many shades of several basic colors. If you are unable to locate all the shades listed, or don't wish to purchase an entire skein to obtain the small amount of necessary yarn, you can make substitutions. For example, you could use lavender-blue throughout instead of buying additional shades of pale lavender-blue and light lavender-blue. Or, you may wish to use up small quantities of Persian yarn left over from previous needlepoint projects. When you make *any* yarn substitution on a project involving small-scale stitches, remember to strive for overall color impact. A good test of color compatibility is to stand back and squint at the proposed colors: if the "blur" looks good to you, any positioning of the colors in the groups will be successful.

1 Square = 1 Inch

Soft-Sculpture Lion

What could be more fun than stitching the king of beasts in needlepoint! And Karut, our soft-sculpture lion, is designed to let you show off all your stitchery skills as well, for he's worked in a stunning array of stitches. Patterns for each section of the lion are on pages 318 to 320.

Materials

60 inches (36-inch-wide) #12-count interlock canvas
⅔ yard (44-inch-wide) purple unclipped corduroy
3x8 inches red suede
3-ply Paternayan Persian yarn, or a suitable substitute, in the following colors and amounts: #321 navy (35 yards), #114 dark brown (48), #145 medium brown (23), #893 mauve (38), #650 violet (31), #958 red-orange (29), #424 burnt orange (37), #645 magenta (42), and #R10 red (3 skeins, 8 yards)
Small amounts of #3 pearl cotton in the following colors: magenta, violet, navy, and orange
1 skein red 6-strand cotton embroidery floss
3 skeins white #3 pearl cotton
4 ounces navy knitting wool
12 inches brass wire (1/16-inch-diameter) for tail
2 orange Shisha mirrors
5 yards coated electrical wire (1/16-inch-diameter) for mane (optional)
Navy and magenta acrylic paints
Paintbrush
Clear-drying white glue
Approximately 15 pounds of polyester stuffing
#20 tapestry needle

Directions

Enlarge the patterns on pages 318 to 320 and transfer them to canvas, following directions on pages 272 and 273. Make sure grain lines on pattern match straight grain of canvas. Do not cut out individual pattern pieces before stitching. Instead, bind edges of canvas with tape; mount canvas in a frame for stitching, if desired.

Work the lion following the color and stitch keys with the pattern. Or substitute your own colors and stitches. If you choose alternate stitches, remember that the lion is a playful piece of needle art; feel free to let your imagination roam, selecting a variety of interesting and unusual stitches from your needlepoint repertoire. Diagrams for Turkey work (the rya-knot stitch) and the Van Dyke stitch, fan stitch, and brick stitch are with the patterns. For an explanation of the remaining stitches, see pages 321 to 323.

The lion's face is worked in two pieces. The pattern is for the right side of the face; reverse it for the left side. Work tent-stitched areas first, then fill areas worked in unusual stitches. Finally, add Shisha mirrors as follows. Glue mirrors in place with white glue. When the glue dries, work five fan-shaped straight stitches across the mirror using six strands of red cotton floss (see photograph). At the end of the mirror closest to the center of the face, work five rows of plain weaving over and under the straight stitches.

The front of the body and the tops of the front legs are worked in a single piece, as are the front side and back side pieces. Note that across the front body there are four squares that spell WORK, just as PLAY and ROAR are spelled on the front side piece and LOVE on the back side piece. If desired, substitute your own words in these squares. Work tent-stitched areas first, then the fancier stitches. On the front side piece, stitch your initials in the triangle to the right of ROAR.

On the tail, work alternate squares of mauve and violet tent stitches. At end of tail, work 1½ inches of navy tent stitches, except work two rows of Turkey loops across the middle. (For how-to for Turkey loops, see page 318.) Make loops between knots approximately ½ inch long by wrapping yarn over a pencil between stitches; leave loops uncut. Finish with 1¼ inches of Turkey work at end of tail, making loops 2 inches long; cut loops open to make a row of fringe.

When all stitching is finished, block the needlepoint, if necessary, and then cut out the individual pieces for the lion, adding ¼-inch seam allowances to all edges.

To assemble the head, stitch face pieces together along center front; overcast-stitch along the seam line using yarn in appropriate colors. Fold seam margin on ears to back of needlepoint; steam-press. Glue seam allowance to the back of ears with white glue. Cut two ear shapes (without seam allowances) from red suede; glue one to back of each ear. When glue is dry, overcast-stitch suede and needlepoint ears together with magenta yarn. Paint any exposed canvas with magenta acrylic paint. Pin ears to face along marked areas, with needlepoint facing front; stitch.

Paint the head back pieces with navy blue acrylic paint. After it dries, stitch the center back seam. With right sides facing, stitch head back to front, leaving lower edge (neck) open. Turn right side out and stuff firmly. Set head aside.

continued

Soft-Sculpture Lion *(continued)*

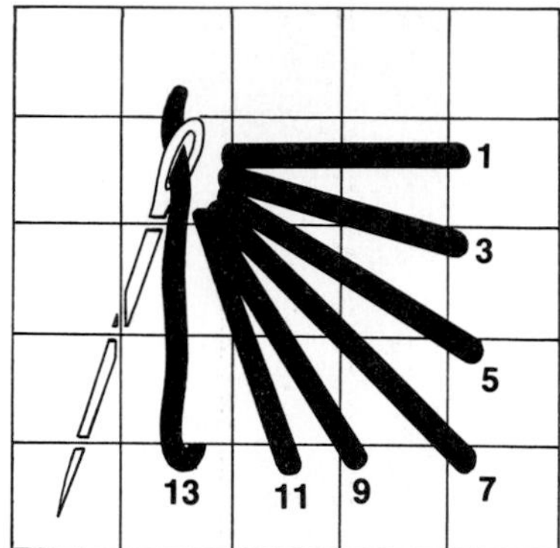

Fan Stitch

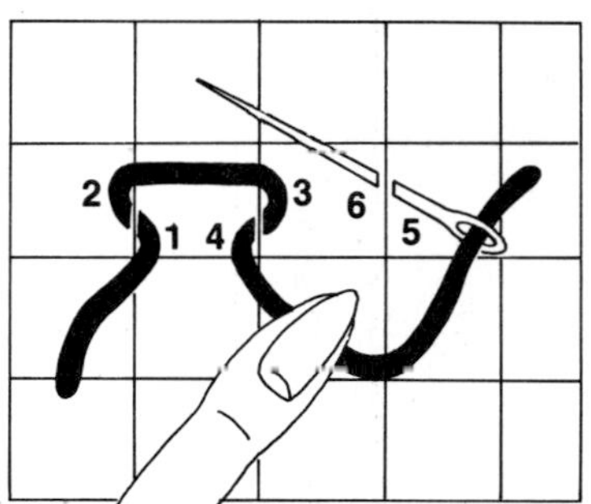

Turkey Loop Stitch

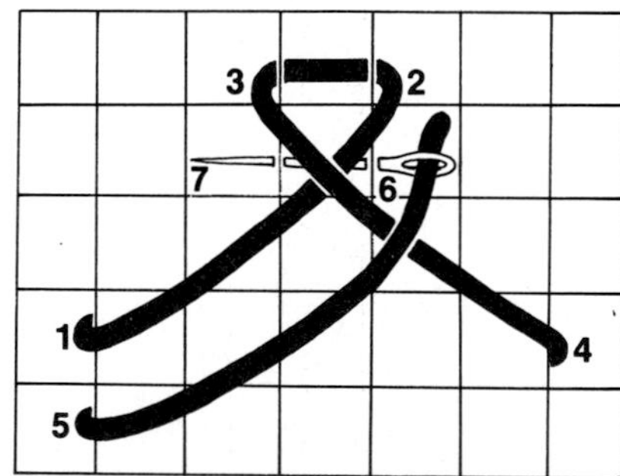

Van Dyke Stitch

For the tail, stitch the long edges together and turn the tail right side out. Sew the navy end together and stuff the tail firmly. Bend a small hook in one end of the brass wire, then insert wire in tail with hook at open end.

To assemble the body, baste the side front piece (side 1) to the front body, matching D to D. Stitch and overcast the seam, if desired, using matching yarns. Baste and stitch the side back piece (side 2) to the front body, matching B to B. Stitch the side front to side back along the top of the body, leaving an opening for the tail. Both the sides and the front are inside at this seam joining.

When adding the bottom, put the right side of the fabric inside and attach at points V, W, S, C, and A. Stitch along the edge of the needlepoint. Clip the seam allowance on the exterior curves and at A, C, S, V, and W. Leave open the spot at which the tail is to be inserted. Turn the stitched pieces and the bottom right side out and stuff tightly. At the neck opening of the body, add a line of Turkey work, making loops 1½ inches long. Clip loops. Insert tail at opening and stitch to body.

For the lion's mane, stitch knitting yarn across back of head in Turkey work, making loops about four inches long. Space rows of Turkey-work stitches about ½ inch apart. If desired, cut electrical wire into 6-inch pieces; fold pieces in half. Then cut 12-inch lengths of knitting yarn. Working with yarn in groups of three, fold yarn lengths in half and wrap or braid over doubled wire pieces. Sew covered wires to head. The wire will make the mane stand up, giving the lion a delightfully wild look. Finish by stitching the head to the body in the direction you'd like the lion to face.

continued

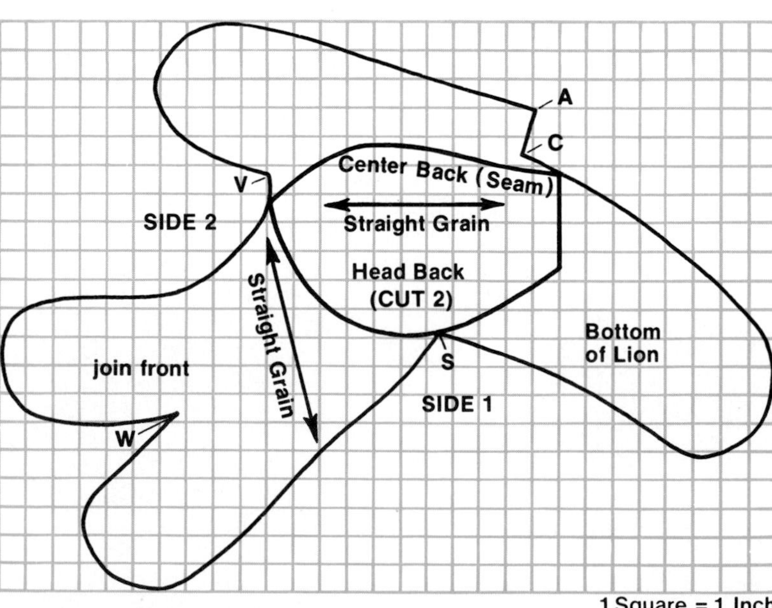

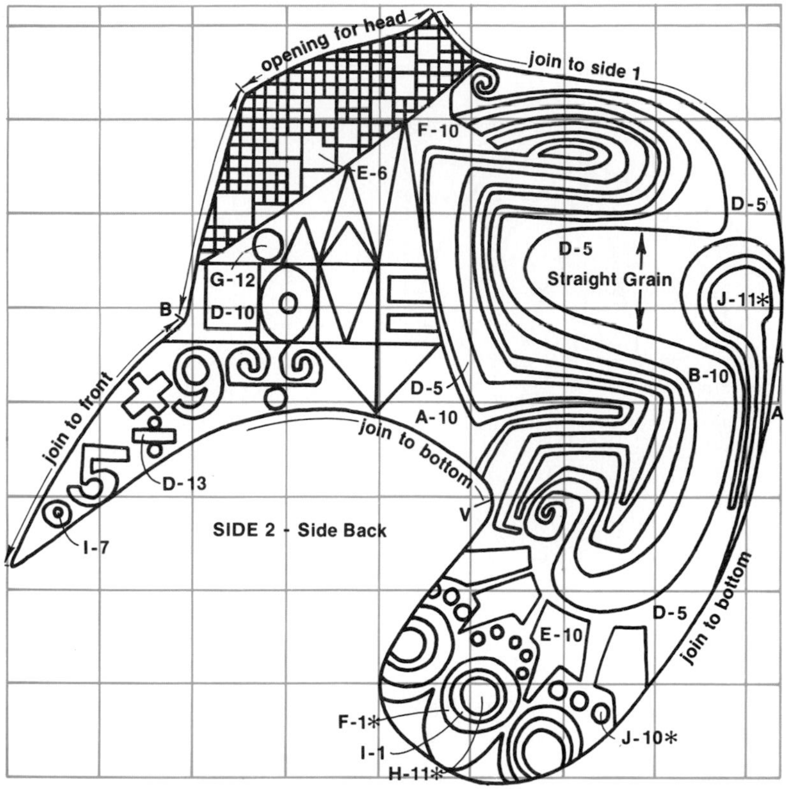

1 Square = 2 Inches

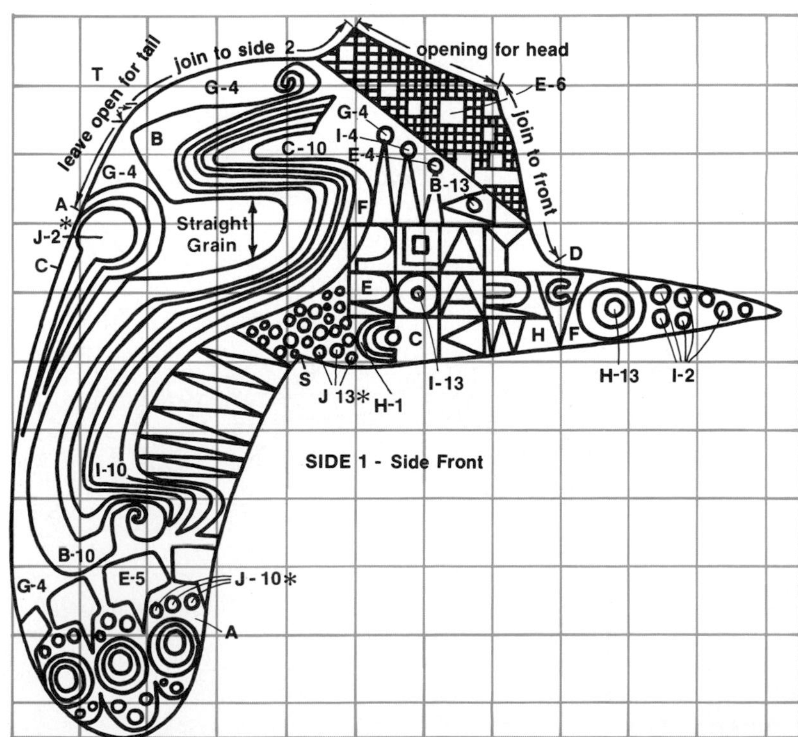

1 Square = 2 Inches

Stitch Key

1. Chain stitch
2. Fan stitch
3. Van Dyke stitch
4. Bargello stitch
5. Brick stitch
6. Scotch stitch
7. French knot
8. Turkey loop stitch
9. Shisha mirror
10. Tent stitch
11. Fan stitch
12. Diamond eyelet stitch
13. Wheat sheaf stitch
14. Double cross-stitch
15. Upright Gobelin stitch

Color Key

A. Navy
B. Dark brown
C. Medium brown
D. Mauve
E. Violet
F. Red-orange
G. Burnt orange
H. Magenta
I. Red
J. White

*pearl cotton

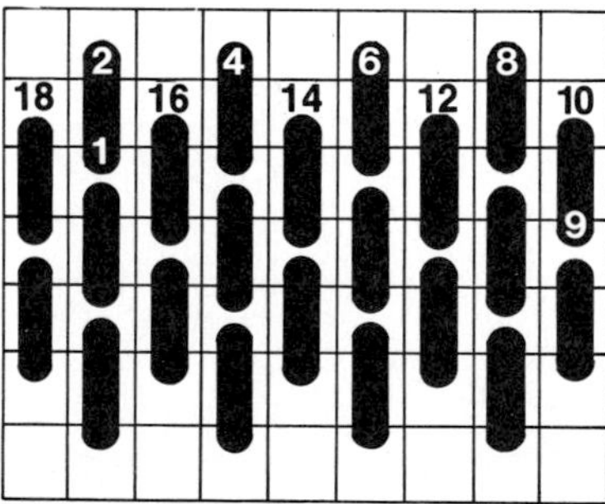

Brick Stitch

Soft-Sculpture Lion *(continued)*

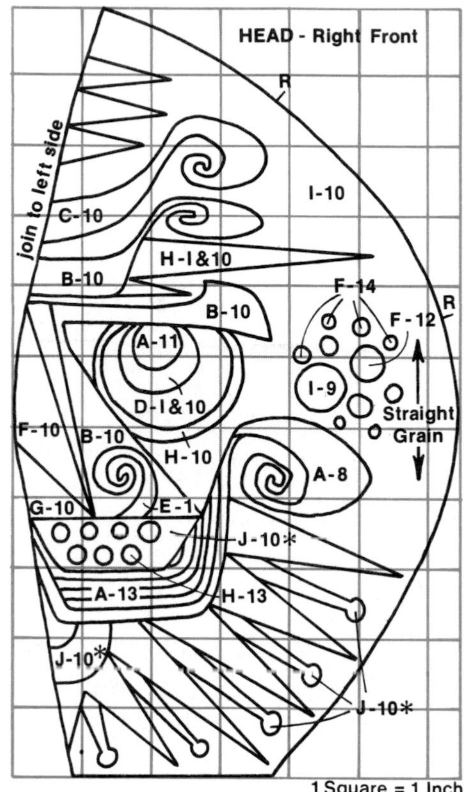

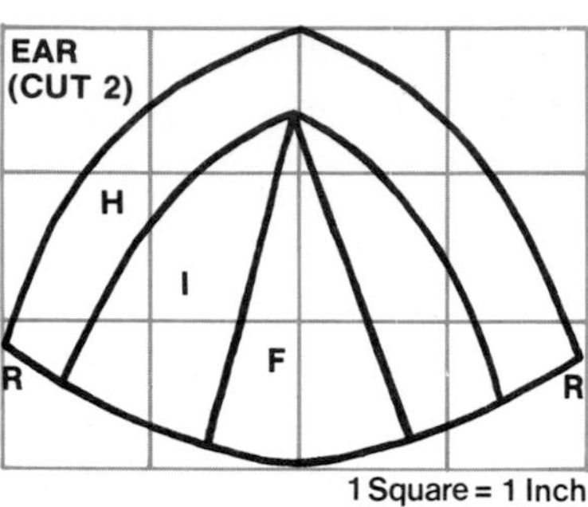

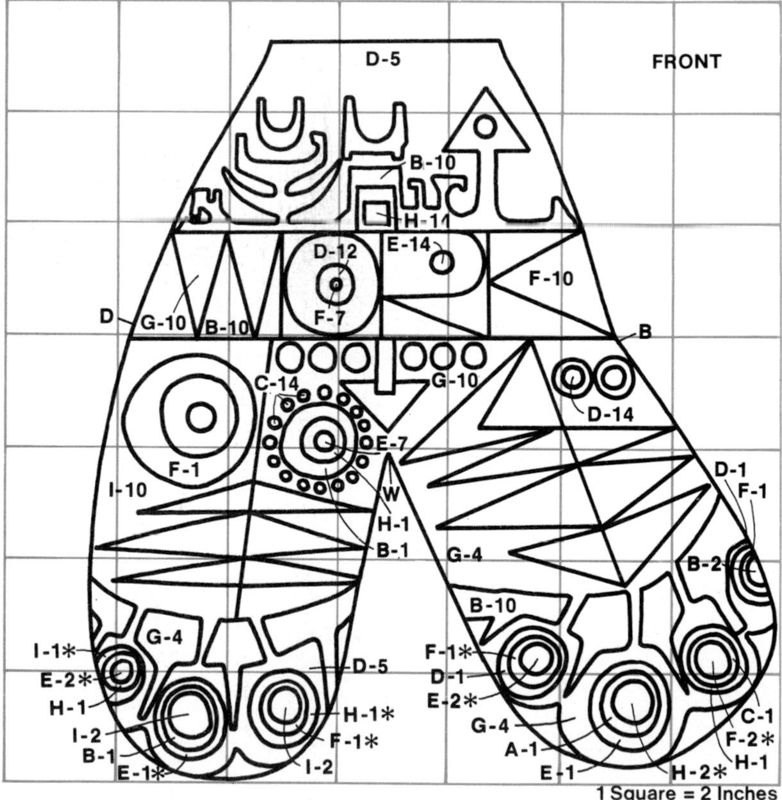

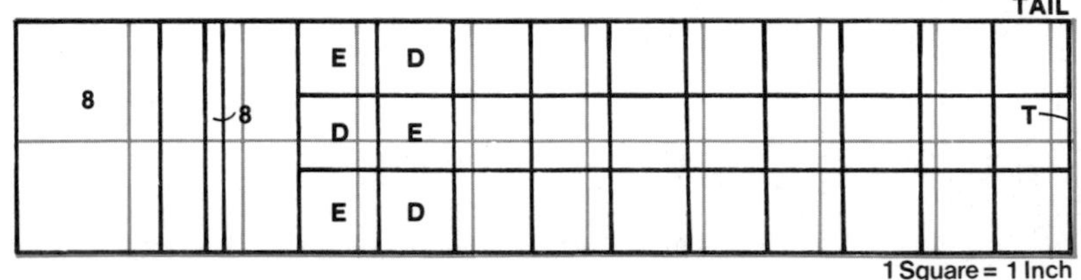

Basic Needlepoint Stitches

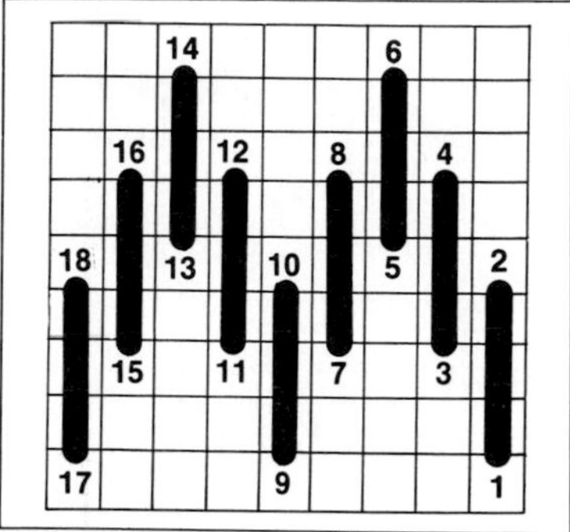

Bargello
(Also called Flame Stitch or Florentine Stitch) Bargello uses long, straight stitches, usually over four threads of canvas, to form a definite design. The stitches are worked horizontally or vertically on the canvas to form a rising and falling pattern. To get the up-and-down effect, stitches are raised or lowered two canvas threads at a time. The key line establishes the pattern and is repeated throughout the entire design. Bargello works up quickly, but requires strict attention to the stitching to make each row identical; otherwise, the design is thrown off balance.

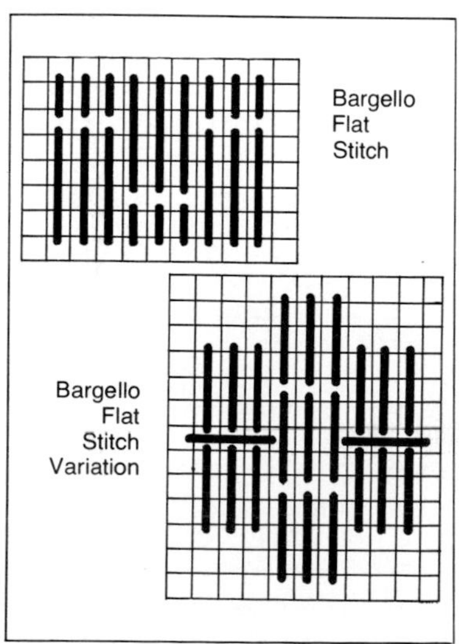

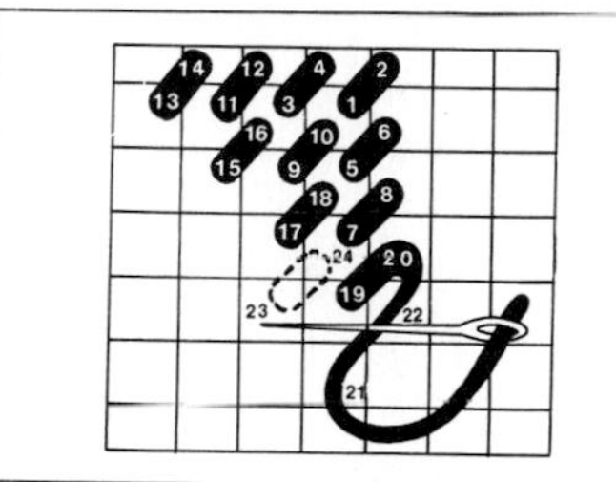

Basket-Weave Stitch
The front of this tent stitch looks like the continental or half cross-stitch, but the back resembles a basket-weave or woven pattern. It is useful for backgrounds and large areas because it does not distort canvas when worked with the grain (see page 241). Begin stitching in the upper right corner and work diagonally, moving the needle vertically on the down rows and horizontally on the up rows. The stitching sequence is indicated by the numbers on the diagram. *(See also, Continental, Half Cross-, and Tent Stitches.)*

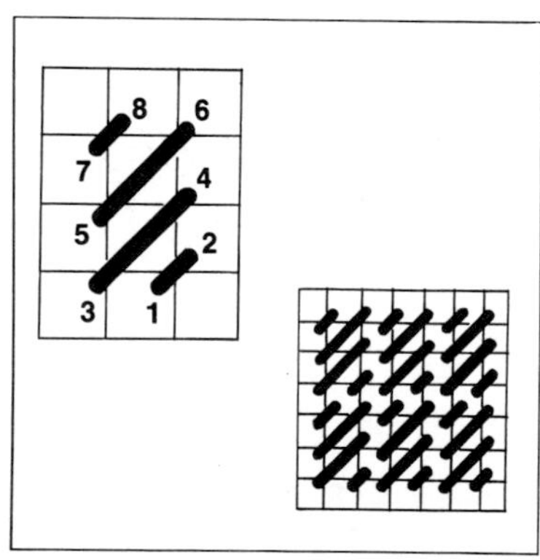

Cashmere Stitch
This stitch, worked in boxes, is made with four stitches per unit. Take the first stitch at the base of the unit and work up. Rows can be worked horizontally, vertically, or diagonally. When used as a background, the cashmere stitch resembles woven fabric. *(See also, Mosaic Stitch.)*

Chain Stitch
See page 406.

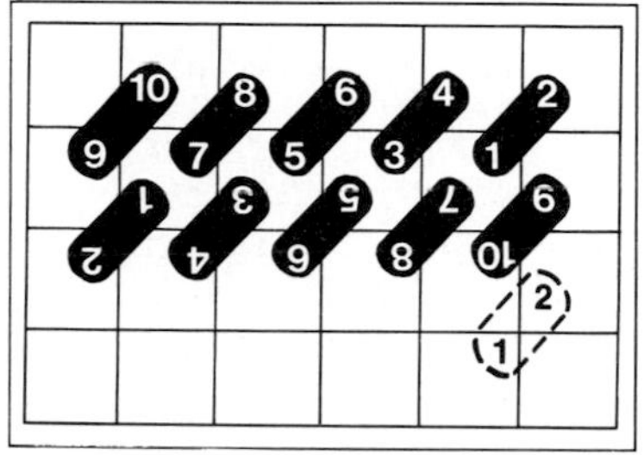

Continental Stitch
The continental stitch is good for outlining and filling small areas. (Avoid using it to fill large areas because it distorts the canvas; use the basket-weave stitch instead.) Work from right to left, turning the canvas on alternate rows. Bring the needle up at 1, down at 2, and up again at 3.

Cross-Stitch
See page 407.

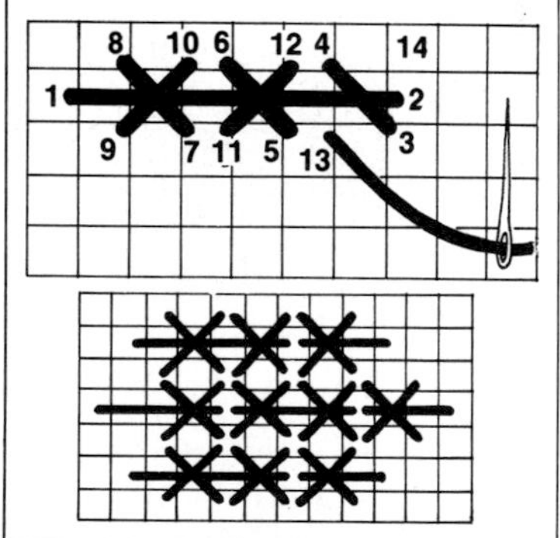

Cross-Stitch Tramé
The cross-stitch tramé is formed with a layer of under-stitching beneath the cross-stitches. Vary the length of the tramé (under-stitches) to avoid a line across the needlepoint. For example, work the tramé stitches over four, six, and then five warp threads. Then cover the under-stitching with cross-stitches.
continued

Basic Needlepoint Stitches *(continued)*

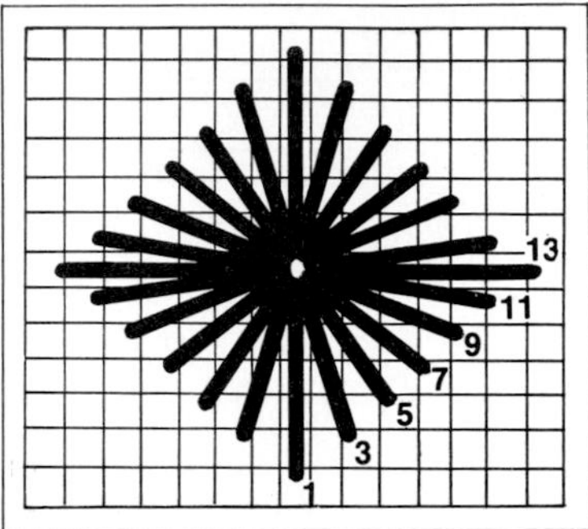

Diamond Eyelet Stitch

(Also called Diagonal Star Stitch) This stitch forms a bold diamond pattern, effective for accenting and highlighting. Work each stitch of the diamond eyelet down through the center hole, pulling snugly to open the mesh. Start at the bottom of the diamond and move counterclockwise, as shown above.

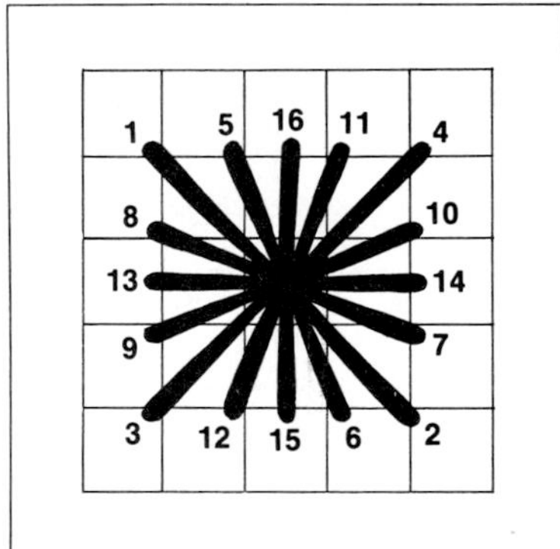

Double Leviathan Stitch

(Also called Leviathan Stitch) A highly textured and decorative box stitch, the double leviathan stitch can be worked singly or in rows. Work a cross-stitch over four horizontal and four vertical threads of canvas. Then cross each arm of the first cross-stitch, making four more stitches as shown. Finally, fill the remaining mesh openings with horizontal and vertical stitches over one thread.

French Knot

See page 408.

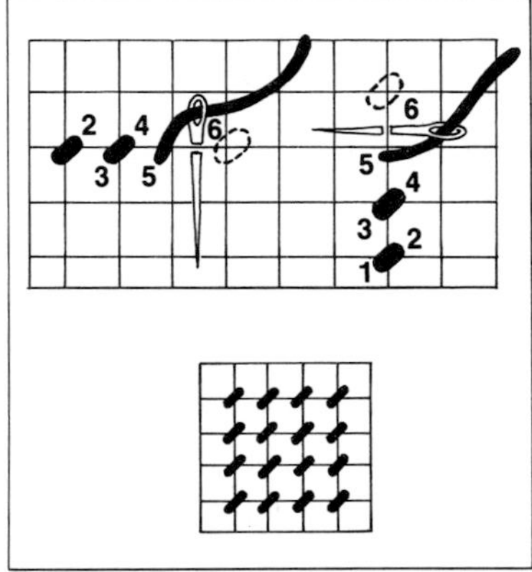

Half Cross-Stitch

This is a tent stitch; it is diagonal on the front but straight on the back, and uses yarn more economically than continental or basket-weave stitches. Use it only with penelope canvas because it distorts mono canvas. Stitch horizontally from left to right or vertically from bottom to top.

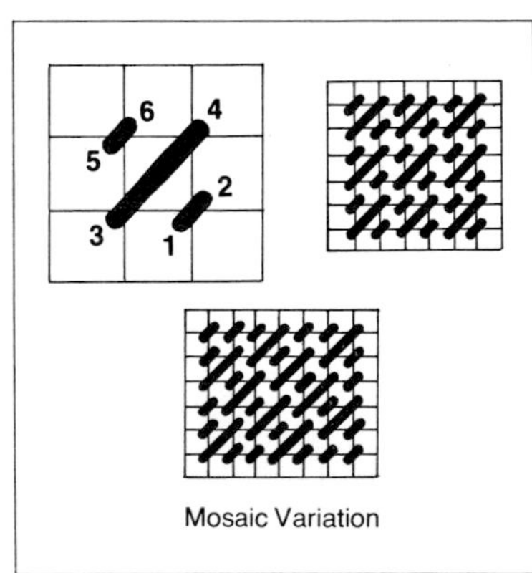

Mosaic Variation

Mosaic Stitch

This square stitch is made with three stitches. The units are worked one at a time in either horizontal, vertical, or diagonal rows. It resembles the cashmere stitch except that there is one less stitch per unit.

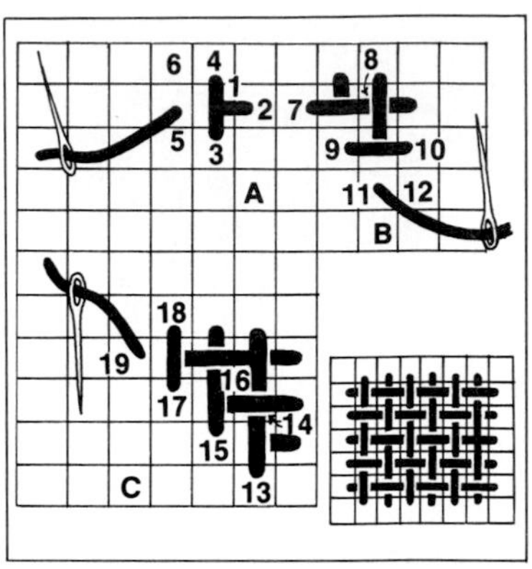

Reverse Basket-Weave Stitch

The woven pattern on the back of the basket-weave stitch appears on the front when working the reverse basket-weave stitch. (Tent stitches appear on the back.) Finish each row with half stitches. *(See also, Basket-Weave Stitch.)*

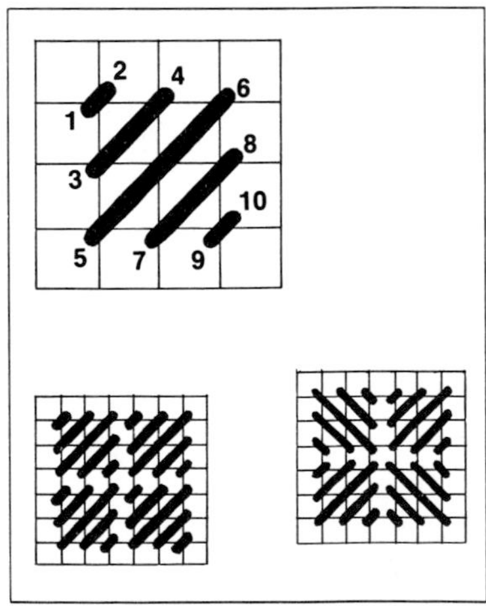

Scotch Stitch

(Also called Diagonal Satin Stitch, Flat Stitch, and Diagonal Flat Stitch) A Scotch stitch is made with either five or seven slanting stitches to form a square unit. It is effective as a border, forming a checkered effect, but distorts canvas when worked over large areas.

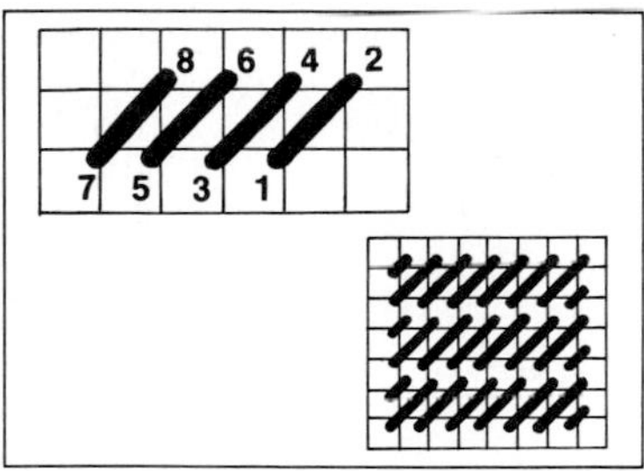

Slanting Gobelin Stitch
(Also called, Oblique or Sloping Gobelin Stitch) This stitch, worked in horizontal or vertical rows, looks like a tent stitch except that it covers two to five horizontal threads of canvas. Take tent stitches at the beginning and end of each row to achieve square corners. This stitch is effective when used for borders and geometric designs.

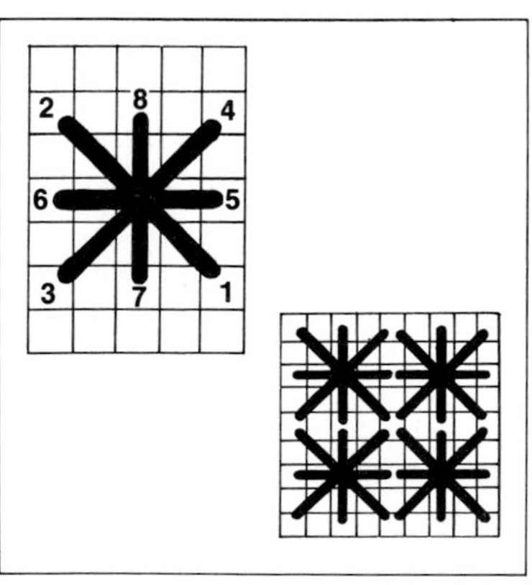

Smyrna Stitch
This starlike stitch is usually used for decorative accents. Work a cross-stitch over two or four canvas threads. Then, cover the first two stitches horizontally and vertically with an upright cross-stitch. When working over two horizontal and vertical threads, the canvas is covered completely, whereas some of the canvas may show when working over four threads. *(See also, Upright Cross-Stitch.)*

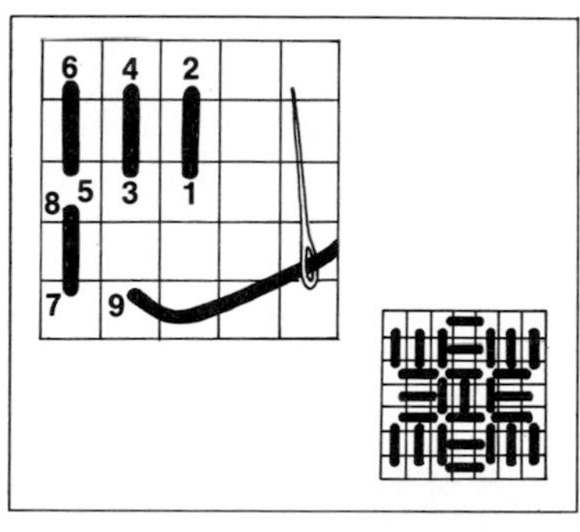

Straight Gobelin Stitch
This is a good border stitch that can be worked horizontally or vertically over two or more canvas threads. Work rows in alternate directions, from right to left and left to right, or from top to bottom and bottom to top.

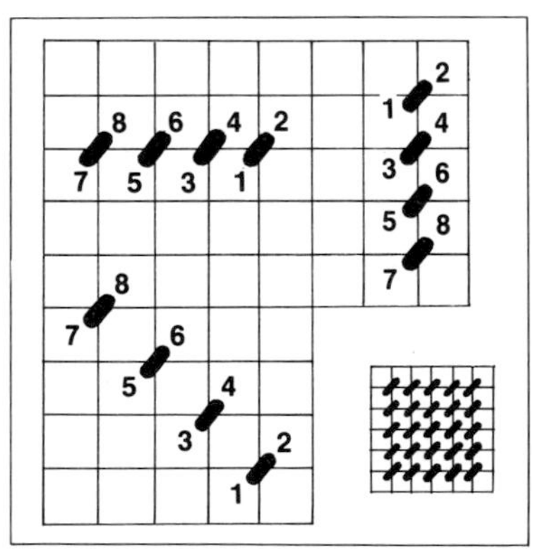

Tent Stitch
"Tent Stitch" is the blanket term used for a slanted stitch that is worked over the intersection of two canvas threads from lower left to upper right, as shown. It can be worked in horizontal, vertical, or diagonal rows. Because it is a small, flat stitch, it is often used for entire designs.

It is only by looking at the back of the needlepoint that tent stitches can be identified as basket-weave, continental, or half cross-stitches.

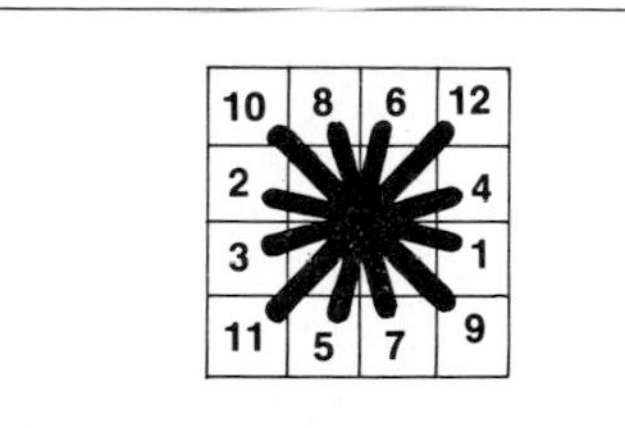

Triple Cross-Stitch
The triple cross-stitch is a square, textured stitch made of three layered cross-stitches. The first one is worked over one horizontal and three vertical threads. The second is worked over three horizontal and one vertical thread. The final cross is made over three horizontal and three vertical threads.

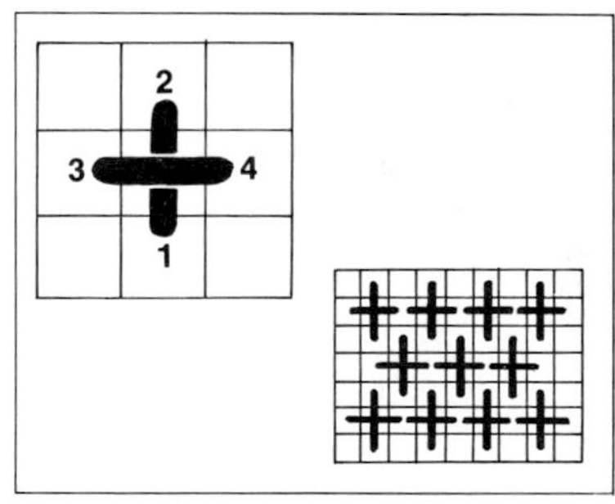

Upright Cross-Stitch
(Also called Straight Cross-Stitch) This textured stitch can be worked singly or in rows. It's a nice background stitch. Make the first stitch a straight Gobelin stitch over two horizontal canvas threads. Then cross the first stitch horizontally so the second stitch covers two vertical threads. For horizontal rows of upright cross-stitches, skip one mesh (two threads) between each vertical stitch. Stagger the position of the crosses from row to row so canvas is covered.

Waste Knot
See page 371.

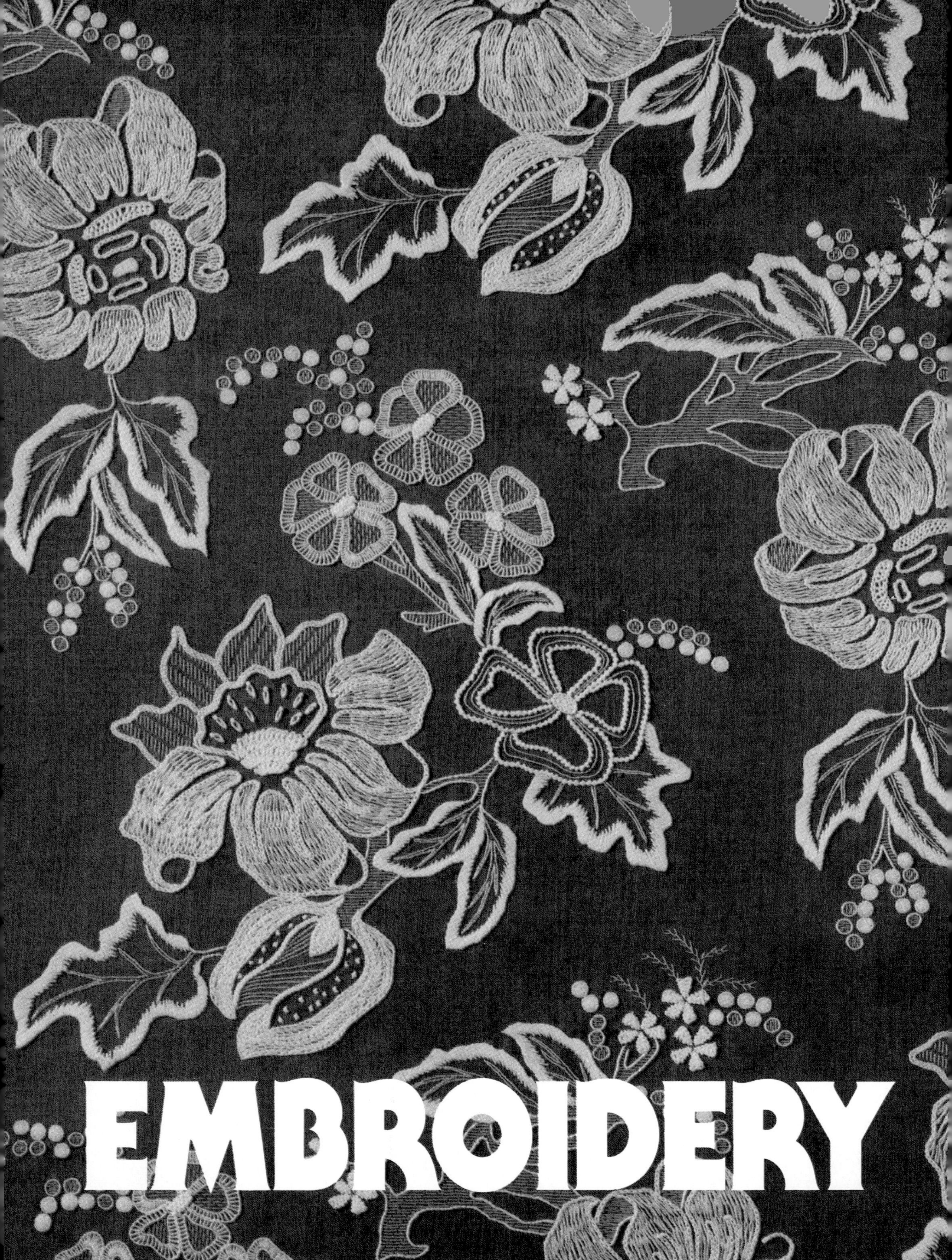
EMBROIDERY

Folk Embroidery

What better way to begin a book about embroidery than with vibrant designs from many different cultures! When you stitch one of these folk embroideries, you will capture the essence of this creative art as it is practiced around the world. The bold motifs on this tablecloth are an appropriate reflection of the happy, exuberant spirit of folk stitchery. In other sections, you will find beautiful projects to make in a variety of techniques that represent the heritage of generations of needleworkers.

So, whether you are an accomplished stitcher or a beginner, you will find much to interest you in this step-by-step guide to many unique, challenging, and useful embroidery projects. Select from our robust section of folk embroidery, or pick a project from our treasure chest of old-fashioned stitchery. If you'd like to be even more adventuresome, try a new, exciting technique like machine embroidery. Whatever you choose, you'll find complete instructions, clear illustrations, and a definitive stitch guide. For how-to instructions for this tablecloth, see page 328.

Hungarian Cloth *(shown on pages 326 and 327)*

You needn't be a long-experienced stitcher to work beautiful embroideries. This Hungarian cloth, with its bold, floral motif and scallops, is worked entirely in one stitch.

Materials

1¼ yards of off-white linen or linenlike fabric, or any length suitable for your table.
#5 pearl cotton in red
Embroidery needle
Embroidery hoop (optional)
Purchased red crocheted edging or size 7 crochet hook (to make your own edging)

Scalloped Edge

Row 1: Make sc with ch 1 between around entire cloth. End with sl st in first sc.
Row 2: *2 sc in first ch 1 sp, 2 hdc in next sp, 2 dc in next sp, 2 trc in next sp, 2 dc in next sp, 2 hdc in next sp, 2 sc in next sp, 2 sl st in next sp. Repeat from * around cloth. End with sl st in first sc.

Directions

The pattern is for one quarter of the tablecloth. Enlarge it according to directions on pages 272 and 273, reversing it as necessary to complete the design, and transfer it to the fabric. Mount the fabric in a hoop or frame, if you wish.

Anchor the thread end with a waste knot (directions are on page 371), and work the entire design in buttonhole stitches. When working the flower petals, centers, and dots, lay the stitches side-by-side, with the loop part of each stitch along the outer edge of the shape, as shown on the petals below. Work stems, scallops, scrolls, and the straight line along the border in double buttonhole stitches, as shown on the stem below. (For an explanation of this stitch, see the Glossary on pages 406 to 409.)

When the embroidery is finished, block it according to the directions on page 400. Turn up a narrow hem and add purchased crocheted edging. Or work a narrow band of hemstitching over 1 or 2 drawn threads, following directions on page 348. Then add a lace edge crocheted from the red embroidery thread for the scalloped edge, following the directions at right.

1 Square = 1 Inch

Embroidered Throw and Floor Pillows

This throw and the matching floor pillows, stitched with crewel wools, feature a sampling of symbolic American Indian motifs.

Directions

Embroider the throw with 9 motifs separated by "goose track" borders. Arrange motifs from left to right in 3 rows as follows: row 1: motifs A, B, and C; row 2: D, E, and F; row 3: G, H, and I. Patterns are below and on page 330.

Enlarge the patterns, following directions on pages 272 and 273. Transfer each design to a 20x20-inch piece of tissue paper and pin the patterns to the blanket. Note that each motif has a 1-inch border around it—making a 2-inch border between motifs when they are transferred to the fabric.

Cut the blanket into a 62-inch square. Using hand or machine basting, transfer the patterns to the fabric. Be sure to include the outlines for the borders. Tear away the tissue paper before you begin the embroidery. Work with fabric in a hoop to prevent puckering.

Using the basting stitches as a guide, work the embroidery with 5-foot lengths of yarn threaded into a large, sharp needle and doubled. Follow the color and stitch keys for the motifs. If you are using a heavier yarn, such as rug yarn, do not double it and buy only half as much. (Refer to the Glossary on pages 406 to 409 for an explanation of the stitches.)

After completing the motifs, remove the basting stitches and steam-press each design with a warm iron. Make sure basted lines for borders are straight and approximately 2 inches apart.

Work the borders in black buttonhole stitches, with three "tracks" positioned every inch (see diagram on page 330). Work the two inner vertical borders first, going from top to bottom. Then work the inner horizontal borders, carrying the yarn under the fabric at each square's corner where the borders meet. Work the inside line of border stitches around the blanket's edge so that the loops of the stitches are 2 inches from the edge. Press gently.

To quilt, lay the blanket facedown and stretch a layer of batting over it, trimming any excess. Piece the lining fabric to make a 66-inch square, and lay it on top of the quilt batting. Allow a 2-inch margin around each edge. Pin the three layers together.

Tie the layers together with black pearl cotton at 3-inch intervals along the border of each square. To tie, insert the needle through the

continued

Materials

1 twin-size gray utility blanket
Twelve 40-yard skeins 3-ply black Persian wool yarn
Three 40-yard skeins 3-ply light gray Persian wool yarn
Three 40-yard skeins 3-ply brownish-red Persian wool
2 large-eyed darning needles
Large embroidery hoop
3⅝ yards black cotton (lining)
1 roll quilt batting (blanket)
Polyester fiberfill (pillows)
#8 black pearl cotton

Stitch Guide

1—Roumanian stitch
2—Satin stitch
3—Couching stitch
4—Laid work
5—Star stitch
6—Buttonhole stitch

Color Key

A Black
B Gray
C Red

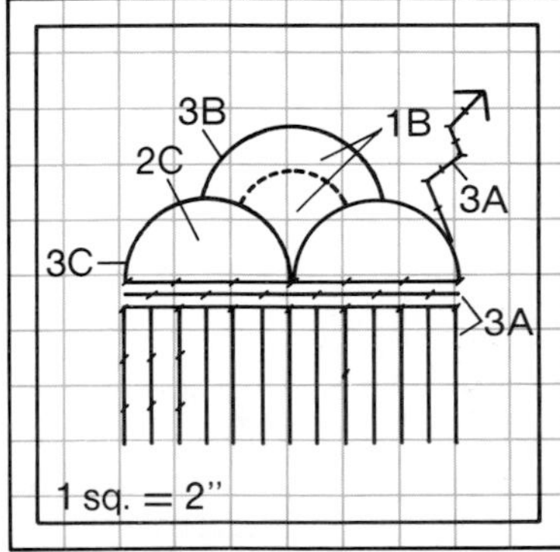

A. Thunderbird

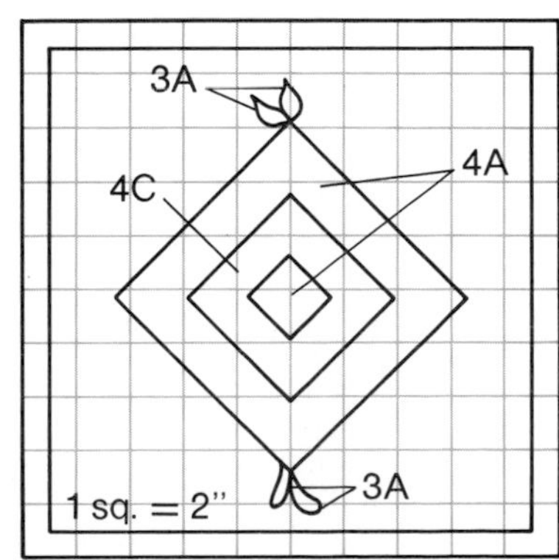

B. Tepee

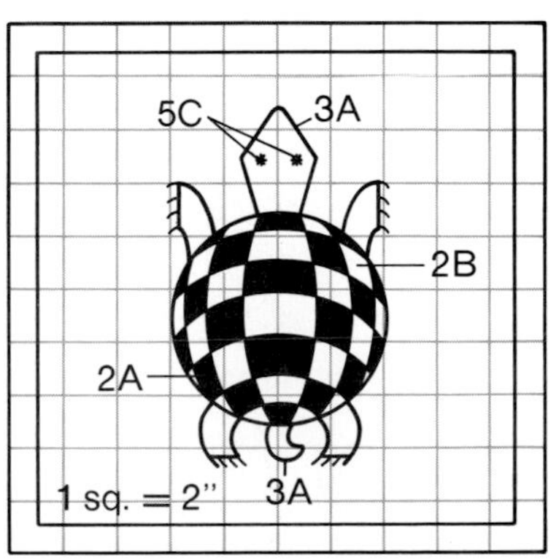

C. Turtle

Embroidered Throw and Floor Pillows *(continued)*

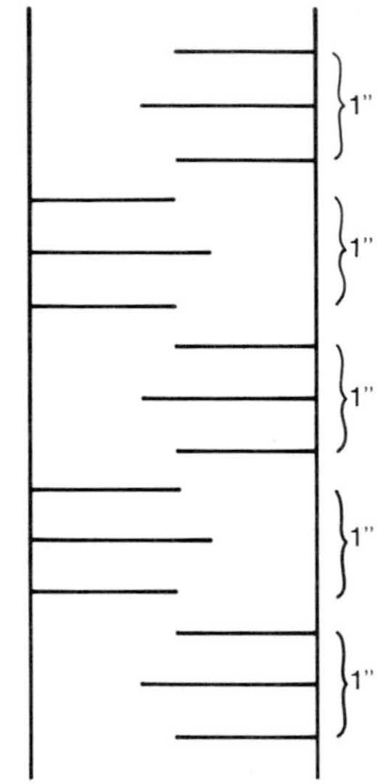

throw from back to front, and take a small stitch on the front side under an embroidered stitch. Pull the thread through to the lining side and double-knot it. Continue along each border on the inside of the throw and around the edges.

After tying, trim the lining to ⅝ inch beyond the edge of the throw. Fold this margin in half and fold again *over* the edge to the front. Miter the corners. Pin but do not stitch.

Add the final line of outer border stitches using a blanket stitch and working through all three layers. Finally, secure the binding by slip-stitching the edge of the lining to the front of the throw with black sewing thread.

Pillows: *Note:* Cut the remaining blanket fabric in half to make two pillow fronts. Enlarge patterns for any two motifs and transfer them to the blanket pieces. Center the designs on the fabric, and enlarge the border to 2 inches. Baste along the design lines, and embroider as for the throw.

Cut back pieces from black lining fabric. With right sides together, stitch front and back together in a ⅝-inch seam. Leave an opening for turning. Stuff the pillows with polyester fiberfill and slip-stitch the openings closed.

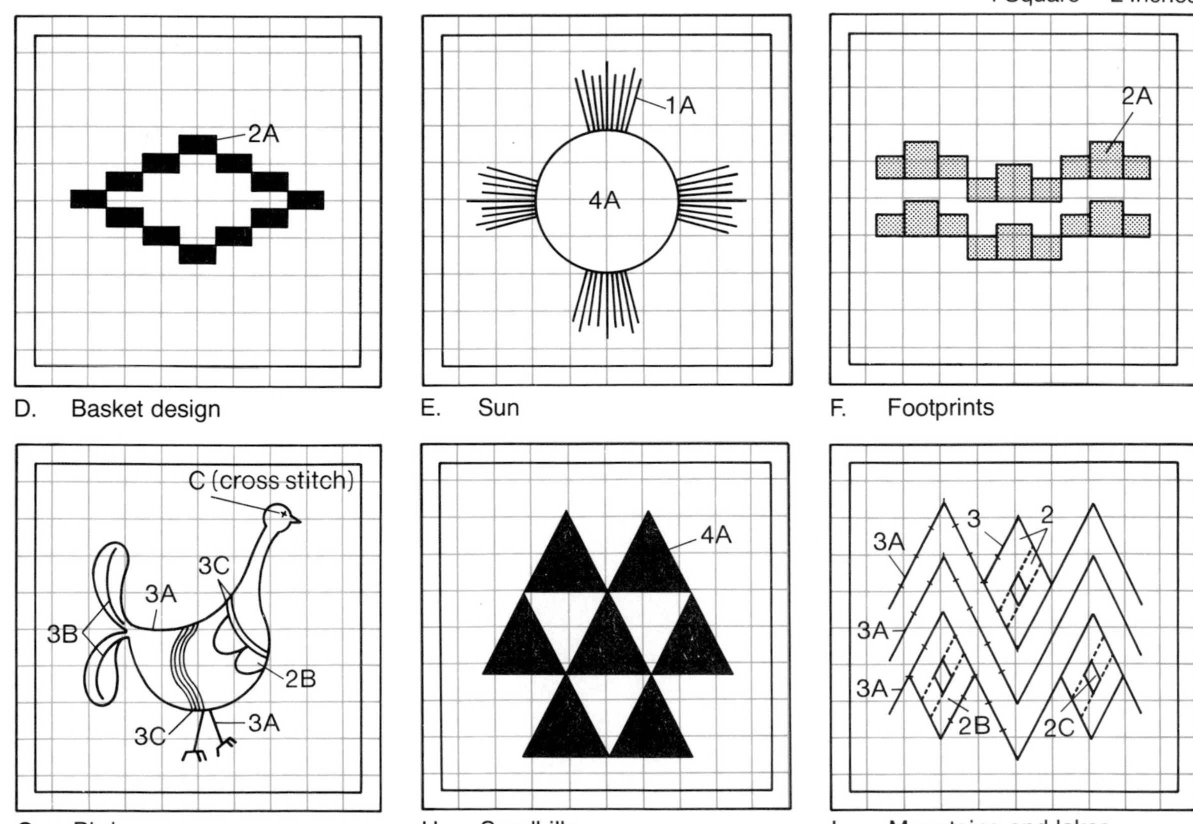

Cross-Stitch Table Runner

Shaded like a mosaic, this cross-stitch design is from the Balkans.

Materials

26x44 inches white #22-count linen, Hardanger, or similar even-weave fabric
Embroidery floss in black, red, orange, light blue, variegated blue, and variegated brown
Small tapestry needle
Graph paper (10 squares per inch)

Directions

To make a colored diagram, use colored pencils to transfer the design below to graph paper. The pattern shown is for one quarter of the corner design and the border motif. Complete the design by reversing the pattern and matching the adjoining sides.

Work the border motif at the lower right of the chart only on the arms of the main motif that extend along the sides of the cloth. Do not work it on the arms that extend toward the lower edges or on the cross in the center of the cloth.

Begin the embroidery by marking a point in one corner of the fabric 6½ inches from two edges. This is the center of the first cross. Stitch with 2 strands of floss throughout, and embroider the cross-stitches first. Work each stitch over 2 threads of the fabric, laying stitches in the spaces between threads. Use a tapestry needle to avoid splitting the threads.

When cross-stitch areas are filled, outline the center octagon and the arms of the cross with black double-running stitches. Omit the black outline around the red octagon. (See the Glossary on pages 406 to 409 for an explanation of the stitches.)

Follow the color key below. When colors are indicated with a slash between them, such as O/B, use the color to the left of the slash (O) in the first and third quadrants of the cross, and the color to the right (B) in the second and fourth quadrants.

Work the border motif for about 24 inches down the length of the cloth, and then repeat the corner motif. Work the border about 5 inches along the short sides, then repeat the corner. Continue completely around the edge of the runner.

Finally, find the exact center of the completed stitchery frame (by counting threads) and repeat the cross motif. Be sure to match the center of the fabric to the center of the design.

Finish with a narrow hem about 5 inches below the border. Work hemstitching, if desired, following instructions on page 348.

Color Key

X Black
R Red
O Orange
P Light blue
B Variegated blue
V Variegated brown

One square equals one stitch over 2 threads. Outline shapes indicated above with black double-running stitches over 2 threads.

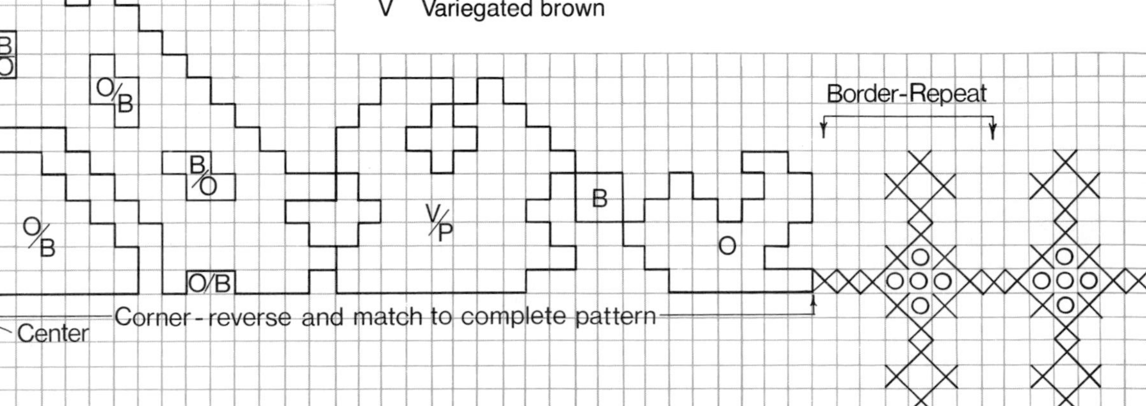

Flowered Tablecloth

Floral motifs are traditionally popular embroidery patterns. These blossoms are outlined in black and sparkle like stained glass. Here, they accent a Central European tablecloth.

Materials

Sufficient even-weave fabric for your cloth (see note at right)
Embroidery floss in black, yellow, red, blue, and green
Embroidery needle
Embroidery hoop or frame

Directions

Note: Our tablecloth is 36 inches square, with the motif embroidered in one corner. On a larger cloth, you may wish to work the motif in all four corners.

Enlarge the pattern below and transfer it to the fabric, following the directions on pages 272 and 273. Insert the fabric into an embroidery hoop or frame so that it will not pucker as you work.

If you wish to pad the dots and satin-stitched areas of the design to give them a rich, raised look, see the directions on page 346. Outline those sections that are to be padded, and pad-stitch them before you begin.

Work the design with 3 strands of floss, following the color and stitch keys on the diagram. After filling in the colored areas of the flowers, outline the dots and flower sections in black outline stitches. Work stems in outline stitches. (For an explanation of the stitches, see the Glossary on pages 406 to 409.)

Block the finished embroidery by steam-pressing it lightly on the wrong side over a padded board.

Machine-stitch 2 inches from the raw edge of the cloth using regular thread in a color to match the fabric. Work a single row of black overcast stitches next to the line of machine stitching. Fringe the fabric between the overcast stitches and the raw edge as shown in the photograph opposite.

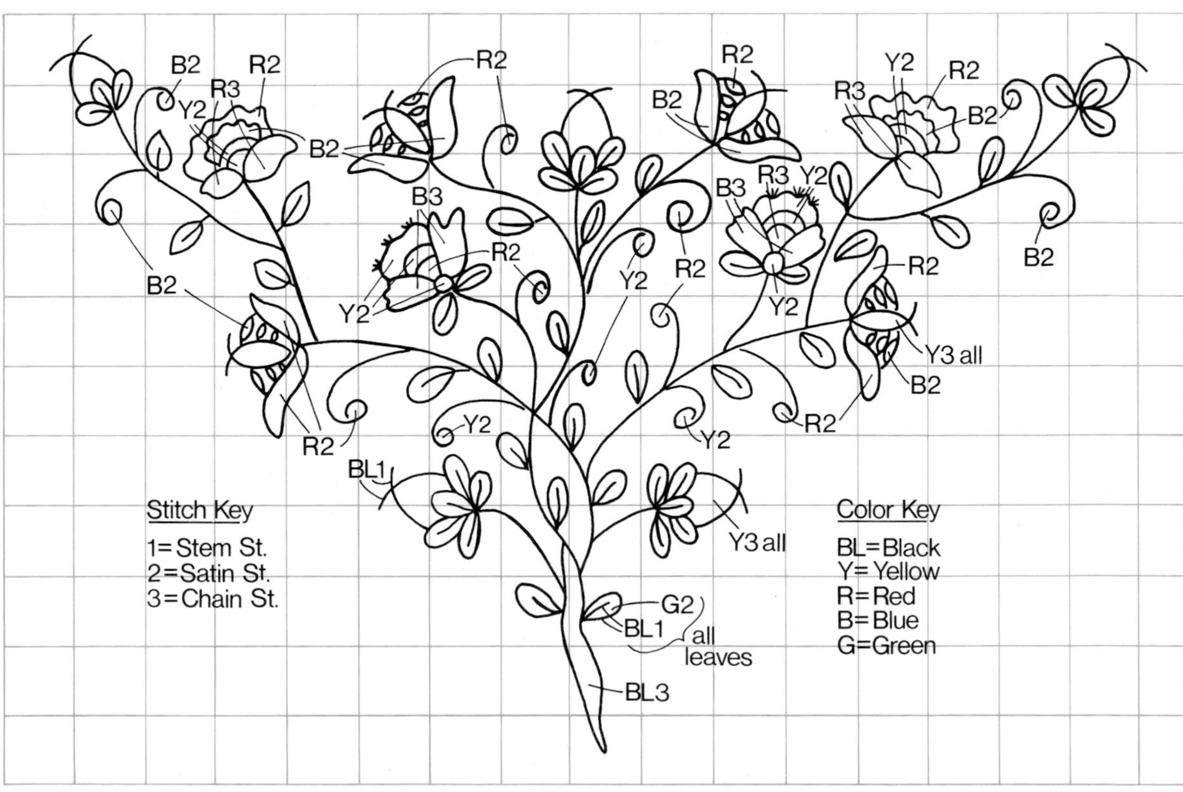

1 Square = 1 Inch

Embroidered Crèche

Embroidered in sampler-like stitches, these crèche figures are just as beautiful and impressive as those gowned in satin and haloed in gold.

To capture the vitality of old-world needlework, we embroidered the familiar hearts and flowers motifs in red and green crewel wool. Needlepoint canvas makes cross-stitching the borders and facial features easy. Halos are made of purchased crochet trim, and the completed figures are stuffed with beans or seeds for stability.

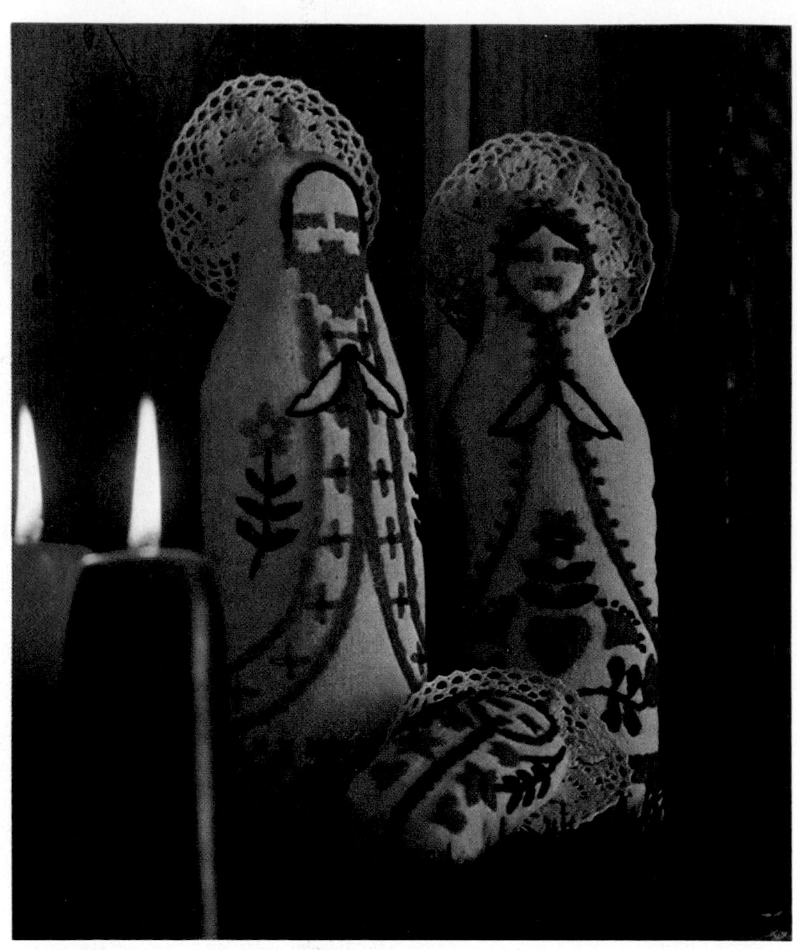

Materials

- ³⁄₈ yard off-white linen or other coarsely woven fabric
- 1 small skein each of red and green Persian yarn
- Embroidery and tapestry needles
- 6-inch square of cardboard
- Embroidery hoop
- ⅔ yard 1½-inch-wide crocheted lace
- White glue
- Scraps of #5-mesh mono-canvas
- Seeds or beans
- Funnel
- Scraps of quilt batting or polyester fiberfill

Directions

Enlarge the pattern pieces, following directions on pages 272 and 273, and transfer the *outlines only* to the wrong side of the fabric. Allow at least 1 inch between each pattern piece (actual seam allowances are ³⁄₈ inch) and keep the patterns far enough away from the edge of the material to allow you to use an embroidery hoop easily. Do not cut out the pattern pieces until the embroidery is finished.

Trace the embroidery details onto the right side of the fabric and mount it in a hoop or frame. Referring to the photograph for colors, satin-stitch the hearts, flowers, and leaves, and stem-stitch the flower stems and hands. Edge Mary's robe with chain stitches and French knots. Joseph's robe has two rows of chain stitches separated by flowers worked in detached chain stitches.

Use 1 strand of yarn for the embroidery.

Work the features and the rows along the base of each figure in cross-stitches, using scraps of needlepoint canvas as a guide. Pin the canvas in position and work the stitches over it. Then dampen the canvas to relax the sizing in it, snip the canvas threads, and gently pull them out one at a time.

1 Square = ¾ Inch

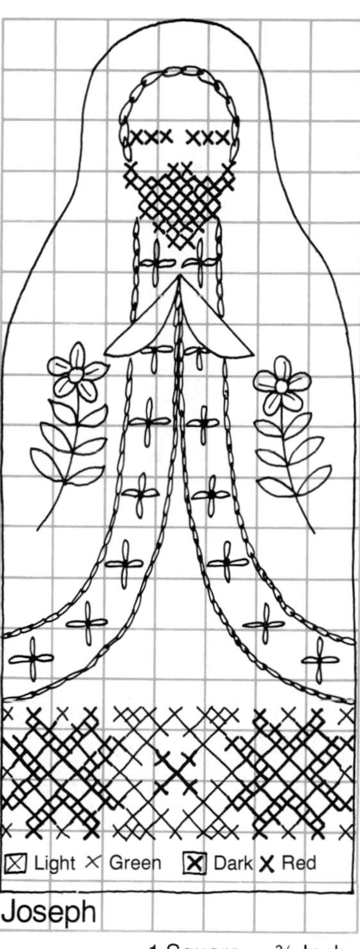

1 Square = ¾ Inch

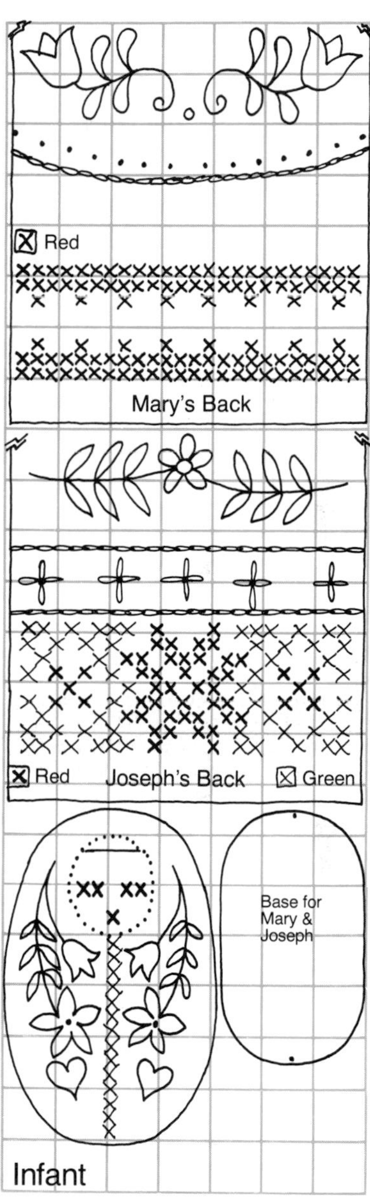

1 Square = ¾ Inch

Cut out pattern pieces, leaving ⅜-inch seam allowances. Cut a linen backing for the infant, using the front as a pattern. Sew fronts to backs, leaving Mary and Joseph open along the bottom and leaving a 2-inch opening in the infant. Clip curves and turn right side out. Press a ⅜-inch hem along the bottom edge.

Cut two cardboard bases for Mary and Joseph. Place cardboard on fabric and trace around edges. Cut out fabric bases, adding a ⅜-inch seam allowance. Glue the fabric bases to the cardboard bases, clipping and turning back the raw edges of the fabric.

Place the side seams of the figures at the dots on the bases and sew the edges to the bases, leaving a 2-inch opening on each.

Insert a funnel into the openings and fill the figures as full as possible with seeds or beans. Slip-stitch Mary's and Joseph's openings. Finish stuffing the infant with batting, then slip-stitch.

Stand Mary and Joseph upright, open the seams along the top of each head, and stuff tightly with batting. Slip-stitch openings.

Gather three 8-inch pieces of crocheted lace for halos and tack onto the heads of the figures.

Stitch Guide

Satin stitch

●● French knots

Outline stitch

Chain stitch

XXX Cross-stitch

Chain Stitch Pillow

Charmingly stylized animals are also popular motifs in folk stitchery. Who can resist this rooster from Afghanistan with his simple lines, bright colors, and homey appeal?

Directions here are for chain stitches with a needle. To learn how to make them with a crochet hook—called tambour work—turn to page 402.

Materials

18x18 inches black linen or cotton
18x18 inches navy or black unclipped corduroy
#8 pearl cotton in white, yellow, red, green, maroon, and blue
Embroidery needle
Embroidery hoop (optional)
Pillow stuffing

Color Key

W White
Y Yellow
R Red
G Green
M Maroon
B Blue

Directions

This design is composed of a single motif surrounded by a border and repeated 4 times. Recreate the design as shown, or if you prefer, work it just once for a smaller pillow or a wall hanging.

Enlarge the pattern and transfer it to the linen fabric, following the directions on pages 272 and 273 for enlarging a design without a grid. Work the entire design in chain stitches, following the color key.

When colors are indicated with a slash between them, such as G/B, use the color to the left of the slash (G) in the first and third quadrants, and the color to the right (B) in the second and fourth quadrants, as shown in the photograph.

Begin the embroidery by outlining each block of color with a single row of chain stitches. Then fill in the remainder of the shape with additional rows of chain stitches worked parallel to the outline. Work from the outside of each shape toward the center. For example, embroider the outer edges of the flower shapes first. Then begin filling the petals with rows of chain stitches until you reach the center of the flower, when the chain stitches should be worked in a spiral, as indicated on the pattern.

Block the finished embroidery and stitch the front to the back, right side together, in a ½-inch seam around 3 sides. Turn and stuff the pillow cover, and slip-stitch the fourth side closed.

Cross-Stitch Runner

This floral runner is from Yugoslavia. Work it in the colors shown, or use threads that match your own decor.

Materials

24x40 inches of #22-count Hardanger or other even-weave fabric
Embroidery floss in dark forest green, medium kelly green, and orange
Embroidery needle
Embroidery hoop (optional)
Graph paper (10 squares per inch)
Colored pencils to match floss

Color and Stitch Key

Cross Stitch	Backstitch
■ Dark Green	| Orange
× Med. Green	⸸ Dark Green
○ Orange	

Directions

To make a colored diagram, use colored pencils to transfer the chart below to graph paper. Use sufficient paper to work out the pattern repeat across the short end of the runner.

To work the embroidery, first find the center of the narrow ends of the fabric. Allowing 2½ inches of plain fabric for hemming, begin working the pattern from the center toward the outer edges. Work each stitch over 2 threads of fabric. Note that the center motif is slightly different from the others. Work this motif only once, then repeat the design that is shown on the left in the chart. The line of backstitches in the center of each motif is a single row; it is not repeated when the pattern is reversed.

When you have finished stitching the motifs along the end of the runner, continue working the side borders to a length of about 35 inches—less if you prefer. Then turn the corner and work the floral motifs across the opposite end of the runner.

Finish your runner with a plain hem or a row of hemstitching, following directions on page 348.

Old-Fashioned Stitchery

Experience a bit of nostalgia by stitching some of our charming old-fashioned designs. Embroidering in the manner of yesteryear can be refreshing and exciting. And to help you re-create these treasured old-time designs, we have simplified your work with easy to follow step-by-step instructions. All of the stitches are explained in the Glossary beginning on page 406, and each project is explained with patterns and graphs.

So if you would like to embroider a design from the past, select a project from this section with that special look of days gone by. Directions for the cloth shown here are on pages 342 and 343.

Embroidered Tablecloth *(shown on pages 340 and 341)*

This lovely tablecloth is made up of only two motifs repeated on the diagonal. You can duplicate our cloth, or experiment with your own design, using only one motif, for example, for a tablecloth, pillow top, wall hanging, or curtain.

Materials

36x50 inches green linen, or sufficient yardage for your cloth
72 skeins white cotton embroidery floss (or sufficient skeins to complete your cloth)
Embroidery hoop or frame
Embroidery needles

Stitch Key

1 Outline stitch
2 Leaf stitch
3 Herringbone stitch
4 Long-and-short stitch
5 Feather stitch
6 Chain stitch
7 Twisted chain stitch
8 Rosette chain stitch
9 German knot
10 French knot
11 Braid stitch
12 Backstitch
13 Open chain stitch
14 Padded satin stitch
15 Chain scroll stitch
16 Running stitch
17 Lazy daisy French knot
18 Cable stitch
19 Herringbone stitch with feather stitch overlay
20 Buttonhole stitch

Directions

To duplicate our cloth, enlarge the patterns on the next page and transfer them to the fabric, following the placement diagram. Directions for enlarging and transferring designs are on pages 272 and 273. When enlarged to full size, motif A is about 11 inches wide by 18 inches long, and motif B is about 15 inches wide by 17 inches long. Mount the fabric in a hoop or frame, if desired. If you intend to launder the cloth, we suggest you pre-shrink the fabric and floss beforehand. Soak skeins of thread in warm water for a few minutes and let them dry thoroughly.

Work the design entirely in white floss, using the number of strands indicated in parentheses on the pattern following the stitch numbers. (Directions for all the stitches are in the Glossary.)

When the embroidery is finished, press the cloth lightly on the wrong side, and hem.

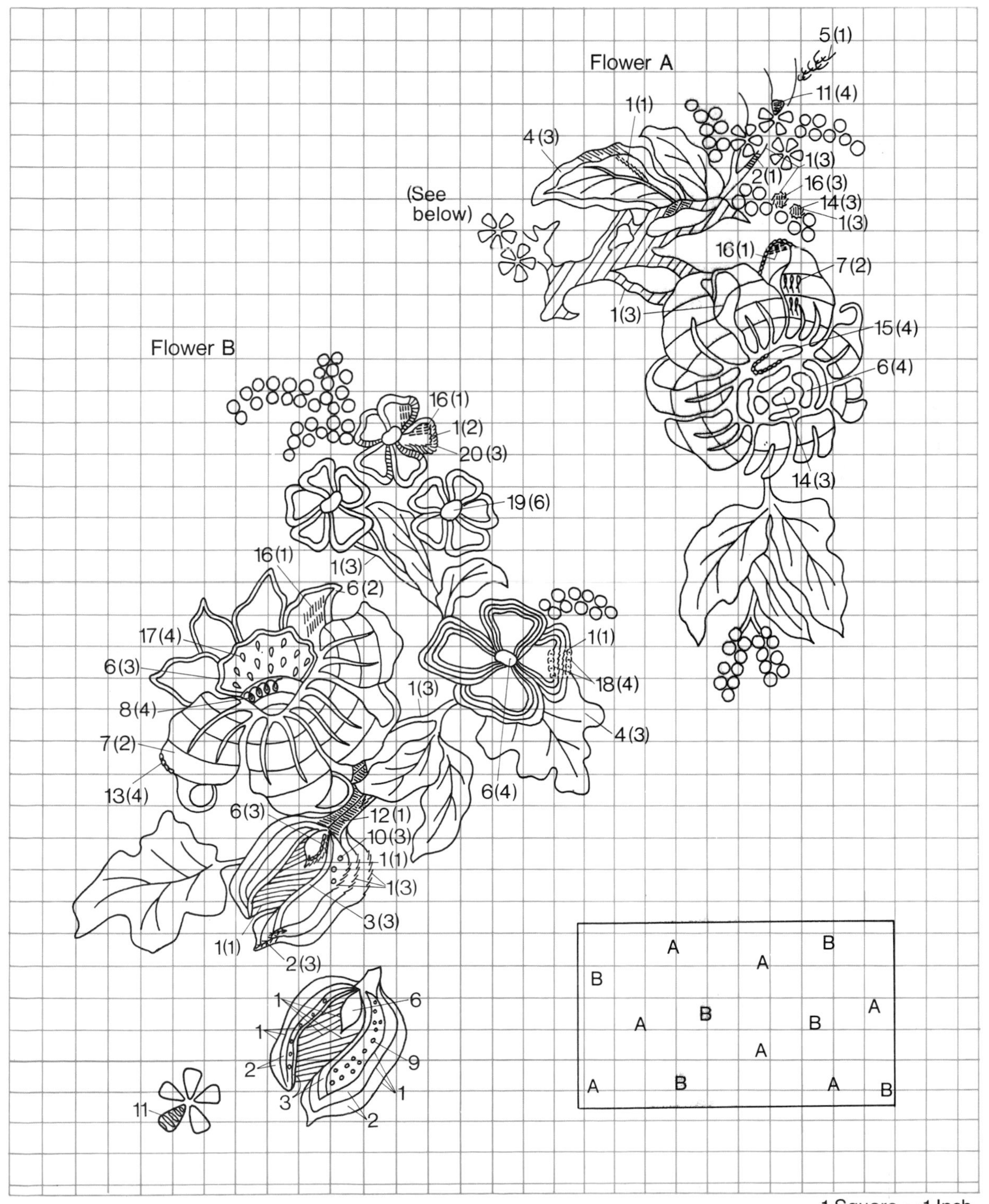

1 Square = 1 Inch

Blue Rose Tablecloth

The heirloom tablecloth shown here is stitched in a form of counted thread work. The rose motif is embroidered using a straight stitch, while the openwork borders and hemstitching are simple drawn thread work.

Materials

Purchased even-weave tablecloth or even-weave linen yardage of desired length
Thread to match fabric
#5 pearl cotton in light, medium, and dark blue
Embroidery needle
Embroidery hoop or frame
Graph paper (optional)
Colored pencils (optional)

Color Key

O Light blue
X Medium blue
△ Dark blue

Directions

The rose motif and openwork border are embroidered once in the center of each side of our tablecloth. The pattern may be worked on any size square or rectangular tablecloth or runner, and repeated as often as you wish.

Our tablecloth is worked on #36-count even-weave linen, and each motif measures approximately 3¼x13 inches. A fabric with a different count (number of threads per inch) will yield a rose of a different size. For example, on #22-count Hardanger fabric, the motif will be about 1½ times larger than on #36-count fabric.

Before plotting out the design for the cloth itself, you might want to embroider one complete motif either with or without the drawn thread border on a scrap of the fabric you intend to use for your tablecloth. In this way, you will be able to determine exactly what size the motif will be on the fabric you have chosen.

The graphed pattern below represents the center rose motif and the oblong extension to one side of it. For a complete pattern, reverse the oblong motif, match it to the center at the points indicated, and repeat it on the other side of the rose.

The proportions of the pattern as shown on the graph are deceiving. Each square on the graph actually represents a long, thin straight stitch, even though we have used squares to indicate each stitch in order to include color indications for the pattern. If you find working from a colored graph easier, you may wish to transfer the design to graph paper with colored pencils.

Embroider the entire design in straight stitches. (If you are unfamiliar with this stitch, see the Glossary.) Work each stitch over 7 threads of the fabric and leave 2 threads between each stitch. Except in the top row, the top of each stitch is worked into the same space as the bottom of the stitch in the row above.

To work the rose motif once in the center of each side of your tablecloth as we did, begin by finding the exact center of each side of the cloth. Mark it with a tailor's tack about 5 inches above the raw edge. Then begin working the rose, starting in the center. After you have finished the rose, work the drawn thread box and border, following the directions on page 346.

continued

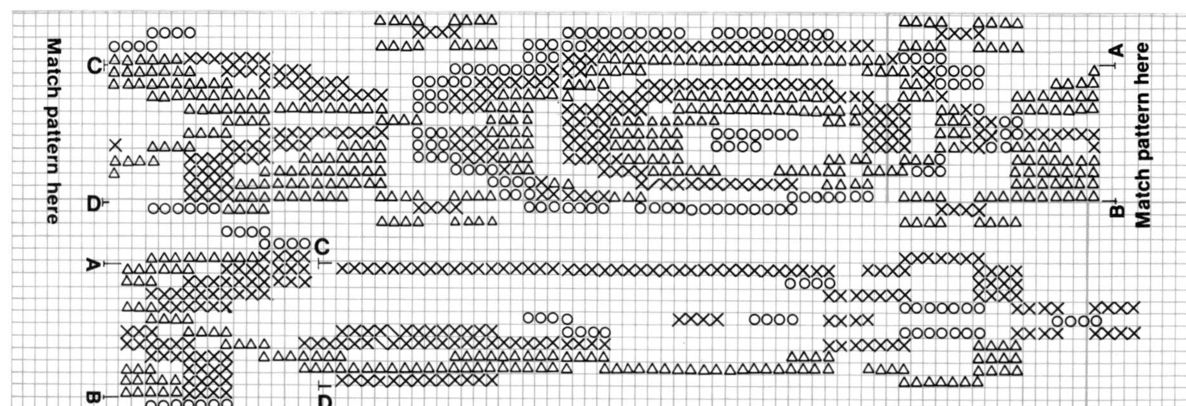

Blue Rose Tablecloth *(continued)*

For the drawn thread work, first plan for the ends of the box to fall about ¾ inch beyond the ends of the rose motif, with the sides about ⅝ inch above and below the sides of the motif.

From the fabric, withdraw about 6 threads that run parallel to the hem (making the drawn area about ¼ inch wide if your fabric is #36-count linen). Then, with thread to match your fabric, bind the remaining (vertical) threads in groups of 4, using the same stitch used for hemstitching. (For hemstitching how-to, see page 348.)

Bind both edges of the drawn area, creating a "ladder" of threads around the rose motif.

Then find the center of the short sides of the box and withdraw an additional 6 threads to make the border that extends around the cloth to join the boxes. In the corners of the drawn area, where warp and weft threads are both withdrawn, work buttonhole stitches to stabilize the edges of the fabric and prevent raveling.

Finish the cloth with a double row of decorative hemstitching. Or simply turn up the raw edge ¼ inch, then turn it up again and press. Blindstitch for a plain tailored hem.

For A Fine Finish—Outlining and Padding

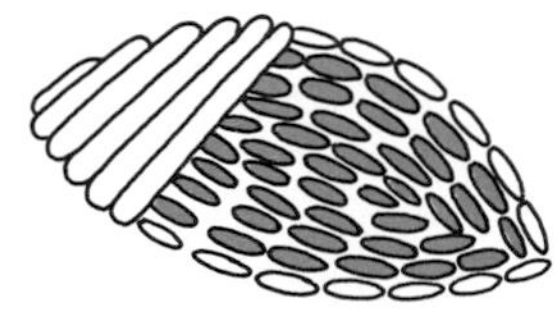

It is time-consuming to outline and pad design areas to be covered with close, fine stitches. But when you take time for this extra step, the result is striking. We recommend you make it a regular preliminary part of your embroidery.

Outlining and padding design elements gives your embroidery neat, crisp edges and lovely rounded surfaces; it enables you to highlight important motifs; and it strengthens raw edges on pieces of cutwork—all hallmarks of fine handiwork.

For both outlining and padding, use the same color thread as you intend to use for the finishing step. You may use exactly the same thread, or you might want to try a slightly coarser and more tightly twisted thread for a firmer edge.

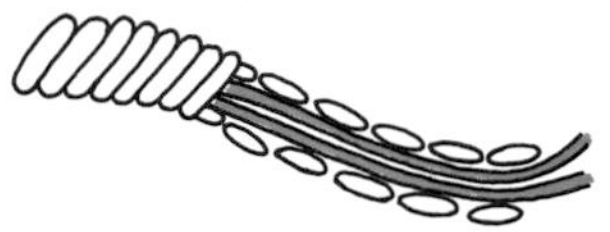

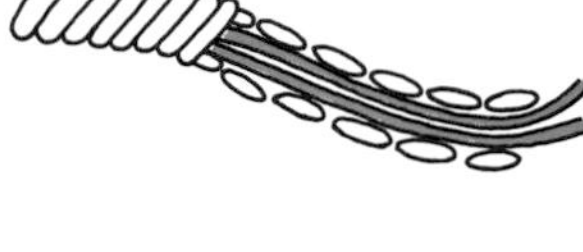

Begin by working an outline around each shape with small running stitches, backstitches, or split stitches. (See the Glossary on pages 406 to 409 for stitch how-to.)

Except on dots or small circles, pad with double running stitches worked back and forth across the shape (parallel to the outline) as shown in the top diagram at left.

Or pad with a cord (or group of cords) laid underneath fine satin or buttonhole stitches, as in the center diagram at left.

For dots or small circles, fill in the outline and pad the center with a single double cross-stitch or star stitch, depending on the size of the circle and the thickness of your thread (see lower diagram at left).

Embroidered Pansy Cloth

Directions

Mark but do not cut out a 52-inch circle on the fabric. Following directions on pages 272 and 273, enlarge the pattern and transfer four pansy clusters to the fabric, spacing them equally around the circle. Add a single pansy motif midway between each cluster. Match the hemline on the pattern to the circle on the fabric.

Work the embroidery in a hoop, using 1 strand of floss throughout. Work leaves and stems in medium blue outline stitches. Use medium blue floss to satin-stitch around the pansies, *except* where petals extend beyond the rim of the cloth. Work these extensions in buttonhole stitches. In the centers of the flowers, work four circles in white satin stitches with a yellow French knot in the middle. Lines radiating from the center are light blue (outline stitches), as are the French knots on each flower.

To finish the cloth, cut away the fabric from the buttonhole-stitched edges of the pansies using small, sharp scissors. Trim remaining fabric to ½ inch below the hem. Turn up a narrow hem and add crocheted edging.

Clusters of pansies on graceful stems and a crocheted edging border this circular linen tablecloth. Embroidered in simple stitches even a beginner will be familiar with, it has a romantic, old-fashioned look.

Materials

54x54 inches white linen or fine percale
Embroidery floss in white, yellow, and medium and light cornflower blue
Embroidery needle
Embroidery hoop or frame
Blue and white crocheted edging, ½ inch wide

1 Square = ¾ Inch

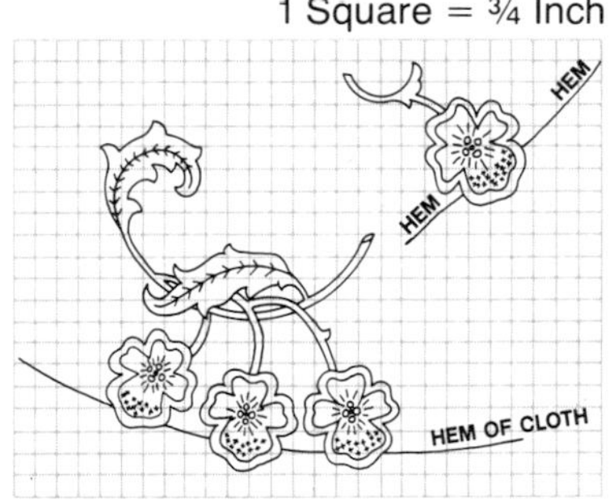

Cross-Stitch Rose Wreaths

Here are two ways to use this delightful cross-stitch rose wreath design. Create a table runner or make tree ornaments that can double as pincushions or sachets.

Materials

Even-weave fabric, such as Aida cloth, Hardanger, or linen (see note below)
#5 pearl cotton in varying shades of red, orange, pink, and green
Tapestry needle
Embroidery hoop
Gold cord
Polyester stuffing

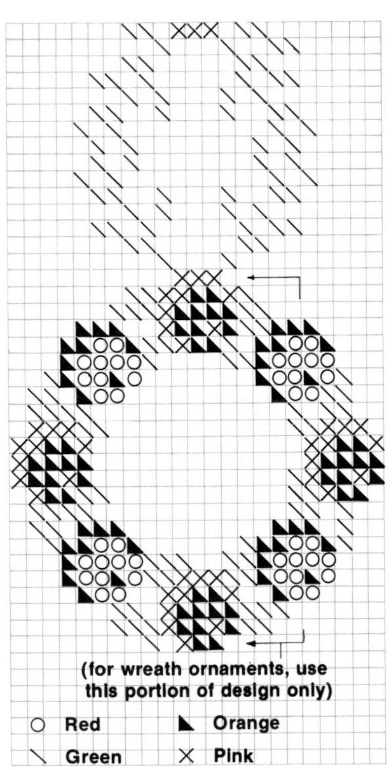

Directions

Note: The ornaments are worked on #24-count Hardanger cloth and the motif measures 2 inches across. The runner is worked on #20-count Hardanger and the wreaths measure 2¼ inches in diameter. With different fabric, work a sample to determine size.

Ornaments: Work in three shades of pink and one of green.

Following the graph, work wreath motif, leaving at least 2 inches of fabric between each for border and seams. Embroider several before cutting them out. Cut out wreaths with a 1-inch margin around the design. Cut matching circle for the back. Stitch front and back together ⅜ inch from edge of wreath, leaving a small opening. Turn, press, stuff lightly, and slip-stitch.

Tack gold cord along the edges of the ornament, tie the ends in a bow (slip-stitch to hold), and add a nylon-thread hanger.

Runner: Cut fabric 2 inches larger than the finished runner will be. Ours is 16x48 inches and has four wreaths across the short side and 13 down the length, with smaller, green wreaths between.

Begin with a rose wreath 2½ inches from the raw edge in the center of a long side. Work toward the short ends, connecting rose wreaths with green ones. On corners, work a green wreath at right angles to a rose wreath. Finish with hemstitching.

For a Fine Finish—Hemstitching

Hemstitching adds a nice decorative touch to delicate embroidery and provides a framework for a fringe on finely woven fabrics.

To work this lovely hem, make sure your edge is perfectly straight by removing a thread and cutting the fabric along the channel that is left. Fold under the raw edge, turn up the hem, and baste.

Turn the cloth so the wrong side faces you, and carefully snip 2 to 4 threads parallel to the hem, *directly above the upper fold of the hem.* Hemstitch with a thread the same size and color as the threads in the fabric, following the diagram at left below.

Slip the knotted thread end under the fold and bring the thread through the hem 2 threads below the drawn area. Insert the needle 3 or 4 threads to the right and in the drawn area. Go under 3 or 4 threads and bring it up again still in the drawn area. Then cross over 3 or 4 threads and reinsert the needle, slipping it under the fold and bringing it out again 2 threads below the drawn area. Pull the thread snug, and repeat.

You may wish to add a second row of stitches along the top of the drawn area, wrapping either the same threads as before and creating a ladder (below, center), or wrapping alternate ones (below, right).

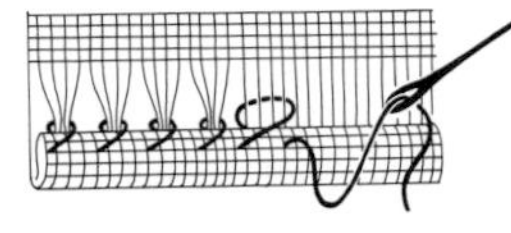

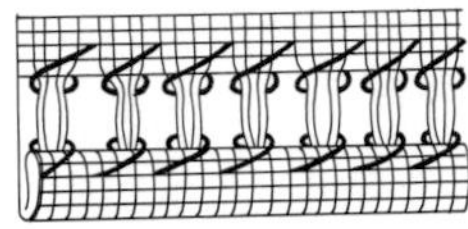

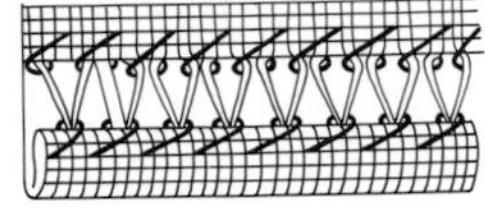

Pillowcases from Aunt Mary's

Beautifully designed and stitched bed linens are among our favorite needlework treasures. The three embroidered pillowcases you see here are heirlooms from the collection of Aunt Mary—a gracious lady who truly loves fine stitchery.

If you don't have someone in your family who hands down elegant, old-fashioned embroideries, create your own with our patterns.

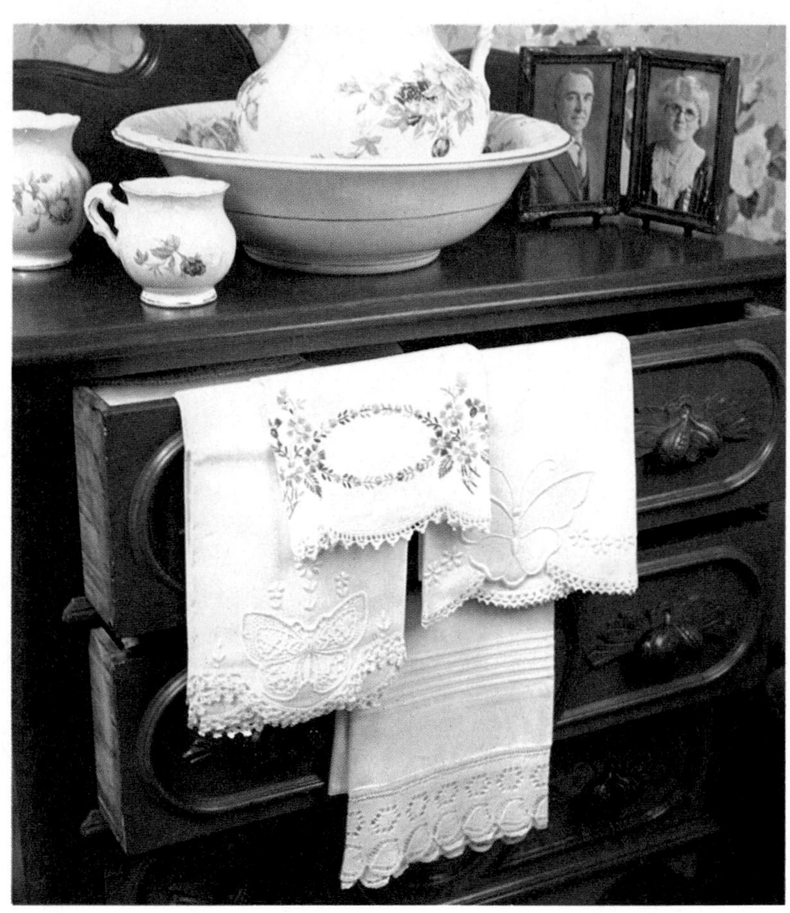

Materials
Pillowcases (see note below)
Sufficient crocheted lace edging for hems of cases
Embroidery needles

Flowered cases
Embroidery floss in white, yellow, and light and medium shades of pink, blue, green, and lavender

Lace butterfly cases
White embroidery floss
Nylon net
Small lace medallions, cut from doilies or lace yardage

Embroidered butterfly cases
White embroidery floss

Directions
Note: Make pillowcases to fit your pillows, or use purchased cases with hems removed. Shape the lower edge according to the pattern.

General instructions: Enlarge the pattern, reversing it to complete the design, and transfer it to the fabric, following instructions on page 166. Embroider according to directions below.

Turn up a narrow hem on the pillowcases, hemstitching if desired. Finish with crocheted edging sewn along the bottom.

Flowered cases: Use 2 strands of floss. Work stems in shades of green outline stitches; small leaves are green lazy daisy stitches. Work flower petals and large leaves in straight stitches, alternating light and dark shades of floss. Use dark green for the laid work base of one flower. Flower centers are white and yellow French knots.

Lace butterfly cases: With 1 strand of white floss, work flower petals and leaves in padded satin stitches, following directions on page 346. For French knots, use 3 strands. Work stems in outline stitches with 2 strands.

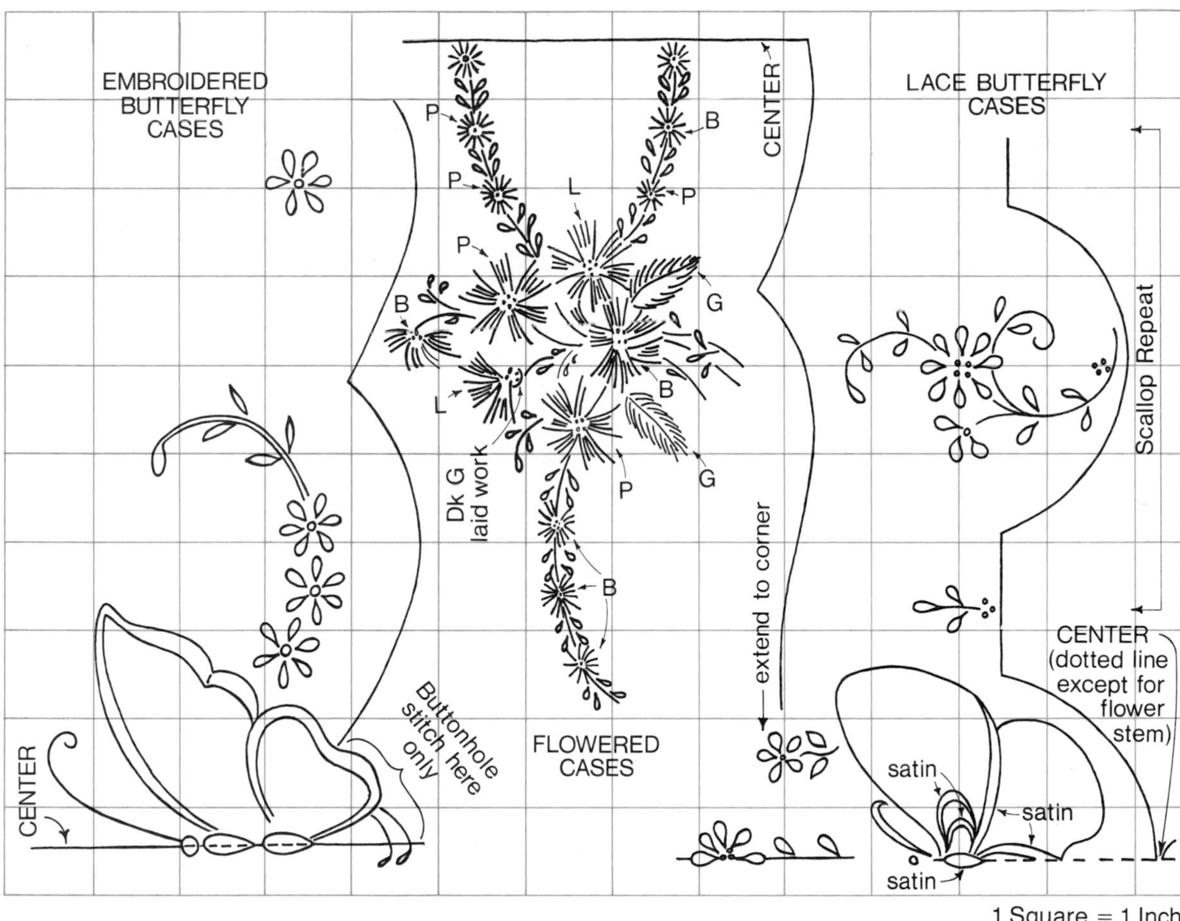

Aunt Mary's butterfly is a combination of embroidery and needle lace. For a close approximation, work the antennae and the body and wing detail shown on the pattern in satin stitches over a padding thread, with 1 strand of floss. Then, with small, sharp-pointed scissors, cut away the fabric interior of the butterfly. Lay a small piece of fine-mesh nylon netting or organdy behind the design, and buttonhole-stitch the netting to the fabric along the outline of the butterfly, working the thread through both the pillowcase and the sheer fabric. Work additional satin stitches over the body and wing detail to join the two pieces of fabric. Finally, appliqué small pieces of lace to the sheer wings.

Embroidered butterfly cases: Using 1 strand of white floss, work the flowers, leaves, and butterfly outline (except at lower edge) in padded satin stitches (see page 346 for directions for outlining and padding). Work the lower edge of the butterfly in buttonhole stitches to bind the raw edge of the fabric. Work antennae and stems in outline stitches, using 2 strands of floss.

Color Key For Flowered Cases

P Pink
B Blue
L Lavender
G Green

Crewel Picture Frame

Set off your favorite picture in this crewel frame, then adapt the designs to embellish a Christmas stocking.

Materials

21x26 inches white linen or any even-weave fabric
3-ply Persian yarn in light, medium, and dark copen blue
17x22-inch piece of ⅜-inch plywood for backing
Quilt batting
Crewel needle
Tape or staples

Color Key

A Dark copen blue
B Medium copen blue
C Light copen blue

Stitch Key

1 Chain stitch
2 Satin stitch
3 French knots
4 Outline stitch
5 Laid work

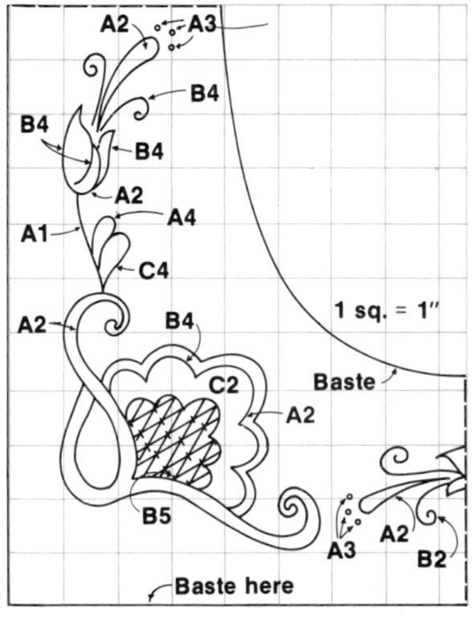

Directions

The pattern at left is for one quadrant of the design. Enlarge it and complete the remaining three quadrants. Extend small flower motifs up sides and across top and bottom, as shown in the photograph. Finally, transfer the design to the fabric.

With regular sewing thread, baste the linen along the inner and outer edges of the frame, as indicated. Embroider the design using 1 strand of yarn and following color and stitch guides. Block the finished embroidery, following directions on page 400.

Cut an oval from the center of the plywood to correspond with the oval on the pattern. Pad wood with 2 to 4 layers of quilt batting and stretch the embroidery over the batting, aligning the basted lines with the frame edges. Cut ovals from the quilt batting and clip the curves on the linen so the fabric lies smoothly.

Tape or staple the linen edges to the back of the frame and mount a picture or mirror in the center.

Embroidery Materials and Equipment

Even-weave fabric

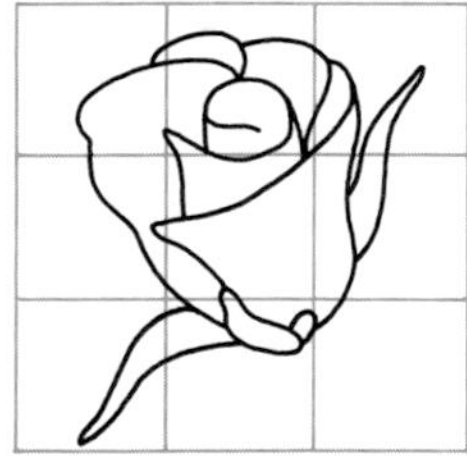

The original pattern

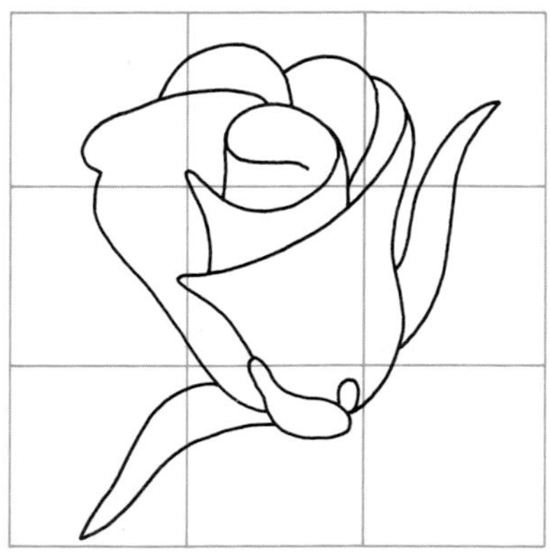

Enlarging on a grid

Materials

Unusual fabrics can make your stitcheries exciting, but the most commonly used ones for traditional embroidery are even-weave cottons or linens and other fabrics with a fairly smooth texture and a regular weave.

An even-weave fabric is one with the same number of horizontal and vertical threads per inch, as shown in the top diagram at left. The advantage of even-weave is that embroidery stitches will be uniform in size, which is an important consideration for cross-stitch and other counted-thread techniques. Aida cloth and Hardanger fabric are among the most widely available even-weave fabrics and each can be purchased with a specific thread count, such as 11 or 22 threads per inch.

Choose a good quality fabric that is firm enough to support the threads and stitches you intend to use.

Many yarns and threads are available for stitchery. Use wool yarns for crewelwork, and embroidery floss and pearl cotton for traditional stitchery. For special effects, try rayon, silk, and metallic threads.

Choose good quality, colorfast threads. If necessary, pre-shrink them by soaking in cool water. Dry thoroughly before stitching.

Cut yarns and threads into pieces about 18 inches long for embroidery. Longer threads will look worn and tired from being pulled through the fabric.

Yarns and threads have a lengthwise "grain" just as fabrics do, and are slightly smoother in one direction (with the grain). Thread the needle so you stitch with the grain and the thread will be attractive-looking longer.

Do not be afraid to use brightly colored yarns and threads. Colors will not be as bright on the fabric as in the skeins.

Store stitchery materials in a plastic bag to keep them clean.

Equipment

Keep both blunt and sharp needles on hand for embroidery. Blunt-end tapestry needles are used for counted-thread work and surface stitchery when the needle is worked into the spaces between threads or does not otherwise enter the fabric. The spiderweb stitch, for example, is worked with a blunt needle.

Use sharp needles for regular embroidery. Be sure the eye of the needle is large enough for thread to pass through easily without breaking. If crewel needles are too small, use chenille needles, which have larger eyes and sharper points.

An embroidery hoop or frame is a real boon to a stitcher. Mount your fabric in a large hoop, lace it into a needlepoint frame, or tack it to artist's stretcher strips assembled into a frame. When it is propped against a table or mounted on a floor stand, both hands will be free for embroidery (one on top, the other underneath). Your work will go faster and the tension on the thread will be uniform, reducing the amount of distortion in the fabric.

Among the small pieces of equipment many stitchers find helpful are *embroidery scissors* with sharp, narrow points, such as stork scissors. They are handy for snipping out mistakes.

A flexible leather thimble is useful to protect your fingers.

Commercial *yarn caddies* are widely available, or you can make one. Divide yarns for each project by color, and sandwich them between two layers of fabric cut into a strip. Baste together the layers between yarn colors, making a pocket for each. When you need a thread, pull it from the pocket. Remaining threads stay clean in their pockets.

Designs from Nature

The world around us is a boundless source of design motifs, and for years, embroiderers have looked upon Mother Nature as master designer. It is hard to imagine more perfect stitchery subjects than a graceful butterfly or the beautifully muted colors and natural symmetry of a delicate flower.

In this section, we offer you a very special selection of designs from nature to stitch in a variety of embroidery techniques. Whether you delight in crewel yarns or richly colored cotton floss, you are sure to find many must-do projects. These beautiful crewelwork pillows are an excellent example of how an embroiderer can forever capture a moment in nature. For complete instructions for these unique pillows, please see pages 358 to 361.

A Walk in the Woods—Wall Hanging and Pillows

Take a stroll through a forest of crewel-embroidered trees and animals and learn many new stitches and techniques along the way.

Whether you are a beginner or a virtuoso with the needle, you can lavish all your creative skill on the samplerlike variety of stitches used in the 30x60-inch wall hanging shown above.

And if you are a saver, you may already have a

workbasket full of brown, green, blue, and gray threads to use in this stitchery. Forty-seven shades of floss and 20 shades of wool were used in the original hanging. But almost any combination of earth-toned wools and cotton floss may be used effectively.

On the next four pages are patterns and stitch suggestions. Feel free to depart from them, though, and improvise in the placement and combination of stitches. Here is a chance to use your own creative impulses to make a stitchery that is uniquely your own.

continued

A Walk in the Woods—Wall Hanging and Pillows *(continued)*

1 Square = 1 Inch

Materials

Wall Hanging

2 yards 36-inch-wide unbleached linen or linenlike fabric
Embroidery floss (see note)
3-ply crewel wool (see note)
Embroidery hoop (optional)
Embroidery needles
30x60-inch artist's stretcher strips or purchased frame

Pillows (shown on pages 354 and 355)

Two 22x22-inch pieces off-white linen or linenlike fabric for each pillow
Embroidery hoop
Embroidery needles
Blunt tapestry needles
DMC embroidery floss in the colors and amounts listed on page 361 or suitable substitutes
Pillow stuffing or 17-inch-square pillow forms

1 Square = 1 Inch

Directions

Wall Hanging

Note: If you wish to purchase yarn or floss, you will need gold, white, black, and ecru. You will also need varying shades—from pale to dark—in the following colors: yellow-green (olive), bronze green (khaki), blue-green (turquoise), blue, reddish-brown, golden brown, gray-brown, gray, orange-red, and yellow.

Enlarge the pattern above and transfer it to the fabric, leaving a 3-inch margin around the edges.

Embroider the design, using the photograph on pages 356 and 357 and these directions as guides.

Animals: All eyes are dark brown. Work in floss except as noted using 3, 4, or 5 strands.

continued

A Walk in the Woods—Wall Hanging and Pillows *(continued)*

Wall Hanging

Owl: Use two shades of beige for chest and face, brown wool for back feathers and face outline, gold for tail feathers and eyes, and white for accents. Work chiefly in long-and-short stitches; tail feathers are lazy daisy stitches; white accents are all open chain stitches.

Bunnies: For the pair, use light orange-red for one, light gold-beige for the other, with ecru accents on both. Work chiefly in long-and-short or twisted chain stitches, but use loose French knots for a fluffy tail. Work lettuce in dark olive wool buttonhole stitches. Work the single bunny in shades of ecru and light gold-beige twisted chain stitches. Noses are dark brown.

Bird: Use two shades of yellow, with a light turquoise neck ring and accents among the feathers. Beak is light brown. Work long-and-short stitches on head and body, leaf stitches on wings and tail, but make knotted chain stitches at tops of wings.

Squirrel: Use two shades of gray-brown, working head and body in long-and-short stitches, the tail in twisted chain stitches. Add loose French knots at top of tail. Outline in dark brown.

Ducks: Work heads and necks in medium and dark blue-green, with a yellow eye-band on one; feathers are shades of gray, turquoise, and dark green, with yellow and white accents. Beaks are gray, tipped in brown. Use long-and-short, twisted chain, leaf, and straight stitches.

Greenery: Use 1 strand of wool, except as noted. Work tree trunks in closely spaced rows of chain, buttonhole, or outline stitches in colors noted below.

For the large tree on the left, use dark gray and khaki green on the trunk. Work leaves in shades of olive and light yellow-green outline stitches. Work vine in gold-brown, with clusters of yellow French knots. For satin-stitched leaves, use two shades of blue-green floss.

For the large tree in the center, use medium and light gray, with accents in olive and black. Work mushrooms in medium reddish-brown; use satin stitches for caps, and chain stitches for stems.

For the large tree on the right, use light and medium gray-brown for trunk. Work wisps of vine in gold-brown outline stitches, and leaves in two shades of blue-green leaf stitches.

Work trunks of smaller trees in the background in brown and reddish-brown chain stitches. Leaves are yellow-green satin stitches, with stem-stitched outlines. Work round flowers at base of trees in two shades of brick-red buttonhole stitches, and leaves in two shades of olive outline and satin stitches.

Work wild strawberries (left) in brick-red wool and long-and-short stitches; outline with stem stitches. For leaves, use outline, feather, and straight stitches in shades of green.

Work pond background in shades of blue running stitches, ripples in blue outline stitches, and edge of water in blue straight stitches. Use brown outline stitches to define the edge of the pond and rocks on the shore.

Work reeds near bunnies in three shades of blue-green, using satin and leaf stitches.

Work large leaves on shore (right) in shades of olive and yellow-green wool, using chain, outline, long-and-short, and twisted chain stitches. Stems are dark brown and green outline stitches.

Work squirrel's branch in outline stitches in shades of brown, with leaves in olive and shades of blue-green satin stitches and long twisted chain stitches. Use dark brick-red wool for berries; pad first (directions are on page 346) and then satin-stitch.

Block the fabric following directions on page 400. Mount on stretcher strips.

Pillows

Enlarge the patterns opposite and transfer to fabric. Refer to the photograph on pages 354 and 355 for suggested distribution and combinations of colors.

Both pillows are relatively simple, and may be worked in any combination of traditional stitches using 2 to 6 strands of floss, depending on the effect desired. However, a more experienced embroiderer may want to experiment with some of the more adventuresome stitches described below.

On both pillows, tails of animals are worked in twisted chain stitches; the end of each is a series of twisted chain ring stitches (using 3 strands of floss) to give it a fluffy appearance.

Some fruit on pillow B is worked in velvet stitches; the rest is worked in spiderweb stitches, both using 6 strands of floss.

Many of the leaves on each pillow are executed in herringbone and fishbone leaf stitches (using 3 or 4 strands of floss).

Try padded satin stitches on the red berries on pillow A to add dimension (3 strands). Outline with chain stitches.

Use 4 strands of floss and a buttonhole picot stitch for the petals of the small coral flowers on the left side of pillow A.

Leaves of the plant at the base of the tree on pillow A may be worked with 3 strands in chain scroll stitches.

Whipped chain stitches (4 strands) are used for texture and dimension on the stem of the plant on the right of pillow B.

Cable chain stitches (4 strands) give an airy texture to the fringe of leaves on the same plant.

When the embroidery is finished, block the pillow top and press gently on the wrong side. Stitch top to backing fabric, turn, press, stuff, and slip-stitch.

DMC embroidery floss

No.	Skeins/Color	
Pillow A		
225	1	Light rose
224	1	Medium rose
368	1	Light yellow-green
732	1	Dark yellow-green
780	1	Dark golden yellow
833	1	Light olive green
401	1	Light red-brown
613	1	Pale burnt umber
734	1	Light bronze green
421	2	Medium tan
3327	2	Dark red
936	2	Light avocado
935	2	Medium avocado
937	3	Medium-dark avocado
434	3	Warm brown
614	3	Light burnt umber
320	4	Medium yellow-green
801	5	Coffee brown
Pillow B		
225	1	Light rose
224	1	Medium rose
732	1	Dark yellow-green
580	1	Dark moss green
834	1	Pale olive
830	1	Dark olive
401	1	Light red-brown
3327	1	Dark red
368	2	Light yellow-green
833	2	Light olive
434	2	Warm brown
613	2	Pale burnt umber
936	2	Light avocado
935	2	Dark avocado
421	3	Medium tan
614	3	Light burnt umber
320	5	Medium yellow-green
937	5	Medium-dark avocado
801	5	Coffee brown

1 Square = 1 Inch

1 Square = 1 Inch

Wildflower Pillow and Crewel Throw

You'll enjoy embroidering our crewel throw and forest-green pillow as decorative accessories for your home. With our designs, you can preserve forever the delicate freshness of wildflowers —clover and violets, black-eyed susans, dandelions, and five other patterns.

Use wool and cotton threads, and when your throw is stitched, add a lacy crocheted edging. Patterns are on the following pages.

Wildflower pillow

Materials

1 yard of green velveteen
5 yards of cable cord
#5 pearl cotton in white, blue, brown, red, medium and light pink, medium and light green, medium and light violet, medium and light orange, and dark, medium, and light yellow
Transfer pencil
Tissue paper
Embroidery hoop or frame (see note below)
Embroidery needle
Pillow stuffing, or 14-inch circular box-pillow form

Directions

Note: Use a hoop larger than the diameter of the finished project to avoid crushing the nap.

On tissue paper, draw a 14-inch circle. Using a scale of "1 square equals ¼ inch," enlarge the patterns on pages 364 and 365. Trace flowers at random on the paper pattern, referring to the photograph for placement suggestions. Scatter flowers to avoid large empty spaces in the circle.

Using the transfer pencil, trace flowers on the front of the pattern. Then iron the pattern on the back of the fabric so the design will be face up when embroidered. Iron lightly over a padded surface, such as a terry cloth towel, to avoid crushing the nap. Go over design lines with chalk if they are hard to see.

Hand-baste along outlines of motifs so you can embroider them from the right side. Otherwise embroidery must be worked from the back of the fabric.

Cut out the fabric circle, leaving an additional 2-inch margin around it so the fabric can be held securely in a hoop.

Embroider the flowers, following the stitch and color guides on pages 364 and 365. (Refer to the Glossary on pages 406 to 409 for an explanation of the stitches.)

When the embroidery is finished, press the wrong side on a padded surface. Steam lightly to avoid crushing the nap.

Cover cording with strips of velveteen cut on the bias, or use purchased cording in a matching or contrasting color. Pin the cording along the edge of the 14-inch circle, and machine-stitch with a zipper foot.

Cut a 3-inch-wide strip of fabric for boxing, and stitch it to the cording, right sides together, in a ½-inch seam. Sew a second row of cording ½ inch from the edge of the other side of the strip.

Cut a 15-inch circle of fabric for the pillow back, and pin it to the boxing strip, right sides together. Using a zipper foot, stitch along the cording seam, leaving 12 inches open. Turn right side out, insert the pillow form, and slip-stitch the opening.

Wildflower Afghan

Materials

2 yards of 44-inch-wide white wool
16 oz. of sweater and afghan yarn to match fabric
Small skeins of Persian yarn in 6 shades of green, 5 shades of orange, 4 shades of blue, 3 shades of violet, and 2 shades of pink, brown, and yellow
Transfer pencil
Tissue paper
Embroidery hoop
Crewel embroidery needle
Size 0 crochet hook

Directions

Draw a 14-inch circle on paper. Enlarge the patterns on the next page (scale is "1 square equals ½ inch"), and draw each wildflower inside the circle once. Retrace the *front* of the flower with a transfer pencil and then transfer the designs to the *wrong* side of the fabric. Center the circle of flowers in one corner of the wool, keeping the designs about 9 inches from the raw edges.

Using regular thread in a contrasting color, baste around outlines so you can work on the face of the fabric.

Embroider the designs, using 2 strands of wool for all the stitches except the French knots. Use 3 strands for French knots. Follow the stitch and color guides given with the patterns on the next two pages.

Finish the afghan with the 5-inch crocheted border, following directions below. Or add a 5-inch fringe.

Crocheted Border

First scallop: Starting at center of scallop, ch 20; join with sl st to first ch to form ring. Work 30 sc in ring, join with sl st to first sc. Work back and forth in rows. *Row 1:* Ch 5, (sk next sc, dc in next sc, ch 2) 5 times; sk next sc. Work (dc, ch 3, dc) in next sc, (ch 2, sk next sc, dc in next sc) 6 times. Ch 1, turn. *Row 2:* Sc in first dc, (2 sc in next ch-2 sp, sc in next dc) 6 times; 3 sc in ch-3 sp at tip of scallop, sc in next dc, (2 sc in next ch-2 sp, sc in next dc) 5 times, ending with 3 sc over turning ch. Ch 1, turn. *Row 3:* Sk first sc, sc in each sc to center sc at tip of scallop, 3 sc in center sc, sc in each sc to end. Working as for Row 3, work Rows 4, 5, 6, and 7. *Row 8:* Sl st in first sc, ch 4, tr in same sc, (ch 3, sk 2 sc, holding back the last lp of each tr, work 2 tr in next sc, yo and draw through 3 lps on hook—tr-cluster made) 7 times; ch 3, (work tr-cluster, ch 3, and tr-cluster in center sc), (ch 3, sk 2 sc, tr-cluster in next sc) 8 times. Ch 1, turn. *Row 9:* Work (sc, 3 dc, sc) in each ch-3 sp around scallop. Break off.

Second scallop: work same as for first scallop until Row 8 is completed. Ch 1, turn. *Row 9:* Work (sc, 3 dc, sc) in each 3 ch-sp around scallop to within last 2 ch-3 sps, (in next sp work sc, dc, drop lp from hook, insert hook on right side in corresponding dc on preceding scallop, draw dropped lp through, work 2 more dc and sc in same sp on new scallop) 2 times. Break off. Continue making and joining scallops in this manner for 36 scallops.

Heading: *Row 1:* Working on the right side across straight edge of scallops, attach yarn with sl st to last sc in Row 9 of first scallop; ch 5, * sk ½ inch on horizontal edge, dc in edge, ch 2. Rep from * across, ending with ch 2, dc in last sc on ch 4, ch 3, turn. *Row 2:* Tr in first ch-2 sp, * ch 1, holding back last lp of each tr, work 2 tr over next ch-2 sp, yo and draw through all 3 lps on hook—tr-cluster made. Rep from * across, ending with tr-cluster over turning ch. Ch 1, turn. In each ch-1 sp make sc, dc, sc. Sl st in first sc; break off.

To finish: Steam-press. Lay fabric on table; pin border in place, using one scallop in corner. Trim fabric to fit. Whipstitch edges of fabric, repin border, and sew to fabric. Press.

continued

CROCHET ABBREVIATIONS

ch	*chain*
sc	*single crochet*
dc	*double crochet*
tr	*triple crochet*
sk	*skip*
sl	*slip*
st(s)	*stitch(es)*
sl st	*slip stitch*
lp(s)	*loop(s)*
sp	*space*
rep	*repeat*
rnd	*round*
yo	*yarn over*
*	*repeat whatever follows**

Wildflower Pillow and Crewel Throw *(continued)*

These multi-purpose patterns are designed for use on the embroidered pillow and throw pictured on page 362. By varying the size of the motifs, you can use them for many other embroideries as well. For example, work one or more motifs on a box in crewel wool or pearl cotton. Or use the motifs for machine embroidery or tambour work.

For directions for these techniques, refer to the Contents pages.

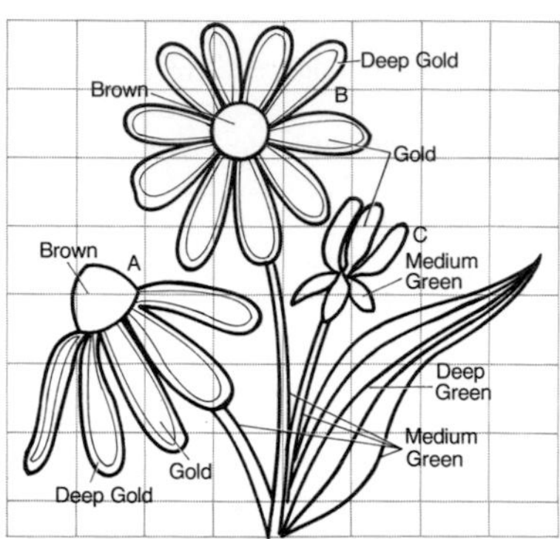

Black-eyed Susan: *For the embroidered pillow*, eliminate flower C. Petals of flowers A and B are double rows of gold chain stitches; centers are clusters of brown French knots; stems are couched and leaves are chain-stitched, both in medium green.

For the crewel throw, work as for the embroidered pillow.

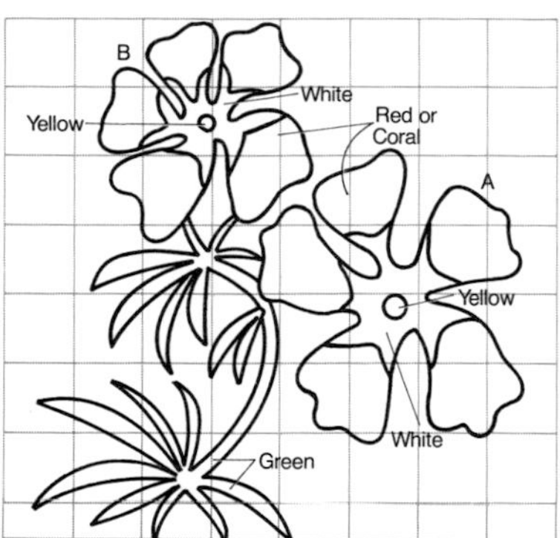

Gilia: *For the embroidered pillow*, use a single bloom of the Gilia (flower A), plus a spray of leaves. Work coral petals in satin stitches and white centers in fly stitches, with one yellow French knot at the center. Narrow leaves are single rows of blue-green chain stitches.

For the crewel throw, work the petals in coral satin stitches and outline stitches. In the centers, embroider a cluster of yellow French knots. Work the stem and leaves in forest green wool, couching the stems with regular sewing thread. Work the leaves in rows of chain stitches.

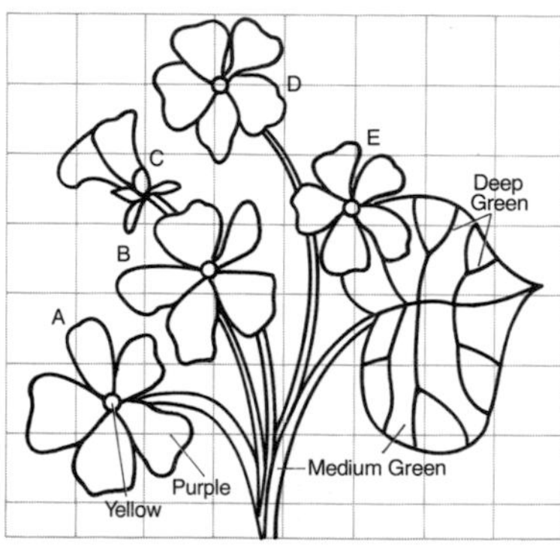

Violet: *For the embroidered pillow*, each petal is a single purple lazy daisy stitch filled with purple satin stitches; centers are yellow French knots; and stems are light green stem stitches. Work the leaf in light green satin stitches with darker green couched veins.

For the crewel throw, work petals in satin stitches. Flowers A, B, and D are deep purple; flowers C and E are medium purple. Centers are yellow French knots. Leaves are medium green satin stitches, with light green couched veins and stems.

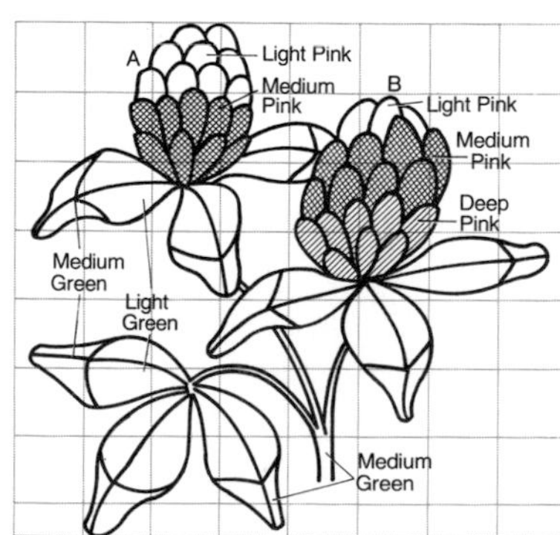

Clover: *For the embroidered pillow*, work both flowers in two shades of pink French knots.

Work stems in stem stitches and the leaves in fly stitches, both in medium green with random veins in darker green.

For the crewel throw, work flowers in two shades of pink French knots. Couch stems in grass green; leaves are grass-green satin stitches with veins of deeper green.

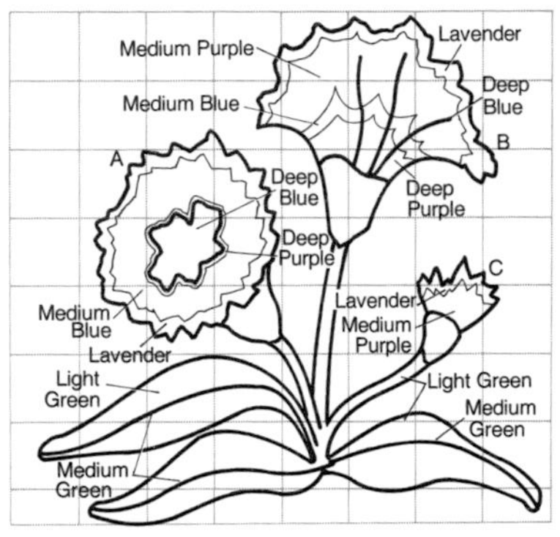

Bachelor's Button: *For the embroidered pillow,* work the flowers in medium blue long-and-short stitches with no shading. Embroider the stems in grass-green stem stitches and leaves in rows of chain stitches.

For the crewel throw, work flowers in purple long-and-short stitches, with flower centers in blue. Embroider base of each in green satin stitches; couch stems with regular thread; work leaves in split stitches.

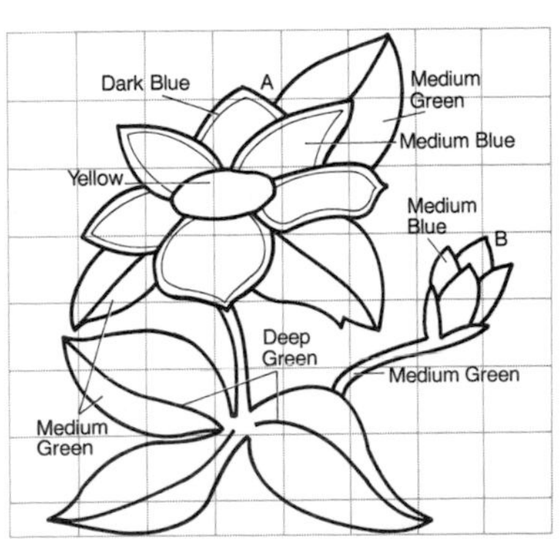

Hepatica: *For the embroidered pillow,* omit the bud (flower B), stems, and lower leaves. Work the petals of flower A in blue satin stitches; the center is pale yellow French knots; the leaves are closely worked rows of pale green satin stitches.

For the crewel throw, omit bud, stem, and lower leaves. Work petals and flower center as for embroidered pillow. Work leaves in green satin stitches.

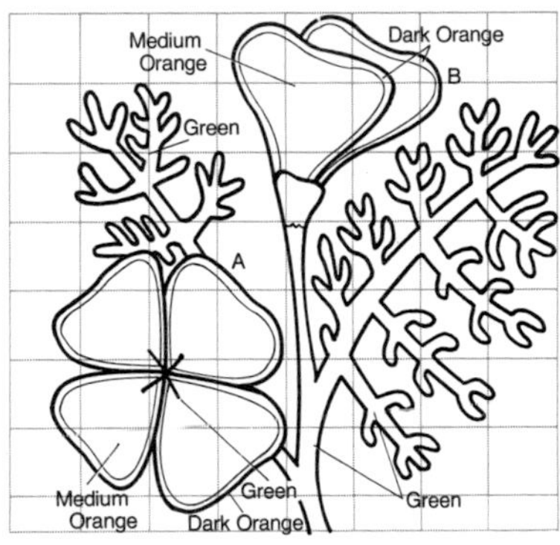

California Poppy: *For the embroidered pillow,* work petals in medium orange satin stitches, stems in green stem stitches, leaves in green fly stitches.

For the crewel throw, outline petals with dark orange stem stitches; work in light orange satin stitches. Work stem in grass-green couching and leaves in grass-green fly stitches.

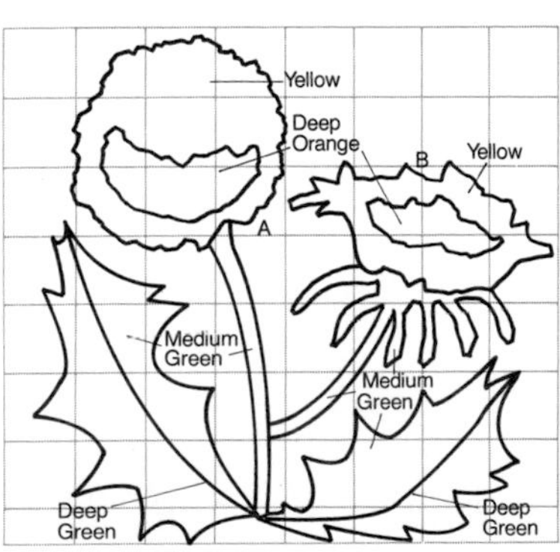

Dandelion: *For the embroidered pillow,* work all three flowers in medium yellow straight stitches (omit orange). Couch the stems in green, and embroider the leaves in tight rows of green chain stitches.

For the crewel throw, add the dandelion to the design, if you wish (it was not used in the afghan shown). Follow suggestions for the embroidered pillow, or work flowers in long-and-short stitches in yellow and dark orange yarn, as indicated on the pattern.

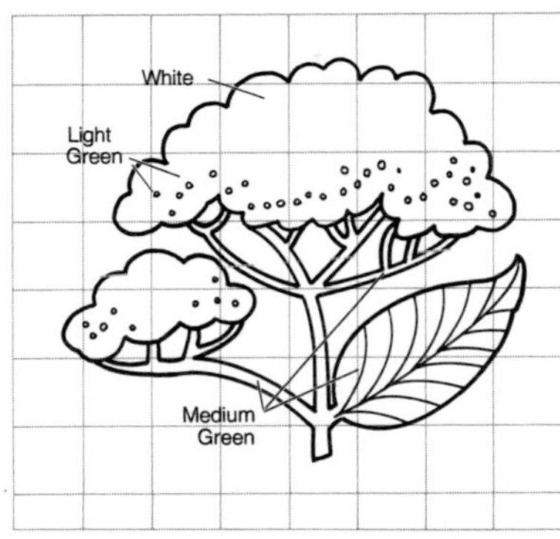

Queen Anne's Lace: *For the embroidered pillow,* work the stems in medium green chain stitches and the leaves in medium green leaf stitches. Embroider the flower heads in white French knots, or a combination of light green and white French knots or seed stitches.

For the crewel throw, add the Queen Anne's Lace design if you wish, following suggestions for the embroidered pillow.

Cross-Stitch and Counted-Thread Techniques

In cross-stitch and counted-thread embroideries, each stitch is carefully sized and placed according to the number of strands in the fabric. The embroidery is developed by counting the number of threads in the material. The result is a beautifully embellished, precise, and well-scaled piece of needlework that is versatile enough to use in any number of ways.

To help you get started in this extremely popular embroidery technique, here is a whole section of cross-stitch and counted-thread project ideas, including a tablecloth, place mats, napkins, and a baby quilt. For how-to instructions for the dramatic and colorful table runner shown here, see page 368.

Auntie Dee's Embroidered Runner

(shown on pages 366 and 367)

An interesting combination of cutwork, needle weaving, and embroidery makes this table runner truly unique. The satin stitching and other details are exquisite, whether seen close up or from far away.

Materials

24x72 inches of #22-count Hardanger cloth
#5 pearl cotton in scarlet, medium blue, light green, and yellow
#8 pearl cotton in white, or white lace thread
Large sheets of graph paper (10 squares per inch)
Colored pencils to match thread
Embroidery hoop or frame
Small tapestry needles
Small, sharp scissors

Color Key

S Scarlet
B Blue
G Green
Y Yellow

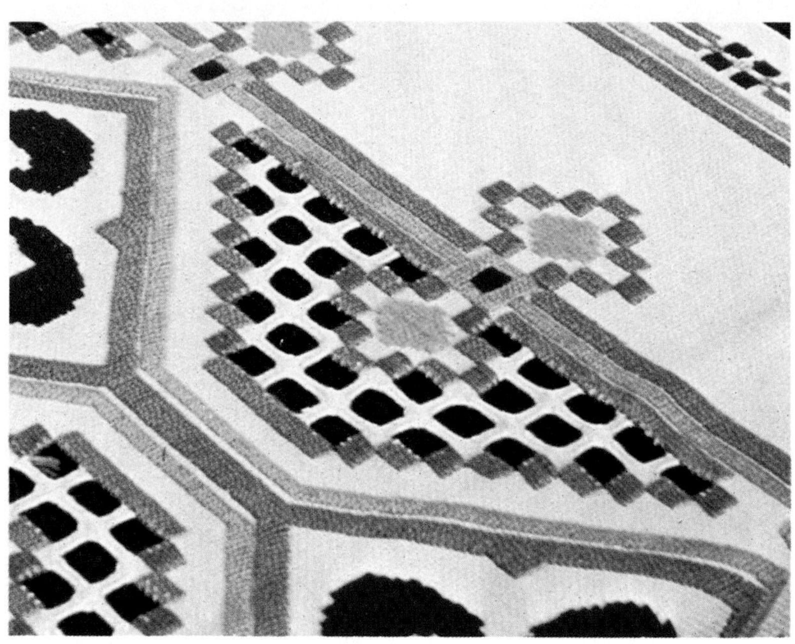

Directions

Use colored pencils and graph paper to make a drawing of the pattern at right. Note that it is for one quarter of the motif only. Transfer it to paper and complete the pattern for the central swirl motif inside the diamond and the cutwork borders separately.

Make the diamond motif, including the central swirl, by lining up side B next to side A, and transferring the design. Continue in this "circular" fashion until the swirl is complete. For the borders and cutwork, reverse the pattern and match the C sides. Then reverse the pattern again on the D side, matching along the center, and complete the upper half.

Begin stitching in the center of the cloth, stretching the fabric in a hoop or frame to prevent puckering. Work the design first in straight stitches over the number of threads indicated. Work from the center of the fabric across the width, omitting the continuous blue line of satin stitches in the lower border at this stage.

After working the motif across the fabric, work the design the length of the runner. Be sure you leave enough fabric at the ends to work the lower border around the corners and across the ends.

Work the design in colored threads before starting the cutwork. For the cutwork, carefully cut away the threads that are missing in the diagram, leaving those that appear as dark lines. Use sharp scissors and work in good light. Then work needle weaving over the threads remaining between colored areas. (See page 376 for specific directions for this Hardanger cutwork.)

When the entire pattern (including the cutwork) is finished, turn up the hem 13 threads below the scarlet blocks and whipstitch in place. Then work the blue line over 5 threads of the fabric and completely around the cloth, catching in the hem margin at the same time. Block the fabric, following instructions on page 400.

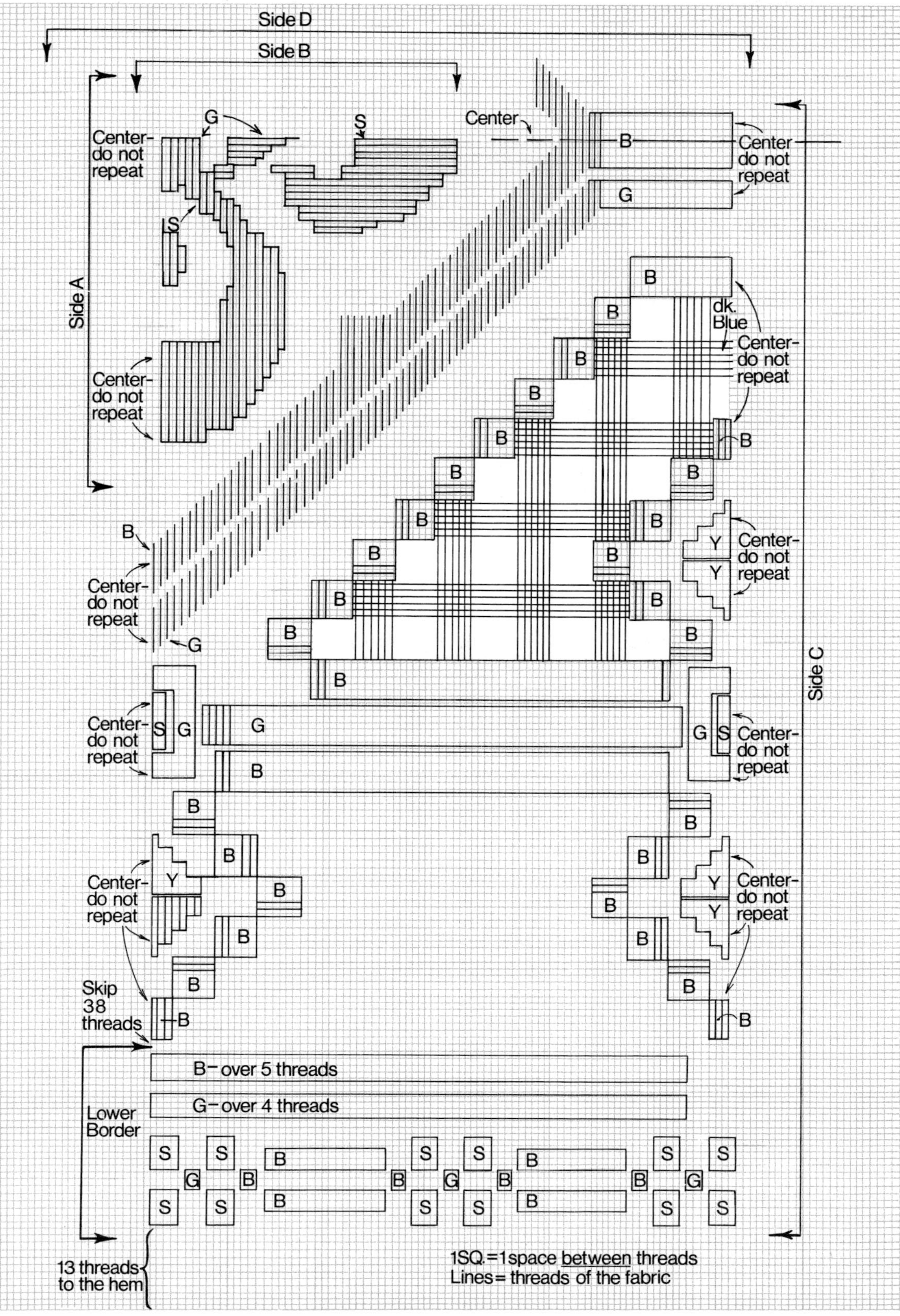
Side D
Side B
Side A
Side C
Center
Center-
do not
repeat
G
S
B
dk.
Blue
Y
Skip
38
threads
B– over 5 threads
G– over 4 threads
Lower
Border
13 threads
to the hem
1SQ.=1space between threads
Lines= threads of the fabric

Auntie Dee's Cross-Stitch Tablecloth

This colorful tablecloth, worked entirely in cross-stitch, is an elaborate-looking design that is actually easy to embroider. The same motif adorns all four corners of the tablecloth, and the border pattern is composed of several simple designs. To further embellish your work, create your own cross-stitched initials for the center of the cloth.

Size your cloth according to our directions so the finished piece will fit your table.

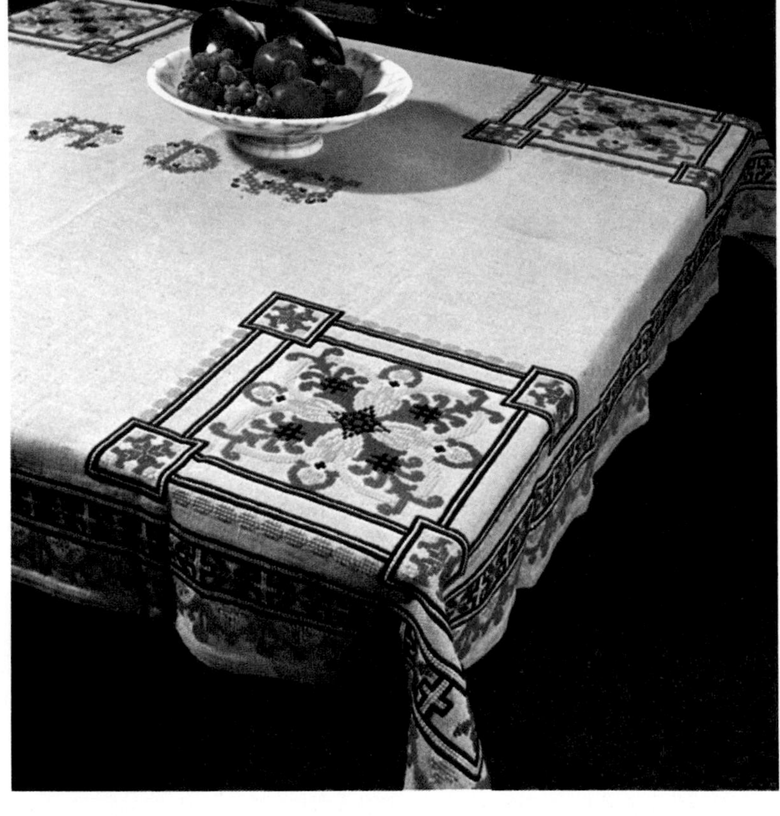

Materials

Sufficient even-weave fabric for your tablecloth (see note below)
#3 pearl cotton in black, gold blue, avocado, and coral
Tapestry needle
Embroidery hoop (optional)
Graph paper (10 squares per inch)
Colored pencils to match thread

Directions

Note: This tablecloth can be worked on 68x68 inches of #18-count linen to be about 62 inches square when finished. If worked on 54x54 inches of #22-count Hardanger cloth, over 2 threads, it will be about 52 inches square when finished.

Using colored pencils, transfer the pattern to graph paper. Begin with the border shown in diagram A, then complete the square corner motif, one quarter of which is shown in diagram B. Note that the inside rows of stitches in the large square are the vertical and horizontal centers of the pattern; they are not part of the repeat.

Stay-stitch the edges of the fabric to prevent fraying. If desired, mount the fabric in a hoop to help prevent puckering.

Before you begin stitching, it is a good idea to make a few practice stitches to decide how many threads of the fabric you want to cover with each stitch. This tablecloth was embroidered with each stitch going over 2 threads of #18-count fabric. If your fabric has a different count, or if you would like a larger design, practice stitching over 3 or 4 threads to see which you prefer. Make a rectangular cloth with this design simply by shortening the border between the corner motifs. When doing this, though, plan the stitch pattern carefully on graph paper before embroidering.

Using a blunt tapestry needle for the embroidery, work pearl cotton through the spaces *between* the threads in the fabric. (Embroider the complete design in cross-stitches.)

Rather than tying knots on the back of your cloth, weave the ends of the threads into the back of the work, or begin and end with waste knots. (To make a waste knot, knot the end of the thread and insert the needle into the fabric from front to back so the knot is on top. Then stitch over the thread end, securing it. Clip the knot and pull the end to the back of the fabric.)

Allowing about a 4-inch margin of fabric around the edges, start the embroidery in one corner. Embroider the border corner first (diagram A). Work the repeat section of the border 20 more times, or as many times as you need for your cloth. Be sure to leave sufficient space at the next corner to work the corner border pattern again. Work the border completely around the cloth.

Work the square corner motifs, allowing ¾ inch between the top of the border and the edge of the corner square.

After the embroidery is completed, block the cloth and press it lightly. Allowing a margin of 4 threads below the coral swag in the border, withdraw 1 thread from the fabric completely around the cloth for hemstitching. Turn up a ⅝-inch hem and finish with hemstitching, following the directions on page 348.

Color Key

- ● Coral
- ⊟ Blue
- ▣ Avocado
- ⊡ Gold
- ☒ Black

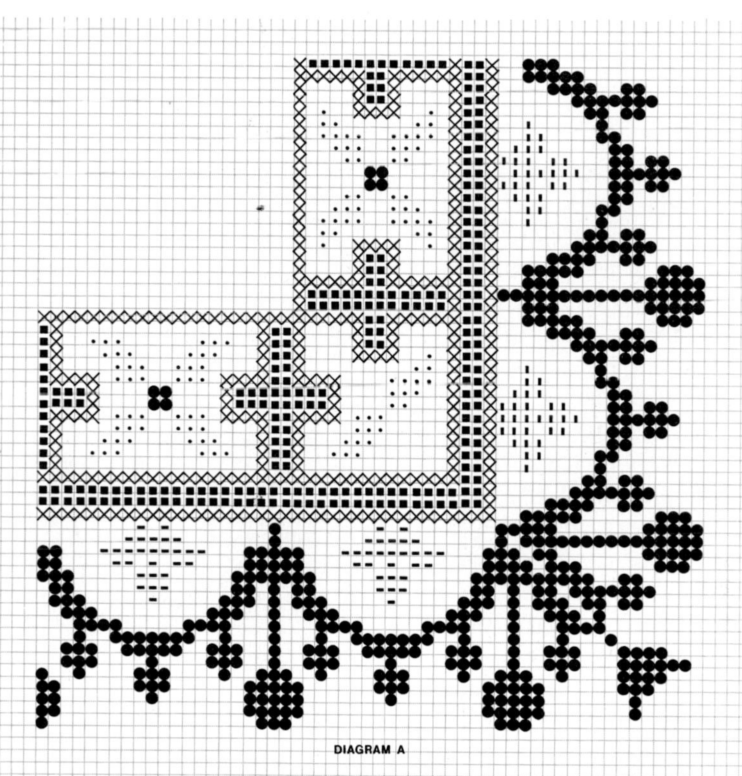

1 square=1 stitch over 2 threads in the fabric

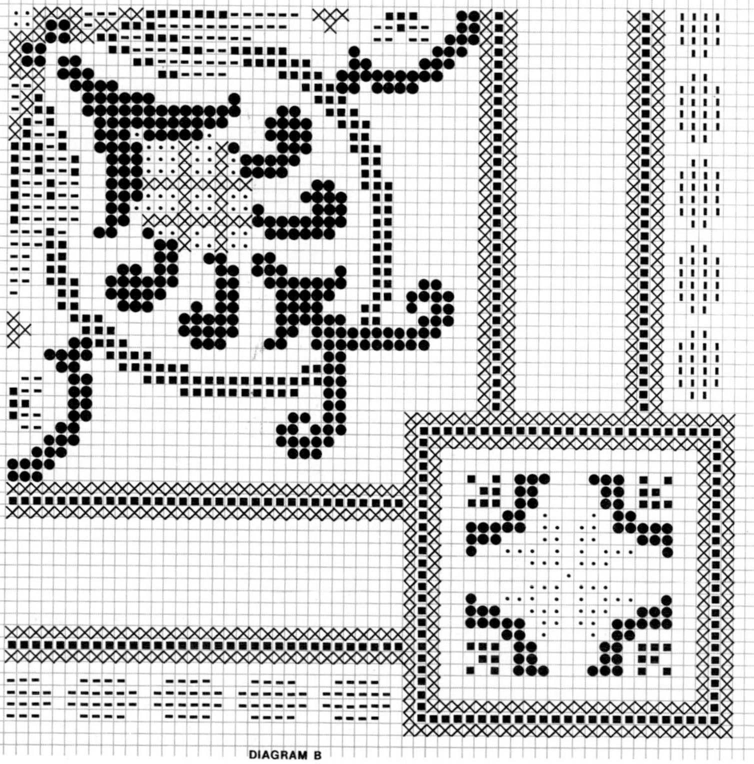

Cross-Stitch Baby Quilt and Embroidered Pillow

To create a keepsake that can be proudly handed down generation after generation, embroider this delightful cross-stitch alphabet quilt. The crib-size quilt can be worked on your choice of fabrics, using any color embroidery floss, although red is traditional. To make your coverlet special, embroider the baby's name and birth date in one of the corners.

Materials

45x45 inches white #40-count even-weave fabric, #22-count Hardanger cloth, or fine percale for quilt top (see note below)
45x45 inches white fabric for quilt back
20x20 inches white fabric for pillow top (same as above)
Two 20x10½-inch pieces white fabric (pillow back)
½ yard muslin
Pillow stuffing
Red embroidery floss
Embroidery or tapestry needle (depending on fabric)
Quilt batting
Embroidery hoop (optional)
#14 mono-canvas (optional)

Directions

Note: If worked on #40-count fabric, the finished quilt will be about 38x38 inches. If worked on #22-count Hardanger cloth, it will be about 41x41 inches. Or, worked through #14 mono-canvas (waste canvas) on percale, it will be about 43 inches square. Depending on the fabric used, there will be similar variations in the size of the pillow top. We tell you how to use all three fabrics, so you can work with the one you prefer. Preshrink fabric and thread, if desired.

On #40-count cloth, use a tapestry needle; work each stitch over 5 threads of the fabric. On #22-count Hardanger, use a tapestry needle; work each stitch over 3 threads. On fine percale, use a sharp needle and baste #14 mono-canvas in place as a guide for stitch placement. Work the design over 2 threads of the canvas. After stitching, moisten the canvas, snip the threads, and gently withdraw each thread from beneath the stitches.

Mark the center of one side of the fabric 1 inch from the edge. Using the chart on pages 374 and 375, work the entire design; start in the center. Follow the placement diagram and stitch chart for the upper left corner to work borders and boxes for the letters, referring to the photograph if necessary. Then work letters shown on page 375, centering them in the boxes. Use 3 strands of floss.

Insert the fabric in a hoop or frame for working, if desired.

When you have finished embroidering the quilt top, outline-stitch the baby's name and date of birth in the lower right-hand corner. Finally, block the quilt top following directions on page 400.

To assemble the quilt, lay the backing on a flat surface. Smooth a 45-inch square of batting on top, and place the embroidered piece on top of that. Pin and baste the layers together.

Quilt with red floss, using one of the following methods: work cross-stitches in center of squares between letters, or cross-stitch over cross-stitches already completed. Or tie double strands of floss in center of squares between letters and clip ends to ½ inch. Or quilt with quilting thread in any traditional pattern. Remove basting threads after quilting is completed.

To bind the edges, trim batting and backing so they extend 1 inch beyond the outermost row of cross-stitches on the front of the quilt. Trim quilt top to ½ inch beyond the edge of backing and batting—1½ inches beyond the cross-stitched border. Turn under the raw edge of the top ¼ inch, fold top over batting and backing, and slip-stitch to the back of the quilt, mitering corners.

To make the pillow, embroider the design, following the diagram on page 374. After blocking, trim pillow top so raw edges fall 2½ inches outside the cross-stitched border. Use two pieces of white fabric to construct a layered back for the pillow, making it a sham. (Dimensions of the pillow front and back will depend on the fabric used for the embroidery.) Measure the completed cover; sew and stuff a muslin pillow to fit.

To care for the embroidered quilt, wash by hand or on the *gentle* cycle in a machine, using lukewarm water and mild soap or detergent. Do not wring out excess water; spin dry or roll in a towel to remove excess water, then dry the quilt flat. Be especially careful when washing to avoid hard machine action; it can pull the batting apart and make the quilt lumpy. If necessary, press the quilt while it is slightly damp, using a warm—not hot—iron.

continued

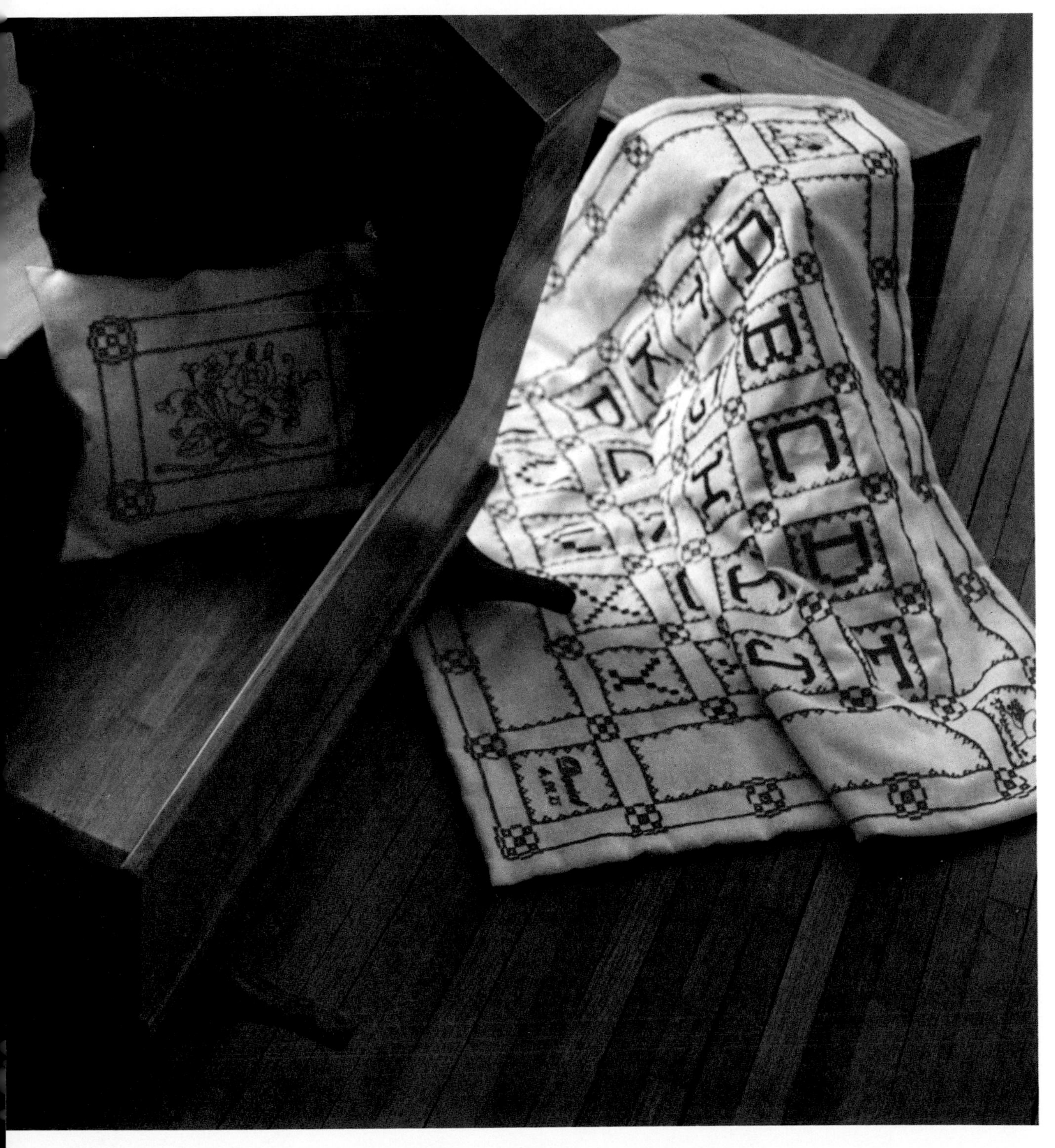

Cross-Stitch Baby Quilt and Embroidered Pillow *(continued)*

Stitch key
1 Cross-stitch
2 Outline stitch
3 Straight stitch
4 French knot
5 Lazy daisy (chain)

Upper right corner

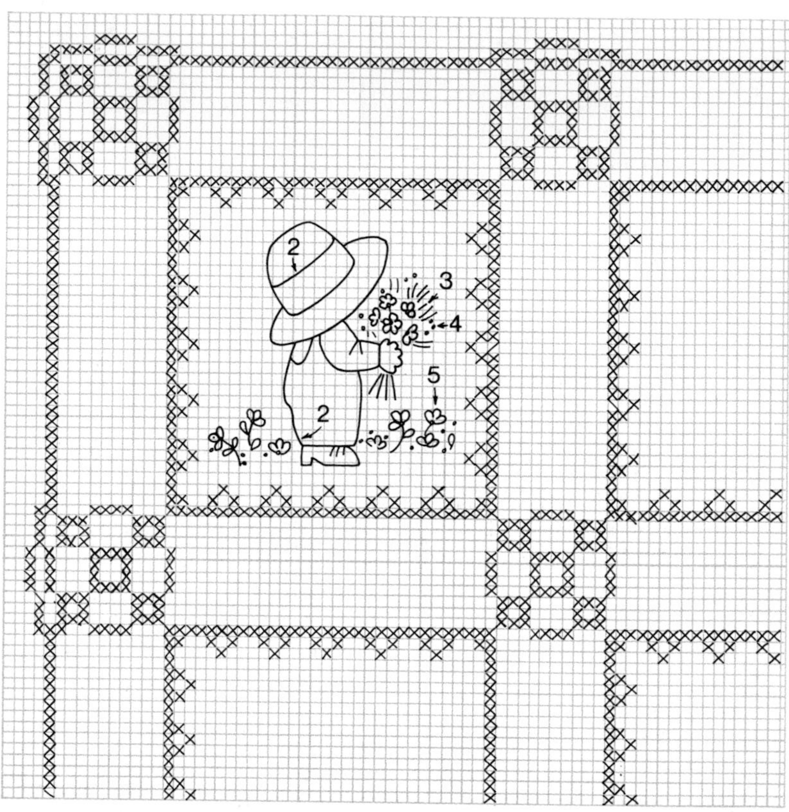

Upper left corner with borders. Below: pillow.

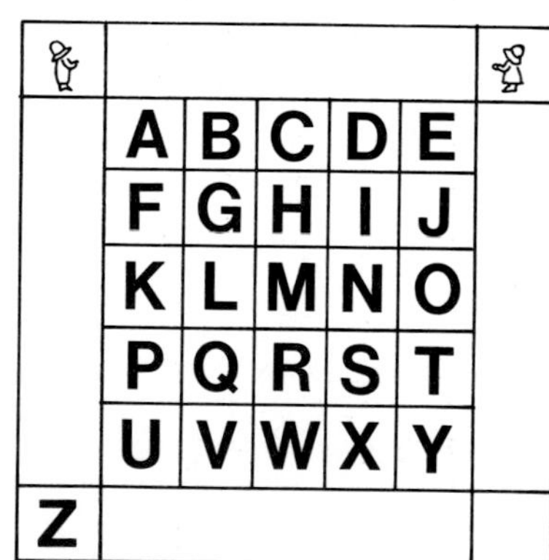

Placement diagram

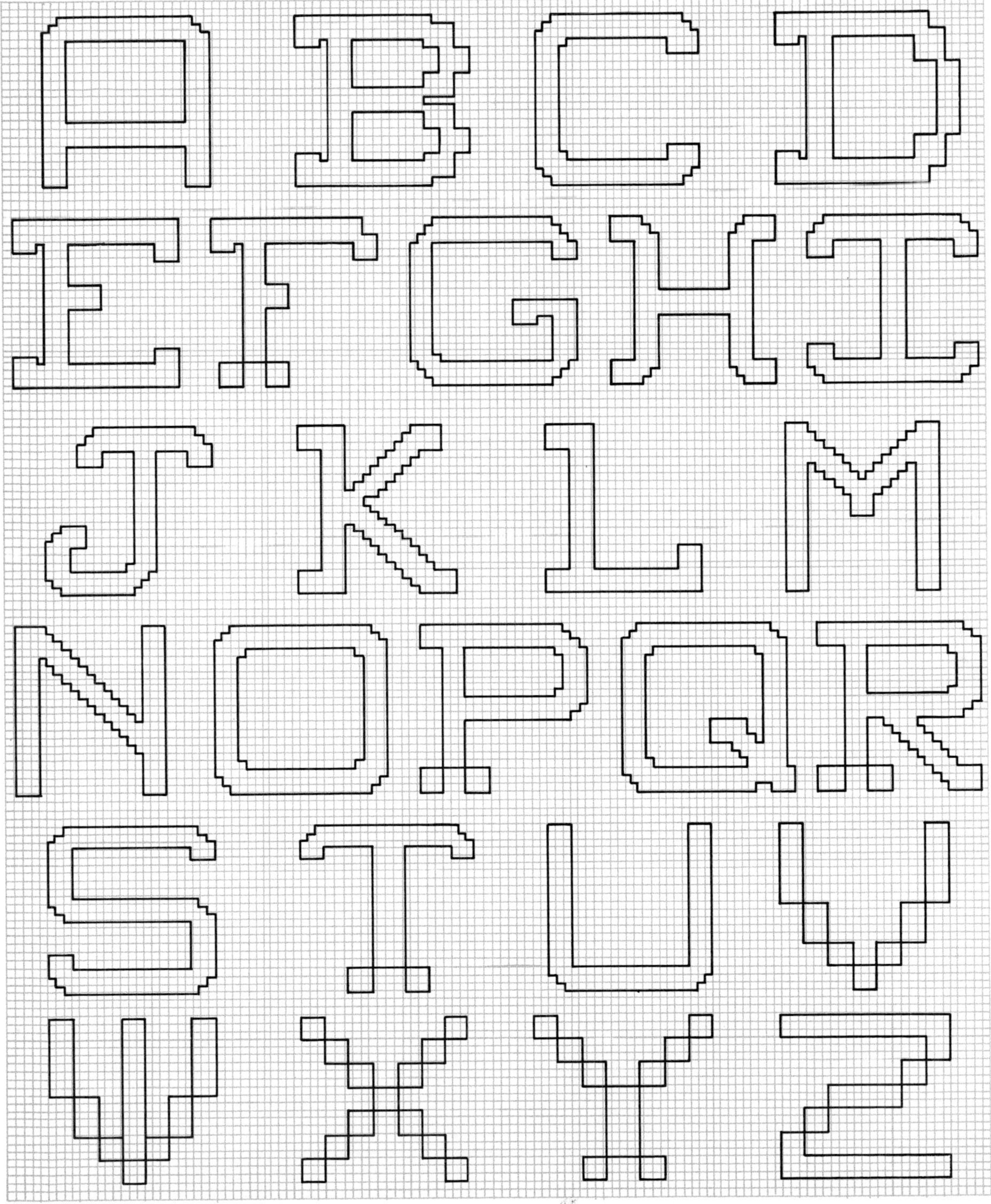

Hardanger Place Mat and Napkin

The table accessories shown here are stitched in a traditional counted-thread technique from the Hardanger province of Norway. Worked on even-weave fabric, the design is embroidered in blocks of satin stitches and accented with cutwork and delicate needleweaving.

We think you will enjoy this challenging and elegant addition to your needlework repertoire.

Materials

17x12 inches #22-count white Hardanger cloth (for each place mat)
16x16 inches #22-count white Hardanger cloth (for each napkin)
White #5 pearl cotton
White #8 pearl cotton or crochet thread
Graph paper (10 squares per inch)
Small, sharp-pointed scissors
Tapestry needles (small)

Directions

The diagram on page 378 is for a portion of the pattern on the place mat, showing part of the corner and side. Transfer it to graph paper, using a large enough piece (or several pieces taped together) so that there are the same number of spaces and lines on the paper as spaces and threads on the place mat. In that way, you can see the exact location of each stitch and be sure that stitches are accurately placed in relation to the total design.

The repeat for the sides of the place mat is marked on the diagram. To complete the pattern, turn the repeat area over so the "A" sides match. When working the corner, reverse the pattern and match it along the diagonal, as indicated.

After working the place mat, graph the design for the napkin by referring to the photograph. Or work a segment of the same pattern embroidered on the place mat.

Before doing any cutwork, embroider the satin stitches using #5 pearl cotton. While stitching, be careful to work the thread through the *spaces* between the threads rather than into the threads themselves. Work blocks of 5 stitches over 4 threads of the fabric—always working one more stitch than the number of threads to be cut, so the cut area is sufficiently bound and will not ravel. Cut areas *must* be edged with satin-stitched blocks.

Work stitches in the sequence shown in diagram A on page 378. When 2 stitches share a space in a corner, bring the thread up through the same space on the inside corner of each block.

When all the satin stitching is finished, do the cutwork. Cut only those threads that are bound with satin-stitched blocks—and indicated on the pattern diagram. Use small, sharp-pointed scissors and cut close to the satin stitching. (The fabric will shrink when washed, and frayed edges will not show.) Cut both ends of block-bound threads and gently lift the cut threads from the fabric with a needle. The fabric will look like diagram B on page 378.

Next, thread a smaller needle with #8 pearl cotton or crochet thread, and anchor the end of the thread under the satin stitching. Bring it up in the center of the threads to be woven—indicated with an "X" on diagram B. Go over 2 threads on the left, wrapping thread around them, and bring the needle up again in the center. Next, go over 2 threads on the right. Continue, pulling threads tightly together as you weave and maintaining even tension.

At the end of a woven area, turn the corner and weave the adjoining threads, always starting with the needle in the *center* of the two pairs of threads. If woven threads are distorted at the end of a block, you have woven too many or too few times over the threads. Make necessary adjustments and continue. Do not end or start a thread in the middle of a row of weaving.

Plan the stitching to weave threads that form a square in either a clockwise or counterclockwise direction. Then, when making the tiny loops joining the pairs of woven threads, work in the opposite direction. To make the loops, weave three sides of the square and half of the fourth. Then make the loops as shown in diagram C on page 378, working the thread through the *center* of the needle-woven pairs, rather than around them. Work one loop on each side of the square, and then finish weaving the fourth side.

When the embroidery is finished, turn up a narrow (¼-inch) hem.

continued

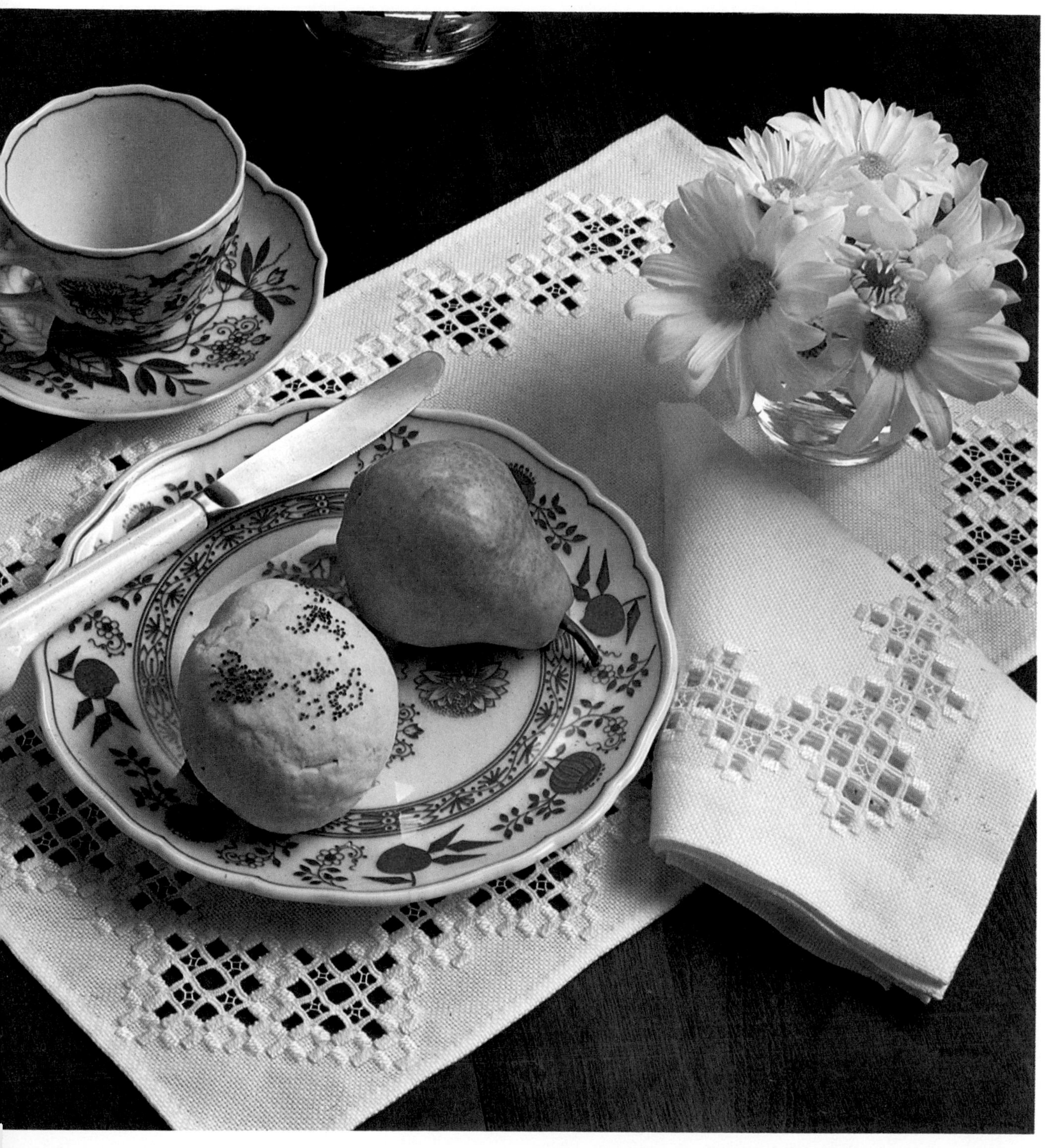

Hardanger Place Mat and Napkin *(continued)*

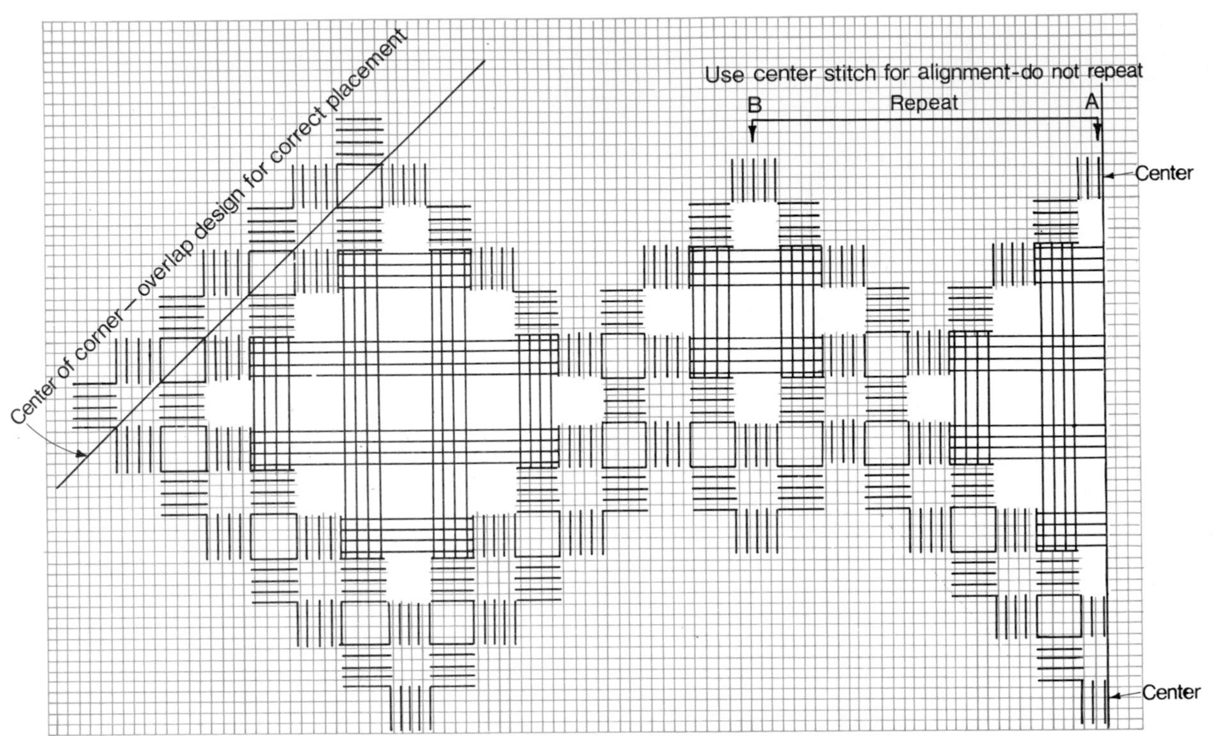

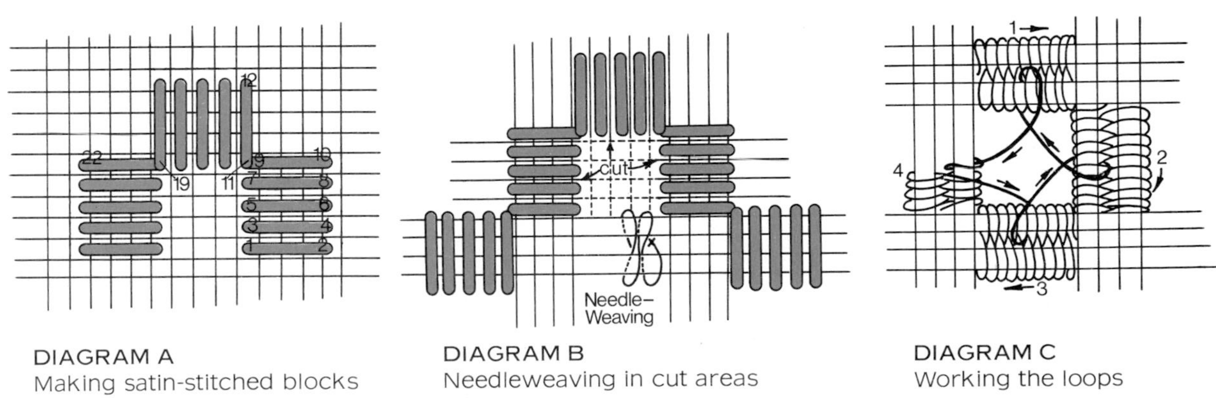

DIAGRAM A
Making satin-stitched blocks

DIAGRAM B
Needleweaving in cut areas

DIAGRAM C
Working the loops

Blackwork Embroidery Scroll

Directions

Enlarge the pattern on the next page and transfer it to fabric.

Work the design by filling numbered areas with stitch patterns shown on pages 380 and 381. Use the number of strands indicated in the chart. Varying the number of strands and the density of the patterns creates shading in the design.

To fill an area, begin in the center and work complete stitch patterns toward the edges. At the edges, work only a portion of the stitch pattern, if necessary. After filling, outline-stitch each shape using 2 strands of floss along the denser side of each pattern and 1 strand along the lighter side. Work the man in outline stitches. Use straight stitches for pine needles and grass.

Block the finished embroidery and stitch it to the satin backing fabric, leaving an opening for turning. Clip corners, turn, and press. Tack to dowels that have been cut to size and painted black. Add black beads at ends of dowels.

continued

Subtle shading is the key to this handsome blackwork embroidery piece, worked on white linen and accented with black details. The stitches are carefully counted and placed so that they gradually fade from dark to light.

Materials

7x10 inches #30-count even-weave linen, or 10x13 inches #18- or #22-count even-weave fabric (see note on page 380)
Black embroidery floss
Tapestry needle
10x13 inches white satin
16 inches of ¼-inch-diameter dowel
4 beads with ¼-inch holes
Black paint

Blackwork Embroidery Scroll *(continued)*

The stitch designs below are fillings to use in the embroidered scroll. Numbers and shading (dark, medium, and light) correspond to numbers and shading on the diagram at left. Use the number of strands of floss indicated on the shading chart, opposite. Embroider the patterns in backstitches, double running stitches, and running or darning stitches, working each stitch over the number of threads indicated by the lines on the chart.

1 Square = 1 Inch

Note: For #30-count fabric, enlarge the pattern to a scale of "one square equals one inch:" for #18- or #22-count fabric the scale is "one square equals 1½ inches." The finished size of the scroll on #30-count fabric is 5x7 inches; on other fabrics, it is about 8x11 inches.

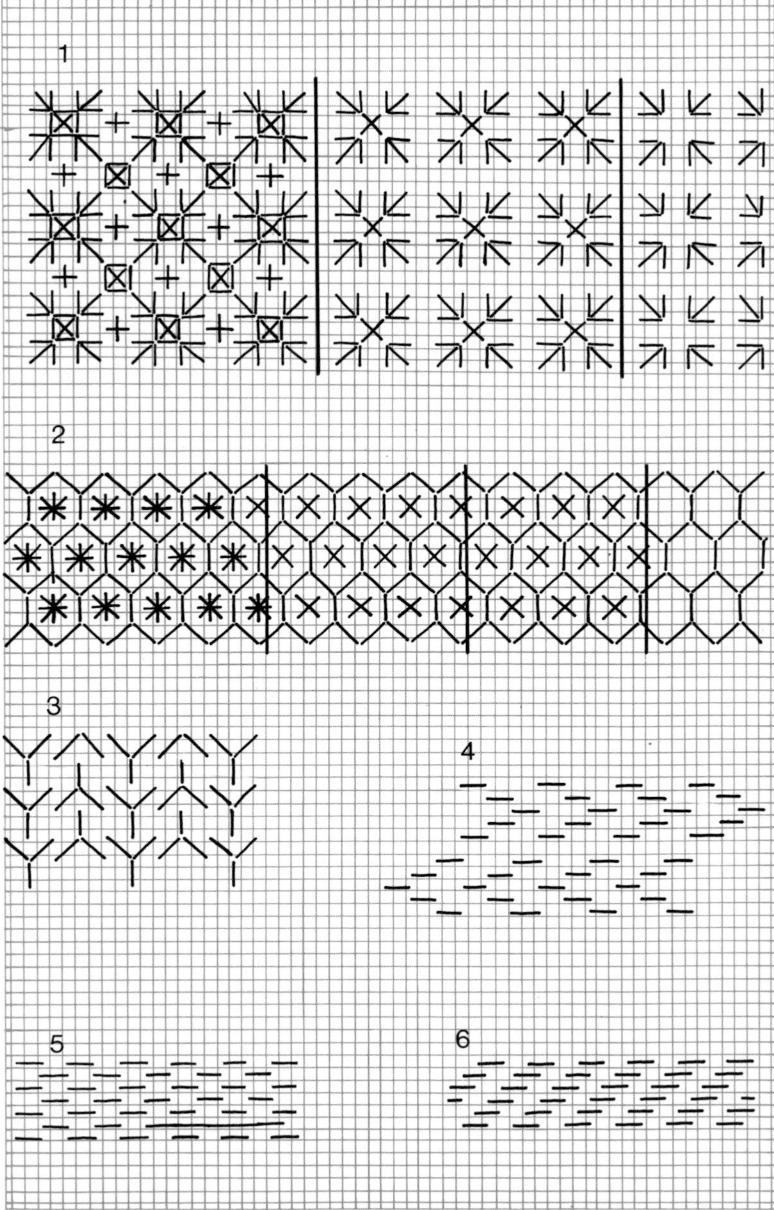

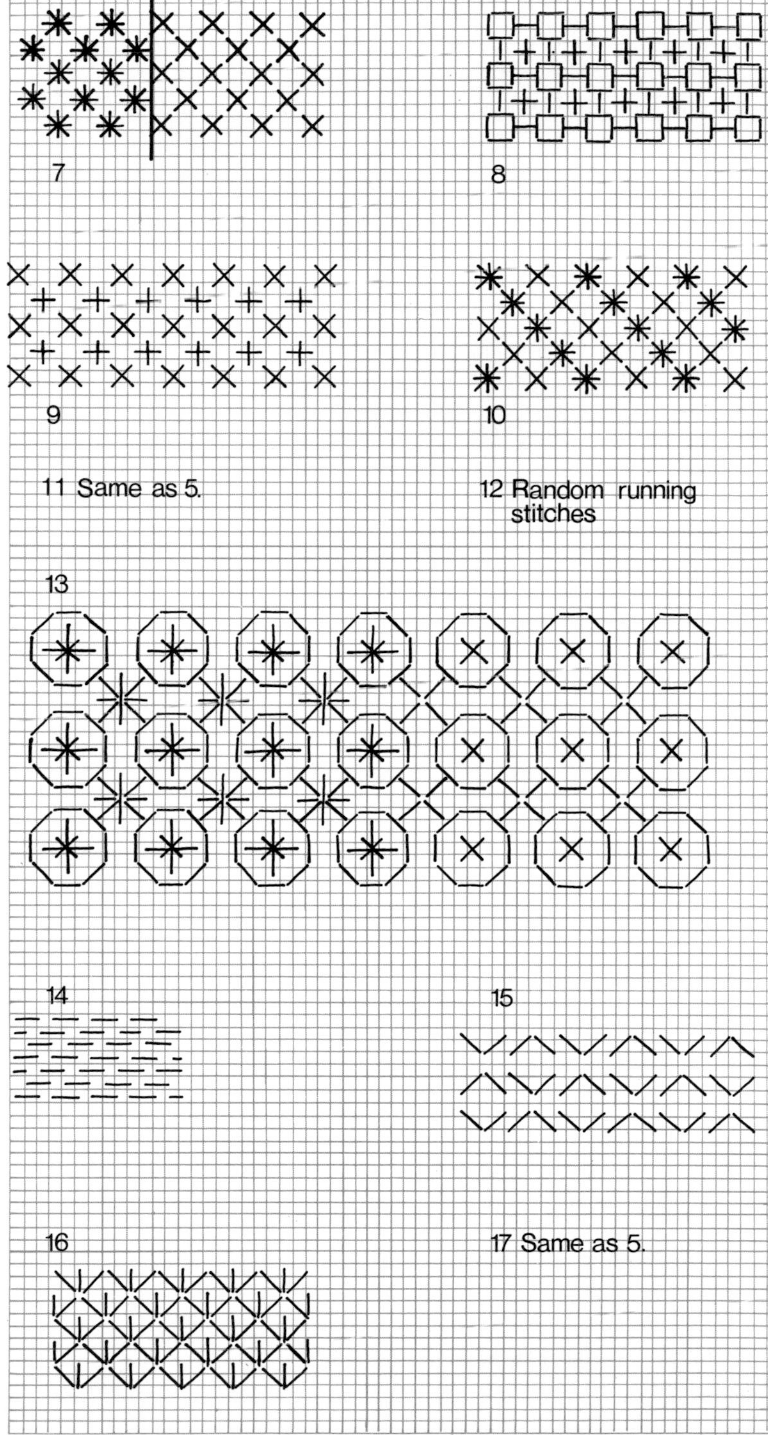

SHADING CHART

Pattern	Shade	Strands
1	Dark	2
	Medium	2
	Light	1
2	Dark	2
	Medium	2
	Medium	1
	Light	1
3		1
4		1
5		1
6		1
7	Dark	1
	Medium	1
8		1
9		1
10		1
13		1
14		1
15		1
16		1

Machine Embroidery

Whatever its make or model, your home sewing machine can stitch up a lot more than an occasional seam. For something new in embroidery, we suggest you try creative machine stitchery to make lovely and exciting accessories for your home. In this section, we have included projects ranging from simple crazy-quilt machine embroidery to the more challenging free-motion work shown in the curtains and pillowcase below. For how-to information, see pages 386 and 387.

Machine Embroidery Basics

If you have access to a sewing machine, you can do machine stitchery and enjoy all sorts of embroidered projects that you might not have time to work by hand. And while we won't deny that practice makes perfect, embroidering on your sewing machine is not difficult once you understand the basics of this kind of needlework.

On these two pages, you will learn some of the basics of machine stitchery that will guide you to successful completion of the projects that follow.

Fabrics

Any fabric can serve as a ground for machine embroidery, although some are easier to stitch on than others. Medium-weight, firmly woven fabrics in particular, such as denim or sailcloth, are easiest to learn on.

Lightweight fabrics, such as broadcloth and sheers, tend to pucker under the needle. Strengthen and stabilize them by backing them with a sheet of typing paper (be sure to pull it away after stitching). If you use iron-on interfacing, test a scrap of fabric with the interfacing before applying it—to be sure the adhesive does not mar the face fabric.

Also back medium-weight fabrics that need extra support with iron-on interfacing or typing paper.

Nubby and napped fabrics, such as terry cloth or velvet, do not take a pattern easily and can be hard to stitch. Solve these problems by drawing the pattern on tissue paper and basting or pinning it to the face of the fabric before inserting it into an embroidery hoop. Stabilize the fabric further with a layer of tissue or typing paper on the back (after stitching, remove paper).

When stitching heavy fabrics, such as upholstery-weight materials, or fabrics with naps that crush easily, do not use an embroidery hoop. Instead, keep the fabric taut with your fingers. Use the thumb and index fingers of each hand to hold fabric and feed it under the needle.

To embroider on knits and other fabrics that stretch, stabilize the back of the fabric with muslin or iron-on interfacing.

Threads

Any thread can be used for machine stitchery, although 100 percent cotton thread is preferable for most projects. Try cotton machine embroidery thread, using a larger thread (such as size 30) on the spool and a smaller thread (size 50) in the bobbin. For most projects, use white thread in the bobbin regardless of the color of the top thread—it will not show.

The heavier thread on the spool has a rich texture and fills the design faster than more slender thread. At the same time the smaller thread in the bobbin eliminates some of the bulk on the back of the fabric for a neater and more even finish.

Rayon, silk, and metallic machine embroidery threads are worth trying for their special effects. When buying metallic thread, though, be sure to choose thread that is smooth enough to feed evenly through the needle.

For some types of machine stitchery, transparent nylon thread is best. With it, you can invisibly couch yarns to fabric (for crewel work on the sewing machine). It is also useful for couching thick threads (including metallics) that cannot be stitched in the needle.

Equipment

Sharp sewing machine needles are a must for machine embroidery. Keep a supply of needles in various sizes on hand and change them often, using a new needle for every project.

For most machine stitchery, use an embroidery hoop to keep the fabric drum-tight under the needle. A round or oval hoop with a tension screw works well. It must be small enough in diameter to move under the needle without bumping the side of the machine. Wrap the inner ring with twill or bias tape to help keep the fabric taut.

Mount the fabric in the hoop upside down—so it will lie flat on the bed of the sewing machine with the design facing up.

Tighten the tension screw to hold the fabric firmly.

There is also an embroidery hoop available that is especially nice for machine work on light and medium-weight fabrics. The inner ring pops into a U-shaped channel in the outer ring.

Adjusting the Machine

Check your machine to see that it is in good working order before you begin. In particular, see that it is well-oiled, for embroidery requires more frequent lubrication of your machine than regular home sewing. Also, clean accumulated lint from the machine often—especially from the bobbin case.

Adjust the tension on the spool and the bobbin, if necessary. You may need to loosen the top tension slightly. To check tension adjustment, lower the presser bar and work some practice stitches on a piece of scrap fabric. Then check the position of the spool and bobbin threads on both sides of the material. The top thread should pull slightly to the underside of the fabric and the bobbin thread should not be visible on the face of the fabric.

Before stitching, check tension with a sample of the fabric to be embroidered to be sure the material does not pucker. If it does, loosen the tension.

Always lower the presser bar to engage the tension on the upper thread when you stitch, even for free-motion embroidery when there is no presser foot in place. Otherwise, thread does not feed properly through the machine and bobbin thread will pile up on the back of the fabric.

For free-motion embroidery, lower or cover the feed dogs under the needle and remove the presser foot. Set the stitch length at zero or fine, and the width on zigzag machines anywhere from narrow to wide, depending on the effect you are striving for.

For more on free-motion work, see page 386.

Working the Stitches

Once you have checked your machine and mounted your fabric firmly in an embroidery hoop, you are ready to begin creative machine stitchery. There are several kinds of embroidery that you may wish to try before you experiment with free-motion.

If you have decorative cams or stitches on your machine, use them in your embroidery. Our crazy-quilt place mats on page 388 are an example of this kind of embroidery.

You also can make attractive and decorative border designs using the fancy stitches on the machine. Simply combine the patterns, working them in complementary colors. See the diagrams at right for suggestions. Use an embroidery, darning, or other lightweight presser foot.

Decorative machine satin stitching makes an attractive edge on appliqué work. For this technique, first stitch the appliqué in place with medium-width, medium-length (10 to 12 stitches per inch) zigzag stitches. Trim excess beyond stitching.

Reset the machine for a wide but closely spaced, fine zigzag stitch (a machine satin stitch) and re-sew around the edges of the appliqué, machine-embroidering it in place. This is one of the techniques used on the tulip wall panel shown on page 390.

You may also wish to try free-motion embroidery using only straight stitches. For this technique, lower or cover feed dogs, remove the presser foot, and set stitch length at zero. Position the fabric under the needle, run the machine at a fairly fast speed, and "draw" with your needle—outlining and filling designs with straight stitches.

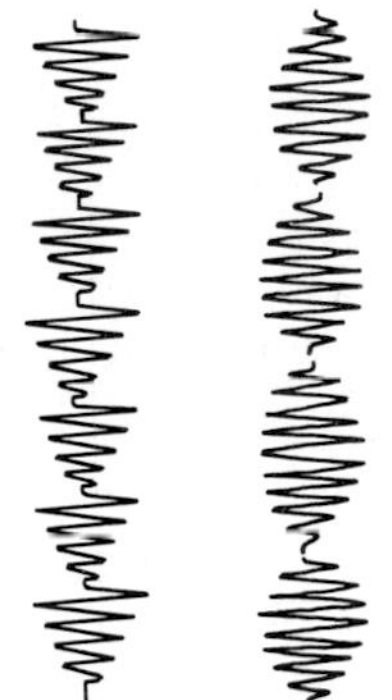

Decorative stitches

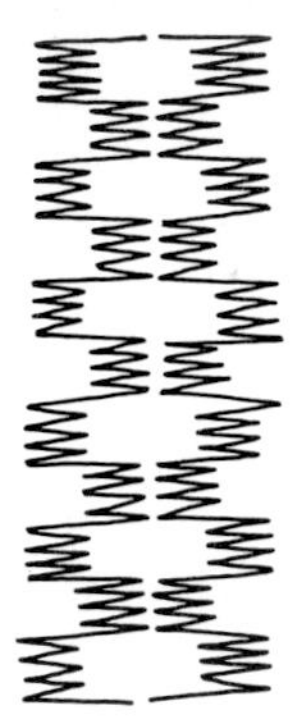

Using one pattern for a border

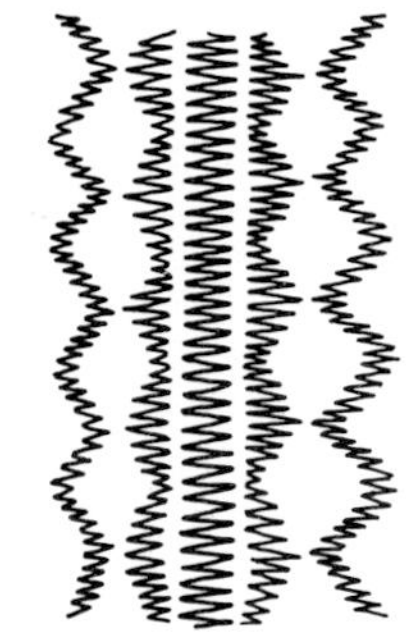

Combining patterns in a border

Machine-Embroidered Curtains and Pillowcase

(shown on pages 382 and 383)

The embroideries on the curtains and pillowcase on pages 382 and 383 are examples of free-motion work on a sewing machine. For this technique, you work without a presser foot, but lower the presser bar to establish tension. Directions here include how-to for the projects shown, plus helpful free-motion stitchery tips.

Materials
Purchased pair of ready-made curtains or draperies
Machine embroidery thread in green, red, yellow, and white
Embroidery hoop
Pillowcase

For a Fine Finish—Free-Motion Machine Embroidery

Whether you have a straight-stitch or a zigzag sewing machine, you can do free-motion embroidery. With either machine, once you lower the feed dogs and remove the presser foot, you are free to move the fabric under the needle in any direction and to draw and stitch creatively with your needle. But, because the position of the sewing machine needle is stationary, the position of the design to be embroidered and the way you move the hoop beneath the needle are important for attractive machine stitchery.

A good guide to get you started is to position and then move the embroidery hoop so the stitches cover the fabric in much the same direction as they would in hand embroidery. For example, to hand-embroider a stem in satin stitches, you would work slightly slanted stitches down the length of the stem. For machine work, then, turn the design slightly at an angle as you slide the hoop under the needle. For a fine line—comparable to outline-stitching by hand—work with the design sideways under the needle.

To fill a shape by hand, you might use long-and-short stitches. For example, in the leaf below at left, hand-embroidered stitches would extend upward from the vein to the outer edge. For machine work, turn the design in the hoop sideways so the machine stitches will fall in the same direction (see diagram below).

When filling shapes, first outline the edges with narrow zigzag stitches. Then cover the inside of the shape with rows of wider zigzag stitches, as shown in the leaf diagram, opposite.

If a shape can be divided, embroider small sections individually—just as in hand embroidery. For example, work the petals of a flower separately. Stitch the top of a leaf first, then the lower half—dividing the shape along the vein (see leaf diagram, opposite). Or divide a star into diamond-shaped sections and stitch.

Always work filling stitches in the same direction as outline stitches. Also, do not rotate or swing the hoop as you stitch; move it back and forth, from side to side.

Moving the hoop back and forth evenly takes some practice. To get used to it, draw a curved line on fabric, mount it in a hoop, and embroider the line without turning the hoop. Or write your name and embroider it—without rotating the hoop.

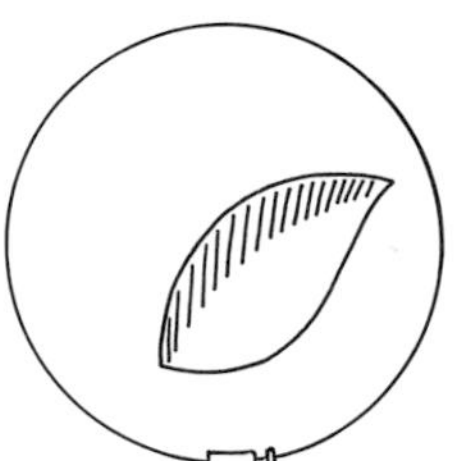

Mark direction of the stitches.

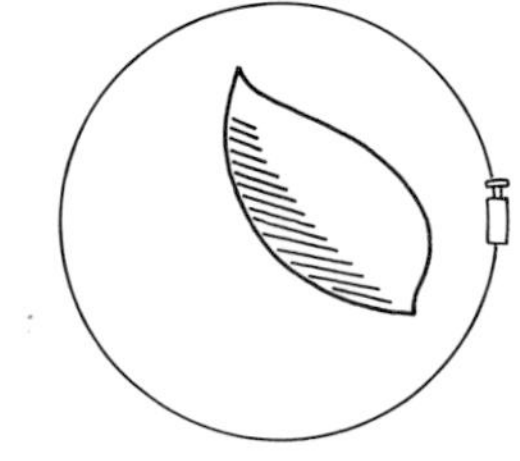

Turn the hoop sideways.

Directions

To embroider the curtains, first remove the hems. Make an iron-on transfer of the pattern below on tissue paper by tracing the design as many times as necessary to cover the width of the curtain. Then iron the pattern onto the curtain, positioning the lowest point in the design 1 inch from the hem fold.

Mount the fabric in a hoop; it must be taut. Place the design area under the needle sideways and work the stem in green thread. Do not rotate the hoop as you stitch—instead, move it back and forth. Work small buds in yellow thread.

With red thread, work the center section of the tulip first. Slide the hoop beneath the needle with the design turned sideways so the stitches fall vertically in the petal, as in the top diagram at right. Work side petals at an angle of about 45 degrees to the center, as shown in the top diagram at right. Finish by working a small circle at the base of the tulip to connect the side petals.

Clip all the threads close to the fabric and press the work into a terry cloth towel or other padded surface.

Replace the hem in the curtain by blindstitching by hand.

Stitch sections individually.

Outline and fill in the same direction.

For the pillowcase, use the pattern opposite. Machine-embroider the design following instructions above. The same pattern may be used along the top of a sheet for a matched set of linens.

Crazy-Quilt Patchwork Place Mats

These crazy-quilt place mats are machine-embroidered the easiest way—by using the decorative stitches or cams on your sewing machine to anchor colorful scraps to background fabric.

Materials

Scraps of cotton fabrics
¾ yard 36-inch-wide fusible interfacing (for 2 place mats)
1 yard solid-color backing fabric
Contrasting bias binding
Steam iron
Embroidery thread in colors to complement fabrics

Directions

Preshrink all cotton fabrics, including the backing fabric. Cut two 13x16-inch ovals from the fusible interfacing and two from the backing material.

Cut interesting shapes from cotton scraps in complementary colors and prints, referring to the photograph for ideas, if necessary. Place them wrong side down on the adhesive side of the fusible interfacing. Overlap the edges slightly. Press with an iron until the scraps adhere to the interfacing.

Set your sewing machine on one of its decorative settings, or insert a decorative cam. Using a contrasting thread color, stitch around each fabric scrap to conceal the raw edges. Combine several decorative stitches, if you wish, or use double needles threaded with same- or different-colored threads.

Place right sides of the place mat's front and back together. Sew a ½-inch seam around raw edge, leaving room for turning. Clip curves, trim seams, and turn right side out. Slip-stitch openings closed. Baste bias binding over raw edges and stitch.

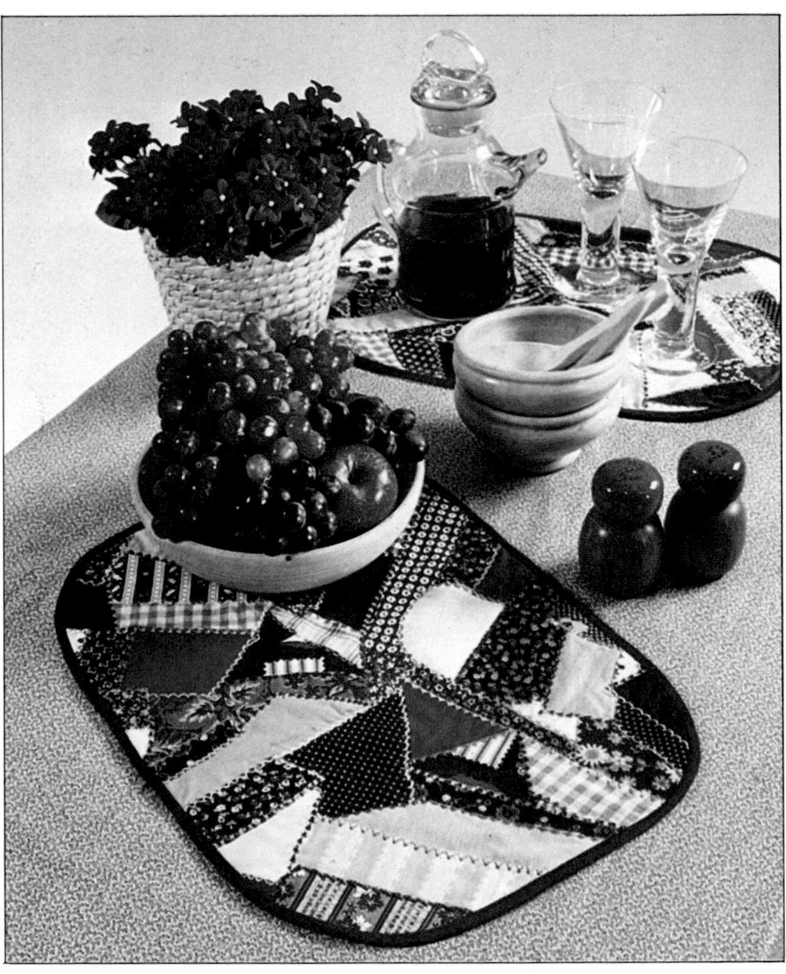

Machine-Embroidered Hardanger Place Mats

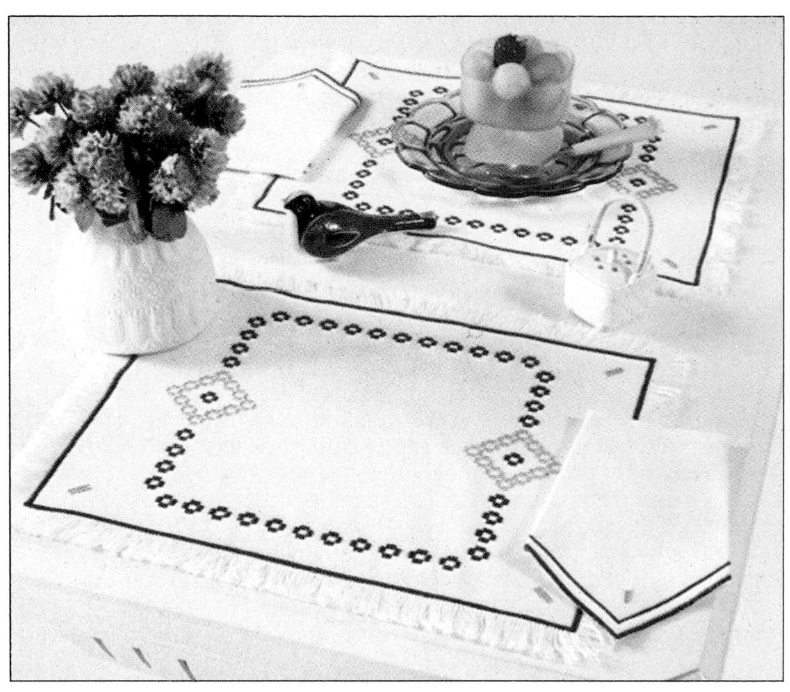

The simple beauty of machine stitchery is well-illustrated by these lovely place mats. Make them by bar-tacking—zigzag stitching back and forth across four threads of fabric, letting the embroidery thread build up on the fabric.

Even-weave fabrics are best for this technique, since their visible, interlocking threads act as a bar tacking guide as you stitch.

Materials

1⅛ yards of 42-inch-wide Hardanger cloth or other even-weave fabric (for 2 place mats and 2 napkins)
Light blue and dark blue embroidery thread
8-inch-diameter screw-type embroidery hoop
Tissue paper

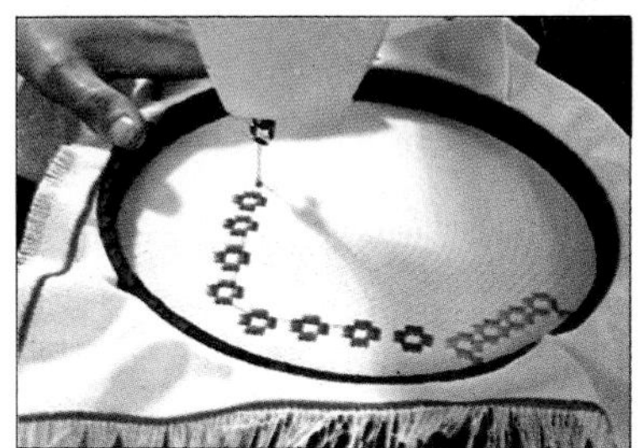

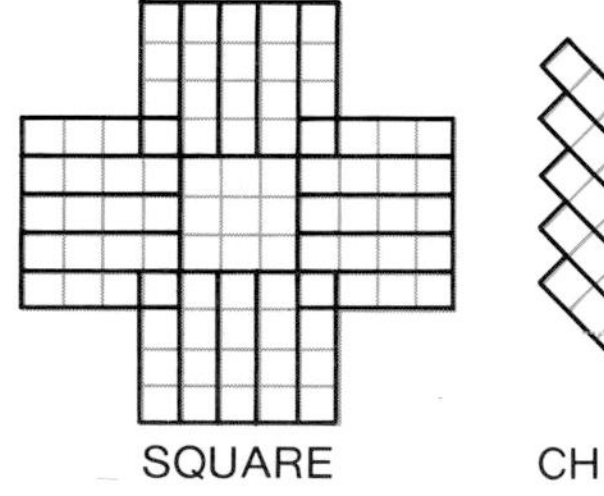

SQUARE

CHEVRON

Directions

Cut two pieces of fabric 16x13 inches for the place mats and two pieces 14x14 inches for the napkins. Set the machine for a wide zigzag stitch, and use dark blue thread on top and white thread in the bobbin. Lower the feed dogs and remove the presser foot.

Wrap inner hoop with bias tape to minimize creasing. Back place mats with tissue to prevent puckering, and clamp fabric in hoop right side up, with paper on the bottom (see photograph at right).

Referring to the photograph above for placement suggestions, follow the diagram at right to form bar-tacked squares and chevrons. Each zigzag stitch should cross 4 threads of the fabric.

Lower needle into fabric, and bring up bobbin thread. Bar-tack across 4 threads, repeating 5 times so threads build up on surface. Stitch 5 bar tacks side by side to form 1 side of the square.

With needle in top of fifth bar tack, pivot hoop so next series of bar tacks is perpendicular to first. Continue stitching and pivoting until there are 4 sets of 5 bar tacks around a common square. When finished, set stitch width to "0" and sew several stitches along side of bar tack to keep it from raveling.

Position needle for next set of bar tacks—about ¼ inch from first set—without cutting thread between bar-tacked squares.

When bar-tacked squares and light blue chevrons are completed, remove fabric from hoop. Sew a satin-stitched border 1 inch from raw edges and fringe, as shown. Trim all thread ends.

For napkins, satin-stitch a dark blue border ½ inch from the edge, with a second border ¼ inch inside the first. Add a light blue chevron in each corner. Trim fabric close to first border.

Machine-Embroidered Wall Hanging

Tulips are in full bloom on this cheerful wall hanging, made with a variety of techniques, including machine embroidery, appliqué, and quilting. The stuffed nylon bulbs add dimension.

Materials

14x20 inches light blue fabric
10x20 inches brown, medium-weight drapery fabric
6x20 inches tulip-red velvet
Embroidery thread in the following colors: light, medium, and dark green, dark red, red to match velvet, yellow, medium brown, and black
12x14½ inches muslin
6-inch and 10-inch narrow embroidery hoops
1 pair medium-brown nylon stockings
Scraps of polyester fiberfill
Two 1x14-inch strips of wood lath
2 brass decorative screw eyes

Color Key

A Dark Green
B Medium green
C Light green
D Red
E Dark red
F Yellow
G Medium brown
H Black

Directions

Lap brown fabric ¾ inch over blue. Set machine for longest stitch and widest bight and sew pieces together with 10 rows of zigzag stitches in three shades of green, overlapping rows to form a band of grass 1 inch wide.

Enlarge pattern onto tissue paper, center it on fabric, and pin and machine-baste outlines of the design. Tear away tissue paper.

Mount fabric in hoop. Using light presser foot, work stems first in medium-wide satin stitches. Refer to tips for free-motion work on page 386, and begin center tulip. Work leaves in rows of wide satin stitches, reducing stitch width as width of leaf decreases and to accent leaf tips. Accent center veins with narrow zigzag stitches.

Make a bulb shape about ¾ inch thick by wrapping stocking around stuffing. Allow some stocking to double over, creating dark and light areas. Pin to background, folding and pleating to form pointed tops of bulbs. Sew down with narrow zigzag stitches. Stitch edges with a second row of medium-wide satin stitches, accenting pointed tips and widening stitches at the base. For inner contours, quilt the fabric with narrow zigzag stitches through all layers.

Embroider roots with narrow black satin stitches. Cut tulip appliqués ½ inch larger than pattern. Pin in place, and mount fabric in embroidery hoop on *wrong* side. Zigzag outlines and inner contours with matching thread. Trim excess velvet on front. Reinsert fabric in hoop. Satin-stitch around petals, varying width of stitch from wide (bulbous curves) to narrow (points). Use narrow zigzag for veins and yellow accents; work stamen in black.

To finish, cut fabric to 18x18 inches. Stitch muslin to sides, right sides together. Turn, press, and turn under ⅛ inch on top and bottom. Turn up 2-inch hem; blindstitch in place. Insert lath through casing at top and hang, or sew curtain rings to corners for hanging.

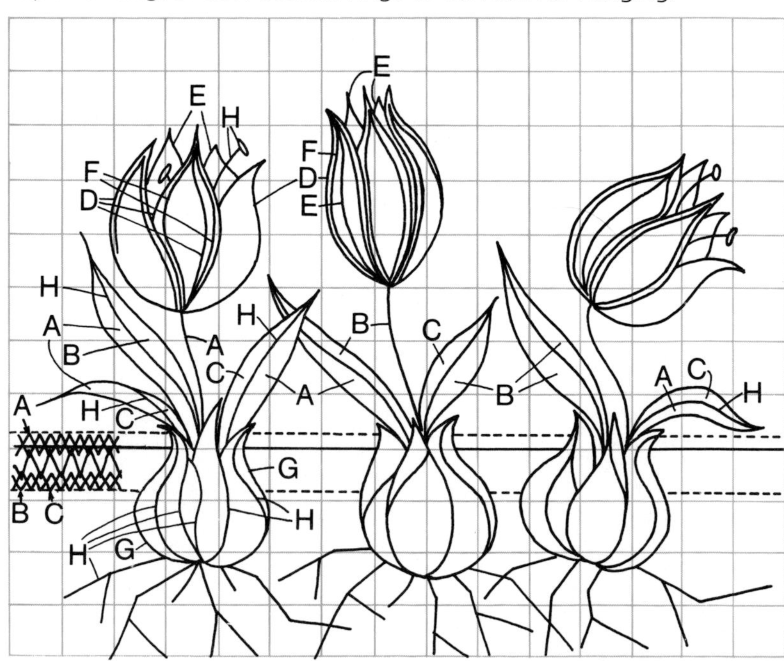

1 Square = 1 Inch

Special Stitchery Techniques

After mastering basic embroidery techniques, it is time to try something new and different. In this section, we go beyond conventional projects and introduce an entirely new repertoire of stitches and ideas. Shisha mirrors, metal threads, and tambour work are only the beginning—the possibilities are endless. Adapt the projects to fit your needs and the materials available to you. And stay flexible enough to incorporate your own ideas into the patterns and stitchery suggestions given here.

Special embroidery techniques are not necessarily more difficult. They simply allow more creativity—and that is what embroidery is all about. For instructions for this richly embroidered shisha fish, please turn to page 394.

Shisha Stitchery—Embroidered Fish

(shown on pages 392 and 393)

Shisha mirrors from India embellish our soft-sculpture fish. Anchored to the fabric with stitchery frames, they are complemented by a variety of simple stitches.

Patterns are on the next two pages.

Materials

½ yard unbleached muslin
⅓ yard brown cotton
¼ yard each of bright orange, beige, and gold cotton
Scraps of rust, burnt orange, and sand-colored fabrics
Quilting thread
Polyester fiberfill
#5 pearl cotton in gold, yellow, bright orange, burnt orange, and brown
36 shisha mirrors
Embroidery needles

Directions

Enlarge the pattern pieces on pages 395 and 396, adding ½-inch seam allowances. Cut pattern pieces in the colors and amounts indicated on the pattern.

Pin the face to the front body piece, turning under the seam allowance on the curve (not the outer margins). Attach a shisha mirror for the eye, following the directions below. Use brown pearl cotton to attach the mirror.

Embellish the fish's eye with additional stitchery, referring to the pattern and to the photograph on pages 392 and 393 for suggestions. Embroider the mouth and the curve of the face. Then set the face and front body piece aside.

Baste together fin #1 and its matching muslin piece (facing). Hand- or machine-quilt the two pieces together along the lines indicated on the pattern. Use pearl cotton for the quilting, in a color that contrasts with the fabric. Add embroidered French knot accents, as shown in the photograph.

continued

Shisha Stitch

1. Hold the shisha mirror in place with your finger or a dot of glue. Bring the thread up at A, close to the mirror, and down at B. Continue, following the diagram at right, to make a square of stitches over the mirror that secure it to the fabric.
2. Repeat the four stitches above, making a second square diagonal to the first. The two squares make the frame holding the mirror.
3. Bring the thread up close to the edge of the mirror and loop it around the threads of the frame making a stitch similar to a buttonhole stitch. Pull the thread tight.
4. Take a small stitch in the fabric along the edge of the mirror, as shown. Hold the thread under the needle.
5. Wrap the thread around the frame again, as in step 3.
6. Tack into the fabric along the edge of the mirror again, placing this stitch next to the stitch made in step 4.

Continue making stitches around the mirror, following steps 5 and 6. Be sure to pull the thread snug with each stitch.

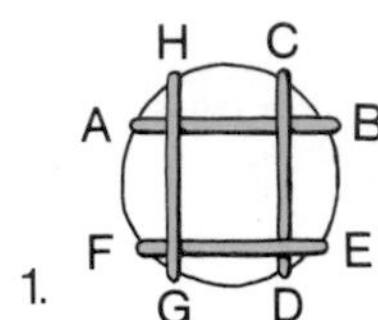

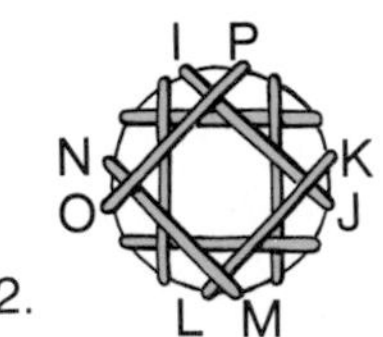

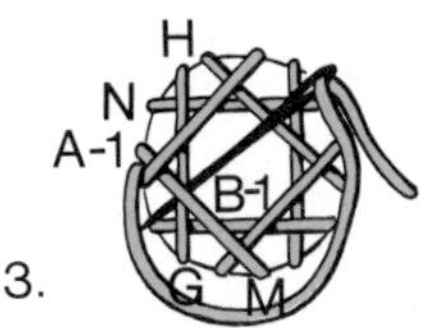

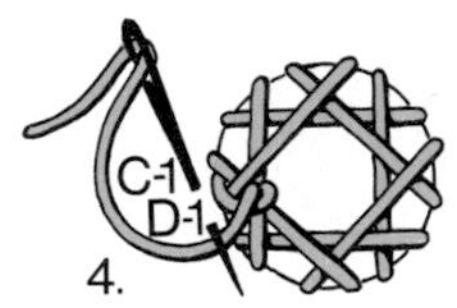

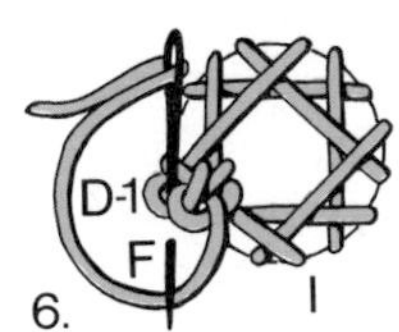

Shisha Stitchery—Embroidered Fish *(continued)*

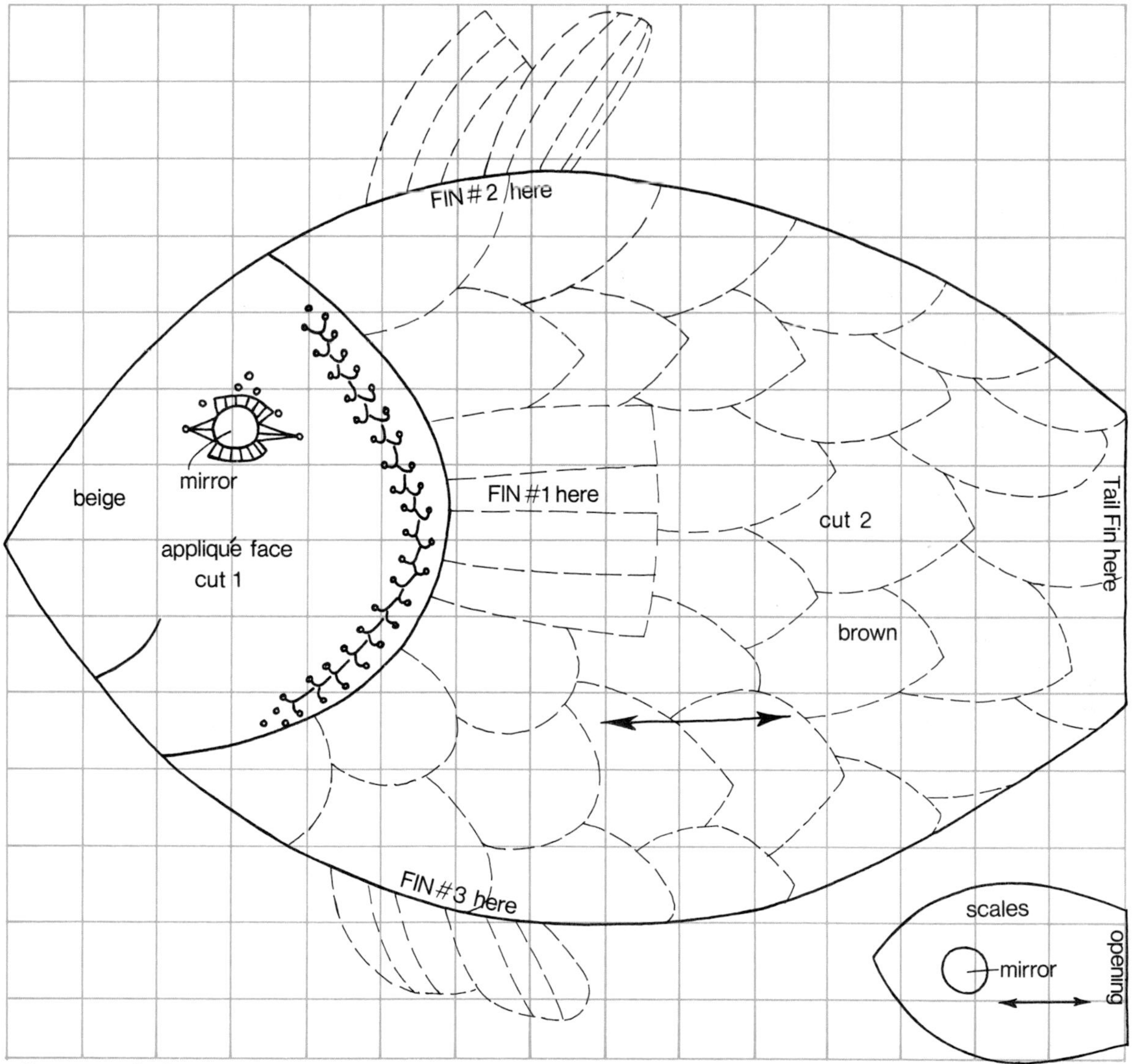

FIN #2 here
beige
mirror
appliqué face
cut 1
FIN #1 here
cut 2
brown
Tail Fin here
FIN #3 here
scales
mirror
opening

1 Square = 1 Inch

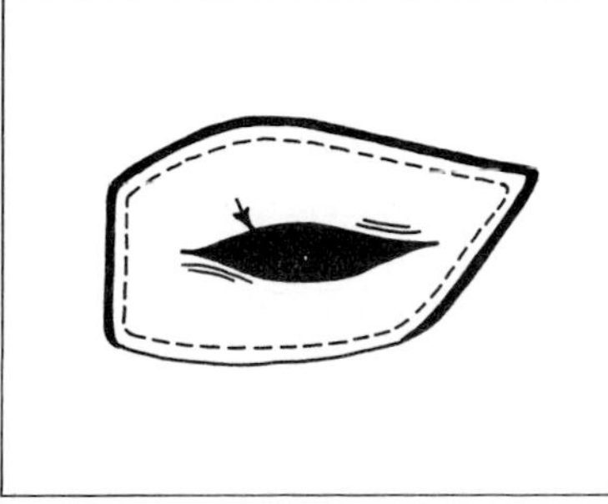

Next, trapunto-quilt individual sections of the fin, referring to the diagram at left, if necessary. In the center of each section, make a slit through the muslin only—not through the face fabric—and stuff lightly. Use an orange stick to push stuffing gently into corners, if necessary. Slip-stitch the opening.

With right sides facing, sew together the front and back fin #1 pieces, leaving the end open. Clip the curves and turn right side out. Stuff lightly and baste the fin closed along the seam line of the opening.

Before stitching the front pieces to the backs, complete fins #2 and #3 and the tail fin in the same manner, adding embroidered accents and shisha mirrors (to the tail fin) as shown on the pattern.

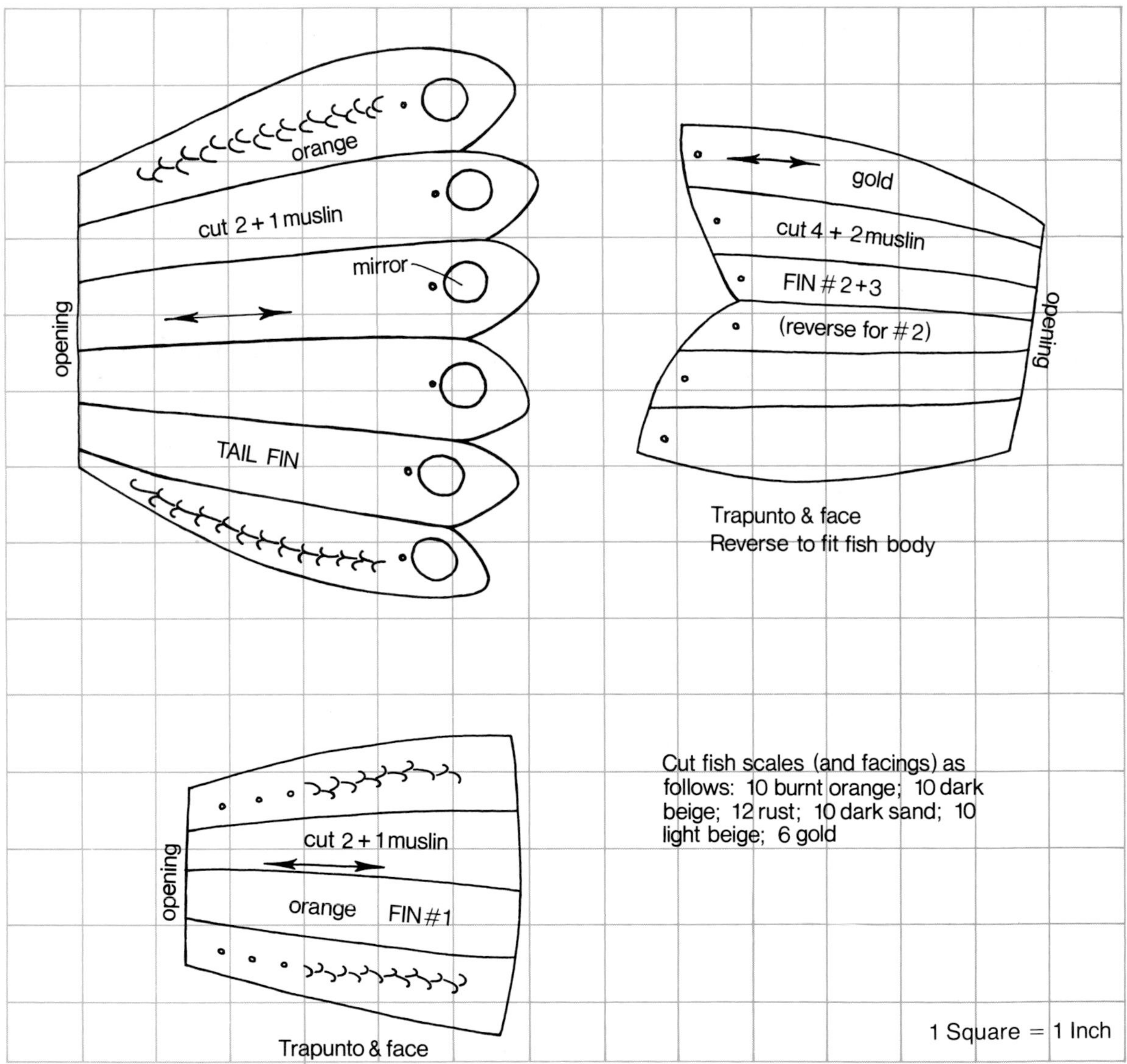

Stitch shisha mirrors to the tips of half of the fish "scales," as indicated on the pattern. Add additional embroidery to highlight the mirrors. We used French knots, buttonhole, lazy daisy, and straight stitches in a variety of colors.

Complete each "scale" by sewing a plain piece to an embroidered one, right sides together, along the curved edges. Turn, stuff lightly, and slip-stitch the openings closed.

To assemble the fish, pin fin #3 under the facepiece, referring to the photograph if necessary. Sew the face to the body with running stitches, catching the fin in the seam. Baste together raw edges of face and body front on the seam line.

Pin the fins to the body front, raw edges even. Sew together front and back body pieces with right sides facing, catching the fins in the seam. Leave an opening for turning. Turn the fish right side out, stuff, and slip-stitch the opening.

Using the photograph on pages 392 and 393 as a guide, tack scales to front, overlapping slightly. Vary placement so that two scales of the same color do not fall next to each other.

Creative Stitchery Sampler—Moon Flowers

(shown on page 399)

Directions

Cut a 36x40-inch piece of brown burlap and hand-baste a 2-inch margin around all four sides to delineate the design area.

Enlarge diagram A on page 398 onto tissue paper and cut each outlined pattern piece from your choice of fabrics and colors. Because this stitchery is meant to be a sampler, a variety of colors and textures in fabrics and stitches will add much to the design. As you choose, bear in mind that the colors you select and the textures of the fabrics will influence the mood of your picture. Also keep in mind the materials you have on hand.

Apply a *thin* line of white glue around the edges of each cut fabric piece to keep them from raveling. It will dry clear.

Assemble a 32x36-inch frame with stretcher strips. Make sure corners are square and then stabilize them with staples or corrugated fasteners to keep the wood from shifting as you work. Using thumbtacks, attach the basted burlap to the frame along all four sides. This provides a sturdy working area as you experiment with the placement of fabric to make a pleasing arrangement of shapes.

Pin the shapes to the burlap as you decide on placement. If you are dissatisfied with the color or placement of a piece, cut a new pattern piece and replace the original.

When all the fabric pieces have been attached, remove the burlap from the frame. Hand-baste the shapes to the burlap, as shown in the top photograph on page 398.

Embroider the large pieces onto the burlap using any appropriate stitch. We used buttonhole, stem, chain, and straight stitches for the tree forms. Leaf forms consist of leaf, satin, buttonhole, stem, and chain stitches. Moon and flower forms contain backstitches and chain, buttonhole, French knot, and straight stitches. Several of the circular shapes contain a series of closely spaced buttonhole stitches that are threaded with a second color yarn. Add as much embroidery as you like, using any number of strands of thread to vary textures and emphasize color and form. Refer to the photographs on pages 398 and 399 for ideas. (Those on page 398 contain close-up views of the stitchery.) See the Glossary on pages 406 to 409 for stitch how-to.

See diagram B on page 398 to determine the outline of completed embroidery areas in our stitchery painting.

These suggestions can form the basis for your own unique stitchery painting, but remember—there is much room here for individual expression. Feel free to combine different stitches and to improvise or change the pattern as desired. Alter the design to suit your own needs and preferences and to use materials you have on hand in your own workbasket of threads and fabrics.

Gently press the finished embroidery on the wrong side.

Place the stitchery right side down on a flat surface. Center the wooden frame on top of the wrong side, using the stitchery's 2-inch basting as a centering guide. Starting in the center of each side, pull the burlap fabric from the front to the back of the frame; secure the fabric with staples. End by stapling along the sides to the corners, pulling the fabric tightly as you move around the frame. Remove all basting stitches.

Protect the front of the stitchery with a light coating of soil-retardant finish. Add a purchased frame if desired, or make a frame of 1x3-inch boards covered with additional burlap as we did.

continued

This delightful 32x36-inch embroidered painting entitled "Moon Flowers" is a challenging sampler piece. Here is your chance to perfect stitches you already know and experiment with new ones.

Use small pieces of purchased fabrics or leftovers from previous sewing projects to create this fantasia of embroidery and appliqué. As you stitch, adapt the design to suit your decor.

Materials

Note: Make use of any leftover fabric or yarn.

1½ yards brown burlap (background)

¾ yard pink fabric

¾ yard coral fabric

Black, brown, and green fabric scraps

Scraps of pink velvet

Green and gold burlap

Pink netting

Assorted fabrics in shades of yellow and green

Off-white, brown, yellow, green, coral, rose, and powder pink pieces of yarn in different plies and textures

Two 32-inch artist's stretcher strips

Two 36-inch artist's stretcher strips

Thumbtacks

Tissue paper

White glue

Soil-retardant spray

Creative Stitchery Sampler—Moon Flowers *(continued)*

Basting the appliqué pieces

Working the embroidery

The finished result

1 Square = 2 Inches

B

1 Square = 2 Inches

Metal Thread Work—Embroidered Panel

To add some sparkle to your stitchery, work with metal threads. While several kinds of silver can be used for embroidery, the stitchery panel shown opposite is worked in a twisted thread that is widely available at a modest price. Small beads and white floss add to the design.

If you have not worked in metal threads before, we think you will find this small project easy and fun to stitch.

Materials

9x15 inches green fabric
3-ply silver thread
1-ply silver thread
White embroidery floss
Black embroidery floss
Embroidery needles
6½x12-inch piece of cardboard
Twelve ⅛-inch-diameter transparent beads
Seventy 1/16-inch-diameter pearly beads

Directions

Enlarge the pattern and transfer it, centered, to the fabric following directions on pages 272 and 273. Work the design in metallic threads and floss according to the color and stitch keys. Numbers in parentheses indicate the number of strands of thread to use.

Mount the finished embroidery on a piece of cardboard, following the directions below. Frame, if desired.

For A Fine Finish — Blocking and Mounting

Blocking and mounting are simple finishing procedures that add much to your embroidery. If your fabric has pulled out of shape while being stitched, straighten it by blocking. Then, if it is a piece that requires mounting, finish it for hanging.

Stitchery worked in a hoop or frame should not need much blocking. Remove it from the frame and steam-press it gently (on low heat) on the wrong side over a thickly padded ironing board. Pin it to the board to hold it in place, if necessary, and use a damp cloth between the fabric and the iron. If colors might run, insert a dry cloth between the stitchery and the damp cloth.

If you have worked the embroidery in your lap, block it on a board with pins, tacks, or staples. Use cork or insulation board and T-pins (used for macrame) or plywood and thumbtacks or staples. Pad the board first with soft toweling. Use 1-inch checked gingham for the top layer of padding—it is an easy reference for straightening the grain of the fabric and sizing the embroidery.

Pin or staple the padding to the board. Lay the embroidery over the padding, facedown, and secure it in the *center* of each side. Then gently stretch it and secure it to the board, working from the center toward the corners. Insert pins or staples into the margins of the fabric only. Keep grain lines straight and fabric taut. Finally, dampen the fabric and let it dry thoroughly.

If the piece is to be mounted and it ravels easily, stay-stitch the edges by hand or machine. Otherwise, finish the edges following directions for your particular project.

Mount the embroidery in one of two ways: use heavy cardboard for small pieces, and artist's stretcher strips or plywood for larger ones. Be sure corners of stretcher strips are square; stabilize them with corrugated fasteners. Mark corners of plywood or cardboard with a T-square to be sure they are right angles.

Soften the appearance of the embroidery against a hard backing by padding with quilt batting, thin foam, or fleece cut to size.

Lay blocked embroidery facedown and center padding over it. (If desired, baste around outlines of the finished piece beforehand for easier centering of padding and backing board.) Center the backing board on top. Pull the edges of the fabric over the board, and staple or tack, starting in the center and working toward the corners. Keep grain lines straight.

When using cardboard, hold edges in place with tape. Then, using heavy-duty thread, sew the raw edges together with long zigzag stitches from top to bottom and side to side. Remove tape.

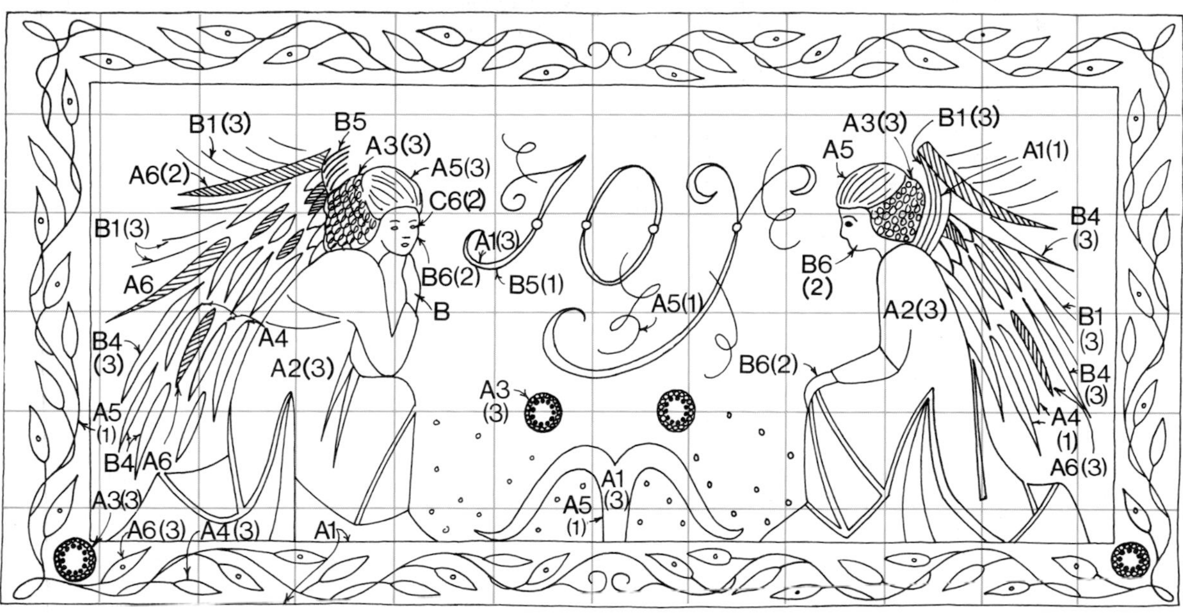

1 Square = 1 Inch

Color Key
A Silver
B White
C Black

Stitch Key
1 Chain stitch
2 Long-and-short stitch
3 French knot (loose)
4 Leaf stitch
5 Outline stitch
6 Satin stitch

Sew transparent beads in clusters of three on the JOY as indicated. Use smaller, pearly beads in circles and between the two angels.

Tambour Work—Mediterranean Pillow

Tambour work is chain stitched embroidery done with a crochet hook. Designs with large areas of solid filling can be worked quickly, easily, and attractively in this unusual technique.

While tambour work is often done with pearl cotton or another twisted thread, this design from Greece is worked in soft wools.

Materials

26x26 inches of white wool
26x26 inches of backing fabric
3-ply Persian wool in the following colors: white, medium and light copen blue, medium and light rose, medium brown, light gray-green, olive, forest green, and light and dark yellow
Embroidery hoop or frame
Size 7 crochet hook
24-inch square pillow form

1 Square = 1 Inch

Directions

The pattern is for one quarter of the pillow. Enlarge it, reversing as necessary, and transfer it to the wool. Mount the fabric firmly in a frame until it is *taut*. Use one strand of yarn throughout, referring to the photograph for color placement.

Anchor the yarn on the underside of the fabric and work with one hand under the frame guiding yarn over the hook, and the other hand on top working the hook. For each stitch, insert the hook into the fabric and draw up a loop ⅛ to ¼ inch long. Drop the loop off the hook. Insert the hook into the top of the loop just made, reinsert it into the fabric, and bring up the next loop. Continue in this way along the line of the design motif.

To master the sequence of motions involved in each stitch, you may want to practice on scrap fabric before beginning the pillow.

Outline each shape first. Then fill shapes by working from the outer edge toward the center in rows of chain stitches. For example, to work the round flower shapes on the pillow, first work the center dot in rose or blue. Next, work the outer edge of the petal shape in one row of white. Fill the space between the center and the white edge with rows of color, as shown in the photograph. Finish by working rows of chain stitches radiating from the central, petaled motif to the outer edge, as indicated on the pattern. Use dotted lines as guides for the length of the narrow "petals." Work rows close together, covering the background fabric.

Block the finished embroidery; sew the top to the back along three sides in a 1-inch seam. Insert pillow form and slip-stitch.

Middle Eastern Pillow

In many tambour embroideries, the background fabric is completely covered with stitches—as in this pillow from the Republic of Kashmir.

For another design to work with a hook, see the pillow on page 338.

Materials
17x17 inches #22-count Hardanger
17x17 inches backing fabric
Size 7 crochet hook
3-ply Persian wool in the following colors: navy blue, cream, brownish-gold, dark and light gold, light nile green, gray, light teal blue, scarlet, dark and light rose, peach, brown, and green
Embroidery hoop or frame
15-inch square pillow form

1 Square = 1 Inch

Directions
Enlarge the pattern at right, reversing it for the opposite side of the design. Following directions on page 166, transfer the design to the even-weave fabric, allowing a 1-inch margin on all sides of the pattern for the seams.

Mount the fabric in a hoop or frame so it is drum-tight. If you are using an embroidery hoop, you may want to wrap the inner ring with bias or twill tape—either one will help the ring grip the fabric firmly when the tension screw on the hoop is tightened. Prop the edge of the hoop against a table while you work the design so both hands are free for the embroidery.

Work the design following the directions for stitching explained with the Mediterranean Pillow, opposite.

Use one strand of yarn for the embroidery and refer to the photograph above for the placement of colors. Fill in the flower shapes and the urn first. Next, work the vines, stems, and leaves.

Add interest to the navy blue background by embroidering some of it in rows of chain stitches that outline the floral shapes and the urn. But work those areas marked with dotted lines on the pattern (at right) in spirals.

Work the cream background of the border in rows that outline the floral shapes, covering the fabric completely.

Block the finished embroidery, following directions on page 400. With right sides facing, stitch the pillow front to the backing fabric in a 1-inch seam. Leave an opening for turning. Turn the pillow cover right side out. Insert the pillow form, and slip-stitch.

Stitchery with Shells and Beads

This shell-and-stitchery wall hanging is made from beachcombing finds. If you do not have an assortment of shells handy, purchase a dimestore collection and work them into this unique design. Most of the fun of this project is in the variety of stitchery techniques you can incorporate in your version of this handsome hanging.

Materials

5 sand dollars
5 half-shells
20 seed pearls
Center shell (or group of shells)
Small mirror
½ yard off-white textured homespun fabric (background)
½ yard medium-weight muslin (interfacing)
¾ yard off-white, closely woven fabric (backing and edging)
Off-white yarn
16½-inch piece of ½-inch wooden dowel
2 large wooden beads
2 smaller wooden beads
2 finishing nails
Embroidery needle
Embroidery hoop
White glue

Directions

Note: The finished size of the wall hanging is 16x15½ inches.

Lay out the background and interfacing fabric (muslin). Assemble your shell collection and divide the shells by size into groups.

Begin laying out the arrangement with the center shell. Then arrange medium-size shells in groups of threes and fives around the center. Fill in the arrangement with clusters of the smallest shells and seed pearls. Leave a 3-inch margin around the design.

Mark the positions of the shells and pearls with pins or light pencil marks and remove the shells.

Set the fabric and interfacing into a large embroidery hoop. Attach the center shell first, as a guide for the placement for the remaining ones. If the center shell has a hole in it, attach a small shisha mirror underneath it (directions for the shisha stitch are on page 394). Glue shells in place before stitching, if desired. Attach them with free-form stitching and couching, using off-white yarn. (For stitch suggestions, see the Glossary on pages 406 to 409.)

Attach shells with holes by bringing the needle through from the back of the fabric, up through the hole in the shell, and returning on the outside of the shell. Follow the natural ridges on the shells for interesting effects.

Hold shells without holes in place in one of two ways. On small shells, work a straight stitch across the width of the shell and bring up the thread again at the edge of the shell. Loop the needle around the straight stitch and reinsert it in the fabric at the rim of the shell, as was done on the half-shells surrounding the center of the hanging. Anchor larger shells, such as sand dollars, with yarn "crosses" or couching, using enough stitches to hold shells securely in place. Attach larger shells first, then add clusters of smaller shells and pearls. Fill in the design with loose French knots, chain ring stitches, long straight stitches—whatever your imagination and the shells themselves suggest by way of shape and size.

When the stitchery collage is finished, remove it from the hoop. Cut a 16x15½-inch piece of backing fabric and trim the face fabric and the interfacing to the same size. Baste all layers together.

Bind the edges with the remaining backing fabric. Cut two 3x16-inch strips for the top and bottom edges, two 3x19-inch strips for the sides, and two 3x5-inch strips for the central hanging tabs.

Fold each tab in half lengthwise, and press. Fold the long raw edges under ¾ inch. Blindstitch the folded edges together.

With right sides together, lay the top and bottom binding strips on the embroidered fabric; pin. Tuck the raw edges of the tabs between the face fabric and the binding strip at the top, positioning them as shown in the photograph. Stitch both top and bottom edges in a ¾-inch seam. Turn the edging back, and press. Turn under the raw edges of the strips ¾ inch on the back and blindstitch in place, tucking in the remaining short ends of the tabs.

Lay binding strips along the sides, allowing ½ inch to extend beyond the bottom of the collage. Stitch in a ¾-inch seam. Finish as for top and bottom binding strips, turning the raw edges under at the bottom. Turn down the fabric remaining at the top to make side hanging loops. Stitch across loops at top, as shown.

Slip finishing nails through small beads and then through larger ones, and drive nails into ends of dowel. Slip the dowel between the tabs for hanging, as shown.

Basic Embroidery Stitches

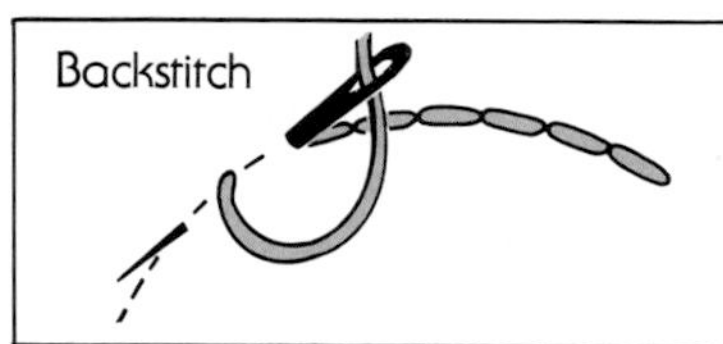
Backstitch

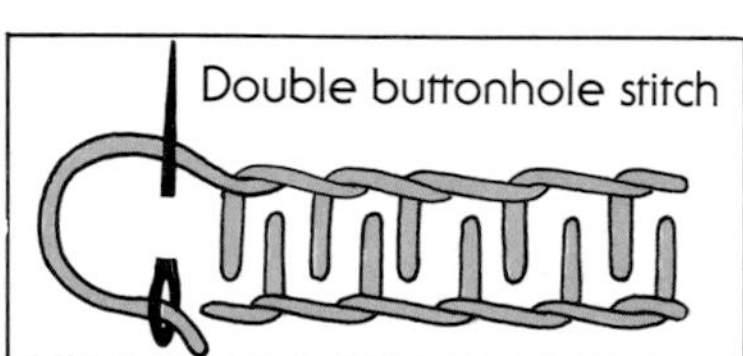
Double buttonhole stitch

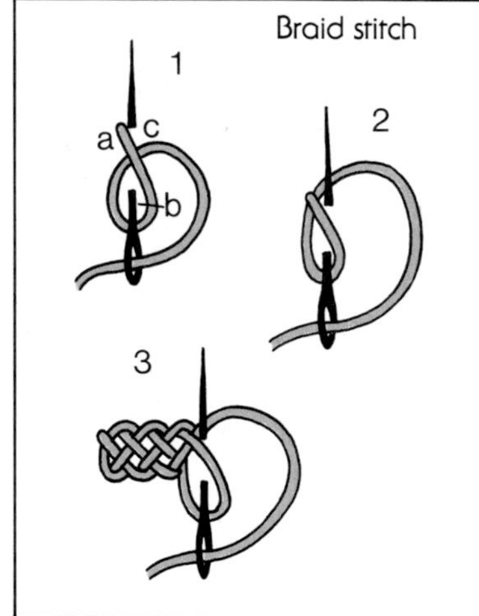
Braid stitch
1
a
c
b
2
3

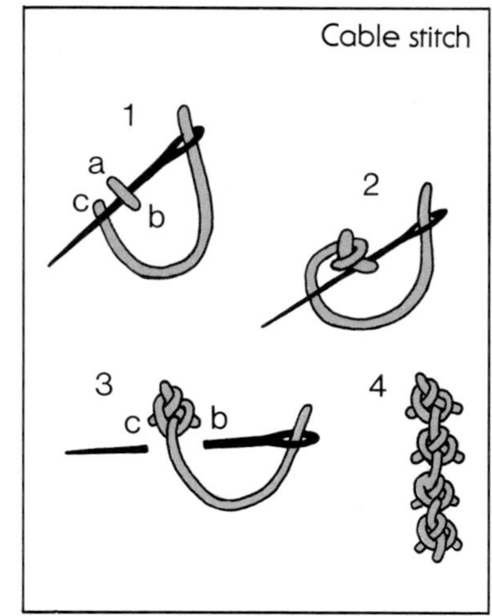
Cable stitch
1
a
c
b
2
3
c
b
4

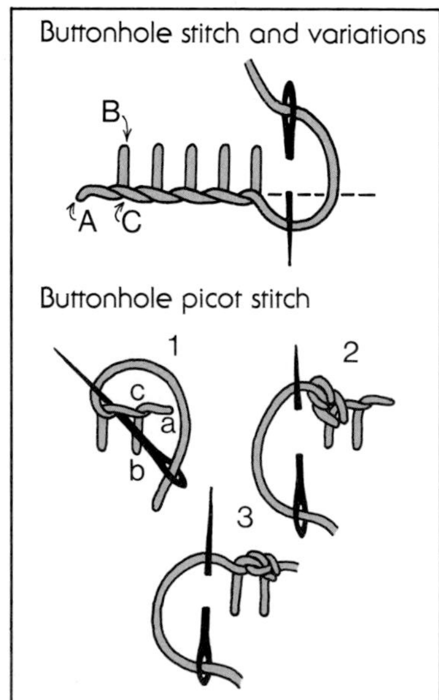
Buttonhole stitch and variations
B
A
C
Buttonhole picot stitch
1
c
a
b
2
3

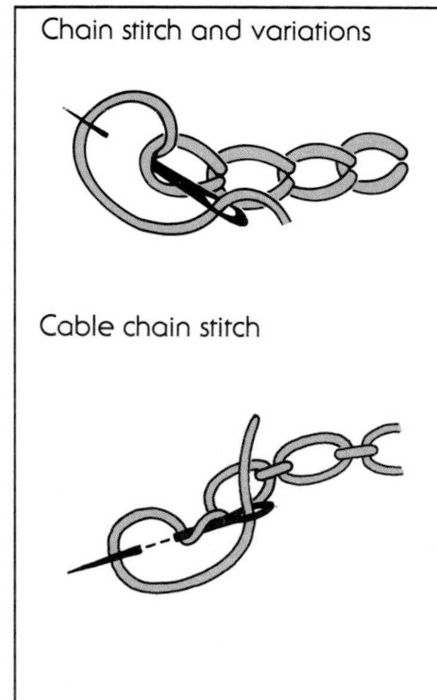
Chain stitch and variations
Cable chain stitch

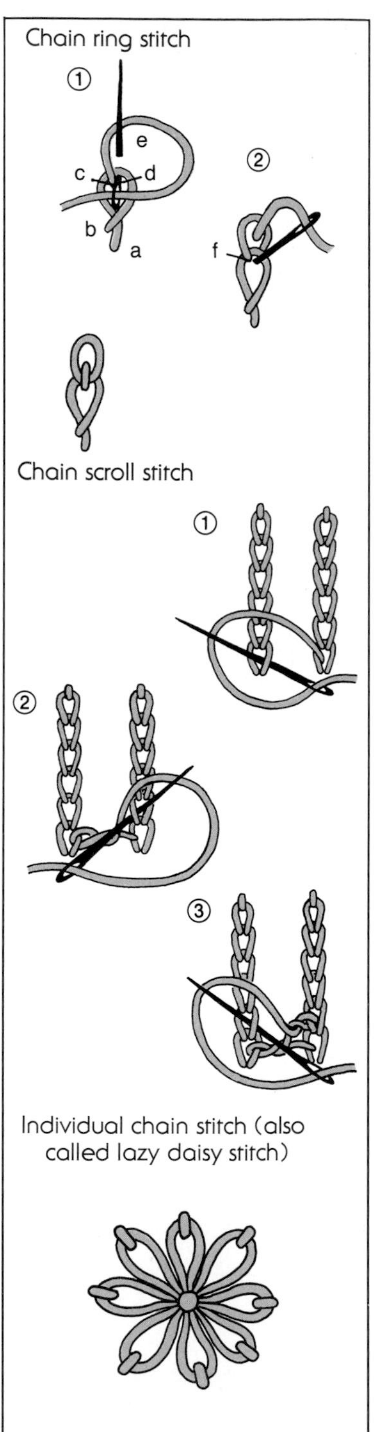
Chain ring stitch
①
e
c
d
b
a
②
f
Chain scroll stitch
①
②
③
Individual chain stitch (also called lazy daisy stitch)

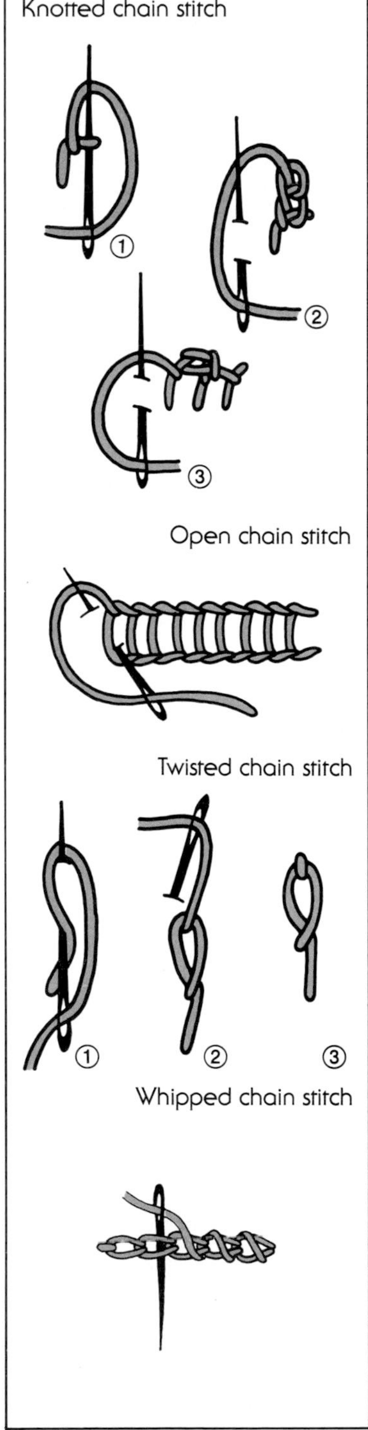
Knotted chain stitch
①
②
③
Open chain stitch
Twisted chain stitch
①
②
③
Whipped chain stitch

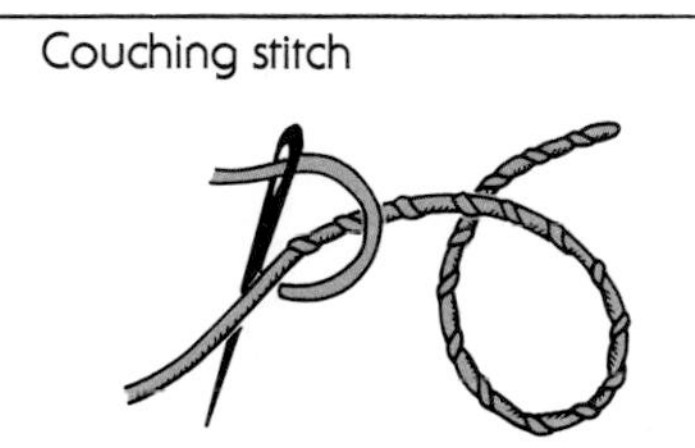
Couching stitch

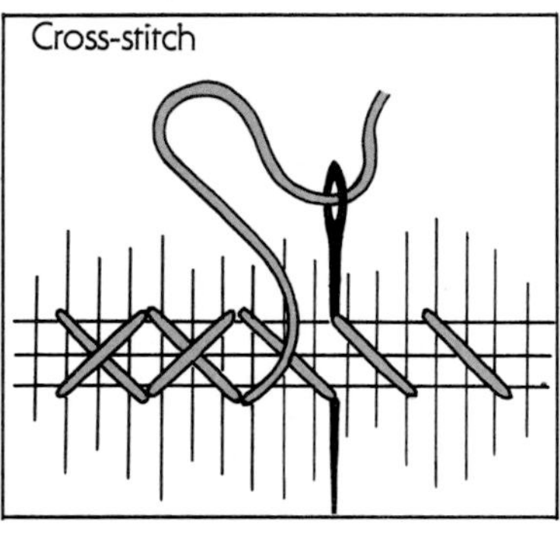
Cross-stitch

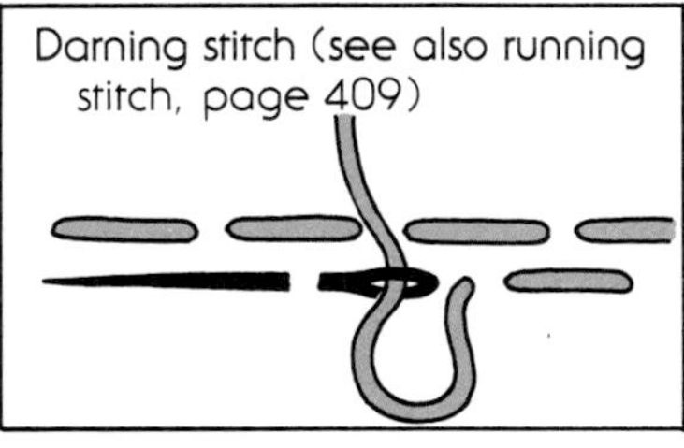
Darning stitch (see also running stitch, page 409)

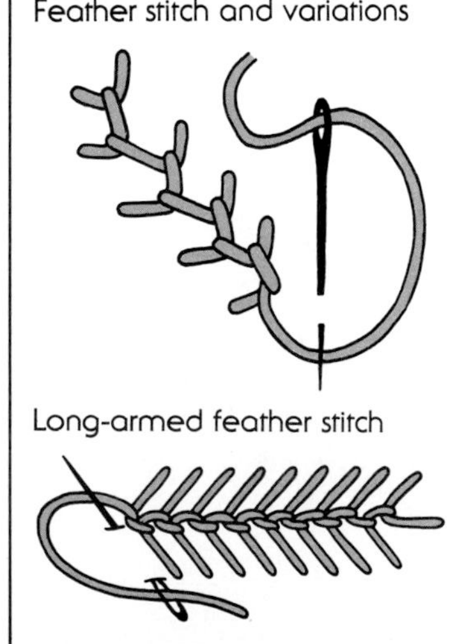
Feather stitch and variations
Long-armed feather stitch

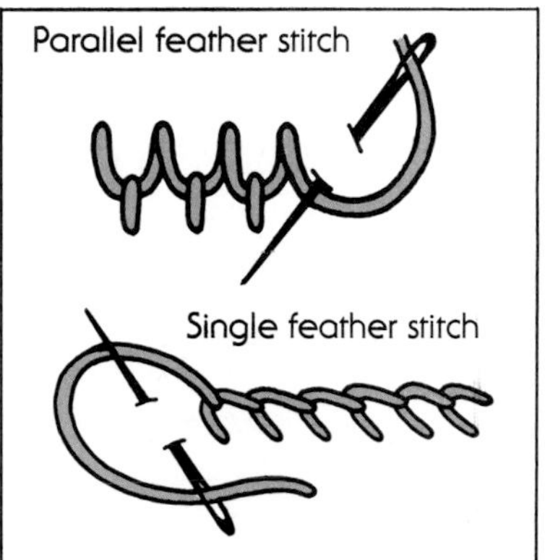
Parallel feather stitch
Single feather stitch

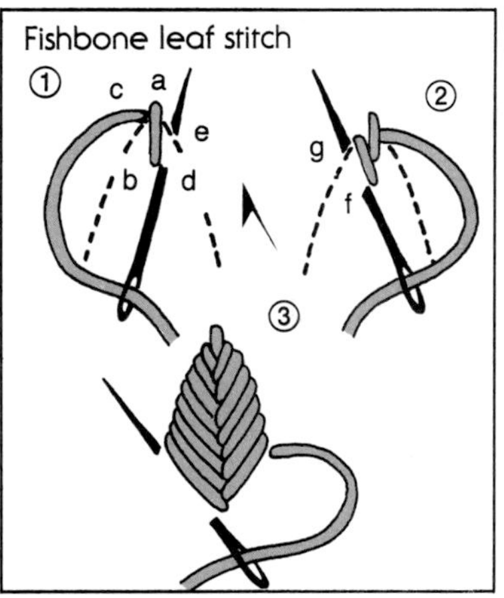
Fishbone leaf stitch
①
c
a
e
b
d
②
g
f
③

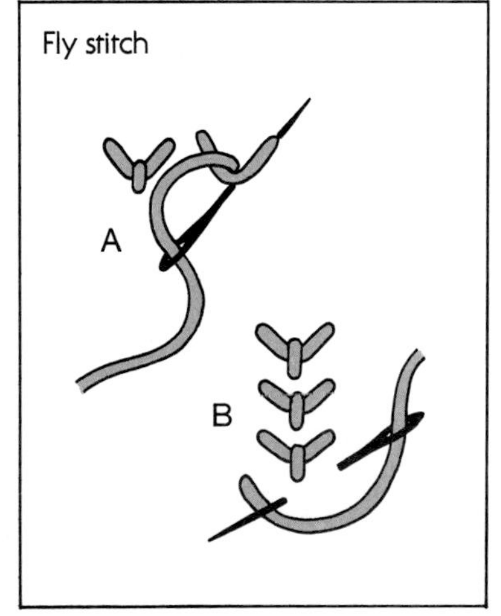
Fly stitch
A
B

continued

Basic Embroidery Stitches *(continued)*

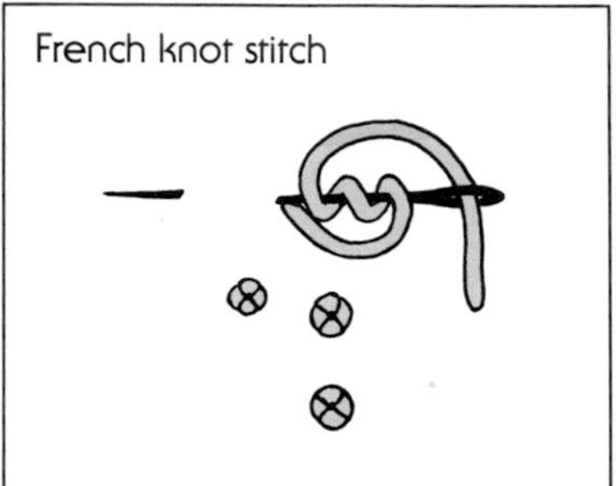
French knot stitch

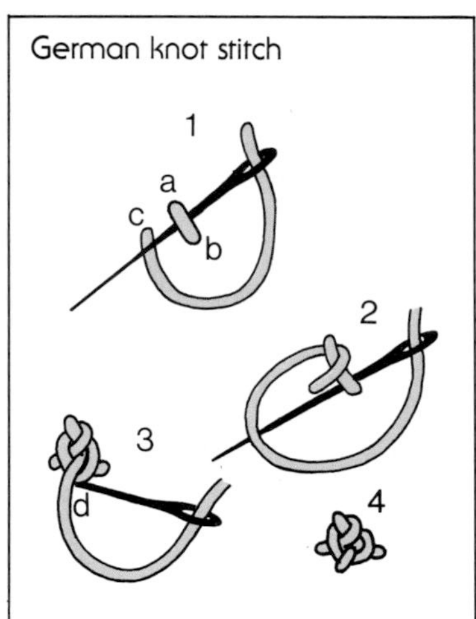

German knot stitch

Hemstitching
(see page 348)

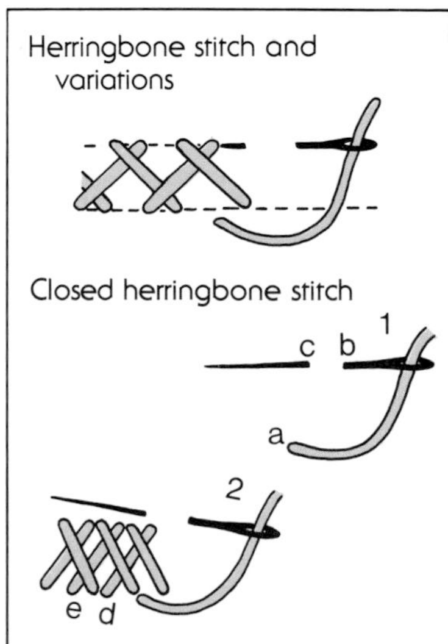

Herringbone stitch and variations

Closed herringbone stitch

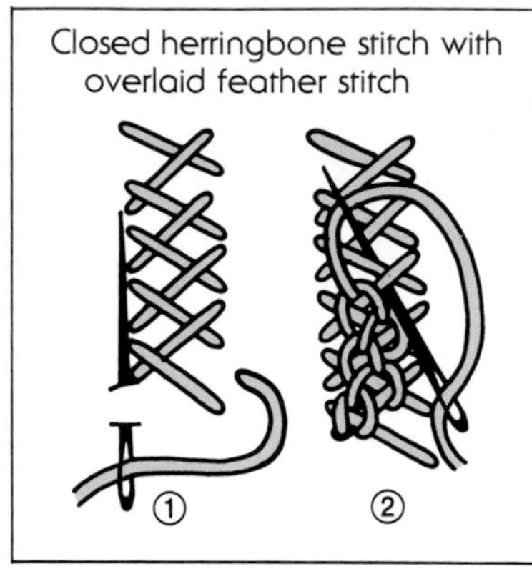

Closed herringbone stitch with overlaid feather stitch

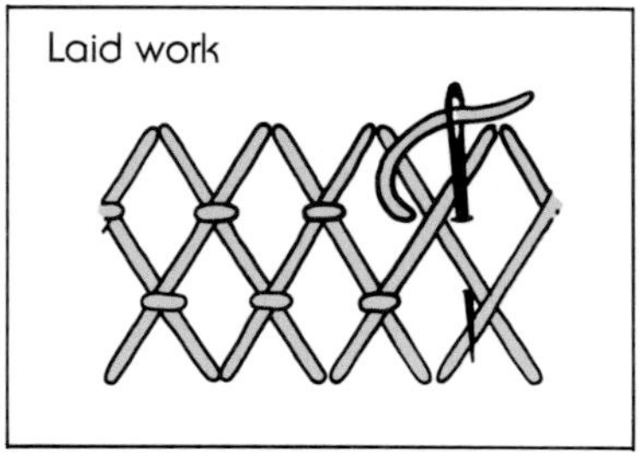
Laid work

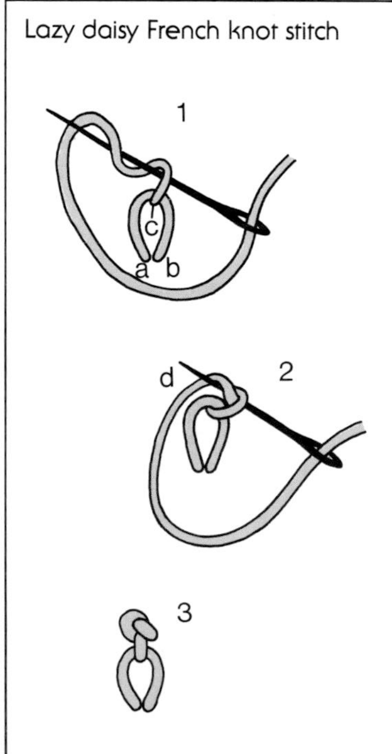

Lazy daisy French knot stitch

Lazy daisy stitch (see also, chain stitch, page 406)

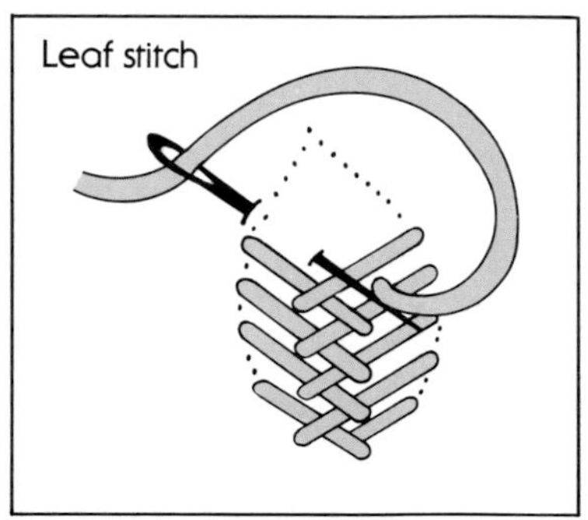
Leaf stitch

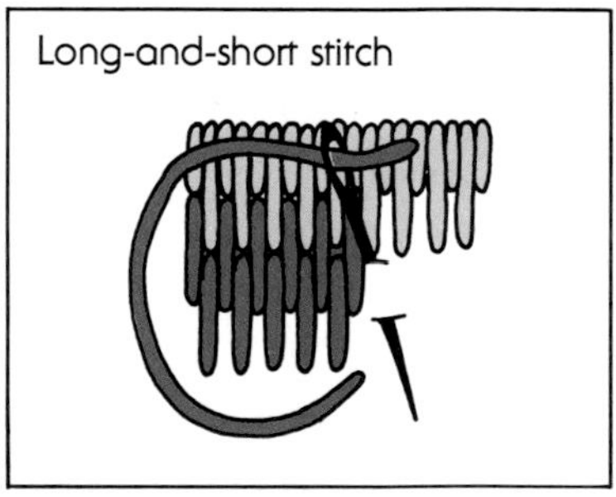
Long-and-short stitch

Needleweaving
(see pages 376 to 378)

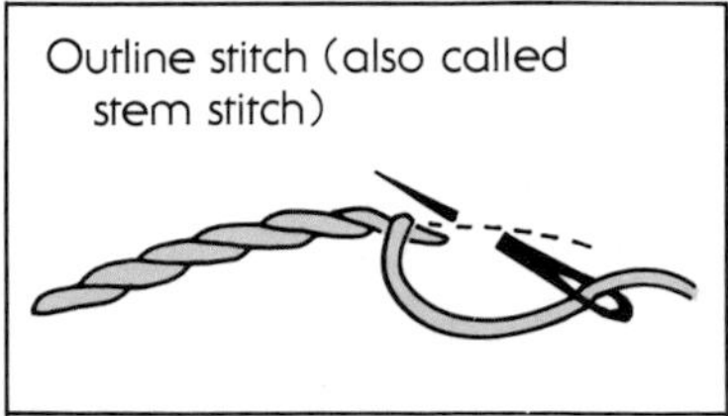
Outline stitch (also called stem stitch)

Rosette chain stitch

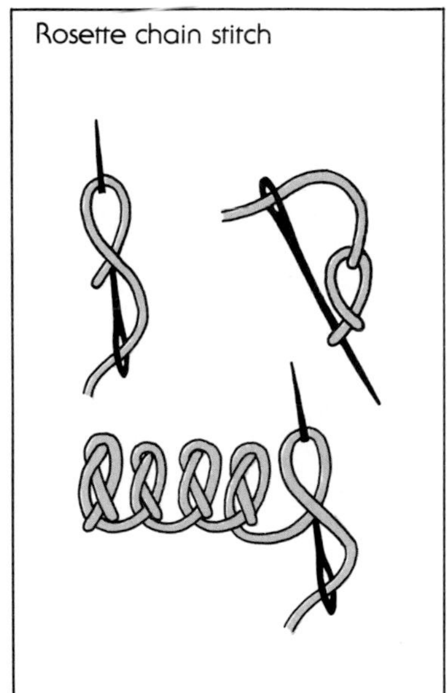

Roumanian stitch

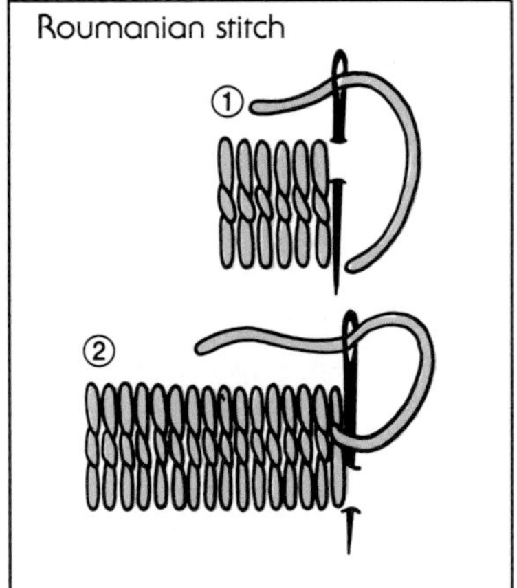

Running stitch and variations

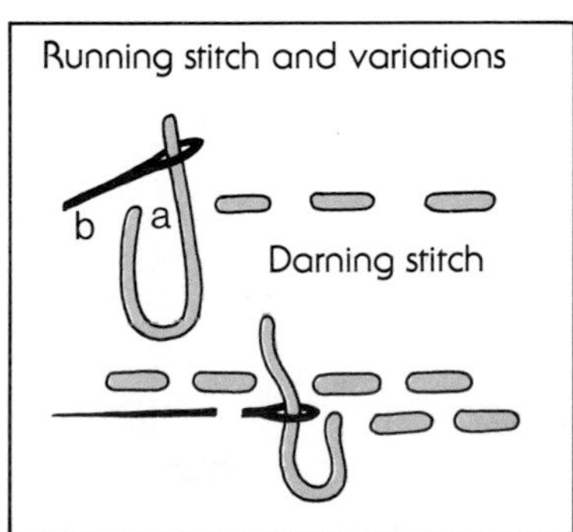

Double running stitch

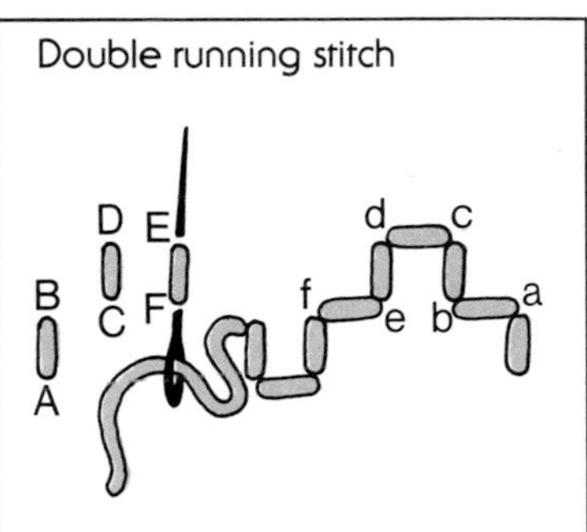

Satin stitch

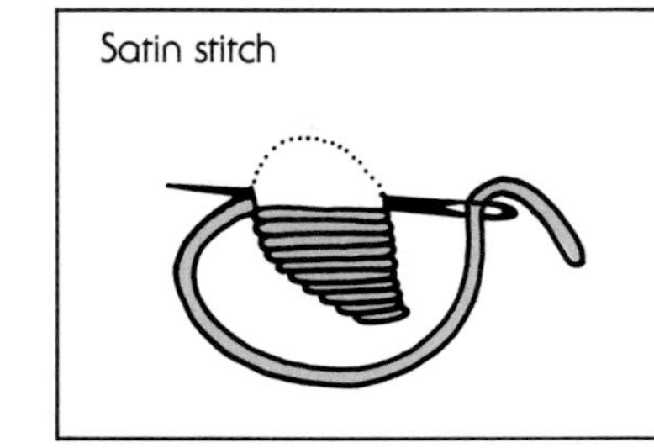

Seed stitch

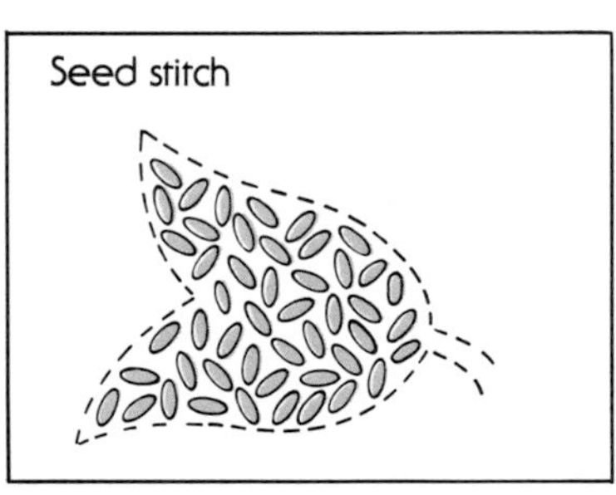

Shisha stitch
(see page 394)

Spiderweb stitch

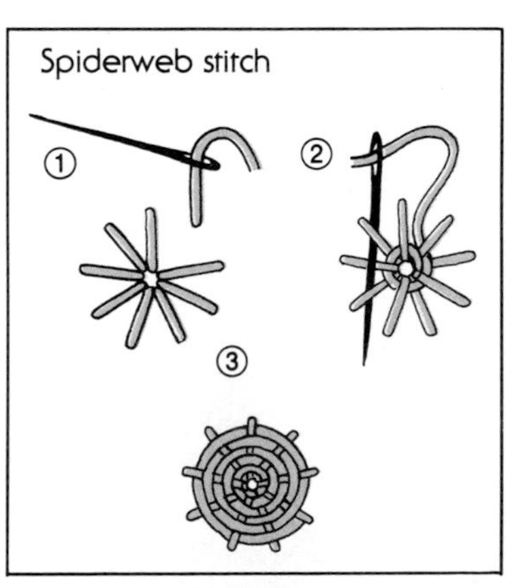

Split stitch

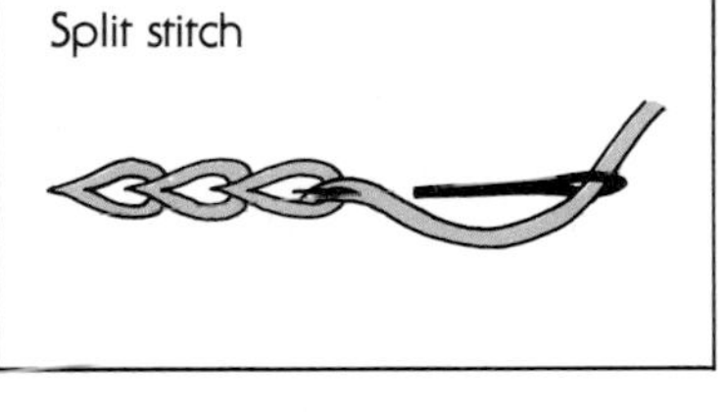

Star stitch

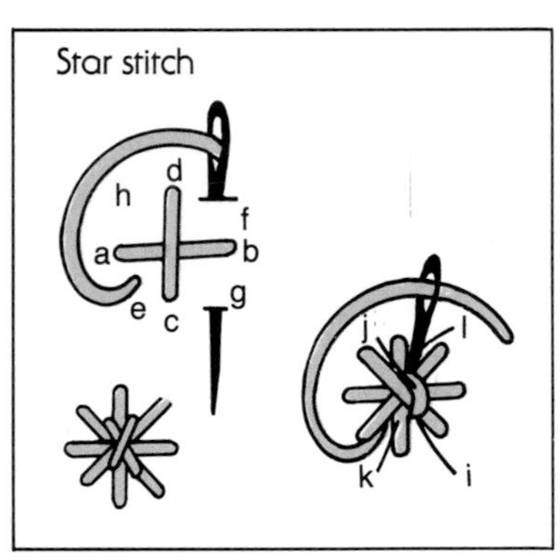

Stem stitch
(also called outline stitch, see page 408)

Straight stitch

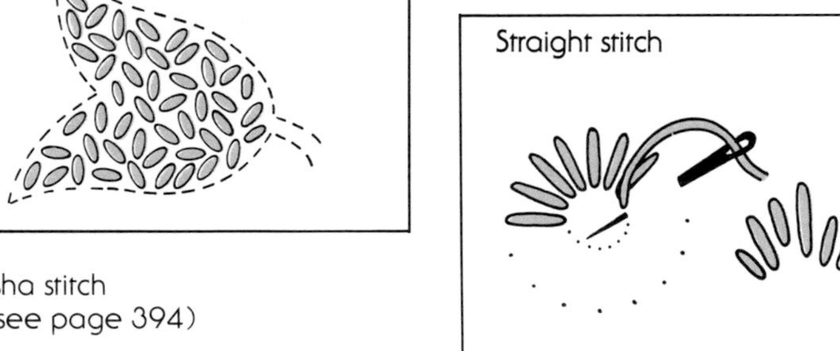

Velvet stitch

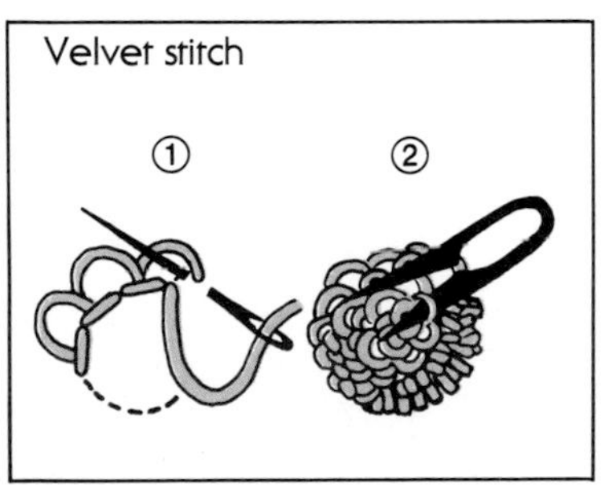

Waste knot
(see page 371)

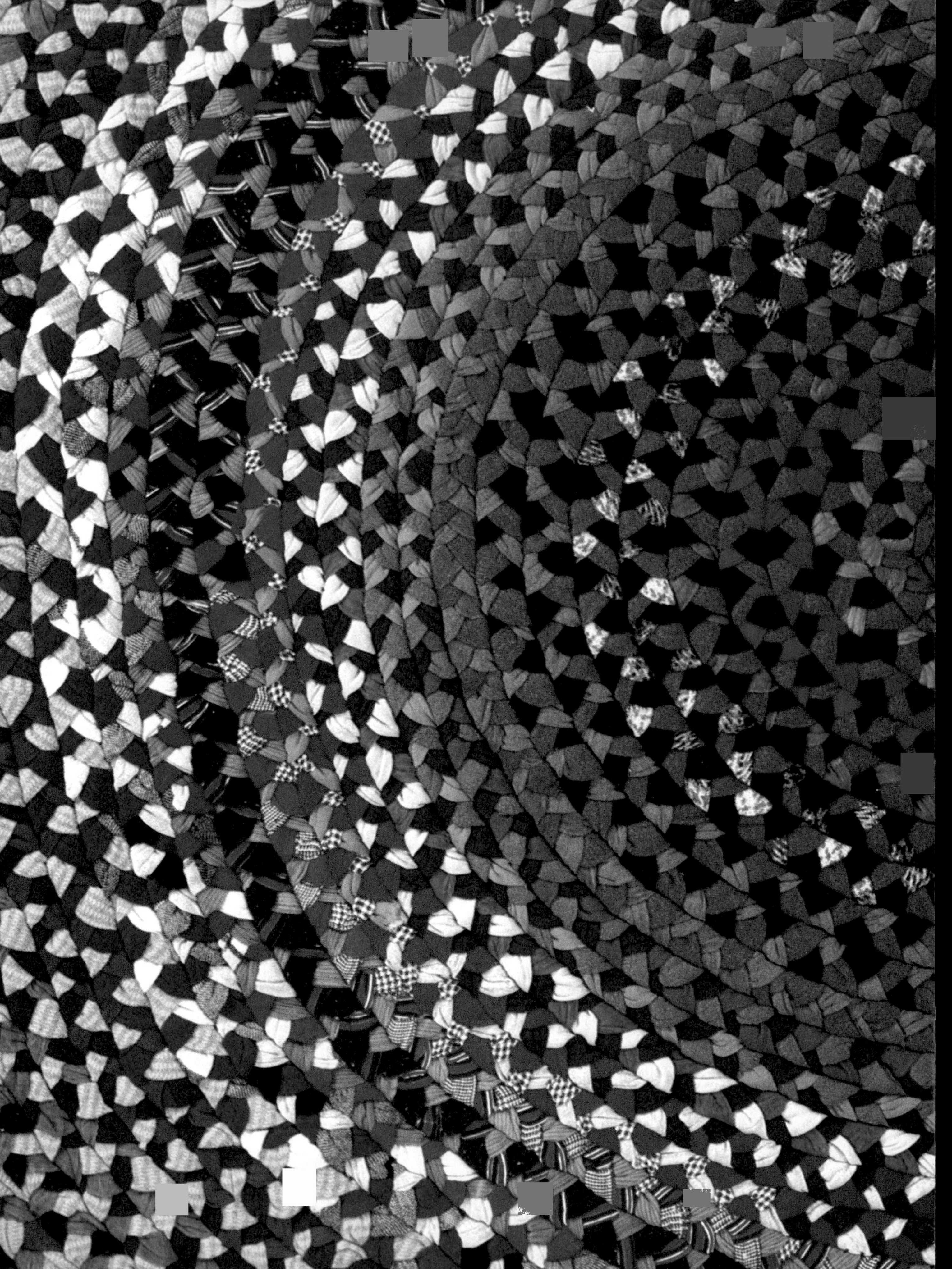

RUG MAKING

Rag & Braided Rugs

There is something wonderfully special about a handmade rug that is warm and appealing and beautiful, however humble its origins. So what nicer way is there to begin this section than with the traditional braid shown here—a genuinely happy marriage of practicality and big impact! And in the rest of our collection, you'll find a terrific selection of rugs to make in a wide variety of techniques and materials—all with easy-to-follow instructions.

To learn to make a braided rug, please turn the page.

How to Make a Braided Rug

What could be more inviting than a soft, warm, and homey braided rug in front of the fire? Or a splendid room-size braid in your dining room? Each can be a wonderfully personal and creative addition to your home.

And you can take pride in your practicality, too, for braided rugs are virtually no-cost. Just gather up used clothing and sewing scraps, cut them into strips, and braid them into a rug that's just the size you want. Here's all you need to know to get started.

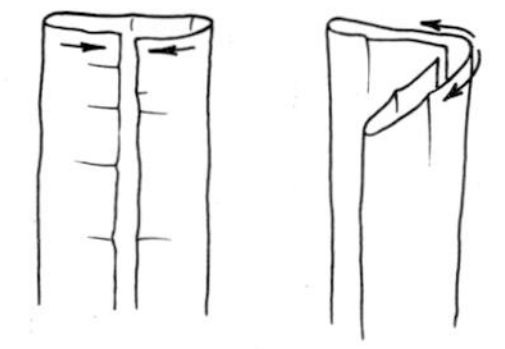

Folding Strips

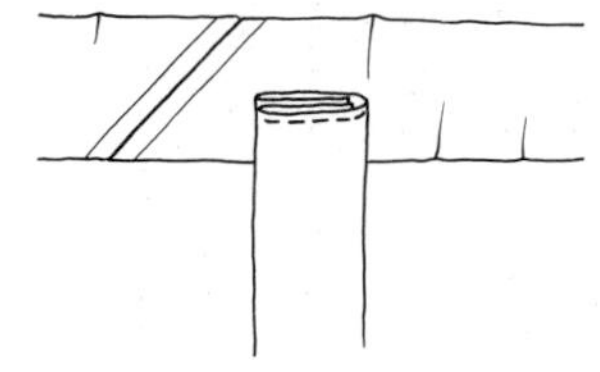

Joining Strips

Fabric and Equipment

The scrap basket is the rug crafter's treasure chest. Look there for worn clothing and remnants from sewing projects to make into rugs. And add to your cache by shopping at rummage sales and second-hand stores for suitable fabrics.

For a traditional braid, choose solid colors, tweeds, and patterns, keeping an eye on their dark and light values so you'll have an interesting mix of shades and textures.

Heavy- or medium-weight wools are best for really durable rugs, although lightweight wools work well in small rugs; cottons, linens, and blends are worth trying for their special effects. Knits, however, stretch so much that they're best avoided. Also avoid mixing light and heavy fabrics; they produce braids that wear unevenly and look lumpy.

Whatever you choose, opt for smooth, closely woven fabrics rather than loosely woven, rough, or loopy ones that may pull, snag, or catch a heel.

For equipment, turn to your sewing basket for safety pins, scissors, a thimble, heavy thread (such as carpet thread), tailor's chalk, and a yardstick. To join braids, use lacers (used to thread elastic) or curved carpet needles.

Estimating Fabric Needs

The amount of fabric needed depends on the size of the rug, the weight of the fabric, the width of the strips cut for braiding, and the tightness of the braid — it's a very individual thing. You can expect to lose between 1 to 2 feet of yardage for every 4 feet that you braid. For the best estimate, cut 3 strips the width you expect to use in your rug, each 2 yards long. Braid, and measure finished length and "uptake" to determine actual requirements.

Cutting Strips

When using old clothing, remove worn spots before cutting. Also remove collars, cuffs, pockets, zippers, and buttons. Open seams.

Cut fabric into strips 2 to 4 inches wide, depending on the weight of the fabric and the desired thickness of the rug. Generally, heavy fabrics are cut narrower than light ones.

Cut or tear strips on the straight grain to minimize stretching. Use a yardstick and chalk to mark cutting lines.

Piecing Strips Together

To simplify braiding, join strips together into 10- to 12-foot lengths using one of the methods illustrated on page 422. The slit-knot method is less satisfactory, though, because raw edges may show. With the "short cut" method, end each cut of the fabric a distance from the edge equal to the width of the strip. For example, on a 2-inch strip, stop cutting 2 inches short of the edge.

Hiding Raw Edges

Fold strips in half lengthwise so raw edges meet in the center; then fold strips in half, as shown at left. Roll each strip into a ball.

Braiding

Begin by unwrapping 4 feet from three balls. Join two strips on the bias, then add a third strip to form a "T," as shown at left. Anchor joined ends to a chair or doorknob.

Braid by bringing the left strip over the middle strip (either by twisting or folding it over). Then bring the right strip over the middle strip, as in the diagram opposite.

The Traditional Braid *(shown on pages 412 and 413)*

Directions

Note: The finished size of the oval braid shown on pages 412 and 413 is 76x90 inches. To make it, you'll need approximately 25 yards of 44-inch-wide dress-weight woolen yardage or the equivalent in worn clothing and sewing remnants. Adjust fabric estimates for a larger or smaller rug accordingly.

Review the general Instructions opposite and below and then select and prepare fabrics for cutting. Cut them into 2½-inch-wide strips and join strips into 3- or 4-yard lengths. Fold strips to hide raw edges and roll them into balls or fold into bundles. To begin, join three strips into a "T" as shown opposite, and braid following the diagram below.

When joining and braiding strips, keep in mind the arrangement of shades, colors, and patterns because a pleasing variation will add much to the beauty of your rug. Refer to the photograph on pages 412 and 413 for ideas, if necessary.

Start shaping the rug around an 18-inch length of braid. This strip forms the center of the rug. If you wish to make your oval rug a different size, determine the length of the starter (center) strip by subtracting the width of your planned rug from its length. For example, for a 3x4-foot rug, the starter strip should be one foot long (4−3=1).

Lace braided strips together as you work, with lacers or a curved needle and thread, following the instructions below.

To care for your braided rug, shake it vigorously to remove loose dirt and have it professionally cleaned when necessary. Use rug beaters with care because they tend to loosen the fibers in a rug and may snag the braids.

Our pioneer ancestors knew the virtue of saving every small scrap of fabric–and the joy of crafting them into useful objects for their homes. Our oval braid is just such a project–easy and economical to make, sturdy and long-wearing, and enormously satisfying to own.

Materials

Wool from worn clothing, or new yardage (see note at left)
Carpet thread
Curved carpet needle or lacers

How to Make a Braided Rug *(continued)*

Keep tension even and avoid stretching the braid. At the end of each 10- to 12-foot length, stitch new strips to working strips and continue braiding. Stagger seams a bit to avoid lumps in the braid.

Shaping the Braid

As you work, shape the braided strips into the rug and lace them together. Starting with the joined end of the braid, begin coiling it into a circle, square, or rectangle. As you progress, gradually wind the entire braid into this shape. Be sure circles are rounded and squares have corners.

To start an oval, see directions above for the traditional braid on pages 412 and 413.

Lacing

Lace braids together side by side using a carpet needle or lacers and heavy thread.

Anchor the thread and draw it through the loop of one braid. Then thread it through the closest loop of the neighboring braid, as shown at right. Work back and forth between braids until they are secure.

Braids should remain flat; do not wind or lace too tightly.

Tapering

Taper the ends of the braid for a smooth finish on the edge of the rug. Cut the final 18 inches to about half the normal width, braid, and slip the ends into a loop of the adjacent coil. Slip-stitch so no raw edges show.

Braiding

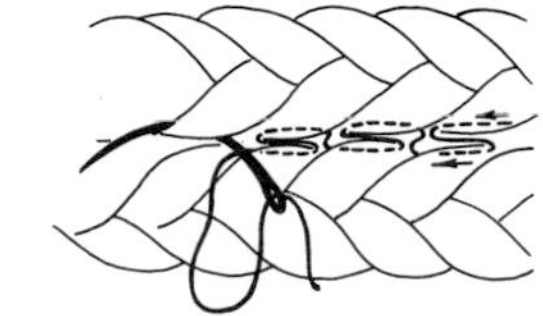

Lacing

Calico Patchwork

Here's a rug with country charm and city sophistication. A braided rug with a new twist, this classy-looking floor covering is worked in squares, patchwork-style. Braid one patch at a time, and then lace the braids together in accordion folds as shown in the diagram below.

Once you've made a few "patches," you can piece them together to use and enjoy while you finish the rest of the rug.

Fabric requirements are for the large, 54x108-inch rug shown here. To estimate fabric needs for a smaller or larger rug, figure about one yard each of three different prints for each 18-inch square.

Materials

20 yards yellow cotton calico
18 yards red cotton calico
9 yards blue cotton calico
9 yards green cotton calico
Carpet thread
Rubber bands or twist ties
Blunt tapestry needle

Directions

Note: This rug is made of eighteen 18-inch squares — nine red, yellow, and blue ones and nine red, yellow, and green ones. Vary the size of your rug by altering the number of squares. The finished size also will depend on the weight of the fabric used and the tightness of the braid.

To prepare strips for braiding, cut the fabric along the lengthwise grain into 3-inch-wide strips about 5 yards long. Sew short lengths together in ¼-inch bias seams.

Press under raw edges of each strip about ¼ inch and fold strips in half lengthwise, as shown in the diagram on page 414. Fold strips into small bundles and secure with twist ties or rubber bands. When braiding, pull ends of strips from the bundles.

For each braided square, join two strips in a bias seam and attach a third strip to make a "T," referring to pages 414 and 415 for specific instructions. Braid the strips in combinations of red, yellow, and green, and red, yellow, and blue. Keep the folded edges of each strip in the center of the braid and keep tension even as you work. Do not taper the strips at the end of the braid for each square; instead, stitch them together, tucking in raw edges.

To make each square, fold the braid back and forth in 18-inch lengths and lace the lengths together side-by-side with carpet thread (see the diagram below). Draw the thread through a loop in one braid and then through the corresponding loop in the braid adjacent to it. Braids should lie flat. Make each braided "patch" 18 inches square. Make nine squares with blue strips and nine squares with green strips.

To assemble the rug, arrange the squares in rows three squares wide and six squares long. Turn every other square so the braids alternate running horizontally and vertically (see the diagram below). Also alternate blue squares with green squares. Lace squares firmly together.

Cut 4-inch-wide yellow bias strips and sew the strips together to make a binding for the rug. Press the raw edges under ¼ inch and fold the strip in half lengthwise. Slip-stitch the binding to the edge of the rug.

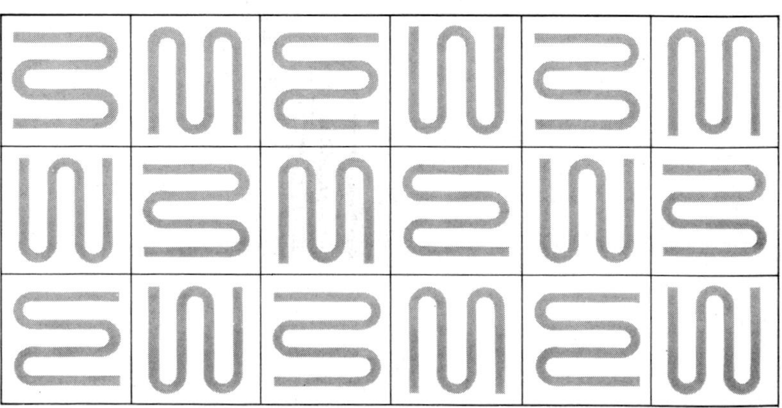

1 Square=18 Inches

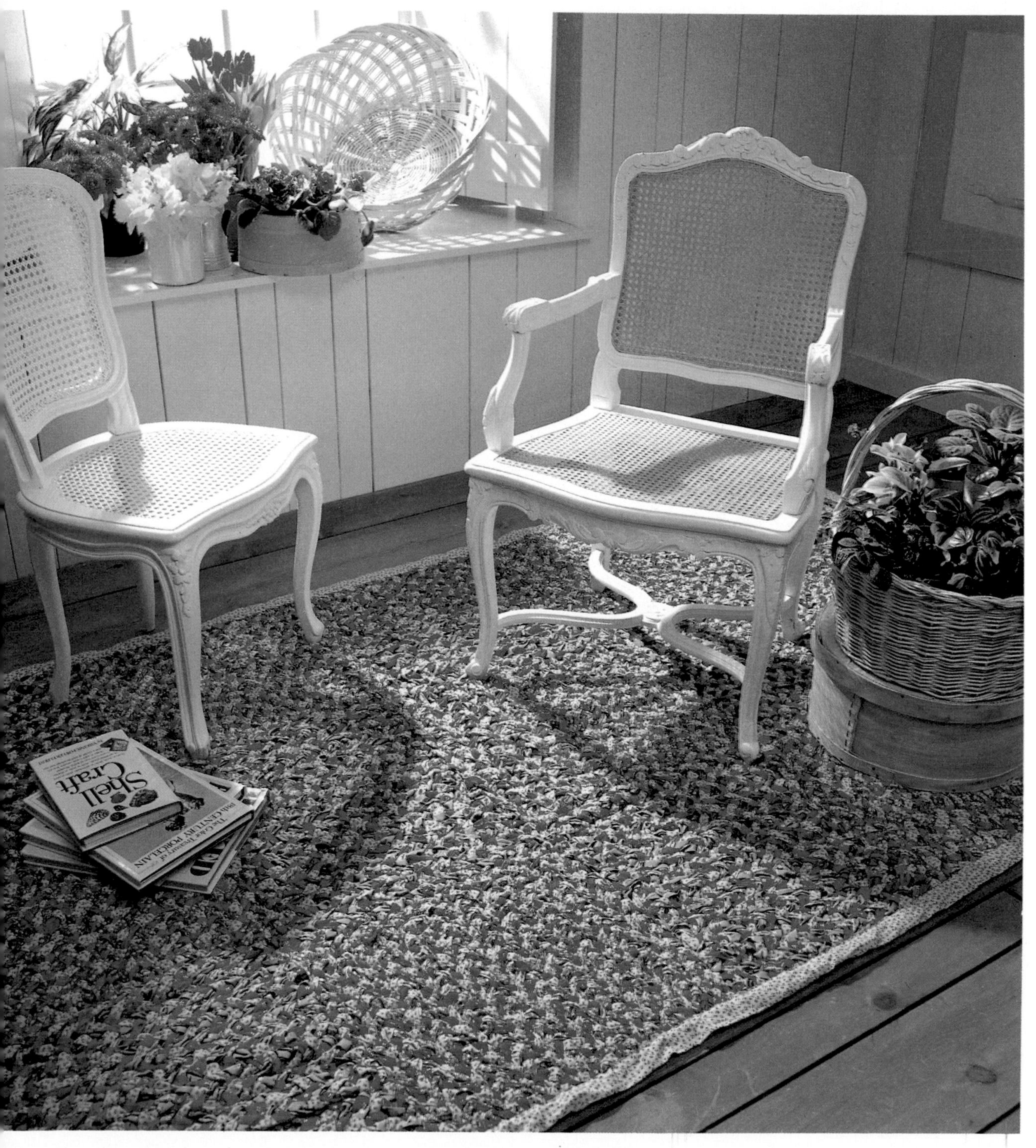
Shell Craft

Cross-Stitch Alphabet Rug

If creative stitchery is your thing, you'll love this unusual "needlepoint" rug made with fabric instead of yarn. Work 2-inch-wide strips of fabric onto a canvas backing in simple cross-stitches for a rug that's wonderfully soft and sturdy.

If this 4x6-foot rug is more than you want to take on right now, why not try this exciting technique on a smaller rug, using the alphabet below to spell out your child's name, initials, or a favorite saying?

Materials

48x72-inch piece of #4-count penelope canvas (see note at right)
Twenty-six ½- to ¾-yard pieces of 45-inch-wide cotton fabric in assorted reds and blues for letters
4 double-bed-size white sheets for background
9 yards 45-inch-wide blue fabric for border
2 yards burlap for backing
Large-eyed tapestry needle
Waterproof marking pen
Masking tape
Carpet thread

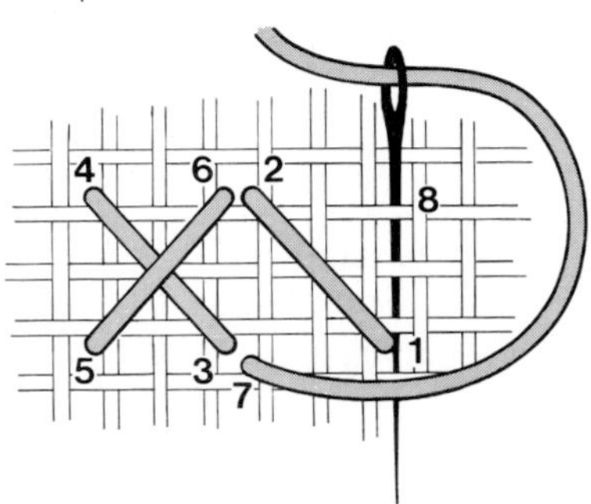

Directions

Note: If 48-inch-wide canvas is unavailable, buy 3½ yards of 36-inch-wide canvas, cut it in half, and piece it together by cutting off the selvage edges and overlapping the two pieces of canvas 1 inch. Whipstitch the two pieces together.

Bind the edges of the canvas with masking tape to prevent raveling. Preshrink the fabric and tear it into 2x45-inch strips.

Turn under the raw edges of the strips by folding and pressing each strip into thirds lengthwise. Use plastic bags to keep fabric clean, and keep the three different sets of fabric separate (letters, background, and borders).

With a waterproof pen, mark the center of the canvas by counting squares. Outline each letter on the canvas as shown on the pattern below. Each square represents one cross-stitch and each cross-stitch covers three horizontal and vertical threads. Keep the pattern centered by marking the inner letters first.

After outlines are complete, work the cross-stitches, referring to the stitch diagram, if necessary. Count the stitches carefully to make sure each stitch covers three threads of canvas. This will keep the pattern aligned.

To begin the cross-stitches, thread the needle with a strip of folded fabric and work the canvas the same way you would with rug yarn. Work half cross-stitches across the canvas in one direction. Then cross them by working back across the canvas in the opposite direction, as shown in the diagram at left. Begin and end the stitches on the back side of the canvas, slipping the loose end through 2 or 3 stitches to secure it. Clip the ends.

Work the letters first, then the background, and finally the border. When finished, trim excess canvas around rug to 1 inch and blindstitch the edges to the back of the rug with carpet thread.

To back the rug, trim burlap to size, adding a 1-inch seam allowance. Turn under raw edges and whipstitch to border.

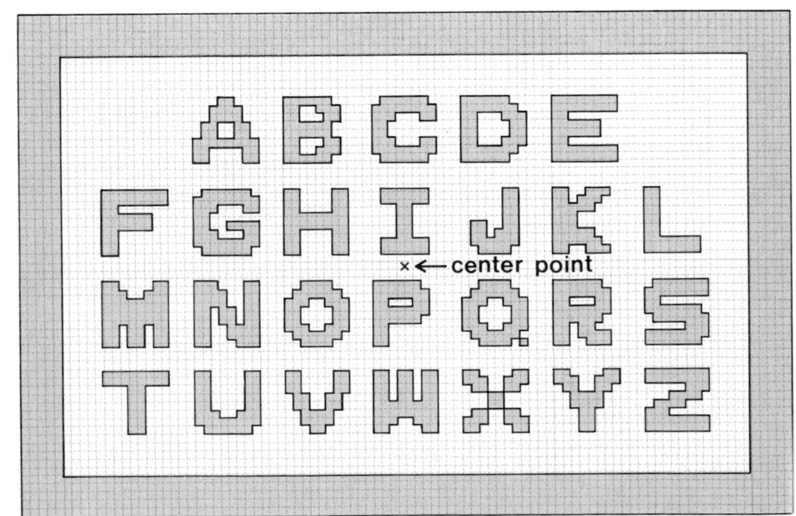

1 Square=1 Stitch

ABCDE
FGHIJKL
MNOPQRS
TUVWXYZ

Contemporary Crocheted Rug

With one easy crochet stitch and a few simple techniques, you can make a rag rug to rival anything that Grandmother used to make. And while the techniques are traditional, the look is "today" when this rug is worked in a variety of fabrics in related colors. Stitch and how-to diagrams are on page 422.

Materials

Sufficient new or used cotton or cotton-blend fabrics for the rug (see note at right)
Size J crochet hook

Directions

Note: Collect rags for the rug by culling old clothes, worn sheets, and other fabrics that are either all cotton or cotton blends. To color-scheme a rug like the one shown opposite, select a good mix of solid colors, patterns, prints, and checks. Ours is worked in blue and white fabrics and is about 8 feet in diameter. A rug about 3 to 4 feet in diameter requires about 9 yards of 45-inch-wide fabric (or the equivalent in salvaged materials). One yard of 45-inch fabric, sheet-weight, yields about 44 yards of 1-inch strips (accounting for seams).

Cut or tear fabric into strips ¾ to 1½ inches wide, depending on its weight. Tear heavy fabrics into ¾-inch strips, medium-weight fabrics into 1-inch strips, and light fabrics into 1½-inch strips. Cut all strips of any given fabric the same width.

Following the diagrams on page 422, join strips by sewing along the bias (diagonal); trim seams. Or join them by folding one end of one strip (A) over 1 inch. Cut ½ inch into the fold, centering the cut in the strip. Fold and cut the other strip (B) in the same way. Insert the cut end of B into the cut end of A, with the right sides of the strips facing the same direction.

Next, slide the uncut end of B through the slit, forming a loop. Gently pull the strip all the way through, at the same time tucking the short end of A through the slit in B. Make sure the joint remains flat. Repeat for all strips. Roll long, connected strips into large balls, as shown in the photograph below.

Work the rug by following the stitch diagrams on page 422. Make a slipknot and 6 chain stitches in one fabric strip (1). Join

continued

MARC CHAGALL

Contemporary Crocheted Rug *(continued)*

1 Chain stitching

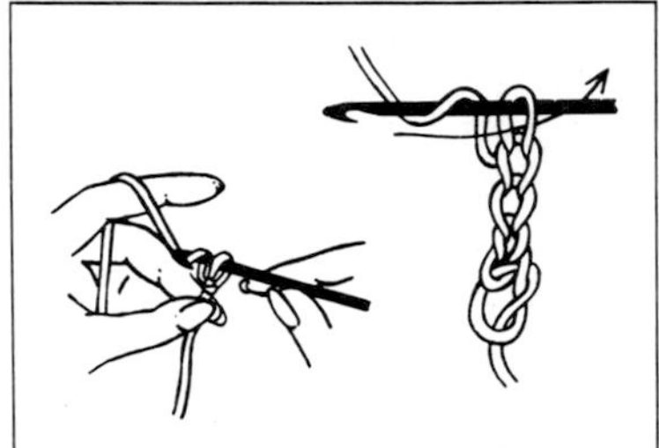

2 Slip-stitch into a ring

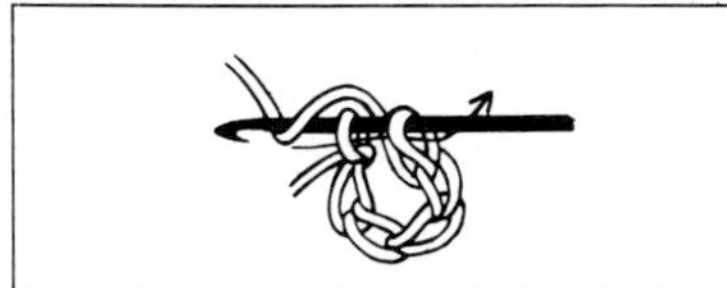

3 Single crochet

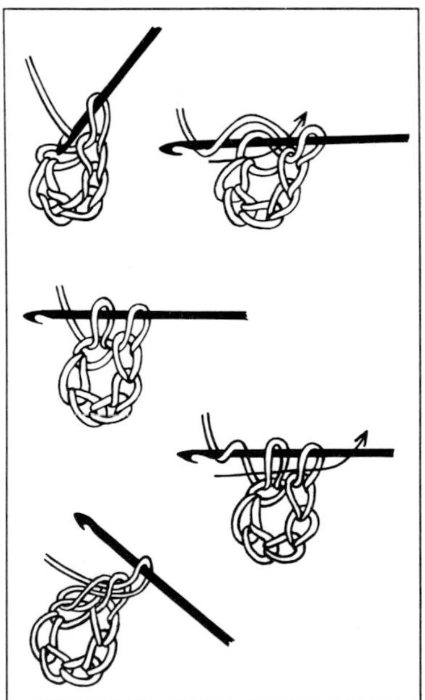

4 Increasing

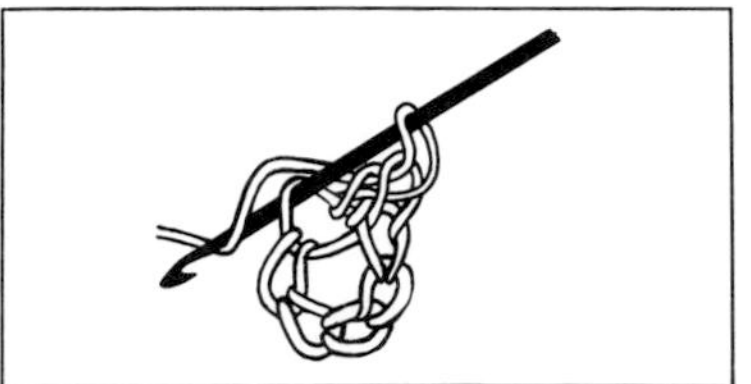

Joining fabric strips

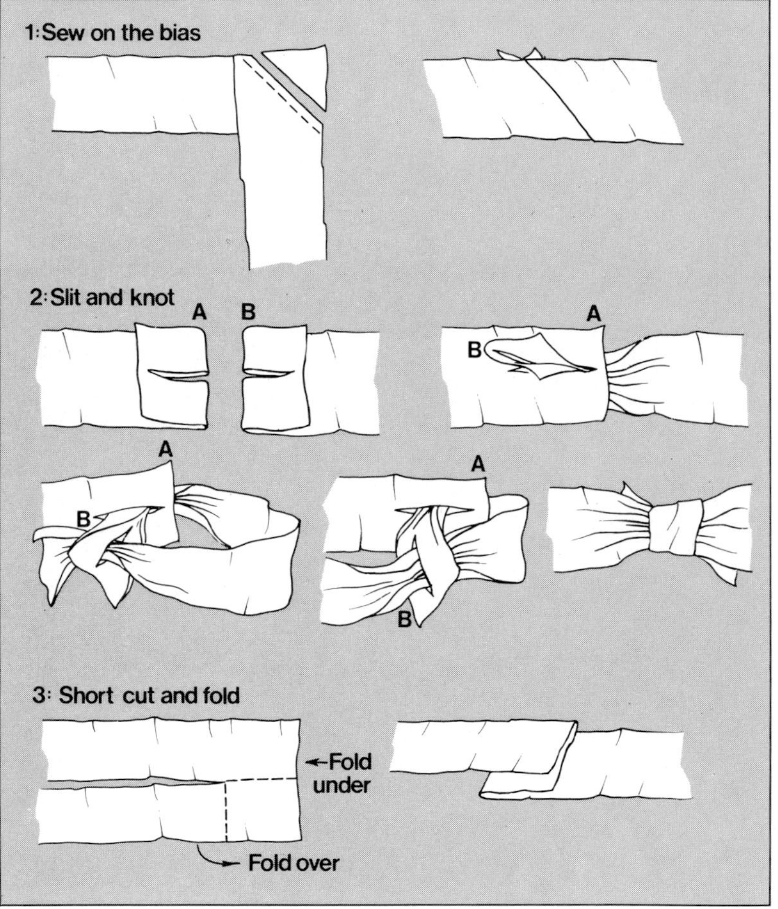

them into a ring with a slip-stitch (2). In the first stitch of the ring, work a single crochet stitch (3). Then work another single crochet in the same stitch so it increases (4). Repeat this procedure in all 6 stitches of the ring.

Thereafter, continue single-crocheting (3), increasing in every other stitch for the second row and thereafter as necessary to maintain the rug's circular shape and flatness.

To change colors or add new strips, join a new strip to the preceding one by hand (by stitching two pieces together along the bias or by slit-joining as shown above). Continue single-crocheting, increasing occasionally and changing colors wherever you choose, until the rug is the desired size.

To finish the rug, cut the last 3 or 4 yards of fabric strips narrower (decreasing to about ⅜ inch wide at the end) so the last round of the rug will decrease in width, ending smoothly. Coat with soil repellent and launder in a heavy-duty machine.

Old-Fashioned Throw Rug

This delightful rug proves that there are no hard-and-fast rules about fabrics for rug making. It's made from an unusual assortment of dress-weight materials, including satin, jersey, and faille, that are transformed into a charming blend of colors and patterns when crocheted into this simple rectangular shape.

Our rug is 28x57 inches. To make yours a different size, see the how-to instructions for the traditional braid on page 415 to determine the length of the starter strip.

For crocheting abbreviations, see page 432.

Materials

Assorted dress-weight fabrics and scraps in a variety of colors, prints, and textures equivalent to about 9 yards of 44-inch-wide fabric (for a rug with an area of 10 to 12 square feet)

Size J crochet hook

Directions

Prepare fabric for cutting, following directions on page 414. Cut strips 1 inch wide and join.

Fold strips to hide raw edges, following directions on page 414. Roll strips into balls.

To make a center, starter strip for the rug, ch 57, or until the strip is about 27 inches long. Follow diagrams opposite.

Crochet into back loops only.

Rnd 1: Starting with second ch from hook, sc in each loop of starter chain. At last loop on chain, make sharp corner by working sc, ch 1, sc, ch 1, sc all in last chain on strip. Work sc in loops of chain back to starting point, sc, ch 1, sc in same loop, sl st to join to last sc, ch 1.

Rnd 2: Sc in each st along the length, (sc, ch 1, sc) in corner ch 1 space, sc in end st(s), (sc, ch 1, sc) in next corner space, sc in each st along the length, (sc, ch 1, sc) in corner ch 1 space, sc in each end st(s), (sc, ch 1, sc) in corner ch 1 space, sl st to ch 1 to join at beg of rnd.

Rep rnd 2 until desired size.

Rugs to Knit and Crochet

Terrific techniques for floors—that's how you'll come to think of crocheting and knitting in this section of our book. With materials like heavy yarns or cords and a crochet hook or knitting needles, you can create not only decorative rugs and runners in a wealth of patterns and textures, but also sturdy and practical floor coverings. The rug shown here, for example, is a popular granny square design worked in inexpensive yarns (directions are on the next page). And it's only one in a wonderful collection of patterns to knit and crochet—all calling for mastery of only a few basic stitches and procedures.

Granny Square Runner *(shown on pages 424 and 425)*

Simple granny squares make a spectacular rug when worked in a rainbow of colors and bordered in black, as shown in the rug on pages 424 and 425. For this 30x62-inch runner, crochet seventy-eight 4½-inch squares to join together into six rows of 13 squares each. To change the size of the rug, alter the number of squares or assemble them differently.

For crocheting abbreviations, see page 432.

Materials

80-yard (2½-ounce) skeins of Belding Lily cotton rug yarn, or a suitable substitute, in the following colors and amounts: 14 black and 20 in assorted colors

Size I crochet hook

Gauge

1 square equals 4½ inches

Directions

Rnd 1: With any color, ch 4, sl st to form ring, ch 3 (counts as first dc), 2 dc in ring, ch 1, (3 dc in ring, ch 1) 3 times, sl st to top of ch 3. Fasten off.

Rnd 2: With another color, join in any corner sp, ch 3 (counts as first dc), 2 dc in corner sp, ch 1, 3 dc in corner sp, ch 1. Continue around square, making a 3 dc group in every sp of previous rnd *and* making a (3 dc, ch 1, 3 dc) group in every corner sp.

Rnd 3: Rep rnd 2, using different color.

Rnd 4: Rep rnd 2, using black yarn for each square.

Assembling—Make 78 squares. Crochet, weave, or sew the squares together, making six rows of 13, using black yarn.

Border—Attach black yarn anywhere along the outer edge, ch 1, make 1 sc in each dc and 1 sc in each joining st around. Do not make sc in sps between dc groups or border will not lie flat.

In corners, make 3 sc in corner sp, join to first ch with a sl st. Rep this rnd two more times using black yarn, change to a color for rnd 4, and finish with two more rnds of black. Fasten off.

Trim and weave in yarn ends.

Tips for Crocheting and Knitting Rugs

Crocheting and knitting are simple craft techniques that produce quick and versatile results. And because of the wide variety of patterns available, they are among the most popular members of the needlecraft family. Here are some tips to help you turn out professional-looking results every time you stitch.

General Tips
Always buy enough yarn to complete your knitted or crocheted rug, and make sure the dye lot of each skein is the same, since dye lots vary and colors may be a shade different.

Familiarize yourself with common terms and abbreviations (on pages 432 and 434) since pattern designers often assume that you know how to work the details. To review basic stitches, see pages 230 to 233.

Before you begin a rug project, check the stitch gauge in the instructions. It specifies how many stitches per inch you should have using a specified crochet hook or knitting needle. Since the size of the rug is dependent upon this gauge, you must adjust your work to the given gauge or your finished rug will not be the size indicated in the instructions.

Since everyone does not knit or crochet with the same tension, it is important to check your gauge before you start working. To do so, cast on or chain about 20 stitches, using the recommended yarn and needles or hook. Work about 4 inches in the specified pattern. Bind or fasten off. Block the swatch (see directions below) and then measure it to see whether rows and stitches correspond to the required gauge.

If your stitch gauge is less than the one given in the instructions, try the next size smaller needles or hook, and again check your gauge. If your stitch gauge is greater (more stitches per inch), try larger needles or hook.

To achieve a handmade rather than a homemade look, block your finished items. Dampen the piece to be blocked by spraying or dipping in water. With rustproof pins, such as stainless steel macrame T-pins, pin the rug in its final shape to a smooth cloth-covered surface that's larger than the piece you're blocking. Allow it to dry slowly, out of sun and away from heat.

If you make a rug larger than 3x5 feet, plan to use a pad beneath it. This ensures a longer life and makes your rug less apt to skid and easier to vacuum.

For small rugs, use non-skid padding underneath, or sew rubber jar rings to the four corners.

Clean large handmade rugs the same way you would commercially made rugs—either professionally or with a rug cleaner.

To care for small handmade rugs, wash or dry-clean, depending on whether the yarns are washable. When washing, however, use cold water and gentle machine action. Avoid tumble-drying with high heat.

Special Crocheting Tips
When crocheting, be sure the yarn is always put over the hook from back to front, and that the number of stitches per row remains consistent.

To change colors without knots, work up to the final step of a stitch. Then take up the new yarn and finish the last step with this color. Pull the yarn ends through to the wrong side of the rug and weave them into the back when the rug is completed.

Special Knitting Tips
When you are joining a new ball of yarn, join at the outer edge whenever possible. With the new strand, make a slipknot around the strand you are knitting with. Then move the slipknot up to the edge of work and continue knitting with the new strand.

When you are working with more than one color, always pick up the color you are about to use from underneath the dropped strand. This prevents holes as you are changing colors.

Scatter Rugs

These small and homey hand-stitched rugs will add instant warmth to any room in the house. The crocheted rug on the left is worked in simple stitches even a beginner can master. And while ours measures about 30x53 inches, it can actually be made any size.

The 29x36-inch checker-board rug is a double knit worked on circular needles.

For an explanation of the abbreviations used, see pages 432 and 434. Stitch diagrams are on pages 230 to 233.

Crocheted Rug

Materials

Eight 70-yard skeins Aunt Lydia's Italian blue rug yarn (A)
Eight 70-yard skeins Aunt Lydia's rust rug yarn (B)
Four 70-yard skeins Aunt Lydia's parchment rug yarn (C)
Two 70-yard skeins Aunt Lydia's medium blue rug yarn (D)
Size I aluminum crochet hook

Gauge

4 dc=1 inch, 10 rows=6 inches

Directions

Note: To make the rug a different size, adjust yarn amounts.

With 1 strand color A, ch 111.

Row 1: Work 2 dc in second ch from hook, 1 dc in each of next 3 ch, sk 2 ch, * 1 dc in each of next 4 ch, 3 dc in next ch, 1 dc in each of next 4 ch, sk 2 ch, rep from * to last 4 ch. Work 1 dc in each of next 3 ch, 2 dc in last ch. Ch 2, turn.

Row 2: Work 2 dc in 3rd loop from hook, 1 dc in each of next 3 dc, sk 2 dc, * 1 dc in each of next 4 dc, 3 dc in next dc, 1 dc in each of next 4 dc, sk 2 dc, rep from * across to last 4 dc. Work 1 dc in each of next 3 dc, 2 dc in last dc. Ch 2, turn.

Rep row 2 for pattern. Work 2 more rows A, 2 rows B, 1 row C, 1 row D, 1 row C, 2 rows B. Rep these 11 rows for entire rug, ending with 4 more rows A.

Clip ends and weave into work.

Knitted Rug

Materials

Seven 70-yard skeins Aunt Lydia's burnt orange rug yarn
Seven 70-yard skeins Aunt Lydia's navy rug yarn
Size 10½ circular knitting needle
Size I aluminum crochet hook
10 ring markers

Gauge

3 sts=1 inch on one side (6 sts of double knit)

Directions

Note: In addition to the basic knitting stitches, you will need to know yf (bring yarn forward), yb (take yarn back), pso (pass stitch over), and pw (purlwise, or as if to purl).

Pattern — double-knit with one color for practice: A: * k 1 (yf), sl 1 (pw) *, rep * to * every row (this gives st st face). B: * k 1 (yb), sl 1 (pw) *, rep * to * every row (for garter st face).

As an exercise, you can make a potholder by casting on 42 sts. Divide into units of 14 sts; * work A for 14 sts, B for 14 sts, A for 14 sts *, rep * to * to desired size.

Pattern for double knit with two colors:

Group No. 1 (first side).

Block No. 1 (navy st st face) —A: * k 1 navy (yf), p 1 orange (yb) *, rep for 18 sts, slip ring to right needle, take navy (yb), orange (yf).

Block No. 2 (orange garter st face) — B: * p 1 orange, k 1 navy *, rep for 14 sts, slip ring to right needle, orange (yb).

Group No. 1 (second side).

Block No. 1 (orange st st face) — C: * k 1 orange (yf), p 1 navy (yb) *, rep for 18 sts, navy (yf), orange (yb).

Block No. 2 (navy garter st face) — D: * p 1 navy, k 1 orange *, rep for 14 sts, navy (yb).

Rep group No. 1 until there are 12 ridges of garter st in orange (block No. 2).

Group No. 2 (first side).

Block No. 1 (orange garter st face) — orange (yf), navy (yb) —E: * k 1 navy, p 1 orange *, rep for 18 sts.

Block No. 2 (navy st st face) —F: * p 1 orange (yb), navy (yb) k 1, (yf) *, rep for 14 sts.

Group No. 2 (second side).

Block No. 1 (navy garter st face) — G: * k 1 orange (yb), p 1 navy (yf) *, rep for 18 sts, orange (yf).

Block No. 2 (orange st st face) — H: * p 1 navy (yb), k 1 orange (yf) *, rep for 14 sts, end with orange (yb), navy (yf).

Rep Group No. 2 until there are 8 orange ridges on each of the sides.

To begin, cast on in two colors using two end of yarn method:

First square: * start with orange (1st st), navy 2nd st), pull 2 orange ends between 2 navy ends and cast on orange, pull orange between 2 navy ends and cast on navy *, rep for 18 sts ending in navy, put on marker.

Second square: * cast on navy, pull navy between orange and cast on orange, pull navy between orange and cast on navy *, rep for 14 sts, ending with orange.

Rep above two blocks 5 times, rep 1st block. This gives you 178 sts on needle.

Follow directions for Groups 1 and 2, rep 7 times, rep Group No. 1, cast off with navy.

To cast off, * k 2 tog, k 2 tog, pso *, rep to end. Cut yarn and pull end through loop. Use this method with one or more colors of yarn.

At each end of rug, work one row of navy single crochet.

For fringe, use four 20-inch lengths of yarn. At each corner, pull 4 ends of orange through, knot the 8 ends tog. At either side of orange, rep with navy. Trim the fringe to desired length.

"Parquet" Rug

Even traditional crochet patterns take on a new look when worked in natural jute – a stunning, contemporary alternative to yarn. These 12-inch blocks work up quickly and easily with only two stitches. Assemble the completed squares according to the diagram below for a parquet look.

For stitch abbreviations and diagrams, please see pages 230 and 432.

Materials

Size J crochet hook

Natural, unbleached 3-ply raw jute (amount depends on size of rug and how tightly you crochet. Work up a sample square and calculate needs accordingly)

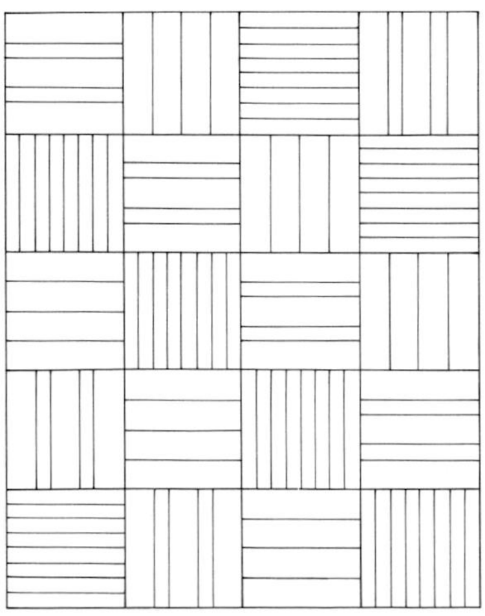

Directions

The rug pictured here consists of 27 single-crocheted squares, 27 double-crocheted squares, and 26 squares of alternating rows of single and double crochet. There are 80 squares in all, each measuring 12 inches square.

The finished rug is approximately 8x10 feet, including the scalloped crocheted border added to the short ends of the rug. The squares are arranged in a parquet pattern (see below, left) to give the rug more texture and reduce stretching.

1. *Single-crochet square:* Work 16 rows of single crochet, 20 stitches per row. Make 27 squares.

2. *Double-crochet square:* Work 8 rows of double crochet, 21 stitches per row. Make 27 squares.

3. *Single/double-crochet square:* Work, alternating 6 rows of single and 5 rows of double crochet, 21 stitches per row. Make 26 squares.

Note: Because you are working with raw jute, the yarn will vary in width and bulkiness, and hence there might be slight differences in the size of each square. Squares can be stretched and blocked to uniform size before joining.

4. *To finish ends of squares:* Cut the two end strings and, using crochet hook, tuck ends under three or four stitches. Tuck both ends under on the same side of square (this will be the wrong side of the rug).

5. *Stitching squares together:* Squares are laid out in a parquet pattern. Arrange squares in ten rows of eight squares each, alternating among the three patterns (single, double, and single/double) and alternating the *direction* of each square (see the photograph opposite and the diagram below left for pattern arrangement).

Join squares together using chain stitches. To avoid numerous bulky loose ends, join two squares together and then, without cutting yarn, move on to the next two squares. Continue until you have joined eight pairs of squares in a row.

End yarn and weave back into rug. Next, join a row of eight more squares to the original set of eight pairs. Proceed until all squares are joined horizontally.

Finally, join squares along vertical rows. Clip yarns and use crochet hook to work loose ends back into the wrong side of the rug so none of the ends show.

6. *To finish rug:* Circle the entire rug with a row of single crochet.

a. Add another row of single crochet to one of the sides with eight squares.

b. To make scallop trim, sc through first stitch on the edge of the rug.

c. Next st is a dc, which will join the first sc with the fourth stitch along border of rug. This fourth stitch will be the center of the scallop, and you will crochet five more double-crochet stitches through this stitch (each scallop thus has a total of six double-crochet stitches).

d. The sixth double-crochet stitch will then be joined by a chain stitch to the seventh single-crochet stitch of the border.

Repeat from *step a* to make scallops along one entire side of rug. You should have about 28 scallops on one side. Repeat procedure for scallop trim on opposite side of rug. Gently steam-press finished rug.

Quick-and-Easy Jute Rug

Here's another traditional crochet pattern – the scallop – looking chic in natural fibers. Heavy, five-ply jute cord in three colors works up quickly into a beautifully textured 45x72-inch rug.

This great contemporary look is simple to stitch, too – it's worked entirely in single crochet. (For diagrams of this stitch, see page 230).

To minimize shedding while working with jute, wind each color into balls and store them in plastic bags.

Materials
540 yards brown 5-ply jute
540 yards bleached white 5-ply jute
190 yards rust 5-ply jute
Size K crochet hook

Directions
Ch 142 with brown jute.

Row 1: 1 sc in second ch from hook and in each of next three ch, 3 sc in next ch, * 1 sc in each of next 4 ch, sk next two ch, 1 sc in each of next 4 ch, 3 sc in next ch; rep from *, ending 1 sc in each of last 4 ch. Ch 1, turn.

Row 2: Sk first sc, 1 sc in each of next 4 sc, 3 sc in next sc, * 1 sc in each of next 4 sc, sk next 2 sc, 1 sc in each of next 4 sc, 3 sc in next sc; rep from *, ending 1 sc in each of next 3 sc, sk next sc, 1 sc in last sc. Ch 1, turn. Rep Row 2 for pat, changing to rust jute for Rows 7 and 8. Rows 9 through 14 are worked in bleached white jute.

Rep entire procedure three more times.

To block finished rug, steam-press so the entire rug lies flat. Shake or beat the rug periodically to remove dirt (5-ply jute will withstand occasional beating).

Crochet Abbreviations

beg .... begin(ning)
ch .... chain
dc ..... double crochet
dec .... decrease
dtr ...... double treble
hdc .... half double crochet
inc .... increase
lp(s) .... loop(s)
pat .... pattern
rnd .... round
sc ...... single crochet
sl st .... slip stitch
sp .... space
st(s) .... stitch(es)
tog .... together
yo .... yarn over

Knitted Patchwork Rug

Deep tones mixed with white make this rug a refreshing accent for your floor. Knit two colors together into 12-inch squares, join them patchwork-style, and surround them all with a wide border.

Materials

70-yard skeins of heavy-duty rug yarn in the following amounts and colors: 32 off-white, 4 cerise, 6 yellow, 5 chartreuse, and 17 turquoise.

Size 11 knitting needles.

Tapestry needle.

Measurements for Blocking

Approximately 4½ x 6½ feet

Knitting Abbreviations

beg .... begin(ning)
CC ... contrasting color
dec .... decrease
dp ..... double-pointed
inc .... increase
k .... knit
MC .... main color
p .... purl
pat .... pattern
psso .. pass slip st over
rem .... remaining
rep .... repeat
rnd .... round
sk .... skip
sl st .... slip stitch
sp .... space
st(s) .... stitch(es)
st st .. stockinette stitch
tog .... together
yo .... yarn over
* ...... repeat from * as indicated

Directions

Make the rug of fifteen 12-inch squares sewn together with a 9-inch border around the edges. To change the size, alter the number of squares and the length of the borders.

Work the entire rug in garter stitch: knit every row.

To make each square, use one full skein each of white and a color, and knit the two together. The border requires about 3½ skeins each of white and turquoise for the short sides, and 5 skeins each for the long sides.

For squares, cast on 29 stitches using two strands of yarn; knit until the piece measures 12 inches. Make 15 knitted squares.

For borders, cast on 21 stitches using two strands of yarn. Knit two strips 36 inches long and two 78 inches long.

When squares are finished, arrange colors in a pleasing design such as the one shown below. Stitch them together with a tapestry needle threaded with a double strand of yarn. Add borders in the same way so all of the pieces are secure.

Whimsical Crocheted Rug

Bright colors trim the "petals" of this whimsical white flower blossom. And because it's worked in only one stitch, it's easier to "grow" than the real thing!

Work single-crochet rounds in three sizes and join them together to make this 38-inch rug.

For stitch abbreviations, see page 432.

For stitch diagrams, see pages 230 and 231.

Materials

13 skeins white 3-ply rug yarn
2 skeins green 3-ply rug yarn
1 skein red 3-ply rug yarn
1 skein yellow 3-ply rug yarn
Row markers
Tapestry needle
Size H crochet hook

Directions

18-inch center circle (make 1):

Rnd 1: With white yarn, ch 4, join with sl st to form ring.

Rnd 2: 8 sc in ring; do not join rounds but use a marker in first st worked to indicate beginning of round.

Rnd 3: * 2 sc in first sc, sc in next sc, repeat from *.

Rnds 4, 7, 9, and 11: Rep rnd 3.

Rnd 5: Sc in each sc around.

Rnds 6, 8, 10, 12, 13, 14, 16, and 17: Rep rnd 5.

Rnd 15: * 2 sc in first sc, sc in each of next 2 scs, rep from *.

Rnds 18 and 29: Rep rnd 15.

Rnds 19 through 28: Rep rnd 5.

Rnds 30 and 31: Sc in each sc, sl st in first sc and cut yarn.

9-inch white circles (make 9): Follow directions for large center circle for 17 rnds.

1½-inch green circles (make 9): Follow directions for large center circle for 3 rnds.

To assemble the rug, position smaller white circles around the center circle as shown in the photograph. Using a tapestry needle and yarn, sew small circles to large one for a distance of seven stitches. Arrange small green circles between the nine white circles and sew in place. Then work edging.

Edging—Rnd 1: Attach red yarn in center sc at top of small green circle, sc in same sp, sc in each sc around.

Sew 7 sc between each circle so circles are joined.

For yellow edging, sc around, *except that at points where circles intersect* sk 3 sc. Complete 1 row. Rep for white (1 row) and green (2 rows).

End off; weave in end of yarn.

To block, steam lightly so rug lies flat. Machine-wash on gentle cycle when necessary.

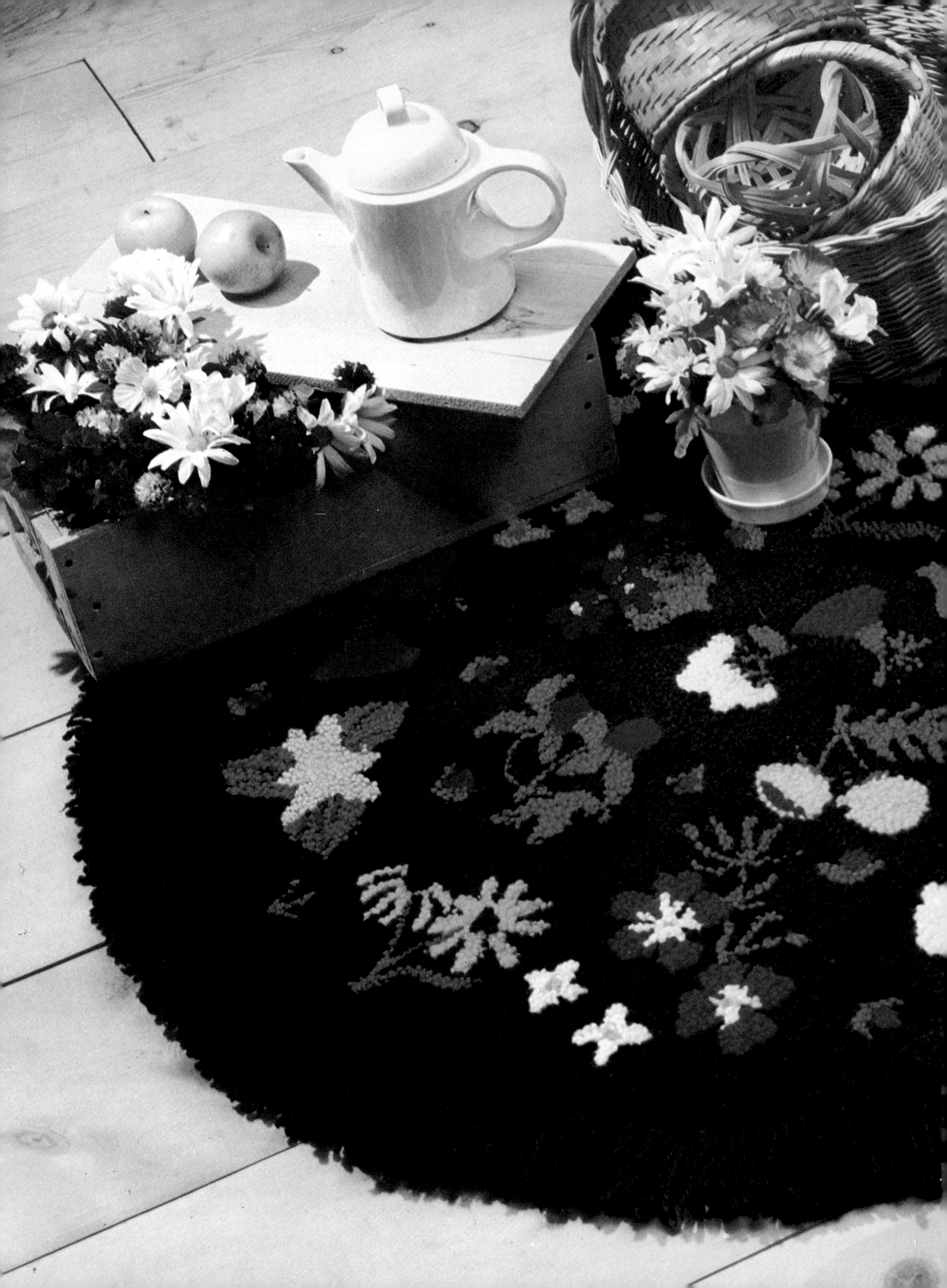

Hooked Rugs

When you hook a rug, you can create a field of flowers for your floor—such as the wildflower bouquet shown here—or any of dozens of other delightful designs.

Working with this technique is different from making braided, knitted, or crocheted rugs in that you sketch your pattern right on the burlap or canvas backing. The design possibilities are limitless, from beautifully simple to wonderfully complex.

The wildflower rug is hooked with a punch needle, and it's just one of our super patterns. To learn to make it, please turn the page.

How to Make a Hooked Rug

To hook a rug like the lovely wildflower design pictured on the preceding pages, you can use either a punch needle or latchet hook. Each tool, however, requires a different set of procedures, materials, and techniques, despite the fact that the end results are quite similar.

For a step-by-step guide to hooking with a punch needle, see the directions at right. For information on latch-hooking a rug, please see page 444.

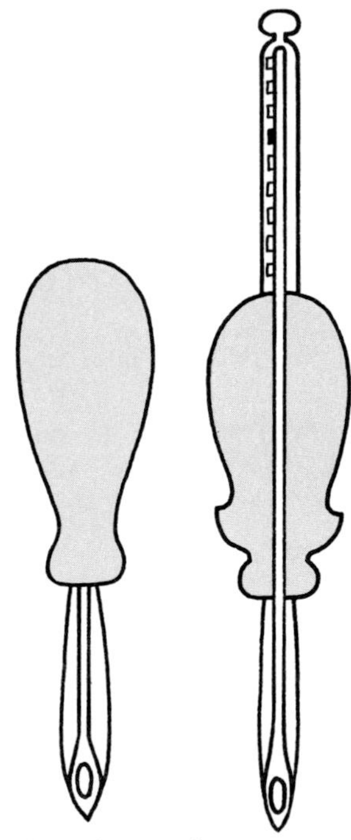

Punch-hooking tools

Materials and Equipment

Several kinds of punch-hooking tools are available for rug making. Some are equipped with needles in assorted sizes to accommodate anything from slender pearl cotton or linen threads up to the heaviest rug yarns. And some are adjustable to let you work everything from traditional low loops to long, rya-like loops for a shag look. In addition, there are several fast-action needles that make loops automatically as you turn the handle.

Choose the needle you find most comfortable and the one best suited to the yarn you plan to use, the design you are going to hook, and the speed with which you like to work.

Backing fabric holds the loops made by the needle. The weave must be tight enough to grip the loops, but loose enough to allow the needle to slip through easily.

Select a firm, long-wearing, even-weave fabric. Heavyweight burlap is popular because it is easy to work, readily available, and inexpensive.

Purchase enough fabric to allow a 3- to 6-inch margin around the design so that when it's mounted for hooking, the needle will not hit the frame.

A frame is essential when hooking a rug; the fabric must be taut or the hook will not work correctly. Use a purchased rug frame or make one from artist's stretcher strips or pieces of 1x2-inch lumber secured at the corners with C-clamps. Be sure corners are square and stable.

Estimating Yarn Requirements

To estimate yarn, see page 453.

Preliminary Steps

Begin by straightening the grain of the backing fabric and narrowly hemming the raw edges. Then transfer the design to the fabric, following directions on page 166. Be sure to reverse the pattern into a mirror image before transferring it since you will work from the back of the design. Finally, with the lengthwise grain of the fabric parallel to the sides of the frame and the design facing up, staple or overcast-stitch fabric tautly to frame.

Working the Design

To hook the design evenly, yarn must move freely through the needle. Thus, it's a good idea to rewind skeins of yarn into balls before beginning. Then thread the needle and adjust it for the length of the loops.

To begin hooking, hold the needle straight up and down over the canvas and push it completely into the fabric until the handle rests on the surface. (On the first stitch, the yarn tail will be on the face of the fabric; trim all tails even with loops after the rug is finished.) Raise the needle back up through the fabric until the tip just touches the fabric, then move it over a few threads for the next stitch. Work with the slot in the needle facing the direction in which you are hooking, and be sure the yarn flows freely. Continue as above, checking the face of the rug occasionally to be sure the pile is dense enough to cover backing.

As you work, outline small design areas first. Then fill them by hooking either in straight rows across each shape or in rows parallel to the outline, depending on the effect desired. The space between rows should be about the same as the space between loops. Hook the background last.

Loops may be left uncut or cut, as desired. If cut, they may be beveled to accent the design.

To finish the rug and secure yarn firmly to fabric after hooking, follow the directions on page 448.

Wildflower Bouquet *(shown on pages 436 and 437)*

Directions

Enlarge the pattern below and transfer it, centered, to backing fabric, following directions on page 166. Go over outlines with a waterproof pen so they are easy to see.

Tack backing fabric to a frame. With the punch-needle tool set to make a loop ½ inch long, fill in flowers, following directions opposite. Work the background last using green yarn.

When hooking is completed, coat the *punched area* of the back with liquid latex, following manufacturer's directions. Trim backing to within 4 inches of the hooked area. Thread tapestry needle with green yarn and sew a row of 4-inch loops ¾ inch from the punched edge using the rya knot stitch. Sew another row of loops between the first one and the punched edge. Clip and trim loops to make a 3-inch fringe.

Turn the rug over and notch and trim the margin to 2½ inches. Apply a band of liquid latex at the edge and press the hem into it with your fingers, making sure it lies flat. Let dry thoroughly.

44 inches

Low loops snugged close together make our wildflower rug a pleasing carpet of blooms. And its 44-inch size makes it large enough to bring the brilliance of springtime into your home.

Materials

60x60 inches burlap or punch-needle canvas
Rug punch tool
Rug frame
#13 tapestry needle
Embroidery transfer pencil
Waterproof pen
Staple gun
Liquid latex rug backing

Multi-craft acrylic rug yarn in the following colors and amounts:

- A Forest green (20 skeins)
- B Kelly green (3)
- C Dark violet (1)
- D Lemon yellow (1)
- E Sun-yellow (1)
- F Emerald green (1)
- G White (1)
- H Red-orange (1)
- I Light violet (1)
- J Brown (1)
- K Blue (1)
- L Pumpkin (1)
- M Medium magenta (1)
- N Dark Magenta (1)

Fantastical Animal Rug

This delightful child's rug is really four rugs in one. You can punch-hook each 24-inch block separately and then stitch them together into a square. Or, work just one in your child's favorite design to make a bath mat or a by-the-bed foot warmer.

Knitting yarns were used for this rug, but rug yarns work just as well.

Materials

4-ounce skeins knitting yarn in the following amounts and colors: 3 orange, 3 yellow, 2 scarlet, 1 emerald, 3 colonial blue, 1 black, and 1 purple
Four 27-inch squares heavy-duty burlap
Liquid latex rug backing
11 yards rug binding
Punch-needle tool
24x24-inch rug frame or artist's stretcher strips
Waterproof marking pen
1½-inch-wide paintbrush
Carpet thread

Color key

B Black
Bl Blue
G Green
O Orange
P Purple
R Red
Y Yellow

Directions

Note: If you wish to use rug yarn rather than knitting yarn, determine the yarn requirements by punching one square inch with the desired rug yarn. Then pull the stitches out and measure the length of yarn used. To determine how much more yarn you will need, figure how many square inches there are in each section of color.

Cut four 27-inch squares from the burlap. Enlarge and reverse the designs and transfer them, centered, to the wrong side of the burlap squares. Go over outlines with a waterproof marking pen. Attach the squares to the frame one at a time with extra-long thumbtacks, making sure the burlap is taut.

Thread the punch-needle tool and adjust it for ¼-inch loops. Punch-hook the designs following the general instructions on page 438, leaving a 1½-inch border of unworked burlap along each side of each square. Make sure the loops are close enough together to cover the backing completely. Begin and end the yarn on the right side, leaving a long tail that can be clipped later.

When all four designs are filled in, sew rug binding to the burlap along the edge of the punched area. Then, turn the binding under and slip-stitch it to the back of each square, making sure the stitches do not show on the front of the rug. Miter the corners.

Join the squares to make a 48x48-inch rug, using an overcast stitch and carpet thread. Brush a layer of liquid latex onto the back of the rug, following the finishing directions on page 448.

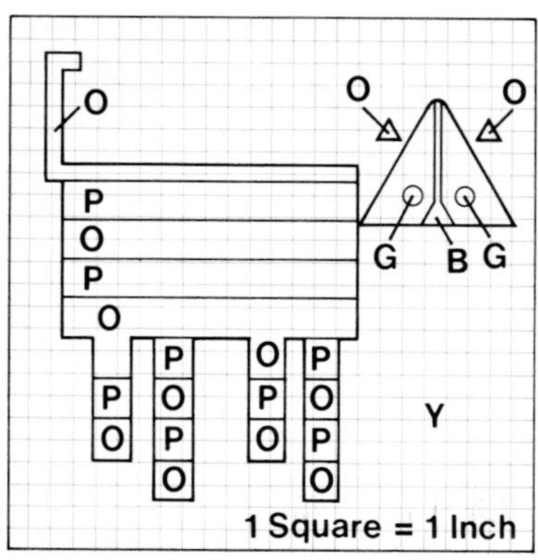

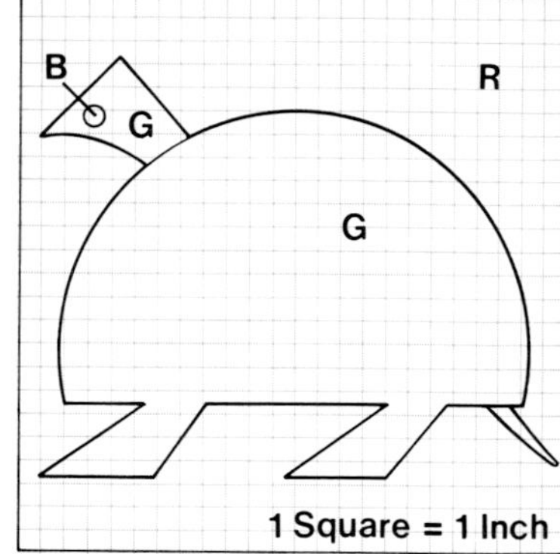

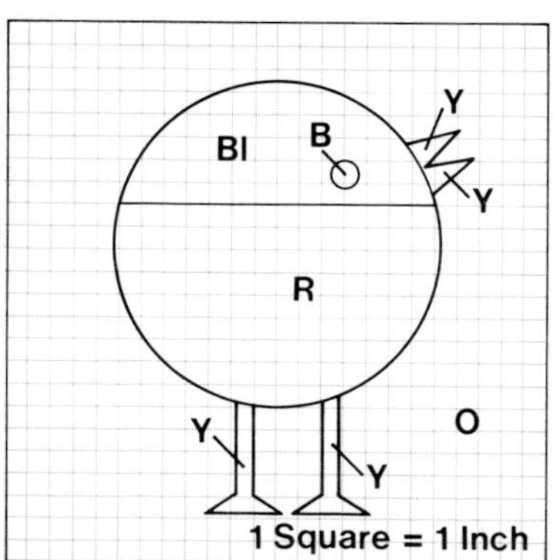

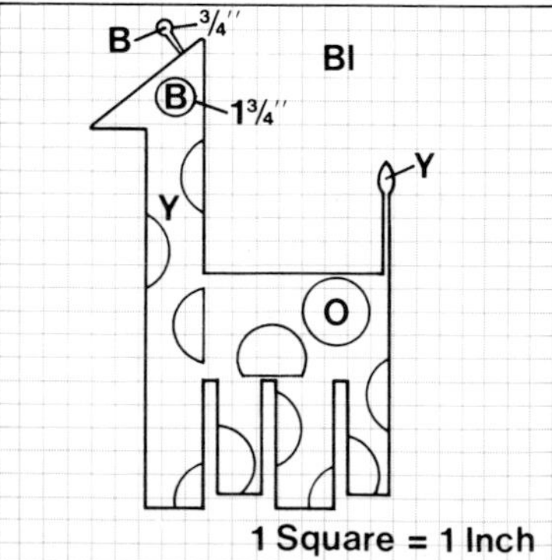

Design-Your-Own Scatter Rug and Pillow

Designing your own rug pattern is lots of fun and not at all difficult, as the small scatter rug and pillow pictured at the right illustrate. Just divide your rug fabric into four-unit blocks and create your own graceful pattern square-by-square. Or if you prefer, use our pattern below.

We worked this rug in earth-tone shades, but the design would be equally effective in six shades of another color, such as blue or green. Just select two light, two medium, and two dark shades of yarn.

Materials
Rug
28x40 inches heavy-duty burlap or punch-needle canvas
6 ounces each of Aunt Lydia's polyester rug yarn (or a similar substitute) in the following colors: cream, peach, burnt orange, rust, brown, and wood brown
Punch-needle tool
Rug frame or artist's stretcher strips
Waterproof marking pen
Liquid latex rug backing
Pillow
16x16 inches rug canvas
16x16 inches backing fabric
Pillow stuffing or 12-inch pillow form
1½ ounces each of Aunt Lydia's polyester rug yarn in the colors listed for rug (above)
Liquid latex rug backing

Directions
Rug
Begin by drawing a 2-inch margin around the rug backing with a waterproof marking pen, making a rectangle 24x36 inches. Divide the rectangle into six 12-inch squares. Then, using dotted lines, segment each square into four 6-inch squares. Draw a wavy line from the center of each of the 12-inch squares into all four corners, making a wavy "X" in each large square, and a wavy diagonal line across each of the smaller squares, as shown in the pillow at right. In the small squares, draw additional wavy lines on both sides of the center line, making stripes of varying widths, as shown in the pattern below. Note that there is a lot of variation in the direction and width of the "waves" in the squares that make up the design.

Or enlarge the pattern below and transfer it to each square of the fabric, rotating it to maintain the effect of the design.

Mount the backing in a frame for hooking. Set the punch-needle tool for ½-inch loops and hook the design, following the directions on page 438. Start by working three rows of loops along the lines dividing the small and large squares, using one of the dark shades (E). (Work one row right on the line, with the other rows on each side of the first one.) Next, punch-hook at least two rows of loops in the other dark shade (F) along the center line that runs diagonally across each small square (making the wavy "X" in the large square). Then, using the remaining four shades (A,B,C,D), work stripes across each block, varying the placement of colors and the width of the stripes from block to block. Punch loops close together, working about four loops per inch and about six rows per inch. Check the front of the rug occasionally to be sure pile is dense and rich-looking.

When all hooking is finished, remove the backing from the frame and finish the rug, following the directions on pages 448 and 449.

Pillow
Cut a 16-inch square of rug backing and draw a 12-inch square in the center. Divide the square into four smaller squares and mark the design, following the directions above for the rug. (Or, enlarge the pattern below and transfer it to the fabric.) Hook the design following the instructions above and on page 438.

To finish, coat the punched area with liquid latex. Sew the pillow front to back, stitching as close as possible to the punched area. Leave one side open. Turn, stuff, and slip-stitch the opening.

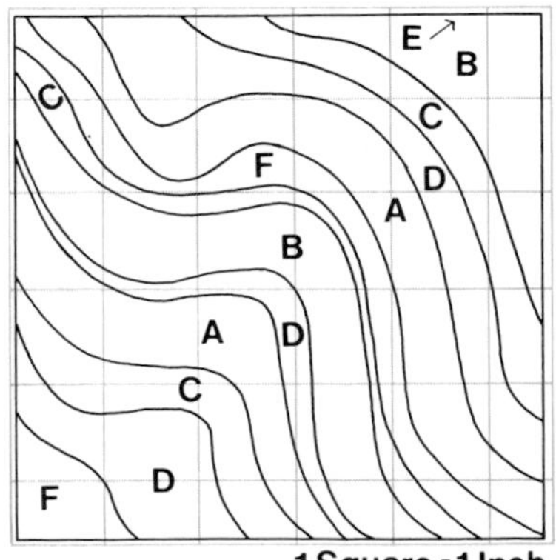

1 Square = 1 Inch

Color Key
A Cream
B Peach
C Burnt Orange
D Rust
E Brown
F Wood Brown

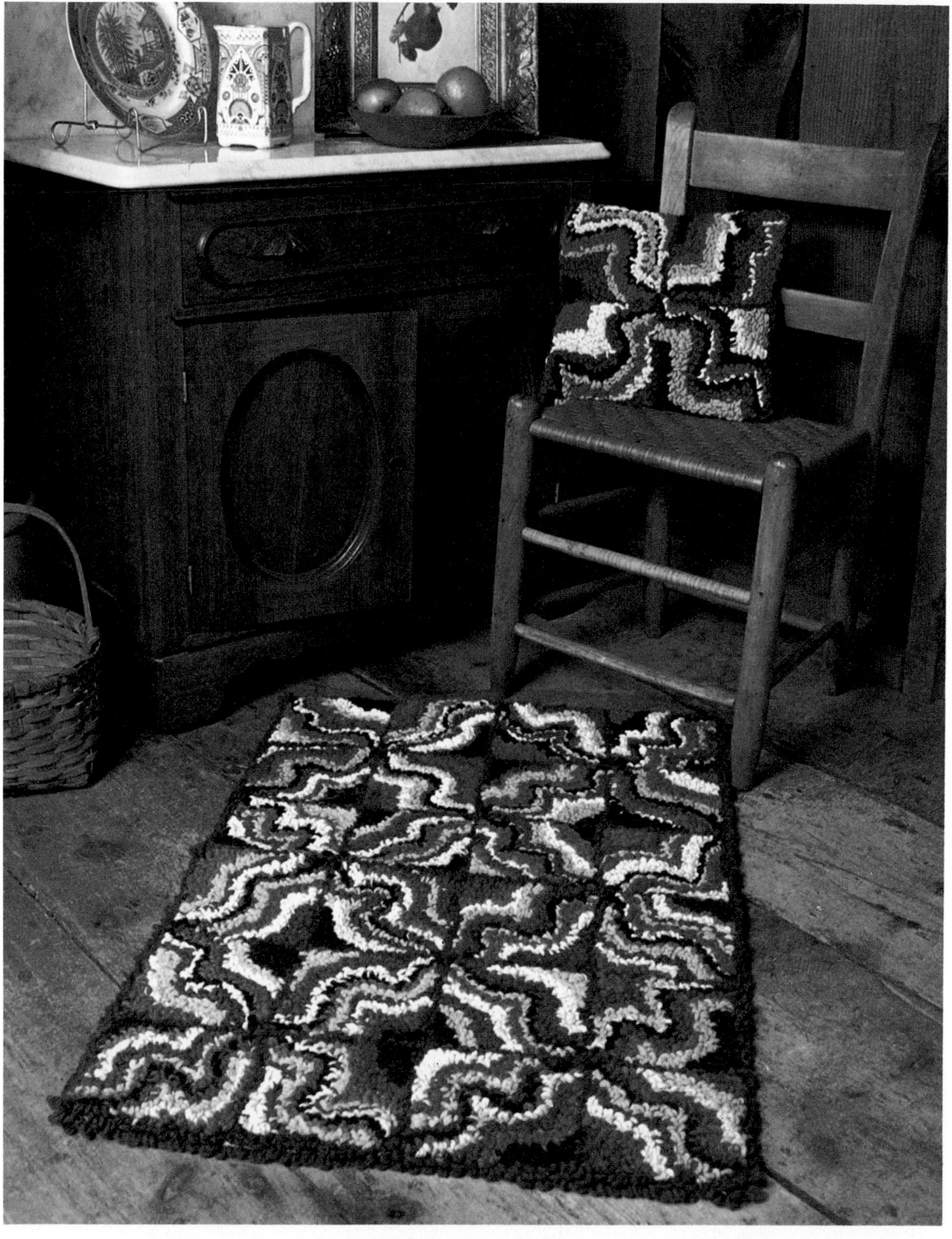

Latch-Hooking: Earth-Toned Rug

To make this attractive circular rug, use a latch hook to knot the yarn into the backing fabric, with the cut ends on the front. The basic instructions help guide your steps.

Materials

68-inch circle #4 or #5 rug canvas (whichever is available and easiest for you to work with)
Washable rug yarn cut in 3-inch lengths, or precut rug yarn in 2½- to 3-inch lengths, depending on desired length of pile
Latch hook
Waterproof marking pen
Carpet thread
Rug binding

1 Square = 2 Inches

Directions

Enlarge the pattern below left for the central motif, and transfer it to the center of the canvas, following the directions on pages 272 and 273. Then add a 10-inch band (brown) around the center, two 1½-inch bands (gold and rust), and a final 3-inch band (green).

Referring to the photograph for colors, work the design following the general instructions for latch-hooking below.

Materials and Equipment

Latch-hooked rugs are worked on penelope canvas — a dual-thread, open-weave backing fabric. It is available in different sizes, designated according to the number of mesh, or spaces, per linear inch. You'll find rug canvas in #3½-, #4-, #5-, and #7-count sizes.

When purchasing canvas, add an extra 4 to 6 inches to the finished dimensions of the rug to allow for blocking and hemming. If you cannot purchase a single length large enough for the rug, piece together several sections. Overlap sections 2 inches, *matching warp and weft threads of both pieces.* (Warp threads are the straight grain of the fabric, parallel to the selvage.) Then, whipstitch sections together.

Bind edges of canvas with tape to keep them from unraveling or tearing yarn as you work.

Yarn for latch-hooked rugs is available precut in 2½- and 3-inch lengths, with 300 to 350 pieces per 1-ounce package. Or, use yarn from skeins cut to the length desired (usually 2 to 3 inches). Fold a 3× 6-inch piece of cardboard in half lengthwise (into a "V"); wrap yarn around it. Then snip along the slot in the "V" with scissors, cutting yarn into pieces.

To determine the amount of yarn required, see page 453.

The latchet hook used to make the rug is a small tool with a hook at one end and a movable latchet bar beneath it. It pulls yarn into a lark's-head knot.

Making the Rug

Transfer design to canvas, following the directions on page 166. Make sure selvages of canvas are on the sides of the design rather than at top and bottom.

To work the design, lay the canvas right side up across a table and work from side to side and bottom to top, completing one row before moving to the next. Knot yarn into *weft* threads only, placing one knot in each square. As bottom rows become full, roll canvas into your lap.

To make each knot, grasp hook in one hand and wrap a piece of yarn around the shank, just below the latchet bar, keeping yarn ends even. Next, insert the hook into one space in the canvas and bring it out again in the space directly above, with the latchet bar open as shown in the diagram below. Then lay the ends of the yarn into the hook, as shown. Finally, pull the hook *back toward* you, out of the canvas. The latchet bar will close, making the knot.

Pull the ends of the yarn to tighten the knot. Continue, making knots across the row of canvas and changing colors whenever necessary.

Block and finish your rug, following directions on page 448.

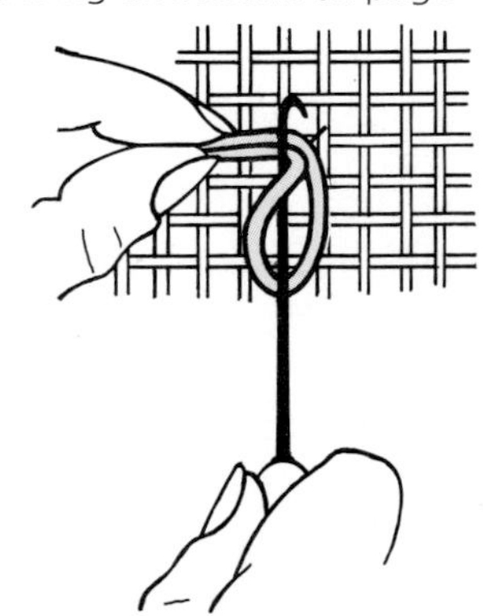

Contemporary Latch-Hooked Runner

Since this contemporary latch-hooked rug is assembled from 12-inch squares worked individually, you can make it any size you wish. After hooking a few squares, stitch them together to enjoy while you finish the others.

Or, work the rug into a 48 × 96-inch runner.

Materials

Thirty-two 16-inch squares of #5-count penelope rug canvas, or canvas pieced up to 52 × 100 inches (see note)
Acrylic rug yarn in bright primary colors (see note)
Latch hook
Waterproof marking pen
Brown wrapping paper
Carpet thread
Rug binding

Directions

Note: This rug is made of thirty-two 12-inch squares that can be worked one at a time and then sewn together. And while our rug measures 48 × 96 inches, you can make yours whatever size you wish simply by altering the number of squares or the way they are joined together. You can even make the rug entirely in one piece. To estimate yarn amounts, see page 453.

If you decide to make the rug in pieces, be sure to assemble the squares so that the large circle in the center of the design is evident (refer to the photograph to see how this is done).

Enlarge the pattern and transfer it to brown wrapping paper. To work the rug one square at a time, cut the rug canvas into 16-inch squares (this allows a 2-inch border of unworked canvas around all four sides) and center the squares on top of the pattern, one at a time. Trace each pattern onto canvas with a waterproof pen. To work the rug in one piece, transfer the designs to a single piece of canvas, leaving a 2-inch margin around the four outside edges.

Referring to the photograph for color ideas, outline each shape and fill it using a latch hook and acrylic rug yarn. (Refer to the latch-hook information on page 444 for basic how-to.) If you use skeins of rug yarn rather than precut pieces, cut the pieces into 2- or 3-inch lengths, depending on how long you want the pile.

To assemble the rug from squares, sew rug binding around each square; turn the 2-inch hem under and slip-stitch the binding to the back of the canvas. Piece the squares together with carpet thread so the rug measures four squares wide and eight squares long.

If you make the rug in one piece, sew binding to the four sides of the rug and turn the 2-inch margin under. Slip-stitch the binding to the back of the rug using carpet thread.

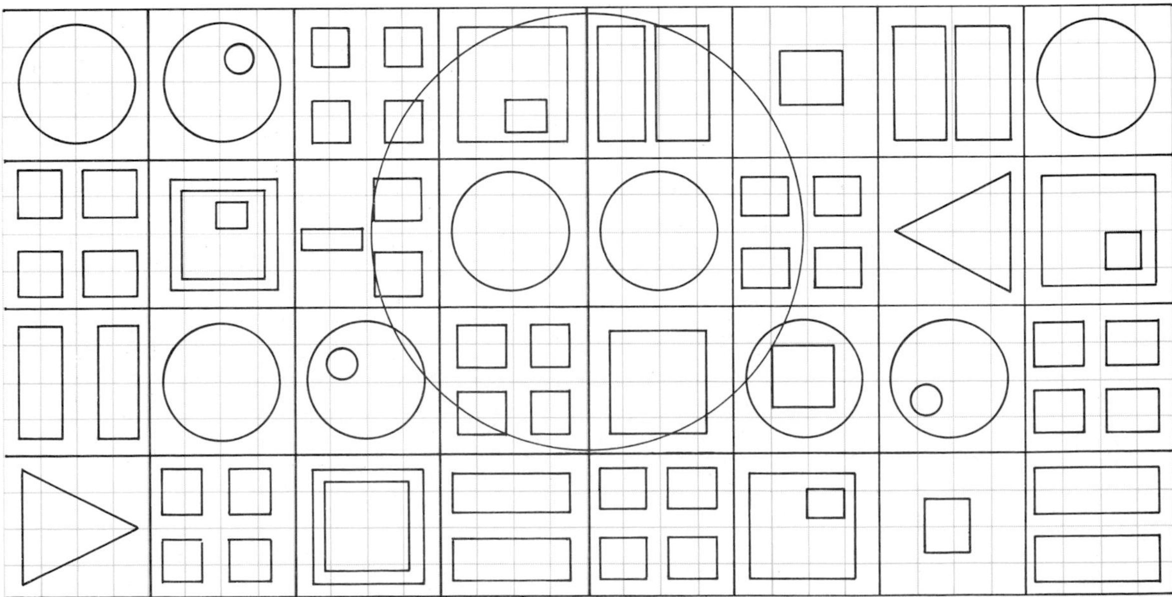

1 Square = 3 Inches

Finishing Techniques: Hooked Rugs

Careful and expert finishing is the final step in crafting a beautiful handmade rug. Here are some techniques for backing, blocking, and hemming hooked rugs that will help you achieve professional-looking results. You can apply the same finishing techniques to needlepoint rugs.

Finishing Punch-Hooked Rugs

Sealing the pile on a punch-hooked rug is essential to preserve its beauty. Otherwise, the loops will pull out, particularly if they've been clipped.

To secure the loops, you will need to coat the back of the rug with liquid latex rug backing – a strong but flexible rubber coating that binds the rug fibers to the fabric backing to hold them in place. It also helps to make the rug skid-proof.

There are two ways to back a punch-needle rug with latex, both of which are explained in the directions below.

One method of preparing a rug for the latex coating requires some tools and equipment: a base at least 2 to 3 inches larger all around than the finished rug (a piece of plywood works well), a hammer and nails, a carpenter's T-square or framing square, and a 1½- to 3-inch-wide paintbrush.

Remove the rug from the frame and lay it facedown on the board. Using the T-square or framing square, carefully align the corners of the rug, *so the lengthwise and crosswise threads of the backing fabric are at right angles to each other.* This is an extremely important step, for if the corners of the rug are not square when the latex is applied, the rug will be permanently distorted. Next, anchor the rug to the backing board with nails, spacing them 2 inches apart and 2 inches from the worked edge of the fabric.

An alternate method of finishing the rug is to apply latex to the back of the hooked area while it is on the rug frame. This is especially practical if the loops of the rug are long. To do this, make sure warp and weft threads of the fabric are at right angles. If they are not, adjust the backing fabric on the frame until they are. Then coat the back of the loops with latex, following the directions below.

Following manufacturer's directions, use a paintbrush to apply liquid latex to the back of the *hooked area only.* If necessary, apply two thin coats of latex rather than one thick coat. Be careful not to paint latex onto unworked areas of the fabric.

Allow the latex to dry undisturbed for at least 24 hours. Then remove the nails from the fabric (or the fabric from the frame) and trim the unworked areas of the backing to within 3 inches of the hooked edge. If desired, add a fringe to the rug at this point by working two rows of rya knots or double half-hitch knots into the margin along the hooked edge.

To hem the rug, carefully apply a 2-inch-wide border of latex to the back of the rug around the hooked edge. Then double-fold the unworked margin and firmly press it into the latex with your fingers, sealing it to the back of the rug. If necessary, notch curved edges so they lie flat and smooth. Let the latex dry thoroughly – at least 24 hours; the rug is then ready to use.

Finishing Latch-Hooked and Needlepoint Rugs

Because latch-hooked and needlepoint rugs are frequently worked in your lap rather than on a frame, they may need to be straightened before they are hemmed. If your rug has lost its shape while being worked, you'll need to block it on a base that is 6 to 8 inches larger than the rug itself; a piece of plywood works well. You'll also need a carpenter's T-square or framing square, nails or staples, towels or other absorbent fabric, and a household sprayer or sprinkler bottle filled with water.

Cover the board with towels or

absorbent fabric and lay the rug facedown over them. Using a sprayer or sprinkler bottle, thoroughly moisten the back of the rug; do not get it soaking wet, however. Also, try not to get the margin on the canvas overly wet; it may pull apart.

Next, nail or staple to the base the margin of canvas along the top of the rug so that the rug edge is parallel to the edge of the base. Space nails and staples 2 inches apart and 1½ inches from the worked area of the canvas.

Pull the bottom edge of the rug into shape, using the T-square or framing square to check that lengthwise and crosswise threads are at right angles to each other. Pull the canvas taut and, starting in the center of the edge, nail or staple it to the board. Repeat the procedure for the sides of the rug, making sure the canvas is stretched taut and is square. Then let the rug dry thoroughly (for two to three days).

If the rug is worked in sections, block each section first, then stitch sections together, right sides facing, with backstitches along the worked areas of the canvas. Be sure to match the designs, and align the mesh of the adjoining sections carefully.

To make the rug skid-proof and to help prevent dirt from working into the underside, you may coat the back of the rug with liquid latex, following the directions above. Do this after the blocked rug is thoroughly dry, but before it is removed from the blocking base.

After blocking, the rug is ready for hemming.

To hem a latch-hooked or needlepoint rug, use 2-inch-wide cotton rug tape. For round or oval rugs, use bias tape. Sew tape around the rug along the canvas margin on the face of the design, stitching the edge of the tape as close to the worked edge of the rug as possible. Use strong thread, such as carpet thread, and small slip stitches or running stitches. Then trim the canvas underneath the rug tape to about ¾ inch.

Turn the rug over, wrong side up, and sew the tape to the back of the rug with overcast stitches or slip stitches. Ease the tape to the rug; do not pull tightly.

Miter the corners to avoid a bulky finish by first cutting a piece from the rug tape, as shown in the top diagram at right. Fold over one side of the tape and overcast-stitch it in place. Then fold over the other side, so the diagonal edges meet. Stitch the tape to the rug and then sew the two diagonal edges together, as shown in the lower diagram at right.

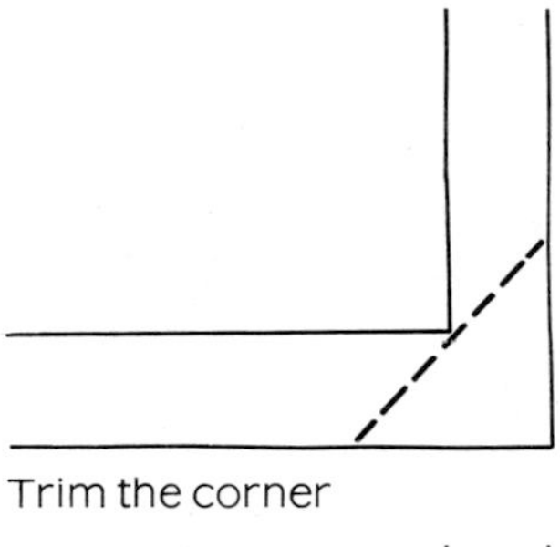
Trim the corner

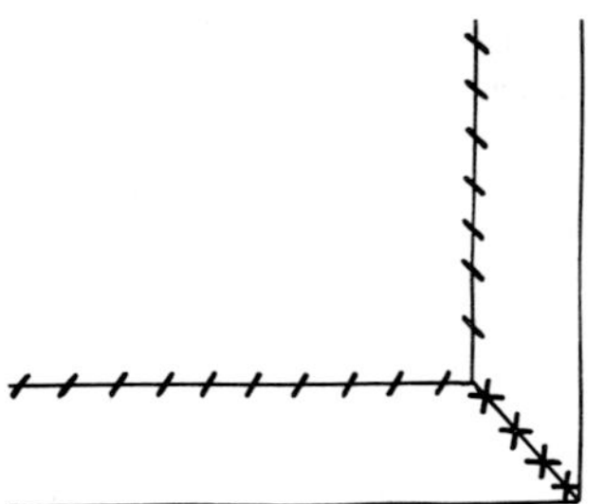
Miter and stitch

Lining a Rug

Occasionally a lining is called for in a handmade rug, usually to keep dirt away from the fibers in the rug. If you wish to add a lining to a rug made on canvas (punch-needle rugs do not need linings), select a firmly woven fabric in a color that complements the colors used in the rug. Purchase fabric equal to the size of the rug plus an inch all around for the hem margin.

Block and hem the rug following the directions above. Then turn under a 1-inch hem on the lining fabric and blindstitch it to the edges of the rug with strong thread. Next, thread a needle with heavy thread that matches the background color in the rug and, working from the front, take tiny stitches through both the rug canvas and the lining. Knot the ends of the thread and clip them close to the knots so they will not show. Take only as many stitches as are needed to keep the lining smooth and even. Make sure the lining is secure.

KNITTING DESIGNS
NOW NEEDLEPOINT
Jan Orr
BOYLES
NEEDLEPOINT STITCHERY
WIRE ART
Boutique

Special Rug-Making Techniques

This enchanting rug is crocheted over a clothesline! And it's just one example of the exciting techniques for rug making you'll find in this section. Here also are rugs to weave, needlepoint, and "hook" on a sewing machine. To learn to make the rug shown here, please turn the page.

"Clothesline" Crochet *(shown on pages 450 and 451)*

What could be more fun than dressing up ordinary clothesline in brightly colored cotton yarns to make an attractive crocheted rug? And it's easy, too, for it's worked entirely in single-crochet stitches. The directions are for a 36x56-inch runner, but you can alter the dimensions just by changing the length of the beginning chain and the number of rows you stitch. Crochet abbreviations are on page 432, and the basic stitches are explained on pages 230 and 231.

Materials

Three 80-yard skeins Aunt Lydia's cotton rug yarn in each of the following colors: red, orange, yellow, light green, dark green, blue, and purple
50 yards clothesline
Size I crochet hook

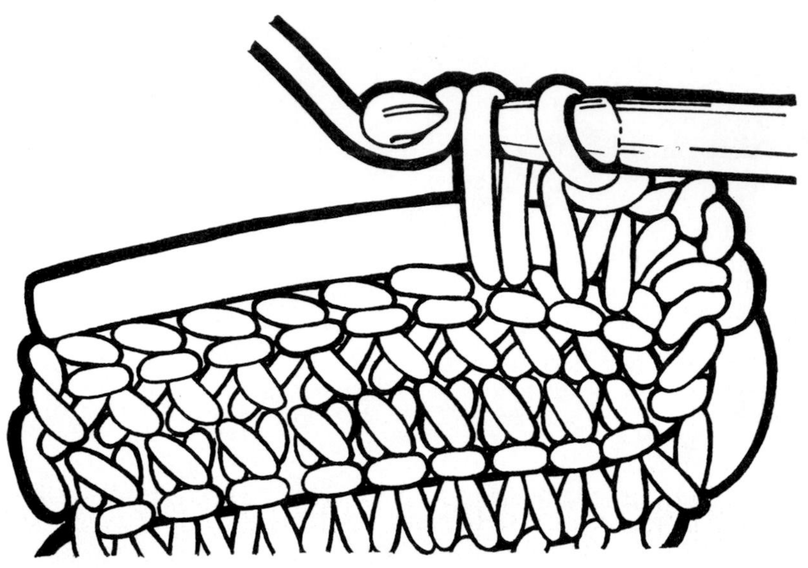

Single crochet over clothesline

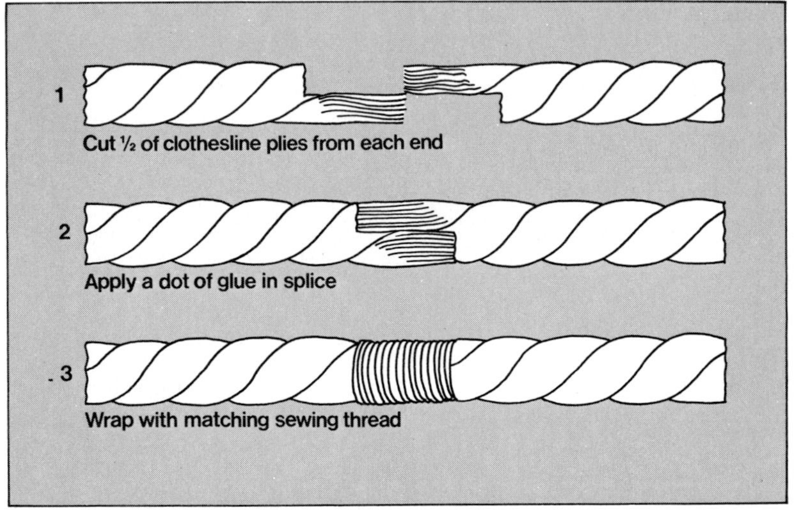
1
Cut ½ of clothesline plies from each end
2
Apply a dot of glue in splice
3
Wrap with matching sewing thread

Directions

With red yarn, ch 101.

Row 1: Sc in second ch from hook, and in each ch across—100 sc—ch 2, turn.

Row 2: Hold end of clothesline next to rug, and sc around clothesline in each sc across, following the diagram above. Ch 1, turn.

Row 3: Sc in each st across—100 sc. Change to orange (crocheting over yarn ends) and repeat these three rows in the following sequence: yellow, light green, dark green, blue, and purple. Repeat these 21 rows six times more, or for length desired; fasten off.

If necessary, splice clothesline by unraveling 1½ inches on end of each piece. Cut out half the ply of each piece, and overlap. Secure with dot of glue and wrap splice with matching color of sewing thread, as shown above.

How to Estimate Materials Requirements for a Rug

If you've found a rug design that you'd like to work in a different technique or material than that called for in the directions, or if you've designed your own pattern, you'll need to estimate the amount of yarn or other materials needed to complete your project.

Here are some tips to guide you in determining these requirements for hooked, needlepoint, and rya rugs. To estimate requirements for rag and braided rugs, see *page 414; for woven rugs, turn to page 471.*

For hooked, needlepoint, and rya rugs, the first step in estimating materials needed for a design is to determine as closely as possible the total number of square inches of each color in the pattern. The easiest way to do this is to enlarge the pattern onto paper marked into one-inch squares, following directions on page 272 for enlarging on a grid.

Next, mark each color area, inch by inch, throughout the design. When a color fills only part of a square, estimate what fraction of an inch that color requires. Finally, total the number of square inches in each color; make a note of the amount.

The second step is to determine the amount of material required to work one square inch of the design in the technique and materials you've selected for your project. Purchase a small amount of each of the materials you intend to use, such as yarn and backing fabric. Then work a sample swatch in the technique you've chosen, following the specific directions below.

Finally, multiply the amount of material needed to work one square inch by the total number of square inches of each color in the design to determine the number of yards or pieces of material required. Then, just to be on the safe side, add a little extra to allow for waste, unless you've already been generous in your yarn estimates.

Punch-Hooked and Needlepoint Rugs

Purchase a small piece of backing fabric and hook or stitch a one-inch square with the needle and yarn you intend to use in the rug. For a punch-hooked rug, determine the length of the loops best suited to the design, and the correct spacing between loops for the best coverage of the fabric (so no backing shows).

Determine the amount of yarn needed to cover one square inch by carefully pulling out the yarn in the finished sample. Measure the length of the yarn (in yards), then compute requirements, following directions above.

Latch-Hooked Rugs

A package of precut yarn, containing 300 to 350 pieces, will cover the number of square inches of canvas shown below:

Canvas Size	300 Pieces	350 Pieces
3½-count	24½	28½
4-count	18¾	22
5-count	12	14
7-count	6	4

To latch-hook a rug with yarn in skeins, determine the number of yards per skein, the length you intend to cut pieces for hooking, and the number of pieces that can be cut from each skein. Referring to the chart above, compute the amount required. For example, with 70-yard skeins cut into 3-inch lengths, you'll get 840 pieces from each skein, and these will cover 52½ square inches of #4-count rug canvas.

Rya Rugs

Transfer the design to rya backing fabric first. Then, compute the number of knots either by counting the knotting spaces or by estimating the number of square inches in each color area.

Work a sample square inch of knots, threading the needle with the number of strands of yarn you intend to use and making loops the desired length. As you stitch, keep track of the amount of yarn used. Compute final requirements by multiplying the amount required for one knot (or square inch of knots) by the total number of knots (or square inches) in that color and yarn.

Off-Loom Weaving

Card weaving is an easy and exciting technique for making strips to stitch into rugs. To make your own cards, cut twenty-two 3½-inch cardboard squares and punch holes in each card one inch diagonally from each corner. Then mark cards with letters as shown below, warp them, and weave this sturdy 24x36-inch rug.

Materials

70-yard skeins Aunt Lydia's polyester rug yarn (or a suitable substitute) in the following amounts and colors: 18 black, 4 brick, and 12 antique gold
22 four-hole weaving cards
Heavy-duty thread

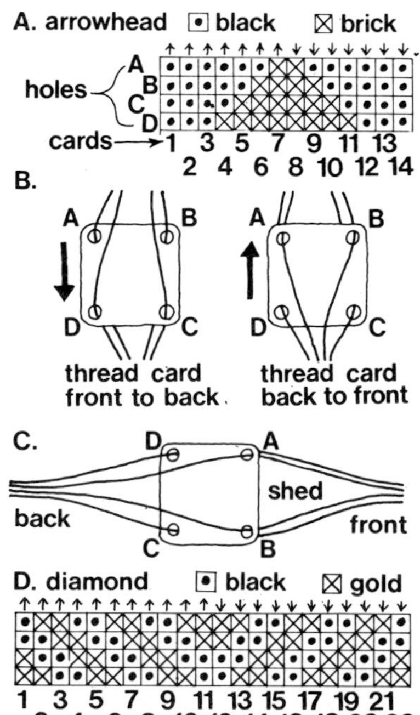

Directions

Start with arrowhead strips. Cut eighteen 5-yard pieces of black yarn and ten 5-yard pieces of brick for warp threads. Tie together all the warp threads in a tight bundle at the center, using one yard of scrap yarn. Anchor the ends of the tie to a doorknob or table leg and spread ends of the warp threads in front of you.

To thread cards for weaving, number 14 cards from 1 to 14. To thread, hold each card at an angle to your body with lettered side facing left. Each hole will be threaded with one strand of yarn. Study diagram A for colors; arrows at the top of the diagram indicate threading direction (up or down). Diagram B indicates how to thread the card in each direction. If the arrow in diagram A points up, thread the card from right (back) to left (front). If the arrow points down, thread from left (front) to right (back).

Following diagram A, begin threading with card 1. Since the arrow is going up, thread each strand of black yarn from the back of the card through to the front. Then pull the yarn strands through the holes about 12 inches beyond the card. Repeat for card 2; then stack 2 atop 1. Continue threading and stacking cards according to the colors and arrows in diagram A. Note that cards 1 to 7 are threaded in one direction (up), while cards 8 to 14 are threaded in the opposite direction (down).

After threading cards, tie a cord around them. There should be 12 inches of yarn in front of the cards; the rest should be in back.

Gather the free ends of the warp in one hand. With the other end of the yarn still fastened to the table leg, pull the free ends until they are taut. Then knot the free ends together tightly with a piece of yarn. Secure this end (the front in diagram C) to your waist around a belt or belt loop. Sit far enough from the table leg so the warp threads remain taut at all times.

To weave, wind four strands of black yarn around a shuttle or into a ball. Hold the pack of cards upright, as shown in diagram C. Draw black weft yarns through the shed (shown in diagram C) between the cards and your body, leaving the first 6 inches of the yarn ball free to weave into the strip when the weaving is complete. Holding the cards as a unit, turn them *forward* to create a new shed. (You started with holes AD on top and, after turning, holes BA will be on top.) Draw the weft through that shed.

If some cards don't turn, make sure they're threaded properly. After each row (one turn of the cards), beat back the weft threads tightly, pushing them toward your body. Also stop periodically to untwist the warp yarns beyond the cards. Continue turning cards in the same forward direction, passing the weft through each new shed until the woven strip is 36 inches long. Then untie the knots and remove the cards, but don't trim the fringe yet. Make three more arrowhead strips in the same way.

For the diamond design, cut twenty-two 5-yard pieces each of black and gold yarn. Thread all cards following diagram D. Prepare warp threads, following directions above. Use black for weft.

To weave, work 14 rows, turning the cards *forward* as you did with the arrowhead strips. Work the next 14 rows, turning the cards *backward*, in the opposite direction. Continue until weaving measures 36 inches. Weave six strips.

To assemble the rug, stitch strips together with heavy-duty thread, using the photograph as a guide. Trim ends of fringe evenly.

Sewing Machine "Hooking": A Quick-and-Easy Rug

"Hook" a rug on a sewing machine? It's easy! Our luxurious 3x5-foot throw, opposite, is made by wrapping rug yarn around a hairpin lace frame, then stitching down the frame's center with nylon thread to form long strips. Position these strips on a fabric backing and stitch them down the center a second time. Then either cut the yarn or leave it looped.

Materials

Sewing machine
Ten 2-ounce skeins white rug yarn
Eight 2-ounce skeins yellow rug yarn
2½-inch-wide hairpin lace frame (available in needlecraft shops)
4-inch-wide hairpin lace frame
Clear nylon thread for spool
White thread for bobbin
1¾ yards washable duck canvas or rug burlap
Liquid latex rug backing
Tissue paper

Directions

Cut rug backing 40 x 64 inches. Draw a 2-inch border around the rug for the hem, and a second border, 6 inches wide, inside the first one for the yellow yarn.

To make white rug yarn loops, use the 2½-inch lace frame. With the curved part close to you, begin wrapping rug yarn around the frame, keeping the loops close together as you wind (as shown in the left diagram below).

Thread the sewing machine with clear nylon thread on top and white thread in the bobbin. Lower the feed dogs. When several inches of yarn loops have been wrapped, stitch the yarn down through the *middle* of the lace frame. Be sure to keep the yarn loops close together without gaps. As the yarn is stitched, let it slide off the open end of the frame; pull the frame toward you, and continue wrapping the yarn around the frame. When you've made a strip of yarn loops 48 inches long, cut the yarn and begin a new strip. Make 27 white yarn strips and 8 yellow yarn strips, each 48 inches long. Also stitch eight 36-inch yellow strips.

Place a large piece of tissue paper or lightweight interfacing *under* the rug canvas to prevent puckering as you stitch. (It tears off easily when you have finished stitching.)

The completed rectangular rug consists of 27 rows of white yarn strips in the center surrounded by 4 rows of yellow strips along each side for a border. To stitch the yarn strips in place, position a long yellow strip along the edge of one side of the backing and parallel to the center panel. Stitch down the center of the yarn strip a *second* time, to secure it to the backing (see the how-to photograph below). For the second row of yellow strips, hold the first row out of the way and stitch the second one alongside. Its center seam will be 1 to 1½ inches from the seam on the first row of yellow loops. Sew a third and fourth row of yellow loops to the backing inside the 6-inch border. Then stitch rows of white loops, spacing center seams only ¼ inch apart. This gives the rug a plush look and hides the backing fabric. Continue stitching strips to the backing until the rug is complete.

Clip the yellow yarn loops with scissors when the rug is finished. Do not cut the white yarn loops.

Turn the 2-inch hem to the back of the rug and press; slip-stitch the hem to the rug back. Apply liquid latex to the back, if desired. Do not use the rug in high-traffic areas.

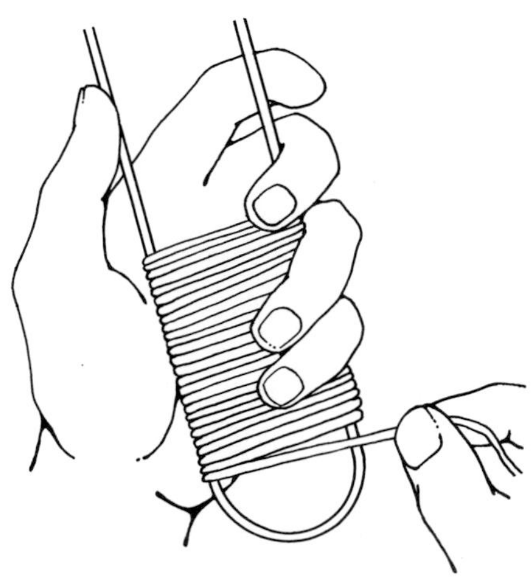

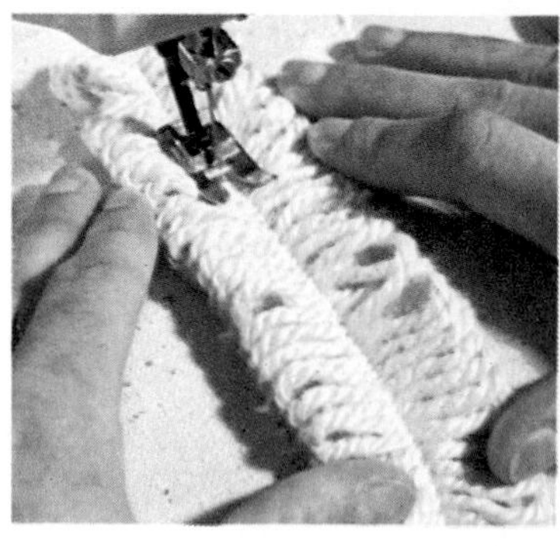

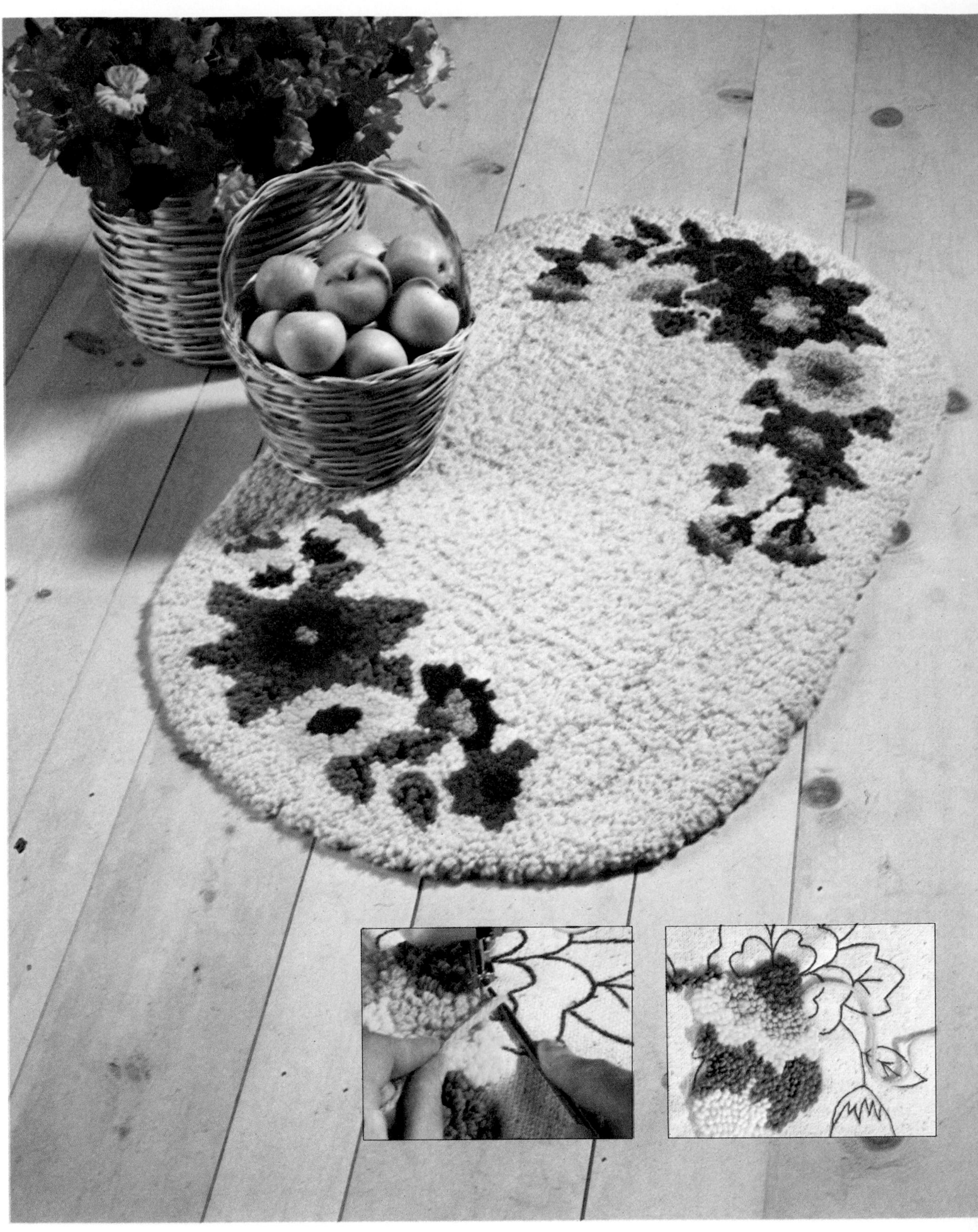

Sewing Machine "Hooking" *(continued):*
Floral Throw Rug

You can "hook" this traditional design on your sewing machine with beautiful results. Our splashy floral rug looks hooked, but is actually worked entirely of closely spaced loops of rug yarn stitched in place by machine.

Materials
1⅓ yards washable duck canvas or rug burlap for backing
Three 2-ounce skeins ivory rug yarn
½ skein rug yarn in each of the following colors: yellow, gold, rust, plum, olive green, and dark green
Knitting needle, pencil, or other instrument for lifting yarn loops
Clear nylon thread for spool
White thread for bobbin
Tissue paper
Dressmaker's carbon paper
Liquid latex rug backing

Color Key
D Dark green
O Olive green
P Plum
G Gold
R Rust
Y Yellow

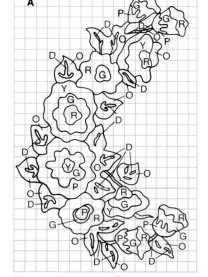

Directions
Note: The finished size of this rug is approximately 26 x 44 inches. Dimensions below allow for a 2-inch hem.

Enlarge the patterns below and transfer motifs to a 48x30-inch oval of backing fabric using dressmaker's carbon paper. Follow the oval drawing for proper placement of the rug motifs.

Place a large sheet of tissue paper *under* the fabric backing to help prevent puckering as you sew.

Thread the sewing machine with clear nylon thread to hide the stitches. Then remove the machine's presser foot and lower the feed dogs. Beginning with the design areas and following the color key, stitch loops of yarn to the canvas backing. It is easiest to stitch one area of color at a time.

To attach yarn loops, first stitch the end of a length of yarn to the material. Pull up a yarn loop using the knitting needle or pencil to the *right* of the sewing machine needle, as shown in the inset photograph at left, opposite. Stitch slowly over the base of the yarn loop to secure it to the backing. Then pull up the next loop alongside the first one and stitch it in place. Continue pulling and stitching loops in this manner to complete each color area, as shown in the right inset photograph. Change yarn color when necessary. Be sure to place the loops close enough that no backing fabric shows through.

To fill in the ivory background areas faster, use several lengths of yarn together and pull up more than one loop at a time. Then, stitch across all loop bases at the same time.

When the rug is complete, turn the 2-inch fabric margin to the back of the rug and press. Slip-stitch the margin in place, trimming excess to eliminate bulk. Apply a nonskid backing of liquid latex, if desired.

(*Note:* Although this rug is sturdy, it is not designed for high-traffic areas. Clean the rug by dry cleaning it.)

1 Square = 1 Inch

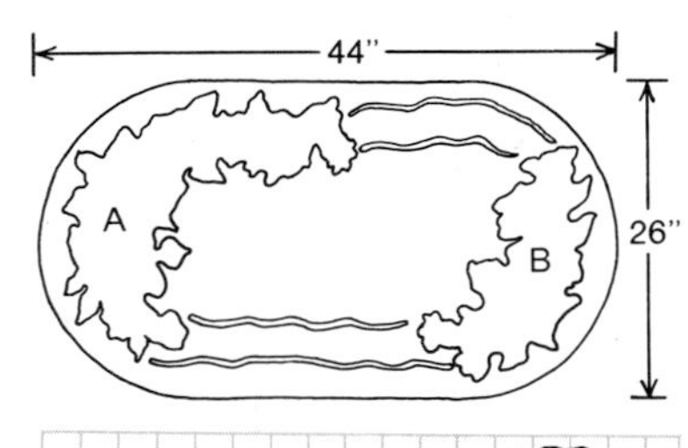

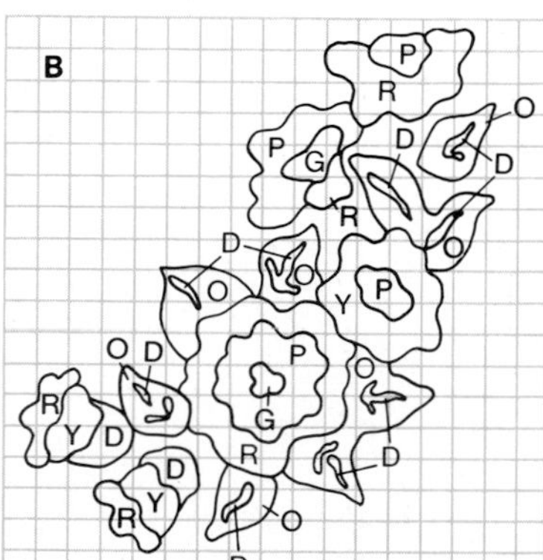

1 Square = 1 Inch

Needlepoint Border

Our 12-inch quickpoint border adds personal pizzazz to a carpet remnant. To make it, work strips of canvas in simple basket-weave and continental stitches. Then join strips together, work the corners, and stitch the borders to a 30x42-inch piece of carpet.

Materials

30x42 inches beige carpeting (purchased)
6¼x4 feet of #5-count canvas
70-yard skeins acrylic rug yarn in the following amounts and colors: 12 white, 8 blue, and 6 brown
Carpet thread
7 yards carpet tape
Large-eyed tapestry needle
Heavy-duty sewing needle

Color Key
☐ brown (3 stitches)
■ blue (9 stitches)
☐ white

Directions

Note: The finished size of the rug is 54x66 inches.

Cut two 70x16-inch strips of canvas and two 34x16-inch strips of canvas. These measurements allow for 2-inch margins of unworked canvas. Bind the raw edges of the canvas with masking tape. Mark the center horizontal and vertical threads on each canvas strip.

Begin the quickpoint pattern in the middle of a 70-inch strip. Starting with brown yarn, work the design following the pattern below. Stop within 14 inches of both ends. Then, work the blue yarn and fill in the background with white yarn, again stopping within 14 inches of the ends. Repeat for the second 70-inch strip, making sure the stitches are worked in the same direction.

Join one of the 34-inch strips to one of the already-worked 70-inch strips by overlapping the top left-hand edge of the 70-inch strip over the bottom two inches of the short side of the 34-inch strip. Line up outside edges to make a right angle. Match the holes and whipstitch the two pieces together. Work the corner, following the pattern and stitching through both pieces of canvas where the strips overlap, keeping the holes aligned.

Work up the left-hand side of the rug to within five inches of the end of the strip. Repeat overlapping procedure on right-hand side and continue working the design as for the left-hand side.

Lay the second 70-inch strip across the top ends of the two short strips, matching corners, holes, and pattern lines. Trim excess canvas if necessary, and whipstitch the strips together where they overlap. Complete stitching on remaining corners, working through two layers of canvas where the pieces overlap.

Block the finished border, following the instructions on page 448. Fold under and press 2-inch margins of unworked canvas along the outside edge of the border. Whipstitch the edges of the back of the border and mask with carpet tape.

Cut a 30x42-inch piece of purchased carpet and whipstitch it to the inside 2-inch margins.

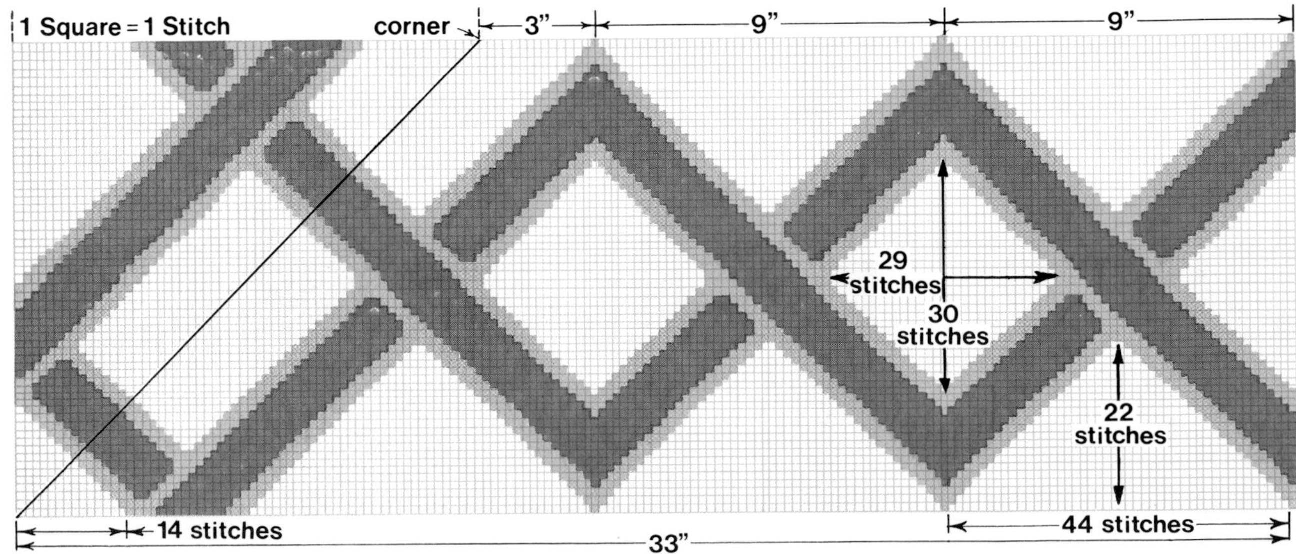

Creative Rug Making

Yes, you can macrame a rug, as our unique rope runner proves! It's simply a matter of turning your talents in new directions. And in this section, you'll find other exciting and unusual rugs to stimulate your creativity. For example, you can think big and weave a stack of small rugs to join into a stairway runner, or think small and stitch a cross-stitch/latch-hook throw rug. You can show off your mastery of many techniques in a single rug, or use just one technique—speed hooking—to work a rug in a hurry. Directions for the runner begin on the next page.

Macrame Rug *(shown on pages 462 and 463)*

The attractive runner shown on pages 462 and 463 features stylized animals and a central Tree of Life design worked with double half-hitch knots in Cavandoli stitches. Separating the panels are bands of alternating square knots. Patterns for the panels are on page 467.

Materials
2-ply jute in the following colors and amounts: 1500 yards natural, 150 yards dark red, 150 yards brown, 150 yards dark green, 150 yards rust, and 150 yards dark blue
18x36 inches of ⅜-inch plywood
Heavy-duty sewing needle
Dental floss or carpet thread
Fast-drying craft glue
Liquid latex rug backing
Staple gun and staples

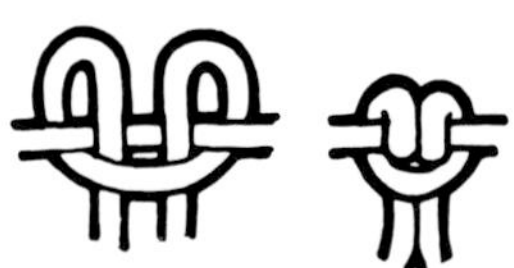

Lark's head knot

Square knot

Directions
Note: The finished size of the runner shown on pages 462 and 463 is 22x68 inches. To make it wider, increase the numbers of knots in multiples of 14, since each animal block is 14 knots wide. (Each block of 14 knots is approximately 2¾ inches wide.) To make the runner longer, increase the depth of the border design or of the alternating square-knot panels. You'll also need to alter the amounts of cord needed for the runner if you increase the size.

To make the rug in the size shown, cut a 36-inch bearer cord from natural jute; then, cut fifty-six 4-yard lengths of natural jute. Fold the 56 pieces in half and attach each one to the bearer cord with a lark's head knot, as shown in the top diagram at left. Staple the bearer cord to the top of the plywood board along the 36-inch side, making sure the ends of the cords are free for tying.

To work the border at the top of the runner, staple a piece of brown jute about 2 yards long to the left side of the plywood so it is perpendicular to the cords at the point where the border design is to begin (just below the lark's head knots). Following the border diagram on page 467, work six rows in Cavandoli stitches, which are explained on page 466. Note that one square on the diagram equals one knot, although each knot is made up of two loops. As you work, push loops of knots close together so they completely cover the bearer cord.

Leave the ends of the cords along the left side of the rug about 4 inches long so they can be turned under and tacked down when the rug is finished. Splice the colored jute as necessary, following the instructions opposite.

Next, work nine rows of alternating square knots in natural jute. Make individual square knots, following the bottom diagram at left and using the center cords of adjoining knots as filler cords. After completing the first row, work a second row of knots using the filler cords from the first row, as shown in the top diagram opposite. Continue until you've tied nine rows of knots.

You are now ready to begin the first animal panel. There are five designs for the animal panels and the center design panel that make up the finished rug. Each row of animals is worked twice, so the lower half of the rug is a mirror image of the upper half. The eight animals in each row are worked in alternate directions so each pair of animals faces each other.

To work the animals, refer to the charted designs on page 467. Work the bird panel first, using dark red cord. Then work the crocodile in dark green, the bull in dark brown, the fish in rust, and the llama in dark blue. Each band, worked in Cavandoli stitches, is 14 rows deep. To begin, staple a length of colored jute about 2 yards long to the plywood and work the first row of the panel entirely in horizontal double half-hitch knots (see diagrams on page 467). On the second row of the panel, begin working the pattern, counting knots carefully so they correspond to the charted designs.

Work the pattern as it is shown in the chart, and then flop the chart so the next animal faces the opposite direction from the first one, as shown in the photograph on pages 462 and 463. Work the entire chart again (in reverse). Continue working the animal blocks alternately across the width of the runner as many times as necessary. Splice cords whenever necessary.

Separate each band of animals with nine rows of alternating square knots, following the directions above. After working six bands of square knots (counting from the top of the runner), work the center.

The Tree of Life design in the center panel of the rug is 33 rows deep. The diagram on page 467 shows the first 16 rows of the pattern and the seventeenth, center, row. It also indicates the first two repeats of the motifs. Work the chart as indicated eight times across the rug, making 16 tree motifs.

Work the first two rows of the center panel in rust, stapling the colored bearer cord to the plywood on the left of the rug immediately below the last row of square knots in the band of alternating square knots that precedes the center design. Work horizontal half-hitches in natural jute over the bearer cord, and vertical half-hitches in the colored cord over the natural cords, as indicated on the diagram.

After the first two rows, work five rows of dark red, five of dark green, and three of dark blue, following the chart on page 467. Work the next two rows of rust to finish the first half of the center panel. To complete the entire design, reverse the order of the first 16 rows and finish the pattern so the bottom half of the panel is a mirror image of the top half. Start colored bearer cords (for the vertical half-hitches) by stapling them to the board at the left side of the runner. Splice cords when necessary.

When the center panel is finished, work nine rows of alternating square knots, following directions above. Then work the second half of the rug as for the first, reversing the order and working the animals from bottom to top so they point in toward the center of the rug, as shown in the photograph on pages 462 and 463. In other words, work

continued

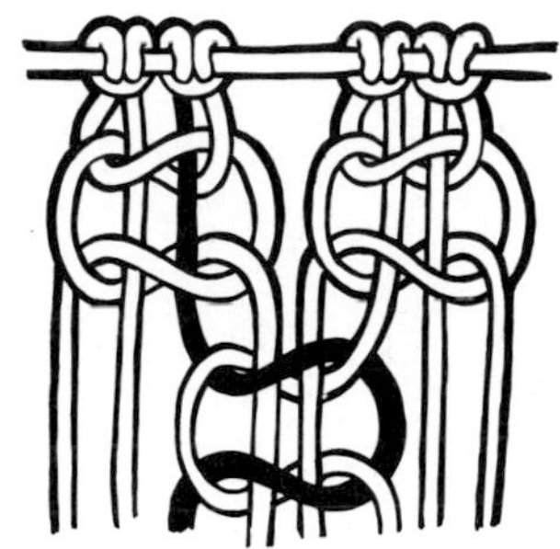

Alternating square knot

Splicing Macrame Cords

Because of the size of this project, it's impossible to work with cords cut to the length of the rug itself. Even tying the cords into butterfly knots (as is usually done) becomes too cumbersome and time-consuming. Instead, work with pieces of cord no longer than 2 yards and splice each cord when it becomes short enough to need replacement. The procedures for adding new cords vary according to the type of knots being tied.

On Cavandoli-stitched bands, when a cord runs short, plan the knotting so you can tie in a new cord when the short cord (the one you're going to drop) *is going to be a knotting cord rather than a bearer cord.* Drop the short cord and tie in the new cord with a double half-hitch, as shown in the center diagram at right. Leave a tail about 2 inches long at the end of the cord to tuck to the back of the rug; tie it to the dropped cord when the rug is finished.

In alternating square-knot bands, replace a cord when it is a *filler cord in a square knot rather than a knotting cord,* as shown in the bottom diagram at right, by simply laying in a new cord. If desired, trim half the ply from the old and new cords, glue, and wrap with thread, as shown in the diagram on page 452.

After completing the rug, turn it over and tie loose ends of all cords; secure the knots to the back of the rug with a dot of fast-drying craft glue. Let dry.

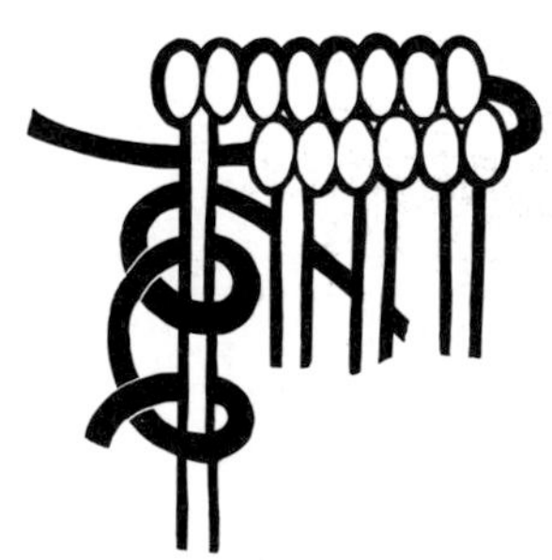

Splicing on Cavandoli bands

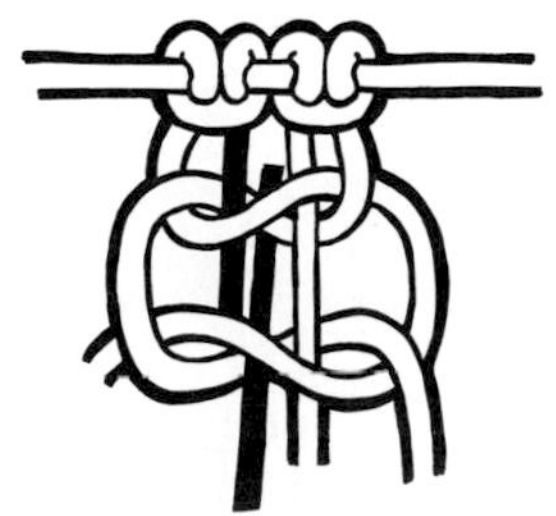

Splicing on alternating square-knot bands

Macrame Rug *(continued)*

the llama band first, then the fish, the bull, the crocodile, and the birds. Work nine rows of alternating square knots between each row of animals and following the birds.

End the rug with six rows of the border pattern used at the top of the rug, working the border also in Cavandoli stitches. Follow directions for the border on page 464.

To finish the runner, fold the ends of all the cords under and tack them to the back of the rug with dental floss or carpet thread. Tie the spliced ends together and secure them to the back of the rug with a dot of glue.

If desired, coat the back of the rug with a light layer of liquid latex rug backing to help keep ends secure and make the rug skid-proof. To apply latex, turn the rug wrong side up and tack it to a plywood base with nails, making sure corners are square and the rug is stretched taut. With a narrow paintbrush, carefully brush a thin layer of latex onto the back, following manufacturer's directions. When coating the bands of alternating square knots, skim the tops of the knots with the latex. Don't saturate them; any latex that soaks through to the front of the knots is apt to be visible on the surface of the rug. Allow the rug to dry thoroughly — at least 24 hours — before removing it from the base. Reapply latex when an area becomes worn.

Horizontal double half-hitch

Vertical double half-hitch

Cavandoli work

Cavandoli Work

Cavandoli work is a knotting technique worked in horizontal and vertical bars so it resembles a solid piece of fabric or tapestry (as in the animal and Tree of Life panels in the macrame rug on pages 462 and 463). It consists of one basic knot, the double half-hitch, and its variation, the vertical double half-hitch (see diagrams at left). Usually worked in two colors, the knotting cords of the background and the contrasting bearer cords make the pattern when vertical double half-hitch knots are combined with regular (horizontal) double half-hitch knots. The background of the design is worked in horizontal double half-hitches, while the colored motif is worked in vertical double half-hitches, as shown in the diagram at left. Thus, the patterns are formed by counting number, color, and direction of knots.

Three or more colors may be worked when the colors are contained within their prescribed rows, as in the Tree of Life panel in the center of the rug.

For Cavandoli work, tie the natural (background) knotting cords to a bearer cord and anchor the bearer cord to a stable base, such as a piece of plywood. Then anchor a cord in a contrasting color beyond the left margin of the rug. Carry the other end of the cord straight across the rug, perpendicular to the knotting cords, and anchor it on the right side so it is straight and taut. Following the charted pattern, use the colored cord as a bearer cord for horizontal double half-hitches to form the background of the square, as shown in the diagram at left. To macrame the pattern, use the colored cord as the knotting cord, tying it in a vertical double half-hitch over a natural cord, forming the patterns shown.

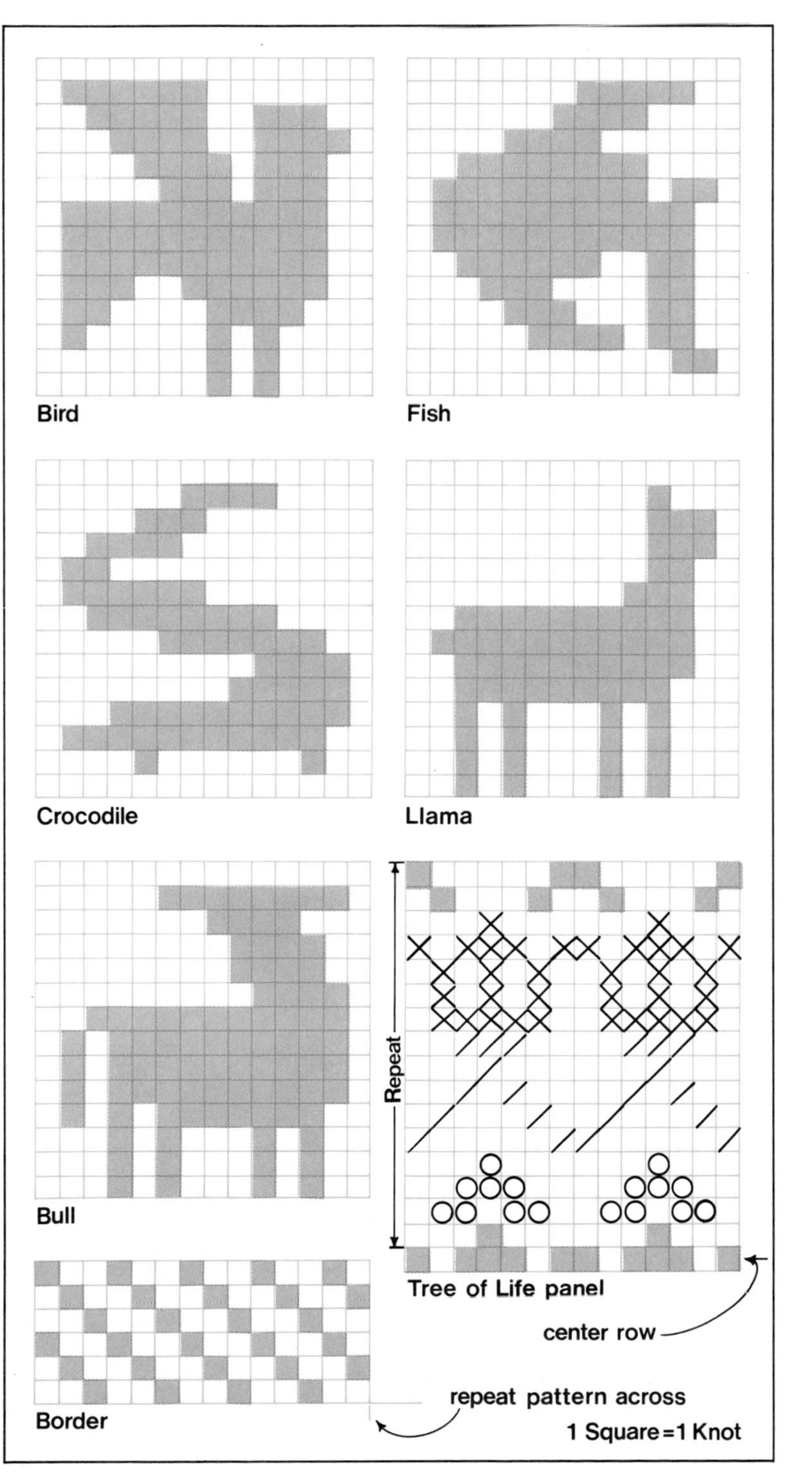

Tree of Life Color Key

- rust
- red
- green
- blue

Woven Stairway Runner

"Rosepath" designs, such as those in the sampler rug, opposite, have been woven in Scandinavian countries for hundreds of years. And while they are traditionally worked on a large floor loom, it's possible to approximate their lovely patterns with a small home-style loom. On pages 470 and 471, there are eight patterns to work into sampler rugs of your own. By making them all the same width but of differing lengths, you can stitch them together into a dramatic stairway runner.

Materials

Two 30-inch artist's stretcher strips
Two 36-inch artist's stretcher strips
8/4 linen thread for warp (see note at right)
Swedish Berga goat hair yarn in brown and yellow, or a suitable substitute (see note at right)
4 corrugated fasteners
1 sheet of 10-square-per-inch graph paper
Transparent tape

Directions

Note: To estimate the amount of materials required to make these "mini" rugs, see the directions on page 471. As a general guide, however, plan on using about 3 cones of 8/4 linen and 12 skeins of each color yarn to make small rugs equivalent to 27x72 inches when added together. Although the loom will be warped to be 30 inches wide, the width of the rug will be only about 27 inches when finished.

To begin, build a 30x36-inch frame from the artist's stretcher strips. Stabilize the corners with corrugated fasteners. The 36-inch sides of the frame will be the top and bottom of the loom, around which the warp is wrapped. Along the top of each of these sides, tape a 1-inch-wide strip of graph paper to help mark the spacing of the warps (10 warps to the inch).

To warp the loom, tie the linen thread securely to the bottom of the loom, about 3 inches inside the corner. Warp only the center 30 inches of the frame, leaving a 3-inch margin on each side to make weaving easier. Carry the linen cord up to the top of the frame, around it, and back to the bottom again. Wrap it around the bottom, and carry it back to the top. *Wrap the warp around the frame in a figure-eight pattern* (when viewed from the side). Continue in this way until you've wrapped the frame 154 times, creating 308 warp threads in the 30-inch space. Pull the warp tightly as you wrap around the frame. Knot the ends of the warp string together when necessary; weft yarn will cover the knots. Knot the end of the last warp securely to the frame. Then, with your fingers, space warps along the lines of the graph paper, so there are 10 warps per inch, except on the outside edges where four warps should be grouped together on each side. Be sure to divide the warp threads evenly.

To begin the first "mini" rug, weave with the warp thread to a depth of ½ inch. On the first row, go over and under two threads at a time to establish 150 double-thread warps, except on the selvages; these should be four-thread warps. On the second row, go over the threads you went under on the first row and under those you went over. Continue until you've woven ½ inch. Then switch to yarn for the border strip.

To weave the border, use brown yarn and weave over and under three pairs of warps (6 threads) at a time to a depth of one inch. Begin and end yarn inside the woven area rather than along the selvage. As you weave each row, beat it down firmly against the previous rows by pushing with your fingers, a large-tooth comb, or a dinner fork, making the weaving snug and firm.

To weave in pattern, follow the charted diagrams on pages 470 and 471. The dark areas in the diagrams represent the brown yarn; light areas are yellow. Repeat each pattern as many times as desired. The patterns in the rug shown opposite vary from 12 to 21 inches long, except for pattern number 4, which is worked only once (and can be woven at the top or bottom of an adjoining pattern). When weaving more than one pattern on the loom, separate them with an inch of brown border, following directions above.

At the top of each pattern, end the rug by working two or three rows of linen thread in plain weave over and under pairs of warp threads. Beat them down snugly against previous rows.

To remove the rug from the loom, carefully cut the warp threads from the loom and knot them tightly together as follows: Cut the

continued

Woven Stairway Runner *(continued)*

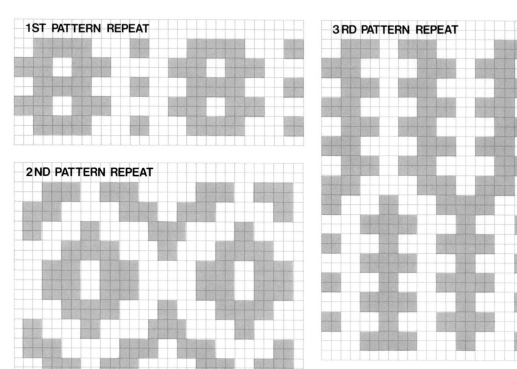

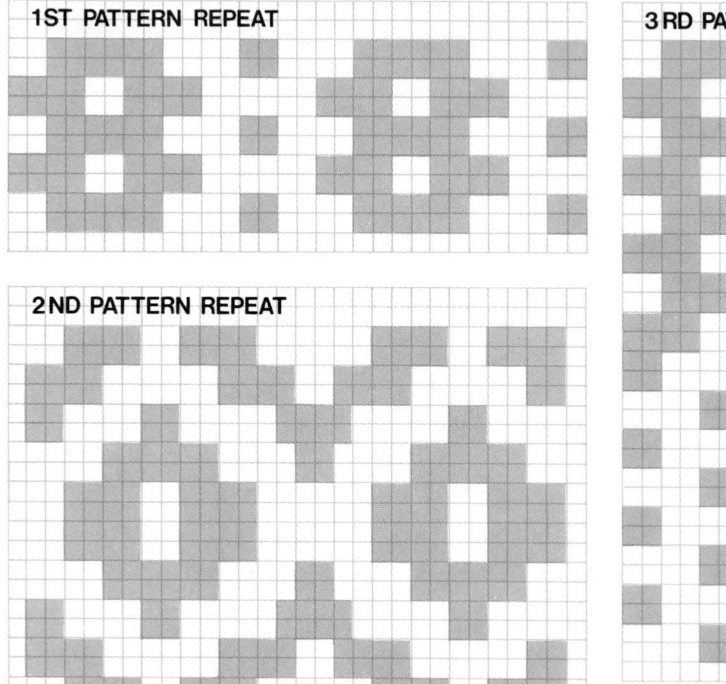

first six threads off the loom. Tie the first five together in an overhand knot. Then cut the next double strands from the loom and tie together one strand from that warp with the one remaining from the previous warp. Continue cutting and tying together strands from adjoining warps until the rug is completely off the loom. Cut threads close to knots, or leave them long for fringe if rugs are not going to be sewn together.

To make the remaining rugs, warp the loom following the directions on page 468. Instead of working ½ inch of linen warp in plain weave, however, work only three rows; then work an inch of brown border, following the directions on page 468. Work the remainder of the rug in pattern, following one of the diagrams.

To assemble the finished samples, stitch them together with strong carpet thread, following directions on page 415 for joining braided rugs. Mount on the stairway with brass rods.

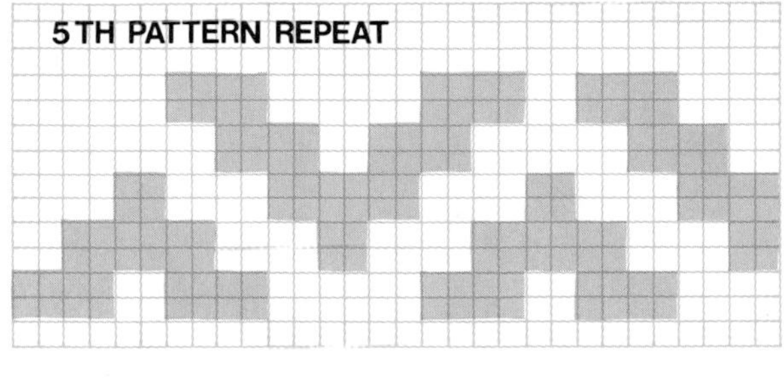
5TH PATTERN REPEAT

6TH PATTERN REPEAT

7TH PATTERN REPEAT

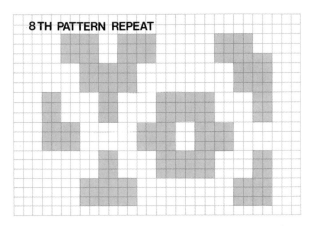

8TH PATTERN REPEAT

1 Row of vertical squares = 1 warp thread

1 Row of horizontal squares = 1 weft thread

How to Estimate Quantities of Yarn for Weaving

To estimate for warp threads: First, count the number of warps (selvage threads) on the loom, or multiply the width of the weaving by the number of warps per inch. Then add to that number any extra threads for special purposes. For example, if you are double-warping the loom, then double the amount you've figured so far. Multiply this number by the length (in inches) of the warp (from the top to the bottom of the loom). Then divide that number by 36 to convert inches into yards. Finally, add a little extra for waste, to get an estimate of the final amount.

To estimate for weft threads, yarn, or fabric: Measure the width of the weaving you plan and add about 25 percent to determine the length of the weft (crosswise thread) you need for one row of weaving. Then estimate how many rows of weft make up one inch of weaving. (Working a small sample at this point helps.) Multiply the width estimate by the number of rows, and then multiply that total by the length (in inches) of the planned weaving. Divide this final sum by 36 for the approximate number of yards of weft yarn or fabric needed.

Family Portrait Rug

This enchanting rug features a happy combination of two techniques. Here the grass, the puppy, and the children are worked with a latch hook, while the lower but slightly textured background is worked in cross-stitches.

By changing the color of the hair, eyes, or clothing, you can make this rug look like a portrait of your own happy family.

1 square=3 inches

Materials

32x43 inches #4-count penelope rug canvas
Three 140-yard skeins (or six 70-yard skeins) Aunt Lydia's polyester rug yarn in light blue, or a suitable substitute
320-strand packages of precut latch-hook yarn in the following amounts and colors: 1 red, 1 gold, 1 yellow, 1 purple, 1 royal blue, 1 denim blue, 1 black, 1 tan, 2 cream, 6 white, 1 medium brown, 2 pink, 1 light green, 1 rose, 1 light gray, 1 dark gray, 1 orange, 8 olive green, 1 kelly green, and 1 dark brown
1 yard ⅝-inch-wide pink grosgrain ribbon
Black waterproof marking pen
Light blue acrylic paint
Large paintbrush
Large tapestry needle
Latch hook
Carpet thread
Masking tape
5 yards rug binding
Brown wrapping paper

Directions

Note: The finished size of the rug is 28x39 inches.

To make the rug as shown, use the pattern above. If you wish to change the design to resemble your own family, adapt the pattern by altering the design or by changing the hair color.

To make your own pattern, take a slide photograph of your family and project the image on a wall covered with paper cut to the same size as the finished rug. Trace the image onto paper with a pencil, then go over the lines with a black felt-tip pen so they are easy to see. Transfer the design to rug canvas, following the directions on page 166.

If you use the pattern above, enlarge it to size, following the directions on page 272, and transfer it to brown paper. Go over the design lines with a black pen.

Center the rug canvas atop the pattern and trace the design with a waterproof marking pen. Draw a border around the design, leaving a 2-inch hem margin along each edge. Bind the edges of the canvas with masking tape.

Using a paintbrush and light blue acrylic paint, paint the sky so the white canvas will not show when the sky is stitched.

To work the design, begin with the sky. Cut a 2- to 3-foot length of light blue rug yarn, thread it into a needle, and work the sky in cross-stitches (see the diagram on page 418, if necessary). To minimize distortion of the canvas, work half cross-stitches completely across the canvas in one direction. Then complete the stitch by working back along the row in the opposite direction. Begin and end the yarn by running it through two or three stitches along the back.

When the sky is finished, work the remainder of the design with a latch hook, referring to the photograph for colors. Begin at the bottom of the design by hooking the grass with olive green yarn, and work toward the sky, completing each row before

moving up to the next one. If necessary, see page 444 for directions for latch-hooking.

When latch-hooking the children, use the colors of your choice for hair and eyes. Also change the patterns on the clothing, if desired. Work the children's skin in white, and the dog in cream and beige (or the colors of your own dog).

After finishing the latch hooking, add the hair ribbons to the little girl's hair. Cut the ribbon in half. Then tie each piece into a bow and run a thin piece of yarn or string through the backs of the ribbons with a large, blunt needle. Use the needle to run the yarn through the canvas to the back. Then tie the yarn in a knot or bow on back of canvas.

Block the finished rug, following the directions on page 449. Then sew rug binding to the canvas along the worked edges. Turn the edges to the back, mitering the corners. Stitch the binding to the back of the rug with carpet thread, making sure edges are secure. Add metal curtain rings for hanging.

Speed-Hooked Rug: Deco Dancers

Our romantic "Dancers" design, opposite, is a punch-needle rug worked with a speed-hooking tool. With this nifty device, you can hook up to a square foot of backing fabric in just an hour or two, making it a real boon to rug crafters with busy schedules.

Materials

Norden Crafts "Eggbeater" speed-hooking rug needle, or a suitable substitute
72x84 inches heavy-duty burlap
Norden Crafts 3-ply wool rug yarn (or a comparable substitute equal in weight to 4-ply knitting yarn) in the following amounts and colors: 18 ounces white, 4 ounces beige, 14 ounces blue, 12 ounces gray, 22 ounces black, 4 ounces green, 4 ounces red, 2 ounces pink, 1 ounce purple, and 12 ounces yellow
Rug frame
Liquid latex rug backing
Waterproof marking pen

Color Key

1 White
2 Beige
3 Light blue
4 Gray
5 Black
6 Green
7 Red
8 Rose
9 Purple
10 Yellow

Directions

Note: The finished size of the rug is approximately 50x75 inches.

Enlarge the pattern below, following the directions on page 166. *Note that the design has already been reversed,* so it can be transferred directly to the rug backing. Transfer it, centered, to the fabric and go over design lines with a waterproof pen so they are easy to see. Mount the fabric, or a portion of it, in the rug frame with the design facing up. The fabric must be taut.

Roll yarn into balls, if necessary, so it will flow freely into the needle as you work. Set the needle for a medium-height loop and thread yarn into it, following manufacturer's directions.

To hook the design, first outline the shapes in the pattern with one or two rows of loops. Then fill shapes with rows of loops hooked back and forth across each area. Work one section of color at a time, following the color key at left.

To work the needle, grasp the handle in your left hand (if you are right-handed) and push the needle into the fabric until the base rests firmly on the burlap. Working with the needle perpendicular to the fabric, turn the handle clockwise, guiding it so it "walks" along the burlap, automatically making loops. When you finish a row, move the needle to the next row, crank the handle counterclockwise, and work back alongside the previous row. With practice, you'll be able to work about a square foot an hour.

Check the front of the rug periodically to make sure that the loops cover the backing completely and that the height is consistent. If you've missed a spot, fill it in when working the next row.

After hooking the rug, remove it from the frame. To finish it, nail or staple it facedown on a base or the floor, *making sure corners are square and fabric is taut.* Apply liquid latex rug backing to the hooked area. When latex is dry, trim excess fabric to within 3 inches of the hooked area. Finish the margin of the rug (making a finished edge), following the directions on pages 448 and 449.

1 Square = 3 inches

Index

Page numbers in italic type refer you to project photographs. Numbers that are not italicized refer to pages with project instructions.

A-B

Afghans, 171–193
Americana pattern, classic, 182, *183*
Brilliant Flower Patch, 184, *185*, *186*
Grandmother's Flower Garden, 180, *181*
granny square sampler, *170–171*, 172–173, *174–175*, 176–177
quick knit patchwork, 188, *189*
star motif, 178, *179*
"windowpane," 190, *191*
See also Throws
Alphabet quilt, cross-stitch, 372, *373–375*
Alphabet rug, cross-stitch, *418–419*
Americana pattern, classic, afghan/coverlet in, 182, *183*
Animal motifs
appliqué
pillow toys, *86–87*
sleeping bag and tote, *156–157*, 158, *159*
hooked rug, *440–441*
in macrame rug, *462*, 464, *467*
soft sculpture, 316, *317–320*, *392–396*
Antimacassars, crocheted, 225–226, *226*, *227*
Apple blossom pattern, knitted lace tablecloth in, 198–199, *199*
Appliqué, 72–167
coverlets
with pillowcases, 88, *89*
wildflower, 146, *147*
curtains, *98–99*
embellishments, 77
fabric for, 74
by hand, 74, *75–77*
headboard, 60, *61*
by machine, 74, 76–77, *77*
patterns, *75*
pillows, *98–99*, *105*, *107*
patchwork, *14–15*
quick-and-easy, *80–83*
shaped, 116, *117*
toys, *86–87*
wildflower, *72–73*, *78–79*
quilts, 128–141
Aunt Mary's Rose Quilt, *132–133*
Appliqué *(continued)*
baby, *84–85*
bird, *104–106*
Blue Grove, *136–137*
butterflies, *142–143*, 144, *145*, 148, *149–154*, 155
Dresden plate, *140–141*
Grandmother's Flower Garden, *62–63*
lace, 126, *127*
quilter's, 64, *65–67*, 68
rainbow, *90–91*, 92, *93*
Rose of Sharon, *138–139*
rose wreath, *134–135*
sampler, *162–166*
tulip, *128–130*
sleeping bag/tote, *156–157*, 158, *159*
techniques, special, 108–127
lace, *125*, 126, *127*, *167*
reverse, 120, *121*, 122–123, *124*, 148, *150*
shadow, *108–109*, 110, *111*
shaped, 116, *117*
trapunto quilting, *69*, 77, *82–83*, *112–115*, *118–119*, *156–157*, 158, *159*
wall hangings and decorations
banners, *100–103*
lace butterfly, *167*
portrait, 160, *161*
reverse, 120, *121*, 122–123, *124*
with stitchery, *94–97*, *118–119*, *390–391*, 397, *398–399*
trapunto quilting, *69*, *82–83*, *114–115*, *118–119*
Attic Windows patchwork pattern, *26*
needlepoint design from, *260–261*
Aunt Mary's Rose Quilt, *132–133*
Auntie Dee's cross-stitch tablecloth, *370–371*
Auntie Dee's embroidered runner, *366–369*
Baby coverlets/quilts. *See* Crib coverlets/quilts
Backing fabric, quilt, border of, 46–47, *47*
Bandanna-design pillow, needlepoint, *264–265*
Banners, appliquéd, *100–103*
Bar-tacking, 290, *291*, 389
Bargello, *321*
bench cover, *252–253*
chair seat, machine-stitched, *290–291*
chrysanthemum pillow, *262–263*
metal threads, 292, *293*, *294*
raffia-stitchery baskets, *296–297*
Basket stitch pillow, 192, *193*
Baskets
crocheted, 228, *229*
needlepoint, *296–297*
Bath mat, patchwork, *25*, 30
Bed canopy, crocheted, 214, *215*
Bed covers
knitted, *206–207*, 208, *209*
See also Coverlets; Quilts; Throws
Bench cover, bargello, *252–253*
Bias binding for quilt, 46
Binding off, in knitting, *233*
Bird pillows, appliquéd, *81*, *105*, *107*
Bird quilt, appliquéd, *104–106*
Blackwork embroidery scroll, *379–381*
Blind stitch for appliqué, *76*
Blocking
embroidery, 400
needlepoint, 241
rugs, latch-hooked and needlepoint, 448–449
yarn articles, 182, 427
Blue Grove Quilt, *136–137*
Blue rose tablecloth, *344–346*
Borders
crocheted, for throw, *362*, 363
needlepoint, for rug, *460–461*
patchwork, for pillow, *81*
quilt, 13
Boxes
lace appliqué, *125*
needlepoint, *278–279*, *293*, 294–295, *295*
Braided rugs
calico patchwork, *416–417*
general instructions, *414–415*
piecing strips for, 414, *422*
traditional, oval, *412–413*, 415
Bride and groom dolls, needlepoint, 280, *281*, *282*
Brilliant Flower Patch afghan, 184, *185*, *186*
Butterflies
appliqué
quilts, *142–143*, 144, *145*, 148, *149–154*, 155
wall panel, *167*
embroidered pillowcases, *350–351*

C-E

Calico patchwork rug, *416–417*
Canopy, bed, crocheted, 214, *215*
Canvas, needlepoint, kinds of, *238–239*
Card weaving, *454–455*
Carpet border, needlepoint, *460–461*
Casting on, in knitting, *232*
Cavandoli work, *466*
splicing cord on, *465*
Chain stitch
kinds, *406–407*, *409*
pillows, *338*
tambour work, *402–403*
Chair pad, patchwork, *19*
Chair seat, machine bargello, *290–291*
Chair set, crocheted, 225–226, *226*, *227*
Checkerboard patchwork pattern, 13
Chinese dollhouse rug, *274–275*
Chrysanthemum bargello design, *262–263*
Cleaning quilts, 131
"Clothesline" crochet, rug of, *450–452*
Coasters, crocheted, 202

Comforters
appliqué, 88, *89*, *104–106*
patchwork, *22*, *23*
Counted-thread work, *366–369*
blackwork, *379–381*
blue rose tablecloth, *344–345*
Hardanger, 376, *377*, *378*
machine-embroidered, *389*
See also Cross-stitch
Coverlets
appliqué, 88, *89*
wildflower, 146, *147*
crocheted, 220–221, *221*
Americana pattern, classic, 182, *183*
for baby, 216, *217*
filet-patterned, 210, *211*, *212*, 212–213
Cozy quilt-patterned throw, *187*
Crayon quilt, 58, *59*
Crazy-quilt place mats, *388*
Crèches
appliquéd banner, *100–101*
embroidered, *336–337*
needlepoint, 310, *311–315*
Crewelwork
picture frame, *352*
throw, *362*, 363, *364–365*
A Walk in the Woods design, *354–359*, 360, *361*
Crib coverlets/quilts
appliqué, *84–85*, 146, *147*
crocheted, 216, *217*
cross-stitch, 372, *373–375*
Crocheting, *230–231*
abbreviations, 230, 363, 432
afghans
Americana pattern, classic, 182, *183*
Brilliant Flower Patch, 184, *185*, *186*
Grandmother's Flower Garden, 180, *181*
granny square sampler, *170–171*, 172–173, *174–175*, 176–177
star motif, 178, *179*
baskets, 228, *229*
bed canopy/valance, 214, *215*
border for throw, *362*, 363
care of items, 182
chair set, 225–226, *226*, *227*
coverlets, 182, *183*, 210, *211*, *212*, 212–213, 220–221, *221*
for baby, 216, *217*
doilies, *203*, *222–223*, 224–225
gauge, 192, 427
hooks for
embroidery with, *402–403*
materials, 228
sizes, 225
measurement, 203
place mats/napkin rings, *200–201*, 202, *203*, 204, *205*
rugs. *See* Rugs: crocheted
table mat, *222–223*, 224–225
tablecloths
filet-patterned, 210, *211*, *212*, 212–213
lace, *194–195*, 196–197, *197*
tools for, 220
Crocheting *(continued)*
hooks, 225, 228
Cross-stitch, *407*
quilt/pillow, 372, *373–375*
rose wreaths, *348 349*
rugs
alphabet, *418–419*
family portrait, *472–473*
stitch diagrams, *321–323*
table runners, *332–333*, *339*, *348–349*
tablecloth, *370–371*
Curtains
appliqué, *98–99*
embroidered, *382–383*, *387*
patchwork, *32–33*
Cutwork, 368, 376
"Dancers" rug, *474–475*
Della Robbia wreath, needlepoint, 306, *307–309*
Design-your-own scatter rug/pillow, *442–443*
Diagonal quilting, 42
Doilies
appliqué using, *167*
crocheted, *203*
star-shaped, *222–223*, 224–225
Dollhouse rug, needlepoint, *274–275*
Dolls, bride and groom, 280, *281*, *282*
Double crochet, *231*
Double half-hitch knots, *466*
Drawn thread work, 346
Dresden plate quilt, *140–141*
Eight-point star pattern (patchwork), *32*
Embroidery
with appliqué, 77
Moon Flowers, 397, *398–399*
pin stitch, 110, *111*
wall hangings, *94–97*, *118–119*, *390–391*
wildflowers, *72–73*, *78–79*, 146, *147*
blocking/mounting, 400
folk, 326–339
knitted throw, *218–220*
materials/equipment, *353*
machine stitchery, 384
nature, designs from
A Walk in the Woods, *354–359*, 360, *361*
wildflowers, *362*, 363, *364–365*
old-fashioned, 340–352
outlining/padding, *346*
special techniques, 392–405
metal thread work, 400, *401*
sampler, 397, *398–399*
shells, use of, 404, *405*
shisha stitchery, *392–396*
tambour work, *402–403*
stitches, kinds of, *406–409*
hemstitching, *348*
Pekinese, *218*, *220*
shisha, *394*
See also Counted-thread work; Cross-stitch; Machine embroidery; Needlepoint
Enlarging designs, *272–273*
Even-weave fabrics, *353*

F-H

Fabrics
for appliqué, 74
for braided rugs, 414
for embroidery
even-weave, *353*
machine stitchery, 384
identifying, 131
for patchwork, 10
Family portrait rug, *472–473*
Felt, for appliqué, 74
Festive REJOICE Banner, *102–103*
Filet crochet chair set, 225–226, *226*, *227*
Filet-patterned coverlet/tablecloth, 210, *211*, *212*, 212–213
Fish, soft-sculpture, *392–396*
Fishpond rug, needlepoint, *300–301*, 302, *303–305*
Floor frame for quilting, use of, 43
Floor pillows, embroidered, *329–331*
Flowers, needlepoint, *276–277*
Folk embroidery, 326–339
Frames
floor, for quilting, 43
mirror, of needlepoint, *242*, 243–244, *244*
for needlepoint, *239*
picture, of crewelwork, *352*
Free-form needlepoint, 298, *299*
Free-motion embroidery on machine, 385, *386*
French binding for quilt, *46*
Fringe for dollhouse rug, 274, *275*
Galaxy (patchwork pattern), *29*
Garden scene, appliquéd, *94–95*
"Gateway to the Sun" wall hanging, 120, *121*, 122–123, *124*
Gauge, for yarn articles, 192, 427
Gift box, lace appliqué, *125*
Grandmother's Flower Garden pattern
afghan, crocheted, 180, *181*
quilt, *62–63*
Granny squares
afghans
sampler, *170–171*, 172–173, *174–175*, 176–177
star motif, 178, *179*
rug, *424–426*
Grids, enlarging with, *272*, *272–273*
Half double crochet, *231*
Half-hitch knots, double, *466*
Hand appliqué, *75–77*
fabrics for, 74
Hand quilting, 43–44, *44*
Hardanger place mats/napkins, 376, *377*, *378*
machine-embroidered, *389*
Hassock, needlepoint, *283–285*
Headboards, appliquéd, *60–61*, *112–113*
Heart pillow, appliquéd, *80*

Hearts and flowers pillow, *14*, 14–15
Hemming rugs, *449*
Hemstitching, *348*
Hexagon Flower; Hexagon Star (patchwork patterns), *31*
Honeycomb throw, 192, *193*
Hooked rugs
machine version, *456–459*
See also Latch-hooked rugs; Punch-hooked rugs
Hungarian tablecloth, *326–328*

I-L

Indian motifs
animal toys, *86–87*
embroidered throw/pillows, *329–331*
wall hanging, appliquéd, 120, *121*, 122–123, *124*
Inlay, needlepoint box with, *293*, *295*
Interfacing for appliqué, 75
Interlock canvas, 238, *239*
Jewel box, needlepoint, *278–279*
Joseph's Coat (patchwork pattern), *27*
Jute
bed canopy/valance, 214, *215*
pillow, 208
place mats/napkin rings, *200–201*, 202
rugs, *430–433*
macrame, *462–467*
King's Cross (patchwork pattern), *30*
Knit stitch, *232–233*
Knitting, *232–233*
abbreviations, 232, 434
afghans/throws
cozy quilt-patterned, *187*
embroidered, *218–220*
honeycomb, 192, *193*
quick knit patchwork, 188, *189*
"windowpane," 190, *191*
bed cover, *206–207*, 208, *209*
care of items, 182
gauge, 192, 427
pillows, 192, *193*, *206–207*, 208–209, *209*
place mats/napkin rings, *200–201*, 202
rugs. *See* Rugs: knitted
tablecloth, lace, 198–199, *199*
tips for, 188, 190, 203
for rugs, 427
tools for, 220
Knots, kinds of, *464–466*
Lace
appliqué, *125*, 126, *127*, *167*
caring for, 126
tablecloths
crocheted, *194–195*, 196–197, *197*
knitted, 198–199, *199*
Lark's head knot, *464*
Latch-hooked rugs, *444–447*
family portrait, *472–473*
Latch-hooked rugs *(continued)*
finishing, 448–449, *449*
materials, 444
estimating requirements, 453
tool and technique, *444*
Latex rug backing, liquid, 448, 466
Laundering
quilts, 131
yarn articles, 182
Linen place mats/napkin rings, *200–201*, 202
Lining rugs, 449
Lion, soft-sculpture, 316, *317–320*
Lisa's Choice (patchwork pattern), *28*
Log Cabin quilt, *40–41*
updated version, *48–49*
Loom-woven rugs, 468, *469–471*
Lounging mat, patchwork, *18*

M-P

Machine appliqué, 76–77, *77*
fabric for, 74
Machine embroidery, 382–391
materials/equipment, 384
technique, *385*
free-motion, 385, *386*
Machine "hooking" of rugs, *456–459*
Machine needlepoint, *290–291*
Machine quilting, *44*, 44–45
Macrame
Cavandoli work, *465*, *466*
rug, *462–467*
splicing cords, *465*
Magic Cubes (patchwork pattern), *30*
Mediterranean pillow, *402*
Metal thread work
embroidered panel, 400, *401*
needlepoint, 292, *293–295*
Middle Eastern pillow, *403*
Mirror frame, needlepoint, *242*, 243–244, *244*
Monkey tote, *156–157*, 158, *159*
Mono canvas, *238*
Monograms, needlepoint, 245
Moon Flowers embroidery sampler, 397, *398–399*
Mosaic-pattern jewel box, needlepoint, *278–279*
Names, in needlepoint, 245
Napkin rings, crocheted/knitted, *200–201*, 202
Napkins
appliqué, *108–109*, 110, *111*
embroidered, 376, *377*, *378*
machine stitchery, *389*
Needlepoint, 236–323
bargello. *See* Bargello
blocking, 241
rugs, 448–449
boxes
metal threads/inlay, *293*, 294–295, *295*
mosaic-pattern, *278–279*
canvas, *238–239*
crèche, 310, *311–315*
design adaptation, *270–273*
Needlepoint *(continued)*
free-form stitchery, 298, *299*
transfer, 248, *273*
dolls, bride and groom, 280, *281*, *282*
equipment, *239*
flowers, *276–277*
frames, 239
free-form, 298, *299*
hassock, *283–285*
lion, soft-sculpture, 316, *317–320*
mirror frame, *242*, 243–244, *244*
pillows, 254–269
assembling, *258*
bandanna design, *264–265*
metal threads, 292, *293*, *294*
paper-doll sampler, *268–269*
quilt-pattern, *260–263*
string, *287*, 288, *289*
variegated yarn, 258, *259*
wedding ring, *266–267*
wildflowers, *236*, 242, *244*
"woven," *254–255*, 256–257, *257*
rug border, *460–461*
rugs
dollhouse, Chinese, *274–275*
from fabric, *418–419*
finishing, 448–449, *449*
fishpond, *300–301*, 302, *303–305*
materials requirements, estimating, 453
string, *286–287*, 288, *289*
WELCOME, 245, *246–247*
wildflowers, *236–237*, 243, *244*
stitches, kinds of, *318*, *319*, *321–323*
stitching guidelines, 240–241
wreath designs
Della Robbia, 306, *307–309*
rose, 248, *249–251*
yarns/threads, 238–239
color schemes, 315
working with, 240
Needleweaving, 376, *378*
Off-loom weaving, *454–455*
Ornaments, cross-stitch, *348–349*
Outline quilting, 42
Panel, embroidered, 400, *401*
Pansy cloth, embroidered, *347*
Paper-doll sampler pillow, *268–269*
"Parquet" rug, *430–431*
Patchwork, 8–39
and machine embroidery, *388*
pieced, patterns and projects for, *24–31*
classic quilts, *34–41*, *48–55*, *128–130*, *140–141*
star pattern, *32–39*
pillow border, *81*
procedure, basic, 10–13, *11*, *12*
projects using, *8–9*, *14–23*
quilts. *See* Quilts
Patchwork afghan, quick knit, 188, *189*
Patchwork-style rugs
braided, *416–417*
knitted, *434*

Pekinese stitch, *218*, *220*
Penelope canvas, 238, *239*
Petit point, 303
Picture frame, crewel, *352*
Pieced patchwork, 24–39
  patterns, *26–31*
    classic quilts, *34–41*, *48–55*, *128–130*, *140–141*
    star pattern, *32–39*
  procedure, basic, 12
Pillow shams, patchwork, *20*, *21*, 39
Pillowcases
  appliqué, 88, *89*
  embroidered, *350–351*
    machine stitchery, *382–383*, 387
Pillows
  appliqué. *See* Appliqué: pillows
  embroidered
    chain stitch, *338*
    cross-stitch, 372, *373*, *374*
    Indian motifs, *329–331*
    tambour work, *402–403*
    A Walk in the Woods, *354–355*, 358, 360–361, *361*
    wildflowers, *362*, 362–363, *364–365*
  knitted, *206–207*, 208–209, *209*
    basket stitch, 192, *193*
  needlepoint. *See* Needlepoint: pillows
  patchwork, *8–9*, *14–15*
    pieced patterns, *24*, *25*, 27, 31, *32*, *33*
  punch-hooked, *442–443*
Pin stitch, 110, *111*
Place mats
  crocheted/knitted, *200–201*, 202, *203*, 204, *205*
  embroidered
    Hardanger, 376, *377*, *378*, *389*
    machine stitchery, *388*, *389*
  patchwork, *8–9*, 15, *16*, *388*
    pieced patterns, *24*, 30
Portrait, appliquéd, 160, *161*
Portrait rug, *472–473*
Pot holders, patchwork, *24*, 29, 31
Puff stitch afghan, 190, *191*
Punch-hooked rugs, *436–437*, *439–443*
  finishing, 448
  materials, 438
    estimating requirements, 453
  speed-hooked, *474–475*
  tool and technique, *438*
Purl stitch, *233*

O-R

Quick knit patchwork afghan, 188, *189*
Quickpoint
  rose wreath, 248, *249–251*
  rug border, *460–461*
  WELCOME rug, 245, *246–247*
Quilt-patterned items
  crazy-quilt place mats, *388*
  needlepoint pillows, *260–263*
  throw, knitted, *187*
Quilting, 42–45, *44*
Quilting *(continued)*
  by hand, 43–44, *44*
  hoop, 44
  by machine, *44*, 44–45
  patterns, 42–43
  trapunto. *See* Trapunto quilting
Quilts, *8–9*, 14, *20*, *21*, 40–55
  appliqué. *See* Appliqué: quilts
  assembling, *43*
  borders, 13
  caring for, 131
  comforter, *22*, *23*
  crayon art, 58, *59*
  cross-stitch, 372, *373–375*
  finishing of edges, 45–47, *46*, *47*
  Grandmother's Flower Garden, *62–63*
  Log Cabin, *40–41*
    updated version, *48–49*
  pieces for, 10–13
  procedure for, 42–45, *44*
  quilter's quilt, 64, *65–67*, 68
  Star of Bethlehem, *50–51*
  star pattern, *34–39*
  Storm at Sea, *52–53*
  tips for, 68
  Tulip Basket, *128–130*
  tying, *45*
  windmill, *54–55*
Raffia-stitchery baskets, *296–297*
Rag rugs
  crocheted, *420–423*
  See also Braided rugs
Rainbow quilt, *90–91*, 92, *93*
Reverse appliqué, 120, *121*, 122–123, *124*, 148, *150*
Rivoli Cross (patchwork pattern), *30*
Rolling Star (patchwork pattern), *31*
Rose of Sharon Quilt, *138–139*
  variation, *132–133*
Rose wreath designs
  cross-stitch, *348–349*
  needlepoint, 248, *249–251*
  quilt, appliquéd, *134–135*
Rosepath-design rugs, 468, *469–471*
Ruffles
  pillow, 15
  quilt edging, 47
Rugs
  braided. *See* Braided rugs
  crocheted
    over clothesline, *450–452*
  granny square runner, *424–426*
    jute, *430–433*
    rag, *420–423*
    scatter, *428–429*
    tips for, 427
    whimsical, *435*
  family portrait, *472–473*
    hooked
      machine version, *456–459*
      See also Latch-hooked rugs; Punch-hooked rugs
  knitted
    patchwork, *434*
    scatter, 428–429, *429*
    tips for, 427
  macrame, *462–467*
  materials requirements, estimating, 453
Rugs *(continued)*
    braided rugs, 414
    woven rugs, 471
  needlepoint. *See* Needlepoint: rugs
  needlepoint border, *460–461*
  woven
    off-loom, *454–455*
    stairway runner, 468, *469–471*
    yarn requirements, estimating, 471
Runners
  floor
    "clothesline" crochet, *450–452*
    granny square, *424–426*
    latch-hooked, *446–447*
    macrame, *462–467*
  stairway, woven, 468, *469–471*
  table, embroidered, *366–369*
    cross-stitch, *332–333*, *339*, *348–349*
Running stitches, *409*
  for appliqué, *76*
Rya rugs, estimating requirements for, 453

S-T

Sampler afghan, granny square, *170–171*, 172–173, *174–175*, 176–177
Sampler piece, embroidered, 397, *398–399*
Sampler pillow, needlepoint, *268–269*
Sampler quilt, appliquéd, *162–166*
Sampler rugs, woven, 468, *469–471*
Satin stitch, *409*
  for appliqué, 76, *77*
Saw-tooth star pattern (patchwork), *32*
Scalloped patterns
  crocheted rug, *432–433*
  quilting, 42
Scatter rugs, *See* Throw and scatter rugs
Schoolhouse pillow, *15*
Scroll, blackwork embroidery, *379–381*
Seams, trimming and pressing, *12*
Shadow appliqué, *108–109*, 110, *111*
Shaped appliqué, 116, *117*
Sheer fabrics, shadow appliqué with, *108–109*, 110, *111*
Shell (scalloped) quilting pattern, 42
Shells, stitchery with, 404, *405*
Shisha stitchery, *392–396*
Single crochet, *230*
Sister's Choice (patchwork pattern), *30*
Sleeping bag, appliquéd, *156–157*, 158, *159*
Slip stitch, *231*
Soft sculpture
  fish, *392–396*
  lion, 316, *317–320*
Speed-hooked rug, *474–475*
Splicing

Splicing *(continued)*
clothesline for crocheted rug, *452*
macrame cords, *465*
Square knots, *464*
alternating, *465*
splicing cords, *465*
Staircase scene, appliquéd, *96–97*
Stairway runner, woven, 468, *469–471*
Star doily/table mat, *222–223*, 224–225
Star motif afghan, 178, *179*
Star of Bethlehem quilt, *50–51*
Star pattern, projects using, *32–39*
Stitch gauge, for yarn articles, 192, 427
Storm at Sea quilt, *52–53*
String needlepoint, *286–287*, 288, *289*
Swan pillow/curtains, appliquéd, *98–99*
Swistraw baskets, *296–297*
Table mat, star-shaped, *222–223*, 224–225
Table runners, embroidered, *366–369*
cross-stitch, *332–333*, *339*, *348–349*
Tablecloths
appliqué, *108–109*, 110, *111*
crocheted
filet-patterned, 210, *211*, *212*, 212–213
lace, *194–195*, 196–197, *197*
embroidered, *340–343*
blue rose, *344–346*
cross-stitch, *370–371*
flowered, *334–335*
Hungarian, *326–328*
pansy, *347*
knitted lace, 198–199, *199*
patchwork, *17*
Tambour work, *402–403*
Throw and scatter rugs
crocheted, *423*, *428–429*
design-your-own, hooked, *442–443*
knitted, 428–429, *429*
machine "hooked," *456–459*
Throws
cozy quilt-patterned, *187*
crocheted, 220–221, *221*
embroidered, *329–331*
knitted, *218–220*
wildflowers, crewel, *362*, 363, *364–365*
honeycomb, 192, *193*
See also Afghans
Tote bag, appliquéd, *156–157*, 158, *159*
Toys, appliquéd, *86–87*
Transfer of designs, 166
to needlepoint canvas, 248, *273*
Trapunto quilting, 77
headboard, *112–113*
sleeping bag, *156–157*, 158, *159*
soft-sculpture fish, *395*
wall hangings, *69*, *82–83*, *114–115*, *118–119*
Tree of Life rug, *462–467*
Tulip Basket Quilt, *128–130*
Tying of quilts, *45*

V-Z

Valance, crocheted, 214, *215*
Variegated-yarn pillows, needlepoint, 258, *259*
Victorian crocheted lace tablecloth, *194–195*, 196
A Walk in the Woods design
pillows, *354–355*, 358, 360–361, *361*
wall hanging, *356–359*, 360
Wall hangings
appliqué. *See* Appliqué: wall hangings
embroidered, *356–359*, 360
machine stitchery, *390–391*
shells, use of, 404, *405*
patchwork, *25*, *26*, 28
Washing
quilts, 131
yarn articles, 182
Waste knots, 240, 371
Weaving. *See* Rugs: woven
Wedding ring pillow, needlepoint, *266–267*
WELCOME rug, needlepoint, 245, *246–247*
Whipstitch for appliqué, *76*
Wildflower designs
appliqué
coverlet, 146, *147*
pillows, *72–73*, *78–79*
embroidered, *362*, 363, *364–365*
hooked rug, *436–437*, *439*
needlepoint, *236–237*, *242*, 243
Windmill quilt, *54–55*
"Windowpane" knitted afghan, 190, *191*
Wools, needlepoint, 239
"Woven" pillows, needlepoint, *254–255*, 256–257, *257*
Woven rugs. *See* Rugs: woven
Wreaths
Della Robbia, needlepoint, 306, *307–309*
See also Rose wreath designs
Yarns and threads
for embroidery, *353*
machine stitchery, 384
needlepoint, 238–239
color schemes, 315
working with, 240
for rugs, 444
estimating requirements, 453, 471
Zoo sleeping bag, *156–157*, 158, *159*

Designer Credits

Patchwork and Quilting
Sonya Barrington; Jan Bowman; Joan Cravens; Janet DeBard; Rosie Fischer; Susannah Flag; Michael Gold; Diana Messerly; Vicki Olivo; Quilts and Other Comforts, Denver, Colorado; Quilts in the Attic, Denver, Colorado; The Rainbow Shop, Beverly Hills, California; Myrtl Thomas; Ciba Vaughan; Erma Wink; Ms. Arthur Woodburn.

Appliqué
Sonya Barrington; Linda Brock; Joan Cravens; Rosie Fischer; Susannah Flag; Patricia Gardner; Susan Hesse; Rebecca Jerdee; Marge Kerr; Carol Lee Knutson; Sherry LeVine; Carol Martin; Jill Mead; Martha Opdahl; Charlotte Patera; Alice Proctor; Cinda Shambaugh; Mimi Shimmin; Ciba Vaughan; Mike Wigg.

Crocheting and Knitting
Bernat Yarn Company; Jackie Curry; May Griffin; Winnie Juhl; Christine Kaczmarczyk; Connie Lidster; Marie Muth; Mary Walker Phillips; Mary Jo Sandahl; Marie Schulz; Susan Toplitz; Unger Yarn Company.

Needlepoint
Curt Boehringer; Gary Boling; Ruth Colt; Joan Cravens; Mary Kay Davis; Sherry DeLeon; Judith Gross; Helen Hayes; Verna Holt; Chieko Hoshiai; Jody House; Emily Lawrence; Janet McCaffery; Margie Poffenbarger; Gay Ann Rogers; Barbara Sample; Ruth and Andy Sheidler; Mimi Shimmin; Ciba Vaughan; Kay Whitcomb; James Williams; Barbara Yost.

Embroidery
Carol Algie; D. J. Bennett; Margot Blair; Joan Cravens; Sara Guiterrez; Verna Holt; Chieko Hoshiai; Ann Levine; Nancy Osborn; Charlotte Patera; Marge Serck; Mimi Shimmin; Charlyne Stewart; Emma Wierson; Mike Wigg.

Rug Making
Alicia Anderson; John Baker; Gary Boling; Joan Cravens; Betty Crist; Dana Ehlinger; Verna Holt; Christine Kaczmarczyk; Laurie Kosky; Donna Leach; Connie Lidster; Nancy Lindemeyer; Ellen Morello; Marjorie Nichols; Mary Walker Phillips; Margie Poffenbarger; Mimi Shimmin; Suzy Taylor; Naomi Thompson.

Acknowledgements
Mary Barton; Blaser-Kimball Art Studio; Gary Boling; Norma Buferd; Charlotte Child; Ruth Colt; Patricia Cooper; Betty Crist; Pat Doviddio; Linda Emmerson; Frederick Fawcett Yarn Company; Heidi Horten; Jean LemMon; Mary Jane Linderman; Living History Farms, Des Moines, Iowa; Jill Mead; Mona Mortensen; Judy Murphy; Elizabeth Perkins; Margie Poffenbarger; Betty Sodawasser; Some Place, Incorporated, Berkeley, California; Grace Towner; Jessie Walker; Mike Wigg.

Photographers
Peter Amft; Mike Dieter; Thomas Hooper; William Hopkins; Frank L. Miller; Bill Wittkowski.